FAULKNER'S WORLD.

A Directory of His People and Synopses of Actions in His Published Works

Thomas E. Connolly
State University of New York at Buffalo

UNIVERSITY
PRESS OF
AMERICA

Lanham • New York • London

Copyright © **1988** by

University Press of America,® Inc.

4720 Boston Way
Lanham, MD 20706

3 Henrietta Street
London WC2E 8LU England

Printed in the United States of America

British Cataloging in Publication Information Available

Library of Congress Cataloging-in-Publication Data

Connolly, Thomas Edmund, 1918–
Faulkner's world.

Includes indexes.
1. Faulkner, William, 1897–1962—Characters.
2. Faulkner, William, 1897–1962—Plots. I. Title.
PS3511.A86Z759   1988   813'.52   88–5439 CIP
ISBN 0–8191–5703–1 (alk. paper)

All University Press of America books are produced on acid-free
paper which exceeds the minimum standards set by the National
Historical Publications and Records Commission.

For Michael, Daniel, Margaret, Katharine, and Nancy

Acknowledgments

I began to form the methodology of this study in the 1950's and early 1960's, and I am indebted to those students, graduate and undergraduate, who from that time participated in discussions of Faulkner's fiction. As a result of these early attempts to grapple with Faulkner's characters and intricate plots, I published two parts of this study as articles in *College English* and I am grateful to the editors of that journal for permission to reprint in expanded form the sections of this book devoted to *A Fable* and *Absalom, Absalom!* and for some remarks in the "Introduction." The original versions appeared as "Faulkner's *A Fable* in the Classroom," *College English*, 21, No. 3 (December 1959), 165-171, and "A Skeletal Outline of *Absalom, Absalom!*," *College English*, 25, No. 2 (November 1963), 110-114.

I resumed this study of Faulkner's fiction in January 1982, during a six-month sabbatical leave, for which I am grateful to the Trustees of State University of New York. My friend and colleague, Dr. Ira S. Cohen, Professor of Psychology at the State University of New York at Buffalo, gave me all sorts of help from beginning to end of this study. I shall always be grateful to him. In the final stages of printing out the text of "Index of Characters." Ms. Glo Aniebo, Assistant to the Chairman of the Psychology Department, SUNY at Buffalo, was most cooperative and helpful.

My daughter Nancy Connolly happily and meticulously helped me in the editorial tasks necessary to make the typescript that came from the computer suitable for the press.

My greatest debt, in producing this book, is to Dr. S. David Farr, Director of the Quantitative Analysis Laboratory, Facuty of Educational Studies, SUNY at Buffalo. He, generously and without any restrictions, gave me access to the computer facilities of his laboratory to an extent far beyond any demands of collegiality. His graduate assistants, Barbara Gordon and Bill Wu, were constantly there to help me out of jams as I tried to master the computer. To them I am most grateful. Dr. Farr's secretary, Nancy Meyers, always offered friendly and efficient assistance, and Patricia Gless, of that office, was also frequently helpful. I am grateful to Ray Volpe of the Computing Center, as well as to Christine Sauciunac.

Finally, this book was supported (in part) by a Research Development Fund Award from the State University of New York Research Foundation for which I am grateful.

Table of Contents

Introduction

William Faulkner crowded his fiction with thousands of characters, named and unnamed (at least 1700 of them have names). Sometimes he was astonishingly consistent, over the period of many years, in telling us about these characters and the communities in which they lived; sometimes he changed a character considerably; sometimes he gave his characters contradictory traits at different times. For example, Mrs. Littlejohn, who runs a boarding house in Frenchman's Bend, is never given a first name and is given only the slightest of characterization, even though she appears in three novels and at least three short stories, and her last name is mentioned in at least three other novels. Ike McCaslin's wife, who vainly tries sexually to persuade him not to repudiate his heritage, and, when she fails, refuses him sex thereafter, is never identified by her given name either. However, though she denies Ike further sex in "The Bear," in "Delta Autumn," as it originally appeared in *Story* and subsequently in the *Uncollected Stories*, she is said to be survived by children, and, in "Lion," as it originally appeared in *Harper's* and eventually in the *Uncollected Stories*, she is said to be survived by a grandchild. Among those characters who undergo considerable change over the course of Faulkner's fiction is Caspey Strother. In the first of the Yoknapatawpha books, *Sartoris* (1929) (which became *Flags in the Dust* in 1973), he is depicted as Elnora's brother. He later becomes her husband in "There Was a Queen." Even Aunt Jenny (Virginia Sartoris DuPre), who is almost always the aunt of Bayard Sartoris [II], becomes his sister in *The Town*, and is called Mrs. Virginia Sartoris in "All the Dead Pilots." Sam Fathers is sometimes the son of the Chickasaw Chief Ikkemotubbe, but sometimes he is the grandson of that same chief. Flem Snopes, however, with eyes the color of stagnant water, who is constantly chewing even after he has taught himself the economical habit of chewing nothing, never changes.

It is not, I think, important that Faulkner, from work to work, treats his characters consistently or inconsistently. What is important, and what always holds, is that, within each work, the characters remain consistent.

In planning this book, I decided to treat each work in chronological order (as best I knew); that is, in the order of conception and/or writing, not necessarily in the order of publication, with the obvious exceptions of the several collections of short stories and of the massive and quaintly named, *Uncollected Stories of William Faulkner*, edited by Joseph Blotner in 1979, in which the stories appear first in the order of revision for later novels, and then as hitherto uncollected and unpublished works. For these stories, I have used dates of composition and publication together with other information from a variety of sources including Blotner's notes. Occasionally, I have added to or deleted material given by Blotner in his notes to the uncollected stories.

A strictly chronological order is impossible because there often was an overlap with one work being started and then interrupted by another which was published first. Sometimes, because of the nature of their publication, these things straighten themselves out, as in the cases of *Sanctuary* and *As I Lay Dying*. Because both texts of *Sanctuary* have been published, it is possible to list *Sanctuary: The Original Text, As I Lay Dying*, and *Sanctuary* in proper order. This is not always possible. See, for example, *Pylon, Absalom, Absalom!*, and *The Unvanquished* which have been listed in order of publication, although, as the headnotes to each novel indicate, there is a good deal of overlapping in their composition. I have also used information gleaned from the following sources to date, as accurately as I could, the composition of these works. James B. Meriwether, *The Literary Career of William Faulkner: A Bibliographical Study* (Columbia, South Carolina: University of South Carolina Press, 1971), which includes the sending schedule. James B. Meriwether, "The Short Fiction of William Faulkner: A Bibliography," *Proof: The Yearbook of American Bibliographical and Textual Studies*, 1 (1971), 293-329; Hans H. Skei, *William Faulkner: The Short Story Career* (Oslo: Universitets Forlaget, 1981); William Faulkner, *Helen: A Courtship and Mississippi Poems*, introductory essays by Carvel Collins and Joseph Blotner (Tulane University and Yoknapatawpha Press, 1981), and Michel Gressett, *A Faulkner Chronology* (Jackson: University Press of Mississippi, 1985).

For each novel and collection of short stories, I list each character in the order of his or her introduction to the work regardless of whether or not the character has been given a name at that point. This listing is followed by a synopsis of the action in which each character is involved. Some minor characters are merely identified either by name only or by some occupation or trait. Only the named characters appear in the "Index of Characters."

I have followed this procedure for several reasons. First, the way in which Faulkner controls time as a device for revealing character, or in maintaining suspense may be discovered by the reader in this analysis and synoptic interpretation of the action. If one follows carefully the page numbers after each item of the synopsis, one can effectively demonstrate Faulkner's use of time to reveal character. Notice, for instance, how early the groom in *A Fable* is introduced and in what unfavorable light he is presented (page 56). Yet, his full story is delayed until the horse-racing story begins (page 151) almost one hundred pages later. The way in which Faulkner uses time as a device for maintaining suspense may be illustrated in a similar manner. Furthermore, the structure of the novel or short story is skeletalized by this method. To use *A Fable* as an example again, the synopsis reveals the envelope structure of the major plot concerning the mutiny in the French army in The Great War by showing how the two sub-plots, one concerning a British air squadron and the other about the racing of the crippled horse, are woven into the novel. The British squadron sub-plot starts with the introduction of Gerald David Levine on page 86 of the novel and ends with the German General and the Generalissimo agreeing to resume the war (pages 306-310). The horse-racing sub-plot is also shown to be sandwiched in by the main plot from the introduction of Reverend Tobe Sutterfield (page 141) to the introduction of the padre in the runner's battalion (page 205) which returns the reader to the main plot about the mutiny in the French army. In addition, the relationships between the characters and the events of the sub-plots and the main plot are revealed by the information collected about each character. To illustrate, the British runner is shown to be the connecting link between the story of the young British aviator, Levine, and the horse-racing story, for it is not enough to establish the relationship of each sub-plot to the principal plot, but the relationship of each sub-plot to the other should also be shown. Finally, the symbolic parallels are underscored but not exhaustively detailed. Thus, the reader is prompted to search out other parallels for himself.

The reader is also able to study the development of themes, not only within the work itself, but also from the first to the last of Faulkner's published works. Thus, such major themes as incest, violence, the ritual initiation to manhood, the hero as Messiah, and miscegenation, for example, may be studied as they appear, reappear, and develop throughout Faulkner's fiction.

I have limited my book to the published fiction because Professor Blotner's massive *Uncollected Stories of William Faulkner* leaves only about eight fragments, most of which are in the libraries of the University of Virginia and the University of Mississippi. These fragments (one of which is not really a fragment but a full short story entitled "Love") are not likely to be available to the general reading public, although they may find their way ultimately into some thesis or dissertation.

I should here say a word about my treatment of a few individual novels or collections of short stories. I have not included an analysis of *Sartoris* (1929), the first of the Yoknapatawpha novels, because, in 1973, Douglas Day edited and published *Flags in the Dust* (Random House) which is the original uncut version that Faulkner had submitted to his publisher, Liveright, who ultimately refused to publish it. Hal Smith persuaded Harcourt Brace to publish it, provided it were cut. Ben Wasson, Faulkner's friend and agent, cut extraneous material from the typescript, and the book was published. In my judgment, *Flags in the Dust* is an inferior novel to *Sartoris*, for it includes such a rambling sub-plot as the affair between Horace Benbow and Belle Mitchell's sister, Joan Heppleton, which detracts from rather than adds to the novel as a whole. We must use *Flags in the Dust* from now on, however, because Random House has allowed *Sartoris* to go out of print. All the characters of *Sartoris* appear relatively unchanged in *Flags*, with one exception: Captain Wylie of *Sartoris* becomes Captain Wyatt in *Flags in the Dust.*

I have included *Sanctuary: The Original Text* (1981) and *Sanctuary* (1931), although there are only minor differences between them, for just the opposite reason. Random House has allowed both versions to remain in print, and some readers may wish to have synoptic access to both volumes.

Faulkner always insisted that *Go Down, Moses* is a novel, although his publisher, Random House, added the words, "and Other Stories" to the title of the first edition, but dropped the last three words from the titles of subsequent issues. The fact remains, however, that "The Bear," is frequently reprinted as a short story in anthologies of short fiction, and "The Old People" has been similarly treated as a short story. Some editors and critics, therefore, consider the volume to be a collection of short stories. I have, therefore, treated it once as a novel and then as a colleciton of short stories.

With *Big Woods*, I have analyzed only the two stories "A Bear Hunt," and "Race at Morning." Faulkner, himself, never gathered these two stories in any other collection of his short stories, and they appear elsewhere only in Blotner's posthumous *Uncollected Stories of William Faulkner*. "The Bear" and "The Old People" are treated elsewhere in this book.

The page numbers I supply refer to the texts listed in James B. Meriwether's "The Books of William Faulkner: A Revised Guide for Students and Scholars," *Mississippi Quarterly*, 35 (summer, 1982), 265-281, and the classification code that appears before the title is that assigned by Meriwether. For those works that either are not mentioned by Meriwether or that appeared after his article was published, I have used the most accessible texts. At the beginning of the analysis of each work, I cite the text to which page numbers refer. After the basic directory of characters and synopses of actions, I have included an "Index of Titles" and an "Index of Characters."

In his fiction, Faulkner mentions hundreds of real people: members of the Confederate and Union armies, American and international politicians and statesmen, athletes, philosophers, authors, historians, criminals, sports heroes, rich men, poor men, and Chickasaw Chiefs. I ignore these people except when Faulkner makes them actual characters in his fiction; such as, William Spratling in several stories, Saint Francis in *Mayday*, Faulkner himself in *Mosquitoes*, Robert Ingersol in "Beyond," and N. B. Forrest,who in The Bear" is mentioned, as is Eunice, in the ledgers, but who appears as an actual character in "My Grandmother Millard." Although I believe in my heart that George Peyton, in *The Reivers* is probably as much a real person as those other real persons, Jim Avant, Horace Lytle, and Paul Rainey, who are mentioned in the same section of the novel as Peyton, I have not been able to prove that he is a real person. Therefore, I list him as a character.

Why, one might ask, another directory of Faulkner characters when at least ten such directories already exist? In his "Introduction" to his own very good index of Faulkner's characters, *William Faulkner's Characters: An Index to the Published and Unpublished Fiction*, Thomas E. Dasher explains very convincingly why the serious student of Faulkner should avoid all other directories and indices that appeared before his own work. I agree entirely with Dasher's conclusion about these previous indices and guides: "Unfortunately, none of these potentially valuable reference works succeeds in satisfying the need for a reliable, accurate, and complete character index of the Faulkner field."[1] It seems superfluous to repeat his arguments here. It remains, simply, to state why we should not just stop at Dasher and not publish this lengthy volume. I think that this work goes far beyond Dasher's in at least four ways. (1) So far as it is possible, this work presents Faulkner's fiction in chronological rather than alphabetical order; and thereby permits the reader to make the kinds of studies that I have already mentioned in this "Introduction." (2) It offers a synopsis of action for each character who is even slightly involved in the plots rather than simply citing the pages on which the characters appear. (3) This book mentions all unnamed characters and gives a synopsis of the function of each in the plot, instead of identifying only a few. The only unnamed characters that I omit are those who have no connection with the plot at all, but serve merely as part of the background scene. (4) I hope that I have avoided mistakes like Dasher's reporting that the great Florenz Ziegfeld (whose name both Faulkner and Dasher misspell) raised horses instead of chorus girls; that Dan Patch is a "man in the horse business" rather than the great pacing horse; that Little Joe is the name of a crapshooter, rather than the number four on the dice; or that Sharps (even though misspelled) is a person and not a rifle; that the Bunden family of "Adolescence" is to be distinguished from the Bundren family of *As I Lay Dying*.

For these reasons I have written *Faulkner's World*.

No doubt mistakes have been made, and, while I hope that I have kept them to a minimum, I assume full responsibility for their presence.

Buffalo, New York

[1]Thomas E. Dasher, *William Faulkner's Characters: An Index to the Published and Unpublished Fiction* (New York and London: Garland Publishing, Inc., 1981), ix.

"Landing in Luck"

Written in 1919; first published in *The Mississippian* **(November 26, 1919).**

Pagination, in parentheses, to the following texts: Early Prose and Poetry, ed., Carvel Collins (Boston: Little Brown, 1962), 134 pp., and the reissue (London: Jonathan Cape, 1963).

_____Bessing (42): flight instructor (42); English (45).

_____Thompson (42): flying cadet (42); makes first solo flight (44); loses wheel on takeoff (46); runs out of gas (47); lands; plane noses over (48); becomes ill (49).

_____: cadet who lands plane alone (43).

_____: orderly (46).

_____: flight commander B flight (46).

_____: three others playing bridge with commanding officer (46).

_____Wharton (47).

_____: cadets in hotel (49).

"The Hill"

Written about 1922; first published in *The Mississippian* **(March 10, 1922).**

Pagination, in parentheses, to the following texts: Early Prose and Poetry. ed., Carvel Collins (Boston: Little Brown, 1962). 134 pp. and the reissue (London: Jonathan Cape, 1963).

_____: man climbs hill (90); descends (92).

Publication details follow the title of each sketch.

Pagination, in parentheses, to the following edition (New York: Random House, 1968), ed., Carvel Collins, 139 pp., and the reissue (London: Chatto & Windus, 1968).

"New Orleans"

Written in 1925; first published in *The Double Dealer* **(January–February, 1925).**

"Wealthy Jew"

_____: wealthy Jew; narrator of "Wealthy Jew" (3); old; makes plaint (3); rails against "mixed races;" loves three things: gold, marble, and purple; splendor, solidity, color (4).

"The Priest"

_____: priest; prays to God and the Virgin in garbled Latin: *"Ave Maria, deam gratiam"* (4–5).

"Frankie and Johnny"

Frankie (5)_____: Johnny's girl; kisses Johnny after he defends her; yellow hair; gray eyes (6).

Johnny (5)_____: young tough; fights drunk who insulted Frankie (6).

_____Ryan: cop (6).

_____: drunk hit by Johnny (6).

"The Sailor"

_____: sailor glad to be on land; thinks of women he has had all over the world (7).

"The Cobbler"

_____: cobbler (7); old; lives in backwater (8).

_____: woman whom cobbler saw dancing on green; his betrothed (8).

"The Longshoreman"

_____: longshoreman; black (9).

_____: woman whom longshoreman hit (9).

"The Cop"

_____: cop; as a boy, dreams of being policeman (10).

"The Beggar"

_____: beggar; lives with his disappointments (11-12).

"The Artist"

_____: artist; can never give the world that within him which is crying to be freed (12).

"Magdalen"

_____: prostitute; wears silk dress; there was once grief (12-13).

"The Tourist"

_____: the tourist (13); sees New Orleans as a courtesan (14).

"Mirrors of Chartres Street"

Written 1925; first published *Times-Picayune* (February 8, 1925).

_____: cripple; on crutches; begs from narrator (15); goes to movie; resists cop; claims rectangle he outlines on sidewalk is his room (16); one-legged; from railway accident (17); taken away in police wagon (18).

_____: first-person narrator; gives cripple a quarter (15).

_____: policeman who arrests cripple (16).

_____: bystanders (17).

Ed (18)   : driver of police wagon (17).

"Damon and Pythias Unlimited"

Written 1925; first published, *Times-Picayune* (February 15, 1925).

_____: "Iowa;" from Winterset (19).

_____: first-person narrator (19); stranger in New Orleans; has not seen races (20); with Morowitz, goes to race track in taxi (22-23); bets on races; wins (25).

_____ Morowitz (20): a round, very dirty man; a Jew; smacks

4

of stables and racing swipes; offers to take narrator to races; says he lives at the St. Charles (21); with narrator, goes to race track in taxi (22-23); his twenty dollar bill is Confederate (25); fights with McNamara over five dollars (27).

_____: taxi driver (21); takes Morowitz and narrator to race track (22).

_____: friend of Morowitz; works at Alhambra Baths (22).

_____ McNamara (25): jockey; has cough; cousin of Morowitz; "a thin lad;" certain death in his eyes; gives them tips on four races (25); admits that five dollars he wants narrator to give him will be his (26); tells narrator to meet him next day with five hundred dollars to make a killing (27).

_____: jockey in hospital (fictitious) (24).

"Home"

Written 1925; first published *Times-Picayune* (February 22, 1925).

_____: man who plays musical saw; passes Jean-Baptiste (32).

Jean-Baptiste (28)_____: has given his word on something apparently criminal (28); an immigrant from southern Europe; in Army (29); has debate with caution (30-31); speaks little English; has learned to handle high explosives after being wounded in war (32); when he hears music from saw, decides not to do what he was planning (33).

Pete (29)_____: friend of Jean-Baptiste (30).

_____: the "General" (29).

Tony (29)_____: "Tony the Wop" (29); friend of Jean-Baptiste (30).

_____: Jean-Baptiste's peasant mother (29).

_____: a policeman (30).

_____: priest who prays and blesses shells (32).

"Jealousy"

Written 1925; published *Times-Picayune* (March 1, 1925).

Antonio (35) '"Tono" (34)_____: restaurant owner (34); in jealous rage; threatens to kill wife (35); jealous of tall waiter; has been jealous for six months (36); questions waiter about him and his wife (37); after being slapped by waiter, threatens to kill him; admits to himself that he does not dare kill waiter; from Sicily; recently married; almost middle-aged; fat; ugly (38); decides to take wife to another city; becomes

5

rational; agrees to sell restaurant to young waiter (39); kills waiter (40).

_____: his wife; knits (34); threatens to leave husband if he has another fit of jealousy (37); young and pretty (38).

_____: waiter; Roman (34); says there is nothing between him and wife (37); slaps Antonio (38); buys restaurant (39); killed by Antonio as he buys farewell gift for wife (40).

_____: father of Antonio's wife (38).

_____: mother of Antonio's wife (39)

_____: policeman (40).

"Cheest"

Written 1925; first published *Times-Picayune* (April 5, 1925).

_____: owner of horses (41).

Jack Potter (42): first-person narrator (41); a jockey; meets girls in movie (42); buys them sodas; likes blonde; he and other jockey take them to dance; takes blonde's garter for luck (43); wears garter in race (44); wins (45).

_____: a swipe (42).

_____: blonde girl Potter meets at movies (42).

_____: blonde's friend (42).

_____: jockey that Potter brings on double date (43).

_____: bouncer at dance (44).

_____: other jockey in race; on favorite (45).

"Out of Nazareth"

Written 1925; first published *Times-Picayune* (April 12, 1925).

_____: first-person narrator (46); a writer (48).

_____ Spratling (46): an artist (46); with narrator, takes youth to lunch (48); gives him money (49-50).

_____: young man who looks like David; from midwest (47); hard worker; likes to sleep in hay; reads *Shropshire Lad* (48); gives narrator a story he wrote (50); 17 years old (53)

_____: first-person narrator in story within a story (50);

spends night in town camp (52-53).

_____: man who picks up this narrator (51).

_____: German doctor or actor in story within story (53).

_____: young Swede in story within story (53).

_____: Arkansan in story within story (53).

_____: son of Arkansan in story within story; 9 years old
(53).

"The Kingdom of God"

Written 1925; first published *Times-Picayune* (April 26, 1925).

_____: man in car (55); brother of idiot (56); fights with man
who hit the idiot; fights with policeman (58); threatens to kill
companion (59); repairs idiot's narcissus; arrested (60).

_____: second man in car (55); takes sack from car to
building (56-57); can not lift second sack by himself; asks idiot to help;
hits idiot (57); sacks contain liquor (59); arrested (60).

_____: idiot in car; eyes blue as cornflowers; holds narcissus
(55); roars when hit (58).

Jake (56)_____: idiot sometimes stays at his place (56).

_____: man in building (56).

_____: policeman (56).

_____: second policeman (58).

"The Rosary"

Written 1925; first published *Times-Picayune* (May 3, 1925).

_____ Harris (61): hates neighbor Juan Venturia and the song
called "The Rosary;" raises chickens (61); becomes ill (62); pneumonia (64);
dies (65).

Juan Venturia (61): neighbor of Harris; unmarried (61); hates Harris;
whistles "The Rosary" when Harris is near; answers ads in magazines in
Harris's name so that he receives goods C.O.D.; owns shop; when Harris
becomes ill, is afraid he will die before he punishes him properly (62);
goes to pawnshop (63); plays phonograph record of "The Rosary" outside
the window of Harris's room (65).

_____ Harris (61): wife or daughter who forces Harris to

7

attend musical functions (61).

"The Cobbler"

Written 1925; first published *Times-Picayune* **(May 10, 1925).**

_____: Italian cobbler; very old; born in Tuscany; tended goats as a youth; met girl daily (66); betrothed (67).

_____: girl who met young goatherd daily (66); betrothed (67); married signor; left rose for youth (68).

_____: "grand signor" with rings (68).

"Chance"

Written 1925; first published *Times-Picayune* **(May 17, 1925).**

_____: man on Royal Street (70); drinks with beggar (71); takes the five dollar gold piece that belongs to newsboy (73); bets the five dollars on a horse named Penny Wise at 40 to 1; it wins; makes two thousand dollars; buys car; drives it into river (74); arrested for speeding; fined ten dollars; has one penny left (75).

_____: man who begs for money (70); a seaman; fights with hero (71); finds penny (71-72).

_____: truck driver (71).

_____: ex-sailor (71).

_____: policeman (72).

_____: desk sergeant (72).

_____: policeman's sister (72).

_____: thief (72); steals five dollar gold piece from newspaper vendor (73).

_____: breathless pursuer (72).

_____: another policeman (73).

_____: newspaper vendor (73).

_____: friend who advises race winner (74).

_____: salesman who sells winner car (74).

"Sunset"

Written 1925; first published *Times-Picayune* (May 24, 1925).

Captain   Wallace (76): National Guard officer (76).

_____: black man; arrives in town; carries shotgun; afraid of traffic (76); seeks river; wants to go to Africa; buys ticket for ferry to Algiers (77); boards second ship; sleeps (79); thinking he is in Africa, climbs fence; shoots at dim figure; climbs haystack (81); sleeps; awakened; is shot; shoots back; wounds a man (82); shoots a watchman (83); found by search group; hallucinates (84); killed (85).

_____: white man who gives black man direction (77).

_____: white man who orders black man off boat (77).

_____: ticket seller (77).

_____: policeman (78).

Bob (78)_____: for whom black man works (78).

_____: Bob's family (78).

_____: white man near second ship (78); puts black man to work (79).

_____: another white man aboard ship; takes four dollars from black man; puts him ashore near Natchez (80); tells him Africa is a mile away (81).

_____: man who passes haystack (81).

_____: man who wakes black man on haystack; speaks a language that black man can not understand (82).

_____: black man who tries to intercept black man (82).

_____: watchman shot by black man (83).

"The Kid Learns"

Written 1925; first published *Times-Picayune* (May 31, 1925).

_____: first-person narrator (86).

Johnny (86) Gray (87): goes to aid of girl accosted by "the Wop;" hits "the Wop;" pulls gun on him (88); follows girl (89); takes her to Mrs. Ryan (90-91); meets "Little Sister Death" (91).

Otto (86)_____: Johnny's friend (86); hits "Wop" with billy (89).

9

_____: "the Wop;" rival of Johnny (87); accosts girl on street (88).

Mary (91)_____: girl accosted by "the Wop;" rescued by Johnny; flees (88-89).

_____Ryan (90): policeman (89) knows Johnny (90).

Mrs._____Ryan (90).

"The Liar"

Written 1925; first published *Times-Picayune* (July 26, 1925).

Ek (94)_____: man on porch of Gibson's store (92); small; with bald head; tells tall tales (93); raised in the hills (95); given first pair of shoes at 21; runs away; treed by hounds (96); observes murder of Starnes (100); shot by stranger (102).

Lafe (96)_____: man on porch of Gibson's store (92).

_____: man on porch of Gibson's store (92).

_____: man on porch of Gibson's store (92).

Will (94) Gibson (92): owner of store; slovenly and comfortable (92).

_____: stranger (92); dark-faced; buys cheese and crackers; sits on porch (94); at spring; whistles (98); kills Joe Starnes; dumps body in sink hole (101); empties box of rattlers on him (102); after Ek tells story of murder of Starnes, shoots him; escapes on passing train (102).

_____Mitchell (93): "Old Man" Mitchell; horse runs away (93).

Mrs._____Harmon (93): horse runs through her house (93).

_____Simpson (95): makers of liquor; brothers (95).

Ken Rogers (95): sheriff (95); goes to hill country with Ek (97).

_____: Ek's father (96).

Lem Haley (96): owns hounds that treed Ek (96).

Tim (97)_____: deputy sheriff (97).

Mrs._____Starnes (97): hill woman visited by sheriff; farmer's wife (97); runs with carpet bag to man at spring; kisses him (99).

10

Joe Starnes (97): hill man; farmer (97); finds wife kissing man at spring; fights with him; is killed (100).

_____: doctor who tends Ek (102).

"Episode"

Written, 1925; first published *Times-Picayune* **(August 16, 1925).**

_____: first-person narrator; from Mississippi (104).

Joe (105)_____: blind man; at least 60; begs at cathedral (104).

_____ : old woman with blind man; at least 60; toothless (104); wife of Joe (105); has had children; poses for Spratling (106).

_____ Spratling (104): wants to sketch woman (104); sketches her (106); face of Mona Lisa (107).

_____ : passerby who helps blind man (105).

"Country Mice"

Written 1925; first published *Times-Picayune* **(September 20, 1925).**

_____: first-person narrator (108).

_____: bootlegger (108); likes to "air off" (drive fast in country); believes it is unlucky to carry a watch (109); Italian (110); tells narrator story (110 ff.); tries to bribe Justice of the Peace (112); pays a thousand dollars for plane (114); afraid of flying (115); flies with pilot and whisky to New Haven (116 ff.); sells plane back to pilot for one hundred dollars (118); finds water in bottles instead of whisky (119).

Gus (112)_____: bootlegger's brother; goes to Montreal for whisky (111).

_____: man who suggests selling whisky at Yale; goes to Montreal for whisky (111).

Joe (115)_____: man who accompanies bootlegger to Yale (111).

_____: highjackers (112).

_____: small town policeman who arrests Gus (112).

_____ Gilman (120): Justice of the Peace (112).

_____ Gilman (120): deputy bribed by bootlegger's partner; twin (113).

_____ Gilman (118): man from Boston; owns airplane; twin

11

brother of deputy (113) wants a thousand dollars for plane (114); buys plane back for one hundred dollars (118).

"Yo Ho and Two Bottles of Rum"

Written 1925; first published *Times-Picayune* **(September 27, 1925).**

Freddie Ayers (122): the mate on the *Diana*; British (122); a great talker; sleeps with eyes open; drunk daily; kills mess boy (123) by accident; a racist (124); hits him with a stick of wood, thinking he was the bosun (125); wants to bury Yo Ho at sea, but crew insists he be buried on land (126); with three others, attempts to kill more of Chinese crew (130).

_____: Captain of the *Diana*; Welsh (122).

_____: Chief Engineer; Scottish (122); drinks whisky intended for Yo Ho's grave (129).

_____: third mate; Eusian [sic, Eurasian?] (123).

_____: owner's agents (123).

Yo Ho (123): mess boy; killed by Ayers (123); body presumably buried by Chinese crew (131).

_____: the bosun (124).

_____: second mate (128).

_____: assistant to engineer (128); finds food and whisky put in baskets to be buried with Yo Ho (129).

Bucky (129)_____.

"Royal Street"

Originally written 1925; revised by Faulkner and dated October 29, 1926; first published partially in 1973, and fully in 1977.

Pagination, in parentheses, to the following text: Leland H. Cox, Jr. Sinbad in New Orleans: Early Short Fiction by William Faulkner: An Annotated Edition; doctoral dissertation (University of South Carolina, May, 1977); pp. 151-163. This is a revision of all but one ("The Tourist") of the eleven sketches of "New Orleans" from The Double Dealer (January-February, 1925) with "Hong Li," which first appeared in the Mississippi Quarterly, 26 (summer, 1973), added. "Hong Li" appeared again in A Faulkner Miscellany, ed., James B. Meriwether (Jackson: University Press of Mississippi, 1974), p. 144.

"New Orleans"

"Wealthy Jew"

_____: wealthy Jew; narrator of "Wealthy Jew;" loves three things: gold, marble, and purple--splendor, solidity, color; harangue on mixed races (151); says no soil is foreign to his people (152).

"The Priest"

_____: priest; has erotic thoughts; prays to Mary in Latin (152-153)

"Frankie and Johnny"

Frankie (153)_____: girl; accosted by drunk; defended by Johnny; kisses him; yellow hair; gray eyes (140).

Johnny (153)_____: young tough; defends Frankie from drunk (139).

_____Ryan (139): a cop.

_____: drunk; accosts Frankie; beaten up by Johnny (139).

"The Sailor"

_____: sailor; glad to be ashore; dreams of all the women he has had throughout the world (155)

"The Longshoreman"

_____: longshoreman; black; has hit a woman (156).

_____: woman hit by longshoreman (156).

"The Cobbler"

13

_____: cobbler; old; lives in backwater; from Tuscany; betrothed to a girl in his youth (157-158)

_____: young girl to whom cobbler was betrothed as a young man (157).

"The Cop"

_____: a cop; as a youth, wanted to be a patrolman (158-160)

"The Beggar"

_____: beggar; thinks of how he viewed life as a boy and contrasts it to the present (160).

"The Artist"

_____: the artist (160); knows that he can never free that which cries within him to be freed (161).

"Magdalen"

_____: a prostitute; thinks of her life (161); once there was love; once there was grief (162).

"Hong Li"

Hong Li (1, 62): thinks how honey becomes oversweet and then bitter; misfortune is man's greatest gift; hapiness rots; thinks bitterly longingly of a woman (163).

"And Now What's to Do?"

Written, perhaps, between 1925 and about 1928 or 1929; first published, in *The Mississippi Quarterly*, **26 (summer, 1973), 399-402; reprinted in** *A Faulkner Miscellany*, **1974, pp. 145-148.**

Pagination, in parentheses, to the following edition, A Faulkner Miscellany ed., James B. Meriwether (University Press of Mississippi: Jackson Mississippi, 1974).

_____: young man; grows up in livery stable (145); skilled at dice; starts to drink as adolescent; at 16, begins to have inferiority complex because of father's business; learns about women by listening to black hostlers; WW I; skilled at dice at 18; makes twenty or thirty dollars each Sunday (146); after girl gets into trouble, leaves on freight train to Ohio; has sex with women but seems repelled by it; meets man in bar who owns pacer (147); drifts south with him (148).

_____: his great-grandfather; came from Tennessee where he had killed a man; killed by pistol (145).

_____: his grandfather; wastes inheritance in politics; lawyer (145).

_____: young man's father; loves horses; owns livery stable (145); every Christmas, gives pints of whisky to blacks who work for him (146).

_____: night man in livery stable (146).

_____: girl who gets into trouble (147).

_____: man whom young man meets in Ohio bar; has pacer (147).

15

Written 1925; originally titled *Mayday;* **first published February 25, 1926.**

Pagination in parentheses for the following editions: (New York: Boni & Liveright, 1926), 319 pp.; (New York: Horace Liveright, 1931); (Garden City, New York: Sun Dial Press, 1937); (New York: Liveright Publishing Corporation, 1951); and (New York: Liveright, 1970), paperback.

Julian Lowe (7): recently a flying cadet of WWI (7) gets drunk on train with Gilligan (19); from San Francisco (23); joins Gilligan and Mrs. Powers in taking care of Mahon; at hotel gets drunk with Gilligan (37); wakes from his drunken sleep in same room with Mahon and romantically envies Mahon his wound, his wings, and his glory (45); 19 years old (50); had forty-seven hours of flying time and would have earned his wings in two more weeks; tries to tell Mrs. Powers of his love for her (50); tells of his romantic envy of Mahon; agrees to go home to his mother after Mrs. Powers comforts him (55); writes to Mrs. Powers from train (internal date of novel, April 2, 1919) (103); writes another letter to her showing a great interest in other girls (153); another letter to Mrs. Powers showing interest in a girl and signed "Your sincere friend" (186-187); sends another letter revealing that the girl he is interested in is being wooed by another (246-247); sends two more letters (277, 280); and then a post card (285); Mrs. Powers's letter about her marriage and Mahon's death returned "address unknown" (315).

Yaphank (7) Joe Gilligan (8): soldier veteran of WWI; drinking on train (7); forces Lowe to drink with him (10); wants to leave train when conductor tells him to behave; throws companion's suitcase out window (13); tries to push his companion out window (15); leaves Hank White on train at Buffalo (20); tells police that two drunken civilians are the two wanted crazy men; runs away with Lowe (21-22); private (23); brings Mahon back to seat with Lowe; promises to take care of him (26); with Mrs. Powers, Lowe, and Mahon, leaves train and takes hotel rooms (35-36); announces that Mahon is not only going blind, but that he is going to die (39); says that Mahon is engaged; has read his papers (40); 32 years old (41); asks Mrs. Powers to marry him (42); sleeps curled up in his clothes at the foot of her bed after they decide to take Mahon home (44); arrives with Mahon to meet his father (93); in love with Mrs. Powers (161-165); reads Gibbons' [sic] "History of Rome" to Mahon (169); accompanies Mahon to Mrs. Worthington's dance (196); watches Cecily dancing with various partners (200); resents Cecily's changing her mind to marry Mahon (250); after Mrs. Powers's marriage to Mahon, he is bitter and sad, but Mrs. Powers appeals to him to continue to minister to Mahon and he loses the bitterness (279); continues to sleep on his cot at the foot of Mahon's bed (282); when he finishes reading Gibbon to Mahon, he begins Rousseau's *Confessions* (285); chases Jones to throw him out of the rectory grounds, but loses him in the garden (290); refuses Mrs. Powers's offer to live without marriage; changes his mind and jumps back on train; when he fails to see her, assumes she got off and gets off too, only to see her on the rear platform moving out of sight (307-309); as he walks, meets fisherman who gives him a drink of corn whisky (310); determines to find her (311); returns to rectory; drags Jones down from wall near Emmy's window; fights him (313-314); offers to stay with the rector; then tells him all about Mrs. Powers (317); walks with rector and hears the yearning of blacks singing in a church (318-319).

Hank White (16): Gilligan's drunken companion on train; sits on floor (9); starts to jump out the window after his suitcase; sobers and comes back in to train (14); passes out on floor; stays on train at Buffalo (19).

Captain   Bleyth (9): RAF pilot (9).

_____: conductor on train (11); tells porter to wire ahead to Buffalo that two crazy men are on the train (15).

Henry (15)_____: the train porter; black (15).

_____ Schluss (16): one of the civilians appointed by the conductor to look after the soldiers (15); sells women's undergarments (16); gets drunk and leaves train at Buffalo (20).

_____: the other civilian (15).

_____: woman on train (19).

_____: policeman in Buffalo (20).

Ed (21)_____: second policeman (21).

_____: porter on second train; refuses to get Gilligan glasses; Gilligan calls him "Claude" and "Othello" (24); Gilligan calls him "Ernest;" tends Mahon solicitously (26 ff.); from Georgia (34).

Donald (34) Mahon (30): young man badly scarred across the brow; wears British flying officer's uniform; met by Gilligan on train (25); from Georgia (26); has withered right hand (27); going blind (28); son of a preacher (43); fails to recognize his father when Gilligan and Mrs. Powers take him home (109); fails to recognize Emmy (110); remembers nothing before his wound (118); is aware that he is going to marry Cecily Saunders (246); married to Mrs. Powers after Cecily Saunders fails to appear for the marriage (278); becomes bedridden (285); has a flashing vision of the day he was shot down; sees his father momentarily and tells him, "That's how it happened." (293-294); dies (294).

Mrs.   Henderson: woman on train who inquires about Mahon's health (31).

Mrs. Richard (36) Powers (34) Margaret (51) Mrs. Mahon (278): woman, companion of Mrs. Henderson on train when she inquires about Mahon (31); returns to join Gilligan in caring for Mahon; takes a drink with them (33); from Alabama (34); wears wedding ring (34); a

18

widow whose husband was killed in France; they had been married for only three days before he left for France; she wrote to tell him marriage was over; leaves the train with Gilligan, Lowe, and Mahon and they take a hotel suite (35-36); when Gilligan asks her to marry him, says she would marry him if she married anyone (42); comforts Lowe; lets him assume they are engaged, but sends him home to his mother; she is 24 (51 ff.); arrives to notify Rev. Mahon that his son is returning (81); comforts Emmy after Mahon fails to recognize her (110); persuades Saunders to have Cecily visit Mahon (118-119); gives Emmy a new dress and other clothes; sits and sews with her and gets her to talk about Mahon (123 ff.); to get specialist to agree to tell his diagnosis to her instead of to the rector, she tells him she is engaged to Mahon (154); she and Gilligan, walking through the woods, see Robert Saunders and two other boys swimming naked (159); tells Gilligan about her marriage; senses that he wants to kiss her; kisses him (161-165); accompanies Mahon and Gilligan to Mrs. Worthington's dance (196); dances with Madden (207) and then with all the other ex-soldiers who recognize her name as that of their former officer but say nothing of her husband (210); threatens to have Gilligan trounce Jones after he tries to seduce her (249); visits Cecily presumably to try to talk her out of the marriage (263-268); watching Emmy feeding Mahon, she realizes that Emmy is the woman for him to marry (277); after Cecily breaks her engagement, tells Dr. Mahon that she is going to marry Mahon herself (277); they are married (278); says that Gilligan and Emmy should have married Mahon because they continue their solicitous care (282); after Mahon's funeral, comforts Dr. Mahon, but refuses to stay (299-300); walks with Gilligan while waiting for her train; kisses him "with slow fire" but refuses to marry him; says that all the men she marries die; asks Gilligan to live with her without marriage; leaves on train (302-307).

Januarius Jones 56): lately a fellow of Latin in a small college (56); stumbles into a scrub pail before lunch with rector (65); changes his wet trousers for a pair of the rector's (66); sees death in the face of Mahon in the photograph shown by his father (67); determines to conquer Cecily Saunders (72); feels her thigh as they move through a door (74); at lunch, shocks her and the rector by talk of sex (74); when rector leaves, tries to feel her breasts; rumples her clothes; she yields coldly to a kiss; then, after he apologizes, she permits him to kiss her (79-80); after Cecily returns, he tries once more to caress her, but she escapes and locks him in the room (91); takes Cecily home after she faints on Mahon's arrival (97); comes upon Emmy in the kitchen and hugs her; she threatens to burn him with the iron; he retreats (134-135); attends the Worthington dance; corners Cecily and tells her that Mahon is there with Mrs. Powers (202-203); after Cecily visits Mahon, tries to make love to Cecily, but she escapes (209); at lunch at the Saunders' home, lets Robert assume that he was a soldier in the war (219); after lunch, carresses Cecily and then proposes to her and assures her that he will not tell about her meeting with George (224-226); asks her to leave him alone and not ask about what he heard of the conversation between her and George (228-229); as he is forcing her to look at him, they are interrupted by Mrs. Saunders who enters the room with innane chatter (230); (Jones has no certain mother and "might have claimed any number of fathers;" he grew up in a

Catholic orphanage) (230-231); as he leaves, tells Cecily that he will return that night (232); he and George Farr fight outside Cecily's house at midnight (239); pretends to go home, but returns to her house only to be discovered there by George who has also returned; they sit on the curb, then sleep until dawn, and go home (241-244); attempts to seduce Mrs. Powers (249- 250); attempts to make love to Emmy, but she slams a door on his hand (253); begins to be obsessed with a desire for Emmy (253); enters the house after the funeral procession starts, finds Emmy in tears, kisses her and leads her off to her room (297); fights with Gilligan who finds him at Emmy's window (313-314).

Dr. (57) Joe (65) Mahon: the rector (56); engages in a rambling talk with Jones and invites him to lunch (64); father of Mahon (67); talks of his son in the past tense (68); implies that Mahon has had an affair with Emmy (68); leaves the lunch table; returns to announce that his son (whom he had thought dead) is to return (81); cannot see that his son is dying (117); Episcopal (261); wakes from a sleep and runs to son's side as Mahon has a vision of the day he was wounded (292); when Gilligan tells him about Mrs. Powers, after she has left, he says, "Circumstance moves in marvellous ways, Joe. God is circumstance, Joe." (317).

Emmy (65)   : servant girl to rector; addresses him as "Uncle Joe" (65); has had an affair with Mahon (68); dissolves in tears when she learns that Mahon fails to recognize her (110); daughter of an alcoholic house painter (120); in despair because Mahon does not recognize her (121); tells Mrs. Powers of her childhood love for Mahon and of the night of their love affair and of her leaving home (124-129); worked for a dressmaker until Dr. Mahon came to take her home after Mahon (who has told him of their affair) had gone to war (128-129); slips up to Mahon and quietly carresses his head (166); slams door on Jones's hand (253); feeds Mahon after his blindness (270); when Mrs. Powers asks her if she would marry Mahon, says no, but then inwardly says yes and vainly waits for her to ask again (273-274); after the wedding, continues to care for Mahon (282); in grief, refuses to attend Mahon's funeral (296); allows Jones to kiss her and lead her to her room (297); visits the pool at night where she and Mahon used to swim (300).

Cecily (66) Saunders (70) Farr (281): was engaged to Mahon before the war (73); lets Jones kiss her (56); tells George of Mahon's return; reveals that she does not want to marry Mahon but feels she must; kisses George (85-87); when she sees Mahon's scarred face, screams and faints; strikes her head on the door jamb (94); completely collapses; Jones escorts her home (96); says she never wants to see Mahon again, but after her father threatens her, decides to visit him (133); at the rectory, rushes in, mistakes Jones for Mahon, and embraces him (137); angered because Mrs. Powers observes her error; visits Mahon and kisses him (138); feels that Mahon is responsible for the error; feels he has humiliated her before Mrs. Powers (138); tells her father that she will not return to Mahon because of the imagined insult; he forbids her to see George Farr; she goes to a neighbor's house to phone George (140-143); meets George downtown (143-144); sends him a note asking him to come to her house after her parents have retired (146); has an affair with him

(147); then avoids him (148); at the Worthington dance, visits Mahon and kisses him in the car, after Mrs. Powers leaves them alone (208); meets George in drugstore by appointment; kisses him; says she loves him, and informs him that she is not pregnant (214); sees Jones as she leaves; wonders how much he has heard; leaves with him (216-218); takes him home for lunch (218); later lets him caress her to learn how much he has heard (224-228); begs him not to return that night (232); after Jones leaves, she wants her father's help (233); lies awake at night, and next day hysterically visits Mahon, embraces him, and promises to marry him immediately (244-245); tells her mother that she has to marry Mahon; then resents her mother's interpretation of the remark (259-261); visits Dr. Mahon; tells him she is going away and that she is not a "good woman" any more (276); leaves in a car (277); is married to George Farr by a Catholic priest in Atlanta (281); returns to town with her husband as Mrs. Powers leaves (306).

George (77) Farr (92): young man who calls for Cecily at rectory (84); persuades her to go with him in the car after she tells him of Mahon's return (85); meets Cecily at night and has an affair with her (147); when they meet in town afterward, she tells him not to touch her (148); enviously watches Cecily dancing with Lee Rivers (195); just as he gives up hope of seeing Cecily again, receives a note and meets her in the drug store 213-214); as he hides outside her house that night, Jones arrives; wrestles with Jones; both hide when Mr. Saunders comes out on the porch above them (239); leaves with Jones; returns; finds Jones has returned; they outwait each other (241-244); has been drunk for a week after learning that Cecily is to be married (268); while drunk, gets a phone call from Cecily asking him to come to her immediately (270); is married to Cecily Saunders (281).

Mrs. Minnie (98) Saunders (95): Cecily's mother; wants Cecily to describe Mahon's scar (96); tries to dissuade Cecily from the marriage (259); interprets Cecily's answer to mean that she is pregnant by Mahon (260).

Robert Saunders (95): Cecily's younger brother; anxious to discuss Mahon's scar (95); goes to rector's house to see scar; Gilligan tells him to try the next day (100-101); brings his friends around to see Mahon's scar (149); threatens to get even with Mrs. Powers for seeing him swimming nude (159); eavesdrops on Gilligan and Mrs. Powers; sees Mrs. Powers kiss Gilligan (160-164); tells his sister that Mrs. Powers loves Mahon and has kissed Gilligan (165); observes the funeral procession (295); suddenly refuses to play ball with a friend, runs home to find his mother, and weeps in the arms of the black cook (298).

Mr. Robert (97) Saunders (96): Cecily's father (96); a Catholic (98); has never wanted daughter's marriage to Mahon but agreed to it (98); after debate with his wife, tries vainly to call off the engagement (114); visits Mahon (115); is persuaded by Mrs. Powers to have Cecily visit Mahon in an effort to inspirit him (118-119); urges Cecily to visit Mahon; when she refuses, treats her roughly and threatens not to let her see George Farr (131-132); after Cecily promises to marry Mahon, visits Dr.

Mahon to object, but his courage fails; they agree to see Mrs. Saunders (254-256).

Tobe (97)_____: black servant of the Saunders (97).

Dr._____Gary (99): another suitor of Cecily (99); likes to waltz; small, bald, dapper; served in French hospital in WWI (166-167); announces bluntly that Mahon is blind (167); attends dance at Mrs. Worthington's (193).

Harrison Maurier (99): from Atlanta, another suitor of Cecily (99).

_____: black male servant of Rev. Mahon (104).

_____: father of Emmy; an alcoholic house painter (120); beats his first wife; is beaten by his second (120).

_____: mother of Emmy, died in childbirth of her fourth son (120).

_____: second wife of Emmy's father; a shrew; beats him (120).

Mrs._____Miller (128): dressmaker in whose shop Emmy works after she leaves home (128).

_____: doctor (perhaps Dr. Gary; see p. 167); general practitioner; predicts Mahon's blindness (129).

_____: stranger with Dr. Mahon (136).

Dr._____Baird (156): specialist from Atlanta (153); says there is no hope for Mahon; that something he has not completed in his past life that he does not consciously remember is keeping him alive and that he will die when the spark is no longer fed (154-155).

[Carolina] Cal'line, Callie (170) Nelson (179): Mahon's former mammy; returns to help nurse him (170).

Corporal Loosh (170) Nelson (171): her grandson; had known Mahon formerly (171); salutes as Mahon's funeral passes (296).

Captain_____Green (173): raised a company; now dead (173); at Brest he is transferred from his company for training (174); thanks Madden for helping him cure venereal disease (175).

First Sergeant (173) Rufus (194) Madden (173): Green's friend from civilian life (178) wounded in battle; loses picture of his girl who had already maried a lieutenant of the staff of a college ROTC unit (179); thinks of the man who killed Lieutenant Powers when Mrs. Burney talks of her son (186); attends dance at Mrs. Worthington's (191); at dance Gilligan introduces him to Mrs. Powers; he remembers the man in the act of killing Lieutenant Powers (202).

_____: orderly who delivers Captain Green's transfer orders (175).

_____: Captain Green's replacement as company commander; former college instructor (177).

Lieutenant (177) Richard (36) Powers (34): shot to death by one of his own men who became hysterical on his first exposure to fighting (179).

_____: soldier who shoots Lt. Powers (179).

_____: boy who dies in shell hole beside Sergeant Madden; had been shoe salesman at home (179).

Mrs. _____ Burney (179): her son's death advances her social status in town; visits Mahon; asks Madden why he did not take better care of her son (185); talks maliciously to Mrs. Powers (258).

_____ Burney: her husband, carpenter (180).

Dewey Burney (181): their son; killed in WWI; had been a friend of Mahon (181); had been indicted for stealing sugar but permitted to enlist (184).

Mrs. _____ Worthington (180): speaks to Mrs. Burney after her son's death (180); sends her car to bring Mahon, Gilligan, and Mrs. Powers to listen to music (187).

Mrs. _____ Wardle (181): speaks to Mrs. Burney about death of her son (181).

Mrs. _____ Mitchell (182): also speaks to Mrs. Burney (182).

_____: Mrs. Worthington's black driver (180).

_____: Mrs. Worthington's "colorless" male cousin; has false teeth and no occupation; hit in the mouth with an ax in a dice game in Cuba during Spanish-American War (187).

James Dough (189): a corporal-pilot for two years in a French chase escadrille (189); has artificial leg; talks to a girl at dance (189); visitor to Charlestown (190); nephew of Mrs. Wardle (192).

_____: black cornetist, leader of dance band at Worthington's (190).

Lee Rivers (190): young man who asks Cecily to dance at Mrs. Worthington's; has had a year at Princeton; asks Madden to talk to Dough to release Cecily for dancing (192).

23

_____: girl at dance; talks to George Farr (195).

_____: companion of George Farr; drinks with him; a soda clerk (195).

_____: short-skirted girl who dances with Dr. Gary (199).

Mrs. _____ Coleman (233): Mrs. Saunders intends to visit her (233).

_____: the Saunders' cook, wife of Tobe (238); comforts Robert (299).

_____: two companions who drink with George Farr (269).

_____: proprietor of dirty restaurant where George drinks; announces Cecily's telephone call (269)..

_____: middle-aged drug clerk who watches George trying to sober up (270).

_____: Baptist minister who marries Mrs. Powers and Mahon (278).

_____: subaltern with three silver V's on his sleeve; part of Mahon's funeral guard (295).

_____: Boy Scout bugler at Mahon's funeral (295).

_____: Robert Saunders' friend with whom he refuses to play after seeing the funeral (298).

_____: black boy whom Gilliigan pays to watch Mrs. Powers's bags at the station (302).

_____: fisherman who gives Gilligan whisky to drink (310).

Willard (318)_____: neighbor of the rector(318).

Action takes place in Charlestown, Georgia.

Written from about August 21, 1925 to sometime after October 15, 1925; first published in 1983. Various drafts were entitled "Elmer and Myrtle," "Growing Pains," and "Portrait of Elmer Hodge."

Pagination, in parentheses, to the following editions: Mississippi Quarterly, 36, No. 3 (Summer, 1983), 337-447, edited with "Note on the Text" by Dianne L. Cox; foreword by James B. Meriwether. Second set of pagination to William Faulkner, Elmer (Northport, Alabama: The Seajay Press, 1983). ed., Dianne L. Cox, with foreword by James B. Meriwether. [Subsequent to printing of the text, The Seajay Press was moved to Columbia, S. C.]

<u>Elmer (343, 3) Ellie (354, 14) Hodge (356, 16)</u>: on freighter approaching Italy (343, 3); Texan; wants to paint 344, 4); fondles tubes of paint (tubes are "virgin yet at the same time pregnant") and brushes "with a brooding maternity;" views the world as "thick-bodied and female;" house burned when he was five; fears red horror; hates to be seen unclothed (345, 5); as a child, sleeps with sister; does not mind being naked with her; sees his sister once after she disappears; youngest in family (346, 6); separated from mother at fire and, naked, comforted by another woman (346- 347, 6-7); adores sister, Jo (348, 8); at 11, still wants to sleep with sister (348-349, 8-9); watches sister undress for bed; has curling yellow hair (351, 11); likes to touch naked sister when she is asleep (352-353, 12-13); with her permission, feels her naked body in bed (353, 13); shocked at Jo's disappearance (354-355, 14-15); receives box of crayons in mail from Jo; when he is 17, sees Jo for last time; refers to ill-fitting uniform and nurses' uniforms, WW I; smokes expensive pipe he does not like (356, 16); on deck, thinks about girls; has bastard son in Houston; met Myrtle at a dance (359, 19); has been in WW I (360, 20); can not dance; proposes marriage to Myrtle (361, 21); returns from war to Houston to find parents gone; note left by mother (362, 22); finds father; learns his mother is dead; visits mother's grave (363, 23); decides that now he can paint; flashback: at 14, in fourth grade, in Jonesboro, "inevitably developed a fine sexless passion for the teacher" (365, 25); adores tall beautiful boy; is cruelly tripped and hurt by him as the boy-God cries, "Fine;" stocky lad inquires of his hurt (366-367, 26-27); in fourth grade, receives box of water colors; paints on wrapping paper and newspaper (367, 27); loses respect for boy-God; transfers devotion to his teacher; she saves wrapping paper for him; walks to school and home with her after school (368, 28); suddenly, she stops him from this activity (369, 29); after boy-God tells him facts of life, is shocked; that evening gets undressed in the dark; decides not to get married (370, 30); at his teacher's invitation, goes to her house at night; flees as she touches him (371-373, 31-33); when family moves again, meets new girl [Velma] (373, 33); goes to Velma's house to borrow cup of sugar; chases her to barn where he finds her in hayloft (374-375, 34-35); flashback: as a child, collects cigar stubs; tells his mother he eats them; takes medicine for hookworm (375-376, 35-36); likes other phallic things: buggy whip and factory smokestack (376, 36); grows big; continues to draw on wrapping paper: smokestacks, armless people and two arms from a pedestal base;

later, when he becomes aware of women, draws "a Dianalike girl with impregnable integrity;" recalls first sex with Velma (378, 38); wounded in war (379-380, 39-40); on troopship, in hand grenade drill, kills soldier next to him, and receives wound in back (381, 41); in hospital, in England, begins to recover, and is sent back home (382, 42); in New York, meets fat woman who gives him entree to art galleries; now walks with yellow stick (382-383, 42-43); goes to New Orleans; sees sister Jo in crowd at Liberty Bond speech; tries vainly to reach her (383-384, 43-44); arrives in Venice (413, 73); lands in jail (414-415, 74-75); flashback: cashes traveller's check for 25,000 lire (416, 76); gets drunk with Second Officer (417-418, 77-78); feels woman's body (418, 78); dances with her; passes out (419, 79); has nightmare (419-421, 79-81); wakes in gondola, accompanied by Second Officer, the woman, and gondolier (422, 82); taken by them to cafe; continues to drink; arrested (423, 83); taken away drunk in gondola (423-424, 83-84); in jail, communicates with one prisoner who takes note from Elmer to Second Officer (425, 85); arrested for stamping on bank note with picture of king on it; released by Chief Engineer (426, 86); goes with Angelo to Milan; vows never to visit Venice again (426-427, 86-87); buys Angelo a new suit and shoes (427, 87); [Break in story.] with Angelo, in Paris, drinks beer on Montparnasse (429, 89); [Break in story.] Elmer is not interested in marrying Myrtle (431, 91); flashback: Elmer's bastard son in Houston; takes girl (Ethel) to movies (432-433, 92-93); has sex with her; when she tells him that she is pregnant, suggests that they marry; is told that she is going to marry Grover (433-434, 93-94); leaves her to go to WW I (435, 95); dreams of finding "a fierce proud Dianalike girl;" marriage, and a child (435-436, 95-96); dreams of going back to mother of his bastard son (Ethel), but does not (436-437, 96-97); pumps gas in gasoline station; meets Ethel as she arrives in car; is introduced to her husband; she gives him address (438, 98); is short-changed twenty-five cents by husband for gas; shocked that his former relationship with Ethel is not resumed; expects her to return to him alone (439, 99); fantasizes her return to him with their child (440-441, 100-101); decides to visit her after she does not come to him; takes trolley to her house, but her husband's face "masking a cruelty feminine and dangerous" comes to his mind; walks past the house; writes her a letter instead, registered mail, return receipt requested; no reply (442-443, 102-103); she and husband return to gasoline station; she asks him why he has not been to see them; then Elmer meets Myrtle; his spine hurts occasionally; Myrtle sails away and he has an image of "a Dianalike girl dark and fierce and proud" (443, 103); visits Ethel; tells her he is going to become a painter (445-446, 105-106,); asks to see her baby (446, 106); sees his son, now five years old; child screams (477, 137). [End of typescript.]

_____: bo'sun (343, 3).

_____: captain of freighter; New Englander; builds model ships, paints ships on backs of charts (343-344, 3-4).

_____: bright cold saleswoman in New Orleans who sells Elmer a book by Clive Bell, Elie Faure's *The Outline of Art* and six novels (344, 4); and a set of oils (356, 16).

_____: Chief Engineer; from Texas; goes to sea in tennis shoes and stiff-brimmed straw hat; works crossword puzzles (344, 4); gets Elmer out of jail (426, 86).

_____: steward on freighter (344, 4).

_____ Hodge (356, 16): Elmer's father (345, 5); an "inverted I O with hookworm and a passionate ambitious wife for gad-fly" (355, 15); after endless moves, inherits two thousand dollars; buys house in Texas, after Elmer has gone to war (378-379, 38-39); notifies Elmer of mother's death (379-380, 39-40).

_____ Hodge (356, 16): Elmer's mother (345, 15; "kind fretful bitter loving woman" (355, 15); dies after Elmer goes to war (356, 16).

_____ Hodge (356, 16): Elmer's older brother (346, 6); deserts family in Paris, Tennessee; gets job in livery stable (347, 7).

_____ Hodge (356, 16): Elmer's eldest brother; leaves family to go to St. Louis (347-348, 17-18).

Jo (346, 6,) Jo-Addie (348, 8) Hodge (356, 16): Elmer's sister (346, 6); sleeps with Elmer; vanishes between two of family's moves; seen once again by Elmer (346, 6); disappears at Jonesboro, Arkansas when Elmer is 11; thin-legged at 16; breast is nil (348, 8); agrees to sleep with Elmer just one night when he is 11 (348-349, 8-9); tells Elmer he does not have to put his hands on folks to like them (349, 9); undresses for bed in front of Elmer; straight black hair (351, 11); gets into bed with Elmer naked (352-353, 12-13); gives Elmer permission to feel her naked body; tells him "when you want to do anything, you do it, Hear?" next morning disappears (354, 14); sends Elmer box of crayons (356, 16); seen by Elmer at Liberty Bond speech in New Orleans (383-384, 43-44).

_____: woman who comforts Elmer at fire (346-347, 6-7).

Lafe (347, 7) _____: companion of woman who comforts Elmer (346-347, 6-7).

_____: man in livery stable in Paris, Tennessee (347, 7).

Mr. _____ Bingham (414, 74): Second Officer on ship (357, 17); ordered by captain not to let "barbers" [vendors of pornographic postcards] aboard ship in harbor of Venice (414, 74); accompanies Elmer and woman (prostitute?) on drinking bout (417-423, 77-83); disappears as Elmer is arrested (423, 83).

Myrtle (357, 17) Monson (361, 21): meets Elmer at dance; vulgar; short legs (359, 19); nose too short, blue eyes too candid, brow too low and broad; two years in Virginia, one year in Texas state university; goes with mother to Europe in 1922 for finishing (360, 20); sips wine at dinner on board ship (388, 48); argues with mother about drinking; getting fat (389-390, 49-50); attracted to ship's officer (391, 51); teaches him American dances; flirts with him at night; after undressing, kisses him through the port (392-393, 52-53); arrives in France (394, 54); from school in Switzerland, notifies mother that she is coming to Rome (408, 68); complains to her mother about life at Lausanne (411, 71).

Mrs.　　　Monson (361, 21): Myrtle's mother (357, 17); goes to Europe with daughter (360, 20); from Kansas; a teetotaller (386, 46); on board ship with Myrtle, drinks two glasses of wine a day (388, 48); argues with daughter about drinking (389-390, 49-50); decides to stay in Rome while Myrtle is in finishing school (391, 51); in Rome decides to join Church of England (395, 55); joins Roman Catholic Church (397-398, 57-58); when Myrtle writes that she is coming to Rome from Switzerland, invites canon (George Bleyth) and his brother (Lord Wohleden) to tea to meet daughter (408, 68).

Mr.　　　Monson (361, 21): Myrtle's father; wealthy from oil; has cabaret performer as mistress (360, 20); accompanies wife and daughter to Europe (386, 46); but [?] remains in America (395, 55).

Joe (358, 18)　　　: helmsman on freighter; college football man (358, 18).

　　　[Hodge?]　　　: Elmer's bastard son in Houston (359, 19).

Ethel (437, 97)　　　: mother of Elmer's son (354, 14); older than Elmer (433, 93); tells Elmer of marriage plans; has sex with him; becomes pregnant; says that she is going to marry Grover (434, 94); meets Elmer at gasoline station where he works; introduces him to her husband; gives Elmer her address (438, 98).

Gloria (360, 20)　　　: Myrtle's father's girl friend, a cabaret performer in New Orleans; has daughter somewhere (360, 20).

　　　: New Orleans barber; trims and waxes Myrtle's father's mustasche (361, 21).

　　　: real estate man in Houston; has note left for Elmer by his mother (362, 22).

　　　: "young pretty jewess smelling of toilet water rather than soap" in real estate office (362, 22).

　　　: tall, beautiful boy-God that Elmer meets when he is 15 (365, 25); has school-yard following; trips and hurts Elmer (366-367, 26-27); after teacher stops Elmer from walking to and from school with her, takes Elmer aside and explains sex to him (369-370, 29-30).

Martha (371, 31)　　　: Elmer's fourth-grade teacher with a noticeable odor (365, 25); unmarried; saves all wrapping paper for Elmer;

28

lets Elmer walk to school with her and home afterward (368, 28); suddenly stops him from walking to and from school (369, 29); invites Elmer to come to her house at night (371, 31); touches him, and he flees (373, 33).

_____: "stocky lad with close-curling crisp hair;" inquires if Elmer has been hurt by boy-God; later becomes "playwright of renown" (367, 27).

_____: elder brother of boy-God from whom he learns facts of life to tell Elmer; young merchant who teaches Baptist Sunday school (369-370, 29-30).

_____: his companion and "favorite satellite," a "fat boy with eyes like bits of broken plate" (370, 30).

Velma (374, 34)_____: girl whom Elmer meets after affair with teacher (373, 33); 16, runs to barn after giving Elmer cup of sugar; presumably introduces him to sex (374-375, 34-35).

_____: sergeant who conducts hand grenade drill on deck of troopship (381, 41).

_____: soldier killed by Elmer in hand grenade drill (381, 41).

_____: soldier in next cot to Elmer in hospital; aviator with broken back and both feet burned off (382, 42).

_____: wealthy fat woman; meets Elmer in railroad station canteen where she is volunteer; wife of dollar-a-year man in Washington; introduces him to art galleries (382-383, 42-43).

_____: dollar-a-year man in Washington (383, 43).

_____: fattish man who makes speech in New Orleans to sell Liberty Loan bonds (383, 43).

_____: young man in New Orleans crowd who hinders Elmer from reaching his sister, Jo (384, 44).

_____: Jewish man in crowd at Liberty Loan speech (384, 44).

_____: soldier in crowd at Liberty Loan speech who bars Elmer's way to sister (384, 44).

Mr. _____ Bryan (386, 46).

_____: captain of ship on which Monsons go to Europe (389, 49).

_____: woman in spiffy green evening dress on board ship

(389, 49).

_____: ship's officer whom Myrtle finds attractive (389, 49); transfers Monsons to his table near the captain's (391, 51).

_____: canon; Anglican clergyman who visits Mrs. Monson in Rome; old man (395, 55).

_____: tall robust girl tennis player in Rome (396, 56).

_____: thin male English tennis player with limp (396, 56).

George (403, 63) Bleyth (398, 58): young male tennis player, "lean and hardbitten as a hound;" son of an English earl and "a Spanish marquisate" (396, 56); destined to be a parson; advises Mrs. Monson to join Roman Catholic Church (397, 57); a canon (398, 58); flashback: at Cambridge, developed "discrimination in wine and a sound tennis game;" becomes churchman (404, 64); reconciles himself to being a country parson in Devon (405, 65); spends two weeks each August with mother's people in Scotland (406, 66); does not like his brother, Lord Wohleden (407, 67).

_____: Italian girl tennis player (396, 56).

Lord (398, 58) Wysbroke (397-398, 57-58): father of George Bleyth; smokes cigars; an earl (396, 56); makes beer (397, 57); advises son to marry Mrs. Monson; receives son's reply (398, 58); goes to London; stays in bed and breakfast (399-401, 59-61); visits son, Lord Wohleden, at his club (402, 62); says Lord Wohleden must go to Rome to marry Mrs. Monson or Myrtle (?) (403, 63).

_____: "I" narrator (397, 57).

_____: New Haven bartender who describes Harkness Memorial to "I" narrator (397, 57).

_____: remote female connection of Lord Wysbroke; writes to him of son's attentions to Mrs. Monson (398 58).

_____: faded companion of above (398, 58).

_____: servant of young canon (398, 58).

_____: servant to Lord Wysbroke; a footman (399, 59).

Henry (399, 59) _____: servant to Lord Wysbroke (399, 59).

Andrew (399, 59) _____:

_____ Jessop (399, 59): farmer (399, 59).

_____ Harris (399, 59): steward to Lord Wysbroke (399, 59).

30

_____: proprietor of the Royal George in Wysborough (399, 59).

_____: attendant who serves Lord Wysbroke tea; loses his cup (400, 60).

_____: Lord Wysbroke's father; lives in Devon; will not die (400, 60); sends George Bleyth one of the "old spade guineas of Charles I" for his birthday and for his mother's birthday (406, 66); can not bear his oldest grandson, Ivor (406, 66).

_____: woman who runs bed and breakfast in London (401, 61).

_____: servant in British club of Lord Wohleden; announces visit of his father, Lord Wysbroke (401-402, 61-62).

Lord Wohleden (401, 61): captain; lost most of teeth; bald (401, 61); son of Lord Wysbroke; thinks servant announces his father's death rather than his visit (401-402, 61-62); ten years older than brother, George Bleyth; thinks him a "clown and a boor" (407-67); visits him in Rome (408, 68).

Jock (402, 62)_____: bet Lord Wohleden twenty to one that his father would live another twenty years (402, 62).

Charles (402, 62)_____.

_____: George Bleyth's servant at Cambridge (405, 65).

_____: George Bleyth's deceased mother (406, 6); a "sparse and gentle aristocrat" (407, 67).

Ivor (406, 66)_____: oldest grandson of Lord Wysbroke's father (406, 66).

_____: woman seen by Mrs. Monson at Rapallo; talks Italian (408, 68).

_____: hulking lad at Rapallo, seen by Mrs. Monson (409, 69).

_____: man at Rapallo, seen by Mrs. Monson (409, 69).

_____: waiter at Rapallo (409, 69).

_____: pilot who meets Elmer's ship in harbor at Venice (413, 73).

_____: man with gray mustache who brings pilot to Elmer's ship (413, 73).

_____: bearded gray man in customs-boat (413, 73).

_____: vendors of pornographic postcards in Venice (414, 74).

_____: three prostitutes on Venetian dock (414, 74).

_____: wireless operator on ship that carries Elmer to Venice (414, 74).

_____: five other prisoners in jail with Elmer (415, 75).

Angelo (425, 85) Marina (427, 87): prisoner in soiled clothes with Elmer in Venice jail (415, 75); communicates with Elmer; takes note to Second Officer; in his absence, gives note to Chief Engineer (426, 86); accompanies Elmer to Milan and then to Paris (426-431, 86-91).

_____: bank cashier in Venice (415-416, 75-76).

_____: manager of bank in Venice (415-416, 75-76).

_____: woman with Elmer in Venice; has an odor (417, 77); gold-filled teeth (423, 83).

Mister Ray (417, 77)_____.

_____: three priests (419, 79) [part of Elmer's drunken dream.]

_____: sleeping beggar with rats eating bread out of hand (419, 79).

_____: gondolier in gondola when Elmer wakes from drunken sleep (422, 82).

_____: two gendarmes who arrest Elmer (423, 83).

_____: boatman in gondola which takes Elmer to jail (424, 84).

_____: police officer who questions Elmer (424, 84).

_____: turnkey in jail in Venice (425, 85).

Grover (434, 94)_____: man who marries Ethel, mother of Elmer's bastard son (434-435, 94-95); shortchanges Elmer in gas station (439, 99).

A 33 *Mayday*

Written in late January, 1926 (dated January 27, 1926); first published, 1976.

Pagination, in parentheses, to the following edition (University of Notre Dame Press, 1976, 1977, 1978), pp. 87. Introduction by Carvel Collins.

Sir (51) Galwyn (47): gazes in "dark hurrying stream" (48); a face appears in water and all the faces he had known (49); "a face all young and red and white" appears in stream; when he questions St. Francis, told to wait (50); rises from floor; puts on armour; mounts horse; rides forth (51); after journeying seven days and slaying a minor dragon, comes to small dwelling; knocks (53); Sir Galwyn of Arthgyl (57); asks Time to show him way to castle where a princess is held captive (59); leaves Time (62); meets Cornish man at arms who defends Yseult (63); kills him and rides on; meets Tristram of Lyonness (64-65); kills Tristram (65); sees Yseult bathing 66); "sojourns" with Yseult when she comes out of water; suggests she put some clothes on; prefers to see her back to her front (69); leaves while she is getting dressed (70); a "milk white doe" appears and asks him to pierce her (71); he does, and she emerges as Elys, daughter of King of Wales; sleeps with her; wakes; leaves her (72); meets Princess Aelia; she takes him in her chariot (73); tells her of Yseult and Elys (75); she rants (76); threatens to jump out of car (77); wakes in forest (79); rides with Hunger and Pain; to meet Hunger's sister (80-81); returns to stream; where paunchy little man tells him to choose; looks in stream (82); choice is to be submerged in waters with no memory or live over one of his experiences (83); at invitation of Lord of Sleep, looks into stream; sees three faces: Yseult, Queen of Cornwall, Princess Elys, and Princess Aelia (86); and finally a face "all young and white;" steps into water; a voice says, "Rise, Sir Galwyn; be faithful, fortunate and brave." Saint Francis identifies the face: "Little Sister Death" (87).

_____: one who came to him at last (47); tells Galwyn, "Rise, Sir Galwyn, be faithful, fortunate and brave." (51).

Hunger (48): "small green design with a hundred prehensile mouths;" "at his right hand" (48); after Galwyn's affairs with Yseult, Elys, and Aelia, tells him there is one more girl to see (80); it is his sister (81).

Pain (4): "small green design with a hundred restless hands, which stood at his left hand" (48).

Fortitude (49): "stark thin face more beautiful than death," appears in water (49).

Ambition (49): "a tall bright one;" face appears in water (49).

Saint Francis (50).

Little Sister Death (87): girl in water (50); Little Sister Death (87).

Sir Morvidus (52): Earl Warwick; in olden times slew giant that had assaulted him (52).

_____: giant slain by Sir Morvidus (52).

Time (56): answers door when Sir Galwyn knocks (53); speaks of destiny (59); tells Sir Galwyn of two princesses (61).

_____: wife of Time, away visiting parents (56).

_____: parents of wife of Time (56).

Princess Elys (61): daughter of Sethynnen ap Seydnn Seidi, the Drunkard, King of Wales (61); appears before Sir Galwyn as a "milk white doe" and requests him to pierce her with his sword (71); as he does, emerges as Elys; sleeps with him (72).

Sethynnen ap Seydnn Seidi (61): the Drunkard, King of Wales (61).

Princess Aelia (61): daughter of Aelian (61); takes Sir Galwyn in her chariot (73); calls Elys a "shocking word" (77); kisses Sir Galwyn and drives her car back to earth (78-79).

Prince Aelian (61): prince among Merovingians and Crown Marshall of Arles (61).

_____: man at arms who stops Sir Galwyn; explains about Tristram-Yseult-Mark (63); is killed by Sir Galwyn (64).

Mark (63): King of Cornwall (63).

Yseult (63): bathing in stream (63); seen by Sir Galwyn (66); emerges and "sojourns" naked with him; goes to put on clothes as he leaves (69).

Tristram (64): in charge of Yseult; nephew of King Mark (64); attacks Sir Galwyn; is killed (65).

Uther Pendragon (65): father of Tristram of Lyonness (65).

_____: "tire- and waiting-woman" to Yseult (66).

_____: the Constable du Boisgeclin (66).

Lord of Sleep (86): paunchy little man; meets Galwyn; high white brow (81).

Fame (84).

_____: gray man who appears with boat at stream (84).

Experience (85): not allowed to leave paunchy little man's domain.

34

A 3 *Mosquitoes*

Begun July-August 1925 in Europe; continued summer to September 1, 1926, and once titled *Mosquito*; first published April 30, 1927.

Pagination in parentheses to the following editions: (New York Boni and Liveright, 1927, 349 pp.); (New York: Horace Liveright, 1931); (Garden City, New York: Sun Dial Press, 1937); (New York: Avon Books, 1942 [paperback]); and (New York: Liveright Publishing Corporation, 1951).

<u>Ernest (34) Talliaferro (9) born Tarver (33)</u>: speaks with a Cockney accent (9); after buying milk for Gordon, meets Mrs. Maurier (16); 38 years old; a widower for eight years; his family originated in northern Alabama; one brother was hanged in Texas; another was a professor of classics in a small college in Kansas; another was elected to a state legislature; a sister disappeared; he becomes a successful wholesale buyer in women's wear; "did Europe in forty-one days;" returned to New Orleans with a precious account (31-33); born Tarver not Talliaferro(33); tries unsuccessfully to speak to Fairchild alone (44); has a drink with the other men before lunch on the yacht (62); is bullied by Mrs. Maurier into staying on deck when the men go below to drink (71); finally gets a drink when Mrs. Maurier retires (97); asks Fairchild's advice about a girl; they return to Fairchild's room to drink (98); sees Jenny asleep in a deck chair; feels her outline through the canvas; attempts to kiss her; is repulsed (127-129); she lures him, later, to a lonely part of the deck; but he flees (189-190); Fairchild sends him to Mrs. Maurier's room under the impression that it is Jenny's (289-290); he becomes engaged to marry Mrs. Maurier (292); visits Fairchild after the cruise; outlines latest plans to conquer Jenny (307-311); returns to tell Fairchild of his failure; tells his neighbor of vain attempt to seduce Jenny (341 ff.); returns to his rooms and contemplates that he is getting old without ever having been successful with women; places his box of contraceptives in a drawer (347); last scene of him is reminiscent of J. Alfred Prufrock (347).

<u>   Gordon (18)</u>: sculptor (9); refuses Mrs. Maurier's invitation through Talliaferro (12); sends Talliaferro for a bottle of milk (13); is quite attracted to Pat Robyn (23); refuses to let her have the marble torso; has red hair and beard (25); refuses Mrs. Maurier's invitation and walks out (29); as he walks, he muses about Patricia Robyn and calls himself a fool (47 ff.); finds Fairchild and Julius at his door when he returns; tells them he's changed his mind and will join the yachting party (49-50); sits at the rail as the others swim (80); lifts Pat from tender to the deck; repeats feat (82); reveals to Mrs. Maurier that he is infatuated with her niece; takes Mrs. Maurier's face in his hands; frightens her (153-154); disappears (201); believed to have drowned (227); appears in a motorboat during search for his body (265); had left boat when Jenny and Talliaferro fell out (266); found man with motorboat; heard of drowning; assumed that it was Fairchild and returned to help find body (266); joyful that Pat has returned (268); spanks her when she calls him the name she learned from Jenny (271); holds her in his lap; feels bones of her face; promises to sculp her face (272-273); after cruise is visited by Fairchild and Julius (317 ff.); had sculped Mrs. Maurier's

head in clay and has caught the truth of frustration behind her silliness (322); learns of her thwarted life from Julius (323 ff.); says his marble torso is not blond but dark; speaks of grief (329); walks with Fairchild and Julius; buys another bottle of whisky; drinks, thinking of Pat (337); borrows some money from Julius and enters a house of prostitution (338).

Mrs. Patricia (17) Maurier (12): is planning a yachting party (19); insists on visiting Gordon (20-21); invites him to party (27); tries to form a bridge party after lunch on yacht; succeeds in getting one table; will not let Talliaferro join the other men below to drink (69-71); first night, she vainly tries to get people to dance (93); after Gordon frightens her, she lies in bed weeping on the second night (163); orders the captain to search Fairchild's cabin, to find the whisky, and to throw it overboard (291); had been forced to marry a wealthy veteran of the Civil War (323); of impoverished northern gentility; came to New Orleans with her father on a government appointment (324); married in a Catholic cathedral (325); never had any children (326).

_____: couple kissing in hall as Talliaferro goes for milk (13).

_____: proprietor of grocery store; sells Talliaferro a bottle of milk (15).

Patricia (17) Robyn (16): niece of Mrs. Maurier; visiting her (16); taken with Gordon's marble torso of a young female figure; 18 years old; wants the torso (24-25); calls Talliaferro Mr. Tarver (31); a twin (46); meets Jenny and Pete downtown and invites them to the yacthing party (56); clad in a suit of her brother's underwear, dives from the wheelhouse; ducks Fairchild and Ayers (80-81); admires Gordon's strength as he lifts her from the tender (82); notices that the steering mechanism is fixed (121); talks to David West about travel; wants to join him in Europe next summer (124-125); plans to go swimming with him next morning (126); repulses Pete when he tries to kiss her (133-134); shares a berth with Jenny (140); plans to use the word learned from Jenny (147); she and Jenny talk about being virgins (147-148); goes swimming with David at midnight (156 ff.); next morning, swims naked; emerges as David watches; goes below (164-166); they pack food and elope; she has taken money from her aunt, Mrs. Wiseman, and Miss Jameson (166-169); insists they go opposite way to that chosen by David (175); she is bitten by mosquitoes (179); they are lost in a swamp (180); faints and recovers (201-202); that afternoon they reach a sign showing them to be going in the wrong direction (207); finally find their way to a house by the lake; pay five dollars to be taken back to yacht (213-214); tries to get Gordon to sell her the statue; calls him name Jenny taught her; is spanked (270-271); after the cruise, has dinner with aunt and Mark Frost; enters brother's room; asks him if he damaged the boat; bites his ear affectionately; retires (313-317).

_____: black chauffeur for Mrs. Maurier (21).

Dawson (33) Fairchild (27): a novelist (33); has told Hooper that Talliaferro is a member of Rotary (36); tells a tall tale of Andrew Jackson crossbreeding horses and alligators (67-68); avoids Mrs. Maurier's bridge game, and takes men below to drink (69); tells another tall tale about Al Jackson's fish farm (86 ff.); urges Talliaferro to make haste in his pursuit of a girl (112-113); had attended a midwest denominational college for one year (115); had been cheated of money on pretense of joining a fraternity; wants to form a stock company to market the pipe Josh has invented (118-120); uses the tender to try to pull boat off beach (193); tells story of his first love and the girl in the outhouse (231-234); reads and comments on Mrs. Wiseman's poetry (246-247); appointed temporary captain (260); leads the others in search for Gordon's body (264); tells another tall story of Jackson's sheep (277 ff.); on fourth night, finally leads the others to the dance (283); as Talliaferro begins to get drunk, he urges him to go to Jenny's room; sends him to Mrs. Maurier's instead (289-290); next morning, wakes with a hangover to find yacht anchored and himself, Ayers, and the Semitic man abandoned by rest (302-304); that night, listens to Talliaferro's latest plan to win Jenny; with Semitic man, visits Gordon (307 ff., 317 ff.); learns of Mrs. Maurier's thwarted life; gets drunk (323 ff.); walks with Julius and Gordon and senses the "Passion Week of the heart" which is central to art (339); vomits (340).

Mrs. Eva (27) Wiseman (55): sister of Julius (65); has discarded her husband; Fairchild and other men like her (103); has published a "tweaky little book" "The syphilis book" (220); it is titled *Satyricon in Starlight* (245).

Dorothy (27) Jameson (55): a portrait painter (101); spent two years in Greenwich Village; took a lover because he owed her money; a musician, he eloped to Paris with another woman; he pawned Dorothy's fur coat on way to boat and mailed her the pawn ticket (102); returned to New Orleans on an allowance from her family; now has Mark Frost for a lover; her affairs with men always end abruptly (102-103); shows an interest in Josh (105); then she turns her attention to Pete (106); tries unsuccessfully to induce Pete to make a date with her (286); after the cruise, Mark Frost visits her; she puts on an embroidered nightdress and waits in vain for him to come to her room (333).

_____ Hooper (34): has iron gray hair (34); assumes that Talliaferro had heard his speech on church attendance at Rotary luncheon (35-36).

Mark Frost (52): tall, ghostly, fair-haired young man (34); a poet (44); claims to be the best poet in New Orleans (44); Dorothy Jameson's lover (102); after cruise, has dinner with Mrs. Maurier (313); later, visits Dorothy Jameson (330); fails to respond to her invitation to go to her room; leaves to catch midnight trolley while she waits for him (333-334).

Julius (49) Kauffman (270): a bald Semitic man (34); speaks pontifically of religion and education (40 ff.); after cruise, visits Gordon with Fairchild; much talk about art (317 ff.); tells the history of Mrs. Maurier (323 ff.); grandson of Julius Kauffman (327).

_____ Broussard (38): owner of and waiter in restaurant where

Fairchild meets Talliaferro (34); Hooper calls him George (38).

Josh (46) Gus (46) Theodore (60) Robyn (45): Patricia's twin brother (46); working on a piece of wood with a saw (46); almost misses the departing yacht (57); at night, seeking a wire rod for his "thing," he takes one from a piece of machinery in the battery room (89-90); heats the rod, using Talliaferro's suitcase to hold the candle, and burns his piece of wood with it (91); he is carving a pipe (104); at breakfast, learns that steering gear is broken (109); without being seen, he cleans and replaces the rod (111-112); pipe is made of cherry wood; he is going to Yale the following year (114); sits with Jenny in deck chair and pets (244).

Walter (46)   : "a yellow negro," servant in Mrs. Maurier's home (46); would not let Josh take Mrs. Maurier's saw to the yacht (58).

David West (122): steward on Mrs. Maurier's yacht, *Nausikaa* (54); jumps overboard to rescue Major Ayers (79); got his job through Dawson Fairchild; not a regular cook; from Indiana; has traveled widely (121-123); admires beautiful scenery (not girls) (129); agrees to swim with Pat (156 ff.); falls in love with her (163); next morning, sees Pat bathing nude; watches her emerge (166); elopes with Pat (169); they get lost in swamp (1800; carries Pat (202); walks all day in wrong direction (207); elopement ends when they hire man to take them back (213); leaves note for Fairchild saying that he is leaving the yacht (236).

Major (61)   Ayers (61): a florid stranger in tweeds (55); loses his teeth in cabin (61); British; announces plan to market salts to constipated Americans (64); can not recognize Talliaferro's accent; thinks he might be native American Indian (65); after drinking in Fairchild's cabin, jumps overboard (79); rescued (79); asks Jenny to go to Mandeville with him (223); after cruise, has an appointment with a business man about his salts (304).

Jenny (Genevieve) Steinbauer (56): blonde girl in soiled green dress (55); is attracted to Josh (75); borrows Pat's bathing suit (80); wakened by Talliaferro's attempt to kiss her; repulses him; returns to sleep (127-129); later, dances with him (129); later, lures him to remote part of ship; he flees (189); falls out of tender and cuts hand (201); agrees to go to Mandeville with Major Ayers (223); sits with Josh on deck and pets (244); returns home by street car with dime given her by Pete (294-295).

Pete (55) Ginotta (296): arrives on yacht with Jenny (55); clutches his hat constantly (58); feels slightly seasick next morning (106); flees below when Dorothy Jameson begins to show interest in him (108); tries to kiss Pat (133-134); finally puts hat down; Mrs. Wiseman accidentally knocks it down and Mrs. Maurier steps on it (277); of Italian descent, the youngest of the family (295); returns to family restaurant (299); eats and then delivers four cases of whisky for his brother (301).

Ed (195)   : captain of the *Nausikaa* (57); returns with tug (261).

_____: helmsman (57); orders Jenny not to hang over rail (74); helps rescue Major Ayers (79); announces bad weather coming (99); goes for tug when boat goes aground (120).

_____: deckhand who helps rescue Major Ayers (79).

Hank (124) Henry (191) Robyn (256): father of Pat and Josh (212).

Thelma (144) Frances (145) _____: Jenny's girl friend (144).

Roy (144) _____: Thelma's "fellow" (144).

_____ Faulkner (145): "a little kind of black man" (white); he comments on Jenny's generous figure (145).

_____: man who tried to pick up Jenny at the Market; he called her word she used in repulsing Talliaferro (146).

_____: man who takes Pat and David back to the *Nausikaa* (213).

_____: man who boards the *Nausikaa* from the tug with captain (261).

Walter (262) _____: one of the *Nausikaa's* sailors; fastens the towline (262).

_____: man who helps Walter (262).

_____: black man who helps Walter (262).

_____: two men in boats who come to look for Gordon's body (263).

_____ Steinbauer (295): Jenny's father; on night force (295).

_____ Ginotta (296): Pete's mother (296); grows deaf (297).

_____ Ginotta (296): Pete's father; owner of Italian restaurant (296); dies after Joe converts the restaurant to a speakeasy (297).

Joe Ginotta (296): Pete's brother; once waiter in family's restaurant; converts it to a speakeasy (296-297); now a bootlegger)301).

_____: girl who comes to restaurant on Pete's return; kisses him (300).

_____: two men on dock to whom Fairchild speaks (303).

Mr. _____ Reichman (304): business man with whom Major Ayers has an appointment, after the cruise, about marketing his salts (304).

_____: man at the typewriter in apartment below Fairchild's (304).

_____ Maurier (323): overseer of plantation; disappeared in Civil War; returned with a fortune (323); becomes owner of the plantation for which he was once overseer (324); engages in shady land deals with Julius Kauffman (324); once married to Mrs. Maurier (325).

Julius Kauffman (324): partner of Maurier in shady land deals (324).

_____: Mrs.Maurier's father; in New Orleans on government appointment (324).

_____: young man with whom Mrs. Maurier was in love before her marriage (324).

_____: man Jenny picks up on dance floor on her date with Talliaferro (343).

_____: woman in bed with Fairchild when Talliaferro calls (349).

Father Abraham

Probably written in late 1926, or early 1927; first published 1983.

Pagination, in parentheses, to the following editions: William Faulkner, Father Abraham, ed., James B. Meriwether (New York: Red Ozier Press, 1983) and to (New York: Random House, 1984).

Flem (14) Snopes (18): banker (13); chews tobacco constantly; never seen with eyelids closed (14); flashback: clerk in Varner's store; marries Eula Varner; given forty acres and Old Frenchman homesite by Uncle Billy Varner; single axiom of social relations: "some men are fools but all men are no honester than the occasion requires;" eyes color of stagnant water; lends money at exhorbitant interest; comes from long line of shiftless tenant farmers (19); moves with wife to Texas (21); saves money in buried tins (21); returns from Texas with varicolored horses and man (22); takes five dollars from Henry after Buck returns it to Mrs. Armstid (49); rides off with Buck (51); when Suratt asks him how much he made from the sale of horses, says they were not his horses (66).

Eula (17) Varner (16) Snopes (18): wife of banker; plump; silk clad (13); flashback: daughter of Billy Varner; "softly ample" girl of 16; body "richly disturbing to the male beholder" (16); attends all social functions; marries Flem Snopes (18); moves to Texas with him; returns with baby (21).

Colonel (13)   Winword (13): talks with wife of banker (13).

_____: original settler in Frenchman's Bend (14); builds huge, colonial house (15).

Will (60) (Uncle Billy) Varner (16): the big man in Frenchman's Bend; beat supervisor, politician, farmer, usurer, present owner of Frenchman homstead; tall, reddish colored; bright blue eyes; mild mannered (16); gives Flem Snopes forty acres of land and Old Frenchman homesite as wedding present (18); called to tend Henry Armstid (60); on way to tend Henry, tells other men that his wife lay naked in moonlight when pregnant to induce a girl (Eula) (62).

_____: son-in-law of Billy Varner; election commissioner (16).

Jody (23) Varner (16): son of Billy Varner; owns store and is postmaster in Frenchman's Bend (16); catches Clarence Snopes (son of I. O. Snopes) stealing candy in store (69-70).

Mrs. Will Varner (16): gray placid wife of Uncle Billy Varner (16); takes charge of Eula's baby (21); while pregnant, lay naked in moonlight to induce birth of girl (62).

_____: suitors of Eula Varner; pay court to her and fight among themselves afterward (17).

41

_____: one of Eula's suitors; leaves suddenly for Texas (18).

_____: another of Eula's suitors; son of well-to-do farmer; moves to Texas (19).

_____ Snopes (20): second Snopes to appear in Frenchman's Bend three years after Flem; works in blacksmith shop; after two years, marries; owns blacksmith shop (20).

_____ Snopes (20): wife of second Snopes (20).

_____ Snopes (20): third Snopes; operates locksmith shop; looks exactly like second Snopes; takes fourth Snopes in home-made perambulator to Methodist church (20).

_____ Snopes (20): fourth Snopes in Frenchman's Bend; baby (20).

_____ Snopes (21): child of Eula Varner Snopes (21).

Buck (25)_____ : man who returns from Texas with Flem Snopes and horses (22); black moustached (23); right ear (off ear) slashed by pony; eats gingersnaps (24); referred to as "owner" of horses by narrator (25); releases horses in livery stable lot (26 ff.); wins $11 in poker game in livery stable (29); with Eck and two others, drives horses into barn to be fed (32 ff.); tries to feed horses "shell corn" (35); announces "arction" to begin after breakfast [37]; starts horse auction; sends Admiral Dewey for more gingersnaps (38); fells horse with butt of pistol; holds it for others to bid (40); offers to give Eck Snopes wall-eyed horse if he will start bidding on second (42); sells horse to Henry (44); tells Mrs. Armstid not to enter lot with Henry (47); after Henry hits wife with rope, enters lot; ejects Henry; gives five dollars back to wife; says Henry did not buy horse (48-49); after Henry gives five dollars to Flem, says Flem will give it back to her tomorrow; offers to swap last two horses and wagon for buggy; trades and rides away (50-51).

_____: casual in overalls on Varner's porch (23).

_____: other casuals on Varner's porch (23).

_____: casual who inquires about stranger's torn ear (24).

Mrs. (26)_____ Littlejohn (26): owner of boarding house in Frenchman's Bend (26); hits wild horse over head with washboard (56); puts Henry to bed after injury (59); starts to tend him; sends for Will Varner (60).

Eck (27) Snopes (28): helps Buck cut horses loose in lot (27); with two others, helps Buck drive horses into barn (32-33); lets Ad stay in lot (34); whips son after horses jump over him (36); after he has been given one horse, offers one dollar, then two for next horse (43); after horses

42

escape, with son, follows horse into Mrs. Littlejohn's (55); appears next morning at Varner's store with son Ad; eats cheese and crackers (67); stretched rope across lane to catch horse; horse broke its neck (69).

Ad (31) Admiral Dewey (33) Snopes (28): Eck's son; yellow hair (28); blue eyes (30); follows father unobserved into lot (33); horses run over him and leave him unharmed (35); gets gingersnaps for Buck (38); as men try to get horses, follows father into lot (53); ordered to get into wagon; does not (53-54); follows father and horse into Mrs. Littlejohn's (55); for third time, horse jumps clear over him (56).

Mrs. Eck Snopes (28): wife of Eck (28); mother of (28) Ad (31).

V. K. Suratt (55): sewing machine agent; lives at Mrs. Littlejohn's (29); as horse runs into his room, leaps from window in underwear (55); later, tells others of Flem's horse deal (64); looks at Flem "with a blend of curiosity and respect" (66); tries to shame Flem for cheating Henry Armstid (68).

_____: two men who help Eck and Buck drive horses into barn (31 ff.).

_____: unidentified man who starts bidding with, "Fo' bits" (38); then bids, "Fo' bits for the lot" (39).

_____: old deaf man at auction (39).

Henry (41) Armstid (65): man in wagon; stops at auction (40); bids three dollars after Eck's two-dollar bid; flings wife aside as she tries to stop him; raises Eck's four-dollar bid to five dollars (43); threatens crowd not to raise his bid (44); after all but two horses are sold, demands his horse (45-46); asks Buck to get his horse; asks others (46); orders wife to accompany him into lot to get horse (47); strikes wife with coiled rope when she fails to head horse (48); ejected from lot by Buck; takes five dollars from wife; gives money to Flem Snopes, when Buck refuses it (49); opens gate to get horse (52); trampled by escaping horses; carried to Mrs. Littlejohn's (59); leg broken (68).

Mrs. Henry (41) Armstid (65): woman in wagon (40); Henry's wife; tries to prevent husband from buying horse; says they have only five dollars (41); that she earned five dollars by weaving (43); follows husband into lot (47); struck by husband (48); given five dollars by Buck (49).

_____ Armstid (65): Henry's children (43).

_____: man who trades buggy to Buck for last two horses (50).

I. O. Snopes (52): clerk in Varner's store; sells ropes to men who bought horses (52); admires Flem Snopes's ability to fleece his neighbors (64-65).

Vernon Turpin (65): farmer in wagon on bridge; run over by Eck's horse (56-57); dragged on face by his own mules (58).

_____ Turpin (65): farmer's wife, daughters, and cousins run over by Eck's horse (58).

Ernest (60)_____ : man sent to fetch Henry's wife after injury (60).

_____: man on Varner's porch with spray of peach tree in teeth (63).

Clarence Snopes (70): son of I. O. Snopes; steals candy from Varner's store (70).

Begun first as *Father Abraham* probably in late 1926 (See *The Hamlet*.), and revised as "The Peasants," and again as "*Aria con Amore*," and renamed "As I Lay Dying," this story was first published in English under its present title in the summer of 1986.

Pagination, in parentheses, to "As I Lay Dying," Mississippi Quarterly, 39 (summer 1986), 369-385.

_____: young boy, first-person narrator; in wagon with uncle; startled by wild horse (371).

_____: narrator's uncle (371); vote gathering (372); judge; tall, loose man in careless clothes; can talk in the idiom of all types (373).

Uncle Billy (376) Varner (371): store owner (371); father-in-law of Flem Snopes (376).

_____: man at whose house narrator and uncle stayed, and who told them about Flem Snopes's horse auction; a farmer (372).

Flem Snopes (372): accompanied by stranger, arrives with twenty-five unbroken range ponies; close-mouthed (372); once Varner's clerk; claims he had nothing to do with the wild horses; known for sharp dealing (374); tubby; eyes color of pond water; wears black felt hat; Varner's son-in-law (376); denies ownership of horses (377); refuses to return Mrs. Armstid's money; says Butch took it with him (384); gives her small sack of candy "fer the chaps" (385).

Buck (373) _____: stranger with Flem Snopes; auctions wild horses; Texan (372); refuses to sell Armstid a horse (379); tells Mrs. Armstid to ask Flem to return the money (382).

Henry Armstid (372): hits wife when she tries to prevent him from buying one of the horses; leg broken (378); others try to prevent him; when Buck refuses to sell him a horse, gives five dollars to Flem Snopes; lets horses escape (379).

V. K. (377) Suratt (372): sells sewing machines (372); asks Flem how much money he made from auction (377); with others, tells story of Henry Armstid (378); asks Flem if he has not already given Mrs. Armstid the five dollars (379); run over by one of Eck's horses (383).

_____: man on Varner's porch (373).

_____: second man on Varner's porch (373).

Ernest (381) _____: third man on Varner's porch (373); lends Armstid tools (381).

_____: fourth man on Varner's porch; peach sprig in mouth

45

(373).

I. O. Snopes (374): fifth man on Varner's porch; sits in chair; face like a nutcracker; scrawny; no particular age (373); Varner's clerk; successor to Flem (374); calls Armstid "Henery" (379); admires Flem's ability to skin others (379).

Vernon Turpin (373): hires lawyer to sue Flem Snopes (373); hurt when Eck Snopes's wild horse ran over his wagon (374-375).

Squire   Whittington (373): lawyer hired by Vernon Turpin (373).

_____: Harvard professor (373).

_____: cane bottom farmer (373)

Mrs. Vernon Turpin (374): in wagon when wild horse overran them (374).

Eck (374) Snopes (375): bought one of the wild horses (374-375); given one to start auction (375); one of his horses ran into Mrs. Littlejohn's (377).

Ad (377) Snopes (375): son of Eck (375).

_____ Turpin (375): women in Turpin's family (375).

Lon Quick (375): catches Vernon Turpin's mules (375)

Mrs.   Littlejohn (375): asks Mrs. Armstid if she has asked Flem Snopes for her money (381).

Mrs.   Varner Snopes (376): Uncle Billy Varner's daughter; married to Flem Snopes (376).

Mrs. Henry Armstid (378): tries to prevent husband from buying horse; is hit by him; knits and weaves by night to earn money; has five children; can plow (378); earned the five dollars that husband gave to Flem (381); asks Flem to return the money (384); when he refuses, accepts small sack of candy for the children; walks away (385).

_____ Armstid: five children of Henry Armstid (378).

_____: blacksmith (380).

Dated by Faulkner February 5, 1927; first published in *The Saturday Evening Post*, 240 (April 8, 1967), 48-53, 57, 58, 60, [61], 62, 63, and by Random House three days later.

Pagination, in parentheses, to the following edition (New York: Random House, 1967), pp. 81, copyright 1964 by Victoria F. Fielden; and to the following reissue (London: Chatto & Windus, 1967).

Dulcie (8)_____: wakes from sleep (5); grows smaller (59); wishes to be home in bed; is (68); wishes to be with others; appears in front of cottage (69); rejoins others (73); all a dream (81-82).

Maurice (6)_____: strange boy who announces birthday from bedside; red hair and yellow-flecked eyes (6); blows up toy ladder for Dulcie to climb to ground from window (10); blows up miniature pony; gives it to Dulcie (14-15); blows up ponies for all the others (16-17); asks little old man for Wishing Tree (20); suggests that they all wish for something to eat; they do and eat (35-37).

_____: Dulcie's mother (7).

Dicky (7)_____: asks for "something" to eat; gets "something" (32-33); grows smaller (59).

Alice (7)_____: black nurse for children (12); constantly objects to little old man (20 ff.); husband (soldier) reappears; throws stovewood at him; tells him to get in cart (43 ff.); grows smaller (59).

George (9)_____: boy who lives across street from Dulcie (9); after they pick leaves from Mellowmax Tree, wishes for sandwich; gets one (32); gets sick from overeating; gets in cart (48); wishes for lion; one appears (55); unwishes; lion disappears (56); wishes he were home; disappears (61).

Egbert (58)_____: little old man with long gray beard (18); knows way to Wishing Tree (20); rides in cart with Alice and Dicky (23); says he was carving a gillypus when they came to him (25); says that the tree they reach is a Mellowmax Tree (35); insists, after they all get what they wish, that it is a Mellowmax Tree (35); after George gets sick and gets in cart, rides George's pony; wishes for candy; gets some (49); wishes for false teeth; gets them (50); wishes for sword; gets one (51); loses gillypus; finds it (57-58); 92 years old (71).

Maggie (21)_____: wife of little old man; throws flatiron, rollingpin, and alarm clock at him (21).

_____: soldier on wall of castle; blows horn (28).

Exodus (45)_____: Alice's husband; corporal in army (41); reappears when Dicky wishes for a soldier (43); after Alice throws stovewood at him, gets in cart (45); says he has been married frequently (54); after they grow small, grows to normal size; puts them all in hat and carries them home (68).

Genesis (45)_____.

Father Francis (74): Saint Francis (74); gives each of them a bird to care for (77).

Completed in September 29, 1927; first published under title *Sartoris* **January 31, 1929.**

Pagination, in parentheses, to the following edition: (New York, Random House, 1973) ed., Douglas Day, 370 pp.

Will (89) Falls (3): "Old Man" Falls (3); gives Bayard [II] his father's pipe; almost 94 (5); never takes money from Bayard (70); tells Bayard how fast young Bayard drives car (71); says he can remove Bayard's wen (72); 93 (209); applies salve to wen; predicts the wen will drop off 9th of July (210); puts his paste on Bayard's wen (215); tells story of Col. John Sartoris killing two carpetbaggers (224).

Colonel (3) John Sartoris (4): built railroad; starts killing folks; kills two carpetbaggers, a robber, and another man; fatality and doom on his brow as he tells his son, "Redlaw'll kill me tomorrow;" and that he'll be unarmed (6); deposed by his men from colonelcy; raises another unit (220); kills two carpetbaggers from Missouri in 1872; apologizes for "exterminating vermin" (224-225).

Louvinia (3): slave of Colonel John Sartoris (3).

Miss Jenny (3) Virginia (12) Sartoris (11) DuPre (12): youngest sister of John Sartoris; brings hamper of glass panes from Carolina to Mississippi (11); widowed at 23; tells story of Bayard Sartoris's [I] death in Civil War (14 ff.); danced a valse with Jeb Stuart in '58 (20); tells shocking stories (25); aunt of Bayard [II] (30); attends marriage of Bayard [III] to Caroline White (46); says Bayard [III] never loved anyone but Johnny (48); when Narcissa shows her letter, says she wants to keep it for flattery (59); notices Old Bayard's wen (74); takes him to Dr. Alford for wen (84); rages when she discovers Will Falls's ointment on wen (219); takes Bayard to Memphis to consult specialist (227); goes to bed for three weeks after Simon's death (361); visits cemetery to view graves of Sartoris men (363 ff.).

_____: aunt of "you;" the one before Miss Jenny came; sister of "Cunnel" (3); full-blooded Sartoris (4).

Colonel (6) Bayard (3) Sartoris [II] (5): 14 when, in Civil War (3), helps his father escape Yankees by holding stallion in willows; "Old Bayard;" deaf; son of Colonel John Sartoris (5); first child (13); reads Dumas; obsessed by keys and locks (30); will not lend bank's money to anyone who owns a car (48); twice a year buys Old Man Falls an outfit of clothing; always has a present of tobacco and candy for him (70); has wen on face (72); knocks Caspey through door with stick of stove wood (73); takes John Sartoris's pipe to chest in attic (79); records deaths of John Sartoris and Caroline White Sartoris and her son in family bible (83); says he can break his neck in peace if he wants to (92); hears of Bayard's accident; takes Dr. Alford to house (205); salve put on wen by Old Man Falls (210); taken to Memphis for wen (227); wen falls off in specialist's office (228) on July 9th (229); gives black delegation check to cover Simon's theft (264); dies in car as Bayard loses control (300-301).

_____: Bayard's grandfather in Memphis (3).

_____: Yankee officer; finds Colonel John Sartoris on porch (4).

_____: Yankee enlisted man who rides to barn (4).

_____: two carpetbaggers killed by John Sartoris [I] for "stirrin' up niggers to vote" (6).

_____: robber and "other feller he kilt" (6).

_____ Redlaw (6): kills John Sartoris (6).

Byron Snopes (71): announces that Simon has come for Bayard [II] (7); book-keeper in Old Bayard's bank (71); attended business college in Memphis (94); writes obscene letter during noon hour (95); lives in Beard's Hotel (96); has promised Virgil Beard an airgun (98-99); dictates note to Narcissa to Virgil Beard (99); buys air rifle (101); haunted by Virgil Beard; changes boarding house; goes to live with I. O. Snopes (217); his lust rises (218); writes another letter to Narcissa (219); tortured by knowledge that Bayard [III] and Narcissa are married (249); drags Virgil across bank floor; gives him five dollars (250-251); pretends to lock vault in bank (252); returns to bank at night; writes final obscene, lustful letter to Narcissa (253); enters Narcissa's house; takes undergarment and package of letters; leaves last letter (255); slashes knee as he escapes; robs bank; gets car from black man; leaves town by way of Frenchman's Bend (257); fails in attempt to have sex with Minnie Sue Turpin on escape route (260).

Simon (6) Strother (23): Old Bayard's black driver (7); announces that Bayard [III] is home (8); feels Meloney's thigh (24); after Bayard hits Caspey with stick of stove wood, says, "Aint we got ez many white folks now ez we kain suppo't?" (74); whips Isom for driving Bayard's car (78); complains to old John Sartoris about the two Bayards riding in the automobile (102-103); goes with Bayard [III] in car; very frightened; turns off switch (104-106); walks home (106); drives twin horses, Roosevelt and Taft (221); tells Old Bayard of his money problems (221-222); leads church delegation to Old Bayard for repayment of money (261); late Deacon and treasurer of proposed Second Baptist Church; absconded with $67.40 (263); forced to repay final 40 cents (265); found killed in Meloney Harris's cabin; head crushed by blunt instrument (361).

Bayard Sartoris [III] (8): returns by train (8); approaches his grandfather late that night; angry and guilty about his brother's death (38); tried to prevent Johnny from flying Camel (39); twin of John (41); thinks of his brother while in bed with wife on last day of leave [suggests mixture of homosexual-incest with epicene heterosexuality] (41); goes to Memphis to buy automobile (48); flashback: swings on rope; dives

50

into swimming pool (61); he and his brother enlist in RAF (65); returns from Memphis with his car (69); drives car fast (71 ff.); takes Simon for ride in car; cruelly frightens him with speed; (104 ff.); terrorizes another black in wagon; feels savage and ashamed (107); drinks with Rafe McCallum (112 ff.); guilt-ridden about John's death; gets drunk (114-115); insults Eustace and Gratton (115-116); rides stallion (119); knocked out as horse falls (120); drinks with Suratt and Hub (124 ff.); returns to town; returns for more whisky with Hub and Mitch (129); removes bandage (131); with Mitch, Hub, and three black musicians, serenades girls' dormitory (132); serenades Narcissa Benbow (138); they visit homes of all unmarried girls (140); taken home by marshal to sleep it off (143); thinks bleakly of rest of life (144); settles to work routine (194 ff.); then, when crop is making, despair returns (196); crashes car in creek (197); broken ribs (200-201); ritually empties chest of Johnny's trophies and burns them (204-205); in despair while Narcissa reads to him (207); screams in sleep as Narcissa sits with him (237-238); holds her wrist while he talks violently about Johnny (238-239); his cast is removed (246); frightens Narcissa by driving her car wildly; she kisses him (248); married to Narcissa (249); essay on mule (267-268); takes Narcissa 'possum hunting with Caspey and Isom (270); Caspey's talk of Johnny sends him into despair (25-276); loses control of car; regains it; grandfather dies (300-301); after grandfather's death, rides to McCallums's on horse (301 ff.); discovers that they haven't heard of grandfather's death (305); suffers guilt about death (306); says he killed Johnny (307); relives day Johnny was shot down and jumped to his death (315); hunts with Buddy McCallum (322); recognizes that he lacks courage to tell them about his grandfather's death (325); leaves McCallums's on Christmas eve (329); spends night in black man's barn (332 ff.); boards train (338); sends postcards to Aunt Jenny (347); in San Francisco; in Chicago (351); drunk (352); sees Harry Mitchell in nightclub (354-355); killed in plane crash while flight-testing it (358); b. March 16, 1893, d. June 5, 1920 (364).

_____: section hand who sees Bayard [III] get off train (8).

John (Johnny) Sartoris [III] (9): killed in WW I (27); flies a Camel; shoots at brother Bayard trying to head him off; shot down by Ploeckner (39); jumps from burning plane to death (40); twin of Bayard (41); goes up in balloon (62) body not returned (63); dies July 5, 1918 (83); killed first bear when he was 12 (204); jumps from plane to his death after being wounded by German pilot (239); killed July 19, 1918 (364). (See contradiction above.)

Elnora (11) Strother (52)_____: tall mulatto woman; servant in Bayard Sartoris's house (11); sister of Caspey; mother of Isom; apparently daughter of Simon [but see "There Was a Queen."] (52).

Isom (11)_____: son of Elnora; nephew of Caspey; apparently grandson of Simon (52); drives Bayard's car; whipped by Simon (78); drives Aunt Jenny to cemetery (363).

_____Sartoris (11): mother of John Sartoris [I] (11).

51

Bayard Sartoris [I] (12): killed before Second Manasas; A. D. C. of Jeb Stuart; brother of Colonel John Sartoris (12); killed by Yankee cook with derringer on anchovie raid (19).

_____ Sartoris (13): third child of John Sartoris [I]; "eldest" daughter; to be married in June (13).

_____ Sartoris (14): younger daughter of John Sartoris (14).

_____: Scottish engineer; helps John Sartoris build railroad (13).

Joby (13): slave of John Sartoris (13); grandfather of Simon Strother; buries silver in Civil War (34).

_____: Jeb Stuart's body servant (14).

_____: fat Yankee staff major captured on raid by Jeb Stuart and Bayard Sartoris [I] (15).

Captain _____ Wyatt (15): one of Jeb Stuart's group; lets captured Yankee major ride behind him (15).

Allan (18) _____: one of Jeb Stuart's men (18).

Caroline (46) White (83) Sartoris (20): wife of Bayard Sartoris [III]; died last October (20); names child Bayard nine months before it is born; epicene (47); dies in childbirth (67), October 27, 1918 (83).

Bayard (47) Sartoris [IV] (20): child of Bayard Sartoris [III]; dies October 27, 1918 (83).

_____: hill man who built Mitchell house in Jefferson (22).

_____: black chauffeur intimidated by Simon (22).

_____: thin black woman in purple turban in Mitchell kitchen (23).

Rachel (24) _____: large black woman in Mitchell kitchen (23); cook (24).

Meloney (24) Harris (361): young light black woman in Mitchell kitchen (24); leaves Mitchell home; opens beauty shop (168-169); Simon found killed in her cabin (361).

Belle (25) Mitchell (26) Benbow (340): plump young woman (25); secretly holds Horace's hand at Mitchell tennis court (170); while Harry plays tennis, takes Horace into house; they kiss (180); tells Horace she wants to have his child (181); as she and Horace plan to marry, asks him if he has plenty of money (243); in Reno for divorce (287); marries Horace Benbow (340).

Narcissa Benbow (26) Sartoris (249): 26 years old (28); visits Miss Jenny (43); wears white (45); shows Miss Jenny anonymous letter (58); says she will destroy the letter; tears it up (59); joins Red Cross in WW I (66); witnesses Bayard ride stallion and crash (120, 135); visited by Dr. Alford (137); serenaded by Bayard and others (138); watched by a man [Byron Snopes] as she disrobes (139-140); meets Horace at station (145); tells Horace that she hates Bayard and all men (150); throughout first night home, hints of incest between Horace and Narcissa (156 ff.); tells Horace that Belle is dirty (190); visits Aunt Jenny; says she's had several more letters (191); tells her of Horace's affair with Belle (192); says, "I wouldn't have treated Horace that way." (193); becomes estranged from Horace over Belle (190-194); calls Bayard a beast (207); visits Bayard and reads to him, but won't talk to him (207); visits Bayard while others are in Memphis (229); frightened by Bayard's scream in his sleep (238); weeps hysterically when Bayard holds her wrists and tells of Johnny's death (239); receives another letter (241); kisses Bayard after he drives her car wildly (248); married to Bayard (249); pregnant (267); goes 'possum hunting with Bayard, Caspey, and Isom (270 ff.); says Bayard doesn't love anybody (282); spends day at old home; regrets not destroying letters (284); feels forewarned of doom awaiting her child when she looks at miniature of Johnny (349).

Harry Mitchell (26): owns fine tennis courts (161); cotton speculator (174); as he gives Horace drink, says he would kill the man that tried to wreck his home (178); brings flowers to Little Belle at her recital (182); in nightclub in Chicago; his diamond stolen (355).

Horace (27) Benbow (26): Y. M. C. A. in WW I (27); brother of Narcissa (62); takes Snopes to WW I with him (66); returns to Jefferson; kisses sister on mouth (145); fusses over glass-blowing outfit (146-147); talks to Narcissa about Belle (159); 7 years older than Narcissa (159); attended Sewanee and Oxford (160); makes one nearly perfect vase; calls it by sister's name (162); Rhodes scholar at Oxford (163); decides to be Episcopal minister on way home from Oxford; practices law in father's office (165); visits Mitchell tennis court; secretly holds hands with Belle (170-171); plays tennis with Frankie (172 ff.); goes with Harry for drink (177); as he kisses Belle, tells her he loves her (180); agrees with Narcissa that Belle is dirty (190); becomes estranged from Narcissa over Belle (190-191); tells Narcissa that he is going to marry Belle Mitchell; more hints of incest (242); discusses his forthcoming marriage with Narcissa; speaks of seething corruption and putrifaction (287-288); has an affair with Joan, Belle's sister, while she is in Reno (290-299); after Joan examines Narcissa's room, feels unclean (297); married to Belle Mitchell (340); meets train every Tuesday; carries package of shrimp to Belle (343); reviews the failure of his marriage (343 ff.).

_____ Sibleigh (39): British pilot in WW I (39).

_____: German pilot shot down by Bayard Sartoris [I] (39).

_____ Ploeckner (40): German pilot who shoots down John

Sartoris [II]; pupil of Richtofen (40).

Caspey (45) Strother (52): returns from WW I; son of Simon; brother of Elnora; uncle of Isom (52); drafted to labor battalion on St. Sulpice docks (52); very aggressive against whites (53); tells others his war stories (54 ff.); says he has had his white women in France and will have them here (56); delays saddling Old Bayard's horse and sasses him; knocked through door by Old Bayard (73); goes hunting with Bayard and Narcissa (270 ff.).

_____ Sartoris (51): wife of Bayard Sartoris [II].

John Sartoris [II] (51): son of Bayard [II] (51); dies in 1901 of yellow fever and old Spanish bullet wound (79).

Lucy Cranston (63) Sartoris (51): wife of John Sartoris [II]; mother of twins John and Bayard (51, 63).

Aunt Sally (58) Wyatt (66): moves into Narcissa's house during WW I (66); not related (155); returns home after Horace returns (161).

_____: balloonist who got sick (62).

_____: carnival man who explains balloon to Johnny Sartoris (62).

_____: black man in wagon; picks up Johnny after balloon flight (62).

Montgomery Ward (154-155) Snopes (66): taken to WW I by Horace Benbow (66) 21 in 1917; turned down by Army because of heart; had travelled to Memphis with plug of chewing tobacco beneath left armpit (155).

_____: country man who moves to Jefferson with family; drafted and sent overseas (66); company cook in SOS (67).

_____: his wife; pregnant (66).

_____: his two infant children (66).

_____: child born after he leaves for Europe (66).

Res (215) _____: cashier in Sartoris bank (76).

_____: bank examiner (77).

Myrtle (84) _____: receptionist in Dr. Alford's office (84).

Dr. _____ Alford (84): newcomer to Jefferson; examines Old Bayard's wen (85); wants to operate immediately (86); calls on Narcissa Benbow (137); treats Bayard for broken ribs (205).

_____: Myrtle's mother (85).

_____: Dr. Alford's aunt and uncle (85).

Doctor Lucius (Loosh) Quintus Peabody (87): fattest man in Yocona County (86); 87 years old, 310 pounds; John Sartoris's regimental surgeon (87); warns Bayard [II] about his heart and riding with Young Bayard (91); bandages Young Bayard's head (121); shows Aunt Jenny newspaper account of death of Bayard [III] (360); courted his wife 14 years (367).

Dr. Loosh (366) Peabody (91): Dr. Peabody's son (91); lives in New York; surgeon (366) visits father; 30 years old; only child (367).

_____: bank director (94).

_____: black youth who delivers cokes (94).

W. C. (150) Beard (96): countryman who owns Beard Hotel and gristmill in Jefferson (96).

Mrs. W. C. (150) Beard (96): his wife; runs Beard Hotel (96).

Virgil (97) Beard (96): their 12-year-old son (96); copies Byron Snopes's letter to Narcissa (99); hangs around bank (215); begins to haunt Byron (217); visits Byron at bank; screams as Byron drags him outside; runs away with five dollars Byron gives him (251).

Doctor (97)   Jones (97): janitor in bank (96).

_____ Snopes (97): Byron Snopes'S cousin; operates restaurant (97, 251).

_____ Watts (99): owner of hardware store (99).

_____: wagon full of blacks; buzzed   by Bayard   with Simon in his car (105).

_____: blind black beggar in Jefferson (108).

Rafe (111) Raphael Semmes (325) McCallum (109): has   six   brothers; meets Young Bayard in Jefferson (109); guarantees horse trader that the horse Bayard rides will be paid for (118); twin of Stuart; 44 years old (310).

Deacon (112) Rogers (142): proprietor   of   store-restaurant   where Bayard and McCallum drink (110).

Houston   (111): black   waiter-cook who brings mixings to Bayard and Rafe McCallum (110).

Henry McCallum (111): makes   moonshine   whisky   (111);   something womanish about him; superintends kitchen; makes good whisky (308); 53

years old; second son (310).

Virginius (305) McCallum (112): father of Rafe and other McCallums (112); in 1861, at 16, walked to Virginia to enlist; widowed; 82 years old [born 1845; gives date of action 1927; time inconsistency here.]

Buddy (112) Virginius (325) McCallum (112): in WW I (112); awarded medal (314); youngest son; 20 years old (325).

Samson (113): neighbor of McCallums (113).

_____: Anzac major and two ladies in Leicester lounge with Bayard (114, 352).

Eustace (116)_____: lawyer (115), insulted by Young Bayard (116).

_____Gratton (115): insulted by Young Bayard (115).

_____: horse trader; horses victims of railroad (117).

Tobe (117)_____: black hostler (117).

_____: small black child that Bayard and horse leap over (119).

_____: white man in wagon in path of Bayard and horse (119).

_____: two blacks, one with pitchfork; Bayard on horse (120).

V. K. Suratt (121): sewing-machine agent; drives Bayard (121) to barn for whisky (123).

Hub (124)_____: youth on fender of Suratt's car (121).

_____: Suratt's grandfather; leg removed by Doc Peabody (125).

_____: four men who hold down Suratt's grandfather (125).

_____Suratt (126): V. K.'s brother; taught him to chop cotton (126).

_____: Hub's mother (127).

Sue (127)_____: Hub's sister (127).

Mitch (124)_____: freight agent at railway station; accompanies Young Bayard and Hub (129).

_____: two of the black musicians; accompany Young Bayard (129).

Reno (133)_____: third musician who accompanies Young Bayard (133).

Buck (141)_____: marshal (141); takes Young Bayard to his room for night (142-143).

_____: station agent (145).

Sol (148)_____: porter (146).

_____: trainhand and baggage clerk (146).

_____: Marine private at railroad station; spits at Horace's feet (147).

_____: English architect who built Benbow's house (151).

Francis Benbow (152): brought lantana tree home from Barbados in '71 (152).

Will Benbow (152): father of Horace and Narcissa (152); takes son to circus (291).

Flem Snopes (154): first Snopes in Jefferson; in restaurant; brings family one by one into town; becomes manager of city light and water plant; becomes vice president of Sartoris bank (154).

_____ Snopes (154): his wife (154).

_____ Snopes (154): his child (154).

Sophia (162)_____: maiden elder sister of Aunt Sally (155).

_____: other sister of Aunt Sally (155).

Julia Benbow (156): wife of Will Benbow; mother of Horace and Narcissa (156); died when Horace was 14, Narcissa 7 (160).

_____: Horace's servant at Oxford (164).

Belle (181) Mitchell (166): Belle Mitchell's 8-year-old daughter (166); called Titania by Horace (175); lives with Horace and Belle (340).

_____: son of carpenter; made a poet by Belle Mitchell; now a reporter on Texas newspaper (168).

_____: besotted young man whom he replaced (168).

57

Mrs. _____ Marders (169): guest at Mitchell house (169).

Frankie (169) _____: young girl at Mitchell tennis court (169); 17 years old (174).

Joe (177) _____: book-keeper in local department store; plays tennis at Mitchell's (172).

_____: youth recently expelled from state university; plays tennis at Mitchell's (172).

_____: gardner-stableman-chauffeur for Mitchells (175).

_____: another youth who plays tennis (179).

_____: Little Belle's music teacher (185).

_____: black man in wagon when Bayard crashes his car (196); takes Bayard home in wagon (199, 202).

John Henry (198) _____: his son (196); pulls Bayard from under car (198).

_____: grandmother of Will Falls (210).

Zeb Fothergill (212): stole horse from Sherman's picket (212).

_____: black woman who works for Beards (217).

I. O. Snopes (217): runs restaurant; takes in Byron (217).

Clarence Snopes (218): son of I. O. Snopes (218).

Mrs. I. O. Snopes (218): swings in porch swing all day (218).

_____: succeeds Colonel John Sartoris as colonel (220).

Mrs. _____ Winterbottom (224): owner of boarding house in which Colonel John Sartoris kills two carpetbaggers (224).

Dr. _____ Brandt (228): specialist in Memphis to whom Dr. Alford and Miss Jenny take Bayard for his wen (227).

Mrs. _____ Smith (228): telephone operator in Brandt's office (227).

_____: youth who drives Bayard's car to Memphis for repairs (247).

_____: black man visited by Byron Snopes (251); supplies him with escape car (257).

58

_____Varner (251)_: owner of store in Frenchman's Bend (257).

Mrs._____Littlejohn_____(257)_: owner of boarding house in Frenchman's Bend (257).

_____Turpin (258)_.

Minnie Sue Turpin (258)_: resists Byron Snopes's sexual advances (260).

Uncle Bird (261)_____: one of delegation of six blacks who want Simon to repay money (261).

_____: leader of delegation of blacks; wears Prince Albert coat (261); reinstates Simon after Old Bayard repays money (264).

_____Moore (263)_: member of black delegation; announces that Simon has absconded with $67.40 (263).

_____: elderly black man who owns cane mill (267).

_____: his grandson who feeds mill (267).

Unc' Henry (270)_____.

Euphrony Strother (277)_: Simon's wife (277).

Abe (279)_____: black man who baits Doc Peabody's line (279).

Eunice (283)_____: Benbows's cook (283).

Joan (293) Heppleton (298)_: woman with bronze hair (290); knows Horace's name (292); Belle's sister (293); visits Horace's house; talks of her lovers; married at 18 to a man three times her age; deserts him in Honolulu; goes to Australia with Englishman; assumes his name; divorced; deserted by Englishman in Bombay; remarries an American in Calcutta; divorced year later; has settlement from first husband (295); has an affair with Horace Benbow; asks him not to talk about love (296 ff.); leaves town without warning (299).

_____: clerk in drugstore; rewraps Joan's package (293).

_____: Joan's first husband; three times her age; deserted by her in Honolulu (295).

_____Heppleton (298)_: Englishman; lover of Joan; deserts her in Bombay (295).

_____: second husband of Joan, American; divorced (295).

_____: Joan's father (296).

_____: Joan's mother (296).

_____: man in Ford car; stalls as Bayard drives past (300).

Mrs. Virginius McCallum (305): first wife of Virginius; now dead (305).

_____ McCallum (305): father of Virginius McCallum; gave son mule on his marriage (305).

Mrs. Virginius McCallum (305): second wife of Virginius (305); mother of Buddy (325).

Mandy (306)_____: McCallums's cook (306).

Lee McCallum (306): least talkative of family (307); in late 30's; keeping company with woman (322).

_____: black man who sneaked Bayard's horse to him (306).

_____: black man who assists Henry McCallum in making whisky (308).

(Richud) Richard_____: one of black men in Mandy's kitchen (309).

_____: another black man in Mandy's kitchen (309).

_____: half-grown black boy in Mandy's kitchen (309).

Jackson McCallum (310): eldest son of Virginius; 55 (310); breeds cross between fox and hound (318).

Stuart McCallum (310): twin of Rafe; 44 (310).

_____: black man in whose barn Bayard sleeps on Christmas eve (331).

_____: his wife (334).

_____: his three children (334).

_____: his brother-in-law (probably does not exist) (335).

_____: mail carrier at station (343).

_____: express agent at station (343).

_____: express car clerk who hands package of shrimp to Horace (343).

_____DuPre: husband of Virginia Sartoris DuPre (350).

_____: woman in Chicago nightclub with Bayard [II] (351).

_____Monaghan (354): aviator in Chicago with Bayard [II] (351).

_____: shabby man in Chicago with Bayard [II]; wants him to fly plane (351).

_____: traffic cop (353).

_____Comyn (354): in WW I (354).

_____: woman with Harry Mitchell in Chicago (355).

_____: waiter with Harry Mitchell in Chicago (355).

_____: man who lends Bayard [II] helmet and goggles; warns him not to fly plane (356).

Benbow (369) Sartoris (358): son of Bayard [III] and Narcissa (358).

_____Sartoris: wife of Colonel John Sartoris (359).

_____: telegraph operator in Jefferson (359).

_____: nurse to Benbow Sartoris (361).

_____Peabody: wife of Dr. Lucius Peabody, the elder (367).

Dr. _____Straud (368): mentioned by young Dr. Peabody.

"Music - Sweeter Than the Angels Sing"

Ghost written for Katherine Hargis, a friend, shortly before first publication in the *University of Missisppi Freshman Theme Review,* **3, No. 11 (Week ending April 28, 1928).**

Pagination, in parentheses, to the University of Mississippi Freshman Theme Review, 3, No. 11 (Week ending April 28, 1928); republished in The Southern Review, 12, No. 4 (October, 1976) to which second pagination refers. The latter publication corrects some misprints in the original, misspells a word, and changes the spelling from Katherine to Katharine.

_____: ticket agent in Jackson, Tennessee (1, 868).

Joby (1, 868)_____: first black train passenger; going to Oxford, Missisippi; likes to hear train whistle (1, 868); injured in train wreck; asks Captain Barr to blow train whistle for him (2, 870); dies (3, 871).

Rastus (1, 868)_____: black companion to Joby; going to Grand Junction Tennessee (1, 868).

Joe (1, 868)_____: brakeman on train (1, 868).

Captain_____Barr (1, 868): train engineer (1, 868); his engine passes over a defective rail joint and cars are wrecked; many are killed (2, 870).

_____: four black brothers on train (1, 868).

Colonel (2, 869)_____Murray (2, 869): owns the Birmingham cut-off road (2, 869).

A 5 *The Sound and the Fury*

Begun as early as 1925, in Paris; written between the fall of 1927 and October, 1928; published October 7, 1929. Originally titled "Twilight."

Pagination, in parentheses, for the following editions: (New York: Jonathan Cape and Harrison Smith, 1929), 401 pp., (New York: Vintage Books, 1963); paperback, with "Appendix: Compson: 1669-1945," pp.403-427. [See Meriwether's cautionary remarks about this issue.] (New York: Modern Library, 1966); (New York: Random House, 1966); (New York: Modern Library, 1967), a "Modern Library College Editions" paperback. In 1984 Random House published a "New, Corrected" edition of The Sound and the Fury with new pagination. The second set of page references, therefore, is to this new edition (New York: Random House, 1984), New, Corrected Edition, 326 pp.

Beginning of Benjy's Section April 7, 1928

Maury (23, 20) Benjy (3, 4) Benjamin (3, 5) Compson (95, 77): the monologuist of part I; watches golfers; 33 years old on April 7,1928 [*ergo*, born April 7, 1895]; must be cared for by a guardian (1, 3); taller than Luster (2, 4); years earlier [1902-1903], at Christmas time, he and Caddy perform a chore for Uncle Maury (3, 5); goes to meet Caddy at gate in winter (4-5, 6-7); to him, Caddy smells like leaves and trees (5, 6); is driven to the cemetery by T. P. to visit graves of his brother Quentin and his father [*ca.* 1914] (9-13, 9-12); by 1914, is as big as the 18-year-old T. P. (9, 9); once had a spotted pony (13, 12); carries Uncle Maury's letter as he and Caddy deliver it to Mrs. Patterson; is sent alone by Maury to deliver a note to Mrs. Patterson; Mr. Patterson intercepts it (14-15, 13-14); Luster thinks that Benjy is not aware that the family no longer owns the pasture (22, 19); once named Maury (23, 20); gets drunk with T. P. on the day of Caddy's wedding [April 25, 1910] (24, 21); cries on the night of Damuddy's death when children hear their mother crying (29, 25); cries when Dilsey sings (33, 28); sleeps at Dilsey's cabin with T. P. at time of Quentin's funeral (34-35, 29); plays at Dilsey's house with Luster and Miss Quentin (both babies) at the time of his father's funeral [1912] (35, 30); sleeps with Luster that night (38, 32); "smells" his father's death and cries (40, 34); is taken by T. P. to the ditch where Nancy's [farm animal] bones lie and where he can bellow without disturbing anyone; voice has changed (40-42, 33-35); climbs on box to look in window at Caddy's wedding; bellows (46-47, 39-40); gets hiccups (48, 40); when Caddy puts her arms about him on her wedding day, can not smell trees at this time and begins to cry (48, 40); earlier [*ca.* 1905-1906], becomes upset when Caddy wears perfume for then she does not smell like trees; accepts her again after she has washed (48-51, 40-43); at 13 [1908] Dilsey decides he is no longer to sleep with Caddy (51-52, 43); becomes upset when he discovers [*ca.* 1908] Caddy in the swing with Charlie; disturbs Miss Quentin and the pitchman in the swing (56-58, 46-48); after Caddy's marriage and departure, goes to gate to look for her; escapes from yard and grabs a schoolgirl (62-64, 51-53); name changed to Benjamin; mother teaches him new name (68, 57); burns hand on stove (72, 59); his mother's complaints about his crying for burnt hand trigger a series of memories of her "sicknesses" and self-indulgence at the time of Damuddy's funeral and his name-changing day (72-78, 59-64); senses that Caddy has lost virginity or is pregnant (84-85, 68-69); cries when he looks for his missing testicles as he undresses (90. 73); with Luster, watches from window as Miss Quentin escapes (90-91, 74); smells death on the night of Damuddy's death (92, 75); [end of Benjy's section]; his pasture sold to send Quentin to Harvard (116, 94); howls at Caddy at the time of Dalton Ames affair (185, 149); [end of Quentin's section]; is one and a half times as tall as Jason (244, 196); [end of Jason's section]; described in 1928 as big, with dead, hairless skin, pale fine hair, clear pale blue eyes; moves with shambling gait (342, 274); "smells" Miss Quentin's escape (359, 288) goes to church with Dilsey on Easter (360 ff., 289 ff.); can manage solid food by himself (376, 301); likes to play with a mound of earth and two bottles of flowers; called his cemetery (393, 317); rides with Luster to graveyard (396, 317); bellows loudly when Luster takes Queenie around the square in wrong direction (399-400, 320); becomes serene after Jason turns Queenie toward home and buildings and other objects are passed in their familiar sequence (400-401, 320-321).

Luster (1, 3)   : Benjy's black attendant in 1928; lost a quarter in the field; wants to go to a show (2, 3); Dilsey's grandson; finds a golf ball (17, 15-16); threatens to whip Benjy (19, 17); son of Frony (35, 30); afraid of seeing the ghost of his grandfather [Roskus] (40, 33); tries to keep Benjy from disturbing Miss Quentin and the pitchman (56, 46); tells pitchman that Benjy is deaf as well as dumb (60, 49); finds cover of contraceptive conainer by swing; shows it to pitchman; speaks of Miss Quentin's other suitors (61, 50); tries to sell golf ball to golfer who steals it from him (65, 53); becomes mean to Benjy; says he will be sent to Jackson as soon as his mother is dead; makes him cry; whispers Caddy's name (66, 54-55); sasses Dilsey (67, 55); eats some of Benjy's birthday cake; continues to torment Benjy (70, 57); asks Jason for a quarter (81, 67); gets his quarter from Miss Quentin (91, 74); [end of Benjy's section]; asks Jason for a ticket to the show; watches him burn them both; (317-318, 255); [end of Quentin's section] [end of Jason's section]; finally goes to the show (334, 268); announces that Jason's window is broken (343, 275); tells Dilsey that he and Benjy saw Miss Quentin climbing out window the night before (357, 286); tries to play the saw in basement (358, 287); wearing new hat, accompanies Dilsey, Frony, and Benjy to church on Easter (360-361, 289); torments Benjy by taking part of his "cemetery" away and whispering "Caddy" in his ear (393-394, 315-316); to quiet Benjy, Dilsey permits Luster to drive him toward the graveyard in T. P.'s absence (396, 317); swings Queenie to left rather than to right at square (399-400, 320).

Caddy (3, 4) Candace (7, 7) Compson (95, 77): Benjy's sister (3, 4); protects him fondly (5, 6); takes Benjy with her to deliver Uncle Maury's letter (7, 8); very devoted to Benjy; takes Uncle Maury's letter to Mrs. Patterson (13, 12-13); on the night of Damuddy's death [1898], gets wet playing in the branch; seven years old [born ca. 1891] (19-20, 17-18); takes off dress; fights with Quentin in branch; both get wet (20-21, 18-19); her name is not mentioned after she sent her daughter home (37, 31); on night of Damuddy's death, leads children in climbing tree to see

66

in window (44-46, 38-39); expects a band for Damuddy's funeral; when she is 14 [1905-1906], starts to wear grown-up clothes and perfume, but, because Benjy does not like the smell of perfume, gives her bottle to Dilsey (48-51, 40-43); when Dilsey puts Benjy to bed by himself, comes to lie down with him until he falls asleep [1908] (53, 44); when [ca. 1908] Benjy gets upset at finding her in the swing kissing Charlie, quiets him by leaving Charlie, promising Benjy that she "wont anymore," and washes her mouth with kitchen soap (56-58, 47-48); cares for Benjy, and continues to try to carry him when his name is changed [ca. 1900], although he is then too big for her to carry (74-75, 61-62); when she loses her virginity or knows she is pregnant, Benjy senses it(84-85, 68-69); feeds Benjy (86, 70); refuses to look at Quentin during his meeting with Sydney Herbert Head (117, 95); the night before the wedding, she asks Quentin to take care of Benjy and Father (131, 106); says she is sick; tells Quentin not to interfere in her marriage (137, 111); makes Quentin promise to prevent them from sending Benjy to Jackson; says she had no control of her action with her lovers (138-139, 112-113); does not know who the father of her child is (143, 115); when Benjy howls after the Dalton Ames affair, runs to branch and sits in water (185 ff., 148 ff.); confesses her love of Dalton Ames (he is the only one she loves) by holding Quentin's hand against her heart (187, 150); finds Quentin after he has attempted to send Ames away; again demonstrates her love for him by having Quentin feel pulse in throat (203, 162-164) [end of Quentin's section]; in letter to Jason, encloses check; accuses him of tampering with letters to Miss Quentin (236, 190); Head casts her off (245, 197-198); returns for father's funeral; no one had notified her of death (251, 202); gives Jason $100 to let her see daughter (253, 203-204); visits her and Ben with Dilsey's help (257, 206-207); distrusts Jason; asks to see the bank statements to find where her money is going; sends money each month; her checks have been coming for fifteen years (272-273, 218-219) [end of Jason's section].

Maury (3, 4) L. (279, 224) Bascomb (127, 279, 103, 224: uncle to Caddy and Benjy (3, 4); drinks (4, 5); gives Caddy a letter to deliver (7, 8); beaten up by Mr. Patterson (52, 43); [end of Benjy's section] [end of Quentin's section]; writes to Jason to draw money from his mother's account (277-279, 223-224) [end of Jason's section].

Versh (3, 5) Gibson (363, 291): black attendant to Benjy in the earliest period (3, 5); carries Benjy (then called Maury) on the night of Damuddy's death (23, 20); gets "Memphis notions" (37, 31); tells Benjy that he is going to become a "bluegum" because his name was changed (84, 69); says Benjy's name was changed because his mother was too proud (86, 70) [end of Benjy's section].

Caroline (4, 5) Bascomb (127, 103) Compson (95, 77): Benjy's mother (3, 5); complains about Benjy worrying her (7, 8); a hypochondriac (8, 8); makes weekly trip to cemetery (9-13, 9-12); cries on night of her mother's death [1898] (29, 25); cries at the death of her husband (40, 34); complains about Benjy disturbing her when he burns his hand; is completely ungrateful to Dilsey about Benjy's birthday cake; full of self-pity (72-74, 59-60); unable to cope with Benjy when he is five (75,

62); locks Miss Quentin in her room at night; asks for hot water bottle (90, 73) [end of Benjy's section]; husband objects to her and Quentin spying on Caddy (118, 96); wants to leave family; take Jason with her after she learns of Caddy's affair with Dalton Ames; says Jason is the only one to whom her heart goes out (126, 102); rejects Bemjy, Caddy, and Quentin in a long tirade, being very conscious of having married above her station, and being also conscious of a sense of sin (126 ff., 102 ff.); it has been her dream that Quentin go to Harvard from before his birth (221, 178) [end of Quentin's section]; forbids the family to mention Caddy's name before Miss Quentin (247, 199); at her husband's funeral, thanks God she is left with Jason rather than with Quentin (249, 200); burns check she thinks is Caddy's (273, 220); thinks she has invested $1000 in Earl's business for Jason (281, 225); when she saw Caddy (at 15) kissing a boy, wore mourning the next day (286, 229-230); says Quentin and Caddy always conspired against her (326, 261); bemoans the loss of family fortune and status (326-327, 261-262) [end of Jason's section]; thinks at first that Miss Quentin committed suicide after her disappearance (352, 283).

Dilsey (9, 9) Gibson (363, 291): Versh's mother (3, 5); Luster's grandmother (35, 30); moans at Roskus's funeral (39, 33); on the night of Damuddy's death, gets all the children out of the tree and into the house (54-55, 45); reprimands Luster for teasing Benjy (68, 57); gives Benjy a birthday cake that she bought with her own money (69, 58); beats Luster for teasing Benjy (71, 59); threatens to have his "pappy" beat him when he comes home (72, 59); on the night of Damuddy's death, puts children to bed in the spare room (89-90, 73) [end of Benjy's section]; [end of Quentin's section]; tries to defend Miss Quentin from Jason; (228-230, 184-185); tells him to hit her rather than Miss Quentin (230, 185); takes over the care of Miss Quentin from the moment Mr. Compson brings her home (246, 198); helps Caddy to see her baby (257, 207); scorns Jason (318, 255) [end of Jason's section]; forgets Mrs. Compson's hot water bottle on Easter morn (337, 342, 270, 275); says Luster has just as much Compson devilment in him as any Compson (344, 277); takes Benjy to church on Easter (360 ff., 289 ff.); says the Lord does not care whether Benjy is smart or not (362, 290); as the preacher's voice becomes more black and his message more emotional, begins to weep; weeping as she leaves the church, says, "I've seed de first en de last . . . I seed de beginnin, en now I sees de endin."(371, 297).

Jason (7, 8) Richmond Compson (95, 77): father of Compson children (7, 8); begins to drink heavily about 1908; belittles Uncle Maury to his wife (52-53, 43-44); whips Jason after he cuts up Benjy's dolls (83, 68); sits with his children when wife is sick at name change (88, 72) [end of Benjy's section]; gives Quentin his own father's watch (93, 76); says that virginity is only a state in which others are left, and that "nothing is even worth the changing of it" (96, 78); says people are not able to do anything very dreadful (98, 80); suggests that Mrs. Compson take Caddy to French Lick to forget "him" [Dalton Ames?] and to allow the talk to die away (126, 102); drinks himself to death (154, 124); explains menstruation to Quentin (159, 128) [end of Quentin's section]; on March 26, 1912, went "up there" and brought Caddy's baby, Miss Quentin, home;

died a month later and was buried on April 22, 1912 (245, 197-198); probably told Herbert Head that Miss Quentin was not his child (246, 198) [end of Jason's section].

T. P. (9, 9) Gibson (363, 291): Benjy's attendant in middle period; 18 years old; drives surrey when Roskus is laid up (9-10, 9-10); gets drunk with Bejny on day of Caddy's wedding (23, 20); calls the champagne "sasprilluh" (25, 21); helps Roskus with milking; son of Roskus and Dilsey; brother of Frony and Versh (34, 29); milked young cow dry [technically: milked lazily and therefore insufficiently so that she ceased producing milk] (36, 30); takes Miss Quentin and Benjy to view the hearse at Mr. Compson's funeral (38, 32); on the night of Damuddy's death, lets Benjy play with his bottle of lightning bugs (43, 36); with Benjy, climbs on box to see Caddy's wedding; both are drunk and fall off (46-48, 39-40); thinks he will blame the dog, Dan, for drinking champagne (47, 39) [end of Benjy's section].

Roskus (9, 9) Gibson (363, 291): by *ca.* 1914, has such bad rheumatism that he cannot drive the surrey (9, 9); early stages of rheumatism [*ca.* 1911-1912] prevent him from milking (34, 28); says there is no luck on the Compson place (34, 29); sees change of Benjy's name as bad luck (35, 29); dies about 1920 (39, 33); sometime before 1912, shoots farm animal, Nancy, when she falls into ditch (40, 33); [end of Benjy's section].

Jason (9, 9) Compson (95, 77): monologuist of part III; head of family after deaths of Quentin and Mr. Compson (9, 9); announces that Uncle Maury is drawing on his mother's account for $50 (12, 12); when the other children play in branch on night of Damuddy's death, plays off by himself (21, 19); other children are sure that he will tell on them (22, 20); as a child, he walks with his hands in his pockets (23, 20); as a child, is fat; tattles on the others (27, 23); cries when no longer allowed to sleep with Damuddy (31, 26); cries when he learns of her death (42, 36); first speaks of sending Benjy to Jackson *ca.* 1911, when Benjy escapes from the yard (63, 52); cuts up Benjy's dolls (79, 65); threatens Miss Quentin for being with the show fellow (82, 67); as a child, chews paper (88, 72) [end of Benjy's section]; was promised a job by Head (114, 91); was treasurer in a child's business of making kites with the Patterson boy (116, 94); his mother says he is more Bascomb than Compson (127, 103); smell of gasoline makes him sick (213, 172); when he and Patterson boy have financial trouble in the kite business, gets an even smaller partner, and remains treasurer (217-218, 175) [end of Quentin's section]; in 1928, still resents Quentin's year at Harvard and father's drinking; calls Miss Quentin a bitch (223-224, 180-181); has sadistic, incestuous attraction to Miss Quentin (225, 181); bullies and is rough with Miss Quentin (227-228, 183-184); finds Luster has not replaced spare tire on car; orders Luster to keep Benjy in rear of house (231-232, 186-187); stubbornly refuses to replace tire himself (232, 187); receives letter with check from Caddy addressed to his mother (236, 263, 190, 212); is anti-semitic (237, 191); speculates in cotton market; pays $10 a month to a New York firm for advice (239, 192); gets letter from girl friend (prostitute) Lorraine; burns it; last time gave her $40 and the maid $5 (240-241, 193-194); at father's funeral bitterly resents Quentin's year at Harvard and lost job (245, 197); takes $100 from Caddy in cemetery for quick glimpse of her baby (253, 204); tries to prevent Dilsey from letting Caddy see her baby and Benjy by telling her that Caddy has leprosy (257, 207); promises Caddy that to give Miss Quentin the check that she sends her (261, 210); lets Caddy visit her daughter once or twice a year; opens her letter; finds $50 money order in it; discovers that she has no more blank checks; puts Caddy's check and money order in desk (262-263, 211); tells Miss Quentin that her money order is for $10 forces her to sign it and gives her cash (264-267, 212-214); insists on going home to lunch; searches for blank checks; forges a chech and puts it in Caddy's letter to his mother and reseals it (269, 216-217); goes through check-burning ritual with mother (272-273, 219-220); wants to send Benjy to Jackson (276, 221); insists on banking salary each month in his mother's name; has her power of attorney (281, 225-226); lies to employer, Earl; says he went to dentist instead of home to lunch (283, 227); says he deposits $160 a month in mother's account (284, 228); sees Miss Quentin and the pitchman (288-289, 231-232); chases them (290, 233); gets telegram saying his cotton account was closed out at 20.62 (292, 234); leaves work in his car; is beginning to get headache [from gasoline]; refuses to take aspirin (293-294, 235-236); gets money from cash box (296, 237); chases Miss Quentin and pitchman (296 ff., 238 ff.); they trick him and let air out of his tire; flee (302, 242); returns to town (305, 244-245); objects to Benjy's Sunday rides (312, 250); does not like Babe Ruth (314, 252); lies in saying he has not seen Miss Quentin since morning (316, 324, 254, 260); burns tickets to show before Luster (317-318, 255); torments Miss Quentin at dinner (321-324, 258-260); says Caddy can not name father of her child; then retracts statement (327, 262); counts money before retiring (328, 263) [end of Jason's section]; complains that his window has been broken (345, 278); has changed lock to room so that no one can enter when he is away; orders Miss Quentin to breakfast on Easter morning (346, 247); while Dilsey calls her, realizes what has happened; rushes to her empty room (351, 281); finds money box empty (353, 283; calls sheriff (354, 284); drives to Mottson (381, 305); fights with circus cook (385-388, 309-311); pays black man $4 to drive him back to Jefferson (391, 313); turns surrey around in square (400, 320).

Miss Quentin (10, 10) Compson (95, 77): [Caddy's daughter] in swing with a man (56, 46); runs to house when Benjy and Luster approach (59, 49); says Benjy should be sent to Jackson; threatens to leave home (85, 69-70); objects to eating with Benjy; says they sent him to spy on her (86-87, 70-71); argues with Jason; pushes Dilsey from her; runs to her room (87, 71); gives Luster a quarter (89, 72); her grandmother locks her in room each night (90, 73); climbs out window and runs away (90-91, 74) [end of Benjy's section] [end of Quentin's section] 17 years old in 1928 [born November 1910] (223, 180); has been skipping school (224, 180); when Jason bullies her, fights back (228, 183); when Dilsey tries to protect her from Jason, hits her hand down and calls her a "damned old nigger" (230, 185); insists that her mother buys her clothes and school books (232-233, 187); says she is sorry she was born (234, 188); defies Jason and, like her mother, says she is bad and is going to hell (235, 189); surprises Jason with her $50 order; almost gets it from his desk

(264, 212); is forced to sign money order unseen and to accept $10 (267, 215); fails to come to lunch (277, 222); lets air out of Jason's tire (302, 242) [end of Jason's section]; breaks window to Jason's room; steals his money; escapes (343-353, 275-283).

Quentin (12, 11) Compson (95, 77): monologuist of part II; brother of Caddy, Benjy, and Jason; fights with Caddy in branch on night of Damuddy's death; they get wet; kicks T. P. into hog trough; fights with him at Caddy's wedding (23-24, 20-21); gives Benjy a hot drink to make him vomit the champagne (25, 22); insists his mother is crying on night of Damuddy's death (30 ff., 25 ff.); in a fight at the time of name change (82-83, 67-68); seems to know of Damuddy's death before other children (90, 73) [end of Benjy's section]; wakes at Harvard; estimates time; hears watch; thinks of St. Francis's Little Sister Death (93-94, 76); turns watch face down (94, 77); thinks of announcement of his sister's wedding and of having confessed incest to his father; recalls conversation with father about Caddy and virginity; dwells on thought of having a sister (95-96, 77); yearns to be in hell with sister; rehearses confession of incest; thinks of Dalton Ames (97-98, 79-80); thinks of suicide and flatirons; says that you commit suicide not when you realize that nothing will help, but when you realize that you do not need any help; twists hands off his watch (98, 80); lays out clothes and packs trunk; dresses in best suit; writes two notes; aware of passage of time; constantly thinks of Caddy's wedding (99-100, 81-82); becomes his own sundial when he becomes aware of his shadow; mails letter to father (101, 82); visits watchmaker's shop (102, 83); buys two six-pound flatirons (105, 85); gets on street car; remembers Christmas trip back home, December 1909 (105-107, 86-87); gets off car at bridge (110, 89); thinking of his own suicide, recalls Benjy's ability to "smell" death; sight of Bland rowing (111, 90) triggers beginning of association with Dalton Ames and khaki shirts, a theatrical fixture once seen, and his sister's rendezvous with suitors (113, 92); thinks of Caddy's wedding announcement and of his meeting with Sydney Herbert Head; in this whole memory, is haunted by thoughts of "little sister" and "had no sister" (113-115, 92-94); returns to Harvard by another street car (116-117, 94-95); remembers packing bags for trip to French Lick (117, 95); recalls father's objection to spying on Caddy and conversation with father in August 1909 (118-119, 96); gives Deacon noter for Shreve; shakes hands in farewell (119-124, 97-100); tells Shreve about note (125, 101); leaves on another trolley (126, 102); changes to another car; changes trolley again and then gets on interurban car (129, 104-105); thinks of interview with Caddy on eve of wedding (130-131, 105-106); recalls interview with Head about cheating and his refusal of both a job and money (132-136, 107-111); associates Bland's rowing with Herbert and Caddy (137-138, 111-112); leaves interurban car; starts to walk (138, 112); recalls being thrown by a horse [ca. 1907]; and injuring broken leg trying to drive off Caddy's early lover [probably the "pimple faced infant"] (139-140, 113); recalls hunting trip [ca. 1908] with Louis Hatcher and Versh (140-142, 114-115); recalls discussion of paternity of Caddy's baby before the wedding and telling his father in August 1909 the story Versh told him of the man who mutilated himself (142-143, 115-116); hides the flatirons under the end of a bridge; yearns for a private hell for him and Caddy; watches a big trout from bridge (144-145, 116-117); remembers telling Caddy that Herbert Head was dropped from his club for cheating at cards and suggesting that Caddy, Benjy, and he go away together (152-153, 123-124); visits bakery; meets little girl (155 ff., 126 ff.); calls her "sister" and unknowingly assumes the Dalton Ames role with her and her brother Julio (155, 126); lies to bakery woman to protect little girl (156, 126); buys girl ice cream (159, 128); tries to find where girl lives (160, 129); runs away (165, 133); recalls time he slapped Caddy for kissing a boy and time he hugged Natalie (166-172, 133-139); climbs wall and finds himself back with little girl (166, 134); attacked by Julio and arrested by Anse for kidnapping girl (172-173, 139); meets Mrs. Bland and others (175-176, 141-142); pays Julio one dollar and a fine of $6 (179-180, 144-145); after he joins Mrs. Bland and others, begins to recall Caddy's affair with Dalton Ames and to transfer his antagonism to Gerald (184 ff., 148 ff.); begins a long recall of Dalton Ames affair (184-203, 148-164); in this reminiscence, he recalls the following events: Caddy talks of Quentin's virginity; he tries to assume the guilt of her affairs (185, 149); follows Caddy to branch, and threatens to kill Dalton Ames (185-187, 149-151); throughout this whole reminiscence, he is haunted by smell of honeysuckle (185 ff., 149 ff.); falsely confesses to having had lots of affairs with girls (188, 151); suggests a suicide pact with Caddy, but can not act (188-189, 152)); is introduced to Dalton Ames (192, 155); after her meeting with Ames, says there is a curse on the family (196, 158); tries to face up to Dalton Ames and make him leave town; faints when he tries to hit him; the key phrase "did you ever have a sister" is here introduced (196-203, 158-164); [This whole Dalton Ames affair is recalled by Quentin while riding in the car with the Blands just after he had played the Dalton Ames role to the outraged Julio (185-196, 149-158)] has fought with Gerald; bathes his bloody face; Shreve helps him (203 ff., 164 ff.); worries about cleaning his vest (204 ff., 165 ff.); before he hit Gerald, had asked him if he ever had a sister (206, 166); sends Spoade and Shreve back to picnic; catches car (207-209, 167-169); has been hit in left eye (209, 169); changes to trolley; returns to Harvard (212, 171); in his room, hope that Shreve followed him begins to grow; decides to leave blood-stained tie to Deacon; tries to clean vest with gasoline (213, 171-172); changes shirt and tie; counts time left for Shreve to reach him; has a vision of himself on trolley going to death and passing Shreve going the opposite way (214, 172); on way to lavatory, recalls trip to bathroom at night as a boy (215-216, 173-174); yearns for death: "And then I'll not be." (216, 174); begins a long reminiscence of several blended periods (216 ff., 174 ff.); it is centered on Dalton Ames and Caddy (216-217, 174-175); recalls discussing suicide with father as well as failure to commit incest (219, 176-177); dresses; gets fresh handkerchief; brushes teeth; leaves room to mail Shreve's letter (222, 178-179); [end of Quentin's section]; suicide by drowning (243, 196) [end of Jason's section].

Mrs.   Patterson (13, 13): woman with whom Uncle Maury is having an affair; he sends letter to her by Caddy and Benjy [1902-1903]; caught by her husband when Benjy, delivering a letter alone, fails to escape notice (14-15, 13-14) [end of Benjy's section].

Mr.   Patterson (14, 13): intercepts letter from Maury to Mrs.

Patterson (14, 13); beats up Uncle Maury (52, 43) [end of Benjy's section].

Damuddy (22, 20) Bascomb (127, 103): grandmother of the Compson children; sick (22, 20); takes meals in bed (27, 23); dies in 1898 (28, 24); Mrs. Compson's mother (29 ff., 25 ff.) [end of Benjy's section].

Frony (34, 29) Gibson (363, 291)_____: mother of Luster (35, 30); daughter of Dilsey and Roskus; sister of T. P. and of Versh (34, 29); informs children of Damuddy's death by mentioning the funeral (39, 33); [end of Benjy's section] [end of Quentin's section] [end of Jason's section]; accompanies her mother, Luster, and Benjy to church on Easter; objects to Benjy's presence (362, 290).

Sis Beulah Clay (39, 33): mentioned by Frony; they moaned at her funeral for two days (39, 33); [end of Benjy's section].

_____: pitchman in swing with Miss Quentin (56, 46); wears red tie (58, 48); learns of Miss Quentin's sexual promiscuity when Luster finds cover of contraceptive container (61, 50-51); [end of Benjy's section].

Mrs._____Burgess (63, 52): mother of girl Benjy knocked down when he got out (64, 52-53); [end of Benjy's section].

_____Burgess (63, 52): schoolgirl knocked down by Benjy (64, 53) [end of Benjy's section].

_____: golfer who takes Luster's golf ball (65, 53); [end of Benjy's section].

Charlie (57, 47)_____: one of Caddy's early boy friends (57, 47) [end of Benjy's section].

_____: Frony's husband, Luster's father (71-72, 59); [end of Benjy's section].

Beginning of Quentin's Section June 2, 1910

[Except for Sydney Herbert Head, all characters from Shreve MacKenzie through Colonel Sartoris exist only in Quentin's section.]

Shreve (95, 77) MacKenzie (182, 146): [See "Genealogy" following text of *Absalom, Absalom* where his name is given as Shrevlin McCannon.] Quentin's roommate at Harvard; wears glasses; warns Quentin that he is likely to be late for chapel (95, 77-78); returns; sees Quentin dressed up; asks, "Is it a wedding or a wake?" [It is both.] (100, 82); when Quentin fails to open Caddy's wedding announcement, assumes it refers to Quentin's sweetheart (115, 93); questions Quentin about package [flatirons] he is carrying; tells him of Mrs. Bland's note (125, 101); interrupts at Quentin's trial (177 ff., 142 ff.); called "Mr. MacKenzie" by Mrs. Bland (182, 146); ministers to Quentin after fight (203 ff., 164 ff.); refuses to let Quentin apologize (207, 167); returns to picnic (208, 168).

_____ Spoade (96, 78): calls Shreve "Quentin's husband;" once tried to induce Quentin to go to a prostitute (95, 78); from South Carolina, a senior; never runs for chapel; never on time for it; attends both chapel and first lecture without shirt or socks; fully dressed at noon (96, 78-79); has five names including the name of a "present English ducal house" (113, 91-92); speaks to calm others at Quentin's trial (177, 143); says Quentin's father is a congregational minister (178, 143).

Dalton Ames (98, 79): has sexual relations with Caddy (98, 79); places pistol in Quentin's hand (98, 79); strong, can lift Caddy to his shoulder (187, 192, 150, 154); wears khaki shirt (197, 158); says if it had not been him with Caddy, it would have been someone else; says women are all bitches (199, 160); shows Quentin how well he can shoot; then hands him gun (199-200, 160-161).

Deacon (101, 82) _____: black man, always appears in parades (101, 82); meets all trains at beginning of school term at Harvard; can tell a southerner at a glance; uses a white boy of 15 to help with their bags (119-120, 97-98); accepts rumor and enlarges on it that he graduated from divinity school (120, 98); turned Democrat three years earlier; looks for patronage (12, 992).

_____: girl who sells Quentin a cigar (102, 83).

_____: two bootblacks to whom Quentin gives cigar (102, 83).

_____ Parker (102, 83): Quentin eats last breakfast at Parker's (102, 83).

_____: watchmaker whom Quentin visits (102, 83).

_____: black man on street car (105, 86).

_____: black man on mule, seen by Quentin from train, December 1909 (106, 86).

Miss Laura (108, 88) _____: Quentin's childhood teacher (108, 88).

Henry (108, 88) _____: Quentin's schoolmate; answers for him (108, 88).

Gerald Bland (111, 90): rows shell wearing straw hat and flannels (111, 90); curly yellow hair, violet eyes, a Kentuckian; has an apartment in town besides his room at Harvard; rows on river while Quentin watches (112, 91); beats Quentin in fight (203 ff., 164 ff.).

Mrs. _____ Bland (111, 90): Gerald's mother; speaks proudly of Gerald's women; dislikes Spoade; likes Quentin (112-113, 91); Shreve calls her "Semiramis" (125, 101); speaks to others of Gerald's beauty (130, 105); calls Shreve "that fat Canadian;" has twice tried to arrange new

74

roommate for Quentin (131, 106); sees Quentin arrested (175, 141); calls Shreve "Mr. MacKenzie" (182, 146).

_____: the "pimple-faced infant," one of Caddy's earliest suitors (114, 92).

Sydney Herbert Head (115, 93): promised Jason job in his bank; meets Quentin at station in April 1910; has given Caddy a car; from South Bend, Indiana (114-115, 93); flatters Mrs. Compson (117, 95); speaks to Quentin privately before the wedding (132, 107); they almost fight over his cheating at Harvard (133-134, 108-109); tries to offer Quentin a job (134, 109) or money (135, 110); dropped from his club at Harvard for cheating at cards (152, 123); [end of Quentin's section.] turns Caddy out and refuses to provide for her child (247, 198) [end of Jason's section].

Louis (114, 93)_____: presumably Herbert Head's chauffeur who has been teaching Caddy to drive (115, 93).

_____Patterson (116, 94): boy, partner of Jason in kite making (116, 94).

_____: 15-year-old white boy who helps Deacon (120, 97).

Louis Hatcher (141, 114): hunting companion [ca. 1908] of Quentin; cleaned his lantern on night of Johnstown flood [May 31, 1889]; thinks he thereby saved the town (141, 114).

Martha Hatcher (141, 114): wife of Louis Hatcher.

Kenny (145, 152, 117, 122)_____: one of three boys that Quentin meets on bridge (145, 152, 117, 122).

_____: little girl Quentin meets in bakery (155, 125); buys a five-cent loaf of bread (157, 126); will not leave Quentin (160 ff., 129 ff.); Italian (161, 129).

_____: woman in bakery (155, 125); dislikes little girl; gives her cake; dislikes foreigners (158, 127).

Doc_____Peabody (159, 128): weighs three hundred pounds (159, 128).

_____: two men in front of store; Quentin asks them about little girl's home (161, 129).

Anse (161, 130)_____: marshall (161, 130); arrests Quentin (173, 139).

_____: man at livery stable (161, 130).

_____: man in frock coat at post office (162, 130).

_____: Italian woman to whom Quentin speaks (163, 131).

_____: the "town squirt" kissed by Caddy when she is 15 (166, 134).

Natalie (166, 134)_____: girl hugged by Quentin in barn [ca. 1906]; (166 ff., 134 ff.); Caddy pushed her down a ladder (167, 134).

Julio (172, 139)_____: brother of Italian girl; leaps on Quentin (173, 139).

_____: referred to as "Squire" by Anse (176, 142); justice of peace; tries Quentin (177, 142-143).

Miss_____Holmes (181, 145): girl in Mrs. Bland's car.

Miss_____Daingerfield (181, 145): girl in Mrs. Bland's car.

Wilkie (184, 148)_____: black servant of Gerald Bland's grandfather (184, 148).

Mike (206, 166)_____: apparently the owner of a gymnasium in town at which Gerald Bland has been practicing boxing (206, 166).

Colonel_____Sartoris (218, 176): presumably Colonel John Sartoris, a contemporary of Quentin's grandfather.

Beginning of Jason's section April 6, 1928

[All characters from Professor Junkin through Burgess exist only in Jason's section.]

Professor_____Junkin (224, 180): Miss Quentin's teacher or principal (224, 180).

_____Beard (234, 188): in whose lot the show tent is pitched (234, 188).

Earl (234, 188)_____: owner of hardware store where Jason works; gives Jason two passes for the show (234, 188); implies that Jason bought his automobile with $1000 his mother thinks she invested in Earl's store (284, 228); says he will not lie for Jason and would permit Mrs. Compson to examine his books (286, 229); says he feels he can rely on Job, but implies he can not rely on Jason (309, 248).

Job (235, 189)_____: black man employed by Earl (235, 189).

_____: drummer, probably a Jew; has coke with Jason (237, 191).

76

_____: Western Union telegraph operator (239, 193).

Doc _____ Wright (239, 193): a cotton speculator (239, 193).

_____ Hopkins (240, 193): a cotton speculator (240, 193).

Lorraine (240, 193) _____: Jason's mistress; sends him letter from Memphis (240, 193); a prostitute (291, 233).

_____: man who made money selling "rotten goods to niggers;" repented and bought Chinese missionary (241, 194).

_____: farmer who buys hame string from Jason (242, 194-195).

Mink (254, 202) _____: driver of livery hack Jason uses to carry baby to Caddy (254, 204).

_____ Rogers (261, 210): owns restaurant where Earl eats (261, 210).

_____ Simmons (269, 216): gives Jason key to opera house where he finds blank checks (269, 216).

I. O. Snopes (271, 218): a cotton speculator (271, 218).

Buck Turpin (287, 231): accused by Jason of accepting $10 to let show come to town (287, 231).

_____: man Jason questions while chasing Miss Quentin (298-299, 239).

Ab Russell (299, 240): farmer (299, 240); lends tire pump to Jason (303, 243).

Parson _____ Walthall (308, 247): objected when men of town shot the courthouse pigeons (308, 247).

Mac (314, 252) _____: man with whom Jason discusses baseball (314, 252).

_____ Burgess (328, 263): father of girl whom Benjy knocked down; knocked Benjy out with a fence picket (328, 263).

Beginning of Dilsey's section April 8, 1928
[All remaining characters exist only in Dilsey's section.]

Rev. _____ Shegog (361, 290): from St. Louis; preacher gives sermon at Dilsey's church on Easter (362, 290); undersized, has "a wizened black face like a small, aged monkey" (365, 293); at first sounds like a white man when he begins to preach (366, 293), but speech becomes more and more emotionally black as he goes on; sermon moves from coldly

77

intellectual to deeply emotional (367-368, 294-295).

_____: regular clergyman at Dilsey's church; huge man of light coffee color (365, 293).

_____: sheriff to whom Jason reports theft (376, 301-302); tells Jason he is responsible for what Miss Quentin did; suspects to whom money belongs (379, 303-304).

Myrtle (376, 302)_____: woman in Sheriff's office when Jason reports theft.

Vernon (376, 302)_____: her husband.

_____: black man who fills Jason's tank and checks his tires (380, 305).

_____: circus cook with whom Jason fights (385 ff., 309 ff.).

_____: man who rescues Jason from cook; owner of show (388, 311).

_____: two blacks who refuse to drive Jason to Jefferson (390-392, 313).

_____: black man who drives Jason from Mottson to Jefferson (391, 313).

The Compson Animals

Horses

_____: spotted pony ridden by Benjy (13, 12).

Queenie (10, 10): first mentioned in 1902-1903 (10); then *ca.* 1912 (33, 28); draws surrey to graveyard for Benjy's Sunday rides [1928] (397 ff., 317 ff.).

Prince (13, 12): first mentioned *ca.* 1902-1903 (13, 12); again <u>ca</u> 1912 (33, 28); Quentin has Prince saddled to meet Dalton Ames [1909]; then does not use him (197, 202, 159, 162).

Fancy (13, 12): first mentioned 1902-1903 (13, 12); [Is this the spotted pony? Probably yes. (see p. 186, 149.)]; next mentioned *ca.* 1912 (33, 28); eating by the branch on night Jason Richmond Compson dies [1912, 35] (42); "blotchy like a quilt," watches Quentin as he runs down to Caddy at branch at the time of the Dalton Ames affair [*ca.* 1909] (186, 149).

Dan (312, 250): Earl's horse, driven by Job (312, 250).

Cows

_____: the big cow [*ca.* 1902-1903] (13, 12); [*ca.* 1912] (33, 28).

_____: the little cow [*ca.* 1902-1903] (13, 12); [*ca.* 1912] (33, 28).

Nancy (40, 33): [might be cow but no real evidence; a farm animal] fell into ditch; Roscus shot her; flesh eaten by buzzards; bones continue to lie in ditch (40, 33); Quentin can not see bones in ditch at time of Dalton Ames affair [1909] (191, 153).

Dogs

Dan: in 1910, howled on the night of Quentin's funeral or death (35, 29); in 1912, howled on the night of Jason Richmond Compson's death (41, 34); in 1910, at Caddy's wedding, T. P. would blame Dan for drinking champagne (47, 39); *ca.* 1908, Dan is present when Benjy finds Caddy in swing with Charlie (56, 46).

"Appendix Compson: 1699-1945"

Written in 1946 for *The Portable Faulkner.* **When, in 1963, the "Appendix" was added to the Vintage Books edition, it was reset, and some changes were made in the text. Apart from changes in punctuation, several changes in action or content were made. The following are the principal changes in content: (1) Jason Lycurgus Compson rode up the Natchez Trace first** (*Portable* p. 740) **in 1820, and then (Vintage, p. 406) in 1811. (2) Originally** (*Portable,* pp. 743, 748, 753, and 755) **Miss Quentin climbed from her room to Jason's room by a rain pipe** (*Portable,* pp. 753, 755) **and entered through the broken window to rob him, and then she climbed down the pear tree and escaped. In the Vintage and in all the other editions cited above, the pear tree disappears (Vintage pp. 410, 417, 426). (3) The place in which Jason hides his money has been changed, and this change may have introduced a serious error in fact to the "Appendix." Originally, Jason keeps his money (saved and stolen) in a locked steel box beneath a plank in his locked closet in his locked room** (*Portable* pp, 751, 752, 754). **This hiding place was changed to a locked bureau drawer in his locked room (Vintage pp. 421, 422, 424). This change may have introduced the incorrect statement that Miss Quentin was locked in her room by Jason at noon (Vintage p. 424). Readers of the novel know that Miss Quentin's maternal grandmother (not Jason) locks her in her room every night. (4) The final change in content introduced in the Vintage version occurs in the section of the "Appendix" titled "Benjamin." There (Vintage p. 423), T. P. follows Benjy along the golf course fence; whereas in the original** (*Portable* p. 753), **Luster follows Benjy by the golf course fence, as he does in the novel. Whether Faulkner or his publisher made these changes is not clear from the published text alone.**

Pagination in parentheses first to the New York editions mentioned above for The Sound and the Fury, *and second to* The Portable Faulkner

(New York: The Viking Press, 1946). Because the 1984 edition (New York: Random House, 1984) does not include "Appendix Compson: 1699-1945," there can be no pagination for that edition here.

Ikkemotubbe (403, 737) Doom (403, 737): Chickasaw Indian chief, "The Man;" granted a square mile of land to Jason Lycurgus Compson I (403, 737).

[Andrew] Jackson: President of the United States [1829-1837] (404, 737).

Quentin MacLachan [Compson I] (404, 738): orphaned son of Glasgow printer; fled after the battle of Culloden [1746] to Carolina; took a claymore and a tarton with him; at 80, fled, in 1779, before British to Kentucky; became neighbor of [Daniel?] Boone (404-405, 738).

Charles Stuart [Compson] (405, 738): son of Quentin MacLachan Compson I; fought in British regiment during Revolution; left for dead in Georgia (405, 738); lost leg; overtakes his father and son in Harrodsburg, Kentucky; gives up schoolteaching to become a gambler; gets involved in the plot to secede Mississippi Valley from the United States and join it to Spain; flees from his former companions in plot; takes claymore, tartan, and son with him (406, 739).

_____ Wilkinson (405, 739): head of the confederation to secede Mississippi Valley from the United States and join it to Spain (405-406, 739).

Jason Lycurgus [Compson I] (406, 740): son of Charles Stuart Compson; rides up the Natchez Trace in 1811 [date given as 1820 in *Portable Faulkner.*] on a small horse that is very fast for short distances; becomes clerk, then partner of Chicasaw agent in Jefferson; trades horse to Ikkemotubbe for square mile of land in center of future Jefferson (406-407, 740).

Quentin MacLachan [Compson II] (408, 741): son of Jason Lycurgus Compson I; Governor of Mississippi; last Compson "who would not fail at everything he touched save longevity and suicide." (408, 741).

Jason Lycurgus [Compson] II (408, 741): Civil War Confederate Brigadier General; failed at Shiloh in 1862 and at Resaca in 1864; put first mortgage on the Compson land; then for forty years sold fragments of it to keep up the mortgage on the rest; died in 1900 (408-409, 741).

Jason [Richmond] [Compson] III (409, 742): [Though Faulkner here calls him Jason III, he is not really III., for in *The Sound and the Fury*, he is called Jason Richmond Compson.] an attorney; an alcoholic; reads Latin classics; sells last of the land to a golf club to get money for Caddy's wedding and to send Quentin to Harvard for one year (409-410, 742).

Dilsey (410, 742) [Gibson]: knows by clairvoyance that Jason is blackmailing his sister (416, 747); lives with Frony in Memphis in 1943; almost sightless (418, 748); refuses to identify Caddy's picture (418, 749).

Candace (410, 742) Caddy (412, 744) [Compson]: knows that Quentin loves death and perhaps in the deliberate marriage pushes him to death; two months pregnant with another man's child at her marriage (412, 744); met Head at French Lick summer 1909; divorced by Head in 1911; married a minor movie magnate in 1920; divorced in Mexico in 1925; vanished in Paris in 1940 with the German occupation; 48 in 1940 (413, 745); in 1943, her picture appears in a slick magazine with a German staff-general (415, 746); this version of Caddy's history says that Caddy brought her baby home in 1911, and left by the next train, never to return (416, 747).

Quentin [Compson] III (410, 742): loves the concept of eternal punishment; tries to isolate himself and Caddy in a private hell where he can keep her forever intact; loves death above all (411, 743); waits to end of school year to commit suicide to get full value of tuition money because Benjy loved the pasture (411-412, 744).

Miss Quentin (424, 753) [Compson]: robs Jason; runs away with pitchman; 17 when she ran away (410, 742); stole almost $7000 (not three) from Jason (424, 754).

Jason [Compson] IV (410, 743): after his mother's death and no longer fearing Dilsey, sends Benjy to the state asylum in Jackson; sells the Compson house to a country man (410, 743); by 1943, owns his own business as a dealer in cotton (414, 745); at first recognizes Caddy's picture (416, 747); then denies it (417, 748); "first sane Compson since before Culloden;" before he sold house, divided it into apartments; attended a Memphis school to learn to class and grade cotton; afraid of Dilsey, but could not force her to leave even when he stopped paying her wages; saved nearly $3,000 which was part of the money stolen by Miss Quentin (420-421, 750-751); had himself appointed Benjy's guardian without his mother's knowledge; had Benjy castrated; goes to movies on Saturday nights with [Lorraine] woman who visits him from Memphis (422, 752); can not report true amount stolen by Miss Quentin because four thousand of it had been legally reported as spent in his reports on his ward, Miss Quentin (424-425, 754); dreams at night of catching her and murdering her (426, 755).

[Caroline Bascomb Compson]: mother of Compson children and widow of Jason III (410, 743); dies in 1933 (422, 752).

_____: country man who buys Compson house; makes it a boarding house (410, 743).

Maury (423, 752) Benjamin (410, 743) [Compson]: sent to state asylum in Jackson after his mother's death (410, 743); renamed by Quentin (423, 753); gelded in 1913 (423, 753).

Melissa Meek (417, 748): county librarian in Jefferson; finds picture of Caddy in June (417, 747) of 1943 (413-414, 745-746); shows picture to

Jason (416, 747); divined that Jason was blackmailing Caddy (416, 747); goes to Memphis to show picture to Dilsey (417, 748); finally gives up after Dilsey refuses to identify Caddy, and realizes that Caddy does not want to be saved (420, 750).

T. P. (423, 755) [Gibson]: goes to Memphis (426, 755).

Frony (417, 748) [Gibson]_____: lives with mother, Dilsey, in Memphis (417, 748); marries a pullman porter and goes to St. Louis; returns to Memphis for Dilsey (426, 755).

[Lorraine]_____: Jason's mistress; after his mother's death, visits Jason on weekends in Jefferson (422, 752).

Maury (423, 752) [L.] [Bascomb]: borrows money from everyone, including Dilsey (423, 752).

_____: pitchman with whom Miss Quentin elopes (410, 743); already a convicted bigamist (426, 755).

Luster (426, 753)_____: aged 14 in 1928 (426, 756).

A 10 Miss Zilphia Gant

Written prior to mid-December, 1928; first published June 27, 1932.

Pagination in parentheses to Miss Zilphia Gant ([Dallas:] The Book Club of Texas, 1932), 29 pp. 300 copies.

Jim Gant (1): horse and mule trader (1); runs off with Mrs. Vinson (3).

_____: hulking halfwitted boy; helps Jim Gant (1); tells Mrs. Gant that Jim has abandoned her, and that he and Mrs. Vinson have gone off together (3); says Gant owes him $1.75 (4); is beaten by Mrs. Gant (6).

Mrs._____ Vinson (3): woman who runs place at which Jim Gant stops (2); runs off with Jim Gant (3).

_____ Vinson (3): man, usually drunk, at place where Jim Gant stops (2).

Mrs. Jim Gant (2): wife of Jim Gant (2); after Gant runs off, leaves daughter with neighbor; borrows pistol from another neighbor; follows Gant (4); returns ten days later; returns pistol with two exploded cartridges; traced them to Memphis (5); beats halfwit when he asks her for $1.75; three months after return, sells house and buys dressmaking shop in Jefferson (6); lives with daughter behind shop for twenty-three years; forced by county health officer to send Zilphia to school (7); walks Zilphia to school morning and afternoon; stays with her in playground during mid-morning recess (8-9); beats woman who suggests that Zilphia go to school (9-10); beats Zilphia (10); when doctor prescribes play with other children for Zilphia, tries to have Zilphia invite girls to her room (11); after surveying town, permits Zilphia to visit a girl from school (12); sits on box in cedars until time for Zilphia to return home (12); when Zilphia reaches thirteen, examines Zilphia's body each month; tells her "what her father had done and what she had done" [presumably killed husband and Mrs. Vinson] (13); sleeps in same bed with Zilphia (13); when Zilphia goes out, goes out to street, meets Zilphia, and returns with her (14); finds Zilphia with boy under blanket; calls her a bitch (14); now lives in frame bungalow; closes shop when painter begins to notice Zilphia (16); becomes ill; locks herself and Zilphia in their house; hides keys (17); had tried to pay painter to leave town (18); greets daughter and husband with shotgun (21); after forcing painter to leave town, dies (22).

Zilphia (7) Gant (2)_____: child of Jim Gant (2); sent to school after seven years in Jefferson (7); found by her mother with boy under blanket in woods (8); 9 at time woman suggests that she go to school (9); beaten by mother; vomits; pole thin; in third year, tries to refuse to go to school because she is ashamed of her mother's presence (10); becomes ill (11); at 13, her mother examines her body every month (13); goes out and is followed by her mother; is found with boy wrapped in blanket in ditch; has been doing this for a month; withdraws from school (14); sits

83

by window and watches schoolmates grow up and pair; makes wedding gown for girl she visited and then dresses for her daughter; sits by window twelve years (14-15); has beau; grows plump (15); dreams of painter (16-17); while mother sleeps, finds keys and leaves house; returns to shop and painter (18); marries him; insists on returning to mother (20); mother forces her to enter house; never sees husband again (21); for six months she waits for him; is "faithful" to him (22); has shop painted; gets partner as shop prospers (23); at night, tosses in bed and tries to conceive without a man; reads story in paper of wedding in neighboring state; name of groom is name of her husband (24); goes to Memphis; hires private detective; dreams of painter; grows plump; gets letters from the detective agency about husband and second wife (25); learns wife is pregnant; becomes ill; says she mistook rat poison for toothpaste; recovers; counts time till birth; goes to hospital (26); weeps at night; absent three years; returns with girl she claims to be her daughter; after ten years begins to dream again; walks daughter to and from school twice a day; dreams now of "negro men;" something happens to her and she "dreamed hardly at all any more, and then only about food" (27); 42 at end of story (29).

_____: neighbor with whom Mrs. Gant leaves her daughter (4).

_____: neighbor who lends pistol to Mrs. Gant (4).

_____: boy with Zilphia in woods (8).

_____: woman client of Mrs. Gant, who suggests Zilphia go to school (9); is beaten by Mrs. Gant (9-10).

_____: doctor who tends Zilphia (10-11).

_____: girl from school whom Zilphia visits (12).

_____: Zilphia Gant's beau (15); tramp painter (16); tells Zilphia that her mother tried to pay him to leave town (18); promises to get Zilphia out of it (19); marries Zilphia (20); forced to leave town by Mrs. Gant (22).

_____: Zilphia's partner in shop (23).

Zilphia (28)_____: girl Miss Zilphia Gant brings back to town and claims as her daughter (28).

A35 *Sanctuary: The Original Text*

Written from January to May, 1929; first published 1981.

Pagination, in parentheses, to the following edition: (New York: Random House, 1981), ed., Noel Polk, 309 pp.

<u>Horace (4) Benbow (23)</u>: passes jail (3); has taken another man's wife and child and then walked out on them; Goodwin's lawyer (5); leaves wife after ten years; takes Ruby and child to his house (6); takes Ruby to hotel (10); flashback: tells Little Belle not to pick up boys on the train (14-15); asks Narcissa not to marry (17); does not attend her wedding (18); leaves his house in Kinston and walks to Jefferson (19 ff.); four days later he arrives at spring (20), where he meets Popeye (21); taken to house; gets drunk (25-26); led to truck by Tommy; rides to Jefferson (30); 43 years old (40); flashback: each Friday, goes to railroad station to get shrimp for Belle (46); says he left his wife because she ate shrimp (56); has taken Little Belle's photograph with him (59); returns to his house; seven years older than Narcissa (61); cleans house (62); thinks of Ruby (65-66); goes to undertaker to see Tommy's body (69); takes train; changes to another train (149-150); reaches Oxford (152); inquires at university Post Office for Temple Drake (153); returns to Jefferson (159); finds that Ruby has been thrown out of hotel; pays her bill (160); argues with sister over Ruby (195 ff.); decides to write to Belle for divorce; told by Clarence Snopes that Temple is in a Memphis brothel; writes to Belle in Kentucky offering a divorce (205); visits Miss Reba's house (206); asks Temple to tell him what happened; interviews her (211 ff.); leaves Miss Reba's (218); returns to Jefferson (219); looks at Little Belle's photo and becomes ill as he thinks of her undergoing what Temple has (220); plans to go to Europe (254); plans to subpoena Temple (255); writes to Narcissa; returns to Belle after trial (281); says he ran after trial (282); asks Narcissa to tell Ruby that he can not continue defense of Goodwin; that he will get her the best criminal lawyer for an appeal (283).

_____: black man who killed his wife, by slashing her throat with razor; sings in jail (3).

_____: his wife (3).

<u>Lee (10) Goodwin (4)</u>: in jail; waits for Popeye to shoot him (4); moonshiner (6); has been cavalry sergeant in Philippines and on the Border and in France; not married to Ruby (55); confident that they can not prove that he murdered Tommy (71-72); will not let Horace tell court that Popeye was on the place at time of murder (74); fears that Popeye will kill him; notified sheriff of Tommy's murder; says Ruby is his wife (75); killed another soldier in Philippines; sent to Leavenworth; let out to fight in war; returned to Leavenworth (105); flashback: drunk, looks for Temple; fights with Ruby (121); slaps her (122); stops fight between Gowan and Van (128); after Popeye and Temple leave, calls sheriff (141); flashback: kills soldier in Philippines; sent to Leavenworth; let out to fight in WW I; sent back to Leavenworth (267 ff.); beats Ruby when she tells of paying lawyer with sex (269); tried for murder; in trial, it is

85

implied that he raped Temple with corncob (273-280); presumably found guilty (280); taken away after Horace leaves (284).

Popeye (4)): meets Horace Benbow at spring; detains him by threat of pistol (21 ff.); has no eyelashes (47); kills dog (53); enters barn where Temple is hiding (123); climbs down into crib where she is; kills Tommy; rapes Temple (140); drives away with Temple; buys sandwich for her; forces her back into car (141); takes her to Memphis to Reba Rivers's house (162 ff.); enters Temple's room; throws back covers; makes whinnying sound (183); burns Clarence Snoopes's neck as he looks through Temple's keyhole (208); picks Temple up as she leaves house (226); holds hand over her mouth (227); takes her to Grotto (228); dances with Temple (229); kills Red (237); goes to Pensacola every year to visit mother (249); paid Minnie $5 a day not to let Temple out of house or to use telephone (252); on way to visit mother, arrested in Birmingham for murder of policeman (285); jury out eight minutes; finds him guilty (287); makes no attempt at defence (287 ff.); hanged (291).

Goodwin (4): child of Goodwin and Ruby (4); sickly (5); boy (9).

Ruby (4)): Goodwin's woman (5); a whore (32); not married to Goodwin (55); called his wife by Goodwin (75); calls Horace to come to town (78); tells him that there was a young girl at the place at time of murder (79); earlier had sex with lawyer while Goodwin was in Leavenworth (105); tells Temple that she would get car for her to leave and never come back (107); takes Temple to barn (114); tries to stab Goodwin with carving knife; is slapped by him (121122); leaves house and goes to spring (122); tells Horace that Temple left with Popeye (141); taken by Horace to hotel; turned out of hotel (160); stays with half-crazed woman (199); thinks that Horace wants sex in return for Goodwin's defense (266); says she earlier got Goodwin out of jail by sex with his lawyer (267); followed him to Leavenworth (268).

Narcissa (8) Benbow (23) Sartoris (20): Horace's sister; scolds Horace for taking Goodwin's case (5); insists that Ruby leave her housse (7); deserted by husband after three months; widow and mother eight months later (16); for a year has received obscene letters; they are stolen (74); argues with Horace over Ruby; tells him to go away (195 ff.); visits Eustace Graham, District Attorney; says she wants Horace out of case (257-258); writes to Belle, saying that Horace will be home (258); in response to Horace's appeal, says that she mailed part of his letter to Ruby; that Lee has been taken away (284).

Jenny (5)): 89 years old; confined to wheelchair after stroke (7); brought plants from Carolina in 1867 (33).

Belle (15) Mitchell (16) Benbow (23): Horace's wife (6); says Horace is in love with his sister (16).

Belle (14) Mitchell (16): her child by previous marriage (5); brings home a boy she met on train (14); calls Horace "shrimp" (15).

Harry Mitchell (16): husband whose wife (Belle) Horace took (5).

_____ Benbow (23): father of Horace (6).

_____ Benbow (23): mother of Horace (6).

Bory (6) Benbow (40) Sartoris (20): child of Narcissa (6); called Johnny by Aunt Jenny (36); 9 years old (44).

Bayard (35) Sartoris (20): father of Bory (6); marries Narcissa; deserts her after three months; dead eight months later (16); Captain; married to Narcissa in Memphis on August 27, 1919 (63).

_____: judge at Goodwin's trial (10).

Isom_____: drives Horace's car (11).

_____: porter in hotel (12).

_____: boy brought home by Little Belle (14).

_____: black cook in Horace's house in Kinston (19).

Tommy (29)_____: barefoot man (26); leads Horace to truck (29); half-wit (49); looks like Christ (52); killed; no one knows his last name (69); flashback: watches Temple through window as she removes dress (130); tells Temple that Lee says it will not hurt her; tells her that he will not let anyone into the crib (138); killed by Popeye (140).

_____: man in truck (29).

_____: second man in truck (29).

Saddie (33) Saturday (44)_____: black servant in Sartoris house (36); twin of Sundy; named Saturday by Horace (44).

Gowan Stevens (33): suitor of Narcissa; graduate of the University of Virginia (33); has date with girl at University of Mississippi (39); going to baseball game with her at Starkville (43); sends farewell note to Narcissa (71-72); flashback: takes Temple to dance (81); drinks heavily (83 ff.); gets drunk; vomits (84-85); passes out (86); meets Temple at Taylor (87); drinks bottle of hair oil; drives Temple toward Starkville; stops at Goodwin's for liquor (88); crashes car into tree (88-89); goes with Tommy to barn for more liquor (94-95); drunk three times in one day (101); beaten unconscious by Van (111-112); wakes after Temple and Popeye leave; goes to spring; gets picked up by car (143-144); had asked Narcissa to marry him (147).

Sundy (34) Sunday (44)_____: twin of Saddie; named Sunday by Horace (44).

Herschell Jones (36): suitor of Narcissa (36).

Temple (81) Drake 100): red-haired girl friend of Gowan Stevens at the University of Mississippi (37); meets Gowan in Taylor (87); when car crashes tries to run but can not (89); finds Pap, old blind man, on porch (92); frightened; says they must leave (96); asks Popeye to drive them to town; he refuses (97); hides behind stove; says her father is a judge (99); on probation at University for slipping out (103); taken to barn by Ruby (114); 17 years old (115); frightened by rat (120); raped by Popeye (140); leaves with him (141); according to Clarence Snopes, sent up North by father (157); in car with Popeye, bleeds; begins to scream (163); leaves car as boy she knows approaches (165); forced back into car by Popeye (166); taken to Reba Rivers's house by Popeye (168); in bed, waits for doctor (172); locks door when Minnie and Miss Reba leave (173); after doctor tends her, locks door (175); unlocks it (177); agrees to let Horace interview her (210 ff.); tells Horace of night in house; how she tried to make herself into a boy (214); tells of Popeye feeling her (216 217); does not seem to tell Horace about murder (217); leaves room; sees Minnie; returns to room (221); hides Popeye's pistol in bed (222); bribes Minnie; leaves house; goes to telephone in drugstore; returns to house (224); that night, leaves house; Popeye in car meets her (226); gets in car; calls Popeye "daddy;" says that Red is better man than Popeye (227); taunts Popeye over impotency; says he watches Red have sex with her (228); dances with Popeye (229); drinks heavily (230-231); calls Popeye "daddy" repeatedly; tries to get his pistol (231); becomes drunk; lusts for Red (232); plays dice; wins; leaves Popeye at dice table; meets Red in room (233); aggressively pushes her body at Red (234); carried out of room by two men (235); appears in court for Goodwin's trial (272); mother dead (276); lies about her rape, implicating Goodwin (277); stares at back of courtroom (278); removed by father and brothers (278-279); with father in Luxemburg Gardens (290).

Johnny (38) Sartoris (20): uncle of Bory; brother of Bayard; went to Princeton (38).

_____: portrait of Confederate colonel in Miss Jenny's room (41).

_____: portrait of man about 60 in Miss Jenny's room (41).

_____: portrait of man in early 1900's; sick (41).

_____: photograph of twin boys in velvet suits in Miss Jenny's room (41-42).

Elnora (44)_____: black cook in Sartoris household; mother of Saddie (Saturday) and Sundy (Sunday); unmarried (44). [See *Flags in the Dust*, in which she is Caspey's brother and "There Was a Queen," in which she is Caspey's wife.]

_____: husband of Aunt Jenny; killed in 1862 on second anniversary of wedding (44).

Pap (75)_____: filthy old man; blind (46); deaf (94).

_____: Popeye's grandfather; Popeye inherited watch from him (50).

_____: Popeye's mother (50).

_____: builder of house in which Goodwin lives (51).

_____: youth who delivers packages to Horace (62).

_____: coroner (69).

_____: Baptist minister (71).

_____ Stevens (73): Gowan Stevens's mother (73).

_____: man who writes obscene letters to Narcissa (74).

_____: sheriff (75).

_____: doctor who tends Ruby's baby (78).

Doc (82)_____: town boy who watches Temple and Gowan leave dance (81).

_____: second town boy (81).

_____: third town boy (81).

Luke (83)_____: moonshiner (83).

_____: man at shack who brings Gowan glasses and cokes (84).

_____: black man at railroad station (86).

Judge (99) Hubert (102) Drake (100): Temple's father; a judge (99); enters courtroom and removes Temple (278-279).

_____ Drake (100): brother of Temple; lawyer (100).

_____ Drake (100): brother of Temple; lawyer (100).

_____ Drake (100): brother of Temple; newspaperman (100).

Hubert (Buddy) (102) Drake (100): brother of Temple; student at Yale (100).

_____: girl who tells dean Temple slips out at night (102).

_____: Dean at University of Mississippi; puts Temple on probation for slipping out (103).

_____: Ruby's brother (104).

Frank (104)_____: Ruby's boy friend; killed by her father (104).

_____: Ruby's father; kills Frank (104).

_____: soldier killed by Lee Goodwin (105).

_____: black woman because of whom Goodwin killed soldier (267).

_____: Lee Goodwin's first lawyer (105).

_____: Congressman who gets Lee Goodwin released from Leavenworth (105).

Van (111)_____: fights with Gowan (111); flashback: tries to have Temple sit on lap (126); fights with Goodwin (132).

_____: man and woman in railroad station (149).

_____: conductor on train (150).

_____: youth on train (151).

Shack (151)_____: youth on train (151).

Marge (151)_____: name mentioned by Shack (151).

Beth (151)_____: name mentioned by Shack (151).

_____: clerk in University Post Office (153).

Clarence Snopes (154): state senator; meets Horace on train (154); tells Horace that Temple Drake ran away (157); takes Virgil and Fonzo to black brothel (193); calls Horace at night; says he has news (201); visits him (202); tells him that Temple Drake in in a "Memphis 'ho-house'" (205); meets Horace outside Miss Reba's (206); neck burned by Popeye as he spies on Temple (208); appears with black eye and bruises; anti-Semitic (259).

_____ Snopes (156): Clarence Snopes's father (156).

_____: porter on train (158).

_____: proprietor of hotel in Jefferson; throws Ruby out of hotel because Baptist women protested (159).

_____: woman who takes Ruby and child into jail after she is expelled from hotel (160-161).

Ed (161)_____: jailor (161).

_____: man who sells Popeye sandwich (165).

_____: mechanic at gas staton (165).

_____: young man in Dumfries (165).

Minnie (170)_____: black maid at Miss Reba's whorehouse (168); brings supper to Temple (178).

Reba Rivers (168): madam of whorehouse (168); tells Temple that all the girls are after Popeye (170); gives Temple glass of gin (172); supports four children (not hers) in Arkansas home (210); tells Horace that Temple will be dead or in an asylum in year, the way she and Popeye go on; says something is funny about it (218); had been with Mr. Binford for eleven years (249); tells friends about Popeye's bringing Red to Temple's room (251).

Dr. (170)_____Quinn (170): sent for to tend Temple (170); says he does not make calls on Sundays (172); arrives after Miss Reba speaks to him (174).

_____: married woman who offers Minnie $25 to get Popeye into same room (170).

_____Binford (178): Miss Reba's man ((178); dead for two years (179).

Virgil Snopes (184): arrives in Memphis (184); looking for hotel with Fonzo; arrives at Miss Reba's (186); to attend barbers' college; rents room (188); thinks whores are Miss Reba's children (189); goes to brothel with another student (191).

_____: prostitute; arrives with man (187).

_____: man who brings prostitute to Miss Reba's; leaves in cab (187).

_____: fellow student; takes Virgil and Fonzo to brothel (191).

_____: blonde prostitute in red dress with Clarence Snopes (192).

Eustace Graham (256): District Attorney (199); club foot (256); introduces corncob with which Temple was raped (274).

_____: half-crazed woman with whom Ruby and child stay (199).

_____: Minnie's husband; has left her; disapproves of her work; went off with waitress (208).

_____: waitress (208).

_____: Memphis lawyer; millionaire; two hundred and eighty pounds; has special bed made for Reba's house (209).

_____: man in cap outside whorehouse (224).

Red (228)_____: Temple hints that he has sex with her as Popeye watches (228); asked for sex by Temple at Grotto (234); murdered by Popeye (237); in funeral melee, coffin knocked over and body rolls out (242).

_____: four men at table (230); two of them carry Temple out of room (235).

Joe (241)_____: proprietor of Grotto (237).

_____: bouncer (238).

Gene (238)_____: invites people at Red's funeral to drink; bootlegger (238).

_____: man at Red's funeral; wants them to play jazz (239).

_____: woman in red dress at funeral (240).

Lorraine (248)_____: thin woman; returns with Miss Reba from funeral (244(244).

Myrtle (246)_____: short, plump woman; returns with Miss Reba from Red's funeral (244).

Uncle Bud (245)_____: small, bullet-headed boy of 5 or 6; returns with Miss Reba from Red's funeral (244); drinks Miss Reba's beer (247); gets drunk; vomits (253).

_____Harris (256): plays poker with Eustace Grimm (256).

_____: Jewish lawyer in Memphis (259); appears at Goodwin's trial (272).

_____: barber to whom Clarence Snopes complains about the Jewish lawyer (259).

_____: black in half-crazed woman's house (262).

92

_____Jones (281): Kinston hack driver (281).

_____: judge who tries Popeye for murder of policeman (286).

_____: bailiff (286).

_____: lawyer appointed by court to defend Popeye (287).

_____: District Attorney who prosecutes Popeye (287).

_____: turnkey in jail to whom Popeye gives $100 (287).

_____: Memphis lawyer who arrives in Popeye's cell (288).

_____: minister who calls on Popeye before he is hanged (289).

_____: sheriff at Popeye's execution (290).

A 6 *As I Lay Dying*

Written between October 25, 1929 and January 12, 1930; first published October 6, 1930.

Pagination, in parentheses, to the following editions: (New York: Random House, 1964) 250 pp., corrected by James Meriwether; (New York: Vintage, 1964), paperback; (New York: Modern Library, 1967).

Darl (3) Bundren (4): very sensitive and observing (10-11); anxious to take the wagon for a $3 hauling job; promises to be back by sundown the next day (16-19); looks at his mother before he leaves (20-21); knows Dewey Dell is pregnant; knows his mother is going to die before he and Jewel return (26-27); asks Jewel if he knows his mother is going to die (38); wagon wheel breaks under the load of lumber (48); senses when his mother dies (51); it takes three days for him and Jewel to return for a new wheel (87); sees buzzards hovering over the house as he and Jewel return; tells Jewel that it is not his horse that is dead; says he can not love his mother because he has no mother; says Jewel's mother is a horse (88-89, 95); second son; people talk about him (107); when he sees his mother at night crying by Jewel's bed, knows [that Jewel is her son by a man other than his father] (129); he and Cash ride the wagon across the ford (134ff.); when wagon overturns, leaps into the water (142); buys cement in Mottson (194); uses it to make a cast for Cash's leg (198); asks Jewel whose son he is (202); at night, he and Vardaman listen at coffin to hear their mother "talking" (202); is missing after fire; found lying on top of the coffin to keep the cat away (214); had set fire to barn and the others decide to send him to asylum in Jackson (222); some men wait outside the graveyard to seize him after the burial; laughs uncontrollably when he is seized (227); taken on train to Jackson; talks to himself about himself on train (243).

Jewel (3) Bundren (4): owns wild horse which he alternately caresses and curses (12); bitterly resents Cash's making the coffin where their mother can see and hear; yearns for the others not to be and for him and his mother to be alone in the world (14-15); resents the Tulls for visiting his mother; his mother's favorite son (17); on way back, when he realizes his mother is dead, curses Darl (88-89); when they carry the coffin from the house to the wagon, is in a fury of despair; hurries so much that the others fall away, so that he practically heaves coffin into the wagon alone (91-93); enters barn as the others leave (97); catches up to the wagon, riding his wild spotted horse (100); the horse he rides is one of the Snopes horses, which he bought from Quick's father (106); tries to pay Samson for feed for his horse (109-110); offers to buy Tull's mule (120); when he was 15, had a spell of daytime sleeping (121 ff.); Darl discovers that he is out every night all night, and assumes he is seeing a woman (124); returns one morning riding spotted horse; was not with a woman; cleared Lon Quick's forty acres to earn money to buy horse (127-128); rides horse ahead of the wagon across the stream (137); snubs the rope and holds the wagon when it overturns (147); dives for Cash's tools (150); the son of Whitfield (169); borrows team of mules from Armstid (172); when he learns of his father's proposed trade for Snopes's mules, rides off on his horse (182); leaves his horse with Snopes for the span of mules (183); rejoins family on foot outside Mottson while they are making a cast for Cash's leg (198); curses Darl when he asks who his father is (202); rescues horse from burning barn (209); returns to get his mother's coffin out single handedly (211); his back is burned; on the outskirts of Jefferson, tries to fight with man they pass on the road (220).

Vernon (10) Tull (4): his family uses New Hope graveyard (28); promises to return to help Anse with his corn (32); returns with Vardaman (69); returns at dawn to his own place, and then takes Peabody's team back (80); refuses to let his mule join the Bundren's team in crossing the river (120); helps them cross the river (130); searches for Cash's tools in water (150);

Cash Bundren (4): good carpenter; making coffin for mother, (4); once fell off a church (15); is scheduled to work on Tull's barn (32); limps from his injury (55); insists on bevelling the boards for mother's coffin (74); finishes coffin in the rain toward daybreak (75); plugs up the holes in the coffin made by Vardaman (82); broke his leg in the fall--28 feet, 4 1/2 inches (85); warns the others that the coffin will not balance on the wagon (85,90); takes his tools on the funeral journey (95); when Jewel was 15, followed him one night (126); stays with wagon as it turns over when the log hits it (141); can not swim; lets horse pull him ashore (148); breaks leg again (156); rides on top of the coffin (172); taken to Armstid's (173); to have his leg set by Uncle Billy Varner (176); Darl makes a cast of cement (198); that night, leg begins to get feverish (203); leg and foot turn black (213); faints as they try to break cast; leg bleeds (214); feels closer to Darl than to the others (224); urges Darl to submit and go to Jackson (227); finally is taken to Doc Peabody (220).

Addie Bundren (4): having coffin made (4); watches Cash making her coffin (8); wants to be buried in her family plot in Jefferson (18); suddenly takes to bed (36); after doctor visits her, sends for husband Anse and calls to Cash (44-45); is told that sons, Darl and Jewel, have gone to make one more load (46); watches as Cash shows her the nearly finished coffin and dies (47); two holes are bored in her face when Vardaman bores holes in her coffin lid (70); buried head to foot in coffin so that her wedding dress could flare out; a mosquito net veil hides the auger holes in her face (83); flashback: when Jewel, at 15, was sleeping, used to hide special treats for him (123); cries by Jewel's bed at night after he returns with the horse (129); had been a school teacher who hated her pupils and sought to make them "aware" of her with a switch; her father taught her that living is just a preparation for being dead; hates her father (161-162); takes Anse for husband merely to get a husband; learns that living is terrible while carrying Cash (163); with respect to Anse, love is just a word to her (163-164); feels that her aloneness has been violated by Cash (164); after Darl's birth, begins to take revenge on Anse; asks him to take her to Jefferson for burial (164-165); considers Anse as dead; takes a lover; thinks of their sin rather than their love; the lover [Whitfield] is a minister (165-166); two months after their affair is over, realizes that she is pregnant with Jewel;

gave Anse daughter Dewey Dell to "negative" Jewel and Vardaman to replace the child she had robbed him of; then she is ready to die (167-168).

Cora Tull (6): has baked cakes to sell in town, but when she delivers them, they are no longer wanted (6); repeats pious cliches to herself (7); once taught school (11); misinterprets the decision to borrow the team (21); has been visiting Addie's bedside for three weeks (21); misinterprets Addie's burial in Jefferson (21-22); once spoke piously to Addie about sin and opening her heart to God (158 ff.).

Miss   Lawington (6): woman in town who advises Cora about chickens (6).

            : woman who orders cakes from Cora and then cancells order (7).

Kate (7) Tull (30): sits by Addie (8); Vernon and Cora's daughter (30); predicts Anse will get another wife before cotton-picking (32).

Eula (9) Tull (30): sits by Addie (9); Vernon and Cora's daughter (30).

Dewey Dell (15) Bundren (4): fans mother (8); says Jewel is not kin to the others, not "care kin" (25); communicates without words with Darl (26); refuses to say, even to herself, that she is pregnant (38-39); wants to ask Dr. Peabody to help her (50); gets supper after mother's death; yearns for help from Dr. Peabody; goes to milk cow (56-58); finds Vardaman instead of Lafe in the barn; thinks he is spying on her (60); gets upset when Samson tries to convince her father to bury her mother at New Hope (108-109); as they pass New Hope cemetery, becomes tense; remembers a nightmare; says to herself that she believes in God (114-116); seventeen; goes to druggist in Mottson for abortion medicine; two months pregnant(190-191); Lafe had given her $10 to buy the medicine (191); just before they get to Jefferson, goes into bushes and changes to her Sunday clothes (218); she tells Mr. Gillespie that Darl set fire to the barn; she leaps furiously at Darl when the men seize him (227); goes to drugstore in Jefferson (231); thinks she is getting abortion medicine and that submitting sexually to Skeet Macgowan in the basement at night will make medicine work (238); afterwards, knows it is not going to work (241); father takes her $10 (245).

Anse (20) Bundren (4): husband of Addie; has splayed feet (11); once a load of wood fell on him (15); humpbacked; avoids work; says he got sick from working in the sun at age of 22 and will die if he ever sweats again; has lost his teeth (17); has promised Addie to bury her in her family plot in Jefferson (18); resents the road that runs before his house; thinks it brought him bad luck (34); when the doctor arrives, Anse says he never sent for him; resents having to pay Dr. Peabody to tend Addie; sees it as interfering with his getting a new set of teeth (36); has not been to town for twelve years (41); when his wife dies, reveals a second motive for taking her to Jefferson: "Now I can get them teeth." (51);

97

forbids Jewel to take his horse (94); shaves every day now (95); muses in pious self-pity; looks forward to his new teeth (104-105); stops in Samson's barn but refuses all offers of beds in the house (110); learning that the next bridge is out, turns around and retraces steps (112); drives to the river near Tull's where the bridge used to be (117-18); with Tull, Dewey Dell, and Vardaman, crosses river by fallen bridge (130-131); rides Jewel's horse to the Snopeses' place to trade for a span of mules (177); to get mules, gives a chattel mortgage on his cultivator and seeder, Cash's $8 Jewel's horse, and the money he has saved to buy his new teeth (180-182); stops at a house in Jefferson to borrow spades (225); returns spades after the funeral (230); takes Dewey Dell's money and says it is a loan (246); gets shave and combs his hair; leaves the others (248); returns with new teeth (249) and new wife (250).

Lafe (25)_____: man who helps Dewey Dell pick cotton; father of her unborn child (25-26); gave her $10 to get abortion medicine (192-193).

Vardaman (29) Bundren (4): youngest in family; has caught a large fish (29); cuts up fish (37); runs outside when his mother dies; thinks Dr. Peabody is responsible for her death (48-52); goes to the barn to Jewel's horse; vomits (53); beats Doc's horses and drives them off; yells, "You kilt my Maw." (53); cries in barn after refusing to milk cow (54-55); reverts to time before he cut up the fish; thinks of it as "cooked and et" (55); is horrified at the thought of nailing coffin shut; thinks his mother went away and someone else lay down; begins to think of his mother having traded places with the fish (62-64); walks four miles in the rain at midnight to Tull's to verify that the fish had existed (66); opens window so that his mother can breathe (69); bores holes in the top of the coffin (70); says, "My mother is a fish." (79); fishes in slough in which no fish have ever been (87); chases the buzzards from his mother's coffin (178); says his mother is a fish; that she got out of the coffin when it was in the water; says his mother does not smell like that (187); watches the buzzards hovering in the sky (185-187); dreams of a train for Christmas throughout the book (206); sees something at night that Dewey Dell tells him not to speak of (205); what he saw was Darl setting fire to the barn (213); waits for Dewey Dell in front of the drugstore (237).

Dr._____Peabody (36): doctor who attends Addie (36); he refrained from going to her at first for fear that there was something he could do to bring her back (40); weighs two hundred and twenty-five pounds (41); seventy years old; must be pulled up path by rope (39, 41-42); confirms that Addie is dying (44); treats Cash's leg (229-230).

Lon, Big Lon (154) Quick (80): finds Peabody's buggy; reports that the river is rising (80); owned spotted horse that Jewel buys (107); it is descendent of Texas ponies Flem Snopes brought to area twenty-five years earlier (127); father of Lon Quick, Little Lon (154).

Lon, Little Lon (154) Quick (80): as the Bundrens pass Samson's, tells them that next bridge is out (107); son of Big Lon (154).

_____Armstid (81)_: puts the Bundrens up after they cross the river (173); gives Anse whisky and offers his team (175).

_____Whitfield (82)_: arrives at funeral to announce that the bridge has gone (83); once struggled to save Addie and prayed for her (159); when he learns that Addie is dying, his conscience urges him to confess his fatherhood of Jewel and ask forgiveness of Anse (169); on the way, learns that Addie has died and piously takes it for God's will that their affair remain secret (171).

Uncle Billy (83) Varner (176)_: one of the mourners (83); sets Cash's leg (176).

Jody (83) Varner (176)_: his son.

_____Varner (83)_: wife of Billy, mother of Jody (83).

_____Houston (83)_: one of Addie's mourners (83).

_____Littlejohn (84)_: another mourner (84).

_____Samson (105)_: tries to talk Anse into burying Addie at New Hope because she is beginning to smell (107); offers Bundrens food and refuses pay from Jewel for feeding his horse (109-110).

[Stuart] MacCallum (106)_: Rafe's twin.

Rafe MacCallum (106)_:

Rachel Samson (108)_: Samson's wife (108); gets upset about their taking Addie to Jefferson (111).

Flem Snopes (127)_: brought spotted horses to area (127).

Lula Armstid (174)_: Armstid's wife; puts Cash to bed (173).

_____Suratt (181)_: was going to sell "talking machine" to Cash for $8 (181).

Eustace Grimm (183)_: brings the span of mules from Snopes (183).

_____Snopes (175)_: supplies mules for Anse's trade (175); nephew of Flem Snopes (183).

_____Moseley (188)_: druggist in Mottson (188); refuses to sell abortion medicine to Dewey Dell (191).

Albert_____: fountain clerk in drugstore in Mottson (189).

_____: Marshal in Mottson who tries to make Anse leave town (193).

_____Grummet (193): owner of hardware store in Mottson where Darl buys cement for Cash's leg (194).

_____Gillespie (206): man at whose place the Bundrens stop on the eighth night (206); barn burns (208); fire set by Darl (222).

Mack (209) Gillespie (206): his son.

_____: man with whom Jewel tries to fight on outskirts of Jefferson (219).

Mrs. _____ Bundren (225): woman from whom Anse borrows spades (225); owns a gramophone; marries Anse Bundren (250).

_____: men who seize Darl to take him to insane asylum in Jackson (227).

Skeet Macgowan (231): works in Jefferson drugstore (231); pretends he is a doctor when Dewey Dell inquires about abortion medicine (232); gives her a glass of turpentine to drink and tells her to return at ten that night for the rest of his treatment; gives her six capsules full of talcum powder, takes her to basement for sex as the rest of the treatment (237-238).

Dr. _____ Alford (231): has office over drugstore (231).

_____: druggist in Jefferson, "the old man" (232).

Jody (232) _____: clerk in Jefferson drugstore (232).

A 9 *Idyll in the Desert*

Written before January 23, 1930; first published December 10, 1931.

Pagination, in parentheses, to first edition (New York: Random House, 1931) 17 pp. Included in Uncollected Stories of William Faulkner.

Lucas Crump (10): mail carrier; carries rifle; tells tall tale about how he once killed a mountain sheep from buckboard (3); carries occasional passengers (4); carries passenger to Sivgut, a rest home for people with tuberculosis (5); Howes's (House's) background; imagines that women have taken care of him all his life (9); cooks for Howes (House); chops firewood for him when he is ill; sends telegram to married woman in New York (10); after Howes (House) leaves the woman, wires her husband, who arrives in Blizzard; takes money husband leaves for his wife and fakes letter from Howes (House) to get money to her (13); two or three times a year, takes her fake letters; writes to husband once a week to report her condition; tells woman that specialist sent by husband is county health officer (14); hires substitute for half salary for a year so that he can camp near woman (14-15); wires her husband; sends her to Los Angeles by train to be met by husband (15); says his name is Sitting Bull; that he was killed a while back (17).

_____: narrator (3).

_____ Painter (4): rancher (4).

Matt Lewis (4): runs livery stable (4); shows Crump newspaper announcing Howes's (House's) wedding (15).

Darrel Howes (House) Dorry (8): male "lunger" (tuberculosis patient at Sivgut); recovers after two years and leaves without his lover (6); they are not married (7); looks like "Hollywood dook" to mail carrier (9); chops wood; insists on paying in advance for his food; stays at Sivgut two years (10); recovers; gains thirty pounds; walks forty miles to Blizzard; takes eastbound train; leaves lover at Sivgut (10-11); flashback: had studied architecture in Paris; 25 when affair begins (11); when he becomes ill, leaves his lover without telling her that he is sick or where he went (12); as former lover leaves, returns to Blizzard with new wife (15); fails to recognize former lover (16).

_____: woman companion of Howes (House); becomes ill (tuberculosis) after he gets well; stays on after he leaves (6); not married to "lunger" (7); flashback: arrives after Crump sends her telegram from Howes (House) (10); stays ten years at Sivgut (10); had left her husband and two children; about ten years older than Howes (House); thirty-five when affair begins (11); chops wood (13); thinks money from husband comes from Howes (House) (13-14); waits for him to come to her (15); as she leaves to die, watches Howes (House) and new wife arrive in Blizzard; has aged (16); dies on train to Los Angeles (17).

_____: her husband (7); ten years older than wife; an

architect (11); after Crump telegraphs him, arrives in Blizzard, but does not visit wife; returns home after leaving money for her (13); fails to recognize her in morgue (17).

Manny Hughes (13): post office employee who helps Crump with the faked letters (13).

_____: eastern specialist sent by husband to attend wife; poses as county health officer; tells her she has one year to live; accepts fee of one dollar (14).

_____: substitute hired by Crump (14-15).

_____: Indian woman hired by Crump to attend the woman (15).

_____: Howes's (House's) new wife (15).

A 7 Sanctuary

Written from January to May 25, 1929; revised from page proofs from mid-November to early December, 1930; first published February 9, 1931.

Pagination, in parentheses, to the following editions: (New York: Jonathan Cape and Harrison Smith, 1931), 380 pp.; (New York: Modern Library, 1932); (New York: Harrison Smith and Robert Haas, 1933); (New York: Grosset & Dunlop, 1946).

Popeye (1)_____: carrying pistol, detains Horace Benbow at spring for two hours (3); takes him to the Old Frenchman Place; frightened by an owl (6); has shot Tommy's dog to death because it frightened him (21); owns the truck used to carry whisky to Memphis (23); is watching with Tommy as Gowan drives car into tree (44-45); refuses to let anyone but Lee drink; does not drink himself (52); refuses to drive Temple and Gowan to town (57); is ordered by Lee not to touch Temple (87); feels Temple's breast beneath raincoat (88); leaves with others in truck (93); sees Ruby and baby at spring next morning and tells her he has had enough and is going to town (116); sees Godwin watching barn where Temple is hiding; tells him he is going to town, but enters the barn from rear (116-117); from loft, enters crib where Temple is hiding while Tommy sits outside the door (120); orders Tommy to open the door and continue watching Goodwin; shoots Tommy (121); rapes Temple (122); drives off with Temple in car (123); buys her a sandwich (166); takes her to Memphis (169); to Miss Reba's brothel (170); has always refused to have anything to do with any of the prostitutes (174); leaves Temple with Miss Reba (174); visits Temple's room, crouches by the bed, and makes a high "whinnying sound like a horse" (191); catches Clarence Snopes looking through keyhole at Temple's door; burns his neck with match (251-252); watches Temple and man in bed at brothel; hangs over bed; impotent (278); takes Temple to the Grotto (280); goes to Pensacola each summer to visit his mother (307); on his way there is arrested in Birmingham for the murder of a policeman; arrested in August for a murder on June 17th the night he had Red murdered (361); born Christmas [1900] with eye problem; walked and talked only when about 4 years old (363); had no hair until he was 5 (368); as a child, ran away from a children's party after cutting up a pair of love birds with scissors; cut up a kitten and was sent to a home for incorrigibles; served five years (370); refuses to send for lawyer; jury out for eight minutes; finds him guilty (373); seems to give up (375-377); is hanged (378).

Horace Benbow (4): meets Popeye at spring (1); an attorney in Kinston (4); accompanies Popeye to Old Frenchman Place (6); eats dinner with Popeye and the others (11); objects when Little Belle brings home a boy she met on train (14); 43 years old (16); after his argument with Little Belle, leaves home without any money and begins journey back to Jefferson, looking for a hill (17); gets quite drunk on porch, telling story of Little Belle and waiting for a ride to Jefferson (18); urges Ruby to go back to the city and start life over; says he lacks courage; says he left his wife because she ate shrimp (18); has been married ten years (19);

103

attended Oxford (27); seven years older than Narcissa; married a divorced woman (126); tells Narcissa and Miss Jenny about the people at the Old Frenchman Place (129); opens up his old house in Jefferson to live there (130); after Goodwin's arrest, takes Ruby and her child to his house; he is Goodwin's lawyer (138); after Narcissa and Aunt Jenny object, takes Ruby and child to hotel (145); refuses to return to Narcissa's house; has Isom drive him home (148); calls Goodwin a coward (152); keeps insisting to Ruby that Temple was all right when she last saw her with Popeye (192,197); knows of Gowan's actions (198); takes train (201) to Oxford (205); inquires for Temple; told she quit school two weeks before (205-206); sees Temple's name on wall of men's room at RR station (27); on train back to Jefferson learns from Clarence Snopes that Temple returned home and was sent to an aunt's in the North (213) pays Ruby's hotel bill (217); repeats that she is not married to Lee (219); agrees to pay Clarence Snopes for information about Temple (247); visits Miss Reba's looking for Temple; meets Clarence Snopes outside (248); asks to see Temple to get her to testify for Lee Goodwin (253); asks Temple what really happened (255); leaves Miss Reba's without the information he sought (264-265); thinks that he and Temple and all the others would be better off dead (265); returns to Jefferson; vomits after looking at Little Belle's picture and thinking of Temple's rape (268); writes to Belle asking for a divorce (313); calls Miss Reba and learns that Temple and Popeye have left (322); is anti-semitic (338); after Goodwin's conviction, cries in car on way to Narcissa's; eats well (350); walks back to town to find a lynch mob (351); lies down at hotel (353) finds Lee Goodwin being burned with gasoline; man who sets fire to Goodwin sets fire to himself (354-355); returns to Kinston (357); calls Little Belle at house party; she dismisses him (360).

Lee (8) Goodwin (9): a bootlegger (8); while a soldier in the Philippines, killed another soldier over a woman; is sent to Leavenworth; released to serve in Army in WWI; awarded two medals; returned to Leavenworth after the war; released by the intervention of a congressman (68); stops Gowan and Van from fighting (79-80); knocks out Van in Temple's room; orders Popeye to leave her alone (87); picks Temple up; puts her on bed by Gowan (90); returns and demands the raincoat; leaves on truck (93-94); next morning watches Temple relieve herself in bushes (109); is drunk and tries to find Temple (113); fights with Ruby; slaps her (113-114); watches barn where Temple is hiding (116); when Ruby returns, tells her that he must get the sheriff (124); had been a cavalry sergeant in the Philippines (129); arrested for Tommy's murder (135); refuses to name Popeye; says state will have to prove his guilt (136); sheriff has destroyed his still (150); Baptist minister has preached against him and Ruby (151); refuses to allow Horace to mention Popeye's presence (152-156); fears retribution by Popeye (156-157); refuses to mention Temple's presence at Old Frenchman Place (157-158); expects Popeye to shoot him while in jail (326); jury out eight minutes after Temple's perjury (349); burned to death by lynchers (355).

Ruby Lamar (9) Goodwin? (48): cooking at Old Frenchman Place (7); from Memphis where she probably was a prostitute (8); mother of small boy (19-20); asks Horace to send her orange stick (20); warns Temple not to stay after dark (56); scorns Temple; tells her of her affair with Frank and how her father shot him (67); tells Temple of Lee Goodwin's past; scorns her (68-69); turned to prostitution to hire lawyer to get Goodwin out of Leavenworth (68); offers to get car for Temple, whom she despises (70); worked nightshift as waitress to see Goodwin while he was in jail (71); flashback: watches inside Temple's room; sees the others as they come in (94-95); takes Temple to barn for the night (97); stays with her until daylight (100); fights with Goodwin to prevent him from going to Temple; after he slaps her, takes child to spring (114-115); returning to get baby's bottle, sees Popeye driving off with Temple (123); calls the sheriff; speaks of dead man (124-125); not married to Goodwin, according to Benbow (130); tells Horace that she has no money for defense (148); sends for Horace; baby is sick; tells him a young woman was at Old Frenchman Place (160-161); tells Horace about Gowan and Temple's visit to Old Frenchman Place (193 ff.); stays at jail (215); thrown out of hotel (216); Horace finds her a place to stay (240); first witness at trial (323); returns to jail that night (325); Horace coaches her for the next day (329); assumes that Horace would want sex as payment; was willing (330-331); tells Horace of her life with Goodwin (332 ff.); had lived with the lawyer for two months before she found that he could not get Goodwin out of Leavenworth (333).

Tommy (20)   : gets whisky from under kitchen floor; feebleminded (10); takes Gowan to barn for drink (54); tries to give Temple food (76); asks Goodwin to tell others to stop pestering her (79); through window, watches Temple remove dress (81-82); after fight, feels protective toward Temple; follows Ruby and Popeye into room (91); next morning, sits outside crib in barn guarding Temple (117); tells Temple it will not hurt her; feels her thigh (118); promises her to keep others from getting to her (118-119); shot in back of head by Popeye (121); no one knows his last name (134).

Pap (116)   : old man with long white beard; blind and deaf (12).

Little Belle (14) Mitchell (126): brings boy home whom she met on train (14); reminds Horace of what he found on train, shrimp (15); Horace Benbow's step-daughter (126).

_____: boy whom Little Belle met on train; attends Tulane (14).

Belle (15) Mitchell (126) Benbow (15): Horace's wife, mother of Little Belle (15); by another husband (17); wires Narcissa to tell her to tell Horace that she has gone back to Kentucky and has sent for Little Belle (127); back in Kinston at end of novel (358).

_____: Ruby Lamar's son; sleeps in box in kitchen (19-20).

_____: two men who drive Popeye's truck; take Horace to Jefferson (23-24).

Narcissa Benbow Sartoris (27): Horace's sister; widow; with son ten years old [internal date for action of novel: Benbow Sartoris born June 11, 1920.] (25); objects to Horace letting Ruby stay in their home (139); 36 years old in 1930 (141); refuses to marry Gowan Stevens (198); refuses to let Ruby stay at house after she is turned out of hotel (218); thinks that Horace is having an affair with Ruby; asks Horace to go away (221); wants him out of Goodwin case at any cost (317); writes to Belle to say that Horace will return to her (318).

Benbow Sartoris (27): son of Narcissa; ten years old in 1930 (25); called Bory by his mother (28).

Jenny (25) [Virginia Sartoris Dupre]: great-aunt of Narcissa's husband (25); teases Horace about leaving Belle (28); tells him to go back (127, 155).

Gowan Stevens (26): walks in garden with Narcissa (25); attended University of Virginia (26); takes Temple to dance at University (33); afterwards, gives lift to three town boys, one of whom dates Temple (34); buys a quart of whisky (36); brags of ability to drink; gets drunk; vomits; passes out (38-39); has date to meet Temple, on train with school group to attend baseball game, and take her from train at Taylor next morning (39-40); drives there after he recovers; meets train; Temple gets off (40-41); has bought cheap work shirt and drinks bottle of hair oil (42); attempting to drive Temple to Starkville, decides to get bottle of whisky at Goodwin's (43); tells Temple he has met her "town" boy friends and has seen her name on lavatory wall (43); drives car full tilt into tree (44); they go to Old Frenchman Place to borrow car (46 ff.); gets Tommy to take him to barn for drink (54); after Popeye intimidates him, goes to barn for more whisky (59); gets drunk three separate times that day (59); after supper drunk again, begins arguing with Van (79); knocked out by Van, is carried to Temple's room (85); next morning, very battered, goes for car (100); begins to feel ashamed and unable to face Temple (101); reaches house and hires car; hires man to drive it and sends it back for her; hitches ride in opposite direction (102); never comes back to town; writes Narcissa a farewell letter (153); had asked Narcissa to marry him (198).

Herschell Jones (26): once courted Narcissa (26).

Temple (31) Drake (62): student at State University at Oxford (31); goes to dance with Gowan Stevens; red haired (33); leaves train at Taylor for date with Gowan (41); after Gowan wrecks car, enters Old Frenchman Place; afraid of Popeye (48-50); tells Ruby that she and Gowan are married (57); becomes terrorized; screams and hides in kitchen near baby until Goodwin finds her (60); father is judge (60); has four brothers: two lawyers, one a newspaper man, one a Yale student; father is a judge in Jackson (62); on probation at college (63) for slipping out at night (65); predicts Ruby's baby will die (73); in room at night, props chair against door; removes dress and puts on coat and raincoat over it; gets into bed (81-83); after the fighting, is taken to barn by Ruby to spend the night

(97); 17 years old (104); unable to use barn as outhouse as others do, relieves herself in bushes; being watched (109) by Goodwin (110); as he enters house, runs to barn; is terrorized by rat (111-112); hides from Goodwin in crib in which she slept (118); without a sound, watches Popeye climb down ladder into crib (120); after rape by Popeye, lies screaming on porch by old man (122); Popeye drives off with her in car (123); in car, is in shock; feels blood seeping (163); screams (164); is taken to brothel in Memphis (170); treated by Doctor Quinn (179); finally eats dinner brought by Minnie (187); visited by Popeye (191); visited in brothel by Horace (255); asks for drink; is now drinking fairly heavily (256); tells Horace of night at Old Frenchman Place (257); but avoids speaking of actual crime (258); said she tried to think herself into being a boy that night to avoid rape (259); says Popeye felt her under coat that night (262); had hallucinations while he stood over her (263-264); fails to tell actual details of rape (264); flashback to time she first got dressed in brothel; hurls new clothes and Popeye's suit into corner; hides gun under pillow (270); bribes Minnie with $10 to let her leave; promises to return; makes telephone call at drugstore; returns to brothel (273-274); gulps large drink; leaves house at night; meets Popeye outside in car (277); in car, tells Popeye he is not a man; reveals that he brought another man to brothel and watched him with Temple (278); at first thought Popeye had actually had sexual relations with her; then discovered that he was impotent (278); at Grotto, dances with Popeye; drinks heavily (281-283); calls Popeye "daddy" (277,284); asks him for his pistol (284); refuses to dance with Red; gets drunk (285); has physical desire for Red; plays dice (286); leaves table; goes to room where Red comes to her; she writhes her loins against him; begs him to take her (287-288); tells Red that Popeye came there to kill him (288); taken from Grotto by two men (288-290); full tale of her relations with Red and Popeye told (311); appears in court on second day (339); had been raped with a corn cob (340); testifies; 18 years old; mother dead; in Miss Reba's brothel since May 12th (342-343); testifies that Goodwin entered crib and shot Tommy; identifies corn cob; gazes at back of courtroom throughout testimony (345); taken from court by father and four young men (348); with father, goes to Paris; sits in Luxembourg Gardens (378).

_____: first town boy who waits outside dance attended by Temple and Gowan (32).

Doc (34)_____: his companion (32); mimics Temple by saying his father is a judge; spreads broken bottle in road for Gowan's car (33); shows others girl's panties; implies he got them from Temple (34).

_____: third town boy (32).

Luke (35)_____: sells Gowan quart of whisky (36).

_____: restaurant waiter (37).

_____: black man who sees Gowan at RR station (40).

Hubert (63) Drake (62): Temple's father (59); judge in Jackson (62); comes to court to remove Temple from stand (346-347).

Buddy, Hubert Drake jr. 63): Temple's youngest brother (63).

_____: Ruby Lamar's brother (67).

_____: Ruby Lamar's father, who kills her lover (67).

Frank (67)_____: Ruby Lamar's lover; shot by her father (67).

Van (76)_____: at dinner, tries to make Temple sit on his lap (76); follows Temple to kitchen; asks her to go for walk (78); fights with Gowan; knocks him out; he and Goodwin carry Gowan's body to Temple's room (85); tears raincoat at Temple's breast (86); is knocked out by Goodwin (87).

_____Tull (100): Gowan hired car at his home; it is from his place that Ruby calls the sheriff (124).

_____Mitchell (126): first husband of Belle M. Benbow (126).

Isom (145)_____: Narcissa's black driver (131).

_____: black man in jail; murdered wife by slashing throat (135); good baritone (136); to be hanged on Saturday (155).

_____: porter in hotel where Horace places Ruby (147); takes Ruby's message to Horace (160).

_____: clerk who sells Popeye sandwich (167).

_____: mechanic in garage (167).

Minnie_____: black maid in Miss Reba's brothel (170); washes Temple's blood-stained clothes (173); brings Temple dinner (184); paid $5 a day by Popeye not to let Temple out of house or use phone (311).

Reba Rivers (170): madam of brothel (170); carries rosary in one hand and tankard of beer in other; has just come from church when Temple arrives (171); assumes Popeye has had regular sex with Temple (173); tells Temple that all the girls have been trying to win Popeye (174); gets doctor for Temple (178); Mr. Binford had been her man, and she named one of her dogs after him; he was landlord of house for eleven years; died two years ago (185); gets drunk after visiting his grave (189); rents Virgil and Fonzo a room in house (232); reluctant to let Horace see Temple (253); supports four children (not hers, she says) in an Arkansas home (253); urges Temple to tell what happened (256); urges Horace to take Temple back to Mississippi and not let her come back; says she will be dead or in an asylum in year, the way she and Popeye behave in room; realizes that something is odd about their actions, but has not found out about it yet (265); attends Red's funeral (300); reveals

108

that police are after Popeye for Red's murder and that he and Temple have disappeared (307); has learned of Popeye's impotence and what he was doing with Temple and Red; claims she knew all the time (307-308).

Dr. _____ Quinn (173): sent for by Miss Reba to tend Temple; refuses to come on Sunday; Miss Reba says she could put him in jail three times over (176); attends Temple (179).

_____ Binford (185): Miss Reba's man; landlord of brothel; now dead (185).

_____: conductor on train when Horace goes to Oxford (203).

_____: youth on train; rides without ticket (203).

Shack _____: his companion (203).

_____: youth in University post office; tells Horace that Temple quit school two weeks ago; asks if he is another detective (206).
Senator Clarence Snopes (208): meets Horace on train; addresses him as Judge Benbow (208); son of a restaurant owner (210); says that Temple ran away (212); finds Virgil and Fonzo at Miss Reba's; takes them to a black brothel (239); calls Horace; says he has information he wants (242); says he has seen Temple; wants to sell information to Horace (246-247); tells Horace she is in a "Memphis 'ho' house" (247); meets Horace outside Miss Reba's; hints that he thinks Horace is there for a prostitute (248-249); had previously visited Miss Reba several times inquiring about Temple (251); Popeye caught him looking through keyhole of Temple's room; burned his neck with match (251-252); appears with black eye; says he was hit by car; makes anti-semitic tirade that reveals he got his black eye trying to sell information to a Memphis lawyer; reveals that Judge Drake and Horace paid him $100 for the same information (319-320); information he sold was whereabouts of Temple Drake (338-339).

_____: porter on train to whom Snopes gives cigar; called "George" by Snopes (213).

_____: taxi driver who meets Horace at station (215).

Mrs. _____ Walker (215): wife of jailor; takes Ruby and child when they are thrown out of hotel (215, 217).

Ed (218) Walker (215): jailor.

_____: proprietor of hotel; expelled Ruby and child when group of church women protested her presence (216).

Eustace Graham (223): District Attorney (222); has club foot; graduated from the State University (314); put himself through college and law school by playing poker (314-315); says Horace has no chance to win Goodwin's case (317); introduces the corn cob in evidence; calls for lynching (340).

Virgil Snopes (226): arrives in Memphis and bluffs that he has been there before; looking for a cheap hotel, he and Fonzo arrive at Miss Reba's brothel (229); wants to rent room and attend barber college (232); goes to brothel with Fonzo (235).

Fonzo (226)_____: companion of Virgil Snopes (226); thinks Miss Reba's prostitutes are her daughters (233); on return from brothel, tells Miss Reba that they have been to a prayer meeting (236).

_____: barber-student who takes Fonzo and Virgil to a brothel (235).

_____: "half crazed white woman" who allows Ruby and son to stay at her house (240).

_____: Minnie's husband; disapproved of her work; a cook in restaurant; left her to run off with waitress; took all Minnie's clothes and jewelry (251).

_____: man in cap who watches Temple leave brothel to phone (273-274).

Red (279)_____: man whom Temple called from drugstore; Popeye is going to kill him (288); is the man whom Popeye brought to the brothel to watch making love to Temple (288); waves to Temple as two men carry her out of Grotto (290); waked at Grotto (291 ff.); when brawl breaks out at funeral, his coffin is knocked over and his corpse rolls out on floor; had been shot in forehead (299).

_____: man chewing gum (282); with companion, takes Temple from Grotto (289-290).

_____: his companion (282).

Joe (297)_____: proprietor of Grotto (291); opposed to having orchestra play jazz at Red's funeral (294); riot breaks out against him (297).

_____: the bouncer at Grotto (292).

Gene (293)_____: supplies punch at funeral; a bootlegger (293).

_____: man at funeral who wants orchestra to play jazz (293).

_____: orchestra leader at funeral (294).

Lorraine (305)_____: thin woman; wears gold nose glasses; returns with Miss Reba from funeral; probably a sister madam (300).

Myrtle (303)_____: short, plump woman who returns from funeral with Miss Reba; probably a sister madam (300); cries (301).

Uncle Bud (301)_____: 5-or 6-year old boy who visits Miss Reba with Lorraine and Myrtle (300); lives on an Arkansas farm (302); sneaks some of Miss Reba's beer; has been drunk before (305); steals bottle of beer from ice box; gets drunk; vomits (312).

_____: Belle Mitchell Benbow's father; lives in Kentucky (313).

_____Harris (316): proprietor of poker game who plays with Eustace Graham (316).

_____: barber to whom Clarence Snopes explains black eye (320).

_____: Jewish lawyer from Memphis; offers Snopes ten dollars for information about Temple (320).

_____: court clerk at Goodwin's trial (339).

_____: bailiff at Goodwin's trial (339).

_____: judge at Goodwin's trial (339).

_____: the sheriff (351).

_____: night marshal (352).

_____: three drummers who discuss corn cob (352).

_____: black porter at hotel in Oxford (353).

_____: Kinston hack driver; a landowner who lost his fortune (356); meets Horace's train (357).

_____: man who set Goodwin on fire; burns himself (355).

_____: Popeye's mother; daughter of a boarding house keeper (361); marries after she is pregnant (362); an invalid (370).

_____: Popeye's father; a professional strike breaker (361); abandons wife after strike is settled; sends her a post card on the day Popeye is born (363).

_____: Popeye's maternal grandmother (363); tries several times to burn Popeye to death as a child (364); leaves him in car (366); borrows match from policeman (367); burns house and herself (368).

_____: old black woman who tells Popeye's mother what is wrong (363).

_____: Popeye's maternal grandmother's second husband; took wife's savings (363-364).

_____: grocer boy who brings olive oil to house (365).

_____: doctor who orders eggs cooked in olive oil for Popeye (365).

_____: woman in whose car Popeye was found as child; provides doctor's care for him and gives party for him (365-369).

_____: her black chauffeur (365).

_____: policeman who lends Popeye's grandmother match (367).

_____: officer who escorts Popeye from Birmingham (371).

_____: judge who tries Popeye (371).

_____: defense attorney appointed by court to defend Popeye (372).

_____: District Attorney (374).

_____: turnkey in Alabama jail; Popeye gives him $100 (374).

_____: Memphis lawyer who arrives in Popeye's cell (376).

_____: minister who prays by Popeye's bed (377).

_____: sheriff who executes Popeye (378).

Seven of these stories were published for the first time in *These 13*. Dates of writing and publication are indicated for each story. *These 13* was published on September 21, 1931. Originally, this collection was called *A Rose for Emily and Other Stories* in the contract for publication.

Pagination, in parentheses, for The Collected Stories of William Faulkner (New York: Random House, 1950), 900 pp.; (London: Chatto & Windus, 1951); (New York: Vintage Books, 1977). See Meriwether A 22. Second set of pagination to (London: Chatto & Windus, 1958-1959), Three volumes, Vol. Two.

"Victory"

Written perhaps as early as 1926 or 1927; published first in *These 13*.

Alec (441, 159) Gray (serial number 024186) (439, 157): tall, white-haired Englishman, a "milord military;" four years after WW I, arrives from Marseilles and travels to the war-ruined village of Rozieres; takes a room in new, cheap hotel (431-432, 149-150); seems either deaf or in daze (432-433, 150-151); flashback: British soldier who says he is too young to shave (439, 157); refuses to say "sir" to Sergeant-Major (440, 158); son of shipbuilder in Clyde, Scotland; enlists in British army (442, 160); does not write home for seven months while in penal battalion (443, 161); after release, considers himself old enough to shave (444, 162); kills the Sergeant-Major (bayonet in throat) and savagely beats his dead face with the rifle butt (446, 164); receives citation for bravery during this battle (446, 164); is hospitalized several months (447, 165); being sent to officers' school (447, 165); is commissioned, sends home his medal; spends his leaves in London in "haunts of officers;" continues to read Bible; as officers of K Company are killed, is promoted to subaltern-captain (448, 166); now inspects men and orders their names taken (449, 167); leads company in capturing several German machine guns; is wounded; receives another citation (449-452, 167-170); hair almost white now; face gaunt; returns home in civilian clothes (453, 171); announces intention to return to England where work was promised and where he has officer friends (454, 172); his awards were the MC (Military Cross) and DSM (Distinguished Service Medal); joins Officers Association; works in London; affects style of the distinguished officer (455-456, 173-174); saves for return visit to France; has completely surrendered to the empire (456, 174); returns to France; finds job gone when he returns to London; savings dwindle; old friends can not help (456-457, 174-175); can not get work of any sort; leaves London to find work; returns (457-458, 175-176); tries begging (459, 177); bathes in river; irons clothes with hot stones prepared for him by tramps (462-463, 180-181); finally seen by Walkley selling matches on London street; though he recognizes Walkley, his eyes are perfectly dead; curses him and refuses help (463-464, 181-182).

_____: porter at Gare du Nord (431, 149).

_____: driver of car that takes Gray to Rozieres (432, 150).

_____: French owner of hotel in Rozieres (432, 150).

_____: his wife (432, 150).

_____: small, rat-faced man, Swiss, who meets Gray at hotel; seems to be guide (435, 153).

_____: man in corduroy coat at bar with hotel owner (436, 154).

_____: nameless women peasants in third-class coach; watch Gray and comment on his search (436, 154).

_____: flashback: Sergeant-Major of Gray's battalion (437, 155); murdered in trench by Gray during raid (446, 164).

_____: British colonel of Gray's battalion; inspects troops (437, 155); orders Gray's name taken because he has not shaved (439, 157).

_____: two British officers (ADC's of colonel) (437, 155).

Sergeant _____ Cunninghame (439, 157): Gray's company sergeant who fails to take his name when ordered (441, 159).

_____: Gray's corporal (441, 159).

Matthew Gray (441, 159): Scotch ship builder of Clyde; father of Alec Gray whom he considers too young to work in shipyard (441, 159); urges son to reject medal and refuse officers' school, for he was not born a gentleman (448, 166).

Alec Gray [I] (441, 159): Scotch, 68-year-old grandfather of young Alec; argues that boy should be allowed to enlist (442, 160); gives up work in shipyard to sit on porch trying to hear guns (443, 161); dies while Alec is at war (447, 165).

John Wesley Gray (442, 160): younger brother of Alec (442, 160).

Matthew Gray (442, 160): youngest brother of Alec Gray (442, 160).

Simon Gray (442, 160): uncle of Alec Gray; received Victoria Cross from Queen Victoria (442, 160).

Annie (454, 172) Gray: Alec Gray's mother (443, 161).

Jessie Gray (443, 161) _____: sister of Alec Gray; marries while he is in London (456, 174).

Elizabeth (447, 165) Gray: infant sister of Alec Gray; born while he is at war (444, 162).

_____: British general who waves to Alec's company as it moves to the front (444, 162).

_____: Alec Gray's batman (448, 166).

_____ McLan (448,167): soldier with dirty rifle (448, 167).

_____ Walkley (463, 181): subaltern, hospitalized with Alec Gray (452, 170); goes to Canada when demobbed; prospers as wheat farmer (463, 181); returns to London; meets Gray on street selling matches (464, 182).

_____: medical officer who discharges Gray (453, 171).

_____ Whiteby (457, 175): a suicide (457, 175).

_____: constable who tells Gray to move along when he is begging (459, 177).

_____: blind man, tramp, ex-soldier (dispatch rider) (459, 177); had been engaged when he enlisted; lost girl's picture; it was replaced by his companions with blank card (460, 178).

_____: four ex-soldiers; tramps; companions of blind man (459 ff., 177 ff.); prepare hot stones for Gray (462, 180).

_____: fiancee of blind man; has scar on left wrist; is unfaithful to him while she gets one of hospital nurses to sit with him at night (460-461, 178-179).

_____: nurse who sits with blind man (461, 179).

"Ad Astra"

Composed by December 21, 1927; on sending schedule March 5, 1930; first published in *American Caravan, IV*, eds., Alfred Kreymborg, Lewis Mumford, and Paul Rosenfeld (New York: Macauly, 1931), 164-181; revised for *These 13*.

_____: narrator (407, 125); an American in British forces, WW I (407, 125).

_____: subadar; an Indian major, squat, small, and thick, a non-drinker (407, 125); a prince in his own country (408, 126); says that all those in generation that fought in the war are dead but do not yet know it (421, 139).

[Bayard] Sartoris (407, 125): twin brother has been killed in war (414, 132); ambushed German pilots; shot down three in week until he got the one that had shot down his brother (414, 132); ends brawl in restaurant by swinging chair at light (424, 142); gets ill; vomits after fight (428, 146).

                    Bland (407, 125): blond, tall Southerner; Rhodes Scholar; transferred to Air Force out of Oxford battalion; when drunk, talks of wife but is not married; has been wounded (408, 126); as drink runs out, cries and speaks of poor little wife (429, 147).

                    Comyn (407, 125): British officer (407, 125); thick, huge man (409, 127); pilot; wants to fight everyone (410, 128); Irish (420, 138); hurls American MP over heads of crowd in brawl (423, 141); with Monaghan, takes German prisoner to French brothel (426-427, 144-145).

                    Monaghan (410, 128): member of RFC; wears American tunic (410, 128); has shot down German officer; wants to take him home; American (412, 130); shanty Irish (414, 132); father made fortune digging sewers; Yale man (415, 133); has killed thirteen Germans; has torn off insignia and medals (416, 134).

                    : has bandaged head; wears short tunic (410, 128); German officer, prisoner of Monaghan (412, 130); comes from Beyreuth; has wife and son (412, 130); has four brothers; at university, learned to seek brotherhood of man; refused barony (417, 135); wife, daughter of peasant musician (418, 136); learns on morning of capture that brother is dead; he is now baron; to avoid barony, destroyed papers and identity disc; intended to be shot down (419-420, 137-138); loses consciousness; is revived (424-425, 143-144); as Comyn and Monaghan take him to brothel, asks narrator to write to wife and tell her that life is nothing (426, 144).

                    : waiter in Cloche-Clos (restaurant) (411, 129).

                    : American MP (412, 130): defies and hits French officer who challenges presence of German prisoner (423, 141).

                    : patronne of the Cloche-Clos; wears steel spectacles (413, 131); wants to hold German prisoner responsible for broken crockery (422, 140).

                    Hume (414, 132):

[John] Sartoris (414, 132): twin of [Bayard] Sartoris; shot down.

Franz (418, 136)   : brother of German officer.

                    : French officer (421, 139); demands explanation for presence of German; has glass eye (422, 140); sets off general brawl (423, 141).

                    : French sergeant (421, 139).

"All the Dead Pilots"

Once titled "Per Ardua" and "Dead Pilots," written by February 5, 1930; on sending schedule April 23, 1931; first published in *These 13*.

_____: narrator; has false leg; censors mail at Wing Headquarters in 1918; experiments with synchronized cameras (512, 194).

_____: gunnery sergeant in Spoomer's squadron (513, 195).

_____ Spoomer (513, 195): holds Guard's captaincy in British Army, an observer; serves as commander of a Camel pursuit squardon; nephew of Corps Commander; decorated with "Mons Star" and DSO; was at Sandhurst in 1914 when war broke out; has dog almost as large as a calf; big, ruddy man with china eyes (513, 195); rival of [John] Sartoris for favors of Kitchener, a camp follower (514, 196); uses rank to assign jobs to Sartoris while he courts the girl (517, 199); does not want dog to eat from enlisted mess: "that's for soldiers." (519, 201); caught by Sartoris in 'Toinette's bedroom (probably hiding in wardrobe); clothes stolen (524, 206); returns to squadron dressed in woman's skirt and shawl; sent back to England to be a temporary colonel at ground school (527, 209).

_____: WW I British Corps Commander, K. G., brigadier in 1914; just returned from India service; Spoomer's uncle (513, 195).

_____ Ffollansbye (513, 195): finds [John] Sartoris drunk; sends him back to airdrome (514, 196).

[John] (521, 203) Sartoris (513, 195): American serving with British Flying Corps (513, 195); vocabulary of two hundred words; lives on Mississippi plantation with great-aunt and grandfather; came to British Army via Canada in 1916; has girl in London whom others call Kitchener "because she had such a mob of soldiers;" does not know this; she leaves others for him; discovers she has gone off with Spoomer; gets drunk; returns to squadron; puts garter on a captain's tunic; puts tunic on corporal; fights him, calling him Cap'm Spoomer (514-515, 196-197); rival of Spoomer for favors of French girl in Amiens; gives her presents; releases Spoomer's dog to learn if Spoomer is courting girl (516-517, 198-199); one day dog goes to Amiens; Sartoris disobeys orders; follows dog; refused entrance to place where Spoomer and girl are; returns to base; wrecks motorcycle trying to run down Spoomer's dog (519-520, 201-202); wants to teach Spoomer to fly to run him out of sky (510, 202); killed in July 1918 (521, 203); as Germans shell Amiens, flies to nearby field; drives French ambulance to estaminet; has drunk bottle of brandy (521-522, 203-204); breaks door to 'Toinette's room; takes Spoomer's clothes; leaves; fights French corporal; dresses drunken French ambulance driver in Spoomer's uniform (523-524, 205-207); places paper with Spoomer's name and squadron number in pocket; drives ambulance back to field; flies back to front, then to aerodrome; stunts plane; crashes; vomits (526-527, 208-209); loses front teeth in crash; reduced to second lieutenant; transferred (527, 209); squadron of night-flying Camels; can not fly Camels even in daytime (528, 210); shot down and killed July 4, 1918 (530, 212).

_____ "Kitchener," Kit (514, 196): London girl friend of [John] Sartoris; goes off with Spoomer; has many other soldiers (514, 196).

_____: British corporal; ex-professional boxer; dressed by Sartoris in a captain's tunic to fight in name of Spoomer (514-515, 196-197).

'Toinette (523, 205)_____: French girl in Amiens, courted by Sartoris and Spoomer; runs a back-street estaminet with older woman (516, 198).

_____: French woman; partner of 'Toinette (516, 198).

_____: French soldier in peasant smock; drives lorry to airfield (519, 201).

_____: British patrol leader; announces fall of Cambrai (520, 202).

_____: French woman working in field near Amiens (521, 203).

_____: French ambulance driver whose ambulance Sartoris steals (522, 204).

_____: French corporal (522, 204) who tries to stop Sartoris from leaving estaminet (525, 207).

_____: Anzack major (527, 209).

_____: British brigadier who sends Spoomer back to England (527, 209).

_____: British Wing Commander (527, 209).

Mrs. Virginia Sartoris (529, 211): Aunt Jenny (529, 211); Sartoris's great-aunt [Here given name Sartoris, not DuPre.]

Elnora (529, 211)_____: mentioned in Sartoris's letter to aunt; knitted him socks which he gave away (529, 211).

Isom (529, 211)_____: also mentioned in letter (529, 211).

[Bayard Sartoris II]: Sartoris's grandfather (529, 211).

Major C. Kaye (530, 212): Sartoris's commanding officer in Camel squadron; writes to Aunt Jenny about Sartoris's death in WW I (530, 212).

R. Kyerling (530, 212): a pilot who could not help Sartoris (530,

212).

"Crevasse"

Written perhaps as early as 1926 or 1927, originally as part of "Victory;" first published in *These 13.*

_____: British captain (466, 184); leads party of soldiers across battlefield into strange valley during WW I (466, 184 ff.); they discover skulls on the floor of valley, as though men had been buried sitting down (470, 188); suddenly ground gives way; party falls into chalk cavern (471, 189) where they discover bodies of Senegalese troop gassed in May 1915 (472, 190); fourteen of the group survive; twelve are missing (472, 190); captain leads men to tunnel; saves them (473-474, 191-192).

_____ McKie (472, 190): subaltern (466, 184) in strange valley, discovers French rifle all decayed (469, 187); discovers skull (470, 188); lost when party falls into crevasse (472, 190).

_____: sergeant (466, 184).

_____: wounded British soldier (465, 183); keeps insisting he is not dead (471, 189, 474, 192).

"Red Leaves"

On sending schedule July 24, 1930; first published in *The Saturday Evening Post,* **203 (October 25, 1930), 6-7, 54, 56, 58, 60, 62, 64; revised for** *These 13.*

Three Basket (313, 77): Indian, about 60; wears enameled snuffbox clamped through one ear (313, 77); dislikes concept of owning slaves; considers them worse than white people; "man was not made to sweat;" cannibal, has once eaten black flesh (314, 78); can not understand why the "savage" slaves cling to life and prefer to sweat rather than to enter the ground with chief (326, 80); he and Berry appeal to Moketubbe to lead hunt for Issetibbeha's missing slave so that he might be killed and buried with chief (324-326, 88-91); finally removes Moketubbe's red-heeled shoes that have put him into coma (327, 91); offers body servant food before he is killed (339, 103); leads black man to his death with Issetibbeha (341, 105).

Louis Berry (322, 86): second Indian (313, 77).

The Man (313, 77) Moketubbe (316, 80): Indian Chief (313, 77); grandson of Doom (316, 80); son of Issetibbeha; as The Man, is entitled to wear red-heeled shoes all the time now (316, 80); at age of 3, becomes fascinated with shoes brought back from France by Issetibbeha (320, 84); although slippers did not fit him at 3, tried to put them on until he was 16; stopped trying in father's presence; at 25, father gave him shoes, remembering that his own father's uncle did not have red-heeled shoes to lure assassin (322, 86); becomes The Man at 30 years; now wears slippers;

two hundred and fifty pounds; height five feet, one inch; has yellow face (325, 89); puts slippers on; in coma (327, 91); joins hunt for body servant; carried in litter; carries red shoes with him (335, 99); faints when he wears slippers too long (337, 101).

Issetibbeha (314, 78): The Man who has just died (314, 78); when his father, Doom, died, debated tribal elders over what to do with slaves; they decide they could not eat them, for there were too many; decides they must do as the white men (319, 83); begins to breed slaves to sell to white men; takes trip to Paris on profits; brings home from Chevalier de Vitry shoes with red heels (320, 84); five years after he gives son shoes, dies after brief sickness (322, 86).

Doom (316, 80): grandfather of Moketubbe (316, 80); father of Issetibbeha (317, 81); hauled deckhouse of steamboat twelve miles for his house (317, 81); had been born a mere sub-chief, a Mingo; one of three children on "mother's side of the family;" takes trip to New Orleans; meets de Vitry; gets involved with young woman, daughter of wealthy West Indian who bears his child after following him to Mississippi (317-318, 81-82); then begins to acquire slaves and to cultivate land in imitation of whites, but never had enough work for slaves to do (318, 82); dies when son is 19 (319, 83) [Ikkkemotubbe].

_____: missing slave of Issetibbeha (316, 88); 40 years old, a Guinea man; taken at 14 by trader; Issetibbeha's body servant for twenty-three years; hides in barn while Issetibbeha is dying (327-329, 91-93); in flight, returns to steamboat to watch preparations for funeral (333-334, 97-98); is bitten by cottonmouth; lets snake slash him several times, saying "Ole Grandfather. It's that I do not wish to die." (334-335, 98-99); eludes pursuers six days, then, injured, hides in swamp (336, 100); when cornered, asks Indian to slay him in dark (337, 101); begins to sing in native tongue (338, 102); accepts food before his death; can not swallow (340, 104); can not drink water before death (341, 105).

Chevalier Soeur Blonde de Vitry (317, 81): man Doom meets on trip to New Orleans; helps pass Doom off as The Man, the Chief, on male side of family; first called him *du homme*, hence Doom (317-318, 81-82); rumored to be friend of Carondelet and intimate of General Wilkinson (318, 82); back in Paris, borrows three hundred dollars from Issetibbeha (320-84).

_____: West Indian girl; mother of Doom's child Issetibbeha; marries Doom shortly before child is born (318, 82); city woman with black blood (321, 85).

_____: brother of Doom's wife; seeks Doom with pistol (318, 82).

_____: black maid to mother of Issetibbeha (318, 82).

_____: itinerant minister; marries Doom and West Indian; rides mule with cotton umbrella and three-gallon jug of whisky (318, 82).

_____: Moketubbe's mother, a black field hand, seen one day by Issetibbeha on way to fish (321, 85).

_____: Issetibbeha's "newest" wife; tells him that Moketubbe, at 25, is still trying to put on red-heeled shoes (321, 85).

_____: tribal doctor in skunk-skin vest; attends Issetibbeha in last illness (322, 86).

_____: old Indian; recalls it took three weeks to catch Doom's slave to bury him with Chief; is accompanied by two women (323, 87).

_____: stripling Indian with "punkah-like fan of fringed paper;" stands behind Moketubbe's throne (325, 89).

_____: headman of slaves (328, 92); gives runaway slave cooked meat (332-333, 96-97).

_____: 14-year-old boy slave; guards blacks' drums in forest; mute (328, 92).

_____: captain of slave ship that brings body servant to America; reads Bible while drunk (330, 94).

_____: one of two men who chase slave (331, 95).

_____: other of two men who chase slave (331, 95).

Had-Two-Fathers (336, 100): Indian who removes Moketubbe's shoes when he is in coma (336, 100); [later called Sam Fathers; called John Had-Two-Fathers in magazine version.]

_____: Indian courier; finds slave in swamp (336, 100).

"A Rose for Emily"

Written at least by October 7, 1929 and perhaps as early as 1927; on sending schedule March 7, 1930; first published in *The Forum*, **83 (April, 1930), 233-238; revised for** *These 13.*

Emily Grierson (119, 9): small fat woman, wears black, looks bloated; refuses to pay taxes; [Time set at 1924--1894 plus 30] 30 years before, she had vanquished town about "smell" (121-122, 11-12); watches the four aldermen [in 1891] throw lime about yard and outbuildings for smell which goes away after week or two (122-123, 12-13); at 30 still a spinster (123, 13); inherits father's house; refuses for three days to admit father died; finally yields (123-124, 13-14); reappears with new hairdo after long sickness; begins to go out Sundays with Homer Barron (124, 14); buys rat poison (arsenic) (125, 15); of Episcopal stock (126, 16); town thinks she is married to Homer Baron; orders man's silver toilet set, initials H. B.; buys set of man's clothing, including nightshirt (127, 17); after Barron's return, fails to appear on streets; when next seen, is fat, hair turning gray; pepper and salt, iron-gray (127, 17); dies at 74 (128, 18); skeleton of Homer Barron lies on her bed (130, 20).

Tobe (121, 11)_____: manservant to Emily Grierson (119, 9); black (120, 10); after she dies, lets visitors in, walks out back door; not seen again (129, 19).

Colonel [Bayard] Sartoris (119, 9): mayor of Jefferson; permitted no black woman to appear on streets without apron (119-120, 9-10); remitted Miss Emily's taxes from death of father in perpetuity on invented tale (120, 10).

_____Grierson (120, 10): Emily's father; clutched horsewhip to dismiss suitor (123, 13).

_____: Mayor of Jefferson in 1924 (120, 10).

_____: woman who complains to Judge Stevens about smell (122, 12).

Judge_____Stevens (122, 12): Mayor of Jefferson in 1892; 80 years old; received complaints about smell (122, 12).

_____Wyatt (123, 13): Emily's great-aunt; completely crazy at end; witnessed dismissal of Homer Barron (123, 13).

Homer Barron (124, 14): foreman of construction company to pave sidewalks in Jefferson; big, dark, big voice, light eyes (124, 14); begins to escort Emily (124, 14); drinks at Elks' Club; says he is not marrying kind (126, 16); disappears after town thinks he has married Emily (127, 17); returns three days after Alabama cousins leave; last seen entering kitchen door at dusk (127, 17); murdered by Emily with arsenic; skeleton still lies on bed in bridal chamber; she had slept beside him (130, 20).

_____: one of two female cousins; visits Emily when she buys rat poison (125, 15); from Alabama (126, 16); departs after Homer leaves town (127, 17); returns for Emily's funeral (129, 19).

_____: other female cousin (125, 15).

_____: druggist; sells Emily poison (125, 15).

_____: black delivery boy; gives package to Emily (126, 16).

_____: Baptist minister; calls on Emily about affair with Barron (126, 16).

_____: his wife; writes Emily's relatives in Alabama (126, 16).

122

"A Justice"

Written by November 29, 1930 and once titled "Justice," "Indians Built a Fence," and "Built a Fence," and "Built Fence;" on sending schedule April 11, 1931; first published in *These 13.*

[Jason Lycurgus Compson II]: grandfather of narrator [Quentin Compson] (343, 107).

[Quentin Compson III]: narrator; denies that Sam Fathers is black (343, 107); takes tobacco to Sam Fathers; talks to him about old days (344, 108); 12 years old at time (359, 123).

Roskus (343, 107) [Gibson]: drives Compson surrey to farm every Saturday (343, 107).

Caddy (343, 107) [Compson]: Quentin's sister.

Jason (343, 107) [Compson]: Quentin's brother.

Sam Fathers (343, 107): clever carpenter, almost 100 years old, called Uncle Blue-Gum by blacks and Sam Fathers by whites (344, 108); says name was originally Had-Two-Fathers; takes over as narrator (345, 109); son of Indian Craw-ford and slave woman (357-358, 121-122).

_____ Stokes (343, 107): manager of Compson farm.

_____: black boy sent by Stokes to accompany Caddy and Jason fishing (343, 107).

_____: whisky trader, first white man seen by Sam Fathers (344, 108).

[Quentin MacLachan Compson II]: Quentin's great-grandfather (344, 108).

Herman Basket (345, 109): at first refuses to take any slaves won by Doom (347, 111); tells Doom that he is not in line to become The Man (348, 112); joins Craw-ford in killing three white men to recover slave woman (351, 115).

The Man (344, 108) Doom (345, 109) Ikkemotubbe (346, 110) David Callicoat (346, 110): sold Sam's mother to Quentin's great-grandfather (344, 108); returns from New Orleans with woman; had won her and five male blacks on steamboat; carries box with puppy in it; mixes bread and poison; kills puppy (345, 109); not born to be The Man; nephew of The Man; adopted name David Callicoat from pilot of river boat; says some day he will own steamboat (346-347, 110-111); name Doom--Doo-um-- given him by French Chief in New Orleans; hints that if he becomes The Man, will reward Herman Basket with six horses (348, 112); brings present of candy for The Man's son and presents for The Man's brother and all his kinfolk; after The Man and son die, and Sometimes-Wakeup refuses to

123

be The Man, Doom becomes The Man (349, 113); forces Indians and blacks to bring steamboat to plantation; finds three white men on it; "buys" steamboat from them by giving them six blacks he won and four others (351, 115); tries to prevent Craw-ford from having woman after he brings her back (351-353, 115-117); gives best cock to her black husband to match against Craw-ford's cock (355, 119); after months, brings steamboat to plantation (357, 121); congratulates slave on "fine yellow" child his wife bears; does not see how "justice can darken him any;" names child Had-Two-Fathers (357-358, 121-122); forces Craw-ford and Herman Basket to build very high fence around slave's cabin (358-359, 122-123).

Craw-ford (347, 111) Crawfish-ford (347, 111): Indian, Sam Fathers's father (345, 109); at first, refuses to take half of slaves won by Doom; then wants only the woman (347-348, 111-112); after Doom becomes The Man, asks for woman again; is reminded of death of puppy (350, 114); with Herman Basket, kills three white men to get woman traded by Doom for steamboat; fills bodies with rocks; sinks them in river (351-352, 115-116); feigns hurt back to remain at plantation with woman while others work (352-353, 116-117); tells woman's husband they will settle for her by cock fight (354, 118); when his cock is being beaten, declares cock fight will settle nothing; his cock is killed and then trampled by frustrated slave (356, 120).

_____: slave woman won by Doom (345, 109); desired by Crawford (347, 111); one of five men is her husband (352, 116); mother of Sam Fathers (357-358, 121-122).

_____: Ikkemotubbe's (Doom's) mother (346, 110).

_____: Ikkemotubbe's uncle, The Man (346, 110); dies suddenly after Doom's return to plantation (349, 113).

_____: son of The Man (346, 110); dies suddenly after Doom's return to plantation (349, 113).

Sometimes-Wakeup (349, 113): brother of The Man (346, 110); lives by himself in cabin; after he witnesses Doom's poisoning of puppy, and after The Man dies, refuses to be The Man (349, 113).

David Callicoat (346, 110): pilot of riverboat whose name Ikkemotubbe adopts (346, 110).

_____: one of the slaves won by Doom (345, 109); husband of slave woman desired by Craw-ford (352, 116); gets Doom's cock to fight Craw-ford's cock to determine who gets woman (355, 119); frustrated when Craw-ford changes rules (356, 120); appeals to Doom for justice; shows him his "son," a yellow child (357, 121); year later shows child of proper color (359, 123); the other of Sam Fathers's two fathers.

_____: first biological son of black slave (359, 123).

124

_____: the Willow-Bearer, apparently the one who notifies the next Man of succession (349, 113).

_____: three white men on steamboat, killed by Craw-ford and Basket (351, 115).

_____: New Orleans French chief (348, 112); probably de Vitry.

"Hair"

On sending schedule March 20, 1930; first published in *American Mercury*, **23 (May, 1931), 53-61; revised for** *These 13.*

Susan Reed (131, 21): an orphan; lives with Burchetts; vaguely believed to be related; some suggest illegitimate daughter; 5 years old when barber Hawkshaw arrives in town (131, 21); yellow-brown hair (132, 22); comes to Hawkshaw for haircuts until grown; grows up too fast (133, 23); at 13, whipped for using rouge and paint; starts to show figure early; men begin to talk of her as bad, but not before Hawkshaw (134, 24); begins to date boys before 14; gossips talk; quits school; works in dime store; painted and grotesque, comes to barbershop but not always to Hawkshaw's chair (135, 25); dyes and gums hair (143, 33); gets "into trouble at last" (143-144, 33-34); marries Hawkshaw (148, 38).

Mrs. _____ Burchett (131, 21): Susan's foster-mother (131, 21); whips Susan for using rouge and paint at 13 (134, 24).

Mr. _____ Burchett (131, 21): her husband.

Hawkshaw (131, 21) Henry (139, 29) Stribling (138, 28): barber in Maxey's barbershop in Jefferson; induces Susan Reed to have first haircut (131, 21); regularly cuts her hair; watches her going to and from school; gives her more candy than he gives other children (132, 22); gives her doll at Christmas, and a gift every Christmas (132-133, 22-23); takes two-week vacations in April (135, 25); bought her sixty-dollar watch last Christmas; keeps it because she is too young for expensive gifts from non-family (136, 26); "was born single and forty years old;" son of Starnes's tenant farmer; became engaged to his daughter; pays for Starnes's funeral (138, 28); starts saving; loves Starne's daughter who dies; cuts her hair as she dies (139, 29); pays interest on mortgage for widow Starnes until she dies; continues afterward to pay it; two-week vacations spent cleaning Starnes place (140, 30); gets name "Hawkshaw" from young tarts in Jefferson (141, 31); never charges Susan for haircuts (143, 33); finally pays off mortgage (145, 35); his wedding license was framed "April 4, 1905" (146, 36); marries Susan Reed (148, 38); paid mortgage in full April 16, 1930 (147, 37).

_____ Maxey (131, 21): owner of barber shop in Jefferson (131, 21); begins to spread rumor that Hawkshaw gives Susan gifts for sexual favors (136, 26).

Matt Fox (132, 22): barber in Maxey's shop (132, 22); married, fat, flabby, pasty face; tired or sad eyes; a funny fellow (133, 23); spreads rumor that Susan Reed is promiscuous (136, 26).

_____: first-person narrator; thinks women are all born bad; has daughter of his own (133, 23); travelling salesman; sells work shirts and overalls (137, 27); formerly bookkeeper in Gordonville bank (144, 34).

Mrs. _____ Cowan (136, 26): Hawkshaw's landlady (136, 26, 142, 32).

Will (146, 36) Starnes (138, 28): owner of house in Division; daughter engaged to son of tenant farmer named Stribling (Hawkshaw); dies (138, 28).

Mrs. Will Starnes (146, 36): his wife; dies April 23, 1916 (146, 36).

Sophie (Sophy 146, 36) Starnes (138, 28): daughter of Will Starnes beloved of Stribling (Hawkshaw) (138, 28); dies; has "hair not brown and not yellow" (139, 29); dies April 16, 1905 (146, 36).

Mitch Ewing (142, 32): depot freight agent in Jefferson; also lives at Mrs. Cowan's (142, 32).

_____: Maxey's brother-in-law; owns barber shop in Porterfield (141, 31).

Gavin Stevens (144, 34): District Attorney; attended Harvard; got narrator his job as salesman (144, 34).

_____: young barber takes Hawkshaw's chair (145, 35).

_____ Bidwell (146, 36): storekeeper in Division who knows so much about Hawkshaw's affairs (146, 36).

"That Evening Sun"

Once titled "Never Done No Weeping When You Wanted to Laugh;" sent to *The Saturday Evening Post*, October 2, 1930; on sending schedule October 6, 1930; first published as "That Evening Sun Go Down," in *American Mercury*, 22 (March, 1931), 257-267; revised and retitled for *These 13*.

Nancy (289, 55) _____: black laundress (289, 55); tall, high, sad face; cooks for Compsons when Dilsey is sick (290, 56); accuses Mr. Stovall of not paying her for sex; is beaten by him; arrested; tries to hang herself in cell; cut down by jailor and beaten; accused of using cocaine (291, 57); pregnant, but says it is not her husband's child (292, 58); after work in Compson home, is afraid to go home; announces that Jesus has left her and is back in town (293, 59); senses Jesus nearby; convinced he intends to kill her; says she would kill Jesus and other woman if he took one (295, 61); finally sleeps on pallet in Compson kitchen; so frightened, moves pallet to Quentin and Caddy's room

(296-297, 62-63); when Dilsey returns, says Jesus will kill her that night (297-298, 63-64); asks to sleep at Compson's again (299, 65); asks Compson children to spend night with her in cabin for protection; they go with her; talks loud and pretends Mr. Compson is with them in lane (301, 67); tells children story streaked with references to her own case (302-303, 68-69); as children want to leave, tells them another story and pops corn; as children increase cries, burns hand but does not notice (303-305, 69-72); begs children to ask father to let them stay or to let her return with them (308, 72); tells Mr. Compson Jesus left sign he will kill her on table; a hog bone with blood on it; adopts fatalistic attitude that nothing can stop Jesus from killing her (307, 73); takes comfort in having "coffin money" (308, 74); sits in cottage; refuses to bar door; makes the sound; waits for death (308-309, 74-75).

Jesus (290, 56)   : Nancy's husband; ordered to stay away from Compson house; short black man; razor scar on face (290, 56); says he can kill father of Nancy's child; resents that white men can come to his house, but that he can be ordered out of white kitchen (292, 58); now missing from his house; ostensibly gone to Memphis (293, 59).

Dilsey (290, 56) [Gibson]: cook for Compsons (290, 56); sick in her cabin (291-292, 57-58); returns to work (297, 63).

Jason (294, 60) [Compson]: father of Quentin, Caddy, and Jason; orders Jesus to stay away from house (290, 56); offers to walk Nancy home (293, 59); tells Nancy to leave white men alone; takes her home each night (295, 61); finds children at Nancy's cottage (306, 72).

Jason (290, 56) [Compson]: 5 years old (294, 60); afraid of lane and of accompanying Nancy home (300-301, 66-67).

Caddy (290, 56) Candace (293, 59) [Compson]: 7 years old (294, 60); not afraid to accompany Nancy (300-301, 66-67); plagues Jason about fears ((302, 67).

           Stovall (291, 57): cashier in bank and deacon of Baptist church; accused by Nancy of having sex with her; knocks her down; kicks her teeth out (291, 57).

           : marshal (291, 57).

           : jailor; cuts Nancy down (291, 57).

Quentin (292, 58) [Compson]: narrator (292, 58); 9 years old (294, 60).

[Caroline Bascomb Compson]: mother of Compson children (292, 58); resents husband taking Nancy home; accuses him of thinking her safety more precious than her own (293, 59); frets each night he takes Nancy home (296, 62); urges husband to call police (299, 65).

Aunt Rachel (294, 60)   : old black woman; white haired smokes pipe; said to be mother of Jesus; sometimes admits it; sometimes denies it (294, 60).

Frony (294, 60) [Gibson]_____:

T. P. (294, 60) [Gibson].

Versh (300, 66) [Gibson].

Mr._____ Lovelady (308, 74): "a short, dirty man who collected the Negro insurance;" has Nancy's "coffin money;" wife a suicide; left town with his little girl; returned alone (308, 74).

_____ Lovelady: his wife (308, 74).

_____ Lovelady: his daughter (308, 74).

"Dry September"

Written by February 5, 1930 and once titled "Drouth;" on sending schedule February 8, 1930; first published in *Scribner's*, 89 (January, 1931), 49-56; revised for *These 13*.

Minnie Cooper (169, 39): rumored to have been attacked by a black man; about forty (169, 39); 38-39 years old; of comfortable people (173, 43); slender, losing ground socially; after hearing former schoolmates talking at party, never accepted another invitation; contemporaries marry; their children call her "aunty;" begins to date widowed cashier of bank, about 40; asks former schoolmates to have children call her "cousin" instead of "aunty" (174, 44); town thinks of her affair with cashier as adultery; begins to drink (175, 45); after lynching, dresses in sheerest underclothing and best dress; goes downtown to enjoy all eyes on her (180-181, 50-51); in movies, watches young couples arriving; begins to laugh hysterically; is led away (181-182, 51-52).

Will Mayes (169, 39): black, rumored to have "attacked, insulted, frightened" Miss Cooper (169, 39); night watchman at ice plant (176, 46); dragged from plant to car (177, 47); quietly submits to handcuffs; briefly struggles; hits men, including Hawkshaw (178, 48); is lynched (180, 50).

Henry (179, 49) Hawkshaw (171, 41): barber; middle-aged, thin, sand-colored; first to connect Will Mayes's name with Miss Cooper; insists Mayes is innocent (169, 39); runs out of shop to prevent lynching (173, 43); tries to persuade McLendon and others not to lynch Mayes (176, 46); goes with crowd to lynching (176-177, 46-47); Mayes hits him; Hawkshaw hits him back (178, 48); wants to get out of car; is invited to jump; jumps (179, 49); watches cars returning from lynching (180, 50).

_____: the "client," customer in barber shop (169, 39); a drummer; stranger; ready to start lynch mob (170, 40).

_____: second barber (169, 39).

Butch (170, 40)_____: "a hulking youth in a sweat-stained silk shirt," in barber shop, ready to fan flames against black (169, 39); accuses barber who thinks Miss Cooper has not been harmed of being a "nigger-lover" (170, 40).

_____: one in barber shop who tries to quiet Butch (170, 40; tries to reason with McLendon (172, 42); ex-soldier (176, 46).

John (177, 47) McLendon (171, 41): (has led troops in France) arrives at barber shop; incites men to violence and to lynch (171, 41); not really interested if a black really did rape Miss Cooper; wants to take measures and not wait until one of them "really does it" (172, 42); is armed (173, 43); returns after lynching; bullies wife (182-183, 52-53).

_____Cooper: Minnie Cooper's mother (173, 43).

_____: Minnie Cooper's aunt (173, 43).

_____: widowed cashier in bank who takes Minnie Cooper driving (174, 44); leaves for Memphis bank; returns once a year for bachelor party (175, 45).

_____: clerk in soda fountain who buys whisky for Minnie Cooper (175, 45).

_____McLendon: John McLendon's wife; abused and bullied by him (182, 52).

"Mistral"

Written perhaps as early as late 1925 or early 1926, surely by November 3, 1928; on sending schedule June 19, 1930; first published in *These 13.*

_____: narrator (843, 215); with companion, has walked from Milan (845, 217); says he does not speak Italian, but reports Don's conversations completely (851, 223); time of Mussolini (854, 226); 22 years old; hints that priest's niece poisoned her fiance (856, 228); to avoid cold wind, seeks shelter and food (though they fear poisoning) at rectory (860-861, 232-233); when priest leaves table during meal, finishes eating, drinks all wine, and is asked to leave by housekeeper; they depart to spend October night in the wind (mistral) (864-867, 236-239); after he and Don leave rectory, they visit cafe where they drink brandy; they witness meeting between priest's niece and Farinzale (869-870, 241-242); American (870, 242); separates from Don; refuses to go back and ask for bed (873, 245); waits for Don on bridge; together, they find priest writhing on stomach behind wall and moaning, outside copse where niece is with Farinzale (875-876, 247-248).

Don (843, 215)_____: speaks Italian; offers cigarette to man by roadside (845, 217); 23 years old (856, 228); Catholic (864, 236); American

(870, 242); had once wooed Tyrolean barmaid until her gigantic boy friend returned (874, 246).

     Giulio Farinzale (848, 220): soldier; passes narrator and Don on bicycle (843, 215); bachelor, has only uncle and aunt; drafted into Italian army (848, 220); suddenly and unexpectedly called to service just after priest discovers secret meetings with niece (849, 221); attends funeral of former rival (851, 229).

     _____: Italian man in corduroy (844, 216); deaf (845, 217); states that priest "looked" at his niece too (850, 222).

     _____: his wife; mother of seven children (852, 224).

     _____: the priest (846, 218); has brought up young girl since she was 6; she is called his niece (847, 219); intends her first for church; then arranged wedding (848, 220); catches niece slipping out to meet Farinzale (849, 221); conducts funeral for niece's fiance in evening (857, 229); at meal, says part of funeral service instead of grace; leaves with housekeeper during meal (864, 236); niece has slipped away to meet Farinzale (865, 237); paces back and forth in garden praying aloud like man bereft; blesses Don and narrator as they leave (867, 239); lies on ground moaning outside copse where niece has met Farinzale (875-876, 247-248).

     _____: priest's niece; father unknown (847, 219); by 14-15, dresses brightly and is very vivacious; postpones arranged wedding for three years (848, 220); from window, sees Don and narrator approach rectory (860, 232); meets Farinzale outside cafe (869-870, 241-242); goes with him to copse (875, 247).

     _____: her mother; a prostitute (847, 219).

     _____: laborer whom priest tries to get to marry prostitute; killed in WW I (847, 219).

     _____: fiance of priest's niece (846, 218); now dead (847, 219); hale man; dies suddenly (851, 223).

     _____ Cavalcanti (870, 242): aunt to Guido Farinzale; serves wine to Don and narrator (854, 226); left church at time her nephew was drafted (871, 243).

     _____ Cavalcanti (870, 242): uncle to Guido Farinzale; joined another parish when nephew was drafted (871, 243).

     _____: priest's housekeeper (860, 232); indeterminate age 25-60 (863, 235); asks Don and narrator to leave after meal (865, 237).

     _____: two peasant musicians outside cafe, a fiddler and piper (868, 240).

_____: waiter in cafe; (868, 240); claims to be an atheist (872, 244).

_____: five young men at cafe; witness meeting between niece and Farinzale (868, 240).

_____: peasant woman with child; listens to music (868, 240).

_____: policeman; comes to town on day of funeral; claims to be shoe drummer (872, 244).

_____: barmaid whom Don woos (874, 246).

_____: her sweetheart (847, 246).

"Divorce in Naples"

Once titled "Equinox," on sending schedule May 21, 1930; first published in *These 13.*

_____: narrator; sailor (877, 249); after visiting several cafes with Monckton, the bosun, and two prostitutes, returns to ship (882, 254).

_____Monckton (877, 249): with bosun and narrator visits taverns with two prostitutes in Naples (882, 254).

_____: bosun (877, 249).

Carl (877, 249) _____: called George's wife by Monckton (877, 249); a girl friend with pants by bosun (878, 250); acts like George's servant, carrying bags, stowing gear, etc; messboy; owns thirty-four serving jackets (879, 251); from Philadelphia; 18 years old; had already been at sea for year when he met George; fourth or fifth child of first-generation Scandanavian-American family of shipwrights; 15 when he went to sea; brought up by mother or older sister (880, 252); stays ashore all night with George (882, 254); goes off with George's prostitute (886, 256); after two days, returns to ship; throws undergarment out porthole; showers; works furiously for several days in parts of ship where George can not appear (888-890, 260-262); finally on way to Gibraltar, he and George are seen talking to each other (890, 262); almost gets sick when George tells him about prostitutes' police health tickets and their smell (892, 264); when he and George are dancing again, asks George to buy him suit of women's underwear a little larger than he would wear (893, 265); (presumably to give to next prostitute).

George (877, 249) _____: Greek; curses Monckton steadily after remark about Carl being his wife (877, 249); second cook (878, 250); joined ship with Carl in Galveston; they dance to victrola for which they have only one record; stays at cafe with Carl and gold-toothed prostitute (879, 251); says Carl is virgin (881, 253); after staying ashore all night, sends note to ship that he is in jail (883, 255); had gotten drunk; gone to lavatory; when he returned, discovered Carl had left with

131

prostitute (884, 256); in brawl; is arrested (885, 257); when released, searches for Carl for two days; finally packs Carl's bag; throws it on deck; eventually returns Carl's clothes to bunk; says he is through with him (886-887, 258-259); they are eventually reconciled (890, 262).

_____: Italian prostitute (877, 249); Monckton's (879, 251).

_____: second Italian prostitute (877, 249); bosun's (879, 251).

_____: third Italian prostitute (877, 249); has gold teeth; about 30 years (879, 251); goes off with Carl; leaves George (884, 256).

_____: waiter (879, 251).

_____: Carl's mother (880, 252).

_____: Carl's sister (880, 252).

_____: Carl's father (880, 252).

_____: a swipe; "some West India docks crum," shipmate of Monckton (881, 253).

_____: ship's cook (882, 254).

_____: steward (882, 254); gets George out of jail (883, 255).

_____: man who brings note from George in jail; an Italian; looks like a Columbia day student (883, 255).

"Carcassonne"

Written perhaps as early as 1926; at the latest by June 18, 1931; first published in *These 13*.

_____: dreams (or thinks) of himself riding the "Flying Red Horse" of the Standard Oil Company; sleeps under strip of tarpaper (895, 267) in a garret (896, 268); dream of "Flying Red Horse" melts into memory of tale from first crusade: riderless horse continues to gallop after it has been cut in two (896, 268); then conceives of skeleton separate from body (896-897, 268-269); words from Gospel of St. John (11:25) about resurrection of Lazarus are mixed with other (apparently) non-Biblical words (897, 269); hears rats in garret; reveals that Mrs. Widdrington expects him to write poetry in return for sleeping in her garret (898, 270); has dialogue with his skeleton; has last dream again of riding "Flying Red Horse" beyond earth (900, 272).

Luis (897, 269)_____: operates cantina; allows him to sleep in garret (897, 269).

Mrs._____Widdrington (897, 269): wife of representative of the Standard Oil Company (897, 269).

Written from August 17, 1931 to February 19, 1932; once titled "Dark House;" first published October 6, 1932.

Pagination, in parentheses, to the following editions: (New York: Harrison Smith & Robert Haas, 1932), 480 pp.; (London: Chatto & Windus, 1933); (New York: Random House, [1940]); [New York: New Directions, 1947]; (New York: Random House, 1967); (New York: Modern Library, 1967), paperback; (New York: Modern Library, [1967?]); (New York: Vintage Books, 1972), paperback.

Lena (1) Grove (15): parents die when she is 12 (2); goes to Doane's Mill to live with brother, McKinley (2); becomes pregnant eight years later (3); climbs out window to find Burch, father of unborn child; on road four weeks (4); given ride by Armstid (9); spends Friday evening with Armstids (10-11); accepts Mrs. Armstid's egg money (20); buys cheese, crackers and sardines (24); enters Jefferson as smoke from burning house rises (26); reaches planing mill Saturday afternoon (45); as Byron Bunch tells her of Brown and Christmas, intuits that Brown is Burch (50-51); wants to live at Burden place to wait for Burch-Brown (288); lives in cabin (296); starts labor Monday morning (372); bears baby (375); tells Hightower she has said "No" to Byron Bunch five days ago (389); shows Burch-Brown her baby; tells him a preacher is there (407); holds him; releases him (409); watches silently as Burch-Brown flees (410); with Byron Bunch and baby, picked up by furniture dealer (469); still following Burch-Brown (474); goes to bed in truck (475); when Byron Bunch climbs into truck with her, says, "Aint you ashamed?" tells him to go and lie down (477); next morning, Byron Bunch is gone; decides to ride in back of truck (478); lets Byron Bunch join her there (479).

_____ Grove (15): Lena's father (1).

_____ Grove (15): Lena's mother (1).

McKinley (2) Grove (15): Lena's brother; takes her to Doane's Mill after parents die (2); twenty years older than Lena (3); 40 years old (4).

_____ Grove (15): McKinley's wife and children (3).

Lucas Burch (4) Joe (48) Brown (32): father of Lena's baby; left Doane's Mill six months ago (4); "found out" he had to leave town night Lena told him about baby (15); appears at planing mill as Brown; has small white scar on face (32); loses first week's pay in crap game (34); noisy prank player (36-37); partner with Christmas selling whisky (38-39); quits mill (40); openly sells whisky (41); lives with Christmas in cabin on Burden place (42): Joe Brown (48); found by countryman at fire; drunk (84); disappears; reappears; says Christmas killed Miss Burden and that he has been living with her as man and wife for three years; claims reward (86); tells sheriff Christmas is a "nigger" (91); goes with sheriff to hunt Christmas (94); flashback to Thursday night: returns to cabin drunk; makes noise; choked and beaten by Christmas when he calls him "nigger"

(95-97); returns and claims reward; jailed (279); taken by deputy to see Lena and baby (400); runs away (402); taken to see Lena (403); claims to have sent her message (406); flees through cabin window (409); fights Byron Bunch; beats him (416); escapes on train; disappears (417).

_____ Armstid (6): gives Lena ride in wagon (9); takes her home (10); gives her Mrs. Armstid's egg money (20); takes her to Varner's store (21).

_____ Winterbottom (6).

Martha (10) Armstid (6): Armstid's wife (10); bore five children in six years; breaks bank to give egg money to Lena (19).

[Will] Varner (11): store owner (11).

Jody Varner (21): his son; tells Lena of Bunch, not Burch at planing Mill (22).

Byron (27) Bunch (22): works at planing mill (22); offers Christmas some of his lunch (31); over 30; works alone Saturday afternoons (42); meets and talks with Hightower at night; rides thirty miles to lead choir at country church (43); falls in love (44) with Lena Grove (50); tells her about Joe Brown and Christmas (50); visits Hightower on Sunday night (70); realizes that Brown is Burch (74); takes Lena to Mrs. Beard's (77); tells Hightower that Christmas is partly black; tells about Christmas, Brown, and killing (83-85); tells Hightower he is going to move Lena (283); tells Hightower of hunt for Christmas (286-287); tells Lena that black man killed woman (287); does not tell her about Burch-Brown; tells her that he is on business for sheriff (288); says Burch-Brown will run when he tells him about Lena (290); tells Hightower he has taken Lena to cabin (296); has pitched tent near cabin to protect Lena (297); tells Buck Conner Lena is expecting Burch-Brown's baby (303); tells Hightower of capture of Christmas (343); brings Hineses to Hightower (348 ff.); tells Hightower Christmas is Hineses' grandson (350); asks Hightower to lie to give Christmas alibi for night of killing (369); Monday morning, wakes Hightower; tells him Lena's labor has begun; going for doctor (371-373); goes to same doctor that came when Hightower delivered still-born black baby (374); when he hears Lena's baby cry, realizes that she is not a virgin; realizes that now he will have to tell Burch-Brown (380); goes to get Burch-Brown (390); quits at planing mill (391); goes to room; finds Mrs. Beard has already rented it and packed his things (396); asks sheriff to send Burch-Brown to Lena (398); watches as deputy brings Burch-Brown to Lena (400); watches Burch-Brown run from cabin (402); chases Burch-Brown to whip him (403); fights Burch-Brown; is beaten (416); at peace (417); rehearses what he will say and do on way back to Lena in cabin (418); meets man in wagon who tells him Christmas has been killed (418); with Lena and baby, picked up by furniture dealer (469); talks to Lena about marriage (475); after Lena goes to bed in truck, climbs in with her; climbs out again after she wakes and rebukes him; walks away into woods (477); waits by road for truck to reach him; says he is not going to quit now; she acquiesces; joins Lena (479).

_____: clerk in Varner's store (23); sells Lena sardines (24).

_____: man who drives Lena from Varner's store to Jefferson (24).

Joe (48) Christmas (29): stranger; appears at mill; assigned to sawdust pile (28); refuses food offered by Byron Bunch (31); sells whisky; lives in former slave cabin on Burden place (32); is seen with Burch-Brown; quits suddenly after almost three years (36); acquires new car (38); partner with Brown in selling whisky (38-39); lives with Brown at Burden's place (42); has been hijacking whisky (74); Brown says he killed Miss Burden after living with her for three years (86); flashback to Thursday evening: beats and chokes Brown for calling him "nigger" (95-97); feels "someting is going to happen to me;" thinks of razor, but Brown is not right white person to kill (97); thinks "God loves me too;" says, "It's because she started praying over me;" (98) thinks of his years of sex with Miss Burden and of her menopause (99); strips and stands naked by road as car passes; shouts "white bastards;" (100) sleeps in barn because horses are not women (101); Friday: spends day by spring reading magazine; destroys whisky (101-105); at night, panics in Freedman's Town with smell and sounds of blacks (107); then tries to assert whiteness by bullying blacks on road; is taken for a white man (109); at midnight Friday-Saturday, loses thought control: "Something is going to happen to me;" (110) flashback to orphanage: Christmas, 5 years old, enters dietician's room for toothpaste; hides behind curtain; eats toothpaste (112-113); vomits; discovered by dietician; called "little nigger bastard;" (114); waits to get whipped; given silver dollar instead (116); children call him "Nigger; found by Charley "that Christmas night" (118); taken from orphanage when 5 by mad janitor (124); flashback to night janitor takes him away (127); is aware of bond of hate between him and janitor (129); taken by train (130); returned to orphanage by policeman (131); almost 5 when adopted (133) by McEachern (134); remains silent through whole procedure (134-136); renamed McEachern (136); time jump: Christmas is 8 (137); refuses to learn Presbyterian catechism (137-139); taken to barn and strapped by McEachern (140); beaten second time (141); collapses; wakes late afternoon (142); prayed over by McEachern (143); first time he sees indentations of knees in carpet (144); dumps food Mrs. McEachern brings him in corner (145); later, eats food; time shift: 14 or 15 years old (146); rejects and beats rural black prostitute (147); beaten by McEachern because he fails to milk and feed; decides to run away--caged eagle image (150-151); time shift: Christmas is 18; buys new suit by selling cow (151); lies to McEachern--first lie; after two blows from McEachern, prepares to hit back (154); flashback: his arrival and Mrs. McEachern's efforts to make him love her; cherishes thought of telling foster mother that McEachern has nursed a "nigger" (155-158); hates the woman's "soft kindness" more than the man's harsh justice (158); leaves house at night by rope; realizes that McEachern has found suit (159); flashback: meeting Bobbie (161); thinks of rural black prostitute after seeing Bobbie (166-167); with dime McEachern gives him, returns to restaurant (166); orders coffee and pie; cancels coffee (169); is ashamed after Bobbie saves face for him; works hard to stave off romantic despair; given heifer as reward (170); given half dollar by Mrs. McEachern next time to town;

returns to restaurant; tries to repay nickel (171); meets Bobbie on street; explains (172); flashback: learns of menstruation (173); ritually kills sheep; rejects menstruation in "his life and love;" meets Bobbie after trying to repay nickel; depends upon her to introduce him to sex (174); hits her when she tells him she has menstrual period (177); cracked urn hallucination (177-178); vomits; meets her next week; first sexual experience; keeps rope behind same loose board that Mrs. McEachern keeps her hoarded coins (178); not knowing she is prostitute, begins to pay Bobbie with money stolen from Mrs. McEachern (179); says name is Joe McEachern when introduced to Max Confrey (181); has never had a drink (182); tells Bobbie "I got some nigger blood in me" (184); steals again from Mrs. McEachern; goes to Bobbie's room two nights a week (185); discovers that Bobbbie is prostitute; strikes her; cries (186); begins to smoke and drink (187); discovered by McEachern leaving by rope (189); knocks McEachern down with chair (192); says that he said he would kill him some day (193); takes McEachern's horse; rides home (194-195); steals money (195); rides and beats horse (196 ff.); returns to Bobbie (200) to marry her; offers her money stolen from Mrs. McEachern (203); as Bobbie rejects him as "a nigger son of a bitch," thinks that he has killed for her (204); beaten by Max and stranger (205); time lapse of thirteen or fourteen years: street image introduced (207); fifteen-year street (210); served four months in army; deserted; never caught (211); when he can not pay prostitutes, tells them he is a "negro;" nearly kills prostitute who does not care if he is black (211-212); sick for two years; fights with white and black men who call him black or white; lives as black with very dark woman (tries to breathe blackness into him) (212); trying to escape himself; 33 years old; arrives in Mississippi near Burden home (213); at night enters house by window; eats; thoughts flash back to Bobbie Allen and McEacherns while he eats (216-217); discovered by woman (217-218); time lapse: one year; has been Miss Burden's lover (219); now lives in cabin (220); second night of his affair with Miss Burden, finds food set out on kitchen table; "set out for the nigger," he says (224); flings dishes at wall; (food, sex, violence) on third day, goes to work at mill (225); start of six-month abstinence from her (226); tells Miss Burden one of his parents was "part nigger," but he does not know it (240); "If I'm not, damned if I haven't wasted a lot of time." (241) sewer image introduced (242); sexual orgies with Miss Burden (242-247); begins to be afraid (246); third phase of relationship begins (247); starts to sell whisky; links Miss Burden with Mrs. McEachern and Bobbie (247); begins to go to prostitutes in Memphis (249); thinks Miss Burden wants marriage when she talks of child (250-251); after two-week separation, she orders him to come to her (252); rejects her plan to manage black schools (254); another note from her, which he does not open (257-258); goes to Miss Burden, note unread (260); when she offers to send him to black school, and to read law in Peebles's office, tells her she is old; strikes her; realizes it is menopause, not pregnancy (262-263); as she begins to pray, remembers McEachern's knee prints; flash forward three months: midnight Friday-Saturday; Christmas about to kill Miss Burden (264); kills her (266-267); flags down car with young couple; holding pistol which he took from Miss Burden (267); realizes that she was going to kill him and commit suicide (270); hits preacher and Pappy Thompson in black church; curses from pulpit (305-307); fractures skull of Roz Thompson

(307); leaves foul note for sheriff (309); fools posse by changing shoes with black woman (311-312); as he laces up black shoes, begins to accept role as black man; "That was all I wanted. . . that was all for thirty years." (313); running, falls in ditch and sleeps all day (315); now hungry (316); thinks of himself now as a brother of the blacks that feed him (317); shaves (318); ready to be captured (319); black shoes become mark on his ankles of "black tide creeping up his legs, moving from his feet upwards as death moves." (321); captured on Friday in Mottstown (322); walked on Main Street until recognized (329); shaves before arrest (331); submits when Halliday hits him (332); flashback: grandchild of Hinseses; their daughter's child; abducted by Doc Hines (350); has not denied any charges against him (399); flashback: escapes; runs to Hightower's house for refuge; is killed (419); escapes, handcuffed, in square (424); runs to Hightower's house; hits Hightower with pistol; is killed (425); another account of escape (433); gets revolver from black cabin (437); runs to Hightower's house (438); shot by Grimm and castrated before death (439).

Simms (31): superintendent of planing mill (28); hires Christmas (28).

Mooney (32): foreman at planing mill (28).

Miss (32) Joanna (238) Burden (32): middleaged spinster (32); has lived in big house since birth; family came from North during Reconstruction; "a Yankee lover of negroes; grandfather and brother killed by ex-slaveowner" (42); discovers Christmas in kitchen at night; in candlelight, looks not much past 30 (217-218); Christmas's lover; advisor to dozen black schools (220); struggles physically like a man before yielding sexually to Christmas (221-222); after six months of truce, meets him in cabin; tells her story; 41 years old; New Englander (227); history of Burden family (228-234); born 1880; fourteen years after her brother was killed (236); father tells her of curse on whites because of slavery (238); explains that her father did not kill Sartoris because of "his French blood" (281); sexual orgies with Christmas (242-247); nymphomania seizes her; embraces Christmas saying, "Negro! Negro! Negro!" (245); begins to get fat (247); third phase of relationship with Christmas (247); begins to talk of child (248); tells him she is pregnant (251-252); tells Christmas of her plans for his future--his management of black schools (254); wants to send him to black school; afterwards to read law in Peebles's office (261); strikes Christmas; is struck in turn (262); leaves notes for Christmas; prays over him (263-264); has gun as Christmas kills her (266-267).

Calvin Burden [I] (228): grandfather of Miss Burden; killed by ex-slaveowner (42); son of minister, Nathaniel Burrington; youngest of ten; ran away at 12 via Horn to California; became Catholic; ten years later, reached Missouri; three weeks later, married a Huguenot; renounced Catholicism; Saint Louis; has son; brings him up as Unitarian; reads to son in Spanish (228); kills man over slavery; moves west; anti-slavery; carries pistol; teaches son to hate two things "hell and slaveholders" (229); lost arm in Kansas fighting (230); late 50's when Nathaniel returns (232); rants about Burdens (himself and son) marrying blacks (Mexicans) (224).

Calvin (233) Burden [II] (231): half-brother of Joanna; killed by exslaveowner (42); child of Nathaniel Burden (231); 20 when killed (235); ring-bearer at father's wedding (237-238).

Colonel (235) [John] Sartoris (235): killed grandfather and [half-]brother of Miss Burden (42).

Rev. Dr. Gail (62) Hightower (43): twenty-five years earlier, was minister of a principal church; only he knows of Byron Bunch Bunch leading country choir (43); 50-year-old outcast; denied by his church (44); inherits small income from father; sends it to home for delinquent girls in Memphis; but halves it when he loses church (52-53); came as minister of Presbyterian church; "wife went bad on him;" went to Memphis because "he couldn't or wouldn't satisfy her;" she dies in Memphis; refuses to leave town (54); manoeuvered his appointment to Jefferson (55); mixes talk of religion and Civil War cavalry (56); so possessed with this mania, neglects his wife (57); when she disappears, says she is visiting relatives (58); wife shrieks at him in church (59); visits wife in sanatorium; still preaches madly (60); preaches day after wife's death; congregation leaves (62); next day brings wife's body home; buries her; asked to resign; refuses; congregation walks out when he next comes to preach (63); preaches to empty church; finally locked out of church; finally resigns; refuses to leave town; buys house (64); offers to return money to church; they refuse it; because of his female black cook, town gossips (65); after female cook quits, hires male cook; threatened by KKK; then beaten; refuses to identify assailants (66); helps black woman in childbirth; delivers still-born child (68); as Byron Bunch is involved with Lena, tells him to leave Jefferson (290); quite upset when he learns Christmas's trail has been found (292-293); after Byron Bunch tells him he has taken Lena to cabin, tells him to go for he is destined either to sin or marriage (298); tirade against women (298-299); regrets having given up prayer (300-301); reads Tennyson (301); becomes angry with Byron Bunch when he tells him of capture of Christmas (343-345); has reverie of past (346 ff.); forsees society executing Christmas in name of Christianity (348); refuses to lie to give Christmas alibi (370); awakened by Byron Bunch as Lena's labor begins (373); delivers Lena's baby (375); walks back to town (382); begins to revitalize (383-385); now reads *Henry IV*; sleeps for six hours (383); walks back to cabin (384); urges Lena to send Byron Bunch away (389); thinks Byron Bunch has abandoned him (396); lies to save Christmas (439); his reverie (441-467); flashback: relives past; an only child; father 50, mother an invalid for twenty years when born (442); 8 years old when he opens trunk and finds frock coat (443); father a stranger to him (450); at seminary, wants call to Jefferson where his grandfather "was shot from the saddle of a galloping horse" (452); does not really see future wife; thinks of marriage as a dead state (454); married (456); on train to Jefferson, tells wife the Romantic version of his grandfather's cavalry raid on Yankee stores in Jefferson (457-458); grandfather killed while stealing chickens (459); back to present: recognizes guilt about neglecting wife and about her death and about his failure in ministry (462 ff.); sees himself as deserving his ouster from ministry (464); recognizes the destructive power of his mad dream about grandfather (465).

Mrs.   Beard (43): keeps boarding house where Byron Bunch lives (43); after Byron Bunch moves to tent, rents his room and packs his things (396).

_____: truck driver who identifies Burden house as being on fire (45).

Watt Kennedy (45): sheriff in Jefferson (45); arrests Burch-Brown (42); fat (271); has black man beaten for information (274-277); takes Christmas from Mottstown to Jefferson handcuffed to himself (337); agrees to send Burch-Brown to Lena (399); when Grimm insists on carrying pistol, makes him special deputy (431).

_____ Hightower (54): Hightower's wife; killed in Memphis (54); after year of husband's mania and neglect, begins to change (57); begins to disappear from town; seen entering hotel in Memphis by parisoner; begins to be seen in church again (58); after one absence, returns; shrieks at husband in church during one of his mad sermons; sent by church to sanatorium (59); returns; acts normally (60); after four or five months, goes away again; stops going to church; jumps or falls from hotel window in Memphis; man in room with her; registered as man and wife (61-62); daughter of minister, teacher at seminary; only child (453); older than Hightower; wants to escape (454); teaches Hightower right way to get call to Jefferson; married when call to Jefferon comes (456).

Gail Hightower [I] (451): Hightower's grandfather; a cavalryman; killed (56); shot from his galloping horse (57); once owned slaves; member of Episcopal church; has not entered any church for long time; discovers son preaching in Presbyterian chapel; laughs (442); owns two slaves; drinks bourbon; on son's wedding day, gives house to son, Hightower's father (445); a lawyer (446); never visits house again (447); killed men "by the hundreds," according to slave cook (452); not an officer (457); killed while stealing chickens (459).

_____: parishoner who sees Mrs. Hightower enter Memphis hotel (58).

_____: man with Mrs. Hightower in Memphis hotel when she was killed; arrested; is drunk (62).

_____: minister who takes book from Hightower at wife's burial (63).

_____: Hightower's black female cook (65); after town begins to gossip, quits, saying Hightower asked her to do something "against God and nature" (66).

_____: black male cook hired by Hightower; beaten by townsmen (66).

139

_____: black man who calls Hightower to tend wife in childbirth (68).

_____: black woman whom Hightower tends in childbirth (68).

_____: doctor, arrives after Hightower delivers still-born black child (68); called by Byron Bunch to deliver Lena's baby; arrives too late this time too (374).

Mr. _____ Maxey (81): owner of barber shop in Jefferson (81).

Captain _____ McLendon (81): talks to Maxey about Christmas and Brown as highjackers (81).

Hamp Waller (90): countryman who finds fire (83); finds Miss Burden killed; carries body out (84-85); tells sheriff about Burch-Brown at fire (274).

_____ Waller (90): his wife (83); reports fire (90).

Jupe (109) _____: one of blacks Christmas tries to intimidate on road (109).

Nathaniel Burrington (278): Miss Burden's nephew who offers one thousand dollars reward (86); lives in Exeter, N. H. (278).

Buck (90) Conner (286): marshal (92); tells Burch-Brown to shut up in jail (286); tells sheriff that Lena and Byron Bunch are living on Burden place (302).

_____ Atkins (133): dietician in orphanage (112); sex with Charley interrupted by Christmas vomiting; 27 years old; gives Christmas silver dollar not to tell (116); becomes mad; goes to janitor (118); begins to plan to have Christmas sent away (120) by revealing that he is part black (121); tells matron that Christmas is black (124); tells matron Christmas will have to be sent to black orphanage (126); acts as secretary in corresponding with McEachern (134); names Christmas (363).

Charley (113) _____: young intern at orphanage (112); sex with dietician (113); finds Christmas on orphanage doorstep on Christmas night (118).

_____: parochial doctor (112).

Uncle Doc (324) Eupheus (329) Hines (322): janitor in orphanage; reads Bible; about 45; religious fanatic (119); hates women (120); forces way into dietician's room; begins to identify with God; confirms that matron will send Christmas to black orphanage (122-123); next morning, disappears with Christmas (124); caught by police in Little Rock where he tried to put Christmas in another orphanage (124); arrested (131); lives now in Mottstown; arrived thirty years ago; crazy (322); holds revival services in black churches; fed by black people (323); preaches white

140

supremacy in black churches (325); downtown when Christmas is arrested (326); hits Christmas with stick; urges crowd to kill him (327); half-hour after being taken home, returns; tries to incite crowd to lynch Christmas (332); takes 2:00 a. m. train to Jefferson with wife (341); says he abducted Christmas on God's orders (351); arrested for fighting on night of Milly's birth; originally brakeman on railroad; then foreman at sawmill (352); after Milly elopes with "Mexican," takes pistol and mystically finds them; kills the man; returns with Milly (355); hits her; thinks God led him to find them (356); tries first to have Milly aborted (356-357); undergoes trial; tries to find doctor to abort Milly; arrested for preaching against blacks and brandishing pistol; beats up doctor in another town (357); watches Milly die (358); disappears; returns and steals baby two days before Christmas; returns; will not tell wife what he has done with baby (359); working in Memphis (360); after five years, returns; takes wife to Mottstown (360-361); says he called Christmas "nigger" at orphanage; watched Charley take Christmas from doorstep (363); tells Charley and Miss Atkins his name is Joseph (364); after birth of Lena's baby, while wife sleeps, goes to town (386); preaches lynching (423).

_____: madam of orphanage (120); matron; past 50 (124); determines to place Christmas for adoption rather than send him to black orphanage (126); refuses to discuss Christmas's parentage with McEachern (133).

Alice (127)_____: 12-year-old girl who mothers Christmas in orphanage when he is 3 years old (127).

_____: policeman who returns Christmas from Little Rock to orphanage (131).

_____: two young women who bathe and dress Christmas before his adoption by McEachern (132).

Simon (155) McEachern (134): adopts Christmas; asks about parentage; has been corresponding with Miss Atkins (133); takes Christmas home (134); thinks Christmas "heathenish" name (135); beats Christmas because he refuses to learn catechism (137-142); beats him because he fails to milk and feed (150); after sale of cow and finding Christmas's new suit, accuses Christmas of whoring; hits Christmas twice with fist (154); makes wife kneel for her lie (155); takes Christmas to restaurant for lunch; he meets waitress (162); vaguely warns Christmas to avoid the place (164); returns six months later; gives Christmas dime (166); gives him heifer (170); discovers Christmas sliding down rope; watches him enter Bobbie's car; follows him on horse (189); intuits where they are; finds Christmas and Bobbie at dance (190-191); is felled by Christmas (192).

Mrs. Simon McEachern (134): his wife (134); watches as McEachern beats Christmas (138-142); brings Christmas food (144-145); says that McEachern had nothing to do with food (145); lies to husband about buying suit for Christmas (155); flashback to Christmas's arrival and efforts to make the child love her (155-158); gives Christmas half dollar

(171); knows Christmas steals from hoard (185); sees husband follow Christmas and Bobbie (189-190); watches Christmas steal money (195).

_____: four boys with Christmas when he beats rural black prostitute (146).

_____: rural black prostitute; rejected and beaten by Christmas (146-147).

Bobbie (168) Allen (180): waitress; over 30; small; smallness due to "some inner corruption of the spirit itself" (161); flashback: meets Christmas (161); lies to save Christmas over coffee (169); meets him for first date (174); has menstrual period that night (175); realizes Christmas is a virgin (177); first sex with Christmas in her room, strips; (183); tells Christmas of her prostitution (186); after Christmas hits McEachern with chair, beats him in face (193); returns to town (194); flings money at him (203); calls him "a nigger son of a bitch" (204); abandons him; goes to Memphis (205).

Mame (175) Confrey (180): blond woman in restaurant (163); wife of proprietor (167); takes money from stocking top and leaves it with Christmas (208).

Max (175) Confrey (180): proprietor of restaurant where Christmas meets Bobbie (166); husband of blond (167); thinks Christmas is trying to buy Bobbie for nickel (172).

_____: five boys hunt with Christmas, including one who arranged for rural black prostitute; talk about girls and menstruation (173).

_____: stranger in Bobbie's room before she leaves Christmas (200); with Max Confrey, beats Christmas senseless (205).

_____: two policemen who subdue Christmas after he beats prostitute who does not care if he is black (212).

_____: very black woman in North who lives with Christmas as man and wife (212).

_____: black boy Christmas meets as he arrives near Burden house (213); says no one would harm Miss Burden (214).

E. E. (278) Peebles (261): black lawyer in Memphis; conducts Miss Burden's business affairs (220).

Nathaniel Burrington (228): minister; father of Calvin Burden (228).

Evangeline (233) Burden (228): wife of Calvin (228); mother of son and three daughters; dies (229).

Nathaniel (230) Burden [I] (228): son of Calvin Burden (228); runs

142

away at 14; does not return for sixteen years (230); kills Mexican who claimed Burden stole his horse; has woman and child; returns to family (231) to get married (233); buries father and son; hides graves; marries second time; father of Miss Burden (235); fifty years old when he sends for second wife (236); tells Miss Burden of curse on whites (239).

[Evangeline] Vangie (232) Burden (229): daughter of Calvin Burden (229).

Beck (232) Burden (229): daughter of Calvin Burden (229).

Sarah (232) Burden (229): daughter of Calvin Burden (229).

_____: two successive messengers who bring news of Nathaniel Burden [I] from Colorado and Mexico; second in 1863 (230).

Juana (233) Burden (231): wife of Nathaniel Burden, Mexican; has child (231); dies; is buried with son (236).

_____ Burden (235): second wife of Nathaniel Burden [I]; mother of Miss Burden (235); from New Hampshire (236).

_____: "our cousin in New Hampshire" who sends Miss Burden's mother to her father (236).

_____: young couple who pick up Christmas after he kills Miss Burden (267); boy tells sheriff on Sunday of event (281).

_____ Buford (276): deputy sheriff who discovers that cabin has been occupied (274); beats black man with strap to get information about Christmas and Joe Brown (276); takes Burch-Brown to see Lena (400, 403); escorting Christmas across square when he escapes (433).

_____: black man who denies knowing who lives in cabin (275); tells about two men in cabin after being beaten (277).

_____: second deputy (275); identifies Christmas and Brown as occupants of cabin (277).

_____: bank cashier; takes Burden's death instructions to sheriff (278).

_____: father of boy who picked up Christmas after killing; seeks reward (281).

_____: proprietor of store where Hightower shops; announces that they have found Christmas's trail (291).

_____: black man who tells sheriff of Christmas's attack on preacher in church (305).

_____: black woman on mourners' bench whom Christmas

knocks down (305).

_____ Bedenberry (305): preacher in black church whom Christmas attacks (305).

Pappy Thompson (306): 70 years old; knocked down by Christmas (306).

Roz Thompson (306): grandson of Pappy Thompson (306); goes for Christmas with razor; skull fractured (307).

Deacon Vines (307): deacon in black church Christmas invades (307).

_____: black woman with whom Christmas changes shoes (311-312).

_____: her child (311).

_____: white woman; Christmas questions her about the day while running; recognizes him (314).

_____: black wagon driver; recognizes Christmas; tells him it is Friday (319).

_____: black youth; drives Christmas to Mottstown (320).

Mrs. Eupheus (329) Hines (322): wife of Hines; lives in Mottstown (322); "dumpy, fat little woman with a round face like dirty and unovened bread, and a tight screw of scant hair" (327); recognizes Christmas before she even sees him (329); asks husband what he did with Milly's baby (330); quiets Hines in town (333); as Christmas is being taken back to Jefferson, confronts him silently (337); tries to rent car to go to Jefferson (338-339); eats supper at cafe by depot (339); waits for 2:00 a. m. train (340); flashback to Christmas's history: knows that Hines has hidden Christmas in Memphis (360); present when Lena gives birth; thinks Lena is Milly and baby is Christmas (376); follows Hines to town (386); finds him preaching lynching; goes to sheriff; visits Christmas; tells him (according to Stevens) that Hightower can save him (423); returns to Mottstown (420).

_____: two men who bring Hines home after Christmas's capture (327).

Milly (330) Hines (322): daughter of Eupheus Hines (330); mother of Christmas (350); 18 at time she elopes with circus man (353); deceives father and elopes (354); is brought back (355); dies in childbirth (358).

_____: new first-person narrative voice that tells of Christmas's capture in Mottstown and subsequent events (330-341).

_____ Halliday (331): recognizes Christmas in Mottstown; hits

144

Christmas in face (331).

            Metcalf (334): jailor in Mottstown (334),

            : sheriff in Mottstown (334).

            Russell (334): deputy sheriff in Mottstown (335).

            Dollar (338): owner of store in Mottstown (338).

            Salmon (338): car rental man in Mottstown, from whom Mrs. Hines tries to rent car to go to Jefferson (338-339).

            : cafe man in Mottstown; serves Hineses dinner (340).

            : train agent in Mottstown; sells Hineses tickets (340-341).

    Miss   Carruthers (346): was Hightower's organist before his expulsion; dead now for almost twenty years (346).

    Lem Bush (352): driver of wagon in which Milly went to circus (352); she is not in wagon when it returns (354).

            : Christmas's father with whom Milly runs off; said to be a Mexican; Hines thinks he is black; with circus (353-354).

            : circus owner; returns for trial; says Milly's man was "part nigger instead of Mexican" (357).

            Gillman (359): owns sawmill where Hines works (359).

            : black man at orphanage; works in yard; plants idea in Christmas's head that he does not know what he is--black or white (363).

            : Lena's baby (375).

    Percy Grimm (400): about 25; captain in national guard (425); regrets being born too late for WW I; superpatriot; fights with ex-soldier (425-426); racist (426); on military holidays, dresses in uniform; marksman; goes to American Legion commander to preserve order after Christmas is returned to Jefferson; wants to form and command vigilante-type platoon (427); when Legion commander refuses to co-operate, raises his own platoon (428); wants them to be armed (429); goes to sheriff who orders them not to be armed, as well as Grimm; Grimm disobeys (430); as Christmas escapes, chases him (433); sights Christmas (436); sees Christmas enter Hightower's house (438); kills Christmas and castrates him before he dies (439).

            : black woman Burch-Brown meets after fleeing Lena (410).

_____: black man who takes Burch-Brown's note demanding reward to sheriff (412); meets Byron Bunch; tells him where Burch-Brown is (413-414).

Gavin Stevens (419): District Attorney in Jefferson; Harvard graduate; Phi Beta Kappa (419); puts Hineses on train back to Mottstown; promises them that he will send Christmas's body by train next day (420); takes over narration of story for time (421); speaks of Christmas's "black blood" and his "white blood" (424-425); (his narration ends on page 425) tells sheriff Christmas will plead guilty and take life sentence (433).

_____: Gavin Stevens's grandfather; knew and hated Burdens; congratulated [John] Sartoris (420).

_____: college professor at State University; Harvard friend of Gavin Stevens (420).

_____: flagman on train that takes Hineses back to Mottstown (420).

_____ Grimm (400): Percy Grimm's father; hardware merchant (425).

_____: ex-soldier of WW I with whom Percy Grimm fights (426).

_____: commander of American Legion in Jefferson (427); refuses to support Grimm's plan (428).

_____: one of Grimm's platoon; does not favor wearing uniforms (429).

_____: Grimm's second in command (431).

_____: night marshal in Jefferson (431).

_____: Western Union boy from whom Grimm takes bicycle (434).

_____ Hightower (442): Hightower's father; 50 years old when Hightower was born; anti-slavery; minister at 21 rides sixteen miles each Sunday to preach in Presbyterian chapel; in hills (442); in Civil War served four years but fired no musket and wore no uniform (443); on wedding day, his father gives him house (445); learns medicine (446); an abolishonist; wounded in Civil War; learned surgery and pharmacy helping doctors at the front (447); turns doctor (449).

_____ Hightower (442): Hightower's mother; twenty years an invalid when he was born (442).

146

_____: two men who carry Hightower's father into home (443).

Cinthy (457)_____: black woman "who was [Hightower's] mother too and nurse" (444); was Hightower's grandfather's slave cook (446); returns to serve Hightower's father and mother (451); talks to Hightower about his grandfather; plants mad notions in Hightower's head (452).

Pomp (452)_____: male slave of Hightower's grandfather; his boy; husband of Cinthy (446); followed grandfather to war; did not come back (450); shot by Yankee officer (451).

_____: furniture repairer and dealer; narrator of last chapter (468); gives Lena and Byron ride to Tennessee (469); camps (471); next morning drives with Lena in back with baby (478); picks up Byron Bunch (479).

_____: his wife (468).

Only two of these stories were published for the first time in this volume. Dates of writing and publication are indicated for each story. *Doctor Martino and Other Stories* was first published April 16, 1934.

Pagination, in parentheses, to Collected Stories of William Faulkner (New York: Random House, 1950), 900 pp. for 12 stories excluding "The Hound" and "Smoke." "The Hound," which originally appeared in Harper's Magazine, 163 (August, 1931), 263-274 and was reprinted in Doctor Martino, 1934, will be treated in Uncollected Stories of William Faulkner below, and "Smoke" will be treated in Knight's Gambit below.

"Doctor Martino"

On sending schedule March 5, 1931 with the title "Martino;" first published, under the title "Doctor Martino," in *Harper's Magazine*, 163 (November, 1931), 733-743.

Hubert Jarrod (565): meets Louise King at Christmas time at house party in Saint Louis; home is Tulsa, Oklahoma; has aura of oil wells and three years at Yale (565); slips from party with Louise King; takes her to another house; returns for her after two hours; returns to party; they kiss (566-567); back at Yale, determined to marry Louise King (568); tells Mrs. King that they ought to marry right away; does not want degree; they are engaged; receives telegram from Mrs. King, "Come at once" (569); learns Louise's and Dr. Martino's past from proprietess (572 ff.); has had brief violent interview with Louise (about riding horse?); goes to Mrs. King (575-576); tries to persuade Louise not to ride horse (576-577); hit in cheek with thrown ring (578); shows Dr. Martino ring (580); gives him rabbit (582); realizes that Louise has not sent rabbit to Dr. Martino (583); drives away with Louise (584).

Louise King (565): a "swamp angel" from Mississippi; epicene (565); takes Jarrod in cab to district of residences and shops; is left there for two hours; returns to party; they kiss (566-567); promises to attend spring prom at Yale; arrives at Yale with mother (568); engaged to Jarrod; does not wear his ring on finger (569); afraid of water; learns to swim after Dr. Martino tells her not to be afraid; swims river (573); wears brass rabbit, given by Dr. Martino, around neck (574); becomes sick; does not return following summer (574); says she is going to ride horse that has killed a man (575); explains why she does risky things: to keep Dr. Martino alive (577); flings ring at Jarrod; hits his cheek with it (577-578); tells mother she and Jarrod have let her down; everyone but Dr. Martino has let her down (579); says she will ride horse if it takes a thousand years; locked in room by mother (580); drives off with Jarrod; says she has lost something (rabbit); urges Jarrod not to stop (583).

Jarrod (565): Jarrod's mother; lives in Tulsa, Oklahoma (565).

Alvina (571) King (566): Louise's mother (565); arrives with daughter for Yale prom (568); agrees to marriage (569); thinks Dr. Martino will get Louise killed; says will not return to Cranston's Wells next summer; does not (574); thinks Dr. Martino urges Louise to ride horse to humiliate her (576); calls Lily Cranston a fool; urges for second time that Jarrod approach Dr. Martino perhaps physically (578); locks Louise in room (580); tells Jarrod to pack bags and be ready to leave; tells him he and Louise will be married in Meridian (581); gives Jarrod rabbit to give to Dr. Martino; she got it while Louise was asleep (581).

Dr. Jules (572) Martino (571): man Louise visits in Saint Louis (566); has been going to Cranston's Wells each summer for more than fifteen years (570); has heart problem (571); sits where he can watch Louise playing; never married (572); tells Louise not to be afraid (573); gives her brass rabbit which she wears around neck to remind her not to be afraid; has great influence over her (574); intuits when Louise is sick (575); when Jarrod shows him ring, says Louise must tell him she is engaged; wants sign (580); Jarrod gives him rabbit (582); tells Jarrod he has been conquered by a woman; has been slain (582); dies (585).

_____: Yale psychology instructor (568).

_____: Jarrod's roommate (570).

Lily Cranston (578): small, gray spinster; owns resort at Cranston's Wells, Mississippi; Louise has spent summers there since she was born (570); thinks Mrs. King a fool (571); tells Jarrod history of Dr. Martino (572 ff.); thinks Dr. Martino wants Louise to grow up to marry her (572); beyond 50 (573); gets note from Dr. Martino (584); finds him dead (585).

Uncle Charley (585)_____: black porter who brings Dr. Martino his meal (571).

_____: the cook (585).

"Fox Hunt"

Written possibly as early as January, 1929, but at least by February 7, 1930; on sending schedule March 7, 1930 and once titled "Fox" and "Foxhunt;" first published in *Harper's Magazine*, 163 (September, 1931), 392-402.

_____: three black men who enter stable; feed horses (587).

Unc Mose (587)_____: black worker for Blair (587).

_____: twelve white men; come on mules to watch fox hunt (588): "the white man;" watches hunt from dyke (590 ff.); the youth; has heard Blair say something to his wife that a man does not say in company (592); they watch Gawtrey and Mrs. Blair; she is putting up her hair; crying (607).

Harrison Blair (598): owner of house and horses (588); has been trying to catch vixen for three years (589); comes down every year to hunt; brings guests (590); chases fox without dogs; born at house; went to New York; became rich; bought house back as wedding gift for wife (593); met wife in England (594); married less than week after they met; once killed dog with one blow of stick for not obeying him; once put hand on Ernie who then threatened to kill him; they get along since then (595); forces wife to ride horse he bought for her (596); finally catches fox (604); tramples it to death (606).

Mrs. Harrison Blair (588): rides past observers with Gawtrey (591-592); has Indian oil money; red-haired; meets Harrison Blair in England, while going to school in Europe (594); from Oklahoma; does not want to ride; Blair forces her (596); breaks collar bone trying to learn to ride (599); has known Gawtrey six months (600); originally rebuffed him; after she reads about Allen and showgirl, admits Gawtrey; kisses him (601); then will not let him in house; dislikes him (603); as husband kills fox, apparently has sex with Gawtrey; crying at end of story (606-607).

_____: head groom at Blair's; black (589).

Steve (600) Gawtrey (589): rides on bay horse with Mrs. Blair (591-592); meets Mrs. Blair in Connecticut; hates horses (600); begins to court Mrs. Blair; originally rebuffed; then admitted; becomes her lover (601); had never owned a horse to sell to Blair (602).

Ernie (594)_____: man in black overcoat and derby; pronounces "Negroes" "Nigras" (593); a New Yorker; employee of Blair (594); once threatened to kill Blair (595); narrates much of story (597); valet-secretary (599); invents story of Gawtrey owning horse (600); tells Blair to let his wife talk to Gawtrey about horse; is hit by Blair (601).

_____: uniformed chauffeur; listens to Ernie's story (593).

_____ Blair (588): Harrison Blair's father (593).

_____: Mrs. Blair's mother (594).

_____ Andrews (595): servant of Harrison Blair (595).

_____ Callaghan (596): tries to teach Mrs. Blair to ride (596-597).

_____ Burke (597): Irish maid of Mrs. Blair's mother; dates Ernie (597); apparently becomes maid for Blairs (601); witnesses Mrs. Blair and Gawtrey kissing (601).

Allen (597)_____: Yale college boy; former sweetheart of Mrs. Blair; married to girl from tank show (597).

_____: show girl Allen marries (597).

_____: Mrs. Blair's father; owned oil wells; dead (597).

_____: Allen's father; owns oil wells (598).

Mr. _____ Van Dyming (600): mythical person invented by Ernie to interest Blair in Gawtrey's non-existent horse (600).

"Death Drag"

On sending schedule December 16, 1930, and once titled "A Death Drag;" first published under title "Death-Drag," *Scribner's Magazine,* **91 (January, 1932), 34-42; revised and retitled for** *Doctor Martino and Other Stories.*

Jock (193)_____: pilot of plane that stunts before it lands (185); tall, in dirty coverall (186); knew Captain Warren in WW I; very nervous (193); has no licenses to fly; hair white; crashed plane, passengers burned to death (194); drinks water (196); refuses Warren's invitation to go home with him (205).

Captain _____ Warren (187): ex-army aviator; (185); meets tall man; takes over narration (193); had not seen tall man in fourteen years (193); tells pilot to ground plane; offers to take him home (204).

_____: group of small boys and some blacks and a white man who witness landing (186); one asks questions (186-193); with two others, one rides to town on running board of Mr. Black's car (189).

Mr. _____ Black (189): drives car (189).

Demon Duncan (190) _____ Ginsfarb (194): short man, in breeches, puttees, overcoat; walks with limp (186); speaks with Jewish accent (187); a Jew (188); jumps from ladder beneath plane to car driven by Jake (196); breaks leg on one jump; tightwad (197); as they perform death-drag, haggles with other Jew in rented car about how much they have been paid before he jumps (200-201); refuses to jump; jumps from ladder; not hurt; lands on barn cuts face (202); asked for one hundred dollars; gets sixty (203); crowd and Captain Warren make up difference (204).

Jake (196)_____: third man; overcoat, civilian suit, cap; a Jew (188); drives car that catches Ginsfarb (196).

_____: three men from town who come to airfield; newcomer (188); driver of car; the oldest one; third a stranger (189).

_____ Jones (190): secretary of Fair Association (188).

_____: editor of newspaper who is to print handbills (190).

_____: taxi driver (191).

_____: second late-comer (192).

152

Vernon _____ : waiter in restaurant (194).

_____: country man who offers to tow plane with mule (199).

_____: country woman (199).

_____: boy who drives rented car (205).

Mr. _____ Harris (205): owner of rental car; cheated by Ginsfarb (205).

"There Was a Queen"

Under title "An Empress Passed," and a cancelled title, "Through (or "Thru") the Window," written by July 2, 1929; on sending schedule March 25, 1930; first published as "There Was a Queen," in *Scribner's Magazine,* **93 (January, 1933), 10-16; reprinted in** *Doctor Martino and Other Stories.*

Elnora (727) [Strother] _____: black half-sister to old Bayard Sartoris [II] (727); coffee-colored; proud of her Sartoris head (728); scornful of Narcissa (729); says she will never be a Sartoris woman (730); thinks Miss Jenny is quality; Narcissa not (732); resents Narcissa's visit to Memphis (733); calls her trash (734); finds Aunt Jenny dead (744).

John Sartoris [I] (727): from Carolina; father of Elnora (727).

Bayard Sartoris [II] (727): son of John [I] (727).

John Sartoris [II] (727): son of Bayard [II] (727).

Bayard Sartoris [III] (727): son of John Sartoris [II]; dead at 26 (727).

Simon (727) [Strother]: Elnora's mother's husband (727).

_____ [Strother]: Elnora's mother; bore Elnora by John Sartoris [I] (727).

Caspey (727) _____: Elnora's husband; in penitentiary for stealing (727); [See *Sartoris* and *Flags in the Dust* in which Caspey is Elnora's brother.]

Joby (727) _____: Elnora's son; gone to Memphis (727).

Virginia Sartoris DuPre (727): sister of John [I]; 90 years old; in wheelchair (727); came from Carolina to Mississippi in 1869; calls Benbow, Johnny (728); Yankees killed her father and her husband (732); arrived on Christmas day (733); when Narcissa receives obscene letter, wants to show it to Bayard [II] (735); sometimes urges Narcissa to remarry; becomes furious at Narcissa's guest at dinner; calls him Yankee (736); has Isom wheel her from table without supper (737); after Narcissa tells her how she recovered letters for sex, interprets sitting in creek as baptism, "In

Jordan" (741); sends Bory for her hat; puts it on; sits by window; refuses dinner (741-742); dies (744).

Narcissa (727) Benbow (742) Sartoris (727): widow of Bayard Sartoris [III]; announces that she is going to Memphis for a day or two; stays two days; walks with son across pasture (728); returns with son; both have been in creek with clothes on (731); has lived in Sartoris house for ten years (733); flashback: receives anonymous obscene letter; refuses to let Aunt Jenny show letter to old Bayard [II]; says she will burn it; an orphan (735); marries Bayard [III]; bears his child; says no more letters have come (736); back to present: three days after visit of Jewish guest, visits Memphis and returns without any explanation; sits in creek with son with clothes on (737); large woman in thirties (738); tells Aunt Jenny she lied about burning letter; received ten more; they were stolen by bank bookkeeper; now that she knows who sent letters, is frantic that they are "out in the world;" has read letters again and again (739); recovers letters from Federal agent in exchange for sex; has burned letters (740-741); has son sit by her at dinner; promises him she will never leave him again (742).

Benbow (728) Bory (729) Sartoris (727): son of Bayard [III] and Narcissa Sartoris (727); ten years old (728).

John Sartoris [III] (728): killed in France in WW I (728).

Isom (728)   : Elnora's son (728); defends Narcissa against his mother (732); serves at table at dinner (734).

Saddie (728)   : Elnora's daughter; sleeps on cot by bedside of Virginia DuPre; tends her as though she were a baby (728).

            Sartoris (732): father of John [I], [Bayard I], and Virginia; killed by Yankees (732).

            DuPre (732): husband of Virginia Sartoris DuPre; killed by Yankees (732).

            Sartoris (732): mother of John [I], [Bayard I], and Virginia; house burned by Yankees (732).

[Horace Benbow]: Narcissa's brother (735).

            : Narcissa's guest; Jew (736); Federal agent; found letters bookkeeper had lost or thrown away; had letters for twelve years (740); gives them back to Narcissa in exchange for sex (740-741).

[Byron Snopes]: bookkeeper in Sartoris bank; stole money; stole Narcissa's obscene letters; ran away (739).

"Turnabout"

Written perhaps as early as October-November, 1931; written after

154

December 10, 1931 according to Skei; first published as "Turn About," in *The Saturday Evening Post*, **204** (March 5, 1932), **6-7, 75-76, 81, 83;** revised and retitled for *Doctor Martino and Other Stories.*

H. S. (509) Bogard (480): American pilot; decorated; captain; over 25 (475); dismisses American M. P. ; takes charge of Hope; calls for his car (480); takes Hope to American airfield (481); tells Jerry to "lay off" riding Hope; takes Hope to quarters for flying togs (485); takes Hope on bombing mission with McGinnis (488-489); accompanies Hope and Ronnie on their boat (497); finally realizes he is riding on a torpedo boat (500); asks them not to go as far as Kiel; takes drink (501); as stuck torpedo comes clear, feels sick; presumably vomits (505); drinks again (506); cited for bravery; bombs castle, hoping to kill all generals--theirs, ours (509).

Claude (488) L. (500) Hope (478): quite drunk; held up by American M. P.; 18 years old (475); Royal Naval officer (476); pilots small boat (477); was sleeping in middle of street (479); sleeps in Bogarld's car (480); has never flown before (486); flies with Bogard and McGinnis; fires Lewis machine gun on bombing run (488-489); tries to warn McGinnis and Bogard of bomb hanging from wing (490); on torpedo run, gives Bogard a drink (501); tells Bogard they are riding through a mine field (502); releases stuck torpedo (504); goes just one down to Ronnie when he mistakenly identifies *Ergenstrasse* (507); missing in action (508).

_____: American M. P. holds drunken British naval officer (475); corporal (476).

_____ Beatty (476).

Darrel (509 McGinnis (485): American lieutenant; pilot (476).

Albert (478) _____: British M. P. (478)

Jamie Wutherspoon (479).

_____: five American pilots at card table at airfield (481); they discuss the purpose of the British fleet of small boats (482); one, named Jerry, rides Hope (483-484).

Ronnie (482) Boyce Smith (508): Hope's commander (482); 20 years old (494); decides to take Bogard to raid Kiel (499); is allowed to pick his own targets (501); sights cruiser near freighter; fires torpedo at freighter (503); torpedo sticks in tube (504); mistakenly identifies *Ergenstrasse* as basket mast (507); missing in action (508).

_____ Burt (483): Boatswain's mate on Hope's torpedo boat; missing in action (508).

_____ Reeves (483): able seaman on Hope's torpedo boat; missing in action (508).

Jerry (483) _____: American pilot (483).

_____ Harper (484): aviation gunner on Bogard's plane; cited for bravery (509).

_____ Hope (478): Hope's father (485).

_____: Hope's tutor (485).

_____: orderly who brings coffee (485).

_____: gunnery sergeant (488).

_____ Collier (491): owns mandolin (491).

_____: British marine at Hope's wharf (493).

_____: orderly from airfield (493); carries package for Bogard from McGinnis (494).

Agatha (497) _____: Hope's aunt; torpedo tube named for her (497).

_____: man who delivers Bogard's case of scotch to Hope (508).

_____ Watts (509): aviation gunner on Bogard's plane; cited for bravery (509).

"Beyond"

Entitled "Beyond the Gate," on sending schedule April 22, 1930; first published as "Beyond," in *Harper's Magazine*, **167 (September, 1933), 394-403; reprinted in** *Doctor Martino and Other Stories.*

Judge (786) Howard Allison [I] (796): man being examined by Lucius Peabody (781); dies; leaves house after Chlory screams; in pajamas, but apparently dressed; (782-783); is "there" to escape someone, not to find anyone (784-785); meets Mothershed "there" (785); agnostic; reads Ingersoll, Paine (787) Voltaire and Montesquiue; talks to Ingersoll (788); may be looking for Him; says he once, after serious suffering, hoped for a hereafter; "a waystation" where he could be told "There is hope," or "There is nothing." (788) Federal judge; Republican (789); mother died when he was 14; 28 when he married; 37 when son was born; ten generations in America (790); invited to wait with woman and child while Howard rides by on pony; says pony died at age 18, twelve years ago; tries to move against crowd to leave; offers half dollar to mother of child with stigmata (795); relives leaving office and visiting cemetery; wipes mud from son's tombstone (796); has vision of himself going home from office while his funeral gathers (797).

Lucius Peabody (781): doctor who treats judge (781).

Chlory (782)_____: black female servant; at bedside of judge; screams when he dies (782).

Jake (782)_____: black male servant (782).

_____: young man met by judge; in morning dress about to be married (783); apparently killed when he swerved to avoid hitting child with car (784); looking for wife he was to marry (783-784).

_____: his fiancee (783).

_____: child almost hit by prospective groom (784).

Howard (794) Allison [II] (796): son of judge; 10 when he died (785); last of his name and race; dies while riding pony (789); born April 3, 1903; died August 22, 1913 (796).

_____ Mothershed (785): curses; an atheist; nihilist; carries pistol (786); suicide (787); had read Ingersoll and Paine while alive (788); has body odor (789).

Robert (791) Ingersoll (788): talks to judge (788); tells him to seek his son (791) (no doubt based on the real person Robert Green Ingersoll, 1833-1899).

Mrs._____ Allison: judge's wife; dies (789).

_____: judge's wife's father (789).

Sophia (798) Allison (796): judge's mother;invalid; dominated by son; died when he was 14 (790).

_____: judge's two aunts (790).

_____: young woman with child; passes judge and Ingersoll on bench (791); tells judge that Howard rides by on pony every day; invites him to stay and wait for him (794-795).

_____: child with young woman; plays with dismembered Roman soldiers; has stigmata (793); cries steadily (793-794).

_____: old gentleman who gave child with stigmata the Roman soldiers to play with (793); other children gave him scars while playing (794).

_____ Pettigrew (796): Judge Allison's attorney (797).

_____: minister who officiates at Judge Allison's wake; has droning voice (797).

"Wash"

Written about late summer, 1933; first published in *Harper's Magazine*, **168 (February, 1934), 258-262.**

Colonel (536) [Thomas] Sutpen (535): 60 years old (535); flashback: sits drinking with Wash in scuppernong arbor on Sundays (538); returns with citation from General Lee from Civil War in 1865, to a ruined plantation (538-539); sets up small store on highroad; drinks there with Wash until Sutpen gets drunk (540); gives Milly ribbons (541); when Wash Jones confronts him about what he said to Milly after birth of child, strikes him twice with riding whip; cut down by Wash with scythe (545).

Milly (535)_____: gives birth to Sutpen's child (535); Wash Jones's grandchild (536, 541); tells her grandfather new dress was made by Judith and her (541); cries as grandfather tends her (546); killed by grandfather (550).

_____: her daughter (535); killed by great-grandfather (550).

Dicey (544)_____: black midwife (535); tells Wash Jones the baby is a girl (543); flees as Sutpen strikes Wash (545).

Wash (536) Jones (542): flashback: stays home when Sutpen goes to war; says he is taking care of Sutpen's place and slaves; gaunt, malaria-ridden; 35 years old; called white trash by slaves (536); taunted by slaves for not being in war (537); drinks with Sutpen; thinks very highly of him; compares Sutpen to God (538); after war, drinks with him in store (539); when Sutpen gets drunk, takes him home; now enters house (540); knows where Milly's ribbons come from; talks to Sutpen about Milly (541); expresses extreme faith that Sutpen "will make hit right" (542); back to present: on morning of birth, still has faith that Sutpen will do right (542-543); hears what Sutpen says to Milly "and something seemed to stop dead in him;" realizes that Sutpen got up early for colt not for Milly's child (544); threatens Sutpen; after Sutpen hits him twice with whip, cuts Sutpen down with scythe (545); after white boy discovers Sutpen's body, cooks food; eats; waits (546-547); finally sees Sutpen's class of men as they are; decides not to run (547); thinks his life has been wasted (548-549); when he hears posse approach, with razor-sharp butcher knife, cuts granddaughter's and great-granddaughter's throats; sets kerosene fire to house; runs toward posse with scythe; is killed by sheriff (550).

[Melicent Jones] (536): Wash's daughter (536).

Mrs. [Thomas] Sutpen (536): dies during Civil War (539).

_____: black slave who tells Wash he can not enter Sutpen's house (537).

[Henry] Sutpen (538): Sutpen's son; youth in school at outbreak of Civil War (538); killed in action same winter as mother died (538-539)

[See *Absalom, Absalom!*].

    Judith (540) Sutpen (539): Sutpen's daughter 539); meets Sutpen and Wash when Wash brings Sutpen home drunk (540).

    _____: half-grown white boy; discovers Sutpen's body (546).

    Major (549) [de Spain]: sees Sutpen's body; calls Wash to come out (549).

    _____: sheriff (549); kills Wash Jones (550).

"Elly"

Written perhaps as early as December, 1928 and perhaps as late as February 23, 1929; on sending schedule March 25, 1930, entitled, "Salvage" and "Selvage;" first published as "Elly," in *Story*, 4 (February, 1934), 3-15; reprinted in *Doctor Martino and Other Stories*.

    Elly (207) Ailanthia (212) _____: asks Paul what she can do to make him marry her; they have just had sex in woods; is in car nearing Mills City (207); flashback: lives in Jefferson, two hundred miles away; necks with many suitors on porch; dismisses them at 11:00 p. m.; hates grandmother (208-209); meets Paul de Montigny at girl friend's house; learns of Paul's uncle killing man who accused him of having "nigger" blood (209); meets Paul that night on veranda; dismisses him at 11:00 p. m.; exults, "A nigger. A nigger;" next day introduces Paul to her grandmother (210); that night, leaves veranda; enters clump of bushes with Paul for sex; is caught by grandmother before act; regrets that she is still virgin and had no chance to sin; does not want any man (211); shouts at grandmother next day; meets Paul in drugstore; asks him to marry her; promises him sex if he will marry her (212) he refuses; says goodbye "Forever;" later, engagement announced to Philip whom she has known since childhood (213); after grandmother decides to visit son in Mills City, calls Paul and arranges to meet him for sex (214); asks Philip not to drive with her to Mills City; tells him she is going with party of people; to trust her (215); meets Paul; asks him to hurry; after sex asks him if he will marry her; he refuses (216); confronts grandmother about Paul (218); waits for Paul in bathroom; again asks him to marry her; asks him to kill her grandmother; he tries to hit her (221); in car with grandmother and Paul, asks him to marry her; says she does not believe or care about story of "nigger" blood; he refuses (222); tries to make car go over cliff to kill them all; succeeds in killing Paul and grandmother (223-224).

    Paul (207) de Montigny (209): has just had sex with Elly (207); tells Elly, "I don't marry them" (212); leaves town (213); when Elly calls him, agrees to meet her, but says he will not marry her (214-215); after sex with Elly near Mills City, again refuses to marry her (216); stays as guest at her uncle's house (218) again refuses to marry her or kill her grandmother (221); is killed by Elly (223).

159

Ailanthia_____: Elly's grandmother (207); catches Elly in bushes with Paul (211); very deaf (212) suddenly decides to visit son in Mills City (214); calls Paul a "Negro" (217); says she has known his name for four generations (218); is killed by Elly (223).

_____: Elly's father (208).

_____: Elly's mother (208).

_____: Elly's girl friend (209).

_____: Paul de Montigny's uncle; Elly's girl friend says he killed a man "that accused him of having nigger blood" (209).

Philip (214)_____: young man to whom Elly is engaged; assistant cashier in bank (213); agrees to let Elly go to Mills City alone; trusts her (215-216).

_____: Elly's uncle in Mills City (214).

_____: his wife (217).

_____: Elly's cousin in Mills City (217).

"Black Music"

Written possibly as early as 1926; on sending schedule July 27, 1931; first published in *Doctor Martino and Other Stories.*

_____:"they" who tell narrator about Midgleston (799).

Wilfred Midgleston (799): 56 years old; lives in Rincon; has been there twenty-five years; has not learned more than ten words of Spanish; no job (799); white (801); has not eaten in two days; has breakfast with narrator (802); used to be architect's draughtsman; sleeps in attic over cantina (see "Carcassonne.") bed is roll of tarpaper (803); seventy-five dollars a week salary; does not plan to return home; did not steal; carries a good amount of insurance (804); was a "farn" (a faun) once for one day in his life (805); flashback: after "they" narrate some of the story (807), takes over and tells narrator story (for a time double "I" then "he") (807-808); lives in Brooklyn (808); sent by Carter to take plans for theatre to Mrs. Van Dyming; Martha packs clothes; on train "It" started; he had been chosen (810); sees a goat-like face; falls down; given whisky by porter and conductor (811); has been thrown down by a curve; helped off train; buys tin whistle (812); removes clothes; drinks more whisky; jumps into water from bridge; thinks his face is like the goat-like face he saw on train; puts clothes on again (813); flash forward: shows narrator newspaper article; it is an account of his drunken chase of Mrs. Van Dyming, and release of bull (his day as a "farn") (815-817); name is spelled Wilfred Middleton in account of his disappearance (819-820); sends letter to *Times* correcting error; sends clipping to wife who remarries after collecting insurance money (820-821).

160

_____: first-person narrator (799); invites Midgleston to breakfast (802); in Part III, narrator resumes narration.

_____: person to whom narrator speaks; thinks Midgleston stole money for someone else (800); thinks a human being will steal whenever he can get away with it (801).

Mrs._____ Widrington (803): wife of manager of company that owns building in which Midgleslton sleeps (803).

Mr._____ Widrington (803): manager of Universal Oil Company that owns building where Midgleston sleeps (803).

Mrs. Martha Midgleston (804): wife of principal character (804); packs husband's clothes for trip (810); after husband disappears, collects insurance; remarries (820-821).

Mrs. Mattie (807) Van Dyming (806) nee Mathilda Lumpkin (807): owner of vineyard (806); born in Poughkeepsie; builds house on vineyard (808).

_____: man from New England who once owned vineyard; has leg broken by ram; can not harvest grapes; moves away (806).

_____: Italian owner of vineyard; gets rich (806); killed when truck overturns (807).

_____: his wife (807).

Carleton Van Dyming (807): buys vineyard for wife (807); little man; plans log house they build (808); after Midgleston's wild faun attack on wife, abandons plans to develop vineyard (818).

Mr._____ Carter (809): the boss, the architect (809); designs theatre for Mrs. Van Dyming (810).

_____: porter on train (811).

_____: conductor on train (811).

_____: two men in wagon; meet Midgleston when train arrives (812).

Elmer Harris (819): chief of police in Virginia (819).

_____: second husband of Martha Widgleston (821).

"The Leg"

Written probably as early as 1925; surely by November 3, 1928; on

sending schedule December 14, 1930; first published as "Leg" in *Doctor Martino and Other Stories*.

Davy (824)_____: first-person narrator (823); student at Oxford, 21 years old in 1914; (825); American (827); wounded in WW I; leg amputated; hallucinates friend George (who is dead) visits him when leg is amputated; tells George to make sure leg is dead before they bury it (830); thinks leg is still alive; sends George to find it; thinks it jeers at him (831); begins to recover; loses George; attends Observers School (832); has wood and leather leg; has dream that George has seen him on river with girl; is awakened by someone (833-834); has one final hallucination of visit by George (834-835); spends week with George's people in Devon, but can not find him again (835); attacked by Jotham Rust (836); stabbed in arm (837); third-person narrator takes over at page 838; resumes first-person narration (840); after padre shows picture of himself given to Everbe Corinthia with an unprintable phrase, says he told George to kill it [the leg] (841-742).

George (823)_____: falls in water when Everbe Corinthia opens lock suddenly (824); student at Oxford; 21 years old in 1914 (825); killed in WW I; subaltern (829); promises Davy to be sure his leg is dead before they bury it (830); looks for Davy's leg (831); can not find leg (832).

Everbe Corinthia (823) Rust (835): pretty girl to whom George and Davy talk; cries when George falls in water (825); dies (836); brother follows her when she leaves home at night; brings her back after hearing man laugh; locks her in room; disappears (839-840); found on towpath; revived; screams all day; dies at sunset (840).

_____: helmsman of yawl; shouts to open lock (823).

Sam'l (825)_____: other man on yawl (824).

Simon (824) Rust (835): Everbe Corinthia's father (824); dies shortly after daughter dies (836).

Jotham Rust (835): man with Everbe Corinthia's father at lock (824); Everbe's brother; works in London (825); tried in court martial for desertion (835); wants no clemency; does not want to live; attacked Davy for no apparent cause (836); saw sister die; hears man laugh once in dark: cause for stabbing Davy; has "other proof" (837); on leave last summer; discovered Everbe leaving house at dusk every evening; one evening finds her and brings her home; thinks he sees man disappearing (839); later, follows Everbe; finds empty punt; hears man laugh; punt disappears; takes Everbe home; locks her in room; in morning she is gone (839-840); after her death, AWOL for one hundred and twelve days, searching for man whose laugh he heard one day (840); presumably executed (842).

_____: boy on towpath (827).

_____: man on barge (827).

162

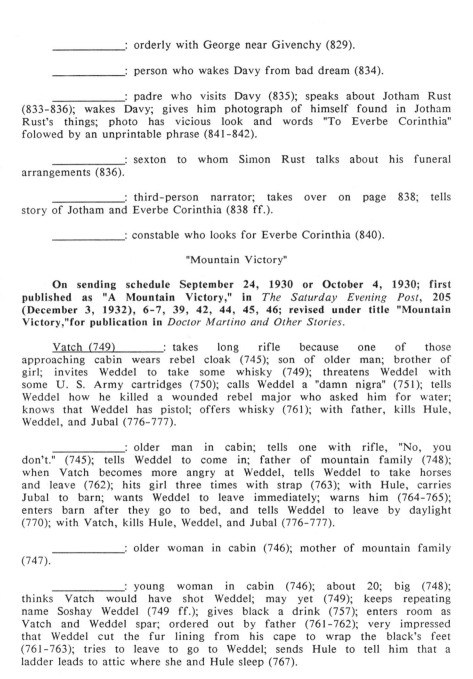

_____: orderly with George near Givenchy (829).

_____: person who wakes Davy from bad dream (834).

_____: padre who visits Davy (835); speaks about Jotham Rust (833-836); wakes Davy; gives him photograph of himself found in Jotham Rust's things; photo has vicious look and words "To Everbe Corinthia" folowed by an unprintable phrase (841-842).

_____: sexton to whom Simon Rust talks about his funeral arrangements (836).

_____: third-person narrator; takes over on page 838; tells story of Jotham and Everbe Corinthia (838 ff.).

_____: constable who looks for Everbe Corinthia (840).

"Mountain Victory"

On sending schedule September 24, 1930 or October 4, 1930; first published as "A Mountain Victory," in *The Saturday Evening Post*, **205 (December 3, 1932), 6-7, 39, 42, 44, 45, 46; revised under title "Mountain Victory,"for publication in** *Doctor Martino and Other Stories.*

Vatch (749)_____: takes long rifle because one of those approaching cabin wears rebel cloak (745); son of older man; brother of girl; invites Weddel to take some whisky (749); threatens Weddel with some U. S. Army cartridges (750); calls Weddel a "damn nigra" (751); tells Weddel how he killed a wounded rebel major who asked him for water; knows that Weddel has pistol; offers whisky (761); with father, kills Hule, Weddel, and Jubal (776-777).

_____: older man in cabin; tells one with rifle, "No, you don't." (745); tells Weddel to come in; father of mountain family (748); when Vatch becomes more angry at Weddel, tells Weddel to take horses and leave (762); hits girl three times with strap (763); with Hule, carries Jubal to barn; wants Weddel to leave immediately; warns him (764-765); enters barn after they go to bed, and tells Weddel to leave by daylight (770); with Vatch, kills Hule, Weddel, and Jubal (776-777).

_____: older woman in cabin (746); mother of mountain family (747).

_____: young woman in cabin (746); about 20; big (748); thinks Vatch would have shot Weddel; may yet (749); keeps repeating name Soshay Weddel (749 ff.); gives black a drink (757); enters room as Vatch and Weddel spar; ordered out by father (761-762); very impressed that Weddel cut the fur lining from his cape to wrap the black's feet (761-763); tries to leave to go to Weddel; sends Hule to tell him that a ladder leads to attic where she and Hule sleep (767).

163

Hule (764)   : younger brother of girl and Vatch (749); helps Weddel take Jubal to barn loft after he becomes drunk (765); returns to barn; tells Weddel that his sister tried to come to Weddel; says she sent him to Weddel to tell him that a ladder leads to attic where she and Hule sleep (767); begins to throttle Weddel; tells him to shoot him (768); asks Weddel to take him with him; says Wedel can marry his sister in Mayesfield; hears father coming up ladder (769); gives Weddel directions; warns him not to pass a laurel copse (772); as Weddel leaves, meets him and tries to show him the escape path (773); again asks Weddel to take him and his sister with him; goes with Weddel down path (774); as Weddel insists on going on, jumps on Thoroughbred, displacing Jubal; says, "They think you will be riding the good horse;" killed by brother and father (776).

Major Saucier (747) Weddel (746): called Soshay by Jubal (746); man on foot leading Thoroughbred (745); Confederate field officer; asks for shelter; offers to pay; says he is on way home to Mississippi (747); takes drink to his black servant (752); 28 years old; takes his pistol (753); says he wants to bathe at well (754); a bachelor (757); missing right arm (758); son of a Choctaw chief (759); after Jubal gets drunk, told to leave immediately; refuses to leave Jubal (764-765); refuses girl's invitation (by way of Hule) to climb ladder to attic where she sleeps (768); tells Hule that he has been freed of Jubal (769); as Hule's father starts to climb ladder to loft, leaves pistol with Hule and goes down to meet father again refuses to leave until Jubal is sober (770); leaves at dawn with Jubal (771); says he has to guess right way one out of three (773-774); again refuses to take Hule and his sister with him (774); as Hule leaps on Thoroughbred, rides down path; killed by Vatch and father (776).

Jubal (764): "something larger than a child" on horseback (745); knocks on door of cabin; black; ex-slave; says Weddel requests sleeping room for himself and boy and two horses (746); says they will pay (747); drinks whisky; 40 years old (753); tells mother and daughter about Weddels (755-756); a stableman (756); gets another drink from girl; says Weddel is not black as Vatch thinks (757); believes Saucier's mother is still alive (760); while Weddel and others spar, takes whisky jug from hiding place and drinks (763); falls headlong on floor unconscious (764); at dawn, leaves with Weddel; rides Thoroughbred (771); killed by Vatch (777).

Francis (755) Weddel (753): father of Saucier Weddel (753); went to Washington to tell president he did not like the way he was treating the people (755); Choctaw chief; son of Choctaw woman and French emigre; met wife and married her in Washington; killed in Mexican War (759).

          Weddel (753): Saucier Weddel's mother (752-753); died in 1863 (760).

Francois Vidal (759): Saucier Weddel's grandfather; named plantation Countymaison, according to Jubal (755); Contalmaison (759); general of Napoleon's and a knight of Legion of Honor (759).

Mrs. Francois Vidal (759): Choctaw woman; grandmother of Saucier Weddel (759).

_____: Indian overseer; full-blooded Choctaw; cousin to Francis Weddel; accompanies him to Washington to protest to President Jackson (759).

_____: rebel major killed by Vatch (760-761).

"Honor"

Written possibly before March 7, 1930 under the title "Point of Honor;" on sending schedule March 25, 1930; first published in *The American Mercury*, **20 (July, 1930), 268-274; reprinted in** *Doctor Martino and Other Stories.*

Buck (554) Monaghan 64): first-person narrator interrupts discussion; resigns; (551); after Armistice, stays in army as test pilot; becomes wing walker; wins twenty-five hundred dollars from White at poker; as civilian, takes job selling cars (552); flashback: given note to Rogers by Jack (553); frequently at Rogers's home; seems to be attracted to Mrs. Rogers; takes them to his place for drink (554); because of storm, they stay overnight at his place (555); after Mildred complains of poverty, offers Rogers a loan; invited to dinner; goes early to see Mildred (556); as affair with Mildred develops, wonders how much Howard knows as he walks the wings (556-557); invited to dinner; kissed by Mildred who says she will live with him (557); asks Howard if he will give her a divorce; says he loves her (558); finally gets away as their divorce is all settled; tells Harris he will not fly with Rogers; then agrees to fly with him (559); as he is on wing, shouts at Rogers to flip him off; loops once; on next loop throws rope at Rogers and holds out arms; as he falls, Rogers dives and catches him on wing (560-561); as he leaves, Rogers gives him letter from Mildred; godfather to Rogers's child (563); resigns job as car salesman because he does not like the women to whom he demonstrates cars (563-564).

Miss _____ West (551): secretary in automobile dealership (551).

_____ Reinhardt (563): man in office; narrator tells him he resigns (551); owner of automobile dealership (563).

_____ Waldrip (552).

_____ White (552): loses one thousand dollars in poker game; fifteen hundred dollars next night; another test pilot; dives wings off speed ship (552).

Mrs. _____ White (552): his wife in California (552).

Jack (552) _____: gives Buck note to Rogers (553).

Howard Rogers (553): good pilot (553); as Buck's affair with Mildred develops, tells Buck not to leave field; invites him to dinner (557); agrees to divorce; offers to walk wings while Buck flies plane (559); as Buck falls off plane, dives and catches him on wing; climbs into front cockpit to hold Buck on wing (561-562); after Buck leaves, returns to Mildred; has son (563).

Mildred (556) Rogers (553): woman whom narrator meets (553); as Buck visits, is crying; says Rogers's insurance rate is too high; complains about poverty; wants him to get regular job (555); visits mother; on return, invites Buck to dinner (556); before Howard, kisses Buck; says she has told Howard everything; wants to live with Buck; says Howard can find another woman (557); after Buck leaves, reconciled with husband; has son (563).

_____: Mildred Rogers's mother (556).

_____ Harris (559): owner of flying circus (559).

_____: flashback: man in Buck's squadron whom he hates and who hates Buck; nevertheless saves Buck's life (562).

_____: Buck's prisoner of war (562).

_____: Indian prince in British Army; Oxford man (562).

_____ Rogers (5): son of Mildred and Howard Rogers (563).

166

"This Kind of Courage," written about 1934, was originally a short story that was expanded to become the novel *Pylon*. It was rejected by May 5, 1934. The novel was written from early November to November 25, 1934; revision was concluded December 15, 1934. The novel was published March 25, 1935.

Pagination, in parentheses, to the following editions and reissues: (New York: Harrison Smith and Robert Haas, 1935), 315 pp.; (New York: Random House, 1965); (New York: Modern Library, 1967).

Jiggs (7)_____: tries to buy pair of boots (8); wants to pay ten percent and pick up boots next day (9); takes bus to airport; Roger Shumann's mechanic (12); aircraft two years old; not fast enough (13-14); has wife and children in Kansas (16); asks boy who his father is today; boy tries to hit him (20); returns to pick up boots (40); steals parachutist's money to buy boots (68); borrows last forty cents from madam in whorehouse (72); next morning, drinks before going to airfield; a drunkard (116); finds reporter on doorstep (119-120); borrows half dollar from man at airport (130); longs for a drink (130-132); has three drinks; pays for two; drunk (146); asks reporter for five dollars; says Laverne sent him for it; implies that reporter can have sex in return (148); hit by Jack Holmes (156); arrested by police (163); released to reporter (181); given sandwich by Shumann; vomits (185-186); after crash, takes money from reporter to Laverne (250); returns money to him (251); visits reporter; tells him he is going with Art Jackson to become parachutist (264); tries to restore boots to return them (271); pawns boots; buys gifts for Holmes, Laverne, and Jack (272-273); takes gifts and money to Laverne (280); says goodbye to reporter (283).

_____: clerk in shoe shop (8).

_____: another clerk in shoe shop; manager; floor walker (9).

_____: driver of bus to airport (12).

Roger Shumann (12): pilot (14); from Ohio (28); in race (32); places second (44); shares wife sexually with Jack Holmes; does not own plane; flies whatever he can get (47-48); when child is born to Laverne, rolls dice to determine who will assume parentage of boy; wins; married by a J. P. (48-49); decides not to check valve stems to save time (156); crashes plane (163); survives crash (164); will fly Ord's plane (165); with reporter, visits Ord to get new plane (167); jokes about reporter fixing him up with Ord's plane so that he can have Laverne after his death (175); buys Jiggs sandwich (185); goes to bed with Laverne (191-194); signs note and signs his father's name to note to buy plane (212); buys Ord's plane; flies it back to airport; lands safely (216-218); crashes as plane breaks up (234); lands in lake; lost (236); body left in lake grave (299).

_____: three men on bus to airport (13).

Colonel H. I. Feinman (14): builder of Feinman airport (14); grants permission for Ord's plane to fly (228).

_____: Jiggs's wife; gets Jiggs's pay before he can collect it (16).

_____: Jiggs's two children (16).

_____: sheriff who helps Jigg's wife get his pay (16).

Jack (71) Holmes (129): taller man repairing plane (19); narrow mustache; delicate, feminine mouth (34); parachutist (32-35); gets twenty-five dollars for parachute jump (34-35); takes sack of flour up with him (35-36); shares Laverne sexually with Roger Shumann (46); rolls dice to determine who will marry her after child is born (48-49); hits, kicks reporter after he accuses him of wanting to sleep with Laverne (103-104); leaves others as they take reporter's money (122-123); turns up at airfield (129); after repairing plane, walks intuitively to Jiggs and reporter; hits Jiggs and reporter (154-156); hurt in jump; apologizes to reporter (164); after crash, finds reporter on beach; gives him twenty-two dollars Roger owed him (257); gives him seventy-five dollars; asks him to send Shumann's body to his father; makes him promise not to send body collect (259); tells reporter they are leaving; says goodbye; says Laverne will never see him again (260).

Laverne (19) Shumann (44): from Iowa (28); married to Shumann; sophomore in high school when married (44); taught to parachute jump (45); shares two men sexually (46); after birth of son, marries Shumann after he rolls high dice (48-49); tells reporter they took money from him (161); returns to reporter's apartment (165); flashback: first parachute jump with Shumann; she climbs back into plane; they have sex in plane; then Shuman tips her out; no underpants as she lands; near riot on ground (195-196); back to present: angry with reporter for helping Shumann buy Ord's plane (221); tells reporter to go away (238); flashback through Jiggs: 14 or 15 when parents die; lives with sister; has affair with her brother-in-law (276 ff.); back to present: takes Jack to Roger's father (305-306); abandons child while he is asleep; says she is pregnant and knows this child's father is Jack Holmes (308-309).

Jack (22) Shumann (44): small towheaded boy (19); fights with Jiggs when he asks, "Who's your old man today?" (20); not more than 6 (21); born in hangar in California (44); taught by mother to fight when asked "Who's your old man?" (49); abandoned by mother (308-309).

_____: tall thin man (20); attacked by boy (21); carries him on shoulders (22); reporter (23); in restaurant with Jack and Laverne (25-26); calleld Lazarus by Jiggs (33); told by city editor to forget sex life of Shumann trio and send flying news (50-51); gives newspapers and coin to man on street (54); meets Jiggs on Grandlieu Street during Mardi Gras (56); goes to Hotel Terrebone where Shumann and others are (58-59); meets Laverne there; flash forward: takes Laverne, Roger, Jiggs, and

168

Holmes to airport and returns to hotel (62-64); telephones his editor after midnight (65); tries to get editor to advance money for Shumann trio; is fired (65-76); visited by editor (89-90); hired with no past, no papers (91); takes Shuman quartet home with him (96-98); gets drunk (100-102); after beating by parachutist, leaves apartment; drinks coffee; gets sick (106-110); next morning found by others on doorstep (119-120); watches silently as others take his money (122-124); brought to apartment by black cleaning woman (134); borrows two dollars (his own money which she took from him) from Leonora (138); infatuated with Laverne; goes to airport (139); thinks the Shumann trio took his thirteen dollars (141); lets other reporter cover air meet (143); wants to let Laverne say they stole his money (145); pays for Jiggs's drink (146); hit by Jack Holmes (156); gives Jiggs seventy-five cents (159); gives Laverne key to apartment; says he is going out of town (160); after Laverne says they took six dollars and seventy cents from him, says rest of money was in his pocket (161-162); calls Hagood; asks for new assignment (162); with Shumann, visits Ord for new plane (167); pleads with Ord to let Shumann fly plane (169); tells Shumann he wants to have sex with Laverne (175); borrows fifty dollars from Hagood; says he can not leave them alone (178-179); pays Jiggs's fine (181); gives money to Shumann (182-183); at newspaper office, types note for purchase of plane (207); sleeps on cityroom floor (209); with Shumann, takes train to buy plane with five thousand dollar promisory note (211-212); flies in airplane as ballast; returns to airport in taxi (216-217); anti-semitic (218); takes care of Jack Shumann during race (229); after crash, told by Laverne to go away; feels numb (238-240); calls story to Hagood (241); dwells on fact that Laverne told him to go away (238 ff.); returns to waterfront with Jiggs (248); watches Laverne eating in diner (250); after midnight, calls paper (253); borrows piece of tarpaulin to keep warm (254); takes money from Jack Holmes; promises to send Shumann's body (not collect) to father (259); returns to apartment (262); watches Jiggs trying to restore boots (264-266); rents car; goes to boneyard; then to Hagood's golf club to borrow money; shows postcard from mother (267-270); gets one hundred dollars; wants to give it to Laverne (272); gives Jiggs drinks; puts one hundred seventy=five dollars in toy airplane, hoping Jack will open it (274); gives Jiggs pair of his shoes (276); after Jiggs tells him of Laverne's affair with her brother-in-law, takes stiff drink; vomits (278); laughs hysterically; cries as he thinks of himself and Laverne (279); takes cab with Jiggs to train; sends Jiggs with money and presents to Laverne (280); waits with other reporters in lunchroom for dawn; listens to them discuss Shumann trio's sex life (289 ff.); denies ever having heard of Shumann's family; lies; says mechanic told him Shumann was an orphan (294); leaves suddenly; finds Jiggs; learns that Laverne and others have gone to Myron, Ohio to leave child with Roger's father (295-296); returns to beach (297); after body is left in lake, returns to town; can not eat; enters bar for drink (298-299); takes bottle to cityroom (301); hallucinates a future time when Jack Shumann would be a grown pilot and he and Laverne would watch him (301); writes story of Shumann's death; goes to Amboise Street to get drunk (315).

Hank (151)   : announcer of races (23); announces that costs of new program will be deducted from prize money (154).

Art (23) Jackson (39): pilot of commercial plane who takes Holmes up to jump (34); Jiggs goes with him after crash (264).

Jules Despleins (27): French pilot (27).

Lieutenant Frank Burnham (27): American pilot (27); killed in crash of rocket plane (52).

Bob (31) R. Q. (60) Bullitt (31): pilot (31).

Al Myers (31): pilot (31).

Mrs. Bob Bullitt (31): wife of pilot (31).

Jimmy Ott (31): pilot (31).

Joe Grant (31): pilot (31).

_____: checker at air games (35).

_____: guard at airport; directs Jiggs to office (38).

Monk (39)_____:

_____ Hagood (62): city editor (41); bald (42); tells reporter he is not interested in sex life of Shumann trio; is interested in news of the air meet (50-51); fires reporter (74); visits reporter's apartment (89-90); lent reporter one hundred eighty dollars; eighteen months ago (96); tells Jiggs to tell reporter to report for work next day (99); lends reporter more money (270).

Vic Chance (47): builds airplanes; but has no money (47).

_____: doctor who tends Laverne in childbirth (48).

_____: Justice of the Peace who marries Laverne and Shumann (49).

_____: elevator operator at paper (52).

_____: man to whom reporter gives papers and coin (54).

_____: madam of whorehouse where Jack Shumann sleeps (70).

_____: little whore in house where Jack sleeps (71).

_____: little whore's fat guy (71).

_____ Renaud (75): ex-senator (75).

_____: man from garage who brings Hagood's car to him (86).

170

_____: waiter in restaurant to which reporter takes Shumann quartet; speaks Italian (83); gives reporter gallon of absinth (84).

Pete (83)_____: owner of restaurant (83).

_____: mamma (83).

_____Hurtz (270): large, fat woman brought to editor by reporter (91); his mother (95); sends him postcard from honeymoon (270).

_____: owner of newspaper (91).

_____: man at airport who lends Jiggs half dollar (130).

Leonora (133)_____: "young lightcolored negress" who finds reporter lying in alley; takes his money (132-133); carries him into house; is reporter's cleaning woman (134); fills her flask with absinth (137).

_____: waitress at airport restaurant; serves reporter (140).

_____Cooper (178): reporter sent by Hagood to air meet; meets reporter with message (142-143).

Jug (142)_____: newspaper cameraman (142); lends reporter dime for phone call (162).

_____: Italian proprietor of bar at airport; argues with Jiggs (146).

_____: wife of Italian bartender (146).

_____: thick-faced man at conference table (150).

_____Leblanc (156): policeman at airport (156).

Matt (169) Ord (165): owns plane Shumann is to fly (165); former pilot (168); refuses to let Shumann fly his plane (169); plane unsafe (170); redesigns plane (172); to fly in race with Shumann (219); tries to ground airplane (227); after crash, shows note for sale of plane to reporter; burns it; calls reporter "bastard" (243).

Mrs. Matt Ord (171): Ord's wife; mother of child (168).

_____Atkinson (168): partner of Ord (168).

_____: owner of plane that Matt Ord redesigns (172).

Mac (226) Sales (173): airplane inspector (173); Federal agent (223).

_____: turnkey at jail where Jiggs is kept (180).

Mac (181)_____: desk man in police station where Jiggs is kept (181).

_____: taxicab driver who takes Shumann and Jiggs from jail (177).

_____: man and woman in store where Shumann buys sandwich for Jiggs (185).

_____: officers who arrest Laverne on first parachute jump (196-197); send her and Shumann out of town (199).

_____: minister who calls mayor when Laverne first arrested (198).

_____: man who lusts after Laverne after first parachute jump (199-200).

_____: copyboy at paper (204).

_____ Smitty (204): newspaperman (204).

_____: proofreader at paper (205).

Joe (205)_____: tavern owner or barkeep (205).

_____: two charwomen at paper (206).

_____: Greek proprietor of Dirty Spoon (210).

Dr. Carl Shumann (212): Shumann's father (212); wanted son to be a doctor; bought him first plane (274-276); lost his country home because of plane repairs; lives in small house in town (304-305); when Laverne leaves son, Jack, with him, insists she never see him again (308); wakes Jack by shaking him and calling him "Roger" (311); in rage, smashes airplane; discovers money (312); throws it in fire; collapses and cries (313).

_____: conductor on train (213).

_____: two mechanics at Ord's factory (214).

_____ Marchand (212): Cajun (215); sells airplane to Shumann in Ord's absence (216).

_____: young man with Feinman at airport hearing on grounding Ord's plane; Feinman's secretary (223).

_____: three reporters at hearing at airport (225).

_____: three oystermen who see plane plunge into lake (237).

_____: bartender who serves reporter and Jiggs (240).

_____: policeman and mechanic in diner with Laverne after crash (250).

_____: diver who searches for Shumann's plane and body (257).

_____ Hurtz (270): reporter's mother's husband (270).

Dr. _____ Legendre (270): doctor to whom Hagood sends reporter for sleeping pills (270).

_____: Laverne's sister; twenty years older; takes Laverne to live with her after parents die (276).

_____: Laverne's sister's husband (276); has sex affair with Laverne (277).

_____: Lavern's parents (276).

_____: taxi driver; takes reporter to airport (283).

_____: four reporters and policeman at salvage scene (285-286); play cards and drink waiting for dawn (288); discuss Shuman trio's sex life (289).

_____: proprietor at lunchstand at salvage site (287).

_____ Grady (291): one of four reporters (291).

_____: clerk at Hotel Terrebone (294).

_____: porter in bar; serves reporter drink (299).

_____: porter in train station in Ohio (302).

_____: cab driver in Ohio (303).

Mrs. Carl Shumann (307): Dr. Shumann's wife (307).

Begun as early as 1931 as a short story entitled "Evangeline," which was first published in *Atlantic Monthly*, 244 (November, 1979), 68-80 and then in *Uncollected Stories of William Faulkner*, 1979; continued in February, 1934 as "A Dark House" and continued in July, 1934; actual writing began March 30, 1935 by rewriting what had gone before; completed January 31, 1936. "Wash," an early version of Sutpen's death was published in *Harper's Magazine*, 168 (February, 1934) (See *Doctor Martino and Other Stories* above.); one segment, "Absalom, Absalom!" was published in *The American Mercury*, 308 (August, 1936), 466-474; published as a novel October 26, 1936.

Pagination, in parentheses, to the following edition and reissues: (*New York: Random House, 1936*), 384 pp.; (*London: Chato & Windus, 1937*); (*New York: Modern Library, 1951*), 378 pp. (*See notes by Meriwether*); (*New York: Random House, 1966*), 378 pp.; (*New York: Modern Library, 1966*), *Modern Library College Editions, paperback, 378 pp.; (New York: Vintage Books, 1972*), 378 pp., paperback.

Rosa (9) Coldfield (7): has worn black for forty-three years (1909-43 = 1866), tells history of Thomas Sutpen (7ff.); county's poetess laureate (11); once engaged to Sutpen; refuses to marry him (13); hates Sutpen for forty-three years; for an insult (14); four years younger than neice, Judith (15); 20 years old when engaged to Sutpen (19); sees defeat of South in Civil War as divine judgment (20); sees her family as cursed (21); as 4-year-old child, visits Sutpen's house with her father on Sundays (26-27); after aunt leaves, keeps house for father (28); moves to Sutpen's Hundred in 1864, after father's death; 20 years old then; born 1845; mother died in childbirth; never forgave father; raised by spinster aunt (59); feeds father secretly at night while he hides from provost marshals; starts to write heroic poetry about Southern soldiers (68); never actually sees Charles Bon dead or alive (74); makes garments for Judith's trousseau; (in Mr. Compson's account, an act of vicarious marriage to Bon) (77-78); writes portfolio of a thousand odes for Southern cause (83); resumes narration (134-172); goes to Sutpen's Hundred in 1864; driven by Wash Jones; hint of affair with his granddaughter; it is the night that Henry murders Charles Bon (134-135); Clytie tries to stop her from entering (140-142); confesses that, without having seen Bon, but only his picture, was in love with him at 14 and loved him better than Judith ever could have (144-148); is not allowed by Judith to see body (149); helps carry coffin (151); stays at Hundred waiting for Sutpen to return (154); lives there with Judith and Clytie from summer 1865 to January 1866, at which time Sutpen returns (158); three months later [April 1866] is engaged to him (158, 164); another reason for wearing black forty-three years shown (167-170); rejects Sutpen when he insults her (168-172); ultimate insult is her successor, Jones's granddaughter (171); tells Quentin that something is living at the Hundred (172); dies January 8, 1910; buried next day (173); flashback: goes to Hundred with Quentin, September, 1909 (174 ff.); Shreve guesses that insult was Sutpen's suggestion that they breed together experimentally, and, if a boy were born, they would be married; ultimate insult is her successor (177); writes Judith's epitaph;

buys and erects her tombstone (211); strikes Clytie down with fist when she tries to stop her from finding Henry at the Hundred in 1909 (350-351); returns three months later with ambulance (374).

Goodhue (212) Coldfield (7): father of Rosa and Ellen (7); Methodist steward; merchant (20); signs bond for Sutpen when he is arrested (48); dies in 1864 (59); nails himself in attic and starves to death (60); changes overnight after war starts; closes store; becomes religious fanatic (81-82); basis for withdrawal is hatred of waste (83); born in Tennessee; arrives in Mississippi in 1828 (381).

Quentin (7) Compson (9) [III]: listens to Miss Coldfield (7); preparing to enter Harvard (9); 20 years old September (10) 1909 (11); has heritage of talk about Sutpen (11); promises to return for her with a buggy (12); sits on gallery with father; discusses Sutpen's history (31); listens to Rosa's version of Sutpen's history (134-172); accompanies her to Sutpen's Hundred in September 1909 (174 ff.); in his thoughts recounts Sutpen's death and burial (181-187); quail hunting with father and Luster, finds Sutpen's graveyard (188); imagines interview between Judith and Charles Etienne St-V. Bon in which she offers to send him north as Henry's son and asks him to call her "Aunt Judith" (208); says that his father acquires knowledge of Bon's black blood from himself after he finds Henry at Hundred (266); believes that Sutpen told Henry on Christmas that Bon was his brother (269); invokes his mother's hell for Bon's incest (347); after he goes to bed, body jerks uncontrollably (360); goes to the Hundred with Rosa (362 ff.); enters room where Henry Sutpen is; interviews him (373).

Colonel (9) Thomas (30) Sutpen (9): nothusband of Rosa Coldfield (7); arrives in Jefferson with "band of wild niggers" (8); builds plantation on hundred square miles of land (8); Sutpen's Hundred (9); arrives June 1833 (11); took land from Indians (according to Rosa); not a gentleman (16); 25 years old in 1833 (17); fights "those wild negroes;" has been in church only three times (20); discovers Ellen in church (21); ceases going to church after minister talks to him about wild rides (24); drinks with Wash Jones in scuppernong arbor (26); has his wild slaves fight for entertainment; even fights them himself with children watching (29-30); forces Henry to watch (29); has short reddish beard on arrival; looks as though he has been sick (32); expert pistol shot (33); acquires hundred square miles of land; records deed with Spanish coin; then disappears (34); returns two months later with captive French architect and twenty male slaves (35, 37); speaks "a sort of French" to his slaves (36); builds mansion (36-37); after house is built, invites groups of hunters to Hundred and stages slave fights (40); borrows first seed cotton from General Compson to start plantation (40-41); refuses offer of loan from General Compson to finish house; first goes to church in 1838 where he sees Ellen Coldfield (41); got land from Ikkemotubbe (44); after deliberate seige of Mr. Coldfield and Ellen, disappears again; returns in two months with a cargo of rugs, mahogany, crystal, etc. to furnish house (43-44); is engaged to Ellen (1838); arrested on suspicion about furniture (47); married in June 1838, two months after arrest (48); desired big wedding (49); refuse is thrown at couple as they leave church (56-57); returns from war in 1866 (61); visits New Orleans summer 1860 (70); about 1858, "the biggest single landowner and cotton-planter in the county" (72); raises regiment with Colonel Sartoris; second in command in 1861; nearly 55 (80); visits New Orleans and (according to Mr. Compson) learns of Bon's association with non-white mistress (92-93); decides to prevent Judith's marriage (93); [from page 92 to end of chapter, constant hints that what Sutpen discovered was the mistress, not that Charles Bon was his own son]; elected Colonel when Colonel Sartoris is deposed by his own officers (126); returns from war January 1866; is engaged to Rosa Coldfield three months later (158); fails at first to recognize Rosa (159); is 59 in 1866; determines to restore the Hundred (160); refuses to join vigilantes (161); is killed by Wash Jones (171-172, 184 ff., 284 ff.); killed in 1869 (188, 381) because he seduced Jones's 15-year-old granddaughter and then scorned her when she bore a girl (183, 185); [discrepancy in date on page 185; Judith is said to be 30 when Sutpen died; thus date of death would appear to be 1871 here.]; buried by daughter, Judith, after coffin falls into ditch (186); Sutpen dies August 12, 1869; ordered his and Ellen's tombstones from Italy while at war (188); born in 1807 in what was to become West Virginia; early life narrated (220-238); formulates "design" after being turned away from front door by black; went to West Indies to start fortune (238); put his first wife aside because she did not fit his design (240); attended school for a few months (241-242); engaged in vaguely described gun battle in West Indies (246 ff.); realizes that he has to learn new language; repudiated wife was West Indian; Sutpen a virgin before marriage (248); subdues natives; is engaged after recovering from wounds (254); also repudiates his child (262); settles his conscience by leaving whole Haitian estate to repudiated wife and child, taking only about twenty blacks (262-263); (according to Quentin) knows instantly on seeing Bon that his design is about to collapse, but attributes it to a mistake (267-268); speaks to Henry on battlefield (276); Quentin's version of seduction of Milly (281 ff.); (according to Shreve) reacts in no way to first meeting with Bon (320); meets son on battlefield (353); tells Henry that Bon's mother was partly black (355).

Ellen (9) Coldfield (7) Sutpen (9): sister of Rosa Coldfield (7); mother of son and daughter (9); asks sister to care for Judith (18); after wild rides to church, substitutes phaeton and tame mare and stableboy for wild slave and carriage (25); accepts fighting of slaves; rejects having children watch (29-30); wears powder to hide tears at wedding to Sutpen (48-49); in her late 30's twenty years after her marriage (68-69); loses her reason about 1852 (69-70); born October 9, 1817; died January 23, 1863 (188); but see contradiction in "Chronology" and "Genealogy" where she is listed as born in Tennessee in 1818 and died in 1862 (379, 381, 382).

Henry (18) Sutpen (9): son of Sutpen and Ellen Coldfield (9); repudiates heritage; murderer and "almost a fratricide" (according to Rosa Coldfield) (15); kills sister's sweetheart (18); two years older than Judith and six years older than Rosa Coldfield [therefore born about 1839] (21); forced by father to watch him fight black slaves; vomits (29); 26 years old in 1864; enters university about 1857 (70); brings Charles Bon home for Christmas 1859) and for a week of summer 1860 (70); brings Bon home following Christmas; disappears with Bon after quarrel with father; formally abjures his father; renounces his birthright (79); private in Confederate Army (87); scarcely 20 when he repudiates father; leaves note for Judith declaring armistice (91); studies law like Bon (102); argument with father takes place on December 24, 1860 (105); meets Bon's mistress and child (114-118); joins company formed at university (119); hopes war will settle problem (120); rescues Bon in battle when Bon is wounded (according to Mr. Compson) (124); kills Charles Bon before his father's house for implied reason that, though he will marry Judith, he will not renounce his mistress (132-133); disappears; (according to Shreve) Henry is wounded, not Bon (344); Quentin imagines him at last accepting the incest (347); meets father on battlefield (353); tells father he will accept incest (354); decides to kill Bon because of miscegenation, not incest, if he tries to marry Judith (355); returns to Hundred four years before Quentin finds him (373).

Judith (15) Sutpen (9): daughter of Sutpen and Ellen Coldfield (9); widow without having been a bride (15); screams when the wild rides to church end; (according to Rosa) urges wild black to make team run away (25); with Clytie, watches father fight wild slave (30); born 1841 (59); gives letter from Charles Bon to Quentin's grandmother (94); buries Bon beside her mother (104); waits four years for Bon with no direct word from him (121); nurses wounded during war while waiting for news of Henry and Bon (125-126); for no apparent reason, gives only letter from Bon to Quentin's grandmother (126-128); after much obliqueness, letter, written in 1865, proposes marriage (129-132); with Clytie, makes wedding gown of scraps (132); meets Rosa outside room where Bon's body lies; holds her own picture in hand (142); refuses to allow Rosa to see Bon's body (149); bursts into tears when she tells father that Henry killed Bon (159); 30 when father dies (185); buries father and reads the service (186); sells store in 1870; uses money from sale to buy headstone for Charles Bon; wrong place of birth put on headstone (190-191); asks General Compson to go to court when Charles Etienne St.-V. Bon is arrested; then 40 years old (201-203); nurses Charles Etienne St.-V., Bon; gets yellow fever; dies before he does (210); born October 3, 1841; died February 12, 1884 (210-211).

_____: French architect; arrives with Sutpen (8); stays with Sutpen two years; from Martinique (35); makes abortive attempt to escape (218); travels through trees for half a mile to elude trackers (239).

_____: small black boy who delivers Rosa Coldfield's note summoning Quentin (10).

[Jason Richmond] Compson (9): Quentin's father (11); takes over narration of Sutpen's history (43); resumes narration (61); knows of "the one before Clytie" (62); speculates on Sutpen's visit to New Orleans (70); shows limitation as narrator when telling about Henry and Bon's break with Sutpen: "Something happened." (79); introduces theme of incest between Henry and Judith (79-80); takes over narration (89-128); in his narration of the story, ignores blood relationship and miscegenation (89 ff.); [from page 92 to page 104 ff. constant hinting that what Sutpen

178

discovered was the mistress, not that Charles Bon is his son]; introduces theme of homosexual attraction between Henry and Bon and vicarious incest between and among Henry, Bon, and Judith (95-96); finally gives up attempt to explain ban on marriage: "It is just incredible. It just does not explain. Or perhaps that's it: they don't explain and we are not supposed to know." (100); reconstructs imaginatively the trip to New Orleans by Henry and Bon; in his version, Mr. Compson imagines that Henry does not tell Bon what his father told him on Christmas Eve; that he knew that what his father told him was true (106 ff.); again homosexual and incest themes are repeated (107-108); imagines that Henry balks at Catholic wedding ceremony rather than the black mistress and child; implies that Henry and Judith knew that Clytie is their half-sister (109); reconstructs meeting of Henry and Bon's mistress and son, and reconstructs scene in which Bon tells Henry of his aquistion of the octaroon (114-118); shows Quentin Bon's letter to Judith (128); takes over narration to tell of visit of octaroon to Charles Bon's grave (192-207).

General (33) [Jason Lycurgus] Compson (9): Quentin's grandfather; nearest thing to a friend that Sutpen had (12); lends Sutpen seed cotton; offers to lend him money to finish home (40-41); signs Sutpen's bond when he is arrested (48); goes to court when Charles Etienne St.-V. Bon is arrested; pays his fine (201-204); gives him money to leave town (204); colonel of regiment in which Henry and Bon's company is a part; lost right arm at Pittsburgh Landing (270); becomes brigadier (276); overhears Wash Jones questioning Sutpen about Milly's dress (284).

_____ Coldfield (16): Goodhue Coldfield's father in Tennessee (16).

_____: Goodhue Coldfield's grandfather in Virginia (16).

_____: Goodhue Coldfield's two blacks; freed when he acquired them (20); women disappear after his death (84).

_____ Coldfield (23): paternal (42) aunt to Ellen and Rosa (23); leaves Coldfield home (28); writes a hundred invitations to the wedding (53); goes from house to house to reinforce the invitations (54); virgin (60); climbs out window and vanishes (64); elopes with horse and mule trader (76); last heard of trying to pass Yankee lines to visit husband in prison (84-85).

_____: Sutpen's wild black slave; driver of carriage that carries Ellen, Judith, Henry, and Sutpen to church (23).

_____: minister who tells Sutpen not to drive wildly to church (24).

_____: black stableboy slave who drives Ellen and children to church (25).

Wash Jones (26): drinks with Sutpen in scuppernong arbor (26);

calls Rosa Coldfield (87); reports killing of Bon by Henry in 1864 (134); makes Bon's coffin (150); has one daughter who had illegitimate daughter who bears Sutpen's child (171-172); kills Sutpen with rusty scythe (172) dies twelve hours after Sutpen (186); supplies Mrs. Sutpen, Judith, and Clytie with game during war (281); questions Sutpen about Milly's dress; knows that Sutpen will "make hit right" (284); kills Sutpen with scythe (285 ff.); has moment of tragic vision of his relationship with Sutpen before he cuts throats of granddaughter and great granddaughter (290-291); runs toward posse with scythe; is killed by Major de Spain (292).

Clytie Clytemnestra (61) Sutpen (9): Sutpen's black daughter (30); should have been named Cassandra (according to Mr. Compson) (62); 74 years old in 1909 (136); stops Rosa from entering room where Judith prepares Bon's body for burial (138 ff.); goes to New Orleans to bring back Charles Etienne St.-V. Bon, December 1871 (195); guards Charles Etienne St.-V. Bon fiercely (200); buries Judith and pays for tombstone for Charles Etienne St.-V. Bon (210); stops Wash Jones from entering house during war (281); opens door for Rosa on night she finds Henry; struck down by Rosa when she tries to stop her (369); sets fire to house; kills Henry and herself (374 ff.).

_____ Holston (31): one of the founders of Jefferson (31).

_____: Chickasaw Indian agent through whom Sutpen acquires land (34).

_____: County Recorder who records deed for Sutpen's Hundred (34).

_____ Akers (36): coon-hunter; discovers one of Sutpen's slaves sleeping in mud (36).

_____ Coldfield (42): Goodhue Coldfield's mother (42).

Ikkemotubbe (44): Indian from whom Sutpen acquires land (44).

_____: sheriff of county; with eight or ten men arrests Sutpen (46-47).

Judge (46) _____ Benbow (46): an early friend of Sutpen (46); leaves baskets of provisions for Rosa Coldfield (170); supports Rosa Coldfield for years by giving her money from mythical estate of her father (212).

_____: justice before whom Sutpen is arraigned (48).

Mrs. [Jason Lycurgus] Compson (54): Quentin's grandmother; wife of General Compson; not a native of Jefferson (54).

Mrs. Goodhue Coldfield (59): Goodhue Coldfield's wife; mother of Ellen and Rosa; dies in childbirth with Rosa; at least 40 when Rosa born

180

(59).

_____: two female slaves that Sutpen brought to Jefferson; one is mother of Clytie (61).

Charles Bon (67): Sutpen's son, "the one before Clytie" (62); visits the Hundred Christmas 1859; summer 1860; home is New Orleans (70); a few years older than Henry; appears to have no parents but a guardian (74); engaged to Judith (75); returns with Henry following Christmas (1860) (78); disappears with Henry after quarrel (79); private in Confederate Army (87); from page 89 to page 128, Mr. Compson's views prevail; has child whose picture Judith finds on his body (90); has non-white mistress; sees mistress as no real barrier to marriage (92); really loves Judith but she is not the first to whom he has been pledged (94); mistress is octaroon (95); seduced Henry "as surely as he seduced Judith" (96); Henry gives him four years to renounce mistress (97); never tries to force engagement or marriage; yet Henry "had to kill Bon to keep them from marrying" (99); reads law at university (102) Mr. Compson imaginatively reconstructs scene in which Charles Bon explains to Henry his marriage to octaroon (116-118); joins company organized at university (119); becomes lieutenant before first battle (124); proposes to Judith in letter (129-132); is killed by Henry (132-133); dies May 3, 1865, aged 33 years and 5 months (134 ff., 190); wounded at Pittsburgh Landing (270); according to Shreve, 28 when he went to university (307); attendance at university arranged by lawyer (311); according to Shreve, recognizes brotherhood on meeting Henry (313-314); after meeting Henry (according to Shreve who changes his opinion), recognizes joint parentage (317); wants Sutpen simply to let him know that he is his son; not to acknowledge him (according to Shreve) (319); vainly waits for some sign from father (326-327); Shreve projects an incest theme/homosexual theme (328); Quentin thinks of Bon yearning for chance at recognition; finally decides to marry Judith and writes letter (347); mother repudiated because of black blood (355); confronts Henry with acknowledgment of black blood; tells Henry, "So it's the miscegenation, not the incest, which you can not bear" (356); tells Henry that he will have to stop him from marrying Judith; offers him pistol (357-358); is killed by Henry.

_____: Sutpen's overseer about 1858; son of sheriff who arrested Sutpen (72).

_____: Charles Bon's legal guardian (74).

_____: horse and mule trader; elopes with Rosa's aunt (76); jailed for offering to trade with Confederates (85).

Colonel (80) [John] Sartoris (80): with Sutpen, raises regiment that departed in 1861 (80); deposed by his own men; replaced by Sutpen (126).

_____ Bon: Charles Bon's octaroon mistress (92); brought to Bon's grave with her son in 1870 by Judith (192-193); stays a week (194); dies about December 1871 (195).

Charles Etienne Saint-Valery Bon (191): son of Charles Bon and octaroon (93); found by Clytie in New Orleans and brought back to Sutpen's Hundred; born 1859; dies 1884 (191); undergoes childhood despair while being tended by Judith and Clytie (198 ff.); begins to associate with blacks; gets into knife fight with blacks; is arrested (201-202); leaves town; returns with black woman; has son (205); constantly defies whites and blacks (206); has yellow fever (see contradiction in "Genealogy."); moved to house by Judith who nurses him and gets same disease (209-210); dies February 1884 (211).

_____: porter who admits Bon and Henry to octaroon's house (112).

Melicent Jones [382]: Wash Jones's child (125); rumored to have died in a Memphis brothel (171).

Milly (185) Jones [383]: Wash Jones's granddaughter (125); unmarried mother of Sutpen's daughter (171); tells her grandfather that Judith gave her dress and helped make it (283); killed by grandfather; throat cut (291).

_____: white man who helps Wash Jones make Bon's coffin (150).

Theophilus McCaslin (152): attends Bon's funeral and gives Rebel yell in lieu of prayer (152).

_____: one or two men who help Sutpen and Jones restore the Hundred (161).

_____: vigilantes who try unsuccessfully to have Sutpen join them (161-162).

Shreve (173) Shrevlin McCannon [383] [named McKenzie in *The Sound and the Fury*]: Quentin's roommate at Harvard (173); fat; wears glasses (181); born in Alberta, Canada (258); 19 in 1910 (294); narrator; tells his version of Bon's mother's vengeance (293 ff.); (according to Shreve) Bon does not know he is Henry's and Judith's half-brother (295); recounts Bon's explanation of marriage to octaroon to his mother (308); like Mr. Compson, posits homosexual/incestuous relationship among Henry, Bon, and Judith (328); moves to believe that Bon knows Sutpen is his father (329); imagines Bon waiting for Sutpen to act before he and Henry depart (329-333); invents an interview between Henry and Bon and Eulalia Sutpen (335); and an interview with lawyer whom Bon slaps and offers to duel (336-339); imagines Henry getting used to idea of incest (340-341); imagines Bon giving Henry a chance to shoot him in battle to settle the matter; insists that it is Henry and not Bon who is wounded (344); believes Bon substituted octaroon's picture for Judith's as a way of telling Judith he was no good (359).

_____: black midwife who tends Milly [called Dicey in "Wash"]

182

(185); found a week later (285).

_____Jones-Sutpen: daughter of Thomas Sutpen; great granddaughter of Wash Jones (185); throat cut by Jones after birth (291).

Luster (187)_____: black servant of Compson family (187).

_____: Sutpen's body servant in war; drives wagon with tombstones (189).

_____: Quentin's aunt and her kinswoman (192).

_____: "gigantic negress" who attends Bon's octaroon (109); visits his grave in 1870 (193).

_____: black boy with whom Charles Etienne St.-V. Bon plays; Clytie curses him out of sight (195).

Jim Hamblett (203): justice before whom Charles Etienne St.-V. Bon is tried for fighting (202-203).

_____Bon: "coal black and ape-like woman;" wife of Charles Etienne St.-V. Bon (205).

Jim Bond (214): son of Charles Etienne St.-V. Bon (205).

_____: county medical officer; tells General Compson that Charles Etienne St.-V. Bon has yellow fever (209-210).

Percy Benbow (212): son of Judge Benbow (212).

_____: wagon full of strangers from Arkansas who stop at Hundred (213).

_____: five boys including Luster and Quentin who approach Hundred and find Jim Bond and Clytie (214).

_____Sutpen: Sutpen's mother (223).

_____Sutpen: Sutpen's father (223).

_____Sutpen: rest of Sutpen's family (223).

_____: first black man Sutpen ever saw (225).

_____Pettibone (231): landowner in barrel-stave hammock whom Sutpen watches (228).

_____: black servant who sends young Sutpen away from front door (229-230).

_____: teacher in one-room school that Sutpen attends for a few months (241).

Eulalia [381] Sutpen: Sutpen's first wife; repudiated by him because she did not fit the design (240); helps Sutpen load muskets in West Indies (247); mother of Charles Bon (256); repudiated because of her black blood (266).

_____: French sugar planter in West Indies (246); father of Eulalia Sutpen (247); not named Bon (266).

_____: Eulalia Sutpen's mother; Spanish (252).

_____: two women servants in seige with Sutpen in Haiti (253).

_____: black groom who carries letters from Jefferson to university (268).

Major [Cassius] de Spain (291): sheriff (291); kills Wash Jones (292).

_____: lawyer (invented by Shreve?) to Charles Bon's mother; keeps record of Sutpen's progress (300 ff.); (according to Shreve) hatches plan to involve Bon with Judith (309-310); in Shreve's account, sends letter of introduction to Henry about Bon (313).

_____: orderly who fetches Henry to meet father (352).

_____: sentry outside Sutpen's tent (352).

Colonel _____ Willow (351): tells Sutpen Henry was wounded (353).

_____: driver of ambulance that comes for Henry (374).

_____: second man in ambulance (374).

Individual stories written from spring, 1934 to mid-1936, and all but "An Odor of Verbena" published in magazines: "Ambuscade," written in spring, 1934; first published in *The Saturday Evening Post*, 207 (September 29, 1934), 12-13, 80, 81; "Retreat," written spring, 1934; first published in *The Saturday Evening Post*, 207 (October 13, 1934), 16-17, 82, 84, 85, 87, 89; "Raid," written late spring, 1934; first published in *The Saturday Evening Post*, 207 (November 3, 1934), 18-19, 72, 73, 75, 77, 78; "Riposte in Tertio," written and revised by late 1934 or early 1935; first published as "The Unvanquished," in *The Saturday Evening Post*, 209 (November 14, 1936), 12-13, 121, 122, 124, 126, 128, 130; retitled "Riposte in Tertio" in the novel; "Vendee," written in September, 1934, and completed October 18, 1934; first published in *The Saturday Evening Post*, 209 (December 5, 1936), 16-17, 86, 87, 90, 92, 94; "Skirmish at Sartoris," written about late 1934 and entitled, "Drusilla;" first published in *Scribner's Magazine*, 97 (April, 1935), 193-200; all revised for *The Unvanquished*; "An Odor of Verbena," written about June-July, 1936, and completed July 24, 1937; first published in *The Unvanquished February 15, 1938*.

Pagination, in parentheses, to the following edition and reissues: (New York: Random House, 1938), 293 pp.; (New York: Vintage Books, 1966), paperback; (London: Chatto & Windus, 1967).

Ringo (3) Marengo (21): slave; born same month and raised with Bayard (7); asks Yankee officer for more mules and food (129); takes over driving wagon (131); is Granny's spy; learns the unit identification and commanding officer's name of Yankee units (141); has drawn map of neighborhood on a shade to keep track of mule deals (142-143); has developed way of not saying "mister" when speaking of white men (143); steals U. S. Army stationery that Granny uses for requisitions (144); when Yankees capture Granny, decoys them into woods; then picks up Granny and Bayard in "borrowed" buggy (149-151); draws picture of Sartoris house as it was before it was burned (160); blames Ab Snopes for telling where mules were hidden (168); whips Ab Snopes (200); stabs Grumby (209); reports carpetbaggers in Jefferson to Bayard (229); brings news to Bayard at college that Colonel John Sartoris has been shot (245); assumes lead in getting Bayard back to Jefferson (245-246); he and Bayard are then 24 (248); wants to bushwack Redmond, but knows Bayard will not (251); follows Bayard to town after John Sartoris's death (282); has pistol in shirt (283).

Bayard (8) Sartoris [II] (26): narrator (3); 12 years old at start (5) son of John Sartoris (6); born same month as Ringo and raised with him (7); with Ringo, transfers stock to new pen (15); mother dies in childbirth (17); with Ringo, watches Loosh for days (23-24); sees him ride off on mule (24); hears him announce that Sherman is about to free blacks; tells Granny (25-26); shoots at Yankee soldier (29); hits horse and it must be destroyed (33); carries some Sartoris dirt to Memphis (62-63); with Ringo, takes old white horse to recover mules stolen by Yankees (68); found by his father (69-70); they find Granny gone (71); on road to find silver and mules, they reach Hawkhurst (97); finds that Yankees have destroyed railroad (100); watches Yankee soldiers beating ex-slaves back from bridge (119); after soldiers blow up bridge, wagon swept into river (122); horses drown; wagon crosses river; Yankee horses put in harness; soldiers take them to camp (123); after Granny's funeral, asks Uncle Buck to lend him pistol (181); with Uncle Buck and Ringo, finds Grumby's horses in Ab Snopes's lot (185); fights Ab Snopes (199-200); shoots Grumby (209-210); he and Ringo nail Grumby's body to compress (cotton press) and his right hand to board over Granny's grave (213); keeps insisting that, because he is only 15, does not know why Mrs. Habersham and the ladies are upset about Drusilla living in cabin with John Sartoris (225); studies law at college for three years (243); intuits that father has been shot (244); is now The Sartoris (247); is now 24 (248); realizes his duty to avenge his father (248); but will not (249); when he was 20, argues with Drusilla about father's dream that includes killing carpet-baggers and others (256-257); after he kisses Drusilla, fails to tell his father (264-265); finally tells him after dinner (266); tells Aunt Jenny he is not going to kill Redmond (276); rides to town next day (282); refuses to let Ringo (and his pistol) accompany him (283); refuses George Wyatt's pistol; tells him to stay out of it (284); confronts Redmond unarmed; lets him shoot at him twice (286-288); returns home to sleep for five hours; wakes up crying (290).

Joby (4): slave; had come to Mississippi from Carolina with John Sartoris as his body servant (18).

Loosh (4): slave; son of Joby, uncle to Ringo (4); son of Louvinia (23); gallops off to Corinth on mule; returns after dark next day (24); announces that General Sherman is going to free "the race" (25-26); shows Yankees where silver is hidden in orchard (84); leaves with Philadelphy, saying that he is free (85).

Philadelphy (4): slave; wife of Loosh (4).

John (6) Sartoris (26): father of narrator (6); returns from Civil War in Tennessee (9); wears captured Yankee trousers and builds stock pen in creek bottom (12-13); buries family silver after fall of Vicksburg (20); leaves to return to war (21); reward is set for him (42); is demoted from rank of colonel by men (56); now leads band of fifty men; steals Yankee horses (60); instructed Granny to go to Memphis (64); taking Ringo and Bayard back home, surprises troop of Yankees; captures them; takes their trousers and boots (76-77); as he sits on porch, Yankee troop rides up (81); escapes on Jupiter (83); returns from war just after Bayard and Ringo murder Grumby (212); works against Reconstructionists (228); leaves cabin to Drusilla; he and Bayard sleep in cabin with Joby and Ringo (231); tells Burdens that election will not be held; they defy him (232); with Drusilla on their wedding day, kills two Burdens with derringer (237); lets Burdens fire first (238); conducts election to defeat black candidate, Cassius Q. Benbow (241); is shot to death (244); marries Drusillaa and rebuilds his house (253); has killed a man who seemed about to rob him (254-255); hates Sutpen (255-256); challenges Sutpen to duel (256); beats Redmond in election for state legislature; partnership with Redmond dissolved; now enemy of Redmond; dictatorial (258); taunts Redmond about not serving in army; when railroad is finished, makes public remark about Redmond (259-260); after Bayard tells him that he kissed Drusilla, does not care; discusses future plans; says he will not be armed next day when he meets Redmond (266); has derringer but does not use it when he is killed (268).

Granny (7) Rosa (10) Millard (118): hides Ringo and Bayard under skirts after they shoot at Yankee (31); lies to protect them (35); washes their mouths for calling Yankees "bastuds" (40); orders Loosh and Joby to dig up silver chest because she dreamed a black man pointed to it; plans to take it to Memphis (42-43); says goodbye to Mrs. Compson (52); John Sartoris's mother-in-law; sister lives in Memphis (64); beats Yankee soldiers with umbrella as they steal mules (66); drives back home with strange horses; meets John Sartoris and boys; they bury trunk again in orchard (80); stole the horses (81); after Yankees burn house, she and boys call them "bastuds" (86); sends Ringo and Bayard to Jefferson to borrow hat, parasol, and hand mirror from Mrs. Compson; now lives in Joby's cabin (88); Yankees have stolen silver (89); they leave to recover silver and mules (90); after several days, they are passed by group of blacks walking the road (95); they pick up black woman and baby (96); leave her at creek; Ringo says other blacks are hiding there (97); after they cross river, demands to see Colonel Dick; demands silver, mules, and "darkies" (124); sent back with ten chests of silver; one hundred and ten mules, and one hundred blacks; says, "It's the hand of God." (128); kneels with Ringo and Bayard to pray after they return with one hundred and twenty-two mules and horses (134); steals back mules Ab Snopes sells to Yankees (137); has printed letterheads and forges requisitions (137); with Ringo, burns out U. S. brands on mules (138); sold back one hundred and five mules to Yankees (139); next time she requisitions mules, Yankees chase her, recognizing forged order; Army has sent out order about her (149); two hundred, forty-six mules stolen; mule trading over (152); next day, goes to church; confesses she has sinned; asks people to pray for her (156); then doles out money she made on last batch of mules (157); Yankee army withdraws from that part of Mississippi (159); after Yankee lieutenant takes last mules, takes Ringo and Bayard to church and prays (167); learns of Grumby's Independents (raiders) from Ab Snopes (170); insists on going alone after Grumby's horses, believing that no man would hurt an old woman (174); Grumby kills her (174-175); is buried (177).

Louvinia (8): slave; wife of Joby; grandmother to Ringo (8).

Uncle Dennison (15) Hawk (231): dead uncle of Bayard (15).

Celia Cook (17): girl who scratches her name on window with diamond ring as General Forrest rides into Oxford (17).

_____ Sartoris (26): mother of Bayard II; dies in childbirth (17).

Simon (18): slave; Ringo's father (18); accompanies John Sartoris to war as his body servant (19); sits by body of John Sartoris (277).

_____ Harrison (34): Yankee soldier who comes to Sartoris place; sergeant (32).

Colonel Nathaniel G. Dick (88): Yankee colonel (34); takes Granny's word that there are no children in the house (35); arranges to give Granny all the silver, mules, and blacks (124-125).

Mrs. _____ Compson (52): arranges for minister from Memphis to preach at Granny's funeral, but Bro. Fortinbride prevents it (178); invites Ringo and Bayard to live with her until John Sartoris returns (180); husband was "locked up for crazy" for shooting potatoes off heads of black children (222) [Evidently not wife of General Compson.]

Theophilus (Buck) McCaslin (52): he and his brother ritualistically lock their slaves in the manor house without windows or a back door; poker players (53); twins; believe people belong to land and slaves earn freedom by working the land; they have land scheme involving white trash small farmers (55-57); they want to volunteer (they are over 70) in John Sartoris's regiment; play cards to see who goes to war (55-57); helps bury Granny (179); joins Ringo and Bayard to hunt Grumby (182); is shot by one of Grumby's men (194); arm gets worse; goes home; takes Ab Snopes with him (201); gives pistol to Bayard (202); praises boys for murder of Grumby (213).

Amodeus (Buddy) McCaslin (52): won card game; became sergeant (57).

[Lucius Quintus Carothers] McCaslin (52): father of Theophilus and Amodeus (52).

_____: Southern captain who accompanies Uncle Buck (58).

_____: Southern officer who meets Granny on road to Memphis; warns her of Yankee patrols (63).

_____: sister of Rosa Millard; lives in Memphis (64).

Uncle Few Mitchell (83): a loony (83).

Denny (98) Dennison (230) Hawk (231): Bayard's cousin (98); later reads law in Montgomery (292).

Jingus (98): slave in Hawk family (98).

Drusilla (100) Hawk (231) Sartoris (253): best horsewoman in county; Bayard's cousin; wears pants (101); saves horse from Yankees by threatening to kill it (103); describes ex-slaves as they march "to Jordan" (104); tells boys of destruction of railroad (109); tells Bayard that she wants to ride with John Sartoris (115); joins John Sartoris in Carolina; rides like a man (170); returns from war with Sartoris (212-213);

188

expresses no grief over death of fiance and father in war (217); dresses as a private (220); cries in Louvinia's arms after ladies visit her (227); is made to wear dress by mother; stops working at mill (231); appointed voting commissioner (238); offers Bayard duelling pistols (252); marries John Sartoris (253); tells Bayard that there are worse things than killing men (261); with odor of verbena in hair, forces Bayard to kiss her; eight years older than Bayard (262); puts sprig of verbena in Bayard's lapel (263); kisses him again and urges him to tell his father (264); hands Bayard duelling pistols beside his father's coffin (273); gives Bayard sprig of verbena next day; crushes other sprig with foot; makes very Romantic speech on beauty of vengeance (274); when she realizes that Bayard is not going to kill Redmond, becomes hysterical (275); before Bayard returns after confronting Redmond, leaves Jefferson to live with brother Dennison in Montgomery (292); leaves sprig of verbena on Bayard's pillow (293).

Gavin Breckbridge (101): engaged to Drusilla Hawk; killed at Shiloh (101).

Louise (105) Louisa (106) Hawk (231): Drusilla's mother; Bayard's aunt; sister of John Sartoris's first wife (105); name most often spelled *Louisa* (170); writes to Granny to find Drusilla (217-218); writes to Mrs. Compson after Drusilla and John Sartoris return (220); upset about Drusilla living in same cabin with John Sartoris (222); arrives with Drusilla's dresses (230); asks John Sartoris to marry Drusilla (233).

Missy Lena (112): in whose cabin Ringo sleeps at Hawkhurst (112).

_____: Yankee officer who gets silver and mules for Miss Rosa (125); gives her ten chests of silver, one hundred and ten Mississippi mules, and offers one hundred blacks (126).

_____: Yankee officer who gives Granny forty-seven more mules (129).

Captain _____ Bowen (132): Yankee officer mentioned by lieutenant (132).

Ab Snopes (135): takes nine of Granny's mules to Memphis to sell for four hundred and fifty dollars (135); John Sartoris told him to look after Granny; sells mules for her (136); tells Yankees where Granny keeps mules (168); convinces Granny to write requisition for Grumby's horses (172-173); Buck, Bayard, and Ringo find him tied to tree (197).

Colonel G. W. Newberry (141): Yankee officer, Illinois Infantry; target of Granny Millard (141).

_____ Fortinbride (152): Methodist non-minister of Granny's church (153); John Sartoris sent this private back home wounded (154); prevents other minister from preaching at Granny's funeral (178); preaches (180).

Dr. Worsham (153): original Episcopal minister of Granny's church (153).

_____: Yankee lieutenant who overtakes Granny and Bayard after last mule requisition (149); arrives at Sartoris place (159); goes to lot where mules are kept; has all forged orders; pays for fence torn down; (164-165); takes mules (166).

_____ Grumby (170): leader of group of white riders who ravage country after Yankees leave (170); carries tattered raiding commission signed by General Forrest (171); kills Granny as Bayard and Ringo chase him; leaves threatening note tied to a hanged black man (203); is captured and tied up by stranger, who leaves him to boys after untying him; throwing pistol at his feet (205-207); tries to shoot Bayard; Ringo stabs him and Bayard shoots him as he runs away (209-210).

_____: minister brought in by Mrs. Compson to preach at Granny's funeral (178).

_____ Snopes (185): Ab Snopes's wife; tells Uncle Buck that Ab has gone to Alabama (185).

Matt Bowden (208): stranger who is also hunting Grumby; bearded, black hair; from Tennessee (189): advises boys to stick to hunting Ab Snopes and leave Grumby to him (193); shoots Uncle Buck (194); adds postscript to Grumby's threatening note (203); captures Grumby; turns him over to Ringo and Bayard (205-207).

_____ Bridger (205): companion to Matt Bowden (205).

_____ Compson (222): husband of Mrs. Compson; shoots sweet potatoes from heads of black children (222).

Mrs. Martha (225) Habersham (215): visits Sartoris place with Mrs. Compson and delegation of ladies in outrage over Drusilla living in same cabin with John Sartoris (223-224); joins Aunt Louisa in planning Drusilla's wedding (234); forces marriage of John Sartoris and Drusilla (253).

Cassius Q. Benbow (228): ex-slave who returns to Jefferson as Acting Marshal; hopes to be elected marshal (228-229).

_____ Benbow (229): family name (229).

[Calvin] Burden [I] (229): from Missouri; sent from Washington to organize blacks (229); killed by John Sartoris (237).

[Calvin] Burden [II] (229): killed by John Sartoris (237).

George Wyatt (237): attempts to hold Drusilla while Sartoris kills Burdens; holds Bayard instead (237); predicts that Sartoris has gone too far in insulting Redmond (260); offers to kill Redmond for Bayard (268); offers Bayard a pistol (284).

Mrs. _____ Holston (237): in whose house Sartoris kills Burdens (237).

_____: Mrs. Holston's black porter (237).

Mrs. _____ Wilkins (243): Bayard boards in her home while reading law (243); lost son in last battle of Civil War (247).

Professor (243) Judge (244) _____ Wilkins (243): breaks news of Bayard's father's death (245).

Jenny (247) [Virginia Sartoris Du Pre]: Bayard's aunt (247); comes to live with brother John Sartoris and Drusilla after their marriage (253); John Sartoris names locomotive after her (259); husband killed at Fort Moultrie; brings colored glass in hamper (271); after Bayard returns from facing Redmond, cries and says, "Damn you!" (292).

_____ Hilliard (250): owner (?) of livery stable in Oxford from whom Ringo gets fresh horse (250).

Ben (266) J. (285) Redmond (251): former partner of John Sartoris in railroad (251-252); had not been soldier in war (258); kills John Sartoris (268); an attorney (285); fires two shots at Bayard, deliberately missing him, and leaves town forever (286-288).

_____ Habersham (253): husband of Mrs. Habersham; works in bank (253).

_____: man killed by John Sartoris along railroad (254).

_____: wife of man killed by John Sartoris; flings money in his face (255).

Colonel [Thomas] Sutpen (255): replaces John Sartoris as Colonel in his first regiment (255); rebuilds plantation; refuses to have anything to do with nightriders; refuses to duel with Sartoris (256).

[Henry] Sutpen (255): son of Colonel Sutpen; kills sister's fiance (255).

[Judith] Sutpen (255): daughter of Colonel Sutpen (255).

[Charles Bon]: fiance of [Judith] Sutpen; killed by [Henry] Sutpen (255).

Judge _____ Benbow (259): arranges for John Sartoris to buy Redmond's share of the railroad (259).

_____ [Du Pre]: husband of Virginia Sartoris Du Pre; killed in

191

Civil War (263).

Bayard Sartoris [I] (271): brother of John Sartoris [I] and Virginia Sartoris Du Pre (271).

Jed (292) White (288): carries news of Bayard's safety home (292).

General [Jason Lycurgus] Compson (282).

The short story, "The Wild Palms," became the first chapter of the novel; written between September 15, 1937 and June 15, 1938, and originally entitled *If I Forget Thee, Jerusalem*; novel published January 19, 1939. Alternate chapters entitled "Wild Palms" and "Old Man."

Pagination, in parentheses, to the following edition and reissue: (New York: Random House, 1939), 339 pp.; (New York: Vintage Books, 1964), 339 pp., paperback.

_____: doctor; 48 years old (3); takes gumbo to woman next door; sees hatred in her eyes; knows her to be sick (10-11); angrily demands to know who performed the abortion; says Harry murdered Charlotte (279-280); calls for ambulance and policeman (282); returns to Charlotte's room with pistol (289).

Martha (6)_____: wife of doctor (3); makes gumbo for neighbors (5); urges husband to send Charlotte and Harry out of town (290).

_____: doctor's father (3); picked out doctor's wife for him; a doctor (4).

Dr. (33) Henry (31) Harry (12) Wilbourne (21): wakes doctor (3); rents cottage next to doctor; wants to use phone to call doctor (14); says he is trying to be painter (18); flashback: intern in hospital in New Orleans where he met Charlotte; youngest of three children; orphaned at 2; raised by older half-sister (31); born 1910 (32); 27 (1937); goes to party (33); meets Charlotte and Rat there (39-40); dines with Rittenmeyers (42); after Rat retires, without any other talk, he and Charlotte declare love for each other (42-43); meets Charlotte five more times at lunch (43); plans to have sex with Charlotte in hotel after asking Flint how to go about it (44-45); she rejects back-alley atmosphere (44 ff.); they depart without sex (50); finds 1278 dollars in wallet in trash bin (51); uses the money to take Charlotte to Chicago (53); takes Charlotte to drawing room on train for first sex (59-60); in Chicago, tries to get employment in hospitals (84); gets job finally as laboratory technician (85); loses job; conceals fact from Charlotte (90-91); fired because of inquiries from detective sent by Rittenmeyer; Charlotte forgot to send monthly report (96); buys food with last hundred dollars; he and she go to McCord's cabin (99 ff.); they stay there; no attempt to find work (99 ff.); feels bored (112); color blind (113); starts to make a calendar based on Charlotte's menstrual period (114); walks twelve miles to town (117); after they return to Chicago, buys typewriter; writes for cheap magazines (121); tells Charlotte he does not want her to work; takes job as mine doctor (127-129); in Utah (131), because he had turned into a husband (132); makes long tirade against respectability (133 ff.); repeats theme of virginity Mr. Compson holds [See *The Sound and the Fury.*] (137); long tirade on sex (136 ff.); says goodbye to McCord as train leaves (141); reaches Utah in winter snow and fourteen degrees (181-182); refuses to abort Bill Buckner (191); aborts Billie Buckner (195); sleeps in same room with Buckners (192); avoids sex (192-193); resumes sex after

Buckners leave (196); tells men of Callaghan's embezzlement; decides to wait for next return of ore train before leaving; invites men to strip commissary (201-202); [no motivation for this decision to stay]; at first, refuses to abort Charlotte; refuses to let another doctor do it either (206); in frenzy, thinks of putting child in orphanage; abandoning it; or setting up as professional abortionist (208); they leave Utah; arrive in San Antonio (209); goes to brothel to get abortion pills (210); thrown out after being hit (213-214); buys abortion pills in drugstore (214); takes Charlotte to dance hall to help abortion pills work (215); pills do not work; wants her to have child in charity ward (216-217); frantically tries to find job; even offers to be doctor's abortionist for half fee; is thrown out (219); finally gets job as WPA school crossing guard; as he starts abortion, hands shake (220); performs abortion; returns with Charlotte to Louisiana to Rittenmeyer's house (221); sits in park and imagines interview between Charlotte and Rittenmeyer (222-227); back to present: admits to doctor he murdered Charlotte (279); deputy calls him Wilson (294); Webster (299); allowed to see Charlotte after operation (305); taken to jail (307); refuses Rittenmeyer's offer to jump bail and leave town ((312-313); stays in jail for several weeks (313-315); tried for manslaughter (317); pleads guilty (318); jury finds him guilty as instructed (322); takes cyanide pill from Rittenmeyer because he realizes that Rittenmeyer had promised Charlotte to give it to him; grinds cyanide pill into powder; with shoe, grinds it into floor (323); "between grief and nothing I will take grief" (324).

Charlotte (20) Rittenmeyer (31): woman in cottage next to doctor's (5); sits all day in beach chair (8); hemorrhaging (14); wants drink (20); flashback: painter (39); not a painter (she lied) but sculptor (40); invites Harry to dinner (41); after husband goes to bed and without any preliminary talk, declares herself to be in love with Harry (42-43); meets Harry for lunch (43); in hotel room, says she will not have sex in back alley (44 ff.); leaves hotel; calls Harry damned pauper (50); accompanied by Rat, joins Harry on train to Chicago (54-55); after she says goodbye to husband, forces Harry to buy ticket for drawing room for sex with Harry (59-60); finds apartment in Chicago (82); calculates their income and expenses (86); makes figurines; sells them (87); after while sales stop (89); inspired by photographer, now makes puppets (90) this project ends (92); begins new project (94); when she learns that Harry has lost job, insists on going out to eat and drink with McCord and others (96 ff.); swims naked each morning at McCord's cottage (110); returns to Chicago with Harry; gets job window dressing in store (119); sends Christmas presents to her children (125); goes on train with Harry to mine in Utah (129 ff.); persuades Harry to perform abortion on Billie Buckner (195); after Buckners leave, runs back to cabin to have sex with Harry (197); to communicate with Polish miners that Callaghan embezzled their pay money, draws picture (200-201); tells Harry she is pregnant (204-205); asks him to abort her (205); in San Antonio, again asks him to abort her at time of menstrual period (209); takes all abortion pills at once; drinks whisky to help abortion pills work; gets sick; vomits; loses two pills thereby; retakes them (215); repeats these actions; pills do not work; they quarrel (216); in third month of pregnancy (217); makes him promise that, if he has not found a good job by the time her next menstrual period arrives (thirteen days), he will abort her (218-219); is aborted by Harry; returns to Louisiana to Rittenmeyer (221); in interview that Harry imagines, meets her children; returns Pullman check to Rittenmeyer; tells him of abortion, hemorrhaging; asks him to do nothing to Harry if she dies (227); after interview, tells Harry to leave immediately to avoid arrest if infection sets in (227-228); as they await ambulance, urges Harry to flee (286); dies (317).

_____ Cofer (11): real estate agent (6).

_____: Portuguese ex-fisherman; owner of grocery store (8).

Francis (225) Rat (21) Rittenmeyer (31): husband of Charlotte (20); Catholic; will not give Charlotte divorce (47-48); accompanies her as she joins Harry on train to Chicago (54-55); on train, gives Harry check made out to Pullman Company for one ticket to New Orleans (57); visits Harry in jail; brings his suitcase and clothes; has paid his bail bond; gives him three hundred dollars (from Pullman check); urges him to jump bail and run away (311); appears in court (318) to enter a plea on behalf of Harry; causes crowd to riot (320-321); reappears in Harry's cell; gives him cyanide tablet because he had promised Charlotte to do it (323);

_____: tall convict; 25 in 1927; feels that he is in jail because of the writers of fiction he has read (23-24); in jail for fifteen years for attempted train robbery (24); in flood, for first time hears sound of the Old Man [Mississippi River] (72); chained to plump, hairless convict; unchained; sent in boat to pick up woman on cypress snag and man on cottonhouse roof (75); after skiff turns over (143), gets back in (144); after skiff hits tree, finds woman on cypress snag (148); holds skiff while she enters it (149); hit on back of head by some object (151); desires only to be free of pregnant woman (153-154); skiff caught on rolling wave of water and carried past Vicksburg (156 ff.); to the Mississippi River (158); another day and night pass (162); eats part of dead hen (163); senses another cresting wave (163 ff.); ten years added to sentence for attempted escape (164); skiff hits boat with three people on it (164-165); refuses offer to put woman on boat and leave her (167-168); carried into Louisiana (172); finally arrives at land with railroad loading platform (173); tries to surrender to soldiers on loading platform; they shoot at him; runs back to skiff (173-174); second wave catches him (175); tosses him on land, an Indian mound (176); woman gives birth (177); cuts umbilical cord with cover of tin can; ties it with shoelace; mound is snake infested (230); spends six days on mound making steering oar for boat (234-235); leaves mound with skiff full of snakes; throws them out (236-237); with woman and baby, is taken aboard steamboat (238); given whisky; fights; has nose broken (241-243); flashback: tried to rob a train (248); with woman and child, put ashore at Carnavron, Louisiana (250); hauls skiff up sixty-foot levee and down other side; finds water; back in skiff; finds house on stilts (251); gives clothes to woman and orders her to wash them (253); becomes partner with Cajun alligator hunter (255); kills alligator with knife (258-259); afterwards hunts alone (262); realizes how good it is to work (264); ignores warning about dynamiting levee; starts to hunt; senses something; returns to house; forcibly removed by four men in motor boat (266-272); taken to armory; fed; clothed; escapes with woman and child; finds way back to Mississippi; turns woman and boat over to deputy sheriff; surrenders (275-278); has been reported dead, drowned (326); charged with attempted escape; ten years added to sentence (331); tells convicts of his return (331 ff.).

_____: District Attorney who sends tall convict to jail (25).

_____: second convict; short, plump, almost hairless; quite white (25); sentenced to one hundred ninety-nine years (26); cooks, sweeps in deputy warden's barracks (27); reads newspapers to other convicts of flood in Mississippi River (28-29); sent with tall convict to rescue woman and man (75); returns with man on cotton house; says tall convict drowned (77-78).

_____: Federal Attorney helps send short, plump convict to jail (26).

_____: State Attorney involved in sending short, plump convict to jail (26).

_____: woman involved in sending short, plump convict to jail (26).

_____: second man in car involved in crime that sent short, plump convict to jail (26); "doubtless the actual murderer" who escaped (27).

_____: two policemen who hold short, plump convict (27).

_____: judge who sentences short, plump convict (27).

_____: trusty in blacksmith shop in prison (27).

_____: deputy who calls convicts to levee (30).

Dr. (31) _____ Wilbourne (21): Harry's father, doctor; worked way through medical school; leaves two thousand dollars for Harry to pay his way through medical school (31-32); dies of toxemia from sucking snake bite on child's hand (32).

Mrs. _____ Wilbourne (21): mother of Harry; second wife of Dr. Wilbourne (31).

_____ Wilbourne (31) _____: older half-sister of Harry; raises him (31); married to clerk in grocery store; helps Harry in medical school with small gifts (32).

_____ Wilbourne (31): other half-sister of Harry (31).

_____: husband of Harry's half-sister; clerk in grocery store

196

(32).

_____: their children (32).

_____: child bitten by snake (32).

_____ Flint (34): fellow intern; opens Harry's telegram in error (34); takes Harry to party (36).

_____ De Montigny (35): apparently another intern (35).

_____ Crowe (36): painter (36); at whose studio the party occurs; plays piano; wears Basque hat and bathrobe (37).

_____: woman kisses Flint at party; hostess (37).

Charlotte (222) Rittenmeyer: elder (222) daughter of Charlotte and Rat (40).

Ann (222) Rittenmeyer: younger (222) daughter of Charlotte and Rat (40).

_____: black maid of Rittenmeyers (42).

_____: black porter at hotel where Charlotte and Harry meet (45).

Ralph (223)_____: Charlotte's brother; sends her twenty-five dollars every Christmas which she saved (48).

_____: nurse in hospital; announces phone call for Harry (52).

_____: conductor on train to Chicago (59).

_____: trusty who drives truck to levee (61).

_____: two guards in truck; take convicts to levee (61).

_____: prison guard who sends tall convict to pick up woman on cypress snag and man on cottonhouse (75).

_____ Buckworth (331): deputy warden; reports tall convict drowned (77); made the victim of the mistake about tall convict (330); transferred to Highway Patrol (331);

Hamp (328)_____: warden of penetentiary (77); orders tall convict's name removed from rolls as drowned (79-80); gives tall convict cigar when he adds ten years to his sentence (331).

_____: man on cottonhouse; rescued by short, plump convict (78).

_____ McCord (88): newspaperman from New Orleans; becomes friend of Charlotte and Harry in Chicago; had known her brother (88); lets Charlotte and Harry live in his cabin after their money runs out (99).

_____: photographer (90).

_____: detective (95); gets Harry fired (96).

Doc (97) _____: part owner of cabin with McCord and Gillespie (97).

_____ Gillespie (97): part owner of cabin with Doc and McCord (97).

_____ Bradley (99): owns cottage near McCord's (99); leaves extra food with Harry and Charlotte as he leaves lake (106-107).

Mrs. _____ Bradley (108): his wife.

_____ Callaghan (182): man who hires Harry to be mine doctor (127).

_____: manager of apartment house in Chicago (129).

_____: woman sitting in cypress snag (148); pregnant; gets into skiff with tall convict (149); about to give birth in skiff (152); hurled by wave and aided by tall convict, lands on Indian mound (176); gives birth (177); travels with tall convict (230 ff.).

_____: mail clerk that tall convict once tried to rob (160).

_____: man with shotgun on boat which skiff hits (164); offers to take pregnant woman on board, but not tall convict (166-167); shoots at tall convict as he leaves (169).

_____: second man on boat which skiff hits (164).

_____: woman on boat which skiff hits (165); puts food into skiff (168).

Buck Buckner (179): manager of mine; from Wyoming (179); asks Harry if he is a doctor (185); tells Harry that there has not been a payroll since September (187); tells Harry about lack of money and desertion of Chinese and Italian miners (187-189); asks Harry to abort wife (190-191); with wife, leaves mine after abortion (195).

Billie, Bill Buckner (179): wife of manager of mine; from Colorado (179); uses expression "get jammed" for being pregnant (180); aborted by Harry (195).

_____: a grimed giant; a Pole (180).

198

_____: another Pole; shorter; pushes ore tram in mine (186); understands Harry; gathers men at commissary (199-200).

_____Hogben (188): engineer who runs ore train (188).

_____: man who brings letter from Buckner (204).

Louisa (211)_____: black maid in brothel which Harry visits to purchase abortion pills (210).

_____: madam in brothel (211); has Harry thrown out (213).

_____: bouncer in brothel; hits Harry; throws him out (213-214).

Pete (214)_____: Mexican servant in brothel (213).

_____: clerk in drugstore; sells Harry abortion pills for five dollars; does not guarantee them (214).

_____: doctor who throws Harry out when he offers to be his abortionist at half fee (219).

_____: pilot of steamboat that picks up tall convict, woman, and baby (238).

_____: mild-spoken man on steamboat that picks up tall convict, woman, and baby (238); Red Cross representative (240); a doctor (241); gives convict whisky; feeds him after fight(241-243).

_____: man who brings whisky to tall convict and woman on steamboat (240).

_____: man in house on stilts; Cajun [Faulkner spells it *Cajan*.] with whom tall convict, woman, and baby live for about ten days (252); alligator hunter (255); tries to tell tall convict that levee is to be dynamited; divides hides; leaves (266-268).

_____: four men in motor launch who forcibly remove tall convict from house before levee is dynamited (271-273).

_____: deputy sheriff to whom the tall convict turns over woman and skiff (278).

_____: ambulance driver who comes for Charlotte (292).

_____: doctor who tends Charlotte in ambulance (293).

_____: deputy sheriff (293).

Dr._____Richardson (294): questions Harry about Charlotte and the abortion; tends Charlotte (296-297).

_____: three nurses in hospital (295-296).

_____: jailor; brings Harry coffee (308).

_____: barber who shaves Harry (316).

_____: officer who takes Harry to court (316).

_____: court-appointed lawyer; defends Harry (316).

_____: bailiff at Harry's trial (317).

_____: judge at Harry's trial (317); tells bailiff to get Rittenmeyer out of town; instructs jury to find Harry guilty; says he will be sentenced to Parchman for not less than fifty years (321).

_____: clerk in court; reads indictment for manslaughter (first real indication that Charlotte died) (317).

_____ Gower (318): District Attorney at Harry's trial (317).

_____: governor of Mississippi (325).

_____: man on governor's staff who visits warden (325); says tall convict is dead (326); has received a discharge as dead (327); charges tall convict with attempted escape; adds ten years to his sentence (331).

_____ Bledsoe (326).

Mrs. Vernon Waldrip (339): tall convict's sweetheart (338); visited him in his third month; now married (339).

200

Six short stories preceded the writing of the novel. "Lizards in Jamshyd's Courtyard" was begun as a story called "Omar's Eighteenth Quatrain," as early as the late 1920's; the story was written before May 16 or 27, 1930 and was first published in *The Saturday Evening Post*, 204 (February 27, 1932), 12-13, 52, 57; it became Book One, Chapter 3 and Book Four, Chapter 2 of the novel. "Spotted Horses" was conceived as early as 1926 in a work then called *Father Abraham* (eventually published under that title in 1983); it was recast under the title "As I Lay Dying," some years later, and still later as "Abraham's Children;" probably by November, 1928, it was submitted to *Scribner's Magazine* under the earlier title, "As I Lay Dying;" first published under this title in the *Mississippi Quarterly*, 39 (summer 1986); rewritten under the title, "The Peasants," it was again submited to *Scribner's Magazine;* it was revised and retitled, "*Aria Con Amore*," and sent to *The Saturday Evening Post* on February 3, 1931; a final revision, under the title, "Horses," was finished by Feberuary 20, 1931; it was first published as "Spotted Horses" in *Scribner's Magazine*, 89 (June, 1931), 585-597; it became Book Four, Chapter 1 of the novel. "The Hound" was written before November 17, 1930; it was first published in *Harper's Magazine*, 163 (August, 1931), 266-274; it was reprinted in *Doctor Martino and Other Stories*, 1934; it became Book Three, Chapter 2 in the novel. "Fool About a Horse" was written probably about March, 1935; it was first published in *Scribner's Magazine*, 100 (August, 1936), 80-86; it became Book One, Chapter 2 of the novel. "Afternoon of a Cow" was written toward the end of 1935 and dedicated to "Joel Sayre/ Xmas," 1935; it was first published in a French translation by Maurice Coindreau as *"L'Apres-midi d'une Vache,"* in *Fontaine*, 27-28 (June- July, 1943), 66-81; it was published first as a short story in English in *Furioso*, 2 (summer, 1947), 5-17. Both these publications as a short story appeared after publication of *The Hamlet* in which this story was incorporated with the story of Ike Snopes. "Barn Burning" was begun on November 7, 1938; it was first published in *Harper's Magazine*, 179 (June, 1939), [86]-96; it was reprinted in *O. Henry Memorial Award Prize Stories of 1939*, selected and edited by Harry Hansen (New York: Doubleday, Doran & Company, Inc., 1939), pp.3-29; it was reprinted in *Collected Stories*, 1950; it was intended to be the opening chapter of the novel, but was not used there. *The Hamlet*, as a novel, was begun in September, 1938, and the structure of the entire trilogy, originally titled *The Peasants, Rus in Urbe*, and *Ilium Falling*, was in mind by mid-December, 1938; *The Hamlet* was finished in late 1939; it was published April 1, 1940. "As I Lay Dying" was eventually published in a French translation entitled *"Tandis Que J'Agonise"* by Jacques Pothier in *Sud*, 48/49 (1983), 9-28.

Pagination in parentheses to the following editions: first (New York: Random House, 1940), 421 pp.; second (New York: Random House, 1964), 366 pp.

Turpin, Haley, Whittington, McCallum, Murray, Leonard, Littlejohn, Riddup, Armstid, and Doshey (4, 4): these are the names of original settlers in Frenchman's Bend.

Will Varner (3, 3): 60 years old; present owner of Old Frenchman Place in Frenchman's Bend (3,3); chief man in county; largest land owner, supervisor in one county, Justice of the Peace in the next, election commissioner in both, farmer, usurer, veterinarian (5, 5), owner of store, cotton gin, gristmill, and blacksmith shop; thin (6, 5); owner, with the exception of Littlejohn's Hotel, of only house in county with more than one story (11, 10); forced by Flem Snopes to pay for his plug of tobacco (61, 54); used to settle his tenants' accounts alone once a year without even Jody's help; now settles them with Flem Snopes's help (69, 60); trustee of local school (119, 105); sets Hoake McCarron's arm (159, 139); has affair with middle-fortyish wife of one of his tenants; does not bother to remove his hat (161, 140); prevents Jody from taking gun after Eula's seducer (164-165, 142-143); shows amazing ignorance of woman's anatomy (162-163, 143); signs over Old Frenchman Place to Flem and Eula Varner Snopes (166, 145); conducts Mink Snopes-Houston trial about scrub yearling (180-181, 158); drives to Mottstown to pick up Eula and baby (302, 263); called to tend Henry Armstid (349-350, 306).

Judge (5, 5)   Benbow (5, 5).

Jody (7, 6) Varner (3, 3): son of Will Varner; manages all family business (6, 5); about 30, unmarried; big man (7, 6); ninth of the children (8, 7); tells father about Ab Snopes wanting farm and barn burning (11, 10); plots to let Ab make the crop and then drive him off with charge of barn burning (12, 10); visits Snopes (22, 19); fear of barn burning makes him give concessions to Ab Snopes; fails to have Snopes sign contract (24-25, 21-22); meets Flem on way home (25, 22); frightened into offering Flem job in store (26-27, 23); explains to his father why he hired Flem; to protect the business (30, 27); now sometimes does not come to store at all (64, 56); one day in September, clerks all day in store; Flem takes over cotton gin (67, 58-59); something in Jody's eyes "between annoyance and speculation and purest foreknowledge" (68, 60); asks Flem how much more it is going to cost him to protect one barn full of hay (76, 67); now takes orders from Flem Snopes (101, 88-89); decides that Eula go to school when she is 8 (109, 97); takes her on back of horse to school (111-112, 99); 27 years old when Eula is 8 (112, 99); as Eula grows up, drives her back and forth for overnight visits to homes of other girls; does not let her attend dances (146-147, 128); insists that she wear corsets (149, 130); wants to shoot man who made Eula pregnant (162-163, 142); catches St. Elmo Snopes stealing candy (363, 317).

_____: Will Varner's blacksmith; makes chair for him out of flour barrel (6, 6).

Mrs. Maggie (89, 77) Varner (3, 3): Will Varner's wife, mother of sixteen children (6, 5); one of the best housewives in county; not now able to read, although she did read a little at marriage (109-110, 97); would lie naked in moonlight before Eula's birth to induce a girl (351, 307);

V. K. (82, 84) Ratliff (7, 6): itinerant sewing machine agent; less

202

than 30 years old (7, 6); tells Jody of second barn burning (14, 12); sells three machines a year; otherwise trades in land and livestock etc. (15, 13); tells history of Ab Snopes (32-33, 29); [an age discrepancy here] was 8 years old at time of Pat Stamper affair (49, 43); now meets Ab Snopes after eight years, but is clearly more than 16 years old (55, 48); it takes five months for him to make his rounds selling sewing machines (62, 54,); sells so many sewing machines on promisory notes he is one hundred twenty dollars in debt to wholesaler (63, 55); follows kinsman to Columbia, Tennessee to mule sale to collect on note and borrow enough to satisfy wholesaler; sells and trades successfully returns home (63-64, 55-56); owns a house in Jefferson kept by his widowed sister; has gall bladder trouble; taken to Memphis hospital for operation (70, 61); owns sleeping-partner's half interest in side-street restaurant in Jefferson; buys contract to sell fifty goats to northerner (77, 67); sells sewing machine to Mink Snopes (83-84, 73); gets exchange of promisory notes from him (85-86, 75); plants story with Flem Snopes about buying goats from Quick (89-90, 78); tells his plan about goats to men on gallery at store (89-92, 78-80); deliberately lets Flem overhear; ignores Bookwright's advice to buy goats immediately (92, 81); mentally congratulates himself on outfoxing Flem about goats (94, 82); visits Uncle Ben Quick and learns that Flem bought fifty goats; has licked Flem (95, 83); bested eventually in his scheme to beat Flem Snopes (99, 86); gives Mrs. Littlejohn money to keep for Ike Snopes (100, 87); witnesses marriage of Flem Snopes and Eula Varner in Jefferson (168, 147); ponders on terrible waste of Eula on Flem (181-182, 159); stops men from watching Ike Snopes make love to cow (224-225, 196); visits I. O. Snopes to stop exploitation of Ike Snopes (228-231, 199-201); sets price of Ike's cow at $16.80 (232, 202); takes Mrs. Mink Snopes and her children into his house (297, 259); buys Mink's children new overcoats (299, 261); sells his old coat to Mrs. Mink Snopes for fifty cents (299, 261); becomes Mrs. Mink Snopes's banker (301, 262-263); predicts that others will be trimmed on sale of spotted horses (315, 276); taunts men from Frenchman's Bend for throwing money away on horses; says Eck Snopes will help in selling them (317-318, 278-279); joins men at night after auction of spotted horses (342, 300); as Eck's spotted horse rushes into his room, leaps out window (346, 303); calls Will Varner to tend Henry Armstid (350, 306); admits that he burned only two of Mink Snopes's notes (366, 320); joins Henry Armstid and induces Bookwright to join them in watching Flem Snopes dig at night at Old Frenchman Place (383-384, 334); gets diviner; returns to field (392, 342); finds sack of coins (397, 346); then two more after being spied upon by someone who gallops off on horse (397-398, 346-347); he and Bookwright find twenty-five dollars in their sacks and decide to buy the land (399, 347-348); intercepts Will Varner and Flem Snopes returning from Jefferson; talks to Flem (404-405, 352); bargains with Flem for purchase of Old Frenchman Place (405-406, 353); three days later, they buy it from Flem: Ratliff pays as his share his half of the Jefferson restaurant; Armstid gives mortgage on his farm; Bookwright pays cash (407, 354); they begin to dig for treasure (409, 356); after he figures out relationship of Eustace Grimm to Flem Snopes (he is a nephew), with Bookwright, examines "seeded" coins to discover that they have been bilked by Flem Snopes into buying Old Frenchman Place (413-414, 360-361); quits digging (414, 361).

Ab (14, 14) Snopes (8, 7): father of boy, two girls; supports wife's sister; farmer (9, 8); rents farm as sharecropper, limps; connected with burned barn (10-11, 8-9); arrested for barn burning (11, 9); believed to have burned second barn (14, 12); steps in horse manure and stains De Spain's rug with it (17, 15); orders daughter to wash rug (18, 15); ruins it (18, 16); takes De Spain to court over rug and twenty-bushel penalty; penalty reduced to ten bushels; believed to have burned De Spain's barn in revenge (19, 16); horse trader (30, 27); uses landlord's goods to trade for horses (35, 31); wears thirty-year-old coat of Colonel John Sartoris that Rosa Millard gave him (37, 33); trades Beasley's horse and his mule to Pat Stamper for pair of mules (42, 37); they do not pull together (43, 38); are doped (44-45, 39); trades team of mules back to Pat Stamper (49, 43); in rainstorm passes out drunk; wakes; learns that Jim and Stamper dyed his own horse black and blown it up with bicycle pump (49, 43); eventually gets span of mules from Jody Varner in exchange for Flem clerking in Varner's store (54-55, 48); accepts whisky from Ratliff (56, 49).

Flem (15, 13) Snopes (9, 8) son of Ab Snopes (9, 8); eyes color of stagnant water (25, 22); wants to get out of farming as soon as he can (26-27, 23); promised job in store by Jody Varner (27, 23,); in return for clerking in Varner's store, his father borrows Varner's mules (54-55, 48); appears to work in store in home-made white shirt, riding mule on saddle belonging to Varner (58, 51); "a thick squat soft man" with beaklike small nose, aged between 20 and 30 (59, 51); inspected at work by entire village (59, 52); makes Will Varner pay for his tobacco (62, 54); never makes mistakes (64, 56); refuses to extend credit to Varner's customers (65, 57); moves to Frenchman's Bend; begins to wear black bow tie; goes to church; will become president of Jefferson bank (65-66, 57-58); takes over supervision of cotton gin from Jody Varner who returns to clerking in store (67, 59); villagers refer to this period as time when he passed Jody (68, 60); begins to help Will Varner settle yearly accounts (69, 60); begins to lend money at interest to villagers (69-70, 61); begins to deal in cattle quite successfully (70, 61); builds new blacksmith shop in Frenchman's Bend (76, 66); hires Trumbull's apprentice; sells new shop to Varner and makes profit all around (76, 66-67); now owns two hundred acres of land with buildings (83, 72); now rides Jody's roan (95, 83); duped into buying fifty goats by Ratliff, but beats Ratliff out of cashing Mink and Ike Snopes's notes (91-101, 80-88); next settles accounts without even Will Varner present (101,88); now gives orders to Jody Varner, who is clerk in store (102, 88); now accompanies Will Varner on Jody's roan to estimate cotton crops, etc. (102, 89); marries pregnant Eula Varner; leaves for Texas (166, 145); will not return to town until after Mink's trial (304, 265); returns to town with spotted horses (309, 271); does not admit horses are his; does not deny that they are (315, 276); joins men at Mrs. Littlejohn's lot after auction of spotted horses (334, 293); when Texan gives back Henry's money, takes it back (338, 296); will not admit ownership of horses (356, 312); refuses to refund five dollars to Mrs. Armstid; says Texan took all money back with him (359, 315-316); gives Mrs. Armstid five cents worth of candy "for the chaps" (362, 317);

refuses to accept summons in suit Mrs. Tull brings against him for damage to her husband (367, 321); refuses to attend trial (371, 324); digs at night in garden (386-390, 337-340); moves with wife and child to Jefferson to live in tent (415-416, 362); on way to town, stops to watch Henry Armstid fanatically digging in field at Old Frenchman Place (420-421, 366).

Mrs. Ab Snopes (9, 8): second wife of Ab Snopes (34, 30).

_____: Mrs. Ab Snopes's sister (9, 8); a widow (15, 13).

_____ Snopes (9, 8): daughter of Ab Snopes (9, 8); very large (54, 47).

_____ Snopes (9, 8): other daughter of Ab Snopes (9, 8); very large (54, 47).

Vernon (12, 10) Tull (10, 9): connects Ab Snopes with burned barn (10-11, 9); visits Ratliff in Jefferson; tells him of considerable herd of scrub cattle on Ab Snopes's rented farm (70, 61); together with Bookwright, tells of replacement of scrub cattle with herd of Herfords said to be owned by Flem Snopes and kept in Varner's pasture (70, 61); run over by Eck Snopes's spotted horse on bridge (345-348, 302-304).

Ike McCaslin (11, 9): lets Ab Snopes and family winter in cottonhouse (11, 9).

_____ Harris (11, 9): his barn was burned (11, 9).

_____ Snopes (15, 13): smaller brother of Flem, not with family now (15, 13); [Probably Colonel John Sartoris Snopes; see "Barn Burning."]

Mrs. (60, 53) _____ Littlejohn (11, 10): hotel owner (11, 10); gives Houston V. K. Ratliff's money for the cow that Ike Snopes fell in love with (224, 195-196); knows that men watch Ike Snopes and cow (225, 197); washes clothes in yard during auction of spotted horses (319-334, 279-292,); hits one with her washboard (346, 303); tells Mrs. Armstid Flem will not return her five dollars (359, 314).

_____: female black cook for Varners (11, 10).

Eula (107, 95) Varner (12, 10) Snopes (166, 145): 13-year-old daughter of Will Varner; sister of Jody (12, 10); last of sixteen Varner children; voluptuous woman at 13; incorrigibly lazy (107, 95); at 8, refuses to walk to school (109-110 97); then Jody takes her on his horse to school (111-112, 99); when Labove first sees her in school, she had "a face eight years old and a body of fourteen with the female shape of twenty" (129, 113); for two years, is the focal point of all the physical attention of schoolhouse (129-132, 114-116); when Labove tries to attack her, knocks him down (137-138, 120-122,); at 14, begins to gather group of youths about her (145-146, 127); at 15, group is made up of farm men

205

(148, 129); men, after sitting on veranda each Sunday night, would eat supper and leave to fight at creek over her (149-150, 131); at 16, is courted by owners of trotting horses and buggies (150, 131); supports Hoake McCarron while they have sex after her father has set his broken arm (159-160, 139); is pregnant (160, 140); is married to Flem Snopes; leaves for Texas (166, 145); returns to town in March with baby (302, 263,).

Major [Cassius] de Spain (15, 13): barn is burned (15-16, 13-14); charges Ab Snopes twenty bushels of corn against his crop for spoiling rug (18, 16).

_____: black servant of De Spain (17, 15).

Mrs. [Cassius] de Spain (17, 15).

Uncle Buck [Theophilus] McCaslin (19, 16): says Colonel John Sartoris shot Ab Snopes in foot for trying to steal his horse (19, 16); after Rosa Millard's death, he, Bayard Sartoris and a black [Ringo] tie Ab Snopes to tree and either whip him or torture him with heated ramrod (33, 29).

Colonel John Sartoris (19, 16).

_____: judge; fines Ab Snopes ten bushels of corn for ruining De Spain's rug (19, 16).

Anse Holland (30, 26): one of earlier landlords of Ab Snopes and Mr. Ratliff [V. K.'s father]. (30, 26).

Rosa Millard (33, 29): Colonel John Sartoris's "ma-in-law," during Civil War in a "horse-and-mule partnership" with Ab Snopes; shot by Major Grumby (33, 29).

Major Grumby (33, 29): shot Rosa Millard (33, 29).

Bayard Sartoris [II] (33, 29): with Buck McCaslin and black [Ringo], tied Ab Snopes to tree (33, 29).

Pat Stamper (33, 29): ended Ab Snopes's horse-trading career (33, 29); horse trader (33-34, 30); trades Ab Snopes his own horse and mule back for mules he traded Ab earlier (49-50, 43).

Jim (47, 41) _____: black assistant to Pat Stamper who can mysteriously transform appearance of horses (34, 30).

_____ Ratliff (30, 26): Ratliff's father; with Ab Snopes rented farm from Old Man Anse Holland (30, 26).

Vynie (35, 31) Snopes (33, 30): first wife of Ab Snopes; from Jefferson; removed (not divorced) by her father from Ab; has had no children (34, 30); takes mule and horse away (50-51, 44); returns; takes cow (51-52, 45); returns with separator (52, 46).

Beasley Kemp (35, 31): traded horse to Ab Snopes that he got from Pat Stamper (35, 31).

Hugh Mitchell (38, 34): tells Ab Snopes that Beasley Kemp paid Herman Short eight dollars for horse he traded to Ab (38, 34).

Herman Short (38, 34): swapped mule and buggy to Pat Stamper for horse that Ab Snopes traded from Pat Stamper (38, 34).

_____ Cain (44, 38): store owner in Jefferson who sells Ab Snopes separator (44, 39).

Doc _____ Peabody (45, 39): sells Ratliff pint of whisky for Ab Snopes (45, 39).

Cliff Odum (51, 45): drives Mrs. Snopes back for cow and returns with separator (51-52, 45).

_____ McCallum (56, 49): Ratliff offers some of his whisky to Ab Snopes (56, 49).

Odum Bookwright (65, 57): together with Tull, tells Ratliff of Flem's cattle dealing (70, 61-62); tells Ratliff of Eula's return with child (302, 263); has bought one of spotted horses (352, 308,); believes that Flem will somehow prevent Mink from being sent to Parchman prison (366, 320); joins Ratliff and Armstid to watch Flem Snopes dig at night (384 ff., 334 ff.); referred to as "that black one" by Uncle Dick Bolivar; ordered off field because he interferes with divining (395, 344); returns to field (396, 345); finds twenty-five dollars in bag (398, 347); a bachelor (407, 354) (but see 78, 68); with V. K., realizes he has been bilked (414, 360-361).

Lon (377, 330) Quick (65, 57): operates saw mill (65, 57); makes first offer for one of the spotted horses (313, 275); buys one (342, 299); leaves gate to lot open to allow horses to escape (377, 330).

_____ Trumbull (67, 58): Varner's blacksmith (67, 58); for twenty years (71, 62);

_____: Trumbull's apprentice (67, 58); farmer; becomes Flem's blacksmith (76, 66).

_____: black fireman in Varner's blacksmith shop (67, 58).

_____: Ratliff's widowed sister; keeps his house in Jefferson (70, 61); mother of at least two boys and two girls (298, 259).

Jack (79, 69) Houston (71, 62): after I. O. Snopes hits quick of horse's hoof, takes horse to Whiteleaf to have it shod (73-74, 64) keeps Mink Snopes's yearling all year (80, 158); awarded three dollars by Varner for keeping Mink Snopes's bull (184, 161); rescues Ike Snopes when cow kicks him (191, 167); childless widower; lives alone with black man to cook (204, 179); notices cow is missing (213, 186); tracks Ike Snopes and cow with hound (215 ff., 188 ff.); lies to Mrs. Littlejohn about safety of Ike; returns home to sleep; continues to track Ike and cow next day (217-218, 189-190); after cow is returned to him, sells it to Mrs. Littlejohn for Ike; accepts money that V. K. Ratliff gave her for Ike (223-224, 195-196); attended same country school as his wife; at 16 quits school; runs away; remains out of county for thirteen years (235, 205); returns to marry girl who was waiting for him (235, 205); at 14, acquainted with whisky; has black mistress two or three years his senior (236, 206); fights other students and strikes down Lucy Pate, his future wife, in schoolyard (238-239, 208); runs away from home at 16 after discovering Lucy Pate had completed his final exams for him; signs note to his father after borrowing all his father's money; sends back money his father gave him (241-242, 210); becomes construction camp timekeeper, locomotive fireman; lives with woman, known as his wife, for seven years after taking her out of Galveston brothel; has been Kansas wheat hand, shepherd in New Mexico, member of construction gang in Arizona and West Texas, and longshoreman in Galveston (246, 211); decides to return to Mississippi to marry; shares money with prostitute-wife (244-245, 213); marries in January; buys stallion (246, 214); kills stallion that killed his wife (247, 215); shot to death by Mink Snopes at 33 years (249, 217).

Eck (73, 63) Eckrum (367, 321) Snopes (73, 63): younger cousin of I. O. Snopes (71, 62); lives in same house with Flem, his cousin or whatever relation (75, 66); marries daughter of family with whom they board; fathers a child ten months later; has five- or six-year-old boy by former marriage (75, 66); becomes apprenticed to Trumbull's former apprentice; then takes over forge (76, 67); I. O. Snopes talks him into paying larger share of cost of Ike's cow (233-234, 204); has paid whole cost of Ike's cow--twenty dollars--and bought him toy cow for twenty-five cents (306 267); helps Buck Hipps get spotted horses into lot (312-313, 274); given horse to start auction (330, 289); buys another one (343, 300); his horse runs into Mrs. Littlejohn's hotel; into Ratliff's room; runs out again (345-346, 302-303); it runs over Tull on bridge (347-348, 304); has caught wild horse (355, 310); it broke its neck (365, 319); at trial, refuses to testify falsely (373, 326); thrice offers to pay damage before judge rules that he never legally owned horse (376-377, 329-330).

I. O. Snopes (72, 63): takes over Trumbull's lease on blacksmith shop (71, 62); proverbist (72, 63); hits quick of Houston's horse's hoof trying to shoe him (73, 64); to teach school in Frenchman's Bend (79, 69); serves as legal advisor to Mink Snopes (184, 161); wife and three children seem to appear (226-227, 199); agrees to stop exploitation of Ike Snopes under vague threat from Ratliff that he might not be schoolmaster (230, 201); says he's single (233, 204); convinces Eck to pay most of cost of Ike's cow (233-34, 204); wife and one child appear; quits as schoolmaster and disappears (303, 264).

_____ Snopes: Eck Snopes's second wife; lives in Frenchman's Bend (75, 66).

<u>   </u> Snopes: Eck's child by second wife (75, 66).

<u>Wallstreet (303, 264) Panic (306, 266) Snopes (75, 66)</u>: Eck's first son-- 5 or 6 years old--by his first wife (75, 66); delivers message to Mink after murder of Houston to come to Lump Snopes in store (617, 227); note to Mink says his wife has money for him (265-266, 231); name explained (306, 266); follows father into lot (320, 280); almost killed by horses (323, 283); escapes injury when horses break out (345, 302); again escapes as horse jumps over him in Mrs. Littlejohn's hotel (346, 303).

<u>   </u> Snopes: Eck Snopes's first wife (75, 66).

Mrs. <u>   </u> Trumbull (75, 66): wife of blacksmith (75, 66).

<u>Mrs. Odum Bookwright (78, 68)</u>: wife of Odum Bookwright (78, 68) [but see 407, 354].

<u>   </u>: counterman in Ratliff's restaurant in Jefferson (78, 69).

<u>   </u>: teacher before I. O. Snopes in Frenchman's Bend (70. (69).

<u>   </u>: fireman in Quick's sawmill, probably black (80, 70).

<u>   </u>: "the other nigger" in Quick's sawmill; has borrowed five dollars from Flem Snopes two years earlier; every Saturday night he pays Flem ten cents and Flem never asks for original five dollars (80-81, 70).

<u>Mink Snopes (83, 72)</u>: as Ratliff tries to sell him sewing machine, signs Flem Snopes's name to twenty-dollar note (86. 75); tries to get Ratliff to deliver message to Flem reminding him of Mink's lot in life (87, 76); allows his yearling to graze on Houston's land (104, 90-91); takes Houston to court (180, 158); must pay three dollars for pasturage to get back his bull (184, 161); kills Jack Houston with shotgun (250, 218); has lived in six other rented cabins since he was married; thinks his cousin, Flem, owns this one (251-252, 219); returns from killing Houston, hits wife; tells her to go (253-254, 221); when baying hound reminds him, returns to Houston's body; drags it through swampy land to dead pin oak; hauls body up tree; puts it inside; almost gets trapped inside tree with body (256-259, 223); sees prints of sheriff and deputies in yard (262, 228); shoots hound which has bayed for three nights; throws shotgun in stream (263-265, 230-231); realizes that buzzards are revealing Houston's body (265-266, 231-232); failed to take Houston's money (268, 233); flashback: at 23, left home on way to sea (270, 235); meets future wife at logging camp (271, 236); after she calls him to her bed, becomes monagomist (273, 238); back to present: throws away ten dollars his wife gave him (275, 240); plays checkers with Lump Snopes, who tries to induce Mink to share Houston's money (281, 245); knocks Lump unconscious; ties and gags him; locks him in barn (285, 248); steals axe from black who found gun; returns to find Houston's body (286, 249); lost

209

in woods (287, 250); finds Lump at tree where he left his axe (288, 251); knocks Lump out again (289, 252); as he tries to chop tree, is attacked by hound he thought he had killed (290, 252); recovers body; beats off dog (291, 254); is captured (292, 255); almost kills himself trying to escape; is jailed (294-295, 256-257); what frustrated him in trying to recover Houston's body was that it came apart in his hands (296, 258); refuses bond and counsel (297, 259); waits for Flem to come to his aid (298, 260); comes to trial after eight months; pays no attention to trial but watches door for Flem (380-381, 332-333); convicted of murder in second degree after jury deliberates twenty minutes; sentenced to life in State Penal Farm (381, 333).

Mrs. Mink Snopes (83, 73): large woman with "incredible yellow" hair (83, 73); first seen by Mink nine years before in doorway of mess hall in south Mississippi convict camp (252, 220); calls Mink a "murdering bastard" (253, 221); leaves him; takes two children (255, 222); casts suspicion on Mink after Houston's horse is found by saying Mink did not do it (267-268, 233); has ten dollars for Mink; is staying at Will Varner's (267, 234); flashback: daughter of camp operator; mother died in chilbirth (271, 236); lives in father's house, but with private entrance; calls loggers to her bed day and night; finally calls Mink (272-273, 236-238); five months later, they marry; her father's enterprise collapses (273, 238); return to present: gives Mink ten dollars she probably got by sleeping with Varner (274-275, 239); visits Mink in jail with children; goes home with Ratliff; insists on doing housework (297, 259); gets job; pays Ratliff's sister one dollar a week board for her children; works in Savoy Hotel for three dollars a week (298-299, 260); attends Mink's trial (381, 333).

_____ Snopes: child of Mink Snopes; towhead (84, 73).

_____ Snopes: child of Mink Snopes; towhead (84, 73).

Isaac (86, 75) Ike (100, 87): Snopes (86, 75): cousin of Flem and Mink Snopes (87, 76); sleeps in Mrs. Littlejohn's barn (93, 81); an idiot; Flem Snopes is his guardian (99, 86); falls in love with cow (188-189, 165-166); tries to approach her; is kicked and rescued by Houston (191, 167); runs to rescue cow in brush fire (193-200, 169-175); taught by Mrs. Littlejohn to descend steps (194, 170); rescued again by Houston (200-202, 175-177); drops half dollar Houston gave him in creek (203, 178); takes cow from barn (204-205, 179); milks cow (206, 180); steals food from barn (206, 180); sleeps with cow in open for several days (212-213, 186); takes cow to Mrs. Littlejohn's barn; makes love to her while men watch through hole in wall (224-225, 196).

Uncle Ben Quick: owns herd of goats (88-91, 77-79).

Sam (30, 27)_____: black manservant of Will Varner; shines Jody's shoes; carries Eula as a child (108, 95); when she is 8, drives her to school in family surrey (111. 98); helps Eck load wagon for Flem's move to Jefferson (415, 361).

_____ Labove (115, 102): teacher in Frenchman's Bend;

210

vanishes (115, 102); football player in college (118, 104); sends home cleated shoes (117, 103-104); takes job of schoolteacher from Will Varner who gives him horse to ride forty miles after playing game (119-123, 105-109); trains students to play basketball; graduates with M. A. and LL. B. in three years (126-127, 112); admitted to bar (112, 113); after graduation, drawn back to Frenchman's Bend by physical attraction of 11-year-old Eula Varner (128, 113); in love with Eula (132, 116); visits brothel in Memphis; agrees to teach another year; thinks of marrying Eula; envisions future husband quite accurately (134-135, 118); despairs of having Eula (135, 118); kneels before her bench for warmth of her body; is discovered by Eula (135-136, 119-120); tries to attack her; is knocked down by Eula who calls him "old headless horseman Ichabod Crane" (137-138, 120-122); when he realizes Eula did not even bother to tell her brother of the attempted rape, leaves town forever (143-144, 126).

_____: the Professor (115, 102); teacher before Labove (114, 101); bibulous (115, 102).

_____ Labove: an incredibly old woman wearing football shoes; Labove's father's grandmother (161, 102).

_____: girl, probably Labove's younger sister (116, 102).

_____ Labove: Labove's father (116, 103); tells Varner his son wants to be governor (118, 105).

_____: football coach who recruits Labove (122, 108).

_____: widow from whom Labove rents room (124, 110).

_____: classics professor who gives Labove original Horace and Thucydides (124, 110).

_____: drummer from city; becomes one of Eula's suitors; takes Eula to dance; beaten by other suitors; chased out of town ; lives in Memphis with wife and family (151, 132).

_____: Hoake McCarron's two rivals (151, 132).

Hoake (154, 135) McCarron (152, 133): successful suitor of Eula Varner (152, 133); orphaned (father shot) at 9 (154, 134); 23 when he woos Eula (154, 135); grew up with black boy one year older; beats him in fight at 6 years; pays black to let him whip him "not severely" with riding crop (154-155, 136); three years in military school, then college; expelled for scandal with wife of minor instructor; returns to oversee mother's plantation (155, 135); warned by displaced suitors (156-157, 137); fights with five suitors; defeats them with Eula's help with buggy whip (157, 137); arm broken (158, 138); arm set by Will Varner; has sex with Eula; rebreaks arm (159, 139); vanishes (160, 140).

Mrs. Alison Hoake McCarron (153, 134): mother of Hoake (152, 133)

McCarron; elopes with Hoake's father (153, 134).

_____ McCarron (152-153, 134): father of Hoake McCarron (152-153, 133); poker player (153, 133); killed in gambling house (154, 134).

_____ Hoake (153, 134): Alison Hoake's father; successful cattle merchant (153-154, 134); leaves property to grandson (154, 134).

_____: black who grew up with Hoake McCarron (154, 135); beaten by frustrated suitors of Eula (157, 137).

_____: "middle-fortyish wife" of one of Will Varner's tenants with whom he is having an affair (161, 140).

_____: 14-year-old boy who spies on Will Varner and wife of tenant while they enjoy sex (161, 140).

The Prince and his Attendants (171-175, 149-153): Flem Snopes appears before him; demands to get his soul back; takes his throne (imagined by Ratliff) (175, 153).

_____ McCallum (185, 162): called "Old Man Hundred-and-One McCallum" by V. K. Ratliff (185, 162).

Launcelot (225, 197) Lump (225, (196) Snopes (184-185, 162): another Snopes; carries Flem's bag when he leaves with Eula (165, 144); new clerk; replaces Flem in Varner's store (183, 160); pried plank off barn so that men can watch Ike Snopes make love to cow, probably for fee (225, 196); sends for Mink after killing (261, 227); lies to protect Mink when black returns shotgun (266-267, 232); plans to force black to confess stealing Mink's gun to have him sent to penitentiary; urges Mink to run away (267, 233); tries to get Mink to tell him where Houston's body is so that he can steal his money (268-269, 234); tries to persuade him to share money (279-282, 243-245); recovers from Mink's blow; meets Mink where axe is hidden; released by Hampton (288-289, 251); lets slip fact that Flem owns horses (354, 310); attends Armstid-Tull-Snopes trial wearing cap that Flem wore to Texas year before (370, 323); swears he saw Flem give Mrs. Armstid's five dollars to man from Texas (374, 327); lives at Winterbottom's (402, 350).

_____: black who cooks for Houston (204, 179); stops Houston from trying to kill stallion with knife (245, 215).

_____: owner of barn from which Ike Snopes steals food for Houston's cow (218, 190); has five children; is past middle age (218, 191); children have all left home: one is professional nurse; one is a ward heeler; one, a city banker; one, a prostitute; oldest simply disappeared (217, 191); orders Houston's black servant to leave as he hunts for Ike (220, 192); next day finds Ike and cow; takes cow home with Ike following (222, 194); returns cow to Houston; gets dollar pound fee (223, 195).

_____: his wife (218, 191).

_____ Snopes (225, 197: mother of Launcelot (Lump) Snopes; school teacher; spent one summer term at State Teachers' College (225-226, 197).

_____ Snopes (226, 197): Lump Snopes's father; steals shoe salesman's sample case (226, 197).

_____ Snopes: wife of I. O. Snopes, "big, tranquil-faced young woman" (228, 199); appears with baby; frightens I. O. Snopes into quitting as schoolmaster and running away (303, 264); follows him out of town (304, 265),

_____ Snopes: little boy trotting along Littlejohn's fence (186, 163); runs to store to tell men when Ike Snopes is about to make love to cow (226, 197). son of I. O. Snopes (228, 199).

_____ Snopes: child of I. O. Snopes (228, 199).

_____ Snopes: infant child of I. O. Snopes (228, 199).

_____ Whitfield (231, 202): minister of village church (231, 201); ordained minister by Will Varner (231, 201); gives formula for curing Ike of infatuation with cow: kill it; cook it; have Ike eat a piece in full knowledge (231, 202).

Mrs. Lucy Pate (238, 208) Houston (235, 205): wife of Jack Houston, an orphan, plain, 24 at marriage; dies six months later; five years younger than Houston (235, 205); deliberately fails in school to be in his class (239, 208); writes his examinations and papers for him (239-240, 209); learns to copy his handwriting (210, 214); killed by stallion (247, 215).

_____ Houston: father of Jack Houston, farmer (235-236, 205); gives son all his money when he leaves at 16 (241, 210); dies (243, 212).

_____ Houston: mother of Jack Houston; taught him to writer his name before she died (236, 205).

_____: prostitute out of Galveston brothel; lives with Houston seven years as his wife (242, 211); offers to live near him when he decides to return to Mississippi to marry (244-245, 213).

_____: black woman; cooks for Jack and Lucy Houston (246, 214).

_____ Hampton (266, 232): sheriff, two hundred and forty pounds (262, 228).

_____: black man who found Mink's shotgun (266, 232).

_____: operator of logging camp at which Mink meets his wife; widower (271, 236).

_____: foreman in logging camp; hires Mink (271, 236).

_____: "magnificent quadroon" with whom logging camp operator lives; most of teeth are gold (271, 236).

_____: Justice of the Peace who issues marriage licence and marries Mink Snopes and wife (273, 238).

George (293, 256) _____: Hampton's deputy; handcuffed to Mink (292, 255).

Jim (293, 255) _____: Hampton's other deputy, his driver (293, 255).

_____: doctor who tends Mink Snopes (295, 257).

_____: Ratliff's nieces and nephews (297, 259).

_____: magistrate who commits Mink Snopes to jail (297, 259).

_____: two officers in court with Mink Snopes (297, 259).

_____: daughter of Eula Varner Snopes and Hoake McCarron (302, 263).

_____ Snopes (303, 264): wife of I. O. Snopes and her baby (303, 264).

_____: grandmother of Wallstreet Panic Snopes (306, 266).

_____ Freeman (309, 271): identifies Flem as he returns to town (309, 271); buys one of the horses (342, 299).

Buck Hipps (310, 272): Texan who accompanies Flem Snopes with horses (309-310, 271) face scarred recently; eats gingersnaps; scarred by barbed wire that holds horses (310-311, 272); knocks one horse down with pistol butt; holds it by the nostrils (326, 287); offers Eck Snopes horse to start auction (330, 289); refuses to get Henry's horse from lot (335, 293); tells Henry's wife not to enter lot (336, 294); removes Armstids from lot; gives her five dollars and tells her to take Henry home without horse (337, 295); tells Mrs. Armstid she can get five dollars back from Flem Snopes next day (339, 297); drives off with Flem after auction (341, 298).

Anse McCallum (316, 277): once bought pair of Texas horses for fourteen rifle cartridges (316, 277).

Henry (331, 290) Armstid (350, 306): arrives at auction (331, 289); bids five dollars for horse; threatens crowd not to raise his bid (333,

292); orders wife to enter lot with him (336, 294); strikes wife with rope because she failed to corner horses (337, 295); after Hipps gives five dollars to Mrs. Armstid, takes money and gives it to Flem Snopes (338, 296); leads men into lot to get horses (343, 300); seriously injured by escaping horses; is taken to Mrs. Littlejohn's hotel (348, 304-305,); suffered broken leg (357, 312); Armstids file suit against Flem Snopes (367, 321); re-broke leg (385, 336); watches Flem Snopes digging at night (388, 338); believes Flem is searching for Old Frenchman's fortune (389, 339); joins Ratliff and Bookwright in search (390 ff., 340 ff.); tries to attack Eustace Grimm after they buy land (408, 355); fanatically continues to dig after Bookwright and Ratliff have accepted fact that they have been bilked by Flem; crowds come to watch him (417-418, 363-364); plagued by boys (420-421, 366).

Mrs. Henry (331, 290) Armstid (350, 306): arrives with husband at auction (331, 2894); wearing sunbonnet and gray, shapeless garment (331, 290); appeals to crowd to stop her husband from bidding five dollars which she earned "weaving by firelight," (333, 291-292); follows Henry into lot for horse (336, 294); asks Flem to return five dollars (360, 315); stoically accepts dismissal of suit against Flem; rides off from trial on mule (374-375, 327); brings Henry dinner pail; returns to farm chores as he digs (419, 364).

Mrs. Vernon Tull (347, 303): Tull's wife (347, 303); Ratliff says she will sue Eck for damage to husband (357, 312); files suit for damages (367, 321); is outraged when she loses her case (378-379, 331-332).

_____ Tull: the four daughters of Vernon Tull (347, 304).

_____: man with peach spray in mouth on store gallery (353, 309); has helped Armstid make his crop in past (357-358, 313).

St. Elmo (363, 318) Snopes (364, 319): "a hulking half-grown boy;" appears before store (357, 312); caught by Jody Varner stealing candy (363, 317); I. O. Snopes's son (364, 319).

_____ Armstid (358, 313): Henry Armstid's oldest girl (358, 313); 12 years old, sleeps with axe, according to Ratliff (358-359, 314).

Mrs. _____ Freeman (365, 319): witnesses Eck's horse break its neck (365, 319).

_____: bailiff; attempts to serve papers on Flem (367, 321).

_____: Justice of the Peace; hears Armstid and Tull cases against Flem and Eck (369, 323); prays before trial (370, 324); dismisses Armstid case after Lump Snopes's perjury (374, 327); rules that Eck never legally owned horse that ran over Tull (378, 330); awards Mrs. Tull ownership of spotted horse and adjourns court (379-380, 331-332).

_____: young lawyer appointed by court to defend Mink (380, 332).

_____: judge who sentences Mink Snopes to life (381, 333).

_____: officer handcuffed to Mink at trial (380, 332-333).

Uncle Dick Bolivar (391, 340): very old man, known throughout county; has no kin (394, 343); makes and sells charms; eats frogs, snakes, insects; a diviner (393, 343-344); helps Ratliff, Armstid, and Bookwright search for treasure; finds three sacks of silver coins (394 ff., 344 ff.); receives dollar fee from Ratliff (400, 348).

Eustace Grimm (400, 348): young tenant farmer living in next county (400, 348).

Mrs. Eustace Grimm (400, 348): wife of Eustace Grimm (400, 348); nee Doshey (413, 360).

_____ Grimm (400, 348): child of Eustace Grimm.

_____ Quick (401, 349): son of Lon Quick.

_____ Winterbottom: owner of boarding house in Frenchman's Bend (402, 350).

Mrs. _____ Fite Grimm: second wife of Eustace Grimm's father (413, 360).

Mrs. _____ Snopes Grimm (413, 360): Ab Snopes youngest sister; mother of Eustace Grimm; wife of Eustace Grimm's father (413, 360).

[These last four names were changed in the 1964 edition, as indicated below.]

Aaron Rideout (417): [original name; in 1956 edition] owner of other half of restaurant in Jefferson; Ratliff once owned other half; now Flem Snopes owns it; cousin of Ratliff (417).

Grover Cleveland Winbush (363): [name changed in 1964 edition from Rideout; see above.] owner of other half of restaurant in Jefferson; Ratliff once owned other half; now Flem Snopes owns it; cousin of Ratliff (363).

_____ Rideout (417): brother to Aaron, cousin to Ratliff (363).

_____ Winbush (363): brother to Grover Cleveland, cousin to Ratliff (370).

Written from 1935 to 1942. **Faulkner began to consider reworking individual stories as a novel about May, 1940; originally titled** *Go Down Moses, and Other Stories.* **(See the treatment of** *Go Down Moses,* **as a series of short stories for writing and publishing details of individual short stories.)**

Pagination, in parentheses, to the following edition and reissues: (New York: Random House, 1942), 383 pp.; (New York: Modern Library, 1955), 383 pp., titled Go Down, Moses and Other Stories; *(New York: Vintage Books, 1973); 383 pp. paperback.*

<u>Isaac (3) Beauchamp (307) McCaslin (3)</u>: Uncle Ike; childless widower, past 70; widower for twenty years; stated to own no property, but owns house (3); lives in Jefferson, supported by Carothers Edmonds (36); story of his repudiation of heritage told, but from point of view of ignorance of motive (105 ff.); son of Theophilus McCaslin (106); gets fifty dollars a month from his cousin McCaslin Edmonds and all succeeding Edmondses; pays Fonsiba's share of inheritance through bank; pays Lucas his share of legacy; arranges for Fonsiba to be paid three dolars a week (107); flashback shoots first deer (163); face marked with blood by Sam Fathers 12 years old (164); 9 when Sam Fathers leaves plantation to live in woods (173); manhood ritual introduced (175); just 12 when they hunt second buck (181); Sam Fathers lets it escape (184); tells his cousin about it; gets lecture on life and is told that Sam Fathers took cousin to see big buck--a symbol of life-- after he had killed his first deer (187); 16 years old (191); comes to initiation ritual in big woods when he is 10 (192) initiation ritual stressed (195); with Sam Fathers, takes the poorest stand in hunt (196); first contact with Old Ben (197); is inspected by Old Ben (198); taken by Sam Fathers to see print of bear (200); alone in woods, feels that bear is looking at him (203); keeps same gun for over 70 years (205); seeks bear without gun (206); relinquishes completely to wilderness; leaves compass, watch, and stick; enters wilderness untainted; is lost (208); finds print of bear; follows prints back to watch and compass; sees bear; passes first manhood test (209); now has killed first buck; face marked with blood by Sam Fathers (209-210); takes fyce to woods and brings bear to bay (211); does not shoot bear; nor does Sam Fathers (212); after Sam Fathers traps Lion, stays on when others return; watches Sam Fathers train dog (218 ff.); conscious of class distinction between Indian parts of Sam Fathers and those of Boon (222); feels there is a fatality in hunting the bear (226); sent with Boon to Memphis for more whisky (226-227); gives Boon dollar (223); rides Katie when Old Ben is killed (237); knows Sam Fathers is going to die (246); as others get ready to leave, says he is going to stay (249); tells Cass to leave Boon alone when Cass asks him if he has killed Sam Fathers (254); at 21, grandson of Carothers McCaslin, relinquishes birthright to his cousin McCaslin Edmonds; begins theory that man can not own land (256); gives Biblical reason for theory (257); says his grandfather and his kind tainted the land with slavery (259); introduces Messianic theme (259 ff.); reads history of his grandfather's and father's and uncle's dealing with slaves in commissary ledgers (261); reads specific tragedy of sexual exploitation

of Eunice and incest with Tomey and birth of Tomey's Turl (266 ff.); 16 at time (267); born 1867 (273); traces Tennie's Jim to Jackson, Tennessee; loses trace of him (273); traces Fonsiba to Arkansas; finds her (276-277); speech on the curse on South (278); leaves Fonsiba's thousand dollars in trust with banker to be paid at three dollars a week for twenty-eight years (280-281); repudiates land; married; no children; unwidowed but without wife; lives in Jefferson (281); long conversation begins in which he repudiates land (282); initiates Messianic theme that God chose his grandfather to sire race that would produce Ike to repudiate his inheritance (282 ff.); develops theory of America being established by God as a refuge from Europe and that whites spoiled it by slavery (284 ff.); believes that because of slavery God put a curse on South (cf. Rosa Coldfield) (286); repudiation takes place in October (289); develops theory that the Negro will endure; great guilt about his grandfather's sexual exploitation of his slave Eunice and about his incest with his slave-child Tomey (294 ff.); vices and virtues of blacks (294 ff.); makes application in the social world of virtues he learned in wilderness from Sam Fathers and Old Ben (295); adopts role of Messiah (299); says, "Yes, Sam Fathers set me free." (300); buys kit of carpenter tools after repudiation (300); born 1867 (301); at 21 opens legacy from Hubert Beauchamp, his uncle; finds silver cup replaced by tin coffee pot and gold coins replaced by IOU's (306-307); accepts "loan" from McCaslin Edmonds; assumes full Messianic role; emulates the Nazarene (309); McCaslin Edmonds pays thirty dollars a month to his account (310); resists wife's sexual seduction to repudiate his heritage (312-315); flashback: at 18 returns with Boon and Uncle Ash for last visit to woods (316 ff.); is shocked at the mechanical advances he sees (318); determines that he will never return to these woods (321); reminisces about his initiation to manhood ritual; and Uncle Ash's desire to kill a deer (323 ff.); visits Sam Father's and Lion's graves (327); almost steps on rattlesnake, "the old one, the ancient and accursed about the earth, fatal and solitary" (329); addresses snake as "Chief," "Grandfather" (330); finds Boon under gum tree hammering at his dismantled rifle (331); almost 80 now (336) thinks that every man and woman at moment of love is God (348); gives his theory about God; role of hunting in man's life (349); can not sleep; reviews story of earlier Big Bottom and killing of first buck (350); reviews the last sex with his wife [cf. "The Bear"] when he repudiated land for son he was never to have (351); wilderness becomes his home (351); hunting companions are more his kin than any; wilderness was his land (352); enunciates principle of land belonging to no man but to all to use well (354); meets granddaughter of Tennie's Jim (357); gives her Roth's message (358); she bore Roth Edmonds's child (358); insists there can be no marriage between Roth Edmonds and granddaughter of Tennie's Jim (358); says she is a "nigger" (361); tells her to "get out of here;" (361) urges her to take the money from Roth; touches her (362); tells her to go back North and marry a man of her own race (363); says that ruined woods do not cry out for retribution because "the people who have destroyed it will accomplish its revenge." (364).

Carothers (7) (Cass) (5) McCaslin Edmonds (3): elder cousin of Isaac McCaslin; grandson of Isaac's father's [Theophilus McCaslin's] sister (3); born 1850; 16 years older than Ike (4); with Uncle Buck, has job of bringing Turl back from visiting Tennie (6); 9 years old at this time (10); when Uncle Buck gets into trouble over getting into bed with Sophonsiba, returns home to fetch Uncle Buddy to help (21); grandfather of Carothers Edmonds (36); built house for Lucas and Molly; allotted specific acreage to Lucas to be farmed as he saw fit as long as he remained on the place (110); owns house rented by Rider (137); 16 years Ike's senior; more his brother than cousin; more his father than either (164); Sam Fathers took him also to see big buck, wild symbol of life, after he had killed his own first buck (187); returns to camp to Sam's burial platform with Boon guarding it (252); takes gun away from Boon; asks Boon if he killed Sam Fathers (253); trustee for McCaslin heritage for children of Tomys Turl (273); orders Fonsiba's future husband off plantation (276); during Ike's repudiation of land, reads Keats's "Ode on a Grecian Urn" to him (296); Truth is one (297); fails to convince Ike not to repudiate his inheritance (299 ff.); gives Ike "as a loan" monthly allowance (308); took Ike to woods for first time (350).

_____ McCaslin (4): deceased wife of Isaac McCaslin; wills house to him urges him to reclaim his heritage (312); strips naked (313); tries to get him to reclaim his plantation by withholding sex; he refuses at first and then agrees; after they have sex, she says that is all he will get from her as she realizes that, even though he agreed before sex, he will not reclaim the land (315).

_____: sister-in-law of Isaac McCaslin; lives in his house (4).

_____: children of sister-in-law of Isaac McCaslin (4).

Theophilus (8) Filus (16) McCaslin (105): Uncle Buck (4); gets necktie to chase Tomy's Turl (5); takes a nap at Beauchamp's before searching for Tomy's Turl (13); hunts Tomy's Turl with dogs (14); bets Hubert Beauchamp five hundred dollars he will take Tomy's Turl home before sundown (15); knocked down by Tomy's Turl (19); after dark, enters Miss Sophonsiba's room; removes trousers; gets into her bed (20-21); plays poker with Hubert Beauchamp: five hundred dollars against Sibbey; one that wins buys either Tennie or Tomy's Turl (24); he loses: three of a kind (threes) to full house (kings over fives) (24-25); twin white son of Carothers McCaslin (105); Ike McCaslin's father (168); member of John Sartoris's horse; rides horse into Gayoso Hotel where Yankee officers sit; escapes scot free (233-234); herds slaves into main house at night, although there is no back door to it (262); twin of Amodeus (263); sold a slave by Bedford Forrest and beaten in trade (273) with brother, increases original thousand dollar heritage from Carothers McCaslin to one thousand for each of three surviving children of Tennie and Turl (273); dies 1881 (274).

Tomy's Turl (4) Terrel (270): has run away (4) to visit Tennie (5); "that damn white half-McCaslin" (6); takes the Jake mule (8); eludes pursuit by Uncle Buck and Cass; disappears (9); when dogs catch up with him, disappears into woods; takes dogs with him (14); when Uncle Buck finds him in Tennie's cabin, runs right over him (19); deals cards in game between Uncle Buddy and Hubert Beauchamp that wins him Tennie; game decided when Hubert, with three threes, refuses to call Uncle Buddy's possible straight (29); son of [Lucius Quintus] Carothers McCaslin; father of Lucas, James, and Fonsiba (105); according to ledgers, son of Thucydides (Thucydus) and Eunice; born 1833; half-brother and nephew of Uncle Buck and Uncle Buddy; outlives them (269).

Amodeus (10) McCaslin (105): Uncle Buddy; cook (4); "never went anywhere, not even to town" (6); goes to Warwick to help Uncle Buck (21); unlike his brother, does not blink, nor does he drink; a little stouter than his brother (26); plays stud poker with Hubert Beauchamp: if he loses, Uncle Buck must marry Sibbey; if he wins, he gets Uncle Buck back and they must buy Tennie (26); he wins (29); wins Tennie in poker game (105); twin white son of Carothers McCaslin (105); uncle of boy narrator (168); uncle of Ike (256); twin of Theophilus (263); urges brother to free Percival Brownlee (264); cook and housekeeper; writes in ledger that Eunice drowned herself (267); with brother, increases original thousand dollar heritage from Carothers McCaslin to one thousand for each of surviving children of Tennie and Turl (273); dies *ca.* 1881 (274).

Hubert Fitz-Hubert Beauchamp (5): owner of Tennie and brother of Sophonsiba whom he is trying to marry off to Uncle Buck (6); after Uncle Buck gets into Sophonsiba's bed, tells him "She is got you at last" (21); loses Tennie to Amodeus McCaslin in poker game (271); Ike's godfather; leaves legacy to Ike (300); silver cup filled with gold pieces (301); according to his sister, Earl of Warwick (302); after sister's marriage, fortunes dwindle (302 ff.); at first insists on having others feel weight of cup full of coins; then he alone holds it as he removes coins (304-305); house burns down (305); replaces gold coins with worthless IOU's (307).

Sophonsiba Beauchamp (5) McCaslin (301): sister of Hubert (5); has a "roan tooth" (10); flatters Uncle Buck (11); talks of marriage to him (11-12); pursues Uncle Buck relentlessly with toddies (14); sends her ribbon to Uncle Buck while he hunts Tomy's Turl (15); screams when Uncle Buck gets into her bed (21); wife of Theophilus McCaslin; mother of Isaac McCaslin; after marriage, moves into big house (301); insists on calling her family plantation "Warwick" (302).

Tennie (5) Beauchamp (263): female slave owned by Hubert Beauchamp (5); bought by Uncle Buck and Uncle Buddy to be married to Turl (29); won by Amodeus McCaslin in poker game in 1859; mother of James, Fonsiba, and Lucas Beauchamp (105); 21 at time of marriage; in 1859; married to Tomy's Turl (271).

Lucius Quintus (266) Carothers McCaslin (36): great-grandfather of Cass Edmonds (6); original owner of the Edmonds plantation (36); got the land from Indians (37); grandfather and father [by his own daughter] of Turl; great-grandfather and grandfather of Lucas, James and Fonsiba Beauchamp (105); Ike's grandfather (359); purchased land from Indians (254); buys Sam Fathers and his mother from Ikkemotubbe for an underbred trotting gelding (263); born in Carolina 1772; died Mississippi 27 June 1837 (266); leaves one thousand dollars in will to his son Turl;

fathered Tomasina by Eunice, and Turl by own daughter Tomasina (270-271); bought Sam Fathers, his mother, and foster-father (166).

Ikkemotubbe (191): Chickasaw chief; sells land to Sutpen (191, 255); father of Sam Fathers; called Doom, corruption of *Du Homme*; son of sister of Issetibbeha; ran away to New Orleans as a boy; returned after seven years with French companion (165); returned with "his foreign Aramis and the quadroon slave woman who was to be Sam's mother" (166); returns with powerful poison with which he intimidates his cousin (166); becomes "The Man" Doom; marries pregnant octaroon to slave (who gave Sam Fathers his name); sold mother, child, and foster father to Carothers McCaslin (166).

_____ McCaslin (7) Edmonds: grandmother of McCaslin Edmonds; sister of Uncle Buck and Uncle Buddy (7).

Jonas (7): slave of Uncle Buck and Uncle Buddy (7).

_____: boy slave who blows dinner horn at Beauchamp's place (9).

_____: young female slave who carries Sophonsiba's fan (10).

_____: slave who brings Sophonsiba's ribbon to Uncle Buck (15).

George Wilkins (33): newly established moonshiner; Lucas's rival (34); sharecropper on Carothers Edmonds's land (34); arrested with Lucas for moonshining (63 ff.); takes money given him by Lucas to repair his house and buys another still (77); not yet 25; marries Lucas's daughter Nat (123).

Lucas (39) Quintus Carothers McCaslin (81) Beauchamp (39): 67 years old, well off; moonshiner (33); dismantles still (33 ff.); for forty-five years farmer on Edmonds's place (35); born on land twenty-five years before Edmonds family owned it; oldest man on Edmonds's plantation; oldest McCaslin descendant on place (36); while hiding his still in an Indian burial mound, finds gold coin (38); spends next five hours looking for more coins; decides that George must go (41); flashback: forty-three years earlier [when he was 24] had intended to kill Zack Edmonds (44); crosses flooded river to get doctor when Carothers Edmonds is born; finds Molly in Edmonds's house nursing both white and black babies (46); demands that Zack Edmonds let Molly return home; thinks he has to kill Zack to prove he returned Molly because Lucas demanded it; not because Zack was tired of Molly (49); says he is a nigger but also a man (47); takes razor; enters Zack Edmonds's bedroom; says he is a "man made McCaslin;" throws razor away; tells Zack to get pistol from under pillow (53); hand wrestles Zack for pistol (55); gains the pistol (56); gives his confused version of Ike McCaslin's repudiation of his inheritance (56); shoots at Zack; gun misfires (57); back to present: can switch from his role as a black to that of "nigger" at will; tries to get George Wilkins arrested to break match with daughter (60); plan backfires; arrested when sheriff finds his hidden still and George Wilkins puts his own still and all his whisky on Lucas's porch (63 ff.); tries to borrow three hundred dollars from Carothers Edmonds to buy machine to divine gold in ground (79 ff.); steals mule from Edmonds to swap for divining machine (83); draws fifty silver dollars from bank; salts the field in two places; then tricks salesman into giving back mule, giving him divining machine, and half of what he finds (90 ff.); then rents machine for twenty-five dollars a night to salesman (96-97); after salesman leaves in disgust, becomes a rabid treasure hunter (101 ff.); flashback: on 21st birthday, apeared to Ike McCaslin to demand rest of the heritage left by Carothers McCaslin to his black children (108); back to present: is willing to give Molly a divorce (119); at last minute, appears in court to call off divorce (128); gives Molly token apology in sack of five-cent candy (130); turns divining machine over to Roth Edmonds (130); Edmonds's oldest tenant; built fire on hearth on wedding day which has burned ever since (138); last and sixth child of Tomy's Turl and Tennie; born about 1875 (274); born March 17, 1874; appears at Ike's home and demands all remaining money in Carothers McCaslin's legacy (281-282); grandfather of Samuel Worsham Beauchamp (373).

Carothers (33) (Roth) (35) Edmonds (33): not yet 45 years old (35); grandson of McCaslin (Cass) Edmonds, Ike's older cousin (36); great-nephew of Ike McCaslin (40); son of Zack Edmonds (43); 43 years old last March (45); after mule is stolen, finds Lucas and George with divining machine; tells Lucas to have mule back in stall by sunup (86-87); once a month as a "libation to his luck" "though actually it was to his ancestors and to the conscience," takes tin of tobacco and sack of candy to Molly Beauchamp, his former nurse (99); flashback: "old curse of his fathers" descends on him when, at 7 years, refuses to share same bed or pallet with Henry Beauchamp, son of Molly and Lucas (111); they never sleep in same room again and never eat at the same table (112); when he announces that he will eat at Lucas's home; is served in kitchen alone; the breach has been made (113-114); realizes that Lucas beat his father (Zack) over Molly (115-116); drives Molly and Lucas to divorce court (125); sets time close to 1939 [in "Delta Autumn"]; has been in WW I (338); small tirade on depression and government control (339); has theory that man behaves only because of presence of police force (346); 40 years old (353); leaves envelope with Uncle Ike to give to messenger along with message "No" (355); had taken woman to New Mexico; sired her child; sends her money to Vicksburg bank; had seen her by road as they approached camp (359); owner of plantation on which Mollie [note variant spelling.] lives (370).

_____: former rival of Lucas Beauchamp as moonshiner; now at state penal farm at Parchman (33).

Molly (45) Mollie (370) Beauchamp: wife of Lucas Beauchamp (34); delivered Roth Edmonds; then kept six months in white house to wet nurse the babies (46); tells Carothers Edmonds she wants a divorce because of divining machine (101); a town woman, not a farm woman (110); reason for objecting to divining machine is religious: what has been buried has been given back to the Lord (102, 122); disappears (124); found unconscious on ground with divining machine (125); grandmother of Samuel Worsham Beauchamp (370); sister of Hamp Worsham (371); intuits that grandson is in trouble; goes to Gavin Stevens for help; repeats that Roth Edmonds sold her Benjamin to Pharaoh (380);

Nat (34) Nathalie Beauchamp Wilkins (72): daughter of Lucas Beauchamp; engaged to marry George Wilkins (34); watches from thicket while father buries his still (40-41); married to George Wilkins in October preceding year; therefore cannot testify against him and Lucas (72); youngest and last of children of Lucas and Molly; 17 years old (73); expecting child (123).

Zachary (Zack) (116) Edmonds (35): now dead (39); son of McCaslin Edmonds; father of Carothers Edmonds (43); refuses to fight Lucas (54); when Lucas holds pistol on him, springs at him and gun misfires (57).

_____ Edmonds (46): wife of Zack Edmonds, mother of Carothers Edmonds; dies in childbirth (46).

Henry (111) Beauchamp: first-born son of Lucas and Molly; nursed by Molly (45) along with Carothers Edmonds and called "his black foster brother" (110).

Aunt Thisbe (50): servant of Zack Edmonds (50).

_____: sheriff of county; Lucas feels he is a redneck (43); arrests Lucas for moonshining (63).

Tom (65) _____: [Federal] commissioner (63).

_____: sheriff's deputy(63).

Judge (71) _____ Gowan (71): dismisses case against both George Wilkins and Lucas Beauchamp for moonshining (74).

_____: U. S. Attorney (71).

Henry (74) _____: deputy marshal (72); ordered to destroy whisky and both George's and Lucas's stills (74).

_____: salesman, not yet 30 (78); came from Memphis with divining machine (81); swaps divining machine with Lucas for stolen mule (82-83); tricked by Lucas into giving him back the mule and ownership of the divining machine (90 ff.); leaves in disgust (101).

Dan (83) _____: one of Edmonds's lotmen (83).

Oscar (83) _____: one of Edmonds's lotmen (83); brought a "yellow slut" from Memphis to plantation; Edmonds sent her back (119).

James (104) Jim (194) Thucydus (272) Beauchamp (39): brother of Lucas (104) ran away at 21 never heard from again (105); Tennie's Jim (194); handles the hounds during hunt (239); goes for Dr. Crawford to treat Boon and Sam Fathers and Lion (243); rides to town; brings Cass and Major de Spain back to woods (252); fourth child of Tomys Turl and Tennie Beauchamp; born December 29, 1864 (272); vanishes December 29, 1885; traced by Ike McCaslin to Jackson, Tennessee; there lost; his legacy returned to McCaslin Edmonds (273).

Fonsiba (105) Sophonsiba (273) Beauchamp (39): sister of Lucas; married and moved to Arkansas; Ike McCaslin puts her share of legacy in bank; daughter of Tomys Turl and Tennie; born 1869 (273); married 1886 (274); elopes with man from Arkansas (276); terribly changed when Ike finds her (277).

Aunt Tomey (105) Tomasina, Tomy (269): mother of Turl by Carothers McCaslin whose daughter she is; grandmother of Lucas, James, Fonsiba (105); daughter, according to the ledgers, of Thucydides (Thucydus) and Eunice; born 1810; dies in giving birth to Turl, June 1833; year stars fell; mother of Turl; unmarried; child fathered by Carothers McCaslin, her father (269); only 23 when Turl was born (270); daughter of Carothers McCaslin (270-271).

Hamp Worsham: brother of Molly Beauchamp whom she has not seen in ten years; lives in Jefferson (117).

Dr. _____ Rideout (125): attends Molly when she collapses with divining machine (125).

_____: Chancellor before whom Lucas-Molly divorce case is heard (126).

_____ Hulett (129): clerk in divorce court (128).

_____: Carothers Edmonds's cook (130).

Spoot (151) Rider (135): black man, over six feet tall and two hundred pounds; boss of sawmill gang; wife has just died (136); rents house from Carothers Edmonds; now 24 years old (137); had been married for only six months (138); sees apparition of dead wife after burying her; wants to go with her; she fades (140); sets plate for dead wife; tries to call her back (141-142); buys gallon of whisky (146); drinks until he vomits; then drinks and vomits three times in succession (149); returns to his aunt's house; refuses to pray (151); joins dice game with white night watchman (152); catches white man with extra pair of dice; as other tries to shoot him, kills white man by cutting his throat with razor (153-154); is lynched (154); tears door off cell before lynching (158).

Mannie (135) Rider: Spoot Rider's dead wife (135).

_____: member of Rider's sawmill gang; offers to take shovel at graveside (135).

_____: Rider's aunt who raised him (136); locked in cell with him (158).

_____: Rider's parents (136).

Acey (136)_____: one of Rider's friends; offers him whisky; says Mannie will be walking yet (136).

_____: black fireman at sawmill (142); gives Rider his lunch pail (143).

_____: white foreman at sawmill (143).

Unc Alec (150)_____: Rider's aunt's husband, Rider's uncle who brings lunch to Rider at mill (144); tries to persuade Rider to stop drinking and to come home (148).

_____: white man who sells gallon of whisky to Rider (146).

_____ Birdsong (155): white night watchman at sawmill (152); throat cut by Rider for cheating in dice game (154); has forty-two relatives on polling list; obvious source of Rider's lynch party (155).

_____: coroner (154).

_____: sheriff's deputy; thinks blacks are incapable of human feelings (154); ironically misreads all signs of Rider's grief (155),

_____: wife of sheriff's deputy (154-155).

_____ Maydew (155): sheriff (157).

_____ McAndrews (156): manager or owner of sawmill at which Rider worked (156).

_____ Ketcham (157): jailor (158).

Sam Fathers (163): 70 years old, son of Chickasaw chief and slave woman; childless son of Ikkemotubbe (165) and quadroon slave (166); got name from slave his mother was later married to; Chickasaw name means Had-Two-Fathers; with his mother and foster father was sold to Carothers McCaslin (166); he is in cage of his own heritage, betrayed into bondage not by Ikkemotubbe [Doom] but by trace of black blood (167-168); tells Ike of the Old People (171); suddenly demands permission to live in the Big Bottom after Jobaker's death (173); addresses giant buck as "Oleh, Chief" "Grandfather," and does not shoot it (184); meets hunting party at edge of wilderness (195); teaches Ike to hunt (195, 198); takes Ike to see his first view of Old Ben's print (200); tells Ike that they do not have the dog yet to bay Old Ben (201); tells Ike that he will not find the bear while he has gun (206); leads party to colt killed by Lion (214); traps Lion (216); says it is the dog that will hold Old Ben

(217); trains dog by starving, then feeding it (218 ff.); near Ike during hunt (239); collapses after Old Ben is killed (242); asks to be left at his hut in woods (245); doctor examines him; says it is exhaustion, maybe shock (246); dies (or is killed by Boon) (253-254); slave of Carothers McCaslin (263); son of Ikkemotubbe (300).

Boon Hogganbeck (164): grandmother was Chickasaw, but has not the blood of a chief (170); divides great fidelity between Major de Spain and McCaslin Edmonds (170); never killed anything larger than a squirrel with gun (176); one of Old Ben's hunting party; becomes infatuated with Lion; takes over feeding him from Sam Fathers (220); sleeps with dog (221); never known to hit anything with gun; shoots at bear five times; misses (225); feels he has failed dog (226); with Ike, goes to Memphis for more whisky (226-227); grandson of Chickasaw woman; sometimes resents Indian blood; sometimes boasts of it; six feet, four; mind of a child; heart of horse (227); 40 years old (228); has shot five times with borrowed pistol at black on street in Jefferson but missed (230); with Ike, goes to Memphis for whisky (226 ff.); borrows dollar from Ike for drink (233); gets bottle of whisky in Memphis (234); drinks; misses train back to camp; Ike gets him on next train; falls asleep (234-235); as Lion hangs on to Old Ben's throat, attacks and kills bear with knife; injured in fight with bear (241); lifts Sam Fathers into and out of wagon (244-245); after Lion dies, caries him to woods to bury him (248); denies he killed Sam Fathers (254); becomes town marshal at Hoke's (316); on last visit to woods, leaves message with Ash for Ike to meet him at gum tree (322); with squirrels trapped in tree, hammers at his dismantled rifle; tells Ike to leave; that the squirrels are his (331); old hunting companion of Ike (352).

Walter Ewell (164): true hunter whose rifle never misses (164); fires at great buck; kills yearling (184-185); old hunting companion of Ike (352).

Major [Cassius] de Spain (164): former owner of camp (344); commander of Ike's father's cavalry regiment (350); returns to his camp; finds Sam Fathers's burial platform with Boon guarding it (252); bought his land from Thomas Sutpen (255); offers Ike a room in his home after he repudiates the land (309); sells camp and woods to logging company (315-316); former owner of hunting camp (344); commander of Ike's father's cavalry regiment (350).

General [Jason Lycurgus] Compson (164): hunting companion of Major de Spain and McCaslin family (194); fires twice; wounds bear (225); insists that Ike ride Katie (237); speaks over Lion's grave "as he would have spoken over a man" (249); decides that Ike can stay behind in woods (250-251); after Ike repudiates his heritage, offers to have him sleep in his own bed (309).

Chevalier Soeur-Blonde de Vitry (165): French friend of Ikkemotubbe (165).

_____: pregnant quadroon slave who was to be Sam Fathers's

mother; after Ikkemotubbe becomes Doom, married to slave; sold two years later with her husband and child to Carothers McCaslin (166).

Issetibbeha (165): uncle of Ikkemotubbe (165); father of Ikkemotubbe (259).

_____: sister of Issetibbeha; mother of Ikkemotubbe (165).

Moketubbe (166): son of Issetibbeha, cousin of Doom; his 8-year-old son dies mysteriously; abdicates when Doom poisons another puppy (166).

_____: grandmother of Boon Hogganbeck; Chickasaw woman (170).

Jobaker (172): full-blooded Chickasaw; friend of Sam Fathers (172).

Uncle Ash (175): black camp cook (198) accompanies Ike on last visit to woods (321 ff.); warns Ike that snakes are crawling (323); after Ike kills first buck, wants to shoot a deer (323 ff.); finds bear instead; gun fails (325-326).

Thomas Sutpen (191): buys his land from Ikkemotubbe (191, 255).

_____: seven strangers who appear in camp when Lion leads pack to hunt Old Ben (222).

Mr. _____ Semmes (227): distiller in Memphis; Ike and Boon sent to him for more whisky (227).

_____ Hogganbeck (227): father of Boon Hogganbeck (227).

_____ Hogganbeck (227): mother of Boon Hogganbeck (227).

_____: conductor on log train (230).

_____: brakeman on log train (230).

Colonel John Sartoris (234): commander of horse, Civil War (234).

_____: man in washroom as Boon drinks (234).

_____: woman restaurant manager; tells Boon not to drink (234).

_____: black waiter in restaurant (234).

_____: black woman shot by Boon accidentally as he tried to shoot black man (235).

_____: black man shot at by Boon (235).

Bayard Sartoris (236): guest in camp before Old Ben is killed (236).

_____ Sartoris (236): son of Bayard Sartoris; guest in camp night before Old Ben is killed (236).

_____ Compson (236): son of General Compson; guest in camp night before Old Ben is killed (236).

_____: two other guests in camp night before Old Ben is killed (236).

_____: swamper who fires at Old Ben during hunt (238).

Dr. _____ Crawford (243): sent for by Major de Spain to tend Boon, Sam Fathers, and Lion (243); sews up Lion (239); then tends Boon; then tends Sam Fathers (246); says Sam Fathers "just quit" (248).

Roscius (263) Roskus (266): male slave of Carothers McCaslin (263); freed by twins on day their father died, June 27, 1837; does not want to leave plantation; dies and buried January 12, 1841; father of Thucydides (Thucydus); husband of Phoebe (Fibby) (266).

Phoebe (263) Fibby (266): female slave of Carothers McCaslin (263); wife of Roscius (Roskus); mother of Thucydides (Thucydus); bought by Carothers McCaslin's father; freed by twins on day their father died, June 27, 1837; does not want to leave plantation; dies August 1, 1849 (266).

Thucydides (263) Thucydus (266) McCaslin (267): male slave of Carothers McCaslin (263); son of Roscius (Roskus) and Phoebe (Fibby); refuses ten acre piece of land provided for him in will of Carothers McCaslin on day after his death (June 28, 1837); refuses offer of two hundred dollars from twins; wants to stay and work it out (266); paid two hundred dollars wages by twins November 3, 1841; sets up blacksmith shop in Jefferson, December 1841; dies; buried in Jefferson February 17, 1854 (267); married to Eunice when she becomes pregnant (269); not a field hand (270).

Eunice (263) McCaslin: female slave of Carothers McCaslin (263); bought by him in New Orleans in 1807 for six hundred and fifty dollars; married to Thucydides (Thucydus) 1809; suicide by drowning in creek Christmas day 1832 (267); not field hand (270); mother of Tomasina by Carothers McCaslin (270); commits suicide when she learns that Carothers McCaslin by incest has made his and her daughter pregnant (271).

Bedford (263) NB (264) Forrest (263): slave dealer (263).

Percival Brownlee (263): slave purchased by Theophilus McCaslin from Bedford Forrest; an anomaly (263); 26 years old; professed to be bookkeeper; not a bookkeeper; purchased for two hundred and sixty-five dollars; can not read; can not plough (264); shoots wrong mule; will not leave; renamed *Spintrius* (name signifies male prostitute) (265); reappears in 1862 leading slaves in prayer meetings; again disappears; reappears in 1866 with Army paymaster, apparently his homosexual companion; finally,

228

twenty years later, "the well-to-do proprietor of a select New Orleans brothel" (292-293).

Amodeus McCaslin Beauchamp (271): son of Tomys Turl and Tennie Beauchamp; born 1859; died 1859; named after Uncle Buddy (271).

Callina (272) Beauchamp (272): daughter of Tomys Turl and Tennie Beauchamp; dies in infancy (272).

_____: child of Tomys Turl and Tennie; born and dies 1863; sex unknown (272).

Carolina (Callina) (272) McCaslin: sister of twins Uncle Buck and Uncle Buddy (implied name on page 272 in the naming of children of Turl and Tennie).

_____: black man wants to marry Fonsiba; dresses, acts, speaks like a white man; owns farm in Arkansas (274); father was slave who served in U. S. Army in Civil War; farm, a grant from government (275); elopes with Fonsiba next morning (276); when Ike finds him and Fonsiba, farm he boasted of is farm only "in embryo" (277); reads book through spectacles without lenses (278).

_____: his father; served in U. S Army during Civil War (275).

Alice Edmonds (276): wife of McCaslin Edmonds; taught Fonsiba to read and write (276).

_____: banker in Midnight, Arkansas with whom Ike leaves Fonsiba's money in trust (280).

Sickymo (291): ex-slave; United States marshal during Reconstruction; name derived because he sold his master's medicinal alcohol beneath a sycamore tree; recalled by Ike during long talk with cousin (291).

_____: half-white sister of Sickymo; concubine of Federal A. P. M. (292).

_____: grandfather of Lucius Quintus Carothers McCaslin (299).

_____: female light-colored black; seems mistress to Hubert Beauchamp; clothed in his sister's dress (302-303); he calls her his cook; sent packing by Sibby (303).

_____: great-grandfather of Tennie Beauchamp (304-305).

_____: father of Hubert Beauchamp (309).

229

_____: partner of Ike McCaslin; "blasphemous profane clever old dipsomaniac" (310).

_____: president of bank (310).

_____: father of Ike's wife (311); gives them lot and house in Jefferson (312).

Daisy (316): Major de Spain's cook (316).

Will (338) Legate (337): accuses Roth Edmonds of having affair with young light-colored black woman (337).

_____: Will Legate's grandfather (344).

Henry Wyatt (347): third speaker at evening meal on hunt (345).

_____: black cook in hunting camp (348).

_____: black cook's helper in hunting camp (348); tends fire in camp heater at night (349).

Isham (348) _____: old black in hunting camp (348).

_____: Ike's wife's widowed niece; keeps house for him; has children(352).

_____: black man; operates skiff that brings granddaughter of Tennie's Jim to hunting camp (357); her cousin (361).

_____: black woman who bore Roth's child (357); had been with him previous November; he also took her to New Mexico for six weeks (358); knows history of McCaslin-Edmonds-Beauchamp family (359-360); is school teacher from Indianapolis; now lives with aunt who takes in washing (360); granddaughter of Tennie's Jim; says Roth Edmonds does not know that she is (361); takes money (362); confesses her love for Roth and departs (363).

_____: child of Roth Edmonds (357) and granddaughter of Tennie's Jim (361); a boy (362).

_____: aunt of granddaughter of Tennie's Jim; lives in Vicksburg; takes in washing (360).

_____: father of granddaughter of Tennie's Jim (360).

Samuel Worsham Beauchamp (369): 26; raised by Mollie Beauchamp (370); sentenced to electric chair (370); known as "Butch" when a youth (372); child of Mollie's eldest daughter; [therefore, his original name was not Beauchamp] who died at childbirth; deserted by father (372); leaves Edmonds's place at 19; arrested for breaking and entering Rouncewell's store; escapes from county jail; sentenced to State Penetentiary for manslaughter (372); uses unmentioned alias; killed Chicago policeman (374); in numbers racket (375); only child of eldest daughter of Mollie and Lucas Beauchamp (376); named for Miss Worsham's father (376).

_____: census taker who interviews Samuel Worsham Beauchamp in jail (369).

Gavin Stevens (370): prematurely white-haired county attorney (370); Phi Beta Kappa at Harvard; Ph. D. from Heidelberg; for twenty-two years has been translating Old Testament into classic Greek (371); raises money to bring home and bury body of executed killer, Samuel Worsham Beauchamp (378 ff.).

_____: officer who arrests Butch Beauchamp for breaking into Rouncewell's store (372).

_____ Wilmoth (375) : editor of county newspaper; tremendously fat (373).

_____ Rouncewell (373): owner of store robbed by Butch Beauchamp (373).

Miss Belle (383) Worsham (374): aged spinster whose father owned Hamp Worsham's ancestors; with Hamp, raises chickens; gives lessons in china painting (374); grew up with Mollie as a sister (375); father's name was Samuel (376); gives Stevens $25 to bring body home (377).

_____: parents of Hamp Worsham (375).

Mrs. Hamp Worsham (374): Worsham's "tremendous light-colored" wife (379).

_____: warden at Joliet prison (375).

_____: District Attorney in Chicago (375).

Samuel Worsham (376): father of Miss Belle Worsham (376).

_____: undertaker in Joliet (377).

A 19 *Go Down, Moses* (as a series of short stories)

Pagination, in parentheses, to the following edition and reissues: (New York: Random House, 1942,) 383 pp., titled Go Down, Moses and Other Stories in its first printing; (New York: Modern Library, 1955), 383 pp.; (New York: Vintage Books, 1973), 383 pp. paperback.

"Was"

Originally entitled "Almost," this story was written sometime before June 1940; revised July, 1940; it was rejected by *The Saturday Evening Post* **July 1, 1940; first published in** *Go Down, Moses*, **1942.**

Isaac McCaslin (3): Uncle Ike McCaslin; childless widower, past 70; widower for 20 years; stated to own no property, but owns house in Jefferson (3); story that follows derives from older cousin Cass.

Carothers (7) Cass (5) McCaslin Edmonds (3): elder cousin of Isaac McCaslin; grandson of Isaac's father's [Theophilus McCaslin's] sister (3); born 1850; sixteen years older than Ike (4); with Uncle Buck, has job of bringing Turl back from visiting Tennie (6); 9 years old at this time (10); when Uncle Buck gets into trouble over getting into bed with Sophonsiba, returns home to fetch Uncle Buddy to help (21).

_____McCaslin (4): deceased wife of Isaac McCaslin; wills house to him (4).

_____: sister-in-law of Isaac McCaslin; lives in his house (4).

_____: children of sister-in-law of Isaac McCaslin (4).

Theophilus (8) Filus (16) [McCaslin]: Uncle Buck (4); gets necktie to chase Tomy's Turl (5); takes nap at Beauchamp's before searching for Tomy's Turl (13); hunts Tomy's Turl with dogs (14); bets Hubert Beauchamp five hundred dollars he will take Tomy's Turl home before sundown (15); knocked down by Tomy's Turl (19); after dark, enters Miss Sophonsiba's room; removes trousers; gets into her bed (20-21); plays poker with Hubert Beauchamp five hundred dollars against Sibbey; the one that wins buys either Tennie or Tomy's Turl (24); he loses: three of a kind (threes) to full house (kings over fives) (24-25).

Tomy's Turl (4): has run away (4) to visit Tennie (5); "that damn white half-McCaslin" (6); takes the Jake mule (8); eludes pursuit by Uncle Buck and Cass; disappears (9); when dogs catch up with him, disappears into woods; takes dogs with him (14); when Uncle Buck finds him in Tennie's cabin, runs right over him (19); deals cards in game between Uncle Buddy and Hubert Beauchamp that wins him Tennie; game decided when Hubert, with three threes, refuses to call Uncle Buddy's possible straight (29).

Amodeus (10) [McCaslin]: Uncle Buddy; cook (4); "never went anywhere, not even to town" (6); goes to Warwick to help Uncle Buck

(21); unlike his brother, does not blink, nor does he drink; a little stouter than his brother (26); plays stud poker with Hubert Beauchamp: if he loses, Uncle Buck must marry Sibbey; if he wins, he gets Uncle Buck back and they must buy Tennie (26); he wins (29).

Hubert Fitz-Hubert Beauchamp (5): owns Tennie; brother of Sophonsiba whom he is trying to marry off to Uncle Buck (6); after Uncle Buck gets into Sophonsiba's bed, tells him "She is got you at last" (21).

Sophonsiba Beauchamp (5): sister of Hubert (5); has "roan tooth" (10); flatters Uncle Buck (11); talks of marriage to him (11-12); pursues Uncle Buck relentlessly with toddies (14); sends her ribbon to Uncle Buck while he hunts Tomy's Turl (15); screams when Uncle Buck gets into her bed (21).

Tennie (5): female slave owned by Hubert Beauchamp (5); bought by Uncle Buck and Uncle Buddy to be married to Turl (29).

[Lucius Quintus Carothers McCaslin]: great-grandfather of McCaslin Edmonds (6).

_____ McCaslin (7) Edmonds (7): grandmother of McCaslin Edmonds; sister of Uncle Buck and Uncle Buddy (7).

Jonas (7): slave of Uncle Buck and Uncle Buddy (7).

_____: boy slave who blows dinner horn at Beauchamp's place (9).

_____: young female slave who carries Sophonsiba's fan (10).

_____: slave who brings Sophonsiba's ribbon to Uncle Buck (15).

"The Fire and the Hearth"

"A Point of Law" (the first chapter of "The Fire and the Hearth" in *Go Down, Moses*) **was written probably by mid-August, 1939; sent to Harold Ober January 4, 1940; first published in** *Collier's*, **105 (June 22, 1940), 20-21, 30, 31. It was revised for** *Go Down, Moses* **and was reprinted in** *Uncollected Stories*, **1979. "Gold Is Not Always" (second chapter of "The Fire and the Hearth" in** *Go Down, Moses* **was written before mid-February, 1939. It was first published in** *Atlantic Monthly*, **166 (November, 1940), 563-570, and was revised for** *Go Down, Moses*. **It was republished in** *Uncollected Stories*, **1979. "The Fire on the Hearth," originally entitled "An Absolution" and then "Apotheosis," was written before late February, 1939. It was first published in** *Go Down, Moses*.

George Wilkins (33): newly established moonshiner; rival of Lucas Beauchamp (34); sharecropper on Carothers Edmond's land (34); arrested with Lucas for moonshining (63 ff.); takes money given him by Lucas to repair his house and buys another still (77); not yet 25; marries Lucas's daughter Nat (123).

Lucas Beauchamp (39) Uncle Luke (124): moonshiner; 67 years old, well off (33); dismantles still (33 ff.); for forty-five years farmer on Carothers Edmonds's place (35); born on land twenty-five years before Edmonds family owned it; oldest man on Edmonds's plantation; oldest McCaslin descendant on place (36); while hiding his still in an Indian burial mound, finds gold coin (38); spends next five hours looking for more coins; decides that George must go (41); flashback: forty-three years earlier [when he was 24] had intended to kill Zack Edmonds (44); crosses flooded river to get doctor when Carothers Edmonds is born; finds Molly in Edmonds's house nursing both white and black babies (46); demands that Zack Edmonds let Molly return home; thinks he has to kill Zack to prove that he returned Molly because Lucas demanded it and not because Zack was tired of Molly (49); says he is a nigger but also a man (47); takes razor; enters Zack Edmonds's bedroom; claims to be a "man made McCaslin;" throws razor away; challenges Zack to get his pistol from under pillow '(53); hand wrestles Zack for pistol (55); gains the pistol (56); gives his confused version of Ike McCaslin's repudiation of his inheritance (56); shoots at Zack; gun misfires (57); back to present: can switch from his role as a black to that of "nigger" at will; tries to get George Wilkins arrested to break match with daughter (60); plan backfires; arrested when sheriff finds his hidden still and when George Wilkins puts his own still and all his whisky on Lucas's porch (63 ff.); tries to borrow three hundred dollars from Carothers Edmonds to buy machine to divine gold in ground (79ff.); steals mule from Edmonds to swap for divining machine (83); draws fifty silver dollars from bank; salts the field in two places; then tricks salesman into giving back mule, giving him divining machine, and half of what he finds (90 ff.); then rents machine for twenty-five dollars a night to salesman (96-97); after salesman leaves in disgust, becomes a rabid treasure hunter (101 ff.); flashback: on 21st birthday, apeared to Ike McCaslin to demand rest of the heritage left by Carothers McCaslin to his black children (108); back to present: is willing to give Molly a divorce (119); at last minute, appears in court to call off divorce (128); gives Molly token apology in sack of five-cent candy (130); turns divining machine over to Roth Edmonds (130).

Carothers (33) Roth (35) Edmonds (33): not yet 45 years old (35); grandson of McCaslin (Cass) Edmonds, Ike's older cousin (36); great-nephew of Ike McCaslin (40); son of Zack Edmonds (43); 43 years old last March (45); after mule is stolen, finds Lucas and George with divining machine; tells Lucas to have mule back in stall by sunup (86-87); once a month as a "libation to his luck" "though actually it was to his ancestors and to the conscience," takes tin of tobacco and sack of candy to Molly Beauchamp his former nurse (99); flashback: "old curse of his fathers" descends on him when, at 7 years, refuses to share same bed or pallet with Henry Beauchamp, son of Molly and Lucas (111); they never sleep in same room again and never eat at the same table (112); when he announces that he will eat at Lucas's home; is served in kitchen alone; the breach has been made (113-114); realizes that Lucas beat his father (Zack) over Molly (115-116); drives Molly and Lucas to divorce court

(125).

_____: former rival of Lucas Beauchamp as moonshiner; now at state penal farm at Parchman (33).

Molly (45) Beauchamp: wife of Lucas Beauchamp (34); delivers Carothers Edmonds; then kept six months in white house to wet nurse the babies (46); tells Carothers Edmonds she wants a divorce because of divining machine (101); a town woman, not a farm woman (110); reason for objecting to divining machine is religious: what has been buried has been given back to the Lord (102, 122); disappears (124); found unconscious on ground with divining machine (125).

Nat (34) Nathalie Beauchamp Wilkins (72): daughter of Lucas Beauchamp; engaged to marry George Wilkins (34); watches from thicket while father buries his still (40-41); married to George Wilkins in October preceding year; therefore cannot testify against him and Lucas (72); youngest and last of children of Lucas and Molly; 17 years old (73); expecting child (123).

Zack (Zachary) (116) Edmonds (35): now dead (39); son of McCaslin Edmonds; father of Carothers Edmonds (43); refuses to fight Lucas (54); when Lucas holds pistol on him, springs at him and gun misfires (57).

Old Cass Edmonds [McCaslin Edmonds] (35): grandfather of Carothers Edmonds (36); built house for Lucas and Molly; allotted specific acreage to Lucas to be farmed as he saw fit as long as he lived or remained on the place (110).

Isaac McCaslin (36): lives in town, supported by Carothers Edmonds (36); story of his repudiation of heritage told, but from point of view of ignorance of motive (105 ff.); son of Theophilus McCaslin (106); gets fifty dollars a month allowance from his cousin and all succeeding Edmondses; pays Fonsiba's share of inheritance through bank; pays Lucas his share of legacy (107).

[Lucius Quintus] Carothers McCaslin (36): original owner of the Edmonds plantation (36); got the land from Indians (37); grandfather and father [by his own daughter] of Turl; great-grandfather and grandfather of Lucas, James, and Fonsiba Beauchamp (105).

_____ Edmonds (46): wife of Zack Edmonds, mother of Carothers Edmonds; dies in childbirth (46).

Henry (111) Beauchamp: first-born son of Lucas and Molly; nursed by Molly (45) along with Carothers Edmonds and called "his black foster brother" (110).

Aunt Thisbe (50): servant of Zack Edmonds (50).

_____: sheriff of county; Lucas thinks him a redneck (43);

236

fat; arrests Lucas for moonshining (63).

_____: [Federal] commissioner (63).

Tom (65)_____: sheriff's deputy(63).

Judge (71)_____Gowan (71): dismisses case against both George Wilkins and Lucas Beauchamp for moonshining (74).

_____: U. S. Attorney (71).

Henry (74)_____: deputy marshal (72); ordered to destroy whisky and both George's and Lucas's stills (74).

_____: white salesman, not yet 30 (78); came from Memphis with divining machine (81); swaps divining machine with Lucas for stolen mule (82-83).

Dan (83)_____: one of Edmonds's lotmen (83).

Oscar (83)_____: one of Edmonds's lotmen (83); brought a "yellow slut" from Memphis to plantation; Edmonds sent her back (119).

James (104) Beauchamp (39): brother of Lucas (104); ran away at 21; never heard from again (105).

Fonsiba (105) Beauchamp (39)_____: sister of Lucas; leaves plantation (105); married and moved to Arknsas; Ike McCaslin puts her share of legacy in bank; arranges for her to be paid three dollars a week (107).

Aunt Tomey (105): mother of Turl by Carothers McCaslin whose daughter she was; grandmother of Lucas, James, Fonsiba (105).

Turl (105): son of Carothers McCaslin; father of Lucas, James, and Fonsiba (105).

Tennie Beauchamp (105): won by Amodeus McCaslin in poker game in 1859; mother of James, Fonsiba, and Lucas Beauchamp (105).

Amodeus McCaslin: wins Tennie Beauchamp in poker game (105); twin white son of Carothers McCaslin (105).

Theophilus McCaslin (105): twin white son of Carothers McCaslin (105).

_____McCaslin (107): wife of Ike McCaslin (107).

[Hamp Worsham]: brother of Molly Beauchamp whom she has not seen in ten years; lives in Jefferson (117).

Dr._____Rideout (125): attends Molly when she collapses with divining machine (125).

_____: Chancellor before whom Lucas-Molly divorce case is heard (126).

_____ Hulett (129): clerk in divorce court (128).

_____: Carothers Edmonds's cook (130).

"Pantaloon in Black"

Written about March, 1940; this story was first published in _Harper's Magazine_, **181 (October, 1940), 503-513. It was revised for** _Go Down, Moses_, **and it was republished in** _Uncollected Stories_, **1979.**

Spoot (151) Rider (135): black man, over six feet tall and two hundred pounds; boss of sawmill gang; wife has just died (136); rents house from Carothers Edmonds; now 24 years old (137); had been married for only six months (138); sees apparition of dead wife after burying her; wants to go with her; she fades (140); sets plate for dead wife; tries to call her back (141-142); buys gallon of whisky (146); drinks until he vomits; then drinks and vomits three times in succession (149); returns to his aunt's house; refuses to pray (151); joins dice game with white night watchman (152); catches white man with extra pair of dice; as other tries to shoot him, kills white man by cutting his throat with razor (153-154); is lynched (154); tears door off cell before lynching (158).

Mannie (135) Rider: Spoot Rider's dead wife (135).

_____: member of Rider's sawmill gang; offers to take shovel at graveside (135).

_____: Rider's aunt who raised him (136); locked in cell with him (158).

Acey (136) _____: one of Rider's friends; offers him whisky; says Mannie will be walking yet (136).

Carothers Edmonds (137): owns house rented by Rider (137).

Uncle Lucas Beauchamp (138): Edmonds's oldest tenant; built fire on hearth on wedding day which has burned ever since (138).

_____: black fireman at sawmill (142); gives Rider his lunch pail (143).

_____: white foreman at sawmill (143).

Unc Alec (150) _____: Rider's aunt's husband, Rider's uncle who brings lunch to Rider at mill (144); tries to persuade Rider to stop drinking and to come home (148).

_____: white man who sells gallon of whisky to Rider (146).

_____ Birdsong (155): white night watchman at sawmill (152); throat cut by Rider for cheating in dice game (154); has forty-two relatives on polling list; obvious source of Rider's lynch party (155).

_____: coroner (154).

_____: sheriff's deputy; thinks blacks are incapable of human feelings (154); ironically misreads all signs of Rider's grief (155),

_____: wife of sheriff's deputy (154-155).

_____ Maydew (155): sheriff (157).

_____ McAndrews (156): owner or manager of sawmill at which Rider worked (156).

_____ Ketcham (157): jailor (158).

"The Old People"

Written about May-June, 1939, and sent to Harold Ober on October 3, 1939, "The Old People" was first published in _Harper's Magazine_, 181 (September, 1940), 418-425; it was reprinted in _O. Henry Memorial Award Prize Stories of 1941_ (Garden City, New York: Doubleday, Doran and Company, Inc., 1941), pp. 155-169; it was revised for _Go Down, Moses_ and was reprinted in _Big Woods_, 1955, and in _Uncollected Stories_, 1979.

Sam Fathers (163): 70 years old, son of Chickasaw chief and slave woman; childless son of Ikkemotubbe (165) and quadroon slave (166); got name from slave to whom his mother was later married; Chickasaw name means Had-Two-Fathers; with his mother and foster father sold to Carothers McCaslin (166); he is in cage of his own heritage, betrayed into bondage not by Ikkemotubbe [Doom] but by trace of black blood (167-168); tells Ike of the Old People (171); suddenly demands permission to live in the Big Bottom after Jobaker's death (173); addresses giant buck as "Oleh, Chief" "Grandfather," and does not shoot it (184).

Ike McCaslin (163): shoots first deer (163); face marked with blood by Sam Fathers; 12 years old (164); 9 when Sam Fathers leaves plantation to live in woods (173); manhood ritual introduced (175); just 12 when they hunt second buck (181); Sam Fathers lets it escape (184); tells his cousin about it and gets lecture on life and is told that Sam Fathers took his cousin to see big buck--which is symbol of life-- after he had killed his own first deer (187).

Tennie's Jim [Beauchamp] (164).

Boon Hogganbeck (164): grandmother was Chickasaw, but has not the

239

blood of a chief (170); divides great fidelity between Major de Spain and McCaslin Edmonds (170); never killed anything larger than a squirrel with gun (176).

Walter Ewell (164): true hunter whose rifle never misses (164); fires at great buck; kills yearling (184-185).

Major [Cassius] de Spain (164).

General [Jason Lycurgus] Compson (164).

McCaslin Edmonds (164): cousin to Ike McCaslin; grandson of Ike's father's sister; sixteen years Ike's senior; more his brother than cousin; more his father than either (164); Sam Fathers took him also to see big buck, wild symbol of life, after he had killed his own first buck (187).

Ikkemotubbe (165): Chickasaw chief, father of Sam Fathers; called Doom, corruption of *Du Homme*; son of sister of Issetibbeha; ran away to New Orleans as a boy; returned with French companion after seven years (165); returned with "his foreign Aramis and the quadroon slave woman who was to be Sam's mother" (166); returns with powerful poison with which he intimidates his cousin (166); becomes "The Man" Doom; marries pregnant octaroon to slave (who gave Sam Fathers his name); sells mother, child, and foster father to Carothers McCaslin (166).

Chevalier Soeur-Blonde de Vitry (165): French friend of Ikkemotubbe (165).

_____: pregnant quadroon slave who was to be Sam Fathers's mother; after Ikkemotubbe becomes Doom, married to slave; sold to Carothers McCaslin two years later with her husband and child (166).

Issetibbeha (165): uncle of Ikkemotubbe (165).

Moketubbe (166): son of Issetibbeha, cousin of Doom; his 8-year-old son dies mysteriously; abdicates when Doom poisons another puppy (166).

Carothers McCaslin (166): bought Sam Fathers, his mother and foster-father (166).

Uncle Buddy [Amodeus] McCaslin (168): uncle of boy narrator (168).

[Theophilus McCaslin] (168): Ike McCaslin's father (168).

Jobaker (172): full blooded Chickasaw without history; hermit, friend of Sam Fathers; dies but no one ever finds his grave (172).

Uncle Ash (175): camp cook (175).

"The Bear"
The first version of this story, "Lion," appears to have been written about March, 1935; it was published as "Lion" in *Harper's Magazine*, 172

(December, 1935), 67-77. This version was reprinted in *Uncollected Stories*, 1979. "The Bear" appears to have been started in the summer of 1941, as Faulkner revised material from "Lion' to become "The Bear" in *Go Down, Moses*. It was first published as "The Bear" in *The Saturday Evening Post*, 214 (May 9, 1942), 30-31, 74, 76, 77 two days before *Go Down, Moses and Other Stories* was published on May 11, 1942. Parts of "The Bear" were used in *Big Woods*, 1955.

Boon Hogganbeck (191): one of the hunting party; becomes infatuated with Lion; takes over feeding him from Sam Fathers (220); sleeps with dog (221); never known to hit anything with gun; shoots at bear five times; misses (225); feels he failed dog (226); with Ike McCaslin, goes to Memphis for whisky (226-227); grandson of chickasaw squaw; sometimes resents Indian blood; sometimes boasts of it; 6feet, 4inches; mind of child; heart of horse (227); 40 years old (228); has shot five times with borrowed pistol at black on street in Jefferson but missed (230); borrows dollar from Ike McCaslin for drink (233); gets bottle of whisky in Memphis (234); drinks; misses train back to camp; Ike McCaslin gets him on next train; falls asleep (234-235); as Lion hangs on to Old Ben's throat, attacks and kills bear with knife; injured in fight with bear (241); lifts Sam Fathers into and out of wagon (244-245); after Lion dies, caries him to woods to bury him (248); denies he killed Sam Fathers (254); becomes town marshal at Hoke's (316); on last visit to woods, leaves message with Ash for Ike McCaslin to meet him at gum tree (322); with squirrels trapped in tree, hammers at his dismantled rifle; tells Ike McCaslin to leave; that the squirrels are his (331).

Sam Fathers (191): meets hunting party at edge of wilderness (195); teaches Ike McCaslin to hunt (195, 198); takes Ike McCaslin to see his first view of Old Ben's print (200); tells Ike McCaslin that they do not have the dog yet to kill Old Ben (201); tells Ike McCaslin that he will not find the bear while he has gun (206); leads party to colt killed by Lion (214); traps Lion (216); says it is the dog that will hold Old Ben (217); trains dog by starving it, then feeding it (218 ff.); near Ike McCaslin during hunt (239); collapses after Old Ben is killed (242); asks to be left at his hut in woods (245); doctor examines him; says it is exhaustion, maybe shock (246); dies (or is killed by Boon) (253-254); slave of Carothers McCaslin (263); son of Ikkemotubbe (300).

Ike McCaslin (229) Isaac (300) Beauchamp (307) McCaslin (300): 16 years old (191); comes to initiation ritual in big woods when he is 10 (192); initiation ritual stressed (195); with Sam Fathers, takes the poorest stand in hunt (196); first contact with Old Ben (197); is inspected by Old Ben (198); taken by Sam Fathers to see print of bear (200); alone in woods, feels that bear is looking at him (203); keeps same gun for over 70 years (205); seeks bear without gun (206); relinquishes completely to wilderness; leaves compass, watch, and stick; enters wilderness untainted; is lost (208); finds print of bear; follows prints back to watch and compass; sees bear; passes first manhood test (209); now has killed first buck; face marked with blood by Sam Fathers (209-210); takes fyce to woods and brings bear to bay (211); does not shoot bear; nor does Sam Fathers (212); after Sam Fathers traps Lion, stays on when others return;

watches Sam Fathers train dog (218 ff.); very conscious of class distinction between Indian parts of Sam Fathers and Boon (222); feels there is a fatality in hunting the bear (226); sent with Boon to Memphis for more whisky (226-227); gives Boon dollar (223); rides Katie when Old Ben is killed (237); knows that Sam Fathers is going to die (246); as others get ready to leave, says he is going to stay (249); tells Cass to leave Boon alone when Cass asks him if he has killed Sam Fathers (254); at 21, grandson of Carothers McCaslin; relinquishes his birthright to his cousin McCaslin Edmonds; begins theory that man can not own land (256); gives Biblical reason for theory (257); says his grandfather and his kind tainted the land with slavery (259); introduces Messianic theme (259 ff.); reads history of his grandfather's and father's and uncle's dealing with slaves in commissary ledgers (261); reads specific tragedy of sexual exploitation of Eunice and incest with Tomey and birth of Tomey's Turl (266 ff.); 16 at time (267); born 1867 (273); traces Tennie's Jim to Jackson, Tennessee; loses trace of him (273); traces Fonsiba to Arkansas; finds her (276-277); speech about curse on South (278); leaves Fonsiba's one thousand dollars in trust with banker to be paid at three dollars a week for twenty-eight years (280-28); repudiates land; married but has no children; unwidowered but without a wife; lives in Jefferson (281); long conversation begins in which he repudiates land (282); initiates Messianic theme that God chose his grandfather to sire the race that would produce Ike McCaslin to repudiate his inheritance (282 ff.); develops theory of America being established by God as a refuge from Europe and the whites spoiled it by slavery (284 ff.); believes that because of slavery God put a curse on South (cf. Rosa Coldfield) (286); repudiation takes place in October (289); develops theory that the Negro will endure; great guilt about his grandfather's sexual exploitation of his slave Eunice and about his incest with his slave-child Tomey (294 ff.); vices and virtues of blacks (294 ff.); makes application in the social world of virtues he learned in wilderness from Sam Fathers and Old Ben (295); adopts role of Messiah (299); says, "Yes, Sam Fathers set me free." (300); buys kit of carpenter tools after repudiation (300); born 1867 (301); at 21 opens legacy from Hubert Beauchamp, his uncle; finds silver cup replaced by tin coffee pot and gold coins replaced by I. O. U's. (306-307); accepts "loan" from McCaslin Edmonds; assumes full Messianic role; emulates the Nazarene (309); McCaslin Edmonds pays thirty dollars a month to his bank account [but see page 107.] (310); resists wife's sexual seduction to reclaim his heritage (312-315); flashback: at 18 returns with Boon and Uncle Ash for last visit to woods (316 ff.); is shocked at the mechanical advances he sees (318); determines that he will never return to these woods (321); reminisces about his initiation to manhood ritual; and Uncle Ash's desire to kill a deer (323 ff.); visits Sam Fathers's and Lion's graves (327); almost steps on rattlesnake, "the old one, the ancient and accursed about the earth, fatal and solitary" (329); addresses snake as "Chief," "Grandfather" (330); finds Boon under gum tree hammering at his dismantled rifle (331).

Major [Cassius] de Spain (191): returns to his camp; finds Sam Fathers's burial platform; Boon guards it (252); bought land from Thomas Sutpen (255); offers Ike McCaslin a room in his home after he repudiates land (309); sells camp and woods to logging company (315-316).

Thomas Sutpen (191): buys land from Ikkemotubbe (191, 255).

Ikkemotubbe (191): Chickasaw chief; sells land to Sutpen (191, 255).

Jim (194) James Thucydus Beauchamp (272): Tennie's Jim (194); handles hounds during hunt (239); goes for Dr. Crawford to treat Boon and Sam Fathers and Lion (243); rides to town; brings Cass and Major de Spain back to woods (252); fourth child of Tomys Turl and Tennie Beauchamp; born December 29, 1864 (272); vanishes December 29, 1885; traced by Ike McCaslin to Jackson, Tennessee; there lost; his legacy returned to McCaslin Edmonds (273).

[Carothers] McCaslin (194) Edmonds (273): Ike McCaslin's older cousin (194); returns to camp to Sam's burial platform with Boon guarding it (252); takes gun away from Boon; asks Boon if he killed Sam Fathers (253); trustee for McCaslin heritage for children of Tomys Turl (273); orders Fonsiba's future husband off plantation (276); during Ike McCaslin's repudiation of land, reads Keats's "Ode on a Grecian Urn" to him (296); Truth is one (297); fails to convince Ike McCaslin not to repudiate his inheritance (299 ff.); gives Ike McCaslin "as a loan" monthly allowance (308).

General [Jason Lycurgus] Compson (194): hunting companion of Major de Spain and McCaslin family (194); fires twice; wounds bear (225); insists that Ike McCaslin ride Katie (237); speaks over Lion's grave "as he would have spoken over a man" (249); decides that Ike McCaslin can stay behind in woods (250-251); after Ike repudiates his heritage, offers to have him sleep in his own bed (309).

Walter Ewell (194).

Uncle Ash (198): black camp cook (198); accompanies Ike McCaslin on last visit to woods (321 ff.); warns Ike McCaslin that snakes are crawling (323); after Ike McCaslin kills first buck, wants to shoot a deer (323 ff.); finds bear instead; gun fails (325-326).

Joe Baker (214): an Indian friend of Sam Fathers .

_____: seven strangers who appear in camp when Lion leads pack to hunt Old Ben (222).

_____: Boon Hogganbeck's grandmother; a Chickasaw woman (227).

_____ Hogganbek (227): Boon Hogganbeck's father (227).

_____ Hogganbeck (227): Boon Hogganbeck's mother (227).

Mr. _____ Semmes (227): distiller in Memphis; Ike McCaslin and Boon sent to him for more whisky (227).

_____: conductor on log train (230).

_____: brakeman on log train (230).

Theophilus (256) McCaslin (254): Ike McCaslin's father; during Civil War, member of John Sartoris's horse; rides horse into Gayoso Hotel where Yankee officers sit; escapes scot free (233-234); Uncle Buck (261); herds slaves into main house at night, although there is no back door to it (262); twin of Amodeus (263); with brother, increases original thousand dollar heritage from Carothers McCaslin to one thousand for each of 3 surviving children of Tennie and Turl (273); dies 1881 (274).

Colonel John Sartoris (234): commander of horse, Civil War (234).

_____: man in washroom as Boon drinks (234).

_____: woman restaurant manager; tells Boon not to drink (234).

_____: black waiter in restaurant (234).

_____: black woman accidentally shot by Boon as he tried to shoot black man (235).

_____: black man shot at by Boon (235).

Bayard Sartoris (236): guest in camp night before Old Ben is killed (236).

_____ Sartoris (236): son of Bayard Sartoris; guest in camp night before Old Ben is killed (236).

_____ Compson (236): son of General Compson; guest in camp night before Old Ben is killed (236).

_____: two other guests in camp night before Old Ben is killed (236).

_____: swamper who fires at Old Ben during hunt (238).

Dr. _____ Crawford (243): sent for by Major de Spain to tend Boon, Sam, and Lion (243); sews up Lion (239); then tends Boon; then tends Sam Fathers (246); says Sam Fathers "just quit" (248).

Lucius Quintus (266) Carothers McCaslin (254): purchases land from Indians (254); buys Sam Fathers and his mother from Ikkemotubbe for an underbred trotting gelding (263); born in Carolina 1772; died Mississippi 27 June 1837 (266); leaves one thousand dollars in will to his son Turl; fathered Tomasina by Eunice, and Turl by his own daughter Tomasina (270-271).

Amodeus (256) McCaslin (254): uncle of Ike McCaslin; Uncle Buddy

244

(256); twin of Theophilus (263); urges brother to free Percival Brownlee (264); cook and housekeeper; writes in ledger that Eunice drowned herself (267); with brother, increases original thousand dollar heritage from Carothers McCaslin to one thousand for each of surviving children of Tennie and Turl (273); dies about 1881 (274).

Issetibbeha (259): father of Ikkemotubbe (259). [See "The Old People" where he is the uncle of Ikkemotubbe.]

Roscius (263) Roskus (266): male slave of Carothers McCaslin (263); freed by twins on day their father died, June 27, 1837; does not want to leave plantation; dies and buried January 12, 1841; father of Thucydides (Thucydus); husband of Phoebe (Fibby) (266).

Phoebe (263) Fibby (266): female slave of Carothers McCaslin (263); wife of Roscius (Roskus); mother of Thucydides (Thucydus); bought by Carothers McCaslin's father; freed by twins on day their father dies, June 27, 1837; does not want to leave plantation; died August 1, 1849 (266).

Thucydides (263) Thucydus (266) McCaslin (267): male slave of Carothers McCaslin (263); son of Roscius (Roskus) and Phoebe (Fibby); refuses ten acre piece of land provided for him in will of Carothers McCaslin on day after his death (June 28, 1837); refuses offer of two hundred dollars from twins; wants to stay and work it out (266); paid two hundred dollars wages by twins November 3, 1841; sets up blacksmith shop in Jefferson, December 1841; dies; buried in Jefferson February 17, 1854 (267); married to Eunice when she becomes pregnant (269); not a field hand (270).

Eunice (263) McCaslin: female slave of Carothers McCaslin (263); bought by him in New Orleans in 1807 for six hundred and fifty dollars; married to Thucydides (Thucydus) 1809; suicide by drowning in creek Christmas day 1832 (267); not field hand (270); mother of Tomasina by Carothers McCaslin (270); commits suicide when she learns that Carothers McCaslin by incest has made his and her daughter pregnant (271).

_____: mother of Sam Fathers; slave of Carothers McCaslin (263).

Tennie Beauchamp (263): slave won by Amodeus McCaslin in poker game (263); 21 at time; in 1859; married to Tomys Turl (271).

Percival Brownlee (263): slave purchased by Theophilus McCaslin from Bedford Forrest; an anomaly (263); 26 years old; professed to be bookkeeper; not a bookkeeper; purchased for two hundred and sixty-five dollars; can not read; can not plough (264); shoots wrong mule; will not leave; renamed *Spintrius* (name signifies male prostitute) (265); reappears in 1862 leading slaves in prayer meetings; again disappears; reappears in 1866 with Army paymaster, apparently his homosexual companion; finally, twenty years later, "the well-to-do proprietor of a select New Orleans brothel" (292-293).

Tomasina, Tomy (269): daughter, according to ledgers, of Thucydides (Thucydus) and Eunice; born 1810; dies in giving birth to Turl June 1833; year stars fell; mother of Turl; unmarried; child fathered by Carothers McCaslin, her father (269); only 23 when Turl was born (270); daughter of Carothers McCaslin (270-271).

Turl (269) Terrel (270): according to ledgers, son of Thucydides (Thucydus) and Eunice; born 1833; actually son of Carothers McCaslin; half-brother and nephew of Uncle Buck and Uncle Buddy; outlives them (269).

Hubert (271) Fitz-Hubert (307) Beauchamp (271): owner of Tennie; loses her to Amodeus McCaslin in poker game (271); Ike McCaslin's godfather; leaves legacy to Ike McCaslin (300); silver cup filled with gold pieces (301); according to his sister, Earl of Warwick (302); after marriage of sister, fortune dwindles (302 ff.); at first insists on having others feel weight of cup full of coins; then he alone holds it as he removes coins (304-305); house burns down (305); replaces gold coins with worthless I. O. U.'s (307).

Amodeus McCaslin Beauchamp (271): son of Tomys Turl and Tennie Beauchamp; born 1859; dies 1859; named after Uncle Buddy (271).

Bedford (263) Forrest (280): Uncle Buck's cavalry commander (272); only man to sell Uncle Buck a slave and beat him in a trade (273).

Callina (272) Beauchamp (272): daughter of Tomys Turl and Tennie Beauchamp; dies in infancy (271).

_____: child of Tomys Turl and Tennie; born and dies 1863; sex unknown (272).

Carolina (Callina) (272) McCaslin: sister of twins Uncle Buck and Uncle Buddy (name implied on page 272 in the naming of children of Turl and Tennie).

Sophonsiba (273) Fonsiba (274) Beauchamp (273) : daughter of Tomys Turl and Tennie; born 1869 (273); marries 1886 (274); elopes with man from Arkansas (276); terribly changed when Ike McCaslin finds her (277);

Lucas (274) Quintus Carothers McCaslin Beauchamp (281): last and 6th child of Tomys Turl and Tennie; born ca. 1875 (274); born March 17, 1874; appears at Ike McCaslin's home and demands all remaining money in Carothers McCaslin's legacy (281-282).

_____: man who wants to marry Fonsiba Beauchamp; dresses, acts, speaks like a white man; owns farm in Arkansas (274); father was slave; served in U. S. Army in Civil War; farm, a grant from government (275); elopes with Fonsiba next morning (276); when Ike McCaslin finds him and Fonsiba, farm he boasted of is farm only "in embryo" (277); reads book through spectacles without lenses (278).

246

Alice Edmonds (276): wife of McCaslin Edmonds; taught Fonsiba to read and write (276).

_____: banker in Midnight, Arkansas with whom Ike McCaslin leaves Fonsiba's money in trust (280).

Sickymo (291): ex-slave; United States marshal during Reconstruction; name derived because he sold his master's medicinal alcohol beneath a sycamore tree; recalled by Ike during long talk with cousin (291).

[Sophonsiba] Sibby (303) Beauchamp McCaslin (301): sister of Hubert Beauchamp; wife of Theophilus McCaslin; mother of Isaac McCaslin; after marriage, moves into big house (301); insists on calling her family plantation "Warwick" (302).

_____: female light-colored black; seems to be mistress of Hubert Beauchamp; clothed in his sister's dress (302-303); he calls her his cook; sent packing by Sibby (303).

_____: partner of Ike McCaslin; "blasphemous profane clever old dipsomaniac" (310).

_____: president of bank (310).

_____: Ike McCaslin's landlady in Jefferson (311).

_____ McCaslin (311): Ike McCaslin's wife (311); urges him to reclaim his heritage (312); strips naked (313); tries to get him to reclaim his plantation by withholding sex; he refuses at first; then agrees; after they have sex, she says that is all he will get from her as she realizes that, even though he agreed before sex, he will not reclaim the land (315).

_____: father of Ike McCaslin's wife (311); gives them lot and house in Jefferson (312).

Daisy (316): Major de Spain's cook (316).

"Delta Autumn"

Written perhaps before May, 1940; received by Harold Ober December 16, 1940; first published in *Story*, 20 (May-June, 1942), 46-55; it was revised for *Go Down, Moses*, and part of it was revised for *Big Woods*, 1955.

Uncle Ike (336) [Isaac] McCaslin (353): almost 80 now; (336); thinks that every man and woman at moment of love is God (348); gives his theory about God; role of hunting in man's life (349); can not sleep; thinks of earlier Big Bottom and killing of first buck (350); reviews the last sex with his wife [cf. "The Bear"] when he repudiated land for son

247

he was never to have (351); wilderness becomes his home (351); hunting companions are more his kin than any; wilderness was his land (352); enunciates principle of land belonging to no man but to all to use well (354); meets granddaughter of Tennie's Jim (357); gives her Roth's message (358); she bore Roth Edmond's child (358); insists there can be no marriage between Roth Edmonds and granddaughter of Tennie's Jim (358); says she is a "nigger" (361); tells her to "get out of here" (361) urges her to take the money from Roth; touches her (362); tells her to go back North and marry a man of her own race (363); says that ruined woods do not cry out for retribution because "the people who have destroyed it will accomplish its revenge." (364).

[Carothers] Roth (336) Edmonds (338): sets time close to 1939; has been in World War I (338); small tirade on depression and government control (339); has theory that man behaves only because of presence of police force (346); 40 years old (353); leaves envelope with Uncle Ike McCaslin to give to messenger along with message "No" (355); had taken woman to New Mexico; sired her child; sends her money to Vicksburg bank; had seen her by road as they approached camp (359).

Will (338) Legate (337): accuses Roth Edmonds of having affair with young light-colored black woman (337).

General [Jason Lycurgus] Compson (344): recalled by Uncle Ash (344).

Major [Cassius] de Spain (344): former owner of hunting camp (344); commander of Ike McCaslin's father's [Theophilus McCaslin] cavalry regiment (350).

[Carothers] McCaslin (351) [Edmonds]: Roth Edmonds's grandfather (344); took Ike McCaslin to woods for first time (350).

_____: Will Legate's grandfather (344).

Henry Wyatt (347): third speaker at evening meal on hunt (345).

_____: black cook in hunting camp (348).

_____: black cook's helper in hunting camp (348); tends fire in camp heater at night (349).

Isham (348) _____: old black in hunting camp (348).

Sam Fathers (350): born slave; son of slave and Chickasaw chief; taught Ike McCaslin how to hunt (350).

[Theophilus McCaslin]: Ike McCaslin's father (350).

_____ McCaslin (351): Ike McCaslin's wife (351).

_____: Ike McCaslin's "dipsomaniac partner" (352).

248

_____: Ike McCaslin's wife's widowed niece; keeps house for him; has children(352).

[Walter] Ewell (352): old hunting companion of Ike McCaslin (352).

[Boon] Hogganbeck (352): old hunting companion of Ike McCaslin (352).

_____: black man; operates skiff that brings granddaughter of Tennie's Jim to hunting camp (357); her cousin (361).

_____: woman who bore Roth's child (357); had been with him previous November; he took her to New Mexico for six weeks (358); knows history of McCaslin-Edmonds-Beauchamp family (359-360); is school teacher from Indianapolis; now lives with aunt who takes in washing (360); granddaughter of Tennie's Jim; says Roth Edmonds does not know that she is (361); takes money (362); confesses her love for Roth and departs (363).

_____: child of Roth Edmonds (357) and the granddaughter of Tennie's Jim (361); a boy (362).

[Lucius Quintus Carothers McCaslin]: Ike McCaslin's grandfather (359).

Uncle Buddy (359) [Amodeus McCaslin].

Tennie (359) [Beauchamp].

[Hubert Fitz-Hubert] Beauchamp (359).

Terrel (359) Tomey's Turl (359).

Uncle Lucas (360) [Beauchamp].

Aunt Mollie (360) [Beauchamp].

_____: aunt of granddaughter of Tennie's Jim; lives in Vicksburg; takes in washing (360).

_____: father of granddaughter of Tennie's Jim (360).

"Go Down, Moses"

Written before July 19, 1940; first published in _Collier's_, **107 (January 25, 1941), 19-20, 45, 46. It was revised for** _Go Down, Moses_, **and it was included in** _Uncollected Stories_, **1979.**

Samuel Worsham Beauchamp (369): 26; raised by his grandmother (370); sentenced to electric chair (370); known as "Butch" when a youth (372); child of Mollie's eldest daughter; [therefore, his original name was not Beauchamp] who dies at childbirth; deserted by father (372); leaves Edmonds's place at 19; arrested for breaking and entering Rouncewell's store; escapes from county jail; sentenced to State Penetentiary for manslaughter (372); uses unmentioned alias; killed Chicago policeman (374); in numbers racket (375); only child of eldest daughter of Mollie and Lucas Beauchamp (376); named for Miss Worsham's father (376).

_____: white census taker who interviews Samuel Worsham Beauchamp in jail (369).

Mollie Worsham Beauchamp (370): grandmother of Samuel Worsham Beauchamp (370); sister of Hamp Worsham (371); intuits grandson is in trouble; goes to Stevens for help; repeats that Roth Edmonds sold her Benjamin to Pharaoh (380); wants whole story of grandson put in paper (383).

Carothers (370) Roth (371) Edmonds (370): owner of plantation on which Mollie lives (370).

Gavin Stevens (370): prematurely white-haired county attorney (370); Phi Beta Kappa at Harvard; Ph. D. from Heidelberg; for twenty-two years has been translating Old Testament into Classic Greek (371); raises money to bring home and bury body of executed killer, Samuel Worsham Beauchamp (378 ff.).

Hamp Worsham (371): Mollie Beauchamp's brother; lives in Jefferson (371).

_____: officer who arrests Butch Beauchamp for breaking into Rouncewell's store (372).

_____ Wilmoth (375): editor of county newspaper; tremendously fat (373).

Luke [Lucas] Beauchamp (377): husband of Mollie; grandfather of Samuel Worsham Beauchamp (373).

_____ Rouncewell (373): owner of store robbed by Butch Beauchamp (373).

Miss Belle Worsham (374): aged spinster whose father owned Hamp Worsham's ancestors; with Hamp, raises chickens; gives lessons in china painting (374); grew up with Mollie as a sister (375); father's name was Samuel (376); gives Stevens twenty-five dollars to bring body home (377).

_____ Worsham (374): Hamp's "tremendous light-colored" wife (379).

_____: warden at Joliet prison (375).

_____: District Attorney in Chicago (375).

250

Samuel Worsham (376): father of Miss Belle Worsham (376).

_____: undertaker in Joliet (377).

First conceived as early as June, 1940; written from January to February, 1948. Faulkner began rewriting the novel at the end of February, 1948, and he finished it on April 20, 1948; earlier titles considered were *Jugglery in the Dust* and *Impostor in the Dust*; published September 27, 1948.

Pagination, in parentheses, to the following edition and subsequent reissues: (New York: Random House, 1948), 247 pp.; (New York: Modern Library, 1964); (New York: Modern Library, n. d.), "Modern Library College Edition," paperback; (New York: Vintage Books, 1972), paperback; (London: Chatto & Windus, 1949).

Hope (40) Hampton (31): sheriff who brings Lucas to jail (3); tremendously big man (43); tells crowd to leave (45); a country man, a farmer (107); quickly suspects, after hearing of digging of grave, that the Gowries are involved (110); calls District Attorney for permission to open grave (111); goes to cemetery (141 ff.); when he reaches grave, says Chick and Co. did not put flowers back (158); had called Mr. Gowrie at 6:00 a. m. to meet him at graveyard (168); finds prints of mule by creek; knows a Gowrie killed a Gowrie (172); finds first body buried in sand (174); after Nub Gowrie finds Vinson's body buried in quicksand, tells him that he was killed by a German Luger that Buddy McCallum traded in 1919 for his son's [Crawford's] foxhounds (179); takes Lucas as bait to catch Crawford Gowrie (218); explains motive for killing (220).

Lucas Beauchamp (3): whole town knows he killed a white man (3); flashback: watches Chick fall in creek (6); takes him home; "son of one of old Carothers McCaslin's, Edmonds' great grandfather's, slaves who had been not just old Carothers' slave but his son too" (7); takes Chick Mallison home, dries him out, feeds him, and sends him on (8 ff.); wears heavy gold watch chain; uses gold toothpick; wears a hat such as Chick's grandfather used (12); at crossroads store, tells white man he is not an Edmonds but a McCaslin (19); keeps scales balanced by sending Chick molasses (22-23); lives alone after his wife's death (23); pays yearly taxes on his land (25); as he enters jail, tells Chick he wants to see his uncle (45); says he wants to hire someone (not a lawyer) to do a job; tells Gavin Stevens (for sake of detective story) only part of what happened (61-62); refuses to say "mister" to white people (62); cause for shooting: one partner was stealing lumber at night and hauling it away (63); asks for tobacco (65); when Chick returns, asks him to go out to cemetery and look at Vinson Gowrie; offers to pay him (68); tells Chick he owns a .41 Colt pistol and that Vinson was not shot by a .41 Colt (69); used as bait to catch Crawford Gowrie (211); after his arrest, gives his gold toothpick to Hampton to keep until he calls for it (240); visits Gavin Stevens's office a week after arrest (May 16th) (241); offers to pay Stevens's fee; then his expenses (244-245); pays two dollars for spoiled fountain pen (including fifty pennies); then asks for receipt (246-247).

Charles (32) Chick (113) Mallison Jr. (68): first one waiting for Lucas Beauchamp to be brought in; 16 at time of action (3);

flashback: goes to Edmonds's place with Aleck Sander to hunt rabbits when 12; in first winter cold snap (4); falls in icy creek (5); watched by Lucas Beauchamp (6); taken home by Lucas; dried, fed, and sent out again (8 ff.); Methodist (9) begins to sense the smell of black people (11); says he will have his dinner at Mr. Edmonds's (13); eats what was to have been Lucas's dinner (13); offers to pay for dinner: seventy cents (half dollar, dime, two nickles); quickly regrets it; shame turns to rage (15); later, misses chance to shoot rabbit; throws coins in creek; realizes that he has a debt to Lucas (17); first reaction as a southern boy: "We got to make him be a nigger first" "Then maybe we will accept him as he seems to intend to be accepted." (18); coins he offered Lucas merge into a symbolic half dollar which represents his debt to Lucas Beauchamp (20); devoted to his uncle (21); waits in square with Christmas package for Lucas and Molly in second attempt to pay off debt (21-22); gives package to Edmonds to give them Christmas morning (23); still feels indebted; sends Molly dress by mail; gets gallon of homemade molasses in return (22); delivered by a white boy on mule; rides pony not horse (23); constantly compares Lucas to grandfather (8, 24, etc.); learns that blacks can grieve (25); finally feels free when Lucas passes him without recognition (26); basis for need to pay and thereby keep the imbalance explained: "not for revenge, vengeance but simply for re-equalization, reaffirmation of his masculinity and his white blood" (26); urge to flee on Highboy (31); urge to flee offset by his "forgetting" to give extra feed to Highboy (34-35); again "forgets" to feed Highboy, Messianic impulse (41); walks to square to wait for Lucas to be brought in (41-42); recognizes that he is forced to give Lucas one last chance to call up the debt (42); returns with uncle to jail evening of Sunday in May (46 ff.); sparsity of vocabulary theme begins (47); when he first sees Lucas asleep in jail, reacts in rage at a "nigger" killing a white man; first phase of Chick's development (58); does not buy Lucas tobacco; returns to jail (66-67); as he returns, has conflicting desire to flee (67); asks Lucas what he wants him to do; when Lucas asks him to dig up Vinson Gowrie, thinks, "So this is what that plate of meat and greens is going to cost me." (68); both grasp bars that separate them (69); agrees to dig up Vinson Gowrie (73); in presence of Miss Habersham tries to tell his uncle what Lucas told him (77 ff.); as he tries to convince his uncle, thinks again of paucity of vocabulary (80); asks Aleck Sander to go with him to dig up grave (86); rides Highboy while Aleck Sander drives pickup truck (91-93); on way to grave, begins to merge into Stage Two (96-97); they dig up grave (102 ff.); finds Montgomery (timber buyer) not Vinson Gowrie in grave (104); returns home before dawn; tells uncle (105); with Miss Habersham and Aleck Sander, accompanies his uncle to Sheriff Hampton's house (107); thinks of Ephraim's coment about women and children (112); served coffee by his mother (127); begins to enter second phase (137); goes to graveyard with his uncle (143); May 9th (147); has daydream of wall separating North and South, but feels divorced from South; idea of homogeneous South introduced (152-153); communicates intuitively with his uncle (153); as they return with the bodies, begins to resent mob (181); Face of mob image develops (182); watches mob leave square after they bring in bodies of Vinson and Montgomery (84); imaginatively pictures Miss Habersham being swept by departing mob miles from Jefferson (188-189); begins to get hysterical in car waiting to break through retreating mob (189); says for first time "They ran." repeats it seven times (190, 191, 192, 196, 197, 198); sleeps and wakes fifteen hours later (196); in his self-righteous condemnation of mob (196 ff.), leaves Tenderfoot Scout stage and moves toward Eagle Scout stage (206); reidentifies with South and enters third stage of development (209); Eagle Scout: "Don't stop." (210); thesis about North: no outsiders can settle the debt (215); repeats theme that South alone must pay the debt (216).

Gavin Stevens (15): uncle of Charles Mallison Jr.; county attorney (3); explains rules of white-black relationship to Chick after they encounter Mr. Lilley (48); treats Lucas harshly when asked to defend him (59 ff.); tells Lucas he will be his lawyer; asks him what happened (60); refuses to do job Lucas wants to hire someone to do (61); always assumes Lucas's guilt (64); persuades Miss Habersham to stay at jail instead of going back to graveyard (118); bachelor of 50 (122); repeats theme of women and children (126); introduces the Sambo theme (149); mentions atom bomb for internal date (149); makes anti-Federal government speech (153); makes speech saying that Sambo must be free; develops thesis that South must pay its debt to blacks (154); proposes a confederation of homogeneous black with homogeneous white in South: We shall prevail (156); after Chick wakes from fifteen-hour sleep, makes sermon on "Thou shalt not kill" and "Thou shalt not kill thy brother" (200 ff.); makes speech against North; says South must pay debt (203-204); accuses Chick of being righteous (204); gives full explanation of killing; Crawford and Vinson partners in lumber deal; Crawford steals from Vinson; Lucas witnesses theft; Vinson finds out; threatens Lucas; Lucas decides to tell Workitt about theft; Lucas tricked by Crawford to meet him at store on Saturday when he carries pistol; Lucas tricked into firing pistol; Lucas arrested (222-228); makes speech about American love of automobiles (238); and on women and sex (239); sends Lucas with Chick to give bouquet of flowers to Miss Habersham (242); refuses to name a fee when Lucas asks for it (244); asks for two dollars expenses to replace fountain pen (245).

Carothers Edmonds (3): Lucas Beauchamp lives on his place (3); flashback: invites Chick Mallison to hunt (3-4); a bachelor (7); in hospital in New Orleans for gallstones (this fact increases burden on Chick) (30).

Joe (7)   : Edmonds's "boy"; son of one of Edmonds's tenants (4).

Aleck Sander (4): Chick Mallison's "boy" (4); asked by Chick to go with him to dig up Vinson Gowrie (86); drives Miss Habersham's pick-up truck (93); at graveyard, hears mule coming down hill (99); asks what he was toting on the saddle (100); does not accompany them when they return to graveyard (141).

_____: Chick Mallison's grandfather (8).

Molly (15) Beauchamp (3): "a tiny old almost doll-sized woman much darker than the man" (10); does not like wedding picture because photographer made her remove head rag (15); dies (23).

Paralee Sander (12): Aleck Sander's mother (12).

[Lucius Quintus] Carothers McCaslin (7): white grandfather of Lucas Beauchamp (7).

[Terrel, Turl]: father of Lucas Beauchamp; slave-son of Carothers McCaslin (7).

_____ Edmonds (8): father of Carothers Edmonds, first cousin of Lucas Beauchamp (8).

Maggie Dandridge (15): Chick Mallison's grandmother (15).

Mrs. Charles (68) Maggie (105) Stevens (15) Mallison (68): Chick Mallison's mother (15); serves Chick coffee (127); goes to jail to sit with Miss Habersham (128).

Squire (34) Adam (228) Fraser (27): owner of crossroads store (18); Vinson Gowrie killed there (27).

_____: three young men in crossroads store; one of whom accosts Lucas Beauchamp (18).

Doyle (37) Fraser (27): son of owner of crossroads store, who saves Lucas Beauchamp from being beaten (20); again gets Lucas away from crowd after Vinson Gowrie has been shot (37).

_____: companion of son of owner of crossroads store (20).

Charlie (32) Charles Mallison Sr. (68): objects to wife serving Chick coffee (127).

_____: white boy on mule who delivers Lucas's molasses to Chick (23).

_____ Beauchamp _____: Molly's and Lucas's daughter (23).

_____: her husband (23).

Vinson Gowrie (27): killed at Fraser's store; shot in back (27); youngest son of Nub Gowrie; 28 at death; first Gowrie to sign his name to a check and have any bank honor it (165).

_____ Skipworth (34): constable who arrests Lucas for killing Vinson Gowrie (27); takes him home; handcuffs him to bedpost (28).

_____ Ingrum (28): family that lives in Beat Four (28); name used to be Ingraham (148).

_____ Workitt (28): family that lives in Beat Four (28); name used to be Urquhart (148).

256

Skipworth (33): wife of constable (33).

_____: deputy; drives car that brings Lucas and Hampton to jail (43).

_____Lilley (48): country man who moved to town last year; owns small grocery whose customers are mostly blacks (47); volunteers to help the lynch mob (48).

_____McCallum (33): family that lives in Beat Four (33).

_____Tubbs (53): jailor in Jefferson (51); angry at Legate for defending Lucas (52); leads Chick and Gavin Stevens to Lucas's cell (53 ff.); very anti-black (53 ff.).

Will Legate (52): finest shot and best deer hunter in county; sits on chair at jail with shotgun; Hampton tells him to sit there (52); Hampton pays him five dollars to do so (53).

_____: city man; architect; drives through window; insists on going to jail; tries to buy door to jail (55).

_____: marshal (55).

_____: owner of plate glass window broken by architect (55).

_____: mayor of Jefferson (55).

Jim Halladay (110): District Attorney (59).

Ephraim (63)_____: Paralee's father (63); finds ring (71); states theme that, unlike men who are cluttered with facts, women and children get things done (71).

Skeets McGowan (66): clerk in drugstore (66).

_____: college roommate of Mrs. Maggie Mallison; exchanged rings with her (70).

_____: her daughter (70).

Mrs. (71)_____Downs (71): fortune teller (71).

_____: man from garage, hired by Charles Mallison Sr. to drive his wife to farm to find ring (72).

_____: overseer of Mr. Mallison's farm (72).

Eunice (92) Habersham (75): oldest name in county (75); kinless spinster of 70; lives with two black servants (76); owns pick-up truck (77); joins Chick and Aleck Sander in trip to graveyard; born with Molly and brought up with her like sisters [*cf.* Miss Whorsham in *Go Down, Moses.*] (87); says Lucas could not talk to Gavin Stevens: "He's a Negro and your uncle's a man;" paucity of vocabulary theme again; women and children theme (89); in truck, goes with Chick and Aleck Sander (90 ff.); at graveyard rides Highboy uphill (99); agrees to stay at jail on Monday while sheriff returns to graveyard (118).

Dr. (75)   Habersham (75): early   settler   in   Yoknapatawpha County (75); grandfather of Miss Habersham (87).

_____ Holston (75): tavern   keeper;   early   settler   in Yoknapatawpha County (75).

_____ Grenier (75): early settler in Yoknapatawpha County; a Huguenot younger son (75); architect (76).

Lonnie Grinnup (76): descendent of early settler, Grenier; lives in hut (76).

_____ Habersham (76): father of Miss Eunice Habersham (76).

_____: male black servant of Miss Habersham (76); Molly Beauchamp's brother (119).

_____: female black servant of Miss Habersham (76).

Nub (79) N. B. Forrest (101) Gowrie (79): one-armed   father   of Gowrie clan (79); arrives at grave as Sheriff is about to have it opened; displays pistol (160); forces sheriff to send black prisoners back to car; has his twin sons dig up grave (163); finds it empty (166); finds Jake Montgomery buried in sand (175); finds son buried in quicksand (177); allowed to rebury body (192).

_____: Molly Beauchamp's mother (87); suckled both Molly and Miss Habersham (87).

[Henry Beauchamp]: Molly's first child (87).

Major [Cassius] de Spain (93): cousin of Chick's grandfather (93).

General [Jason Lycurgus] Compson (93).

Ike McCaslin (93): still alive at 90.

Boon Hogganbeck (93).

_____: Boon Hogganbeck's mother and grandmother (93).

Sam Fathers (93).

_____: Sam Fathers's father, a Chickasaw chief (93).

Amanda Workitt Gowrie (101): dead wife of Nub Gowrie; 1878-1926 (101).

Jake Montgomery (104): dead man found in Vinson Gowrie's grave; timber buyer (104); was buying lumber that Crawford stole (229); murdered by Crawford (229-230).

Mrs. Hope Hampton (107): wife of sheriff; in Memphis with daughter waiting for her baby to be born (107-108).

_____: her daughter (108).

_____: woman who washes Hope Hampton's dishes (108).

Judge   Maycox (110).

Mrs.   Tubbs (118): wife of jailor (118).

_____: groom who delivers Highboy to Chick (125).

Willy (140) Ingrum (136): town marshal (135).

_____: two black convicts whom Sheriff Hampton takes to graveyard (139).

Littlejohn, Greenleaf, Armstead, Millingham, Bookwright (149): names of other early settlers (149).

Vardaman Gowrie (165): with twin brother on mule with Nub Gowrie in graveyard (159); son of Nub Gowrie (162) about 30 (163); with brother, digs up grave (166).

Bilbo Gowrie (165): twin of Vardaman (163).

Forrest Gowrie (164): oldest of six Gowrie sons; manager of delta cotton plantation (164).

Crawford Gowrie (164): second son of Nub Gowrie; drafted November 2, 1918; deserts November 10, 1918; serves year in Leavenworth; fights off federal agents with German automatic (note) that he trades to a McCallum for a brace of Gowrie foxhounds (164-165); deals in timber and cattle (165); kills brother Vinson (179); kills brother to keep him from finding out that he has been stealing lumber from him and Uncle Sudley Workitt (220); suicide; somehow obtains Luger pistol with one bullet in it while in jail (237).

Buddy (179) McCallum (164): trades German automatic from WW I to Crawford Gowrie for brace of foxhounds (164-165).

Bryan Gowrie (165): third son of Nub Gowrie (165).

_____: coroner (180).

_____: undertaker (181).

Uncle Hogeye Mosby (184): epilectic from poorhouse (184).

_____: town's night marshal (212).

Uncle Sudley Workit (220): Crawford Gowrie had been stealing lumber from him and Vinson Gowrie (220).

_____ Varner (234).

Individual stories were written from 1930 to 1948; novel first published November 27, 1949.

Pagination, in parentheses, to the following edition and reissue: (New York: Random House, 1949), 246 pp.; (New York: Vintage Books, 1978), 246 pp., paperback.

"Smoke"

Written probably in January and certainly before February 5, 1930; first published in *Harper's Magazine*, **164 (April, 1932), 562-578; reprinted in** *Doctor Martino and Other Stories*, **1934; second version reprinted in** *Knight's Gambit*, **1949.**

Anselm (3) Old Anse (4) Holland (3): arrives in Jefferson from unknown source; within three years, marries only daughter of owner of best land in county; father of twin sons; father-in-law dies; land in name of wife; wife dies while twins are still children; known to be violent; sons leave home on reaching maturity (3); dragged and presumed killed by horse; had been digging up graves of his wife's family plot; orders son, Virginius, to leave (7); lets taxes lapse; they are paid by mail two days before place was to be sold (8); lets place go completely (9); will leaves land to Virginius [(elder son *sic*)] provided chancellor can prove he paid taxes on land (10).

Cornelia Mardis (17) Holland (3): dead wife of Anselm Holland (3).

_____: father of Anselm Holland's wife; owns two thousand acres of some of best land in county (3).

Virginius (4) Virge (17) Holland (4): twin son of Anselm Holland (3); 40 when his father dies (4); takes father's side in inheritance dispute (5); offers to pay brother's fine; farms land (5); wants share of land; never loses temper (6); when father orders him to, packs and leaves (7) to live with cousin (7); uses savings to disencumber cousin's farm (8); visits father five or six times a year (9); passes old Job on day judge is murdered

Anselm (Young Anse) Holland (4): twin son of Anselm Holland (3); 40 when father dies; his mother's favorite; runs away from home in late teens; stays away ten years; returns; demands his share of land (4-5); after violent fight, never speaks to father again (5); arrested for making whisky after living alone for fifteen years; refuses to plead; assaults brother for offering to pay his fine; sent to jail on own demand; pardoned eight months later (5); says he killed his father (21).

_____: first-person-plural narrator "We" (6); member of jury (26).

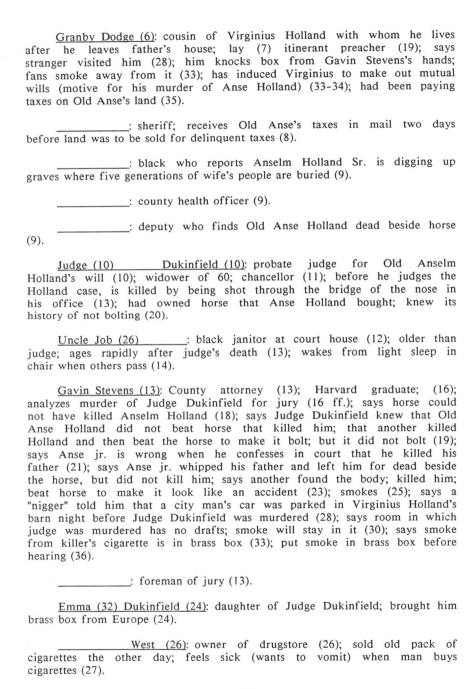

Granby Dodge (6): cousin of Virginius Holland with whom he lives after he leaves father's house; lay (7) itinerant preacher (19); says stranger visited him (28); him knocks box from Gavin Stevens's hands; fans smoke away from it (33); has induced Virginius to make out mutual wills (motive for his murder of Anse Holland) (33-34); had been paying taxes on Old Anse's land (35).

_____: sheriff; receives Old Anse's taxes in mail two days before land was to be sold for delinquent taxes (8).

_____: black who reports Anselm Holland Sr. is digging up graves where five generations of wife's people are buried (9).

_____: county health officer (9).

_____: deputy who finds Old Anse Holland dead beside horse (9).

Judge (10)   Dukinfield (10): probate judge for Old Anselm Holland's will (10); widower of 60; chancellor (11); before he judges the Holland case, is killed by being shot through the bridge of the nose in his office (13); had owned horse that Anse Holland bought; knew its history of not bolting (20).

Uncle Job (26)_____: black janitor at court house (12); older than judge; ages rapidly after judge's death (13); wakes from light sleep in chair when others pass (14).

Gavin Stevens (13): County attorney (13); Harvard graduate; (16); analyzes murder of Judge Dukinfield for jury (16 ff.); says horse could not have killed Anselm Holland (18); says Judge Dukinfield knew that Old Anse Holland did not beat horse that killed him; that another killed Holland and then beat the horse to make it bolt; but it did not bolt (19); says Anse jr. is wrong when he confesses in court that he killed his father (21); says Anse jr. whipped his father and left him for dead beside the horse, but did not kill him; says another found the body; killed him; beat horse to make it look like an accident (23); smokes (25); says a "nigger" told him that a city man's car was parked in Virginius Holland's barn night before Judge Dukinfield was murdered (28); says room in which judge was murdered has no drafts; smoke will stay in it (30); says smoke from killer's cigarette is in brass box (33); put smoke in brass box before hearing (36).

_____: foreman of jury (13).

Emma (32) Dukinfield (24): daughter of Judge Dukinfield; brought him brass box from Europe (24).

_____ West (26): owner of drugstore (26); sold old pack of cigarettes the other day; feels sick (wants to vomit) when man buys cigarettes (27).

262

_____: drummer who leaves two packs of cigarettes in West's drugstore years ago (27).

_____: clerk in West's drugstore (27).

_____: man in city clothes who wants to buy cigarettes in West's drugstore; on dope; buys old pack of cigarettes (27); on way back to Memphis, runs down child; has pistol with silencer on it (29-30); kills Judge Dukinfield (31).

_____: black whom Granby Dodge sent to Gavin Stevens for information about wills (34).

"Monk"

Written before January 21, 1937; first published in Scribner's, **101 (May, 1937), 16-24; reprinted in** Knight's Ganbit, **1949.**

_____: first-person narrator (39).

Monk (39) Stonewall Jackson Odlethrop (45): a moron; perhaps a cretin; in jail (39) for murder; does not even know whom he killed; five years later, makes speech on gallows; about 25 (40); as a child, digs into grandmother's grave; neighbors cannot catch him; they leave food at deserted house; lives with Fraser from 8 to 18; then goes to Jefferson (42); learns to make whisky; kills warden in penitentiary five years after he was first arrested (43); has no conception of death; killing sets him to talking (44); has been to school for one year (45); sentenced to life in prison (46); not guilty (46); pardoned (47); does not want to leave prison where he is devoted to warden; in jailbreak, kills warden with warden's own pistol (47); hanged after saying he is going "to get out into the free world, and farm" (49); finds warden's pistol and returns it (50).

_____: District Attorney (39).

_____: lawyer appointed by court to defend Monk (39).

_____: man whom Monk is convicted of killing (40).

_____: deputy who arrests Monk (40).

_____: jailor (40).

_____: Justice of the Peace who arraigns Monk (40).

_____: sheriff of county (40).

Mrs. _____ Odlethrop (41): Monk's grandmother (41); dead for a week before anyone discovers body (42).

_____: Monk's father; her son (41).

_____: woman Monk's father brings home after ten years; Monk's mother (41).

_____ Fraser (42): childless widower with whom Monk lives as a child for ten years; dies (42).

C. L. Gambrell (50): warden of penitentiary; killed by Monk (43).

_____: two men there when Monk is said to have killed man (44); five years after Monk is sentenced, one of the two, while dying, confesses that he killed the man and put the gun in Monk's hand (46).

Gavin (46) Stevens (52): narrator's uncle (45); gets Monk pardoned (47); starts to solve mystery; says they did not hang man who murdered Gambrell; solves mystery by accident and tells no one but the narrator (50); delegate to Governor's meeting of Pardon Board (51); accuses Terrel of killing Gambrell and framing Monk (53); gets permission to talk to Terrel (55); after Terrel confesses, tells him he will go free (58); returns to Governor; asks him if he wants to hear the true story; is refused; returns home as Terrel is freed (59-60).

_____: Governor who pardons Monk (47); "a man without ancestry" (50); convenes Pardon Board (51); asks Gavin Stevens to send Bill Terrel away so that he can speak to Gavin privately (52); refuses Gavin's request to keep Terrel in jail (59); refuses Gavin Stevens's offer to tell true story of Gambrell's murder; pardons Terrel (59).

_____ Gambrell (47): wife of warden; teaches Monk to knit (47).

_____: conductor on train that takes Monk to jail (48).

_____: warden's black cook; beaten in effort to find missing pistol (50).

_____: a trusty; beaten in effort to find pistol (50).

Bill Terrel (52): elected representative of prisoners who appear before Governor and Pardon Board; sentenced to twenty years for manslaughter; makes same speech as that made by Monk before execution (52); on manslaughter conviction, accused of killing man by throwing him under train; tried to blame son and involve daughter (55-56); suddenly confesses to Gavin Stevens that he induced Monk to kill Gambrell because he laughed at him (56-57); pardoned by Governor (59).

_____: brakeman on train; testifies that two men threw a body under train (55).

_____: other man involved with Terrel in throwing man under train (55).

264

_____: man thrown under train (55).

_____ Terrel (56): Bill Terrel's daughter (56).

_____ Terrel (56): Bill Terrel's son (56).

"Hand upon the Waters"

Written about May-June, 1939; first published in *The Saturday Evening Post*, **212 (November 4, 1939), 14-15, 75, 76, 78, 79; reprinted in** *O. Henry Memorial Award Prize Stories of 1940*, **selected and edited by Harry Hansen (New York: Doubleday, Doran & Company, Inc., 1940). reprinted in** *Knight's Gambit*, **1949.**

_____: man who carries gunny sack (63); finds Lonnie Grinnup drowned on his own trot line (65).

_____: youth less than 20 (63).

Joe (63)_____: runs fish line (63); deaf and dumb (64); orphan, adopted by Lonnie Grinnup (66); disappears; reappears as Boyd Ballenbaugh threatens to kill Gavin Stevens; jumps him; kills him and puts him on trot line like Lonnie Grinnup (80).

Lonnie (63) Grinnup (65): runs fish line (63); drowned on his own trot line (65); actual name should be Louis Grenier (66); middle 30's; touched; had taken in Joe, an orphan, ten years earlier (66).

Gavin (71) Stevens (65): county attorney (65); Harvard Phi Beta Kappa (67); attends inquest into Lonnie Grinnup's death; offers to help with cost of burial (68); begins to investigate drowning by questioning youth about oar of boat (69); in Mottstown, Ockatoba County seat, finds insurance policy for five thousand dollars double indemnity for accidental death issued to Lonnie Grinup; benificiary Tyler Ballenbaugh (72); arranges with agent to set trap for Tyler Ballenbaugh (73); visits Lonnie Grinnup's camp (74); finds Tyler and Boyd Ballenbaugh ransacking his hut; tells them it is all up (75); tells Tyler he wants indictment for murder (77); is shot by Boyd; graze wound in head (79); refuses to tell sheriff how Boyd was put on trot line (80); says paddle in boat was clue for murder of Lonnie who never used paddle (kept it in house) when he worked his trot line (81).

_____: coroner (65).

Louis Grenier, Holston, Stevens (66): early settlers who came from Carolina to settle in Jefferson while it was still a Chickasaw Agency post (66).

_____ Mitchell (68): holds Lonnie Grinnup's burial money at store (68).

265

Ike (68)_____: eldest of four who take Lonnie's body for burial (68).

Pose (68)_____: takes Lonnie's body (68).

Matthew (68)_____: takes Lonnie's body (68).

Jim Blake (68): takes Lonnie's body (68).

Tyler Ballenbaugh (70): farmer, known for self-sufficiency and violence (70); after disappearance, returns; marries; deals in cotton futures (70-71); has taken out five thousand dollar double indemnity insurance policy on Lonnie Grinnup and paid premiums on it with himself as beneficiary (72-73); when found ransacking Lonnie Grinnup's camp, stops brother from attacking Gavin Stevens (76); takes brother outside; gives him pistol, expecting brother to shoot himself (suicide) as he commands; is shot instead (78); wounded in shoulder; somehow also breaks leg (80).

Boyd Ballenbaugh (71): younger brother of Tyler Ballenbaugh; was armed guard in textile strike; in hiding on brother's farm; arrested for brawling (71); drives truck with Okatoba license plates (72); takes Lonnie Grinnup's body to his house for burial (71-72); indirectly admits killing; instead of committing suicide, shoots Tyler (78); then jumped by Joe, shoots Gavin in head (78); and brother in shoulder (80); body found dead on trot line; presumably killed by Joe and put there by him to avenge Lonnie Grinnup (80).

_____: two officers who arrest Boyd Ballenbraugh in Jefferson (71).

_____: insurance agent who insures Lonnie Grinnup (72).

_____: doctor who examines Lonnie Grinnup for insurance; never saw him before but knew Ballenbaugh (72).

Nate (74)_____: black man to whom Gavin says he is going to Lonnie Grinnup's camp; if he is not back by daylight, he is to notify store (74).

_____: his wife (75).

_____: sheriff (79).

"Tomorrow"

Written before August 5, 1940; first published in *The Saturday Evening Post*, 213 (November 23, 1940), 22-23, 32, 35, 37, 38, 39; reprinted in *Knight's Gambit*, 1940.

Gavin (85) Stevens (91): uncle of narrator (85); 28 at time of action; a year out of state university law school; in private practice; graduate of

266

Harvard and Heidelberg; takes Bookwright case; loses though he thinks right is on his side (85); after his defense, jury is hung (88); visits Fentry; rebuffed; visits Pruitt; inquires about Fentry; receives history of Fentrys (95); reveals that Buck Thorpe was child Fentry raised (105).

Chick (88) Charley (88)_____: first-person narrator (85); climbs tree to listen to jury deliberating (89); accompanies Gavin to visit Fentry; a boy of 12 (90).

_____: narrator's grandfather; apparently a lawyer (85).

_____ Bookwright (85): farmer; tried; mistrial; then acquitted; husband and father; from Frenchman's Bend (85); wakes Will Varner at 4:00 a. m. to confess killing Buck Thorpe (86).

Buck Thorpe (85) "Bucksnort" (85): "a swaggering bravo" (85); kinless brawler and gambler in Frenchman's Bend; killed by Bookwright for seducing his daughter (86); raised as child by S. J. Fentry (105). [See Jackson and Longstreet Fentry.]

_____ Bookwright (85): country girl of 17; elopes at midnight with Buck Thorpe (86).

Will Varner (86): Justice of the Peace in Frenchman's Bend (86); owner of store (97).

Isham (97) Quick (86): neighbor of Bookwright; first on scene of murder; found Buck Thorpe with half-drawn pistol (86); tall, gangling man in mid 40's (97); tells Gavin history of Jackson Fentry working for his father (98 ff.); accompanies Thorpe brothers in search for sister's baby who was reared by S. J. Fentry (101).

_____ Thorpe (86): woman who claims to be Buck Thorpe's wife (86).

_____: clerk of court; reads indictment of Bookwright for Thorpe's killing (86).

_____: District Attorney; conducts case through assistant (86).

_____: assistant D. A.; conducts Bookwright's case (86).

Judge_____ Frazier (88): hears Bookwright's case (88); dismisses jury; orders retrial (90).

Mrs._____ Rouncewell (89): owner of boarding house into whose back room jury has been moved (89).

_____ Holland (89): foreman of jury (89).

_____: another member of jury (89).

Stonewall Jackson Fentry (89): member of Bookwright's jury; one man of jury who votes guilty for Bookwright (89); flashback: takes job in sawmill in Frenchman's Bend (92); returns thirty miles for Christmas; walks back to Quick's sawmill; returns third year for good with goat and baby in hired buggy (93); raises boy; makes his clothes (94-95); with boy, disappears; returns after five years (96); when asked if the boy died, says "What boy?" (97); attacks Thorpe brothers with ax to prevent them from taking boy away (102); reason he would not free Bookwright for killing Buck Thorpe: Buck Thorpe was the grown man Jackson and Longstreet Fentry whom he had tried to raise (105).

_____: narrator's mother (90).

G. A. Fentry (90): father of Stonewall Jackson Fentry (90); orders Gavin and Chick off land (91); orders Pruitt off land (96).

Rufus (103) Pruitt (91): neighbor of Fentry (91).

Mrs. _____ Pruitt (91): Rufus's mother (91).

_____ Pruitt (92): her husband.

Captain _____ Stevens (91): father of Gavin Stevens (91).

_____: black man who helps S. J. Fentry's father work place while he is in Frenchman's Bend (92).

Ben Quick (93): owner of sawmill in Frenchman's Bend (93); father of Isham Quick; hired Fentry to work in sawmill (98 ff.).

Jackson and Longstreet (95) Fentry (94): raised by Fentry (94); taken away by his uncles Thorpe (102-103); raised as Buck Thorpe; killed by Bookwright (105).

_____: midwife who taught Fentry to diaper the baby (94).

Mrs. Stonewall Jackson Fentry (100): mother of baby; died shortly after childbirth; maiden name said to be Smith (95); married to Fentry just before she dies (100).

_____ Thorpe (100): brother of wife of S. J. Fentry (99); with brother, comes to find sister's baby (101); takes boy from Fentry; gives him money purse and thanks him for taking care of boy (102).

_____ Thorpe (100): brother of wife of S. J. Fentry (99).

_____ Thorpe (100): father of wife of S. J. Fentry; tried to keep daughter from marrying father of her baby (99).

_____: husband of wife of S. J. Fentry (101); father of baby born by wife of S. J. Fentry; deserted her (99).

<u>   Whitfield (100)</u>: preacher who marries S. J. Fentry and wife just before she dies; helps bury her (100).

                 : deputy or bailiff who accompanies Thorpe brothers (100).

"An Error in Chemistry"

Written about October, 1940; first published in *Ellery Queen's* *Mystery Magazine*, **7 (June, 1946), 4-19; reprinted in** *The Queen's Awards*, **(Boston: Little, Brown and Company, 1946); reprinted in** *Knight's Gambit*, **1949.**

<u>Joel Flint (109)</u>: tells sheriff he killed his wife; Yankee operator of pitch in carnival; after carnival leaves; marries dim-witted fortyish spinster (109); middle 40's; drinks whisky straight (110); killing was not an accident; jailed (111); says he killed wife for insurance (112); there is an insurance policy; disappears from jail (116); leaves scrap of paper from The Billboard at his house (118-119); killed Pritchel and buried him under stable; he had made Pritchel up to look like Flint who escaped from jail (128).

<u>Hub (124)   </u>: sheriff (109); big man; little hard eyes (111); says Flint killed wife because he wanted to be locked up; says Flint was never afraid (112); says the wrong one was killed (114); visits Pritchel with Gavin and narrator (125).

<u>Ellie (126) Pritchel Flint (109)</u>: Joel Flint's wife (109).

<u>Bryan Ewell (117)</u>: sheriff's deputy (109); sent by sheriff to Pritchel's home to watch him (117).

<u>Wesley Pritchel (109)</u>: Flint's father-in-law; builds house for Flints; sees them once a week; dislikes son-in-law (109); locks himself in room after his daughter is killed (113); has clay-pit on farm (114); drives Bryan Ewell away with shotgun (120); tells insurance adjustor how daughter was killed accidentally by her husband (122); 74 years old; buried wife and four children (126); mixes whisky wrong way by putting sugar in first before disolving it in water (127); revealed as Joel Flint (Signor Canova) ex-carnival escape artist (128).

<u>Gavin (111) Stevens (123)</u>: county attorney; prematurely white-haired; Harvard Phi Beta Kappa (111).

                : narrator; nephew of Gavin Stevens (111).

                : Pritchel's neighbor; sent for by sheriff to stay in house with Pritchel (114).

                : his wife (114).

                : other neighbor of Pritchel (114).

_____: three northerners who want to buy Pritchel's farm (115); when insurance adjustor arrives at Pritchel's, they are buying his farm (123).

Ben Berry (117): sent by sheriff to Flint's house (117).

_____: two neighbor women who cook meat for Pritchel (119).

_____ Workman (121): a city man; insurance adjustor (121).

_____: black youth in Flint's truck (124).

_____ Stevens (127): Gavin Stevens's father; grandfather of narrator (127).

"Knight's Gambit"

First written as a short story by January, 1942; revision started by about February 23, 1946, and expanded to novella length by about November 24, 1948; first published in *Knight's Gambit*, **1949.**

Max (178) Harriss (135): brings sister to Gavin Stevens (135); wants Captain Gualdres out of his house; does not want him to marry his mother (137); angry with Stevens for not taking the case; threatens him (139); returns from Europe with mother *ca.* 1939 (161); expert at fencing (162); rides with Captain Gualdres (172); beaten by Gualdres at riding and fencing (181-182); wants engagement to Cayley girl kept secret; Gualdres courts her too (184-185); leaves for Memphis to establish alibi (192); missing from Memphis (198); passes Stevens and Chick in car to the Memphis road (204); has bought McCallun's horse (207); has placed it in stable to kill Gualdres (214 ff.); returns to Jefferson (222); 21 not 19; told by Stevens to enlist (224); leaves through window to enlist (226).

_____ Harriss (135): sister of Max Harriss (135); says she is not engaged to Gualdres, but she loves him (138); told a lie (174); returns to Stevens's room (177); says Gualdres is in danger (178); says she loves Gualdres (179); wants him deported (180); says Max is going to kill Gualdres (181); says Max hates Gualdres because he beat him at riding and fencing (181-182); calls Stevens to have him meet her brother on corner (202-203); marries Captain Gualdres (226).

Gavin (210) Stevens (136): uncle of narrator (135); county attorney (137); refuses to take Harriss case (138); premature white hair; Phi Beta Kappa (140-141); continues chess game after Harriss boy interrupts and threatens him (141); flashback: returns to Heidelberg to finish Ph. D. in 1919 (146); brother of Charles's mother; spent three years as stretcher bearer in French army in WW I (147); tells Mrs. Harriss he hopes she will be happy when she returns; she blushes (164); back to present: stops Harriss and Cayley girls from fighting (187); gives ring back to Cayley girl so that she can return it (188); wires Markey to use police on Max Harriss if necessary to escort him out of town (204); translates Old

270

Testament "back into classic Greek" (207); after learning of sale of horse, gets McCallum and, with Chick driving, goes to Harriss home (210-212); with McCallum, shows Gualdres that the killer horse, not the blind mare, is in the stable (214 ff.); tells Max Harriss to enlist (224); says goodbye to the Gualdreses (228); drives with Chick to Harriss house (229); flashback to time he was 30 and Mrs. Harriss was 16: asked her for a date; asked her father to let him be betrothed to her (234 ff.); gave her a ring before he went to Heidelberg (235); wrote letters to her and to Russian woman with whom he had had an affair; gets letters mixed up (236); back to present: meets Mrs. Harriss (238); marries Mrs. Harriss (241).

Charles (137) Chick (187) Mallison (177): nephew (135) to Gavin Stevens (136); not quite 18 (139); cadet lieutenant colonel in high school ROTC (195-196); Romantic passage on WW II (196-197); goes to movies as uncle orders him to (205-206); on way to movies, asks McCallum who bought horse (206); disturbs uncle while translating to tell him Max Harriss bought horse (208); after Max and Gualdres leave, drives uncle to Harriss home (229); after Pearl Harbor, in flight training; returns to Jefferson on way to Texas (240-241).

Captain (136) Sebastian (178, 180) Gualdres (136): was engaged to Harriss daughter, according to her brother; now wants to marry the mother (138); Argentine (142); rides across square; described as epicene (165); at one with horse; knows the county thoroughly (166); whole county assumes he is Mrs. Harriss's lover (166-167); loves horses; visits them at night; builds an even better steeplechase than Harriss built (167); buys nearly blind horse with Mrs. Harriss's money (168-169); asks people not to come out to watch while he trains it (170); beats Max at riding and fencing (181-182); refuses to leave when Harriss girl warns him about Max's hatred of him (189); marries Harriss girl (226); says goodbye to Stevens (227); joins U. S. Cavalry after Pearl Harbor; renounces Argentine citizenship (242).

Mrs. Harriss (137): mother of Harriss children (137); wealthy widow millionairess in late 30's (142); married at 17 a man whom nobody had heard of; rumored to have been engaged to someone else before her marriage (144); takes children to Europe (153); sends Christmas cards to six friends from the Academy (159); returns from Europe about 1939 (161); leaves for South America two months later (162); impervious to change (161-163); returns with Argentine cavalry captain (163); marries Gavin Stevens (241).

Maggie (163) Mallison (177): Charles's mother (141).

_____ Mallison (142): Charles's father (142).

_____: Charles's grandfather (142).

_____: Charles's grandmother who bought the books in family library (142).

Clarissa, Judith, Marguerite, St. Elmo, Roland, Lothair: first   names
of friends of Charles's grandmother (143).

_____: Mrs. Harriss's father (143); reads Roman poets in Latin
(144); dies (152).

_____: Mrs. Harriss's mother; dies in childbirth (144).

_____ Harriss (144): husband of Mrs. Harriss (144); more than
twice her age (146); has Midas touch (147); returns to New Orleans to his
business for five years after marriage (149); returns for Christmas and
New Year's day; bootlegger; successful (150-151); after father-in-law's
death, makes arrangement with black tenants to run plantation (152);
converts plantation to horse farm (154-155); rebuilds house; brings friends
to house (155); installs polo field and steeplechase (156-158), and pack of
hounds (158); dies sitting at his desk; shot to death (160) in 1939 (161).

_____: black man who drives Harriss's Victoria (149).

_____: black chauffeur for Harriss (151).

_____: light-colored black nurse for Harriss child (151).

_____: man from Memphis who rents Harriss's plantation
(153).

_____: caretaker of Harriss's house; from New Orleans; fat
Italian or Greek (155); pays farmers for stock killed by cars of Harriss's
friends (156).

_____: Charles's great-aunt (161).

Rafe McCallum (168): horse breeder (168); has unrideable stallion
(201); has sold stallion (202) to Max Harriss (207).

_____: barber who speculates on what Captain Gualdres is
training the blind horse to do (170).

_____: his client (170).

Paoli (182)_____: apparently riding instructor who teaches Max
Harriss to ride (182).

_____ Cayley (184): farmer's daughter to whom Max Harriss
gives ring (183); courted by Gualdres (184-185); slaps Harriss girl with
ring; cuts her face (186-187).

Mrs. Hence Mossop Cayley (184): mother of Miss Cayley (184).

Hence Cayley (184): father of Miss Cayley; does not think Max is
any good (184).

272

Robert Markey (192): lawyer in Memphis called by Stevens to put private detective on Max Harriss (192-193).

Captain   Warren (197): served in Royal Flying Corps in WW I (197).

Melissa Hogganbeck (199): Chick's high-school teacher in World Affairs (199).

_____ McCallum: twin McCallum nephews; enlisted in war (200).

Hampton Killegrew (203): night marshal (203).

_____: black plow-hand who drives the young Harriss girl to town (233).

_____: Russian woman with whom Gavin Stevens had an affair in WW I (236).

_____: black butler in Mrs. Harriss's house (237).

Benbow Sartoris (239-240): after Pearl Harbor, commissioned officer in England (239-240).

_____ McWilliams (243): conductor on train on which Charles meets his mother (243).

See *These 13*, 1931, for the following stories: "Victory," "Ad Astra," "All the Dead Pilots," "Crevasse," "Red Leaves," "A Rose for Emily," "A Justice," "Hair," "That Evening Sun," "Dry September," "Mistral," "Divorce in Naples," and "Carcassonne."

See *Doctor Martino and Other Stories*, 1934, for following stories: "Doctor Martino," "Fox Hunt," "Death Drag," "There Was a Queen," "Turnabout," "Beyond," "Wash," "Elly," "Black Music," "The Leg," "Mountain Victory," and "Honor."

Pagination, in parentheses, to following edition of Collected Stories of William Faulkner (New York: Random House, 1950) for the following stories: "Barn Burning," "Shingles for the Lord," "The Tall Men," "A Bear Hunt," "Two Soldiers," "Shall Not Perish," "Centaur in Brass," "Uncle Willy," "Mule in the Yard," "That Will Be Fine," "A Courtship," "Lo!," "Pennsylvania Station," "Artist at Home," "The Brooch," "My Grandmother Millard," and "Golden Land."

Collected Stories was published August 21, 1950. See individual stories for details of writing and publication.

"Barn Burning"

Begun on or before November 7, 1938; first published in *Harper's Magazine*, 179 (June, 1939), [86]-96; intended originally to be used as the opening chapter of *The Hamlet*, 1940; it was reprinted in *O. Henry Memorial Award Prize Stories of 1939* (Garden City, N. Y.: Doubleday, Doran & Company, Inc., 1939), pp. 3-29; reprinted in *Collected Stories*, 1950.

_____: Justice of the Peace (3); shabby, collarless, graying man in spectacles (4); reduces Ab Snopes's penalty to ten bushels of corn as payment to Major de Spain for spoiled rug (19).

Colonel Sartoris (4) Sarty (13) Snopes (4): boy (3) not called upon to testify (5); fights with boy who called his father "Barn burner!" (6); 10 years old (8); very impressed when he first sees Major de Spain's house; thinks that people that rich are safe from his father (10); when De Spain charges his father twenty bushels of corn, says he will hide crop and not give him it (16); works very hard; builds pens for shoat and cow; hopes that his father has changed; does not like being pulled two ways (17); in court, blurts out "He aint burnt. . ." (18); sent by father to get oil from barn; wants to run away but can not; forced to bring oil can to father (21); breaks away from mother and aunt (22); runs to Major de Spain; warns him; runs away (23); sobs, "Father! Father!" as he hears shots; filled with grief and despair (24); "He did not look back." (25).

Colonel [John] Sartoris (4).

Abner (9) Snopes (5): father of Colonel Sartoris Snopes (3); wounded in heel during Civil War; called "Barn burner!" (5); hits son because he knew he would have told on him; says, "You got to learn to stick to your own blood or you ain't going to have any blood to stick to you." (8); on way to Major de Spain's house, steps in fresh horse manure (10); pushes black butler aside; strides across pale rug, soiling it with manure (11); vents hatred toward the house (12); with son Sarty, returns ruined rug to front veranda (15); charged twenty bushels of corn (16); sues De Spain (18); has penalty reduced to ten bushels (19); had been horse trader (20); orders wife to hold Sarty so that he can not tell Major de Spain (22); takes oil can to burn De Spain's barn (22).

_____ Harris (3): "our enemy" (3); impounded Snopes's hog; after he gets message "wood and hay kin burn," barn burns (4); refuses to question Colonel Sartoris Snopes (5).

_____: black who delivers message to Harris "wood and hay kin burn" (4).

_____ Snopes (4): older brother of Colonel Sartoris Snopes (4).

Net (22) Snopes (4): sister of Colonel Sartoris Snopes; big (6); with sister, under father's supervision, washes Major de Spain's rug with harsh, homemade lye (13); they ruin it (14); they are twins (23).

_____ Snopes (4): sister of Colonel Sartoris Snopes; big (6); twin (23).

Lennie (22) Snopes (4): mother of Colonel Sartoris Snopes (6); tries to get Ab Snopes not to ruin Major de Spain's rug (14); tries to stop husband from burning Major de Spain's barn (20).

Lizzie (22) _____: aunt of Colonel Sartoris Snopes; sister of his mother (6).

_____: black butler at De Spain's house; tries to keep Ab Snopes from entering (11).

Lula (11) de Spain (12): Major de Spain's wife (12).

Major [Cassius] de Spain (12): owner of big home and rug that Snopes ruins (12); returns rug to Snopes to be cleaned (12-13); charges Snopes twenty bushels of corn for ruined rug (16).

_____: black youth who carries rug on horse behind Major de Spain (12).

_____: Justice of the Peace.

_____: village blacksmith (19).

_____: man in blacksmith shop (19).

276

"Shingles for the Lord"

Written about June, 1942; first published in *The Saturday Evening Post*, **215 (February 13, 1943), 14-15, 68, 70, 71; reprinted in** *Collected Stories*, **1950.**

_____ Grier (36): narrator; son of Pap (27).

Res (40) Grier (36): Pap; borrows froe and maul from Killegrew (27); argues with Quick and Bookwright about being late (29-30); cuts shingles angrily and drives froe into ground each stroke; owns good squirrel dog with Vernon Tull (31); leaves at lunch time; returns; agrees to give dog to Quick for finishing cutting shingles (35); has traded with Tull for his half of dog in return for pulling old shingles off church (37); borrows crowbar from Armstid and returns with son to remove old shingles from church (38); sets church on fire; carries whole water barrel to fire; falls and knocks himself out (39); called "arsonist" by Whitfield (41); determines to go back and rebuild church (43).

_____ Killegrew (27): fox hunting all night (28); 70 years old (30).

_____ Grier (36): Maw (27); cleans husband's head wound; gives him toddy (43).

Reverend _____ Whitfield (27): calls Res Grier an "arsonist"; calls on people to build new church after old one burns (41).

Solon Quick (27): owns school bus truck (27); tried WPA but disillusioned (29); argues with Pap about being two hours late for shingling church roof (29-30); wants to buy squirrel dog from Pap and Vernon Tull (33); offers to finish shingling in exchange for dog (33).

Homer Bookwright (27).

Mrs. _____ Killegrew (28): deafer than her husband (28).

_____: her cook (28).

Vernon (32) Tull (31): to nail shingles on roof tomorrow (31); with Pap, owns good squirrel dog (32).

_____ Snopes (31): to nail shingles on roof of church tomorrow (31).

Will Varner (31).

_____ Armstid (34): a farmer (34).

Mrs. _____ Armstid (39).

277

<u>   Tull (41)</u>: rest of Tull's family (41).

"The Tall Men"

Written in March, 1941; first published in *The Saturday Evening Post*, **213 (May 31, 1941), 14-15, 95, 96, 98, 99; reprinted in** Collected Stories, **1950.**

<u>   Pearson (47)</u>: state draft investigator (45); insists on serving warrant (53); carries amputated leg (58).

Doctor   <u>Schofield (45)</u>: amputates Buddy McCallum's leg (58).

<u>   Gombault (47)</u>: old deputy marshal (45); tells Pearson to be quiet (53); keeps Pearson so that he will miss train; carries amputated leg out of room; gives it to Pearson; goes to bury it (58); talks steadily about abuses of government trying to control men's lives (55-60); buries Buddy McCallum's leg; then ready to go back to town (61).

<u>Lee McCallum (45)</u>.

<u>Rafe (47) Raphael (54) McCallum (47)</u>.

<u>Buddy (47) Anse (54) McCallum (47)</u>: caught his leg in hammer mill (47); blue-eyed (49); wants doctor to amputate his damaged leg (52); asks his twin sons to enlist in the Sixth Infantry in which he served in WW I (53); refuses to abide by government crop regulation; can not sell his crop and the next one (56); gives up raising cotton; starts raising whiteface cattle; refuses to take money from government (57).

<u>Stuart (50) McCallum (49)</u>: white haired (49).

<u>Jackson (50) McCallum (49)</u>: thin; about 70; "something delicate in his face" (49); the eldest (51).

<u>Anse (50) McCallum (49)</u>: blue-eyed twin son of Buddy McCallum (49); kisses his father; leaves for Memphis to enlist (54); with twin, went for year to agricultural college to learn about whiteface cattle (55).

<u>Lucius (50) McCallum (49)</u>: blue-eyed twin son of Buddy McCallum (49); kisses his father; leaves for Memphis to enlist (54); with twin, went for year to agricultural college to learn about whiteface cattle (55).

<u>Old Anse McCallum (54)</u>: dead for fifteen or sixteen years (54); walked to Virginia to enlist in Confederate Army (54).

<u>   McCallum (47)</u>: wife of Buddy McCallum; mother of twins (55); buried with her own folks (60).

<u>Gavin Stevens (56)</u>: lawyer (56).

_____: county agent's employee who tries to pay Buddy McCallum for not raising cotton (57).

Mrs. Anse McCallum (60): buried in family plot (60).

"A Bear Hunt"

Written about November-December, 1933; first published in *The Saturday Evening Post*, **206 (February 10, 1934), 8-9, 74, 76; reprinted in** *Collected Stories*, **1950; revised for** *Big Woods*, **1955.**

_____: narrator of first four pages (63).

_____ Ratliff (63): sewing machine agent; used to drive team; now drives model T Ford (63); after few pages, narrates story of Provine (66 ff.); beaten by Luke Provine for setting Indians on him (66-67); says he was only trying to cure Luke's hiccups (68); tells Luke Provine to go to John Basket for cure for hiccups (71-72).

Major [Cassius] de Spain (63): owns hunting camp (63); supports Provine's family (64).

Mrs. _____ de Spain (63).

_____: her married daughter (63).

Lucius (63) Butch (64) Luke (66) Provine (63): 40; most teeth gone (63); makes no effort to support family; arrested selling whisky (64); flashback: with his gang, returns from dance; burns celluloid collars on all black men at a black church picnic (65); back to present: beats Ratliff (66); has hiccups (68 ff.); goes to Indian mound for cure by John Basket (71-72); rushes back to camp, saying Indians were going to burn him to death (75); beats up Ratliff for sending him to John Basket (76).

_____ Provine (63): Lucius's dead brother (63).

Jack Bonds (63): dead member of the Provine gang (63-64).

_____ Provine (64): wife of Lucius Provine (64).

_____ Provine (64): three children of Lucius Provine (64).

Old Man Ash (67)_____: black helper in Major de Spain's hunting camp (67); leaves camp after Luke Provine; goes to Indian mound (74); gets to mound ahead of Provine and tells Indians that he is a new revenue agent; urges them to scare him; they pretend to burn him (78); motive was to get even with Provine for burning his celluloid collar many years before (79).

_____: narrator's companion who spent night with him on Indian mound (66).

Uncle Ike McCaslin (69): one of the hunters; sends Luke away from his stand (69).

John Basket (71): Indian (71).

_____ Fraser (73): one of the poker players in De Spain's camp (73).

_____: black man; helper to Uncle Ash (74).

"Two Soldiers"

Sent to Harold Ober January 29, 1942; first published in _The Saturday Evening Post_, **214 (March 28, 1942), 9-11, 35, 36, 38, 40; reprinted in** _Collected Stories_, **1950.**

_____ Grier (94): first-person narrator (81); almost 9 years old (82); with brother Pete, outside Old Man Killegrew's house, listens to radio news about Pearl Harbor and WW II in Pacific (81-82); after brother Pete goes to Memphis to enlist, walks twenty-two miles to Jefferson to follow Pete to Memphis (89); threatens to cut hand off ticket salesman at bus depot (90); bus fare paid by Mrs. Habersham; given sandwich by Foote; leaves on bus for Memphis (92); goes to Army enlistment center (93); cuts soldier with pocket knife (94); reunited with Pete; agrees to return home (96-97); cries as soldier drives him home (99).

Pete (81) Grier (94): nearly 20 years old (81); listens to war news on radio at Killegrew's (81-82); wants to enlist (84); goes to Memphis to enlist (87); reunited with brother (95); sends him back home (96).

_____ Killegrew (81).

_____ Killegrew (81): deaf wife of Old Man Killegrew (81).

_____ Grier (94): Maw (81); does not want Pete to go to war but mends and packs his clothes (85-86).

_____ Grier (94): Pap (81); never got caught up (82); drafted in WW I; sent to Texas for eight months (85).

_____ Tull (83): neighbor; father of girls (83).

_____ Tull (83): daughters of Tull; courted by Pete (83).

Marsh (84) _____: brother of Maw; served in WW I (84); wounded in France (85).

_____: Maw's mother; grandmother of narrator (84).

_____ Foote (89): the law; questions narrator in Jefferson (89); gives him sandwich before he boards bus (89).

Mrs.   Habersham (89): gives ticket seller dollar for ticket to Memphis for narrator (92).

_____: bus ticket seller in Jefferson; will not trade ticket for shrikepoke egg (90).

_____: young woman with Mrs. Habersham (91).

_____: bus driver who takes narrator to Memphis (93).

_____: recruiting sergeant (94).

_____: officer in recruiting station (94); orders Pete returned from train to Little Rock (95).

_____: other soldiers in recruiting station (94).

Mrs.   McKellogg (99): woman who takes narrator home to dinner before he returns to Frenchman's Bend (97).

_____: black man; elevator operator (97-98).

Colonel   McKellogg (98).

_____ McKellogg (98): Colonel and Mrs. McKellogg's son; in school in East (98).

_____: black waiter (98).

_____: soldier who drives narrator back to Frenchman's Bend (99).

"Shall Not Perish"

Written early 1942; received by Harold Ober April 24, 1942; first published in *Story*, **23 (July-August, 1943), 40-47; reprinted in** *Collected Stories*, **1950.**

Pete (101) Grier (102): enlisted right after Pearl Harbor (102); killed in WW II in April; ship sank (102); place of death unknown (104).

_____ Grier (102): narrator's father (101); farms seventy acres (102); returns from town with news that Major de Spain's son has been killed in WW II (103).

_____ Grier (102): first-person narrator; 9 years old (101); with brother Pete, used to listen to radio at Mr.Killegrew's house at time of Pearl Harbor [See "Two Soldiers."] (103); with mother, rides Quick's bus to town; carries shoes and socks; puts them on at outskirts of town (106); story ends with tribute to America (114-115).

_____ Grier (102): narrator's mother (101); with son, rides bus to town; washes feet before putting on shoes and stockings (106); visits Major de Spain (107); tells him to weep (108); takes pistol from table; returns it; tells him to weep not for his son but for those who survived (109); waits in town museum for return bus to Frenchman's Bend (111).

Homer Bookwright (102): owns cattle truck; takes Grier to town (102).

Major _____ de Spain (103): son of Major [Cassius] de Spain; not a real major; inherited title from father (107); banker (107); makes speech to Mrs. Grier condemning the country and war as caused by usury; "by the folly and rapacity of politicians, for glory and aggrandisement of organized labor" (108); offers to send Mrs. Grier home in car (110).

_____ De Spain (103): son of second Major de Spain; aviator; killed in WW II (103).

_____ Killegrew (103).

Solon Quick (106): built and operates school bus (106).

Major [Cassius] de Spain (107): father of present De Spain(107).

_____: black servant of Major de Spain (104); removes pistol (that Major de Spain was presumably going to use on himself) from room (110).

_____: Mrs. Grier's brother; served in WW I (109).

_____: Mrs. Grier's mother (109).

_____: Mrs. Grier's grandfather who went to war (109).

_____: his mother (109).

_____: woman who built town museum (110).

Mrs. Solon Quick (111).

_____: narrator's father's grandfather (111).

Colonel [John] Sartoris (112).

Mrs. Rosa Millard (112): Colonel Sartoris's mother-in-law (112).

"Centaur in Brass"

On sending schedule as "Centaur," August 11, 1931; first published in _American Mercury_, **25 (February, 1932), 200-210; revised for** _Collected_

Stories, 1950; reappears, revised, in Chapter One of *The Town*, 1957.

_____: first-person-plural narrator (149); for town "we" think of adultery when "we" think of Mrs. Snopes and Hoxey together (151); becomes first-person-singular narrator(155); [Point of view varies from third-person narrator to first-person, to Harker as first-person narrator.]

Flem Snopes (149): has monument in brass to himself; only four persons know that it is his monument; comes to Jefferson from country; first a clerk in country store; marries store owner's daughter on same day three of her suitors left county [See *The Hamlet*.]; moves to Texas after wedding (149); returns from Texas one month after wife and baby with stranger and half-wild mustang ponies; gets bill of sale for Suratt's half of restaurant; soon eliminates partner; prospers (150); after Hoxey's election, becomes superintendent of municipal power plant (151); has no friends; eyes color of stagnant water; chews steadily (152); builds monument slowly by stealing brass safety valves and replacing them with steel plugs (153); five months later orders Tom-Tom to bring pieces of brass to his office (155); tells Tom-Tom that Turl wants his day-shift job; that Turl is planning to steal iron from plant; tells Tom-Tom to take pieces of brass to his cabin to hide them; says as soon as he gets evidence, will fire Turl (155); pays city auditors and city clerk $304.50 for missing brass (158); now tells Turl that Tom-Tom thinks that Turl wants to fire the day shift; tells Turl that for two years Tom-Tom has been stealing brass from plant to lay it on Turl and get him fired; tells Turl to get brass during day from Tom-Tom and bring it to him (159); first mistake was to pick Turl to do task; second mistake was to forget about Tom-Tom's "high yellow" wife (160); spies on Turl as Turl has affair with Tom-Tom's wife (161); after Tom-Tom and Turl remove brass from Tom-Tom's barn, told by Turl that Tom-Tom told him he had no brass; sends for Tom-Tom who denies he has brass (166); frustrated when Turl and Tom-Tom put brass in water tank; pays extra $200 for missing brass (167); resigns from power plant; stares at his monument (168).

_____ Harker (153): white man who knows of monument (149); night engineer; finds three brass safety valves replaced by plugs capable of pressure of one thousand pounds (153); for eight paragraphs, Harker becomes first-person narrator (153-154); assumes first-person narration again (157-158); becomes narrator again at page 160 and again at page 166.

Tom-Tom _____ (149): black man who knows of monument (149); day fireman of power plant; two hundred pounds; 60 years old; married for a year to third wife (152); on Snope's orders, takes brass pieces to his own house; repeats; has been firing boilers for forty years (156); finds out that Turl and his wife have been having an affair; takes day off; puts on wife's nightgown [!]; lies on cot as Turl approaches (162-163); leaps on Turl's back with butcher knife; drops butcher knife (164); they fall in ditch; talk; fix all blame on Flem Snopes (165); with Turl, removes brass from his barn (166); puts it in water tank from which Snopes cannot remove it (167).

283

Turl (153)_____: second black man who knows of monument (149); night fireman (153); tells Harker that Snopes removed brass valves (154); agrees to Snopes's order to steal from Tom-Tom's house during day and bring it to Snopes; just past 30 (159); has reputation for tom-catting (160); can not find brass (161); has affair with Tom-Tom's wife; finds Tom-Tom on cot instead of his wife (162); carries Tom-Tom on back; tries to knock him off against trees (164); falls in deep ditch; they talk and fix all blame on Flem Snopes (165).

_____ Snopes (149): Flem Snopes's wife (149); works in restaurant (150); listens to Major Hoxey as he drinks coffee; gossip about them (151).

_____ Snopes (149): her daughter (149).

_____ Suratt (149): sewing machine agent who used to own half-interest in back-street restaurant in Jefferson (149); gives bill of sale to Snopes for one half of restaurant; never gives reason (150).

_____: owner of country store whose daughter suddenly marries Flem Snopes (149).

_____: stranger from Texas; returns with Flem Snopes and horses (150).

_____: Suratt's and Flem Snopes's partner in restaurant (150).

Major_____Hoxey (151): middle-aged bachelor; graduate of Yale; soon to be mayor of Jefferson (151).

_____: black third wife of Tom-Tom; young (152); "high yellow" (160); gets ill on whisky and old watermelon; confesses to Tom-Tom about her affair with Turl (163).

_____: two city auditors who look for missing brass parts (157); return with Buck Conner and city clerk, to say that a recheck of books shows missing brass was worth $525 (167).

_____: city clerk (157).

Buck Conner (159): city marshal (159).

"Uncle Willy"

Written early in 1935; first published in the *American Mercury*, **36 (October, 1935), 156-168; reprinted in** *Collected Stories*, **1950.**

_____: first-person narrator (225); with other children, watches Uncle Willy shoot dope (226); about 14 (227); gets letter from Uncle Willy after he escapes from Keeley; meets him in Memphis; admires him greatly; would do anything for him; breaks into store to steal alcohol

(239); camps with Uncle Willy in tent in Renfro (242); after Uncle Willy is killed, feels he helped him (247).

<u>Uncle Willy (225) Bubber (230) Christian (227)</u>: not anybody's uncle; has no kin except sister in Texas who is married to oil millionaire; lives by himself (225); takes dope; pharmacist who no longer makes prescriptions; gives prizes to baseball teams; shoots dope in their presence (226); goes to Sunday school with school children; "they" make him quit dope after he has been using it for forty years (227); after "they" keep him off dope from Sunday through Wednesday, escapes and returns to store; boys help him get dope fix; is recaptured by Rev. Schultz, Mrs. Merridew and other ladies (230); finally gives up; taken to Memphis hospital; sick for long time (231); returns; has to relearn names of boys who used to watch him shoot dope (233); tells new clerk to rehire Job (234); with boys, breaks into store; takes three gallons of alcohol; drives to Memphis every Saturday in car sister gave him (235); returns drunk with big woman in car; claims to be married to her (236); after she is sent back to Memphis, Mrs. Merridew moves in and sends Willy to Memphis to "the Keeley" (an alcoholic institute) (238); everyone thinks he is crazy (239); gets out of Keeley; sells house in Jefferson; sends letter to narrator to meet him in Memphis (239); when narrator meets him, has car and tent and Job is with him (240); takes narrator to airport where he has bought an airplane (241); plans to have Secretary teach him to fly and to take all four of them to California (241-242); begins to learn to fly; has not taken drink since he bought plane (244); aghast at thought that Secretary can fly and he can not; has graduated from university (245); after Job calls Mrs. Merridew, flies plane; crashes; is killed; taken back to Jefferson for burial (246-247).

_____: Uncle Willy's sister; lives in Texas (225); comes from Texas when he is being forced to give up dope (229); returns to Texas (233).

_____: her husband; oil millionaire (225).

<u>Job Wylie (226)</u>: black cook who helps Uncle Willy in drugstore (226); refuses to be fired by new clerk (232); sits on curb opposite store (233); disappears from town (239); with Uncle Willy in car in Memphis (240); telephones Mr. Merridew (245).

<u>Hoke (233) Christian (226)</u>: Uncle Willy's father; established drugstore (226).

_____ Barbour (227): Sunday school teacher (227).

<u>Reverend _____ Schultz (227)</u>: removes Uncle Willy from Sunday school to begin withdrawal from dope (228).

_____ Miller (227): leader of men's Bible class (228).

<u>Miss _____ Callaghan (228)</u>: school teacher (228).

285

Darl (229) Bundren (228): taken to asylum at Jackson handcuffed to fat deputy (228).

_____: fat deputy; takes Darl Bundren to asylum (228).

_____: narrator's father (228); a lawyer (237).

Mrs. _____ Merridew (228): takes Uncle Willy home with her after church (229); sends for Uncle Willy's sister; stays with him until sister arrives (229); determines to restore Uncle Willy body and soul (232); calls Willy's wife a whore (236); wires to Willy's sister who sends one thousand dollars; with narrator's father, gives Willy's wife money and car to return to Memphis; moves in with Uncle Willy; sends him to the Keeley (238).

Mrs. _____ Schultz (229): wife of minister (229).

Mrs. _____ Hovis (229): takes turn staying with Uncle Willy while forcing him to give up dope (229).

_____: town marshal; breaks down door to Uncle Willy's drugstore (230).

_____: clerk hired by Mrs. Merridew and Rev. Schultz to run Uncle Willy's drugstore; tries to fire Job (232); disappears (236).

Sonny Barger (234): keeps store at which Uncle Willy buys Jamaica ginger (235).

Secretary (235): "a burr-headed nigger boy" hired to drive Uncle Willy's car (235); disappears from town (239); reappears at airport flying a two-cylinder plane (241); after trying to reach Renfro, runs out of gas and lands in right field (242-243); finally tells Uncle Willy that he will never learn to fly plane (245).

Lorine, Billie, Jack (236): names in Uncle Willy's notebook (236).

Mrs. Willy Christian (236): big woman brought home by Uncle Willy; claims to be his wife; has marriage license (236-237); returns to Memphis after she is paid one thousand dollars and given the car; a "Manuel Street" whore (238).

_____: narrator's mother (236).

_____: the mayor (237).

Robert 239) _____: narrator's uncle (239).

Captain _____ Bean (241): flight instructor who teaches Secretary to fly (241).

"Mule in the Yard"

Written probably in mid-December, 1933 or early spring, 1934; sent to Morton Goldman early, 1934; first published in *Scribner's*, 96 (August, 1934), 65-70; reprinted in *Collected Stories*, 1950; included in Chapter 16 of *The Town*, 1957.

Old Het (249)___: at least 70; black (249); joins in attempt to get Snopes's mule out of yard (250 ff.); offers Snopes ten dollars for mule from Mrs. Hait (259).

Mrs. Mannie Hait (249): about 40-odd; wears hat of ten-year-dead husband and man's high shoes (250); with Old Het, chases mule in yard (250-251); paid $8500 for death of husband by railroad; takes cash; paints house red (same as RR stations) (253); her house burns down during mule chase (257); salvages money and, with Old Het beside her, sits in rocker on porch opposite house as it burns; says she wants to buy mule that knocked scuttle of live coals into cellar and burned house down (258-259); sends Old Het with $10 to I. O. Snopes to buy mule (259); says railroad paid Snopes $60 for each mule killed and that he paid Hait $50 for tethering mules on track, but did not pay him for last job when he died; hence cost of mule = $60 less $50 = $10 (261); lets Snopes give her back $10 and tells him where she left mule (262); shot mule (264).

___Hait (250): late husband of Mannie Hait (250); killed with mules by freight train (252).

I. O. (258) Snopes (252): owner of mules killed by freight trains; deathly afraid of mules (252); stops tethering mules on track after Hait is killed; involved in chase of mule in Mrs. Hait's yard (254); when Mannie Hait wants to buy mule, says it costs $150 (259); visits Mrs. Hait after she took mule (261); gives her back $10 (262). finds that she shot mule (264).

___: person who talks with I. O. Snopes about being sued by Mannie Hait (258).

___Spilmer (262): Mrs. Hait has placed I. O. Snopes's mule behind his house (262).

"That Will Be Fine"

Written probably in spring, 1935; first published in the *American Mercury*, 35 (July, 1935), 264-276; reprinted in *The Best Short Stories 1936 and The Yearbook of the American Short Stories*, ed., Edward J. O'Brien (Boston and New York: Houghton Mifflin Company, 1936); reprinted in *Collected Stories*, 1950.

Georgie (272)___: narrator (265); offers to tell Rosie what her Christmas present is for a nickel (265); 7-year-old boy (266); is paid a nickel by Uncle Rodney to watch for Mr. Tucker while Rodney has an affair with Mrs. Tucker; had been paid a quarter by Rodney for being lookout for his affair with woman in Mottstown (268); goes with mother and father in carriage (instead of by train) to Grandpa's for Christmas (270); tells sheriff that Uncle Rodney is out of town; thinks constantly of money (278); takes screwdriver to Uncle Rodney nailed up in Mandy's cabin (279); promised twenty quarters to go to house, throw gravel at window and tell whoever answers that Rodney will be there in buggy in ten minutes, and to bring "all the jewelry" (281); as he is about to throw gravel, sees woman and is grabbed by man; gives man the message; told to go back and bring Rodney back (283); thinks Rodney on window blind is side of beef (286); after the shooting, taken by Rosie to sleep at Mrs. Jordan's house (287).

Sarah (277)   : narrator's mother (265); says Grandpa is too old to get presents (265).

_____: narrator's grandfather; distributes Christmas presents to family; too old to get presents any more (265).

Rosie (265)   : narrator's family's cook (267); arrives in Mottstown by train; cooks for missing Mandy (276); after shooting of Rodney, takes Georgie to Mrs. Jordan's to sleep (287).

Rodney (265)   : gives Rosie dime on Christmas morning (265); uncle to narrator (266); involved in theft of $500; usually unemployed (267); pays nephew as lookout for husbands while he "does business" (has affairs) with Mrs. Tucker and other women (268); works for Compress Association (270); tells sister he needs $2000 (271); forges father's signature; theft involves mother's road bonds (272); leaves town (273); nailed in Mandy's cabin by Fred and George; sends Georgie to bring screwdriver after dark; promises him ten quarters (276); changes promise to twenty quarters (280); sends Georgie with message to woman (281); shot to death (286).

George (271)   : narrator's father; works at livery stable (266); lent Uncle Rodney $500 to cover theft (267-268).

Mrs.   Tucker (266): has affair with Uncle Rodney (268).

Louisa (267)   : narrator's aunt; lives with Grandpa; wife of Fred; mother of Louisa, Fred, and baby (267); arrives in town from Mottstown; met by narrator's mother; cries (270); gives Mr. Pruitt her word that Uncle Rodney will not leave town; he does (273).

Fred (267)   : husband of Aunt Louisa; father of Cousin Louisa, Cousin Fred, and baby (267); with George, breaks into Mandy's cabin but does not know that Rodney is in it; nails cabin shut (276).

Fred (267)   : cousin of narrator (267).

Louisa (267)   : cousin of narrator (267).

_____: baby of Aunt Louisa and Uncle Fred; cousin of

narrator (267).

Mandy (274)_____: Grandpa's cook (267); disappears; cabin locked from inside (275).

_____Tucker (268): husband cuckolded by Rodney (268).

John Paul (269)_____: black driver of hack (269-270).

_____Pruitt (271): president of Compress Association; arrives with sheriff at Aunt Louisa's; gives her until day after Christmas to repay Rodney's theft; shows her check that Rodney forged with grandpas's signature (271).

_____: sheriff (271); inquires about Rodney from Georgie who tells him he is out of town (278).

_____: mother of Louisa whose road bonds Rodney stole (272).

Mrs._____Pruitt (274): probably woman in Mottstown with whom Rodney is having an affair (274); "traipses" up and down town in buggy (274).

Mrs._____Church (274): visits Mrs. Pruitt; finds her without corsets and smelling of liquor (274).

Emmeline (274)_____: Aunt Louisa's baby's nurse (274).

_____Watts (277): sheriff in Jefferson (277).

_____: man who grabs Georgie and his own wife when he attempts to deliver Rodney's message (285); shoots Uncle Rodney (286).

_____: presumably his wife who is about to run off with Rodney and "all the jewelry" (283).

_____: six men who carry Uncle Rodney on window blind (285).

_____: man who takes Georgie back to Grandpa's (286).

· Mrs._____Jordan (287): woman to whom Rosie takes Georgie to sleep after killing (287).

"A Courtship"

Written about spring and early summer, 1942; first published in *Sewanee Review,* **56 (Autumn, 1948), 634-653; reprinted in** *Prize Stories of 1949: The O. Henry Awards***; reprinted in** *Collected Stories,* **1950.**

Issetibbeha (361): The Man (361); old enough now to be allowed just to sit in sun and criticize degeneration of the People (362).

Ikkemotubbe (361): Issetibbeha's nephew (361); son of sister of Issetibbeha (362); leaves plantation with David Hogganbeck; returns over year later with Soeur-Blonde de Vitry and eight new slaves; has poison with which he poisons puppies; after Moketubbe's son dies suddenly, becomes The Man; now called Doom; with David Hogganbeck, courts Herman's sister; races horses past porch where she sits (363); considers various schemes to win Herman Basket's influence in his courtship (365); he and David Hogganbeck try to outrun each other to win her (368-369); tries involved horse racing scheme with no success (369); 22 years old; defeated in eating contest by Hogganbeck (373); final contest: race to cave one hundred and thirty miles away (376); after roof of cave falls on David's back, escapes; returns to save David (378).

David Hogganbeck (361): white pilot of steamboat; with Ikkemotubbe, courts sister of Herman Basket (361); plays violin as steamboat approaches (366); likes dancing; bigger than any two; eats and drinks more than rest (366-367); refuses to return to Natchez with steamboat; fired (368); enters various contests with Ikkemotubbe to win Herman Basket's sister (See Ikkemotubbe.) (368 ff.); in final contest, when cave falls on him, urges Ikkemotubbe to escape; saved by Ikkemotubbe (378); sails steamboat down stream with him after they have lost courtship to Log-in-the-Creek (380).

Herman Basket (361): declines to commit himself to Ikkemotubbe in courtship of his sister (365).

_____: sister of Herman Basket; courted by Ikkemotubbe and David Hogganbeck (361); very beautiful; does not walk unless she has to (362); shells corn or peas into silver wine pitcher (363); ultimately marries Log-in-the-Creek (379).

_____: first-person narrator; one of "us" "The People" [Indians] (361).

_____: white man who disappeares; believed to have been eaten by Indians (361).

_____: Ikkemotubbe's mother; Issetibbeha's sister (362).

Moketubbe (363): son of Issetibbeha; becomes The Man at father's death (363).

Soeur-Blonde de Vitry (363): white friend who returns with Ikkemotubbe and eight slaves (363).

_____: eight new slaves (363).

_____: small son of Mokketubbe; dies suddenly after Ikkemotubbe returns with poison (363).

_____: father of narrator (363).

Owl-by-Night (363): an Indian.

Sylvester's John (363): an Indian.

Sylvester (363): an Indian.

_____: Herman Basket's aunt (362); inherited silver wine pitcher from great-aunt of her second cousin (363); threatens Ikkemotubbe and David Hogganbeck with shotgun (369).

_____: dead uncle of Herman Basket (368).

_____ Colbert (363): great-aunt of second cousin of aunt of Herman Basket; leaves silver wine pitcher to aunt; wife of David Colbert (363).

David Colbert (363): the chief Man of all the Chickasaws in the section; looks down on Ikkemotubbe's family (365).

Log-in-the-Creek (363): no-account Indian; can not dance or drink; plays harmonica; marries Herman Basket's sister (379).

_____: whisky-trader (364).

Captain _____ Studenmare (366): owner of steamboat (366).

_____: boy slave who steers steamboat (366).

_____: 10-year-old Indian boy who runs once around race track before Ikkemotubbe and David Hogganbeck begin eating contest (372).

"Lo!"

Possibly written before July 20, 1933; first published in *Story*, **5 (November, 1934), 5-21; reprinted in** *The Best Short Stories 1935 and The Yearbook of The American Short Story*, **ed., Edward J. O'Brien (Boston, New York: Houghton Mifflin Company, 1935); reprinted in** *Collected Stories*, **1950.**

_____: President of U. S. (381); with companion, leaves grounds on horseback (385); wants Secretary to persuade Indians to wear pantaloons (388); has decreed that Indians wear beaver hats, frock coats, and pantaloons; in return, they have presented him with uniform (389); must try Weddel's nephew in person (393); orders nephew's trial at Secretary's house (394); declares nephew innocent; orders him never to do it again (396-397); reads ten of Petrarch's sonnets in Latin; frees Weddel's nephew (400); when Weddel reports second murder of white man by nephew over ford, sends Army to stop Indians from coming to Washington (402-403).

_____: man squatting in corridor outside President's office; Indian (382); wears beaver hat, frock coat, and woolen drawers; carries pantaloons (382); Indians have been there three weeks (393).

_____: man squatting in corridor outside President's room; Indian (382).

Francis (400) Frank Weddel (383) Vidal (390): claims to own all of Mississippi west of a certain river; father is French; mother presumably Indian (391); "obese mongrel despot and patriarch" of Indians (393); says nephew should be punished if guilty of murder (395); will not say which is his right name, Weddel or Vidal (396); disappointed that trial is not held in White House (397); after President finds nephew not guilty, says Indians will wait until rest of their people arrive (398-399); chief in Chickasaw nation (400); writes to President that another white man has been killed in race with nephew over ford; threatens to return to Washington (401-402).

_____: wife of President (384).

_____: man who gives President cloak and hat (384); calls him General (384); leaves grounds on horseback with him (385).

_____: the Secretary; visited by President to whom he serves breakfast (386).

_____: horseman in Secretary's house as President arrives (386); says Indians kill deer by slitting throats with knife (387).

_____: Secretary's secretary (386).

_____: farmer near Gettysburg who demands that Government pay in gold for slave, cow, barn, hay destroyed in fire that results from Indians suddenly appearing before his slave in barn (386-387).

_____: his slave (386).

_____: Weddel's or Vidal's French father (391).

_____: Weddel's or Vidal's Indian mother (391).

_____: white man murdered by Indians (391); buys land from Weddel; only entrance to ford; fences it (392); builds toll gate; acquires horse to race against Weddel's nephew's horse: ford and toll gate against one thousand acres of land; nephew loses; that night man is killed (392); skull is split (393).

_____: Weddel's nephew; loses horse race; kills white man (392-393).

_____: Indian agent who does not stop Weddel (393).

292

_____: another white man who appears and wants to control ford (401); drowned in race for control of ford with Weddel's nephew (401).

_____: Weddel's nephew's father (401).

_____: secretary to President (402).

_____: Secretary of War; sent for by President (402).

"Pennsylvania Station"

Written before November 3, 1928; first titled "Bench for Two," and "Two on Bench," and "2 Bench;" on sending schedule September 12, 1930; first published in American Mercury, **31 (February, 1934), 166-174; reprinted in** Collected Stories, **1950.**

_____: old man; looks 60; might be 48-58 (609); one of eight children; had sent Danny railroad fare from Chicago to Jacksonville after his trouble (611); gets letter from sister's neighbor eight months after he sent money, saying mother thought boy was with man (he is not); after he finds Danny in jail, telephones Mrs. Zilich to have sister send money (618-619); sends letter to sister saying that Danny is getting along fine (620).

_____: young man who wears new Army overcoat (610).

Danny (610) Gihon (615): not bad, but wild; now in Chicago where he has good job; sends expensive wreath to mother's funeral (611); on his own; wires uncle from St. Augustine, Fla.; in jail (618), for grand larceny and for killing policeman; says he was framed; was in Orlando when policeman was killed (619); released from jail; gets job in Chicago (621); steals mother's funeral money (623).

Mrs. Margaret Noonan Gihon (615): sister of old man; mother of Danny; now dead (611); puts funeral money aside with Mr. Pinckski (612); can read a little; pays fifty cents a week for fifty-two weeks for coffin to be set aside with her name on it (615); each year gets better coffin with nameplate; brings others to admire it (616); goes to Mr. Pinckski to get coffin money to help Danny; discovers he has already taken $130; says she signed note (623); dies soon after (625).

_____: lawyer in Jacksonville who gets Danny good job in Chicago (611).

_____: Danny's boss (611).

_____: woman who accuses Danny of stealing clothes off clothes line (611).

_____ Pinckski (612): collects funeral money (613).

_____: alderman in Chicago; looks after Danny (614).

_____: priest of Mrs. Gihon's parish (615).

_____: old man's landlady (615).

_____: man who rents Danny's room (615).

Mrs. Sophie (620) Zilich (617): lady next door to Mrs. Gihon; writes letters to old man from Mrs. Gihon (615).

_____: Danny's lawyer in St. Augustine (618).

_____: man in uniform of railroad company (620); asks for tickets (623).

"Artist at Home"

On sending schedule March 16, 1931; first titled "An Artist at Home;" first published in *Story*, 3 (August, 1933), 27-41; reprinted in *Collected Stories*, 1950.

Roger Howes (627): fattish, 40, from Mississippi valley, writes advertisements in New York; married; novelist; sells book; buys house in Virginia; visited by friends from New York (627); comes upon wife and John Blair as they embrace (636); when Blair tells him about kissing Anne, gets somewhat angry (637); after Anne locks him out of bedroom, begins to write (638); sleeps on porch; continues to write (639); agrees to take Anne back (640); prevents wife from going in rain to meet Blair (641); after wife leaves him, has Blair's poem published; finishes and publishes story about three of them; uses money from story to pay Blair's funeral expenses and buy fur coat for Anne and winter underwear for self and children (644); reads story to Anne (645).

Anne Howes (627): wife of Roger (627); after Blair kisses her, walks away, and then asks him to kiss her again (636); after Blair leaves, locks bedroom against husband (638); goes to meet Blair; returns; still locks door (639); continues to see Blair; returns; says affair is ended; asks Roger to take her back; apparently cuts telephone wire (640); gets letter from Blair; prevented from seeing him by Roger (641); leaves Roger; returns (644); gives fur coat to Mrs. Crain (645).

_____ Howes (627): children of Roger and Anne (627).

_____: man at station (telegraph and station agent) (628).

John Blair (629): poet in sky-blue coat (628); visits Roger Howes (629); goes home with Pinkie for dinner; attends black prayer meeting (633); kisses Anne (635); tells Roger of kiss; says he will do it again (637); speaks to Anne; leaves (638); returns in rain; stands outside ("The Dead?") (642-643); disappears (643); sends Anne poem; dies (643-644), in

September (644).

_____: Anne Howes's father; minister; lives in Connecticut (630).

Pinkie (630) _____: black cook for Howeses (630).

_____: woman guest who bathes nude in creek (631).

Amos Crain (631): farmer who lives across creek (631).

Mrs. Amos Crain (631): his wife; sends word about woman in creek (631).

_____ Crain: Crain children (631).

_____ Blair: John Blair's mother (636).

_____: Anne Howes's mother (644).

"The Brooch"

Written before January 23, 1930; on sending schedule as "Fire and Clock," January 23, 1930; on sending schedule as "Brooch," January 29, 1931; rewritten about July, 1935; first published in Scribner's, **99 (January, 1936); reprinted in** Collected Stories, **1950.**

Howard (649) Boyd (647): wakened by telephone; only child; graduates from University of Virginia (647); name changed after father deserts family (648); girl shy; meets Amy (648); asks her to marry him despite mother (650); spanks Amy at dance; takes her to next town to be married (651); after birth and death of child, urges Amy to go to dances; deceives mother; pretends to go with Amy to dances (652 ff.); sleeps in separate bed (653); lies to mother about Amy; says she lost ring, not brooch (656); after Amy leaves, reads Green Mansions in bedroom (663); begins drinking after mother's stroke; drinks heavily after child's death (664); suicide by shooting pistol in mouth (665).

_____ Boyd (647): widow; mother of Howard; goes to college with son (647); refuses to let father have marriage annulled; changes son's name after husband deserts; has stroke; learns about Amy; insults Amy to son (648); after marriage, gives Amy brooch (651); catches Amy coming home after Howard said she was in bed; orders her to leave immediately (658).

_____: travelling man with letters to minister and future wife's father; father of Howard Boyd; deserts wife and son (647).

_____: minister (647).

_____: father of Mrs. Boyd (647); dies; leaves property to daughter and grandson (648).

Amy Boyd (648): daughter of conductor killed in wreck; lives with aunt (648); afraid of Mrs. Boyd (650); engaged to Howard, but sits out dances with other men and drinks (650); tells Howard that, because they are engaged, sitting in cars with him is no fun (651); has child that dies a year later (652); with husband's knowledge, goes out Saturday nights without him (652); one night visits mother-in-law's room on return (657); after mother-in-law tells her to leave, begs Howard to leave his mother; described as epicene (659); lies to Howard about being brought home by Rosses (660); packs bag; cries; leaves in cab (662).

_____: dead father of Amy (648).

_____: Amy's aunt; keeps boarding house (648).

_____ Boyd (652): child of Howard and Amy Boyd; dies at one year (652).

Martha Ross (654): calls to tell Howard that Amy left brooch in her car (655).

Frank Ross (660): husband of Martha (660).

"My Grandmother Millard and General Bedford Forrest and
the Battle of Harrykin Creek"

Written spring, 1942, at least before March 30, 1942; first published in *Story*, 22 (March-April, 1943), 68-86; reprinted in *Collected Stories*, 1950.

[Bayard] Sartoris [II] (673): first-person narrator (667); buries silver after Yankees leave (677); takes soap and water to cousin Philip; gets flowers so that Philip can woo cousin Melisandre (679); asks Philip why he does not change his name (682).

Rosa (Rosie) (691) Millard (675): narrator's grandmother (667); practices burying family silver (668); tells Lucius he is free (670); at last minute puts silver in outhouse with cousin Melisandre (676); keeps horses Ab Snopes put in her lot; forces him to ride one of her horses (686); sends for General Forrest to meet her for breakfast and to bring Philip (688); repeats invitation (690); visited by Forrest (691); writes order reporting death of P. S. Backhouse and appointment of Philip St-Just Backus (696); forces Forrest to give John Sartoris leave to give away bride (697); after wedding, holds one final rehearsal of burying silver (699).

Melisandre (667) _____ Backus (699): narrator's cousin (667); in outhouse with silver when Yankees knock it down (676-677); screams when Philip enters dining room (681); can not stand to hear Philip's last name (693); marries Philip in dress her aunt and grandmother wore at their weddings (699).

Colonel (667) John (697) Sartoris (673): narrator's father; voted out of colonelcy in Civil War; comes home for three months; organizes cavalry troop for General Forrest's command; returns to war (667).

Ringo (667): slave companion to narrator; sent to warn others when Yankees arrive (674).

Joby (667): slave.

Lucius (667): slave son of Louvinia; says he and other slaves will be free when Yankees take Yoknapatawpha County (669); sent twice by Granny to invite General Forrest (688, 690).

Louvinia (667-668): slave, wife of Joby (667-668).

Philadelphia (668): slave, wife of Lucius (687).

_____ Sartoris: mother of Colonel John Sartoris (670).

Philip (672) St-Just Backhouse (681) Backus (696): marries Melisandre (672); rides into yard after Yankees; disperses them (677); falls in love with Melisandre (678); from Tennessee; in Forrest's command (680); after dinner, rides away (683); returns with troop to say goodbye (691); placed under arrest by General Forrest for leading attack when ordered to fall back (692); 22 years old (694); renamed Backus by Grandmother Millard (696); married to Melisandre (699).

Ab Snopes (673): member of Colonel Sartoris's troop (673); brings news that Yankees are near Jefferson (674); puts horses in Granny's lot; forced to ride her horse (684-686).

_____ Compson (675): wife of General Compson; sits on basket of silver in outhouse when Yankees raid Jefferson (675).

General [Jason Lycurgus] Compson (675).

Dr. _____ Holston (675): sends slave to warn Mrs. Compson of Yankees (675).

_____: Dr. Holston's slave (675).

Roxanne (675): slave of General Compson; guards outhouse while Mrs. Compson sits on basket of silver (675).

_____: six Yankee soldiers who knock outhouse to pieces (677).

_____ Savage (681): Philip's comanding officer (681).

_____: grandfather of Philip (682).

_____ Backhouse: Philip's father (682).

_____ Millard (688): husband of Granny; owned supply house (688).

General _____ Forrest (691): visits Rosa Millard (691); arrests Philip (692).

_____: four Confederate officers; accompany General Forrest (691).

_____: provost who catches Philip (692).

_____: Philip's uncle; defeated for Governor of Tennessee; on staff of General Bragg (693).

_____ Sartoris (698): narrator's mother (698).

_____: chaplain who marries Philip and Melisandre (699).

_____: four Confederate soldiers at wedding (699).

"Golden Land"

Although mentioned in a letter as early as August, 1934, written before January, 1935; first published in *American Mercuury,* **35 (May, 1935), 1-14; reprinted in** *Collected Stories,* **1950.**

Ira Ewing [II] (702): 48 years old; starts day, after night of drinking, with two aspirin tablets and half glass of raw gin (701); at 14, ran away from home in small Nebraska town named for father (702); spends ten years (14-24) as half tramp, half casual laborer; married at 30 to daughter of carpenter; father of son and daughter; spends $50,000 a year; in real estate; each morning carried into house by Filipino chauffeur and put to bed; lives in Beverley Hills (703); visits mother every day; fully supports her (704); beats drunken son with wet towels because he found him wearing women's underclothes (706); argues with wife (708-709); attacks son and wife (709); decides gardner showed his mother paper about daughter's trial (711); tells mother of sex orgy daughter engaged in (713); visits mistress (717); wishes all young female flesh were blasted from the earth (718).

Ira Ewing [I] (702): father of Ira Ewing II; farmer and preacher; died twenty years ago (702).

Samantha (706) Ewing (702): wife of Ira Ewing [I]; mother of Ira Ewing II (702); brought by son to California (703); supported completely by son (704); uncharacteristically telephones son (707); indirectly asks son for money to return to Nebraska (714-715); flashback: watches grandchildren steal money from mother's purse (723); makes candy and cake; sells them to grandchildren; hides coins to buy ticket to Nebraska

(725); back to present: gives up hope of returning to Nebraska (726).

_____ Ewing (702): wife of Ira Ewing II; daughter of carpenter (703).

_____: father of Ira Ewing II's wife; carpenter (703).

Voyd (705) Ewing (702): son of Ira Ewing II; brought home drunk; discovered to be wearing women's underclothes; beaten with wet towels by father (706).

Samantha (706) Ewing (702) April Lalear (705): daughter of Ira Ewing II (703); involved in scandal about sex orgy (705); found naked with man and other woman; accused of blackmail to get part in movie (713).

Philip (710) _____: Filipino chauffeur of Ira Ewing II; carries him home each morning and puts him to bed (703); drives Ewing to apartment of mistress (717).

_____ Kazimura (712): Japanese gardner for Ewing's mother (704); shows her newspaper about granddaughter's sex orgy (711, 721).

_____: servant who supplies Ira Ewing II with wet towels to beat son (706).

_____: man with Samantha in sex orgy; casting director (713).

_____: other woman in sex orgy (713).

_____: Ira Ewing II's male secretary (715).

_____: photographer who takes Ewing's picture in courthouse (716).

_____: reporter at courthouse (716).

_____: doorman (717).

_____: elevator boy (717).

_____: Ira Ewing II's mistress; divorced mother of daughter of 14 (717); keeps postponing drinks he asks for (718 ff.).

A 23 *Notes on A Horsethief*

Writing began as early as May, 1940; continued in August, 1947; finished October-November, 1947; once titled "Dangling Participle from Work in Progress;" published February 10, 1951 (although the date in the volume is 1950); pp. 151-204 of *A Fable*; entitled "Notes on a Horsethief," published in *Vogue*, 124 (July, 1954), 46-51, 101, 103, 104, 105, 106; revised for *A Fable*, 1954, pp. 151-189.

Pagination, in parentheses, to the following limited edition of 975 copies: (Greenville, Mississippi: Levee Press, 1951), 71 pp.

_____: English sentry; in 1912, had gone to America as groom to an exceptional running horse; three things happen to change life and character; returns to England in 1914 to enlist (1); included in sale of horse because of strange affinity between him and horse; after groom meets horse, it sets phenomenal race records (2); three things happen to him after train wreck: becomes member of small protestant sect [Baptist (6)]; becomes a Mason; becomes skillful at dice; vanishes for twenty-two months with horse and black groom after train wreck (3); steals RR block and tackle from train wreck (9, 10); next night buys or steals pirogue and gets food and plaster for cast for horse (10); sets broken bone; waits months on small island while horse heals (11); supports group at dice tables in New Orleans (12); somehow escapes and races three-legged horse in Weatherford, Texas, and then all over the country (12 ff.); shoots horse; is arrested (20); curses steadily while ex-deputy questions him about motives for killing horse (20 ff.); disappears from jail with two black companions; freed (21) by reason of being a Mason (23).

_____: Argentine hide-and-wheat prince who buys horse; millionaire (1).

_____: U. S. oil baron who buys horse from Argentine (2); refuses to give up search; offers Federal deputy huge sum to find horse, deport English groom, and bring his black groom back in handcuffs (17-18); has offered reward for capture of black groom whom he thinks has all the money won by the horse (28).

_____: black groom; vanishes with English groom and horse after train wreck (3); a preacher (11); arrested after horse is shot (20); disappears with grandson and English groom (22); knocks on back door of jail; is rearrested (32); carried, with turnkey, by crowd to courtroom (35-36); says English groom is going back to England (53-54); says he bears witness to man, not to God (54); sent out of town (71).

_____: British consul in New York to whom the English groom reports to enlist in WW I (3).

_____: Federal deputy marshal who arrests English groom and black groom beside body of dead horse (3-4); arrives in Weatherford, Texas a day late (12); finally sees English groom, preacher, and horse as romantically pursuing man's ancient ideal (15); poet; failed at Harvard and wasted two years at Oxford; finally sees the truth about theft of horse; visits owner of horse in New York; tells him to give up pursuit; offers check to owner for expenses of pursuit; offers to buy horse with note (17); tears up check; resigns as Federal deputy; joins pursuit of horse as private individual (18); finally catches up with them just after they have killed the horse; a lawyer (20); questions English groom about motive for killing horse (20 ff.); gives reason, "So it could run etc." (21); leaves signed blank check with sheriff to cover English groom's bail (23).

_____: the other pursuers (7 ff.).

_____: sheriff's man (7).

_____: black RR work gang with whom the English groom shoots dice (10).

_____: the jockey; preacher's grandson or perhaps great-grandson; 12 years old, at most 14 (13); after arrest, disappears with grandfather and English groom (22).

_____: witness in Weatherford, Texas who informs Federal deputy of the race (13).

_____: father of Federal deputy (16).

_____: secretary to owner of horse (18).

_____: lawyer sent by ex-deputy to defend English groom (21); tells confidential clerk to find black groom and grandson (27); "a man not only tall but big" (36); internal date, April 1914 (39); tells turnkey and crowd in courtroom that black groom has been illegally arrested and that he has a right to a lawyer (40); tells turnkey to let black groom go (47-48); tells turnkey to take him to next jail and charge him (49); unlocks handcuffs; wants him charged with vagrancy (50); says black groom has no money (51); makes long speech against New York capitalists and New England factory owners (61 ff.); sees Irey, black groom, and jockey in square (64); long thought about power of man; predicts that man will survive his wars (64 ff.).

_____: lawyer's chauffeur (21); mulatto (31); murderer; served year and a day in jail (58).

_____: sheriff (22).

_____: black porter at hotel who tells lawyer how black groom and grandson disappeared (22).

Irey (34)_____: jailor, turnkey (22); rearrests black groom (32); "small mild ordinary man" (33); carried, with black groom, by crowd to courtroom (35-36); takes pistol from sheriff's desk (52); draws pistol as crowd comes near him (69); crowd takes pistol away from him (70).

_____: jailor's wife (22); favorite sister or other connection of the sheriff (23).

_____: justice of peace who arraigns English groom (24).

_____: confidential clerk of lawyer (27).

_____: circuit judge whose chambers the lawyer uses (29).

_____: man from Department of Justice (29).

_____: man from company holding sheriff's bond (30).

_____: two men; sheriff's local bondsmen (30).

_____: president of local bank (30).

_____: tax assessor (43).

_____: circuit clerk (43).

_____: woman murdered by lawyer's chauffeur (58).

_____: father of lawyer (60).

_____: son of lawyer (60).

_____: grandson of lawyer (67).

_____: man who sends black groom and jockey out of town; owns sawmill; sole support of mother, three sisters, wife, and two daughters (70-71).

_____: his mother, three sisters, wife, and two daughters (70).

"A Name for the City"

Written about July 1, 1950; first published October, 1950.

Pagination, in parentheses, to Harper's Magazine, 201 (October 1950), pp. 200-214. Revised and entitled "The Courthouse (A Name for the City)" in Requiem for a Nun.

Gavin (220)_____: middle-ageing county lawyer; uncle of narrator (200).

_____: first-person narrator (200).

Issetibbeha (200): Chickasaw king (200)

Ikkemotubbe (200): successor to Issetibbeha (200).

_____: militiamen who arrest gang in Jefferson (201).

_____: gang arrested (201).

_____: sergeant in charge of militia (201).

Alexander Holston (202): one of first settlers in Yoknapatawpha County; brings lock from Carolina; half groom, half bodyguard to Dr. Samuel Habersham; half nurse, half tutor to his 8-year-old motherless son; first publican; founder of Holston House (202); childless bachelor (204); orders return of lock (208).

Dr. Samuel Habersham (202): one of first settlers in Yoknapatawpha County; settlement first named for him (202).

_____ Habersham (202): 8-year-old motherless son of Dr. Habersham; at 25 marries one of Issetibbeha's granddaughters and emigrates with Chickasaws to Oklahoma; first Chickasaw agent (202).

Mrs._____ Habersham (202): wife of son of Dr. Habersham; granddaughter of Issetibbeha (202).

Louis Grenier (202): one of the first settlers in Yoknapatawpha County; Huguenot younger son; brought first slaves and granted first big land patent; first cotton planter (202).

Thomas Jefferson (214) Pettigrew (208): man who carries mail pouch with Holston's lock to Jefferson (202); weighs less than 100 pounds (204); hairless, toothless (208); says the lock belongs to Uncle Sam not Holston (212); town named after him; from Virginia (214).

_____ Compson (206): swaps race horse with Ikkemotubbe for a square mile of what was to become the most valuable land in Jefferson; protects robbers from lynch mob until they are jailed; presides over town meeting about reward for prisoners; adds laudanum to whisky sent to

305

militia men (206); searches for missing lock (208).

Dr (206) _____ Peabody (200): successor to Dr. Habersham (206); tells Pettigrew they are going to build courthouse (213).

_____Ratcliffe (206): post trader (206); suggests putting the lock "on the Book;" i. e. charge it to the U. S. (210); suggests they give Holston $50 until new lock is made (212).

_____: black cook; one of Holston's slaves (208).

_____: husband of black cook; one of Holston's slaves; says Holston wants Compson to produce the missing lock (208).

Mohataha (210): mother of Ikkemotubbe; sister of Issetibbeha (213-214).

Pettigrew (208): mother of Thomas Jefferson Pettigrew (208).

Idea first reported October, 1933; begun as short story December 17, 1933; continued as a play in collaboration with Joan Williams, February 13, 1950 and following months; Faulkner began to consider it a novel and not a play May 19, 1950; first draft finished May 22, 1950 (by this date, he separates "mine" from Williams's); finished June 9, 1951; "The Jail" published in *Partisan Review,* 18 (September-October, 1951, 496-515, 598-608); published September 27, 1951; part used in *Big Woods,* 1955.

Pagination, in parentheses, to the following edition: (New York: Random House, 1951), 286 pp.

_____: three or four Natchez Trace bandits who break out of jail; not the Harpes (5); crowd wants to lynch them (13); take three horses and the Holston lock when they escape (16).

_____: band of militia which captures bandits; one is sergeant (6).

Alexander Holston (7): one of founders of Jefferson; bodyguard to Dr. Habersham (7); founded tavern still known as Holston House (8); first official Chickasaw agent; resigns to become publican; owner of lock whose history is traced in opening forty-eight pages (8); childless bachelor (12); orders immediate return of his lock (17); refuses to witness signing away of Indian land (217).

Dr. Samuel Habersham (7): one of founders of Jefferson (7).

_____ Habersham (7): motherless 8-year-old son of Dr. Habersham (7); at 25, marries one of Issetibbeha's granddaughters; in 30's, emigrates to Oklahoma (8).

Louis Grenier (7): early settler; Huguenot younger son; brings first slaves into the county; granted first big land patent; first cotton planter (7); his plantation is Frenchman's Bend (33); refuses to witness signing away of Indian land (217).

Issetibbeha (8): Chickasaw chief (8).

_____ Habersham (7): wife of son of Dr. Habersham; granddaughter of Issetibbeha (8); granddaughter of Mohataha (217).

Sartoris, Stevens, Compson, McCaslin, Sutpen, Coldfield (9): family names of second wave of settlers (9).

Ikkemotubbe (13): successor to Issetibbeha; swapped square mile of land to Compson for race horse (13); son of Mohataha (21); accompanies son-in-law Habersham to west (217).

Thomas Jefferson (28) Pettigrew (19): rider who brings mail to Jefferson (9); settles argument about replacement of Holston's lock by quoting absurd Federal statutes (23 ff.); named for President Jefferson; town named for him (28-29).

_____ Pettigrew: mother of Thomas Jefferson Pettigrew (29).

Jason (215) Compson (13): arrives in settlement with race horse that he swaps to Ikkemotubbe for a square mile of the most valuable land in future town of Jefferson; saves bandits from lynching (13); gets militia and lynch mob drugged and drunk and puts them all in jail (16); decides to pay Alec Holston for lost lock (19); leads men in rebuilding jail; building courthouse to establish Jefferson (31-33); becomes co-owner of Ratcliffe's store (220).

_____: messenger who rides to Natchez with news of capture of bandits and to get reward (14).

Doctor _____ Peabody (15): Dr. Habersham's successor (15); tells Pettigrew that, instead of charging the lock to the Bureau of Indian Affairs, they are going to pay for it themselves (28).

_____ Ratcliffe (15): post trader (name eventually becomes Ratliff) (15); suggests they pay Holston for lock by putting "it on the Book" (20); i. e., charge it to the U. S. government (21); conscience bothers him about charging cost of lock to government (36); "son of a long pure line of Anglo-Saxon mountain people;" father of a "line of white trash farmers who never owned a slave" (42).

_____: one of Holston's slaves; husband of cook (16).

_____: another of Holston's slaves; Holston's cook (16).

Mohataha (21): sister of Issetibbeha; mother of Ikkemotubbe; signed Indian land away (21, 216).

_____ Whitfield (28): whose cabin is the church [Usually Whitfield is the minister in Frenchman's Bend, appointed by Will Varner.]

_____: slave belonging to German blacksmith (30).

_____: German blacksmith (30); a private who deserted from a Pennsylvania regiment in summer of 1864 (233); father of family of daughters (233).

_____: female slave child who holds parasol over Mohataha (30).

_____: slave coachman of Louis Grenier (33).

_____: slave footman of Louis Grenier (33).

_____ Sutpen (37): newcomer to Jefferson; brings Parisian architect and thirty-odd slaves, who speak Carib-Spanish-French (37).

_____: Parisian architect whom Sutpen brings to Jefferson (37); teaches community how to build, make brick, etc. (38); courthouse is built of brick (40).

Gavin Stevens (40): defense lawyer for Nancy Mannigoe; about 50; bachelor; descendent of pioneer Yoknapatawpha family; Harvard and Heidelberg (49); private practice as well as being County Attorney (49-50); uncle to Gowan (55); returns with Temple and Gowan after sentencing (55 ff.); tells Temple that Nancy told him nothing (64); tells Temple that he knows that there was "a man there that night" (64); points out to Gowan that Nancy Mannigoe was a worthless human being until he and Temple picked her out of gutter (69); reduces size of Gowan's drink (70); says Gowan added "and loved it" to his account of Temple in whorehouse; says that is what he can not forgive (73); asks him if that is why Nancy Mannigoe must die; asks Gowan what else happened in brothel; leaves after Gowan threatens to hit him with bottle (75); scene starts March 11th (76); has sent for Temple to return to save Nancy from hanging (79); says Temple Drake, not Mrs. Gowan Stevens, will have to save Nancy Mannigoe (85); says he wants justice (88), truth (89); says they are going to the governor that night (90); tells Temple that she will have to tell everything (94); leaves when she refuses (95); tells governor of Popeye bringing Red to Temple in brothel (144 ff.); makes long speech of revulsion to governor about Popeye's being impotent (145-146); after a year Gowan began to doubt paternity of his and Temple's child (156); interrupts Temple's account to tell of Alabama Red's younger brother; the letters; blackmail (160 ff.); says that Red's younger brother at first wanted to blackmail Temple for money (167); says that he was going to take Temple, money, and the 6-month-old baby; tells involved story of Red's brother blackmailing Temple (168 ff.); admits to Temple that the governor had decided Nancy's fate a week ago (210); tells Temple she came to governor's office to affirm "that little children shall be intact" (211); has been singing hymns with Nancy Mannigoe in her cell (265); with Temple, visits Nancy in jail (267); says that, even in heaven, Nancy Mannigoe can do the menial work (279).

_____: Sutpen's slave who runs down the architect (40).

John Sartoris (44): newcomer with slaves and money [contrary to other accounts] arrives after Sutpen (44); becomes colonel (45); raises regiment (230); deposed from colonelcy after Second Manassas; joins Forrest with small troop of cavalry (231); with Redmond and General Compson, builds a railroad; with Redmond, buys out General Compson's share; killed from ambush by Redmond (238).

Nancy Mannigoe (50): prisoner; black woman about 30; domestic servant and nurse to two white children; killed second of them by smothering the infant, two months ago; now on trial for life; tramp, drunkard, casual prostitute; probably had married at least once (50); sentenced to be hanged (51) on 13th of March (63); name derived from Norman name of Maingault (118); realizes that Temple has taken money and jewels for Red's younger brother; hides them from Temple (172);

returns to house; witnesses Pete and Temple embrace (178); tells Temple that Pete will blackmail Gowan if she runs off with him (182); accuses Temple of being ready to allow her baby to die either at home or when Pete kicks her out (186); says she tried to prevent Temple (187); when Temple insists she is going to take baby and leave with Pete, murders the baby (192-193); visited by Temple and Gavin for last time (270 ff.); says she accepted death before she lifted hand to kill baby (273); tells Temple to trust God (276); discusses God with Temple (277); says people can not help sinning (278).

_____ Stevens (51): murdered infant child of Gowan and Temple Stevens (50); a girl (92); 6 months old (185); buried day after her murder (196).

Bucky (64) Stevens (51): surviving child of Gowan and Temple Stevens (51); taken by father to grandparents in New Orleans (172); in California, asks mother if they will stay there until Nancy is hanged (78).

Judge (51)_____.

Gowan Stevens (51): father of child killed by Nancy Mannigoe (51); intends to take a drink after eight years (59); offers Gavin drink; says if he "could raise his arm to defend a murdering nigger," he can raise it to take a drink with the victim's mother (60); tells Gavin to go home or to hell (69); pours large glass of whisky (70); rehearses history of his drunkenness leading Temple to a Memphis whorehouse [See *Sanctuary.*] (71-72); adds "and [she] loved it" (73); threatens Gavin with bottle (74); calls his Aunt Maggie and asks that Gavin call him (97); takes older child to parents in New Orleans while he goes on fishing trip (172).

Mrs. Gowan (51) Temple (53) Drake (67) Stevens (51): child killed by Nancy Mannigoe; wife of Gowan (51); mid 20's (53); called "Boots" by husband (55); talks beligerantly to Gavin Stevens; wants to know what he wants from her (56-57); calls Nancy Mannigoe a "nigger dope fiend" that murdered a "white baby" (58); questions Gavin about how much Nancy Mannigoe told him [about Temple] (63); March 11th; has given Gowan a sleeping pill; talks to Gavin; has been recalled from California by telegram from Gavin (77); says all they need to save Nancy from execution is affidavit that she has been crazy for years (82); has changed her mind (without telling reason) and wants to prevent Nancy's execution (84); would commit perjury to do it (87); tells Gavin that Temple Drake is dead (93); refuses to tell all (95); after Gavin leaves, calls Maggie to ask Gavin to return call (96); when he calls back, agrees to go to governor (96); visits him with Gavin (113); insists on speaking of Temple Drake of the Memphis sporting house (116); asks governor to save Nancy (118); says she took Nancy in to have someone to talk to (120); with Gavin Stevens, tells governor of the events of *Sanctuary* (124 ff.); confesses she perjured herself to save the murderer [Popeye Vitelli] and convict an innocent man [Lee Godwin] (128); says she has not come to save Nancy Mannigoe but to let Temple Drake suffer (132-133); says Temple Drake liked evil (135); thinks Gowan is at home; that she gave him a sleeping pill (139); tells of being taken to Memphis brothel (140 ff.); kept there in case the murderer needed an alibi (142); says she fell in love (144) with Alabama Red (146); wrote letters (147); does not want Gowan to see those letters (150); letters are now being used to blackmail her; her only way of paying is by sex (151-152); flashback: marries Gowan in Paris (154); begins long speech to governor of her married life in Jefferson; Nancy Mannigoe hired as nurse and confidante of Temple (157 ff.); story of her being blackmailed by Pete, Red's brother (160-168); flashback to September 13th: says Nancy has disappeared (175); no money for Pete; she is packed to leave with Pete and her baby; starts to burn letters, but does not (177-178); slaps Nancy after she says that Pete will blackmail Gowan (182); implies that Gowan is not Bucky's father (184); acknowledges that Nancy tried to hold family together (188); refuses Nancy's plea not to run away with Pete; screams when she finds her baby murdered (192-193); long soliloquy on blacks' hands and what they do; blends to history of black man destroyed by wife's death [See Spoot Rider of "Pantaloon in Black."] (196-199); tells Nancy that she thought all she had to do was tell her she had to die (274); expresses her guilt and need for suffering; says she knows what she has to do, but wants God to tell her what to do (275); questions God's demand for suffering (277); asks Nancy to tell her what to believe (283).

_____: bailiff at Nancy Mannigoe's trial (51).

Maggie (67)_____: aunt to Gowan Stevens (97).

Henry (113)_____: Governor of Mississippi (112); refuses to stay execution of Nancy Mannigoe (207).

_____: man who kicks Nancy Mannigoe as she lies in gutter; pillar of church, cashier in bank; kicks her because she asks for her two dollars for prostitution (121); kills her unborn baby (280).

Popeye Vitelli (144): murderer (126); kidnapped Temple and took her to Memphis brothel (127); "a little black thing with an Italian name" "a hybrid, sexually incapable" (140); brings Red to have sex with Temple in brothel (144); owns nightclub where Red is bouncer; hanged in Alabama for murder he did not commit (145); would watch Temple and Red have sex (149).

_____: person murdered (126).

_____: lawyer for man accused of murder (127).

[Lee Goodwin]: man falsely accused of murder; convicted because of Temple's perjury (128); moonshiner (136).

_____Drake: Temple Drake's father and brothers (136).

_____: madam of brothel in which Temple is kept (141).

_____: black maid in brothel (141).

_____: chauffeur who drives murderer, Temple, and madam up and down back alleys of red-light district (142-143).

Alabama Red (144): young man brought to Temple in brothel (144); bouncer at nightclub; killed by Popeye with same pistol used in Mississippi murder (145); killed while trying to have sex with Temple without Popeye in room (153).

_____: lawyer who defends Popeye Vitelli (149).

_____ Stevens (172): grandparents (Gowan's parents) of Bucky Stevens whom he visits (172).

Pete (173)_____: Alabama Red's younger brother; criminal (160); blackmails Temple for letters she sent to Red (168 ff.); flashback to September 13th: offers Temple letters (176); after Nancy returns, picks up letters; leaves with bags to wait for Temple in car (180-181).

_____: female slave; holds Mohataha's crusted shoes (216).

_____: Federal land agent; receivesland from Mohataha (216).

_____: Federal land agent's marshal (216).

_____ Farmer (229): jailor or turnkey in Jefferson (228).

_____ Farmer (229): jailor's wife; cooks meals for prisoners (228).

Cecilia Farmer (229): their daughter; scratches name with a diamond on jail window, April 16, 1861 (229); [Fort Sumter was attacked on April 12th and surrendered on April 14, 1861.] rides on mule with husband (257); to bear twelve boys (258).

_____: Baptist minister; offers prayer when John Sartoris's regiment is sworn in (230).

_____: Richmond mustering officer who swears in John Sartoris's regiment (230).

_____: Cecilia Farmer's grandmother whose diamond ring she used (232).

_____: soldier whom Cecilia Farmer sees (232); returns after Civil War to marry her (235 ff.); paroled cavalry subaltern on way to farm in Alabama (257).

_____ Redmond (233): carpetbagger from Missouri; comes to Jefferson (233); by 1876, with Colonel Sartoris and General Compson, has built a railroad (238); kills John Sartoris from ambush (238).

General_____ Compson (237): "the first Jason's son" (237); with

312

Colonel Sartoris and Redmond, builds railroad; interest bought out by the others (238). [Elsewhere "the first Jason's son" is Quentin MacLachan Compson and not a general. Quentin MacLachan Compson's son is the Brigadier General Jason Lycurgus Compson II. See "Appendix" to *The Sound and the Fury*.]

Mrs. Virginia Sartoris Depre (239): sister of Colonel John Sartoris; dedicates statue of Confederate soldier in square on Confederate Decoration Day 1900 (239). [Elsewhere (in *Sartoris* and *Flags in the Dust*) name is Du Pre.]

_____: architect; designs statue of Confederate soldier (240).

Bayard Sartoris [II] (242): banker, son of Colonel John Sartoris; killed in auto accident; grandson drives automobile (242).

[Bayard] Sartoris [III] (242): grandson of Bayard [II]; combat veteran of WW I; grandfather killed as car skids on icy [?] road (242).

"Uncle Pete" Gombault (242): U. S. Marshal (242).

"Mulberry" (242) _____: black; U. S. Marshal during Reconstruction (242); name derived from selling whisky cached under a mulberry tree (243).

_____: Mulberry's former owner; owns drugstore (243).

_____: Federal brigadier who sets fire to Jefferson (249).

_____: Federal provost-marshal (249).

_____: Governor of Mississippi who was sentenced to thirty days jail in Jefferson for refusing to testify in paternity suit against one of his lieutenants (249).

_____: lieutenant against whom paternity suit is brought (249).

Mrs. _____ Tubbs (266): wife of jailor in Jefferson (253).

_____: twelve sons of Cecilia Farmer (258).

_____ Tubbs (266): modern jailor (263); talks about Gavin singing hymns with Nancy Mannigoe (265 ff.).

_____: Nancy Mannigoe's unborn baby; aborted when man kicks her in stomach (280).

_____: preacher for whom Nancy asks (283).

Idea conceived in spring, 1943; writing began August-September, 1943; first version, titled *Who*, sent to Ober in mid-November, 1943; by January, 1945 writing continues; fifteen thousand words written by mid-March, 1945; finished early November, 1953; published August 2, 1954.

Pagination, in parentheses, to the following edition and reissue: (New York: Random House, 1954), 437 pp., and (New York: Modern Library, 1966).

_____: town major (5); witnesses execution of Stefan (384).

_____: officer in charge of cavalry in Place de Ville (5).

_____: sergeant major in charge of cavalry (5).

_____: officer of the day (6).

_____: orderly (6).

_____: batman (6).

_____: adjutant (6); witnesses execution of Stefan (384).

_____: runner (6).

_____: infantry commander who sends infantry to Place de Ville (6).

_____: platoon sergeant; sees girl faint; thick man of 40; husband and father (7); internal date May 1918 (8); examines papers of tall man (11).

_____: man who helps sergeant raise girl who faints (7).

_____: girl who faints from hunger on Wednesday morning (7); as lorry with corporal in it passes, tries to overtake it (18); joins Marthe and Marya (213-214); wife of Stefan (216); Generalissimo seems to know her origin (Marseille) and that she has been a whore (285); returns to Marseille brothel to support her grandmother after Stefan's death (430); (She converts the Virgin Mother's role to that of wife with overtones of Mary Magdalene, but see notes for Marthe, Stefan's half-sister.)

_____: tall man who questions sergeant on Wednesday morning (8); roles of soldier vs. mankind stated at outset (9-10); announces that the whole regiment mutinied; asks why Germans did not attack when French regiment mutinied (10); says that whole front--except for the artillery--stopped at noon yesterday (Tuesday), German, French, American, British (11).

<u>Major (54) General (12) Charles (28) Gragnon (12)</u>: general of Division wants to shoot mutinous regiment (12); at some point in his career, something happened to deny him opportunities; Pyrenean orphan; private at 17; sergeant at 21; sent to officers' school at 24; by 1914, a colonel of Spahis (Algerian native cavalry); brigadier in France *ca.* 1916; now a major general (21); feels abandoned by destiny (23); realizes that he has been given attack doomed to failure (23); always watches attacks from most forward observer's post; contemplates desertion (24); instead of a military failure, has mutiny (25); orders artillery commander to lay down a barrage on trench containing mutinous troops (26); wants to shoot entire mutinous regiment (28); formally requests permission of Group Commander to shoot regiment (34); calls Group Commander *"Mama Bidet,"* "Monsieur the General Cabinet" and "soon-to-be *Marshal d' Aisance*" (35); sent back to headquarters; disobeys goes to front (36); cannot comprehend that the men have caused cease-fire (40-41); receives message from Corps Headquarters confining him until he is taken to Chaulnesmont on Wednesday (43); reads *Gil Blas* (47); that night, returns to see Group Commander (48); to resign (49); says he will not go to Chaulnesmont (for court martial); offers resignation (52); it is refused and he is ordered to Chaulnesmont (53); relieved of sword (229); formally requests from Generalissimo permission to execute regiment (230); major general (376); killed by American sergeant with German pistol; foils attempt to shoot him from front; turns head so that it will be clear that he was shot by own men (376-380).

_____: Generalissimo (12); supreme commander of all allied armies (13); "slight gray man with a face wise, intelligent, and unbelieving, who no longer believed in anything but his disillusion and his intelligence and his limitless power" (13); bilingual (234); informed of arrival of German general (238); flashback: disappeared from Army for thirteen years; reappeared as brigadier general (244-245); flashback: entered St. Cyr at 17 with locket; only nephew of cabinet minister, godson of munitions maker; orphan; last male of his line; entered St. Cyr in 1873 (245-247); (He was therefore born <u>ca.</u> 1856; dates throughout book conflict; for example, batman is said to be with him over fifty years, but Generalissimo is only 62 in 1918.) graduates first in class; earns highest marks ever given at St. Cyr; refuses Quartermaster captaincy (249-250); goes to African outpost as sublieutenant (250); serves six years at African outpost (254); loses camel and soldier (256); retired as lieutenant colonel on March 29, 1885; goes to Tibetan lamasery (265); as WW I breaks out, becomes Generalissimo (271); has thirteen soldiers brought before generals as British, French, and American officers identify Stefan (274 ff.) interviews women (283); revealed as father of corporal (287); says to Marthe (Magda); that when his son dies he will "inherit from me at thirty-three what I had already bequeathed to him at birth" (301); tells Quartermaster General that one of Stefan's squad betrayed him (330); explains to Quartermaster General the necessity of his son's death (331-332); offers corporal chance to flee (343-345); sets up basic dichotomy betweeen them: he, champion of mundane earth--Stefan, champion of man's baseless hopes and passion for unfact; offers to acknowledge him as his son (348); tells coprporal of Mississippi murderer (350-351); predicts that man will not only survive, endure his own inventions of destruction, but will prevail not because of any heavenly immortality, but because of a stubborn folly, a will to prevail (353-354); dies; is buried (433).

_____: provost marshal's adjutant (12).

General (13)_____: British supreme commander (13).

General (13)_____: American supreme commander (13); does not usually drink after dinner (302).

_____: three sentries (French, English, American) in front of Hotel de Ville (15).

Stefan (399)_____: object of vituperation by crowd; corporal; exchanges stares with Generalissimo (17); with squad of twelve soldiers inspires mutiny; not French by birth; only one of four who are not native born who speaks French (126); middle-European (128); born in cow-byre behind roadside inn; mother dies in childbirth (287); born on Christmas eve (290); now 33 (291) served in French army before WW I; twice declines marriage; marries a whore (297-300); after serving his required hitch in army, reenlists after WW I breaks out (299); serves twelve at Last Supper (335); removed from room (340); enters car with Generalissimo (341); taken to hill above the city (342-343); tempted by Generalissimo; refuses offer to escape (343-345); Zsettlani (346); will not desert his squad (345-346); calls Generalissimo "Father" as he returns to prison (356); celled with two thieves (357); visited by priest (362); can not read (363); as regiment is brought to witness execution, the eleven break ranks and kneel before execution posts (383); *Medaille Militaire* removed by sergeant major (384); speaks to good thief; is shot; falls backward and gets crown of thorns before *coup de grace* (385-386); body given to sisters (388); pass signed by Generalissimo (389); buried under beech tree on sisters' farm (397); name finally revealed: Stefan (St. Stephen was the first Christian martyr.) (399); body resurrected by barrage; reburied nearby by blast (401); re-resurrected by Picklock to become Unknown Soldier (423).

Captain_____De Montigny (282): young aide who opens door for three generals (18); 28-30 (235); bilingual (236); ordered to find spoon (273-274).

_____: colonel; regimental commander who recommends Sgt. Gragnon to officers' school (21).

General_____Lallemont (22): French corps commander; sends for Gragnon; his only friend in France; had been subalterns together (21); gives Gragnon attack doomed to fail (23); takes Gragnon to French army commander; expresses notion that French and German armies need each other to survive (28); first to express notion that man is the enemy of the military clique (30).

General (23)_____: *"Mama Bidet;"* French group commander

(27-28); responsible for giving Gragnon assignment doomed to fail; hopes to earn baton (promotion to marshal) with attack (23); "General Cabinet" *"Marshal d'Aisance"* (32); dismisses Gragnon from hearing abruptly; refuses Gragnon's request to shoot regiment (34); says Gragnon has come a long way from Africa; calls him Sergeant Gragnon (34); called by Gragnon "Monsieur the General Cabinet" and "soon-to-be *Marshal d'Aisance*" (35); says Gragnon is trying to make him court martial him; sends Gragnon back to his headquarters and says he will be sent to marshal (Generalissimo) at Chaulnesmont (36); refuses to accept Gragnon's resignation; orders him to Chaulnesmont for court martial (53); repeats man vs. military clique argument (54).

_____: artillery commander (24); ordered by Gragnon to lay down barrage on mutinous regiment (26).

_____: colonel; commander of regiment that mutinies (25).

_____: aide in observer's post with Gragnon (26); explains to Gragnon the remand to cease fire; Germans are doing same thing; says it is the men in the ranks who brought it about (39).

_____: Gragnon's driver (27).

Henri (34)_____: French army commander (28), of the army that contains mutinous regiment (31).

_____: guard at chateau on running board (31).

_____: other French army comander (31).

_____: third French army commander (31).

_____: English chief of staff; wears corset (31).

_____: American colonel; Boston shipping magnate; liason to French army (31).

_____: junior American officer in British-made American uniform (32).

_____: captain of silent artillery (38).

_____: major of artillery; asks why cease-fire was ordered (38).

_____: man who originally owned Gragnon's divisional headquarters; his country house; millionaire (43).

_____: his Argentine mistress (43).

_____: now dead former member of Gragnon's staff; tall, thin, orphan, whose sexual proclivities Gragnon doubted; Judge Advocate

General; former couturier in Paris (44); wants to become playwright (45); killed by bomb (46); owned *Gil Blas* which Gragnon reads (46-47).

_____: wealthy American expatriate; widow; only son in French air squadron; supports asylum near Paris for war-orphaned children and a staff-major (46); middle-aged in rich furs; partially supports French air squadron in which her son is pilot; appears with Sutterfield; supports Sutterfield's *societe* (200).

_____: staff-major supported by American widow (46).

_____: wealthy American widow's son (46); now dead (200).

_____: Gragnon's batman (47).

_____: private who admits Gragnon to group commander (49).

_____: wife of *"Mama Bidet,"* the group commander (50).

Mistairy (150) Harry (151)_____: British private (56); sentry; horse groom in private life (57); men without dependents make him beneficiary of their life insurance (58); kicks runner unconscious for suggesting how the war can be ended (84-85); denies that he knows Sutterfield or that he was ever in Missouri (141); insurance agent for battalion (142 ff.); flashback to 1912: goes to America as groom for horse; three things happen to change his life and character; in 1914, returns to England to enlist (151); an affinity develops between him and horse (152); becomes Baptist, a Mason, and a skillful dice player (153); after wreck of train, takes horse to swamp; steals RR block and tackle; sets broken bone with plaster of Paris; supports group at dice tables (154-155); kills horse to prevent its capture; jailed (162); vanishes; freed with Sutterfield and grandson; release contrived by Masons (163-164); returns to valley where he first raced horse and joined Masons (189 ff.); helps blacksmith; refuses job; takes job on farm (196); leaves Tennessee to enlist after he reads of the battle of Mons (197); baptised by Sutterfield; makes Sutterfield a Mason (198); back to present: presently private in combat battalion of Northumberland Borderers (202); forced by runner to join battalion that goes over the top to seek peace; is killed by barrage (320-322).

_____: British private (56); battalion runner; peacetime architetect, "an aesthete and even a little precious" (60); among first London volunteers; led platoon at Loos (60); sent to officers' school; second lieutenant after five months, 1916; tries to resign as officer (61); when denied, takes publicly a street walker; then is allowed to resign and return to front as enlisted man (62-64); when he returns to front, asks to be runner (St. Paul figure); (64); placed in same company with ex-groom (65); carries unloaded rifle; learns of Stefan and his squad of twelve (66); sent to corps headquarters as courier (71); learns of mutiny (72); realizes that whole front is silent (72); tells sentry about mutiny (76); flashback: runner watches men substitute blank ammunition for live ammunition (82); tells sentry that he can end war by walking out into no man's land; gets kicked (84); unconcious (84-85); reports to battalion as runner (141); observes ex-groom conduct insurance scheme (142-143); gets ten bob from ex-groom to join insurance scheme (146); borrows ten pounds from ex-groom to go to Paris in April 1917 on leave; seeks former residence when student at Sorbonne (141); finds Sutterfield's society (149); after hearing horse racing story, leaves Sutterfield (204); sees Stefan and twelve in British zone (205); back to present: wakes after Harry's beating; two teeth lost (207); witnesses arrival of German general; hit by Levine's false tracers (209-210); revisits *Les Amis* in stolen uniform of gendarme; AWOL (210-211); tells Sutterfield of false AA shells and visit of German general (310-311); hopes to use Masonic sign to induce battalion to meet Germans unarmed (312); leads battalion over the top (320); they are shelled (321); loses leg, arm, eye, and ear; visits Marthe's farm for Stefan's medal; accompanied by Polchek (Judas) (426-427); does not want to see Stefan's grave (431); hurls Stefan's medal at Generalissimo's caisson; laughs, and is beaten by mob; says he will never die (436-437).

_____James (64): colonel of sentry's battalion; summoned to Whitehall to report on sentry's insurance scheme (58); runner returns to his outfit (64).

_____: sergeant major of sentry's battalion (58).

_____: staff-major in sentry's battalion (58).

_____: orderly sergeant to colonel (59).

_____: runner's company commander when he was an officer (61); refuses to approve runner's resignation as officer (62).

_____: 27-year-old brigadier; less that four years out of Sandhurst; much decorated; refuses to let runner resign as an officer; suggests he shoot himself in foot (62).

_____: amateur street walker, taken publicly by future runner so that he can be permitted to resign as an officer (62-64).

_____: staff officer in Knightsbridge barracks; accepts future runner's resignation as an officer (63).

_____: corporal who meets runner on Boulogne quai (64).

_____: lieutenant (RTO) to whom runner reports on return to duty as enlisted man (64).

_____: Army Specialist Corps British private; more than 60 years; lay preacher; formerly porter in law firm; son enlists to avoid prison; enlists to find him; son reported missing at Mons; tells runner about thirteen French soldiers (67); tells runner about blank ammunition (74).

_____ Polchek (330): one of twelve soldiers led by corporal (67); not French by birth (67, 427); middle-European (128); Judas of the twelve; betrayed Stefan and twelve on Sunday night (330); his warning gave Generalissimo chance to approach enemy "to offer him too an alternate to chaos" (331); sits to the corporal's right at Last Supper; "He had a knowing, almost handsome face, masked, composed, alert" (337); is removed from Last Supper; says he was promised brandy (339): Zsettlani (346); Marya says he is looking for a tree; visits Dumont farm with runner (426); flings twenty-nine coins on floor and supplies thirtieth from pocket (428-429); worked for coins to give them to the sisters; pockets them when they refuse them; seen figuratively hanging in doorway (432-433).

_____: one of the twelve soldiers led by corporal (67); the witty apostle (334).

Paul (340) _____: one of the twelve soldiers led by corporal (67); "a squat powerful weathered man with the blue eyes and reddish hair and beard of a Breton fisherman, captain, say, of his own small tough and dauntless boat" (335); placed in charge when corporal is removed from room (340); (The name *Paul* assigned to this man seems to be a deliberate confusing of the parallel with story of Christ and twelve apostles. Compare it with the deliberate blending of Martha and Mary Magdalene and with the conversion of the Virgin Mary into the wife of Stefan.)

Luluque (336) _____: one of twelve soldiers led by corporal (67); "very dark, his jaw wrenched by an old healed wound;" a Midian; wants someone to say grace at Last Supper (335).

_____: one of twelve soldiers led by corporal (67); "He looked like a scholar, almost like a professor" (335); this apostle says grace (336).

Jean _____: one of twelve soldiers led by corporal (67); sits to corporal's left at Last Supper (seat of the beloved apostle) (337).

Pierre Bouc (339) Piotr (356): one of twelve soldiers led by corporal (67); not French by birth (67, 346); middle-European (128); fourth of the mountain men, not quite so tall as others (338); denies that he belongs in group at Last Supper; his name (because it was changed) does not appear on sergeant's list; removed from room by sergeant (339); Zsettlani (346); returns and fights to be readmitted to cell (355); another name Piotr (356).

321

_____: one of twelve soldiers led by corporal (67); not French by birth (126); middle-European (128).

_____: one of twelve soldiers led by corporal (67).

_____: one of twelve soldiers led by corporal (67).

_____: one of twelve soldiers led by corporal (67).

_____: one of twelve soldiers led by corporal (67).

_____: orderly who summons runner to headquarters (71).

_____: corporal; tells runner of mutinous regiment (72).

_____: sergeant-major at Corps Headquarters in charge of couriers (73).

_____: acting sergeant of couriers (73).

_____: officer in trench with sentry and runner (77).

_____: sergeant in trench with sentry and runner (77).

_____: driver of lorry with blank shells (80).

_____: corporal who orders runner back to lorry (82).

Gerald David (88) Levine (89): British pilot (86); general in RE 8 (Royal Aircraft Factory [England]); orders him to land; 18 years old; in RAF (not RFC) (87); his tunic is "a little epicene;" an only child; a romantic about air warfare (88); belongs to B flight; decides to write a last letter to his mother to be found among his gear (91); a hopeless romantic (92-93); ordered to his hut by Collyer, disobeys and goes to hangars (95-96); Jewish; asks Bridesman to explain what happened (97); next day sits in mess hall waiting to be told what is to happen (99); bathes in a wallow of romantic agony over glory missed (101 ff.); goes on patrol with Bridesman and Major, the wing commander (104); flies through fake anti-aircraft ammunition; sees German two-seater plane (105); fires tracers at it (106-107); fires his tracers at his own artillery (107); has Bridesman fire tracers from his gun at him (111 ff.); his Sidcott burns; takes his pistol from burning Sidcott (113); rolls up Sidcott and carries it to hut (114); despairs (119); in romantic despair, a suicide (326).

_____: general in RE 8 (Harry Tate) who orders Levine to land (87); speaks to men at lunch after mutiny (99).

_____: pilot of RE 8 (Harry Tate) (87).

_____: mechanic who orders Levine to mess hall on landing (87).

Major (87)_____: announces that French have declared an armistice; squadron commander (90).

Mrs._____Levine: Gerald David Levine's widowed mother (88).

_____Bridesman (89): Levine's flight commander; B flight (91); tells Levine of mutiny of French regiment (97); tries to persuade Levine to ignore armistice, fake ammunition, German general, etc. (110).

_____Witt (91): British flight commander of C flight (91).

_____Sibleigh (91): British flight commander (91).

_____Conventicle (91): flight sergeant (91).

_____: corporal (91); reads *Punch* (92); calls Levine to go on patrol (101-102).

_____Collyer (93): squadron adjutant; former observer; wounded; Mons star ribbon; tells Levine the war stopped at noon (92); orders squadron to stay in quarters and out of hangars; orders Levine to his hut (95).

_____Monaghan (93): American pilot in British squadron in B flight (93); tries to attack German general after he shoots his pilot (109).

_____: private on guard at hangar who calls corporal of the guard when Levine tries to find out what is going on (96).

_____: corporal of the guard (96).

Captain (97)_____Cowrie (97): shares hut with Bridesman (97).

_____: infantry officer at mess hall on day all flights are cancelled (99).

_____Thorpe (99): British aviator (99).

_____Osgood (99): British aviator (99).

_____De Marchi (99, 323) Demarchi (117): Levine's hut mate (99).

_____: German (Prussian) general in two-seater plane (107); arrives at British airfield (108); kills his pilot (109); arrives during truce to discuss terms with Generalissimo and allies; condemns politicians; proposes military alliance to dominate world; has monacle in eyeless socket (302-304); makes an "out-of-character" speech presumably damning the English, but actually praising them (305); lieutenant general (306); a soldier first, then a German, then a victorious German (307); came to insist on defeat of his country; they agree to resume war (306-310).

_____: German general's pilot (108); killed by general (109).

Madame _____ Milhaud (116): restaurant owner (116).

_____ Burk (116): Levine's hut mate (116).

_____ Levine (118): Levine's father; dead for ten years; managed American cotton firm (118).

_____: army group commander's chief of staff; escorts Gragnon to headquarters; "tall scholarly-looking man" (134); carries Gragnon's sabre to signify that he is under arrest (134-135).

_____: driver of car in which Gragnon reports under arrest (134).

_____: orderly in same car (134).

_____: brigadier in battalion that runner joins (141).

_____: captain in battalion that runner joins (141).

Reverend Tobe Sutterfield (141) Tooleyman (149): visits ex-groom, British private; black (143); head of *Les Amis Myriades et Anonymes à la France de Tout le Monde* (146); known as "Monsieur Tooleyman" (149); wears French infantry corporal's uniform (150); tells runner story of three-legged horse (151); flashback to 1912: on Sunday a preacher, a groom for rest of week; meets Harry and horse; in train wreck (153); arrested with Harry after he shoots horse (162); never reaches jail (164); surrenders in horse theft after others disappear (168); tells lawyer that he bears witness to man, not God (180); released by sawmill owner; takes train to next station (188-189); walks with grandson from Missouri to Tennessee (197); explains to runner reason for racing horse (198); baptizes Harry in creek; Harry makes him a Mason (198); goes to France to find Harry (199); goes with runner when battalion is wiped out; presumed dead (313).

_____: orderly in battalion that runner joins (143); corporal; gives runner Sutterfield's name and address in Paris (146).

_____: uniformed driver in staff car that brings Sutterfield to former groom (143).

_____: French staff captain in staff car that brings Sutterfield to former groom (143).

_____: British staff captain in staff car that brings Sutterfield to former groom (143).

_____: thin black youth with Sutterfield at front (143); wears uniform of French sub-lieutenant (150); grandson to Sutterfield (152); at 12, was jockey to horse (153); arrested with grandfather after Harry kills horse (162); speaks French with good accent (199); after America enters war, wears uniform of American captain (206).

_____: French high cabinet secretary; appears with Sutterfield (143).

_____: private who explains insurance scheme to runner; each month ex-groom pays each man ten bob and men repay him six pence a day for next thirty days; if he dies, ex-groom gets insurance (144).

_____ Gargne (149): owner of house in which runner lived as student in Paris (149).

_____ Gargne (149): his wife (149).

_____: woman receptionist in Sutterfield's society (149).

_____: Federal deputy marshal (parallel to runner figure in main plot) (151); "head man of folks chasing us" [Sutterfield, grandchild, and Harry] (151); leads Federal, state, railway, insurance company, and oil baron's search parties for sixteen months (153); arrives in Weatherford, Texas one day late in pursuit (157); directly compared to British runner (158); born to wealthy New Orleans family; failed at Harvard; spent two years at Oxford; suddenly sees truth of the horse racing, resigns; offers to buy horse from owner (159); lawyer (162); gives reason for theft of horse, "so that it could run" (163).

_____: lawyer from New Orleans sent by Federal deputy marshal (151); finds Harry, Sutterfield, and grandson have disappeared from jail; released (163-164); says Sutterfield illegally arrested second time (173); tells Irey to get Sutterfield in jail somewhere else (176); unlocks the handcuffs (177); "wifeless and childless" [see *Notes on a Horsethief*] (183); talks about "Wall Street and millionaire owners of New England factories" (184); as crowd leaves courtroom, sees Irey, Sutterfield, and his grandson in square (186).

_____: "Argentine; hide-and-wheat prince," owner of horse (151); millionaire (152).

_____: U. S. oil baron, buys horse and sends it to New Orleans (152); offers ex-deputy large check to find horse, deport Harry, and bring Sutterfield back in handcuffs (160); offers reward for capture of Harry, Sutterfield, and grandson (166).

_____: black RR work gang with whom Harry plays dice (155).

_____: father of Federal deputy (159).

_____: Federal deputy marshal's second in command (159).

_____: secretary to owner of horse (160).

325

_____: lawyer's chauffeur (163); a mulatto murderer who spent a year and one day in penitentiary (182).

_____: ex-deputy's Federal successor (164).

_____: local sheriff (164).

_____: lawyer's confidential clerk; ordered to try to find fugitives (165).

_____: circuit judge whose chambers lawyer takes for headquarters (166).

_____: barber and his client (166).

_____: investigator from Department of Justice (167).

_____: investigator from sheriff's bonding company (167).

_____: two men who are sheriff's local bondsmen (167).

_____: two reporters (167).

_____: president of local bank (167).

_____: woman murdered by lawyer's chauffeur (182).

_____: father of lawyer (183).

_____: wife of Irey (168); related to sheriff (170).

Irey (170)_____: jailor; arrests Sutterfield (168-169); disarmed (170); takes gun from sheriff's desk (178); tries to stop crowd with pistol again (187); again disarmed (188).

_____: relatives of Irey (174-176).

_____: owner of travelling sawmill; went to work at 15; supports widowed mother and three unmarried sisters; in 1912, 40 years old; married with two daughters and one granddaughter; releases Sutterfield (188).

_____: his mother, three sisters, wife, two daughters, and one granddaughter (188).

_____: preacher in church in which Harry appears after release from jail (189).

_____: man from the Gap who warns Harry and Sutterfield of approaching pursuit (191).

_____: local sheriff in first pursuit party (191); when valley people ruin pursuit car, takes up collection to repair it (193).

_____: man who brings lame horse (196)

_____: blacksmith (196).

_____: childless farm couple for whom Harry works (196).

_____: mail rider who brings papers with news of battle of Mons (197).

_____: mother of Sutterfield's grandson; born in New Orleans; teaches son French (199).

_____: young man with patch over eye and cork leg; helps wealthy American woman find Harry (200);

_____: older man in French consulate (200).

_____: padre in runner's batallion; speaks of thirteen "doing harm" to speak of peace (205).

_____: gendarme in Villeneuve Blanche whose uniform runner wears on return to *Les Amis* (210).

_____: old man; crippled and led by blind woman (214).

Angelique (216) _____: blind woman who leads crippled man (214); takes child from Marthe (216).

Marthe (214) Magda (285) Demont (423) Dumont (427): non-French peasant; can speak French; carries child not hers (214); half-sister to Stefan (216); offers to share food in exchange for place at fire (219); married farmer of Vienne-la-pucelle (282); reveals that Generalissimo is father of corporal and underscores Father-Son roles (286-287); says that Generalissimo came to their valley "to create a son for one of you to condemn to death as though to save the earth, save the world, save man's history, save mankind" (287); at 19, arrives in Beirut with Marya and Stefan; quickly marries Frenchman for passport for all three (293); holds locket that identifies Stefan as Generalissimo's son; tells Generalissimo that her demand on the locket [presumably pardon for Stefan] will be in vain (294); expresses to Generalissimo hope that he and corporal could save France (299); throws locket at Generalissimo (300-301); says to Generalissimo "So he must die" (301); resumes name *Marthe* after she takes her brother's body for burial (390); with others helping, buries brother beneath beech tree (397); puts his medal on mantel (398); thinks: "between grief and nothing only the coward takes nothing." (399). [Compare *Wild Palms*.]

Marya (284) _____: elder sister of Marthe; appears much younger; "peaceful face of the witless" (214); carries basket (217); after crowd abuses them and they find a stable, takes bread from "empty" basket (219-222); returns spoon to Generalissimo (284); idiot (290).

_____: blue-eyed child carried by Marthe (214).

_____: woman with spoon at fire; calls Marthe and others "the murderer's whores" (218); throws spoon at them (219); appears before Generalissimo about spoon (272).

_____: mayor (223); at meeting of generals (271); Generalissimo asks him to find quarters for three women (Marthe, Marya, Stefan's wife) (273-274).

_____: guard who comes for thirteen (226); provost-marshal sergeant (227).

_____: batman to Generalissimo (230); for more that 50 years except for thirteen years Generalissimo had disappeared (244); walks behind Generalissimo's caisson (433).

_____: chauffeur to Generalissimo; six and a half feet tall Basque "with the face of a murderer of female children" (230).

Quartermaster General (271) _____: young man, 22 in 1873; attends St. Cyr with future Generalissimo; graduated second in class (246-247); a Norman; son of a Caen doctor; grandfather was disciple of Camille Desmoulins, and was executed by Robespierre (254); although ill, applies for and is granted permission to succeed future Generalissimo at African outpost (257); seeks post for its purpose: "the honorable disposal of that which is self-proven to have no place in the Establishment of Man" (258); makes long speech analyzing motives of future Generalissimo; sees him in stage of preparation for role as savior of mankind; kisses his hand (261-264); returns to France with tuberculosis (264); tries to defend sacrifice of Legionaire (268 ff.); when called, twenty-five years later, to be Quartermaster General, still believes Generalissimo to be savior of mankind (271); is horrified at complicity between enemies to bring German General to conference and at decision to destroy peaceful batallions; shares guilt (327); disillusioned in General; tries to return his warrant (328); appears with runner at funeral of Generalissimo (437).

_____: grandfather of Quartermaster General; executed by Robespierre (254).

_____: staff officer, captain, who, with three others, meets future Quatermaster General by chance at Quai d'Orsay anteroom; five years out of St. Cyr (255); discusses future Generalissimo (256); visits future Quartermaster General in hospital (264); tells story of relief of future Generalissimo (266-268).

_____: three other officers who listen to discussion of future Generalissimo (255-256).

_____: cutthroat soldier at African outpost; had murdered woman before joining Legion (256); vanished along with camel (257); caused death of Riff woman and almost a war of retaliation; tricked into going for relief; sent as sacrifice by future Generalissimo to avoid war by appeasing Riff chief (266-268).

_____: Quartermaster General to whom Norman applies to succeed future Generalissimo in Africa (257).

_____: groom who disappears with cutthroat and camel; brings message from Riff chief (266).

_____: Riff chief (266).

General _____ Martel (269): Grand commander who awards future Generalissimo a rosette; parchment twice mysteriously destroyed (269).

_____: his clerk, amateur Alpinist; spills ink on parchment (269).

_____: nurse who tends future Quartermaster General in sanatorium (271).

Colonel _____ Beale (275): British colonel (274); identifies corporal as British soldier named *Boggan* whom he saw killed at Mons (276).

Major _____ Blum (279): French major (274); speaks English (279); identifies corporal as French soldier who collected money for wedding (279 ff.).

Captain _____ Middleton (279): American captain (274); identifies corporal as American soldier named *Brzewski* who died of flu and was buried at sea (277); 24 years old (279).

_____: Amerian soldier; impregnates girl; marries her with help of man identified as corporal (280 ff.).

_____: French girl married with help of man identified as corporal (280 ff.).

_____ Demont (423) Dumont (427): husband to Marthe (282); married her in Beirut (292); meets corpse and women (395); dies same summer as Stefan (423).

_____: mother of Marya, Marthe, and Stefan; mistress of future Generalissimo (286); dies in childbirth in a cow-byre behind roadside inn (287); with Marthe and Marya, left husband to bear Stefan (290).

_____: father of Marya and Marthe; husband of mother of Stefan (286).

_____: grandmother of whore who marries Stefan (300);

_____: guard knocked out by runner (315).

_____ Horn (316): British orderly officer knocked out by runner (316).

Lieutenant _____ Smith (317): knocked out by runner (317).

Sergeant _____ Bledsoe (317): knocked out by runner (317).

_____ Hanley (323): RAF aviator (323).

_____:lieutenant who phones Polchek's information to army headquarters (331).

_____: sergeant who supervises setting of Last Supper; picks teeth with gold toothpick (333); removes corporal from room of Last Supper (340); takes him to Generalissimo's car (341).

_____ Lapin (357): the bad thief with whom corporal is jailed before execution (357); tries to steal corporal's lighter; is first to use name _Jesus_ in novel (358); tells of murder for which he and Horse will die (359); explains on grotesque level what Generalissimo held: you join the Army to free yourself from the human race (359); executed with corporal (385).

Casse-tete-Horse (357): the good thief; can barely talk (357); just before his execution, asks to go to Paris (Paradise) and corporal assures him that he will (cf. "This day thou shalt be with me in Paradise") (384-385).

_____: NCO, sergeant, priest who comes to give last rites to corporal (361); tells him that Gragnon will die (362); preaches Generalissimo's sermon, urging corporal to render unto Chaulnesmont and not die; advances argument that Rome, by the martyrdom of Christ, actually established (with the help of the realist, Paul) Christianity (364); actually uses three temptations of Christ to dissuade Stefan from accepting martyrdom (365); suddenly admits that Generalissimo sent him to corrupt corporal to life and begs corporal to save him; asks him to read the office of the dying for him (366); borrows bayonet from sentry (369), and commits suicide because, long before, he had heard corporal and twelve and has now betrayed them (370).

_____: French driver who brings Americans to murder Gragnon (370).

_____: young American soldier with trustful brown eyes; father raises hogs in Iowa; volunteered for job without knowing what it involved; a sightseer (371); marks places he has been on map for girl friend in Iowa (373).

330

_____ Buchwald (372): American soldier; speaks French (371); grandfather was rabbi of Minsk; killed by Cossak; father was a tailor; born in Brooklyn; will later become bootleg king; has pale almost colorless eyes (372); knocks out Iowan before he kills Gragnon (379); stuns Gragnon and shoots him behind ear as Gragnon turns his head (380); sends for candle to plug hole so that he can shoot him in forehead (381).

Philip Manigault Beauchamp (374): black American private; third man assigned to kill Gragnon (372); from Mississippi; intends to become an undertaker in Chicago after war (375). (He is the one link with Yoknapatawpha County in the novel.)

_____: girl in Iowa (373).

Sergeant _____ Wilson (375): sergeant known by Iowan soldier (375).

_____: American sergeant major; explains execution of Gragnon (375 ff.).

_____: sergeant major (383); removes corporal's *Medaille Militaire* and gives *coup de grace* (384-386); gives Stefan's medal to half-sisters (389).

_____: three men who help Marthe and Marya take Stefan's body in cart (387).

_____: French sergeant who meets Marthe and the cart; transfers body to coffin and sends them by train to St. Mihiel (392).

_____: American sergeant who gives women coffee and accompanies them in train to St. Mihiel (393-394).

_____ Landry (417): sergeant in charge of squad of twelve sent to find body of unknown soldier (402).

Picklock (413): French private; first steals brandy from sergeant (403); sells original body of unknown soldier to old woman for only one hundred francs in rare moment of conscience (417); helps dig up corporal's body (422).

_____: old woman (403); mother of Theodule who was killed in war; wants to accompany squad to Verdun to recover body (404); when squad opens coffin, identifies unidentifiable body as her son (416); buys body (417).

Theodule (404) _____: son of old woman; killed in war (404).

_____: corporal in lorry to Verdun (405).

_____: driver of lorry (405).

331

_____: two soldiers removing bodies at Verdun (407).

_____: corporal with flashlight; leads squad to recover body of unknown soldier (410).

_____Morache (413): member of squad who owns watch (413); his watch pays for body of Stefan; he had murdered wounded German colonel in shell hole to get watch (421).

_____: man in bar (419); supplies Picklock with body of Stefan in exchange for watch (419).

_____: hired man on Marya's and Marthe's farm (425).

_____: poet of France who speaks at burial of Generalissimo (435).

"Mississippi"

On December 20, 1944, Doubleday asked Harold Ober to seek a piece on Mississippi. This semi-autobiographical piece was requested by *Holiday* magazine sometime before September, 1952; by February, 1953, Faulkner was still planning to write the piece; written by March 25, 1953; first published by *Holiday*, 15 (April, 1954), 33-47; part revised for prelude to "Race at Morning" in *Big Woods*, 1955.

Pagination, in parentheses, to "Mississippi," Essays, Speeches, and Public Letters, William Faulkner, ed., James B. Meriwether (New York: Random House, 1966); (London: Chatto & Windus, 1967).

Mr. Bill (35) William (40)_____: the boy (11); plays with black child born in same week (17); as young man, at 19, becomes tramp; becomes interpreter for lawyer; goes with him to Memphis; meets Sells Wales (22); accompanies Wales to baseball games; accepted in hunting club (24); now a man, works on a trawler; becomes one of crew of five amateurs in racing sloop; commanded power launch owned by bootlegger (30); now middle-aged; profession: fiction writer (35); goes sailing with Arthur (36); flashback: as youth, shared in the annual ritual of Old Ben (37); at midnight, drives thirty to forty miles for ice cream for Caroline (41).

Sartoris, De Spain, Compson, McCaslin, Ewell, Holston, Hogganbeck, and Sutpen (12): family names in Yoknapatawpha County (12).

_____: the boy's grandfather; at First Manassas (16).

Caroline (16)_____: family servant in the boy's family; ex-slave; does not accept full pay (16); calls Mr. Bill, "Memmy;" says Mr. Bill owes her eighty-nine dollars; wears white headrag; hairless (40); suffers stroke (41).

Murry (39)_____: the boy's father (16).

_____: brother of boy's father; uncle (17).

_____: sister of boy's father; aunt (17).

_____: black, born in same week as boy; Caroline's grandson (17); now a free farmer (19).

_____: Natchez doctor (17).

_____Wylie (18): owns hand-powered ferry at Wylie's crossing (19).

_____: tall lay Baptist preacher (18); converts those at Wylie's crossing by fighting (19).

Mulberry_____(19): black Federal Marshal at Jefferson; later

333

town's bootlegger (19).

Doctor (19)   Habersham (19): owner of drugstore in Jefferson (19).

_____ Redmond (19): ex-carpetbagger who brings money for railroad to Jefferson (19); kills Colonel Sartoris on Jefferson street (20).

_____ Redmond (19): his children (19).

Colonel (20 [John] Sartoris (20): with Redmond, builds railroad; killed by partner, Redmond, for arrogance; CSA colonel; demoted by own men (20).

_____ Sartoris (20): daughter of Colonel Sartoris (20).

_____ Sartoris (20): daughter of Colonel Sartoris (20).

_____ Sartoris (20): daughter of Colonel Sartoris (20).

_____: lawyer; referee in railroad bankruptcy (21); family friend of young man's family (22).

Sells Wales (22): owns large plantation; owns baseball team (22); buys hotel to get room; buys Cadillac (23); has special train (24).

_____: catcher on Wales's baseball team (22).

_____: base-stealing shortstop on Wales's baseball team (22).

_____: 340 hitting outfielder on Wales's baseball team (22).

_____: room clerk in hotel bought by Wales (23).

_____: owner of Cadillac bought by Wales (23).

_____: owner of shallow-draught steamboat; a farmer (27).

_____: mechanic on steamboat (27).

_____: bootlegger (30).

_____: black cook-deckhand-stevedore on bootlegger's launch (30).

Pete (30)   : bootlegger's younger brother; 21; Italian; yellow eyes; carries pistol (30).

_____: captain of bootlegger's boat (30).

_____: bootlegger's mother (31).

_____: first-person narrator; "We called them" (32).

_____: revenue officer (33).

_____: kinsman of young man; bachelor (33-34); wears spats, homburg hat; atheist; joins two others to get gallon of whisky over Alabama border (34).

_____: two who invite kinsman to drive to Alabama for whisky (34).

_____: doctor; friend of young-to-middle-aged man; son an undergraduate at Harvard (35).

Arthur (35)_____: undergraduate at Harvard; building boat (35); takes Mr. Bill for sail; made own sails (36).

_____: taxi driver (35).

_____: young man in taxi; father vanished in West (35); father a bank president (36).

_____: bank president; father of man in taxi (36).

_____: town clown (36).

_____: Arthur's mother (36).

Boon Hogganbeck (37): youth's father's stable foreman; kills bear "Old Ben" with knife (37).

Captain Joe Thoms (37): Delta planter who, after a bad crop, pays his tenant farmers two hundred dollars each (37).

Jim (37)_____: black tenant farmer of Joe Thoms (37).

Mary (38)_____: Mr. Bill's first sweetheart (38).

Minnie (38)_____: Mr. Bill's next sweetheart; granddaughter of moonshiner (38).

Ned (39)_____: black slave, born in 1865 in yard of great-grandfather of Mr. Bill; talks a great deal; 84 now; wants Murry to preach his funeral sermon (39).

_____: Mr. Bill's great-grandfather (39).

_____: youngest daughter of Mr. Bill; 5 years old (40).

_____: cook in Mr. Bill's (William's) house (40).

335

_____: houseman in Mr. Bill's house (40).

_____: children, and grand-children, and great-grandchildren of Caroline (41).

_____: mother of Mr. Bill (41).

_____: three younger brothers of Mr. Bill (40-42).

Hestelle (42) _____: Mr. Bill's wife (42).

Details of writing and publication appear before each story.

Pagination, in parentheses, to the following edition (New York: Random House, 1955) 198 pp. For "The Bear" (sections 1, 2, 3, and 5) and for "The Old People" see A 19 Go Down, Moses. Compare "A Bear Hunt" here to the unrevised version in A 22 Collected Stories of William Faulkner.

A Bear Hunt"

"A Bear Hunt" was written about November, 1933; first published in *The Saturday Evening Post,* **22 (February 10,1934), 8, 9, 74, 76; revised and republished in** *Collected Stories,* **1950; revised again for** *Big Woods,* **which was published October 14, 1955.**

_____Compson (145): narrator of first four and a half pages; grandson of General Compson (145); at 15, spent night on Indian mound with companion (149).

_____Ratliff (145): sewing machine agent; used to drive team; now drives model T Ford (145); after four and a half pages, narrates story of Lucius Hogganbeck (149 ff.); beaten by Lucius Hogganbeck for setting Indians on him (150); says he was only trying to cure Luke Hogganbeck's hiccups (151); tells Luke Hogganbeck to go to John Basket on Indian mound to cure hiccups (155).

Major_____de Spain (145): owns hunting camp (145); son of "Old" Major [Cassius] de Spain; banker; called Major in memory of father; supports Hogganbeck's family (146).

Mrs._____de Spain (145).

_____: her married daughters (145).

Lucius (145) Butch (147) Luke (149) Hogganbeck (145): one of Boon Hogganbeck's children (145); 40; most teeth gone; with two brothers named Provine, formed Provine gang; once terrorized town; makes no effort to support family; sells whisky; supported by Major de Spain (146); flashback: with gang, returns from dance; burns celluloid collars on all black men at black church picnic (147); back to present: beats Ratliff (149); has hiccups (151 ff.); takes lantern and shotgun; goes to Indian mound for cure by John Basket (157); rushes back to camp, saying Indians were going to burn him to death (160); beats Ratliff for sending him to John Basket (160-161).

_____Hoganbeck (145): wife of Lucius Hogganbeck (145); earns money from Major de Spain by sewing (146).

Boon Hogganbeck (145): loyal but unreliable man-Friday to "Old" Major de Spain and McCaslin Edmonds (145).

Major [Cassius] de Spain (145): "Old" Major de Spain; original owner of hunting camp (145); along with McCaslin Edmonds, supports Boon Hogganbeck all his life (146-147).

McCaslin Edmonds (145): along with Major de Spain, supports Boon Hogganbeck all his life (146-147).

Isaac McCaslin (145): hunter (145); sends Luke away from his stand (152).

Walter Ewell (145): hunter (145).

General [Jason Lycurgus] Compson (145): hunter; grandfather of first narrator (145).

Ash Wylie (145): "Old Ash," father of present Ash; cook in hunting camp (145).

Ash Wylie [II] (145): also called "Old Man Ash;" black helper in De Spain's hunting camp (149); leaves camp after Luke Hogganbeck; goes to Indian mound (159); gets to mound ahead of Luke Hogganbeck; tells Indians that Hogganbeck is new revenue agent; urges them to scare him; they pretend to burn him (163); motive was to get even with Hogganbeck for burning his celluloid collar many years before (164).

_____ Provine (146): part of Provine gang (146).

_____ Provine (146): part of Provine gang (146).

_____ Hogganbeck (146): three children of Lucius Hogganbeck (146).

_____: companion who spent night on Indian mound with narrator (149).

John Basket (155): Indian (155).

_____ Fraser (158): one of poker players in De Spain's camp (158).

_____: black man; helps Uncle Ash (159).

"Race at Morning"

Written September, 1954; published in *The Saturday Evening Post*, 227 (March 5, 1955), 26, 27, 103, 104, 106; revised for *Big Woods*, 1955.

_____: first-person narrator; sights swimming buck (175); 12 years old (176); hunts with Mr. Ernest (178); as he and Ernest are caught in grape vine jumping bayou, crawls so that he lands on top of Ernest (185).

338

Ernest _____: deaf; wears hearing aid without battery (176); tries to jump horse across bayou; gets caught in grape vine; hurled off horse (185); finally catches up with buck; shoots three times; forgot to load his gun (190-191); adopts narrator when his parents desert him (192); farmer (194); stays in camp with boy narrator one day after others leave (195); decides to send boy narrator to school (196); unloaded gun before shooting at buck to preserve him to run again (197).

Roth Edmonds (175): hunter.

Willy Legate (175): hunter.

Walter Ewell (176): hunter.

Simon (177) _____: camp cook (177).

Ike McCaslin (177): hunter.

_____: narrator's mother; went off with "the Vicksburg roadhouse feller" (192).

_____: "the Vicksburg roadhouse feller" (192).

_____: narrator's father (192).

_____: Ernest's wife; died three years ago (194).

"By the People"

Written sometime prior to October 19, 1954; first published in
Mademoiselle, 41 (October, 1955), 86-89, 130, 131, 132, 133, 134, 135, 136,
137, 138, 139.

*Pagination, in parentheses, to Mademoiselle, 41 (October 1955),
86-89, 130-140. This short story was revised for The Mansion.*

V. K. (138) Ratliff (86): sewing machine salesman (86); now sells
organs as well and radios and T. V.'s after WW II (87); bachelor (88);
tells Gavin and narrator about dog thicket (which all dogs in county mark
with urine); and how someone (himself) taught Devries's twin nephews
how to make dogs urinate on Clarence Snopes; makes trade with Will
Varner to have Snopes withdraw; in return, he will not tell about dogs
(138).

Uncle Billy (88) Varner (86): owner of store and sawmill in
Frenchman's Bend (86, 136); has annual picnic at which candidates
announce political candidacies (136).

Gavin (88)＿＿＿: uncle of narrator; M. A., Harvard; Ph. D.,
Heidelberg; bachelor; then married during WW II; County attorney (88);
makes cynical speech about American politics (134).

Charles (140)＿＿＿: first-person narrator (88); in Army in WW II;
had been a major (140).

＿＿＿: Gavin's wife (88).

Clarence Eggleston Snopes (88): Mississippi state senator; announces
his candidacy for Congress, but withdraws it; distant kin to Uncle Billy
Varner (88); as a youth, a bully; then, on Will Varner's order, appointed
constable; change in life style; becomes defender of civic mores, but is
hard on blacks (89); savages former gang lieutenant; joins Ku Klux Klan;
officer in Klavern; then the Dragon or Kleagle; announces candidacy for
state legislature (134); wins liberal votes by denouncing Ku Klux Klan;
continues to preach hatred of "Negroes and Catholics and Jews;" joins
Silver Shirts as soon as they come to Mississippi (131); teaches Baptist
Sunday school; aims to become governor of state; refuses offer to run for
Lieutenant Governor because he wants to run for Congress (132);
announces that he will not run for Congress; says that Devries was so
attached to blacks that he led them twice in battle; thereby insures his
own victory (135); at Will Varner's annual picnic, does not appear;
withdraws from race; will retire from politics (137).

＿＿＿Snopes (88): president of Merchants' and Farmers' bank
in Jefferson (88).

＿＿＿: Justice of the Peace in Frenchman's Bend; on Will
Varner's order, appoints Clarence Snopes constable (89); Clarence Snopes's
grandmother's distant cousin by marriage (130).

_____: second in command in Clarence Snopes's old gang (89); savaged by Snopes after he becomes constable (130).

Colonel _____ Devries (134): announces candidacy for Congress opposing Clarence Snopes; much decorated officer in National Guard in WW II; commanded black troops in WW II and Korean War; full colonel; loses leg; awarded Congressional Medal of Honor for almost single handedly saving a battalion; carries wounded black sergeant out; wounded; rescued by another black from Arkansas; gives him his medal (134).

_____: black sergeant with Devries in Korean War; wounded; carried first by Devries and then by another black (134).

_____: black runner with Devries in Korean War (134).

_____: gigantic black soldier who rescues Devries and black sergeant; given medal by Devries (134).

_____: twin sons of Colonel Devries's sister (137); cut switches from dog thicket and wipe them on Clarence Snopes's pants to cause all the dogs to urinate on him (138).

_____: sister of Devries (137).

Eck Grier (137): swaps dog with Bookwright (137).

_____ Bookwright (137).

_____: narrator's father (140).

The plan of this trilogy was outlined December, 1938; the original title of this part was *Rus in Urbe*; title settled as *The Town*, October, 1939; the actual novel was begun December 2, 1955; dated by Faulkner as written from November, 1955 to September, 1956; published May 1, 1957. Final episode of *The Town* was published as "The Waifs," *The Saturday Evening Post*, 229 (May 4, 1957), 27, 116, 118, 120, and was originally titled, "Them Indians;" "Centaur in Brass," extensively revised from the 1932 edition and from *Collected Stories*, was incorporated in Chapter One of *The Town*. "Mule in the Yard," revised from the 1934 edition and from *Collected Stories*, was incorporated in *The Town*.

Pagination, in parentheses, to the following edition (New York: Random House, 1957), 371 pp., and to the following reissue (New York: Vintage Books, 1961), 371 pp., paperback. (See Meriwether's warning about changes in editions).

Charles (3) Chick (111) Mallison (3), Jr. (49): narrator of part one; cousin of Gowan; nephew of Gavin (3); tells town's belief in affair between De Spain and Eula Varner Snopes (14-15); narrator of part three (45 ff.); given shotgun by Gavin; jumps out of tree into briar patch to pay off debt to Aleck Sander (54); burns hunting coat (55); narrates part seven (103 ff.); takes Gowan's place in relaying news of Gavin to Ratliff (111); narrates part ten (154 ff.); narrates part 12 (178 ff.); witnesses Matt beating Gavin; tries to hurt Matt; sent out of room with Linda (191); narrates part fourteen; (198 ff.); narrates part nineteen (301 ff.); tells of revelation of eighteen-year affair between Eula Snopes and Manfred de Spain and the town's moral outrage and De Spain's ouster as president of bank (301 ff,); sees Eula Snopes emerging from beauty parlor (309); receives letter from her for Gavin Stevens (310); gives it to Gavin 311); narrates part 21 (336 ff.); narrates part twenty-four (356 ff.).

Gowan (3)   : 13 years old; grandfather was brother of grandfather of Charles Mallison Jr.; lives in Washington, D. C.; comes to live with Mallisons while parents are abroad (3); joins Harker's night shift at power plant; Tomy's Turl's helper (16); goes to Jefferson High; prep school in Washington; University of Virginia (45); at 13, sits in ditch behind Flem Snopes's house to see if Gavin Stevens is watching Eula Snopes (52); with Top, spreads tacks to blow out Manfred de Spain's tires (64); when nothing happens, they put rake in road (65 ff.); they sharpen rake and then tire blows (66-67); goes to Christmas ball with Gavin and others (72); after parents return, goes back to Washington to prep school (111).

Gavin (3) Stevens (30): uncle of Charles Mallison jr. (3); at Harvard for M. A.; intends to attend University of Mississippi Law School to be grandfather's partner; will attend Heidelberg (4); has M. A. from Harvard and law degree from Mississippi; city attorney (16); narrator of part two (30 ff.); says the missing brass cost Flem Snopes $242.33 (31); acting city attorney (44); twin of mother of Charles Mallison Jr. (45); early attracted to Eula Snopes (47); asks his sister to visit Eula Snopes (46); stops talking about Snopeses; begins to talk to his sister about women they have known all their lives; members of the Byron Society and the Cotillion Club call on Eula Snopes (52); elected County Attorney after return from Heidelberg (53); tries to get sister to persuade Cotillion Club not to invite Manfred de Spain to Christmas Ball (57); waits in dark for Manfred de Spain to ride by with cut-out (61-62); gives Gowan a box of tacks to spread on road (63); sends corsages to all ladies of Cotillion Club (70); after De Spain dances with Eula Snopes and all others stop and stare, takes De Spain to alley to fight; is beaten badly (75-76); files suit against De Spain's bonding company for malfeasance in office and criminal connivance (83); wants to drain water tank to find brass Flem Snopes stole (84); narrates part five (88 ff.); meets Eula Snopes at his office at night (88-90); six feet tall (90); after Eula Snopes offers him sex, opens door for her to leave; as she tells him to close the door, says, "Don't touch me." (93); thinks Flem Snopes is impotent (94); refuses her sex, saying, "I wont buy Flem." (95); withdraws suit against Manfred de Spain (98); asks his father ("Papa") what he must do now (99); leaves for Heidelberg (101-102); stretcher bearer in WW I with French army behind Verdun; in American hospital with pneumonia (103); returns to Jefferson (104); goes back to France as Y. M. C. A. secretary with American troops; takes Montgomery Ward Snopes with him (104); returns home for two weeks after WW I; returns to Europe on committee for war rehabilitation (112); returns from Europe; elected County Attorney (120); attracted to Linda Snopes (131); narrates part eight (132 ff.); begins to court 16-year-old Linda Snopes (179); communicates with his sister intuitively (181); stops seeing Linda (188); beaten by Matt Levitt (190); narrates part thirteen (192); asks Linda if she wants to marry him; says she does not have to marry anyone (192-193); buys Linda Snopes a travelling case for graduation from high school (199); narrates part fifteen (202 ff.); sends book to Linda by Chick Mallison (205); in love with Linda (202 ff.); Jefferson has three thousand inhabitants (209); has college catalogues sent to Linda; avoids her for six months; never meets her anymore (210); writes Linda letter; tears it up (213); telephones and leaves message with her mother to have her meet him at drugstore (214); meets Linda who is all dressed up; walks with her as she tells him she can not leave Jefferson for college (216-218); visits Eula to persuade her to let Linda go away to school (219); blurts out that Linda is not Flem's child (223); bastard (224); analyzes Flem's motives for not letting Linda go away to college; says he is blackmailing Eula by threatening to tell Linda that she is a bastard (224-225); agrees to represent Mannie Hait (245); thinks Flem Snopes is trying to induce him to take a loan to get control of him to stay away from Linda (286-287); gets letter from Eula Snopes (311); narrates part twenty [time set in 1927-1928; Faulkner has shifted time in this novel back twenty years. In *Intruder in the Dust*, Chick is 12-16 years old after atom bomb. Here he is 12 in 1927-1928.] discusses adultery of Eula Snopes and Manfred de Spain with Mr. Garraway (312-315); drives to ridge, waiting for appointment with Eula Snopes; views Yoknapatawpha County; history of its families (316 ff.); meets Eula Snopes in office at night (319 ff.); swears that if it is absolutely necessary, he will marry Linda (333); drives Eula home (334); narrates part twenty-two; swears Flem is Linda's father (346); with Linda's help, finds picture of Eula; sends it to Italy to be carved into a medallion for her monument (349); trustee for Linda's trust (351); asks Ratliff why Eula committed suicide; begins to cry (358-359).

_____: father of Gowan; works for State Department; lives in Washington; sent to China or India for two years; sends son to live with Mallisons (3).

_____: mother of Gowan; goes to China or India (3).

_____: grandfather of Gowan (3).

Judge Lemuel Stevens (48): grandfather to Charles Mallison Jr. (3); lawyer (4); father of Margaret Mallison and Gavin Stevens (61); appointed by Judge Dukinfield to hear case against Manfred de Spain (97); dies during last year of WW I (113).

Margaret (46) Maggie (67) Stevens (45) Mallison (3): mother of Charles Mallison jr. (3); twin of Gavin Stevens (45); agrees to visit Eula Snopes (48); visits her (51); catches Gowan with tacks, but lets him spread them on the roadway (64); sends Top with cup of coffee to De Spain after tire blows (67); now tries to protect her brother from Linda Snopes (179); when Gavin buys Linda a graduation present, insists on signing four names from family (200).

Charles (49) Mallison Sr. (3): father of Charles (3); argues with Gavin about Eula Varner Snopes and Manfred de Spain (47).

V. K. (3) Vladimir Kyrilytch (322) Ratliff (3): owns restaurant with partner (3); drives buckboard; sewing machine salesman (3-4); Snopes gets his share of restaurant (4); tells Gavin history of Snopes (4-5); tricked by Flem Snopes, with salted ground, into trading his half of restaurant for Old Frenchman Place (8); tells Gavin that Eula still flirts with men (8); says that Flem has not caught De Spain and his wife because, "He dont need to yet." (15); says Flem is farming Snopeses (moving them up socio-economic ladder step by step) (31); jumps out window without pants when spotted horse enters his room (34); narrates part four (78 ff.); narrates part six (97 ff.); says Flem is the only one of the three men in Eula's life who understands her (99); recalls account of Eula's first sex with McCarron in Frenchman's Bend (100 ff.); trades team and buck board for Model T; tells Chick Mallison what Montgomery Ward Snopes did to get Gavin so angry (113 ff.): opened the Y. M. C. A. canteen back room with a prostitute (114); assumes role of knowing everything that goes on in Jefferson (141); lends Wallstreet Panic Snopes money to save his business; becomes partner; they plan to set up a wholesale grocery (149); tells Gavin that Flem Snopes wants to be president of the bank, and will use his wife to become president (151-152); narrates brief part nine (153); narrates part eleven (177); tells Gavin that Flem is afraid Linda will marry if she goes away and then Eula (and one quarter of old Will Varner's property) will leave him (227-229); says that Flem Snopes now wants only one thing--respectability; that he has to be president of the bank (259); tricked by Flem into buying Old Frenchman Place (271); drives Flem to Frenchman's Bend (296); name revealed (322); one child in each generation named Vladimir Kyrilytch; name is their luck (323); narrates part twenty-three (347 ff.).

Flem Snopes (3): arrives in town in mule-drawn wagon with wife and baby; appears next day in Ratliff's restaurant (3); gets Ratliff's share of restaurant (4); flashback: becomes clerk in Varner's store (5); marries Eula Varner; leaves for Texas; returns next summer with wife and baby (6); and with wild horses (6-7); eliminates G. C. Winbush as partner; replaced in restaurant and tent by another Snopes; moves to rented house; superintendent of town power plant (9); appointed by De Spain who is having an affair with Eula Snopes (13); cuckolded by Mayor Manfred de Spain (15); removes brass safety valves from boilers; puts them in water tank (17); receives three new valves C. O. D. (19); separates all discarded brass fittings in plant from iron, and has Tom Tom place them in his office; tells Tom Tom that Turl wants his day job and plans to steal iron from plant and blame it on Tom Tom (19); orders Tom Tom to take brass home and hide it (20); after auditors find that brass fittings are missing, pays $218.52; tells Turl that Tom Tom thinks he wants his job (22); says Tom Tom has been stealing brass and claimed Turl was stealing it; convinces Turl to go to Tom Tom's house during day shift and get brass back (22-23); discovers Turl climbing in window to Tom Tom's wife (24-25); threatens to tell Tom Tom to spur Turl to find brass (25); after brass incident, resigns as superintendent of power plant (29); according to Gavin Stevens, brass cost Flem $242.33 ; was paid $50 a month (31); fires Eck Snopes from restaurant (33); invited to Christmas Ball by Cotillion Club (56); impotent, according to Gavin Stevens (94); has been buying stock in Sartoris bank; becomes vice president after Sartoris's death (118); begins to spend most of day at bank (137); gives up checked cap for black hat; begins to learn how books are kept (138); suddenly leaves lobby of bank (139); does not keep his own money in his bank (141-142); tries to buy into Wallstreet Panic Snope's business or lend him money to expand (146); again offers him personal loan, before he blocks the loan from the bank (147); according to Ratliff, wants to be president of bank; will use his wife to become president (151-152); visits Gavin Stevens (166); wants Montgomery Ward Snopes to go to penitentiary (167); fails to try to bribe Gavin Stevens because he will not send Chick out of room (170); either he or someone he hired, plants whisky in Montgomery Ward Snopes's studio so that he will be charged with possession of whisky, not the pornography; according to Ratliff, has found civic virtue (175); returns key to Snopes's studio to Gavin Stevens (176); has chosen the furniture in his house (221); has bought his house (223); it is he who will not let Linda leave for college (223); visits Gavin Stevens to have him take case; then gives him ten dollars to be witness (245-246); gives Mrs. Hait the mortgage on her house (251-252); buys six of seven mules from I. O. Snopes for one hundred and fifty dollars each; promises to buy seventh, on condition that I. O. go back to Frenchman's Bend and never return to Jefferson (252-253); has sold Hotel Snopes too (253); moves money from Sartoris bank because it was robbed by Byron Snopes (262); decides to run Manfred de Spain out of town for cuckolding him (270); has salted Old Frenchman Place to trick Henry Armstid and V. K. Ratliff into buying it (271); reviews his marriage and the giving of his name to Linda Snopes and Eula's cuckolding him (271-272); attributes

346

latter to "a nymphomania of gland" (272); reviews Manfred de Spain's efforts to pay him for Eula (273 ff.); reviews Manfred de Spain's repaying what Byron stole in return for his getting Varner's votes to make De Spain president (274-275); recalls persuading Will Varner to vote for Manfred de Spain (276-277); decides to get De Spain by moving the money out of the bank (278); by gossip and innuendo, gets all little farmers to transfer money from Sartoris bank (280-281); sees Gavin's interest in Linda's education as a threat (285-286); tries to get others to vote De Spain out of presidency (290); finally gives permission to Linda to go to State University (290), only after he forces Eula to sign over to him one half of what she will inherit from her father (291); goes to Mrs. Will Varner; claims to be about to divorce Eula; gets Will Varner to vote De Spain out of presidency (295); has Ratliff drive him to Frenchman's Bend (296); visits Mrs. Varner (297); according to Ratliff, tells her that Eula has been having sex with De Spain for eighteen years (300); has been a good father to Linda (323-324); tells Linda he was wrong about college; offers her her choice (325); buys De Spain's bank stock (329); becomes president (330); secretly buys De Spain's mansion (339); commissions Eula's monument (349); buys automobile (352); deacon in Baptist church (359); lives in De Spain's mansion (360); pays five hundred dollars for dog that Byron Snopes's children ate (364).

Grover Cleveland Winbush (4): Ratliff's partner in restaurant (3); ousted by Flem Snopes (8); night marshal (88); visits Montgomery Ward Snopes's photograph studio; reports to Gavin Stevens that there was no drinking or gambling going on; according to Ratliff, likes "female excitement" (125-126); tells Sheriff Hampton that Montgomery Ward Snopes is running a club (161); sends his mother a dollar's worth of food each Saturday (167); after he is fired as night marshal, becomes night watchman at brick yard (297).

Colonel [John] Sartoris (4): Confederate cavalry commander (41).

Eck (31) Snopes (8): replaces Flem Snopes in restaurant; from Frenchman's Bend (8); not a Snopes, according to Gavin Stevens (31); has broken neck; sired by a man other than his titular father Snopes (31); broke his neck at Will Varner's sawmill (32); fired by Flem from restaurant for saying there is no beef in hamburgers; becomes night watchman at Renfrow's oil tank (33); got job through Masons (36); works in Varner's blacksmith shop as I. O. Snopes's assistant (36); blows up oil tank; destroys himself (109-110); a Mason; his neck brace is buried (110).

Eula (6) Varner (5) Snopes (3): Flem Snopes's wife (3); daughter and youngest child of Will Varner (5); has "just too much of what she was for any one female package to contain and hold" (6); town believes that she is having an affair with Manfred de Spain (14-15); called "Semiramis" by Margaret Mallison (50); visited by her and then by all the other "ladies" of the Byron Society and the Cotillion Club (51-52); invited to Christmas Ball by Cotillion Club (56); dies (74); sends Gavin a letter to arrange a night meeting at his office (88); almost as tall as Gavin (90); offers to have sex with Gavin in his office (91); tells him to close the door (93); says she offers him sex because he is a gentleman (94); tells Gavin that

Linda is a bastard (224-225); tells Gavin that Linda would not believe him if he told her; tells him to marry her (226); emerges from beauty shop (although she never uses one); gives Chick a note for Gavin (310); note asks Gavin to meet her in his office at 10:00 p. m. (313); tells Gavin that Flem took Linda's will out to Mrs. Varner: will gives whatever Linda will receive from Eula to Flem (320); tells Gavin of scene between Linda and Flem about college (321-322); tells Gavin V. K. Ratliff's real name (322-323); asks Gavin to marry Linda (330, 332); says Flem is impotent (331); commits suicide by pistol (336-337); 38 years old at death (344); 1889-1927 (355).

Linda (50) Snopes (3): child of Mrs. Flem Snopes (3); a little larger than one would expect at 3 months (6); attracts Gavin Stevens's attention when he returns to Jefferson (131); 13 or 14 when he sees her (132); courted by Gavin (179); arrives at Mallisons' for Sunday dinner with torn sleeve (185); leaves soon after dinner (187); after Matt Levitt beats Gavin Stevens, cries (190); says she wants to marry Gavin; says she does not want to marry anyone; says she loves Gavin (192-193); class valedictorian (198); visits Gavin's office (204); sends note to Gavin by Chick that she will be late meeting him at drugstore (215); arrives very well dressed (216); says she can not leave Jefferson to go to college (217); does not know and would not believe that Flem Snopes is not her father (286); given permission to go to State University (290); makes will leaving everything to Flem (320); accepts some things from Flem; refuses others: "She could accept the daughter's due but not the enemy's bribe." (324); after her mother's funeral, visits Gavin (345); says Flem is not her father (346); says she knew of Eula's and Manfred de Spain's affair; says, after Gavin Stevens lies about her father, that she hated her mother and Manfred while she thought Flem was not her father; now glad because she wants her mother to have loved (346); to go to Greenwich Village after her mother's monument is complete (349); to find a husband (350); leaves for Memphis and train to New York after monument to Eula is unveiled (355).

Ab (5) Snopes (4): a member of Colonel Sartoris's cavalry in 1864 (4); raids Yankee picket lines for horses; caught raiding Confederate line; believed hanged; reappears with son Flem to farm Will Varner's poor farm (5); believed hanged by Confederate provost-marshal (41); once shot John Wesley Roebuck in back (55); last Snopes to come to town; lives in little house a mile from town with daughter and Vardaman and Bilbo Snopes; has watermelon patch (129); shoots at boys stealing melons (130); shoots John Wesley Roebuck (130).

Will Varner (5): owns most of Frenchman's Bend; rents farm to Ab and Flem Snopes (5); sends word to Masons to get Eck Snopes a job (36); owns one of the biggest blocks of stock in Sartoris bank (117); despises, fears, and hates Flem Snopes (276); arrives at Flem's house at 4:00 a. m. (299); outraged when Flem shows him Linda's will so that his own intention to cut Flem out of will is frustrated (328); did not know of Eula's affair with De Spain (329); turns over as a trust for Linda what would have been a good part of Eula's inheritance (351).

348

Jody Varner (5): Will Varner's son (5).

Mink (78) Snopes (5): takes over farm when Ab Snopes moves to Frenchman's Bend to live with Flem (5); first Snopes in Jefferson; kills Zack [note] Houston; after months in Jefferson jail, sent to Parchman (78); mean; kills Houston while Flem Snopes is still in Texas (79); waits for Flem to come back and save him; outraged to think that Flem stayed away from Frenchman's Bend to avoid helping him; on way to jail, tries to escape (80); indicted by grand jury; tried; calls for Flem in courtroom (81-82).

_____: three of Eula Varner's suitors who leave town at time she is married (6).

_____: man who returns with Flem and wild horses (7).

Henry Armstid (7): tricked with Ratliff by salted ground (8); lets spotted horses out of lot (34); tricked by Flem Snopes into buying Old Frenchman Place (271); now locked up for life in a Jackson asylum (292).

_____ Harker (9): operates power plant (9) at night (15-16); discovers that valves are not tied to water tank float (18); arrives Tom Tom's house just in time to see Turl enter and run out with Tom Tom on his back (26).

Joe (18) Buffaloe (12): electrician in power plant (9); makes first auto in town (11); made city electrician by Mayor de Spain (13).

Major Manfred (13) de Spain (10): mayor of Jefferson; graduate of West Point; has been in Cuba as second lieutenant; wounded (10); squelches rumor about scar by threatening to fight Theron Adams with axe; elected mayor thereafter (12); buys first "real automobile" in town, an E.M.F. roadster; starts first garage and automobile agency in Jefferson (14); narrator relates the town's belief in an affair between De Spain and Eula Snopes (14-15); plans to create office of power plant superintendent and place Flem Snopes in it as part of cuckoldry plan (15); used his father's money to become one of first stockholders and director of Sartoris bank (43); races Lucius Hogganbeck (58); rides past Mallison house in car with cut-out out to annoy Gavin in rivalry for Eula Snopes (59); forces Gowan and Top to change his tire (67); when Gavin Stevens sends corsages to all ladies of Cotillion Club, he does same (70); on eve of Christmas Ball, sends Gavin rake head in corsage box with two flowers tied to it with a used condom (71-72); after Eula Varner's death, leaves town wearing mourning (74); beats Gavin in fight after he dances with Eula Snopes (75-76); can not enlist in WW I; organizes Home Guard (108); elected president of bank after Colonel Sartoris's death; resigns as mayor; sells automobile agency (118); money Byron Snopes stole "made good by the voluntary personal efforts of the president" at same time Flem Snopes becomes vice president of bank (120); removed as president of Sartoris bank by Will Varner because of his eighteen-year affair with Eula Snopes (304); according to Eula, if she does not leave town with him, he will have to fight (331); leaves town after appearing at Eula's funeral in mourning (339).

Major [Cassius] de Spain (10): father of Manfred de Spain (10); owns one of the biggest blocks of stock in bank (117).

_____ Adams (11): mayor of Jefferson (11).

Mrs. Eve Adams (11): called "Miss Eve Adam," wife of mayor (11).

Colonel (11) [Bayard II] Sartoris (11): banker; team bolts at sight of first automobile; gets board of aldermen to ban automobiles from town (11); sends Byron Snopes to business college in Memphis (41); twin grandsons join RFC (104); rides in car with grandson; dies of heart attack; owns one of biggest blocks of stock in bank (117).

Theron Adams (12): son of mayor (12).

Uncle Ike (58) McCaslin (12): owner of hardware store (12).

_____: Major de Spain's cook (14).

_____: Major de Spain's houseman (14).

Tomy's Turl (15) Tomey [sic] (142) Beauchamp (15): black night fireman in power plant (15); 30 years old; sent by Flem Snopes to Tom Tom's house to find brass and return it to Flem; tom catter (23); has affair with Tom Tom's wife (24); with Tom Tom on his back, falls into ditch (27); in ditch, they talk and blame everything on Flem Snopes (28); with Tom Tom, puts brass in water tank (29).

Tom Tom Bird (15): black day fireman at power plant (15); reads guages; two hundred pounds; 60 years old; married to fourth wife (16); catches Turl entering his house; rides on his back with butcher knife (26); in ditch, blames everything on Flem Snopes (28); with Turl, puts stolen brass in water tank (29); finds Eck Snopes's neck brace after explosion (110).

_____ Bird (15): wife of Tom Tom (16); light colored; has affair with Turl (24).

_____: city auditor who finds brass fittings are missing (21).

_____: other city auditor (21).

_____: city clerk (22).

Buck Connors (23): town marshal (23); arrests Bayard Sartoris for speeding (116); day marshal (195).

_____: Tom Tom's Sunday substitute in boiler room(25).

Otis (25) Harker (195): nephew or cousin of Harker; takes over when

350

he has night off (25); succeeds Grover Winbush as night marshal (195); speaks to Gavin Stevens about Snopes-De Spain affair (318-319).

_____ Snopes (31): "cast a leglin girth" (had an illegitimate child--O. E. D.); mother of Eck Snopes (31).

_____ Snopes (31): titular father of Eck Snopes (31).

_____: biological father of Eck Snopes (31).

_____: black man; imbecile; works with Eck Snopes at Varner's sawmill; dropped log and broke Eck Snopes's neck (32).

_____ Renfrow (32): owns oil tank; hires Eck Snopes (33).

Wallstreet Panic (34) Wall (127) Snopes (34): that horse boy; son of Eck Snopes (34); jumped over by one of spotted horses [sic] (35); moves to Jefferson and with brother, Admiral Dewey, attends kindergarten; advances rapidly; wants to go to school because he wants to learn how to count money (127); works in grocery store (128); gets paper routes and employs brother and another boy to deliver (128); takes one thousand dollars his mother got from oil company for father's death; buys half interest in grocery; graduates from high school (128); married at 19 (144); proposed to Miss Vaiden Wyott, the second grade teacher, who tells him she is already engaged (145); and who introduces him to the girl he marries (146); refuses to let Flem Snopes buy into his business or lend him money (146); overbuys his stock; goes to bank for help; refused by Flem; turned down by Jefferson bank too (147); saves his business; expands and becomes owner of first self-service grocery in Jefferson (148-149).

Mrs. Eck Snopes (34): mother of Wallstreet Panic Snopes (34); now landlady of boarding house, Snopes Hotel; restaurant moved to hotel (40); after husband's death, given one thousand dollars by oil company (110); lets son Wallstreet Panic Snopes use money to buy grocery store (128); keeps house for son and daughter-in-law (146).

Mrs. _____ Littlejohn (34): boardinghouse keeper (34).

_____ Bookwright (35).

I. O. (36) Snopes (5): blacksmith for Will Varner (5); succeeds Eck Snopes behind counter in restaurant; replaces Trumbull as Varner's blacksmith; schoolmaster; bigamist; proverbialist (36); quicks Houston's horse; thrown in cooling tub; becomes teacher, Professor, in Frenchman's Bend; marries a Frenchman's Bend girl; fathers a child; then twins; first wife and 5-year-old son arrive in town (37); disappears out back door of Varner's store; appears in Jefferson in restaurant (38); five of his mules killed with Hait by railroad (232); deathly afraid of horses and mules (235); in Mrs. Hait's front yard with mules (238); wants $150 from Mrs. Hait for mule (243); takes $10 from her from Old Het (244); says Flem Snopes negotiated with railroad for Mrs. Hait and took half of the $8500 awarded and paid I. O. $100 (249-251); hoping to sell all seven mules to Flem, gives Mrs. Hait her $10 back (253); returns to Mrs. Hait and demands $10 after he finds his mule dead (256).

_____ Trumbull (36): runs Varner's blacksmith shop for fifty years; replaced by I. O. Snopes (36).

Zack Houston (36): throws I. O. Snopes in cooling tub after he quicks his horse (77); killed by Mink Snopes; farmer (78). [Elsewhere named Jack.]

_____ Snopes (37): wife of I. O. Snopes; second wife--bigamy; mother of Clarence, Bilbo, and Vardaman Snopes (37); Mrs. Vernon Tull's sister's niece by marriage (38); stays with children in Frenchman's Bend (39).

Clarence Snopes (37): son of I. O. Snopes and second wife (37); takes in Byron Snopes's children; trains them as hunting dogs (368); almost burned at stake by them (369).

_____ Snopes (37): "vast gray-colored" woman; first wife of I. O. Snopes; appears in Frenchman's Bend (37); reappears five years later in Jefferson in rocking chair on gallery of boardinghouse (39).

Montgomery Ward Snopes (37): "vast gray-colored five-year-old boy;" son of I. O. Snopes and first wife (37); joins Gavin Stevens in Y. M. C. A.; goes to France (104); sets up prostitute in back room of Y. M. C. A. canteen (115); fired by Gavin; opens house of prostitution in Paris (115); does not go back to Jefferson for two years (116); returns to Jefferson; opens Atelier Monty (120), a photograph studio (121); Sheriff Hampton and Gavin Stevens raid his club; find he has album of French post cards and pornographic slides (162-163); arrested by Hampton on old Sartoris law against driving car in Jefferson (164-165).

Bilbo Snopes (37): son of I. O. Snopes and second wife; twin of Vardaman (37).

Vardaman Snopes (37): son of I. O. Snoes and second wife; twin of Bilbo (37).

Mrs. Vernon Tull (38).

Vernon Tull (38).

_____: sister of Mrs. Vernon Tull. (38)

Admiral Dewey Snopes (40): second son of Eck Snopes (40).

_____ Snopes (40): "the actual Snopes schoolmaster" (40); but "no schoolmaster himself either" (41); caught with a 14-year-old girl in cotton house; tarred and feathered out of county (41).

Byron Snopes (41): son of "the actual Snopes schoolmaster;" goes to Memphis to attend business college (41); returns to work in Sartoris bank (43); drafted in WW I (106); back in Jefferson in three weeks and two days; robs bank and escapes to Mexico; gets discharged by placing plug of chewing tobacco in left armpit to raise his temperature (107); sends four children back to Jefferson (359).

Virgil Snopes (41): son of "the actual Snopes schoolmaster."

_____: girl found in cotton house with Snopes (41).

Aleck Sander (45): son of Guster (52); jumps in frozen creek for $4 (53).

Guster (41) Sander (52): mother of Aleck and Top (52); cook for Mallisons (54).

Melisandre Backus (50)_____: had been to school with Margaret Mallison (50); now married to and widowed from rich New Orleans bootlegger; has two children; millionairess (178).

_____ Backus (50): father of Melisandre Backus; drinks; reads Latin poetry (50).

Top Sander (52): Aleck Sander's older brother; son of Guster; called Little Top (52); with Gowan, spreads tacks to blow out Manfred de Spain's tires (64).

Top Sander (52): husband of Guster; father of Top and Aleck; called Big Top (52).

Buck Connors (54): one of three white boys who hunt rabbits with Chick and Aleck Sander (53); jumps in frozen creek to pay off debt to Aleck (54).

Ashley Holcomb (54): one of three white boys who hunt rabbits with Chick and Aleck Sander (53); climbs tree and jumps off to pay off debt to Aleck (54).

John Wesley Roebuck (54): one of three white boys who hunt rabbits with Chick and Aleck Sander (53); lets Aleck Sander shoot him in back to pay off debt to Aleck Sander (54-55); once shot in back by Ab Snopes (55).

Lucius Hogganbeck (58): son of Boon Hogganbeck; gets either Roth Edmonds or Manfred de Spain to sign note to buy model T Ford as a jitney; races Manfred de Spain and charges passengers a nickel each to ride in race (58).

Boon Hogganbeck (58).

Roth Edmonds (58).

353

McCaslin Edmonds (58).

Uncle Willy (154) Christian (60): owner of drugstore in Jefferson (60); store robbed and drugs taken (154); bachelor, almost 60; supplies baseball team (155).

Uncle Noon Gatewood (65): blacksmith who lets Top and Gowan sharpen tines of rake (65-66).

Jabbo Gatewood (68): son of Uncle Noon Gatewood; gets drunk three or four times a year and is jailed; best mechanic in county (68); sent for to repair De Spain's car (69).

General [Jason Lycurgus] Compson (69): Confederate brigadier; for two days Governor of Mississippi (69).

Mrs.   Rouncewell (70): runs the flower shop; buried two husbands (70).

_____ Kneeland (70): runs tailor shop; rents dress suits (70).

Grenier Weddel (70): sends corsage to Margaret Mallison; turned down by Sally Hampton who married Maurice Priest [becomes Parsons in 1964 printing]; sends corsage to her too; given black eye by Maurice (77).

Mrs. Maurice (70) Sally Hampton (77) Priest   [becomes Parsons in 1964 printing] (70): has eye blackened by husband (77).

_____: Mrs. Rouncewell's delivery boy (70).

Maurice Priest (77): fights with Grenier Weddel; gets bloody nose; blackens his wife's eye [This character becomes Maurice Parsons in 1964 printing.] (77).

Letty Bookwright Houston (78): Zack Houston's wife; youngest child of Cal Bookwright; school teacher; killed by stallion (78). [Elsewhere Lucy Pate.]

Cal Bookwright (78): father of Letty Houston (78).

_____: sheriff; searches for Houston after his horse rides up to Varner's store (80).

_____: lawyer appointed by court to defend Mink Snopes (82).

_____: man from bonding company (83).

_____: another man from bonding company; has gold toothpick (83).

_____: alderman at bonding hearing (85).

Henry Best (85): alderman at bonding hearing (85).

Judge (87) _____ Dukinfield (87): agrees to hold hearing about missing brass (87); excuses himself and appoints Judge Stevens (97).

_____ Stevens (89): mother of Maggie Mallison and Gavin Stevens; now dead (89).

_____ McCarron (100): father of Eula Snopes's baby (94); with broken arm, fights five or six men for Eula (94-95); according to V. K. Ratliff, did most of Manfred de Spain's work for him (100).

_____: five or six men whom McCarron fights for Eula (94-95).

Job (97) _____: Judge Dukinfield's janitor (97).

_____ Samson (97): hotel porter; carries bonding man's grip (97).

_____ Samson (97): Samson's least boy (97).

[John] Sartoris (104): twin grandson of Colonel Sartoris; joins RFC (104); shot down in France (116).

Bayard (116) Sartoris (104): twin grandson of Colonel Sartoris; joins RFC (104); returns to Jefferson with racing car; arrested for speeding (116); kills his grandfather (117); killed testing aeroplane in Ohio (118).

Jackson McLendon (104): raises Jefferson company in WW I; elected captain (104).

Hub Hampton (104): sheriff who warns Ab Snopes (130); questions Grover Winbush (159-160).

Mrs. _____ Nunnery (108): mother of Cedric Nunnery; present when Eck Snopes explodes oil tank (109).

Cedric Nunnery (108): her son (108).

_____: Baptist preacher at Eck Snope's funeral (110).

_____: French prostitute set up by Montgomery Ward Snopes in Y. M. C. A. canteen (114).

_____: soldier from McLendon's company; wounded; returns to Jefferson with wound stripe (116).

Mrs. Jennie (139) Du Pre (117): sister [not aunt] of [Bayard II]

Sartoris; keeps house for him (117); again listed as sister; puts rubber plant in Sartoris bank (139).

Narcissa Benbow Sartoris (117): wife of Bayard [III] Sartoris (117).

_____: black family almost run down by Bayard Sartoris (117).

Doctor (117) _____ Peabody (117): Colonel [Bayard II] Sartoris's doctor; warned him of heart (117); treats Uncle Willy (156).

Compsons, Benbows, Peabodys (118): family names in Jefferson; all owned stock in Sartoris bank (118).

Miss Eunice Habersham (71): peddles vegetables (71); owned stock in Sartoris bank (118).

_____: two auditors who appear at Sartoris bank after change in presidency (118); discover Byron Snopes's robbery (119).

_____: last two Jefferson soldiers who return from WW I (120).

Miss Vaiden Wyott (127): Wallstreet Panic Snopes's teacher (127); refuses his proposal of marriage; introduces him to girl he does marry; resigns from Jefferson school to take teaching post in Bristol, Virginia (146).

_____ Wall (127): fictional Confederate general (127).

_____: owner of grocery store; hires Wallstreet Panic Snopes (128); sells half share to Wall Snopes; sells rest and retires (128-129).

_____: two boys hired by Wall Snopes to deliver newspapers (128).

_____: boy hired by Wall Snopes to sweep out grocery (129).

_____ Snopes (129): Ab Snopes's old maid daughter (129).

Tom (139) _____: can not read note drawn by Colonel Sartoris (139).

Mrs. Wallstreet Panic Snopes (146): helps in store and delivers groceries; sees that Admiral Dewey Snopes goes to school (146); stops Wallstreet Panic Snopes from going for Flem (148); fights to beat Flem Snopes (149).

_____: drummer who persuades Wallstreet Panic Snopes to overbuy (147).

_____: father of Mrs. Wallstreet Panic Snopes; small farmer (148).

Jason Compson (151): collects rent for his mother on Montgomery Ward Snopes's photography gallery (151).

Mrs. [Jason Richmond] Compson (151): Jason Compson's mother; owns building that Montgomery Ward Snopes rents (151).

_____: two strangers who rob Uncle Willy Christian's drugstore (154).

Walter Christian (155): black janitor in drugstore; drinks medicinal alcohol (155).

Skeets McGowan (156): Uncle Willy's clerk and soda jerk (155).

_____: two boys with Skeets after robbery (155).

_____: Uncle Willy's grandfather (159).

_____: Walter Christian's grandfather (159).

Whit Rouncewell (160): saw two men robbing Willy Christian's drugstore (160); boy with Linda in drugstore (212).

Judge (165) _____ Long (165): Federal district judge (165); six and a half feet tall (168).

_____: deputy who takes Montgomery Ward Snopes's pictures as evidence (165).

_____ Gombault (165): U. S. marshal (166).

Mrs. _____ Winbush (167): mother of Grover C. Winbush; lives in Whiteleaf (167).

Wilbur Provine (168): lives in Frenchmn's Bend; runs a still (168); sent to penitentiary by Judge Long (169).

_____ Provine (168): his wife (168).

Jack Crenshaw (172): revenue field agent (172); finds whisky in Montgomery Ward Snopes's studio; tells Hampton (173).

_____: his assistant (173).

Miss Elma (174) _____: office deputy in Hampton's office; widow of former sheriff (174).

_____: husband of Melisandre Backus; rich New Orleans bootlegger; killed by bullet in middle of forehead (178).

_____: two children of Melisandre Backus (178).

357

Matt Levitt (183): Linda Snopes's beau; Golden Gloves champion in Ohio (183); rebuffed by Linda, drives past Gavin's house blowing horn (186); fights with Gavin in office (190); after Linda jilts him, drives car through town fast with cut-out out (195); leaves town after fight with Anse McCallum (197).

_____ Birdsong (183): preacher; fought with Matt Levitt (183).

_____: country girl dated by Matt Levitt (195).

Anse McCallum (196): has fight with Matt Levitt; has another fight (196).

Buddy McCallum (196): father of Anse; has cork leg (196).

_____ Wildermark (198): owner of luggage store in Jefferson (198).

Miss Eunice Gant (199): clerk in Wildermark's store (199).

_____ Bishop (212): boy with Linda in drugstore (212).

_____: girl with Linda in drugstore (212).

_____: man who sold Flem Snopes furniture (221).

_____ Snopes (222): Flem Snopes's grandfather (222).

Old Het (231) _____: in the poorhouse; very old; dark chocolate color (271); gives Gavin ten dollar bill; has already given one to I. O. Snopes from Mannie Hait (244).

Mrs. Mannie Hait (231): gets $8000 from railroad for husband's death; chops own firewood and works garden (232); childless; house painted same color as railroad stations (233); when told that mule is in yard, carries scuttle full of live coals outside (233-234); says husband was sole owner of I. O. Snopes's mules (235); sets scuttle down at cellar entrance to chase mule (238); scuttle knocked into cellar by mule; house burns to ground by noon; saves most of $8500 (242); asks I. O. Snopes to sell her mule (243); has taken Snopes's mule (250); because railroad paid $60 a head for dead mules, sends I. O. Snopes $10 because he owed Lonzo Hait $50 (251); gets mortgage for house back from Flem Snopes (252); tells I. O. Snopes that she tied his mule to a tree (253); shot it (256).

Mrs. [Jason Lycurgus] Compson (231): wife of General Compson; gave Old Het purple toque forty or fifty years ago (231).

Lonzo (248) Hait (232): killed by train with five mules (232).

_____: railroad claims adjuster; awards Mrs. Hait $8000 (233).

358

_____: depot agent who, Ratliff claims, sent I. O. Snopes a private train schedule through the mail (235).

_____: black man hired by I. O. Snopes to lead mules from depot to stable lot (236).

Benbow Sartoris (244).

_____ Spilmer (253): Mrs. Hait ties mule to tree behind his house before shooting it (253).

Sartoris, De Spain, Compson, Grenier, Habersham, McCaslin (271): more family names in Yoknapatawpha history (271).

_____ Varner (276): Will Varner's wife (276); dominates her church (292); visited by Flem Snopes (297).

_____: three mulatto concubines of Will Varner (276).

_____: their children and grandchildren (276).

Melissa Hogganbeck (288): history teacher in Academy in Jefferson (288).

Mrs. Henry Armstid (292).

_____: Varners' black cook (293).

_____: minister taken from a field and ordained by Mrs. Will Varner (293).

_____: driver hired by Flem Snopes (293); imagined (295).

Mrs. _____ Ledbetter (295): buys sewing machine from Ratliff (295).

_____: Varners' black driver (299).

_____ Riddell (310): highway engineer newly arrived in Jefferson (301).

_____ Riddell (310): his wife (301).

_____ Riddell (310): son of highway engineer; enters second grade; has polio; sent to hospital in Memphis (301).

_____: Chinese laundryman in Jefferson; attends Methodist Church (306).

_____: one of two Jews in Jefferson; runs clothing store; trained in Russia to be rabbi; speaks seven languages; works geometry problems for relaxation; attends Methodist Church (306).

_____: other Jew in Jefferson; runs clothing store (306); brother of first Jew; attends Methodist Church (306).

Doctor _____ Wyott (306): president emeritus of Academy in Jefferson; reads Greek, Hebrew, and Sanskrit; beats senior Wildermarck at chess; militant atheist (306).

_____ Wildermark (306): senior Wildermark (306).

_____: Doctor Wyott's grandfather; founded Academy in Jefferson (306).

Issetibbeha (307): Chickasaw chief (307).

_____: sister of Issetibbeha; mother of Ikkemotubbe (307).

Ikkemotubbe (307): called Doom (307).

_____: delivery boy from Christian's drugstore who arrives at bank at closing time every day with four Coca-Colas (309).

Miss _____ Killebrew (309): teller in Sartoris bank (309).

_____ Hovis (309): cashier in Sartoris bank (309).

_____: one of two girl book-keepers (309).

_____: other girl book-keeper (309).

_____ Garraway (312): owns grocery store at Seminary Hill; curses Calvin Coolidge; first to move his account from Sartoris bank in moral outrage when Manfred de Spain became president; moves it back in a few years (312); inherits store from his father (313); moves his money again the day the Snopes-De Spain affair broke (314); says they must both go (314- 315).

_____ Garraway (313): his father (313).

Sutpen, Sartoris, Compson, Edmonds, McCaslin, Beauchamp, Grenier, Habersham, Holston, Stevens, De Spain (316): family names of white plantation families recalled by Gavin Stevens (316).

McCallum, Gowrie, Frazier, Muir (316): family names of hill country people who travelled from Culloden to Carolina to Yoknapatawpha (316-317).

_____ Ratcliffe (323): Russian ancestor of V. K. Ratliff; ensign in British Army that surrendered in Revolution; sent to Virginia; escaped; married; had son; learned to speak English; became Virginia farmer (322-323).

_____ Ratcliffe (323): his wife (323).

_____ Ratcliffe (323): their son (323).

Vladimir Kyrilytch Ratliff (323): grandson of ensign in British army; came to Mississippi with Doctor Habersham and Alexander Holston, and Louis Grenier and founded Jefferson (323).

_____ Stone (326): lawyer in Oxford who draws up Linda's will (326).

_____ Stone (326): the older Stone (327).

_____: Methodist preacher; offers to conduct Eula's funeral (343).

_____: Baptist preacher; offers to conduct Eula's funeral (343).

_____: Presbyterian preacher; offers to conduct Eula's funeral (343).

_____ Thorndyke (342): Episcopal minister; offers to conduct Eula's funeral (343).

_____: Methodist minister from Frenchman's Bend who had Christened Eula; conducts her funeral (344).

_____: two black men who carry Eula's medallion (352).

_____: black driver who drives Linda to Memphis (354).

_____ Gowrie (357): Mallisons' bootlegger (357).

Clefus (357) _____: sweeps Gavin's office (357).

_____: conductor on train that brings four Snopes children to Jefferson (359).

_____: flagman (359).

_____: black porter (359).

_____ Snopes (361): girl; sent by Byron Snopes, El Paso, Texas to Flem Snopes (359); Byron's child (361); with others, eats dog (364).

_____ Snopes (361): Byron's son (361).

_____ Snopes (361): another son of Byron Snopes (361).

_____ Snopes (361): third son of Byron Snopes (361).

361

Dink Quistenberry (360): married to a Snopes; now owns or runs Jefferson Hotel (formerly Snopes Hotel); meets children of Byron (360).

_____ Quistenberry (360): his wife; former Snopes (360).

_____ Snopes (361): Byron Snopes's wife; a Jicarilla Apache squaw from Mexico (361).

_____ Widrington (362): engineer who moves to Jefferson; owns dog eaten by Snopes children (362).

_____ Widrington (362): his wife.

_____: man from insurance company (362).

Dewitt Binford (365): married to a Snopes; takes in Byron Snopes's children in Frenchman's Bend (365); slashed on face by one child (367).

_____ Binford (365): his wife.

Clarence Snopes (365): name changed from Clarence Snopes to Doris Snopes in 1961 (365).

Miss Emily Habersham (370): calls Travellers' Aid to get rid of four Snopes children (370).

Page one of the manuscript is dated November 8, 1956; typing of first draft started in January, 1958; final typescript was finished March 9, 1959; published November 13, 1959. "By the People," revised from *Mademoiselle*, appears in Chapter 13; "Hog Pawn," sent to Harold Ober in January, 1955, was rejected by magazines, and was revised for Chapter 14; "Mink," published in *Esquire*, 52 (December, 1959), 226-227, 228, 229, 230, 247, 248, 249, 250, 252, 264, appears in Chapter 1.

Pagination, in parentheses, to the following edition (New York: Random House, 1959), 436 pp. and to the following reissue (New York: Vintage Books, 1965), paperback.

Judge   Brummage (43): sentences Mink Snopes to life (3); circuit judge (45).

Mink (3) M. C. (88) Snopes (3): sentenced to life; cousin of Flem Snopes; obsessed with desire to get in touch with Flem (3); envious of Flem's getting Eula and Old Frenchman place; knows Flem would not be there to help him (4); feels that Houston injured him by forcing him to kill him while Flem is away; does not believe in any "Old Moster" (God) (5); looks for some crude form of justice from "them" (6); resents Houston's money, horse, hound, etc. (7-8); pays fifty-cent bull fee to black; but cow fails to conceive (8); cow gets into Houston's feed lot; hopes it will winter there and be serviced by one of Houston's bulls; claims cow was sold to Gowrie (10); enjoys massive envy and hatred of Houston (10-12); plans to give Houston $8 for cow after wintering (12-13); tries to reclaim his cow from Houston; fails (14-15); goes to Will Varner, justice of peace, to get cow back; fails (16); refuses Houston's offer to buy cow (19); when Varner returns with cow, refuses unless extra seventy-five cents is paid to Houston (20); returns at night to build Houston's fence (21); finishes his fence-building chore; waits in vain for cow to be returned (23); "they" have thrown him off balance (24); after Houston demands two days more work for pound fee, walks to Varner's store (26) to ask about law on pound fees; refuses Varner's offer of a dollar; works one day more and returns at midnight to finish (29); takes cow home; uses last $5 to buy 10-guage buckshot shells to kill Houston; loses $5 on way to Jefferson (30); accuses mail carrier of stealing; is knocked down (30-31); tries to borrow two shells from Ike McCaslin (32); spends night in Jefferson (33 ff.); takes shotgun to ambush prepared to kill Houston (38); feels "they" aint satisfied yet as he kills Houston, not for the thirty-seven and a half days of work, but for the dollar pound fee (39); on third day of trial, after sentencing, finally admits that Flem is not coming to rescue him; now at peace (42); inquires what he must do to be paroled after twenty to twenty-five years (43-44); says he has something he has to do when he gets out [kill Flem Snopes] (44-45); fights lawyer who calls him crazy (47); actually thinks that he has to "go back home and kill Flem" (51); sent to Parchman in 1908 (66); as he escapes Parchman, dressed as a woman, realizes he has been betrayed by Flem and Montgomery Ward Snopes (85); captured; tells Montgomery Ward Snopes after his capture that he will just have to wait (86); tried to escape September 7 or 8, 1923 (88); believes he is a born failure (90); small monologue on how the land wears his kind out (90-91); gets twenty more years for attempted escape; learns all the news from Frenchman's Bend; will get out in 1948 (93); realizes he and Flem will be old men when he gets out (93-94); has fatalistic attitude; chained with ten other men who plan to escape (94); screams so that guards come (95-96); begins to count time left; gets threatening note from Stillwell (98); thinks God will kill Stillwell (100); born in 1883; in prison at 25 in 1908 (102); finally released after petition reaches Governor; with $13.85, plans to go to Memphis to buy pistol (103); thirty-eight years in prison (102); remembers shooting a squirrel to feed his foster-mother (105-106); 63 years old when released (106); released from jail; hitches toward Memphis (259); wants to buy pistol; plans to get work to increase his $13 (264); starts working for Goodyhay (269); robbed of $10 by Dad (273); arrives in Memphis (285); buys pistol and three bullets (292); flashback: leaves Parchman without Linda's money to stay out of Mississippi (376); gives money to trusty to return it to warden after he leaves (386); flashback to Monday morning: Mink leaves shop with pistol intending to kill Flem (396); "Old Moster jest punishes; He dont play jokes." (398, 407, 414, 416); picks cotton with black family before entering Jefferson (399-400); learns that Linda really is deaf (401); sleeps in cotton truck (402); has theory about earth trying from birth to draw one into it (402 ff.); test fires pistol (406-407); asks black boy directions to Flem Snopes's house (408); kills Flem Snopes after pistol misfires (415-416); throws pistol at Linda who offers it to him (416); after Gavin gives him money, walks west; feels free now (434); more theory of earth (435) as Mink falls asleep (436).

Jack Houston (3): after stallion kills his young wife, kills stallion and buys another; owns bluetick hound; arrogant man (7); prevents Mink from claiming his cow; offers to buy her for $8; rebuffs Mink (14-15); offers Mink fifty cents a day for fencing pasture; thirty-seven and a half days (17); offers Mink $18.75 to buy cow (18); when Mink returns at night to continue to dig post holes, orders him off land with shotgun (21); adds final outrage to Mink by charging him one dollar pound fee (25); killed by Mink (39).

Flem Snopes (3): cousin of Mink; marries Eula Varner; son-in-law of Will Varner; gets deed to Old Frenchman place (4); wants Montgomery Ward Snopes sent to Parchman (52); according to Ratliff, wants to take over Montgomery Ward Snopes's pornographic shop; took over cafe from Ratliff and Grover Winbush; now banker and vice president; third person inside Baptist church every Sunday (57); plants whisky in Montgomery Ward's shop so that he will be sent to Parchman rather than Atlanta (60); posts bond to free Montgomery Ward Snopes from jail (61); visits him in jail before he goes to Parchman; asks him to perform a task; they bargain (67 ff.); finally intimidates Montgomery Ward Snopes by producing pornographic photo in cancelled envelope to Grover Cleveland Winbush to threaten him with Federal offence (68-69); flashback: brings wild ponies from Texas (123); moves to former Commercial Hotel; becomes superintendent of power plant (128); vice president of bank; sells cap to black boy; buys black hat (135); sold Old Frenchman place to V. K. Ratliff, Odum Bookwright, and Henry Armstid (138); according to Ratliff, threatens to expose De Spain affair if Eula lets Linda go away to college (139); changes mind to allow Linda to enter University of Mississippi; becomes president of bank; lives in De Spain's rebuilt mansion (141); pays Ratliff four bits to drive him to Varner's store in Frenchman's Bend; takes Linda's will (142); forces Will Varner to force Manfred de Spain to resign as president of bank (145); lives with Linda; has bought an automobile (148); bank is now called Merchants and Farmers Bank (152); uses only one room in mansion to sit in (155-156); according to Gavin Stevens, stole Linda's communist party card (240); in 1943, owns what is left of Compson place (322); flashback: calls up mortgage on what is left of Compson place (324); tricked by Jason Compson into purchasing Compson place and golf course (324-325); triumphs over Jason by turning golf course into housing (326-327); builds housing for veterans on old Compson place (332); tries to buy, then tries to give Meadowfill thirteen feet of land to complete sale of land to oil company (335); unmoved when Gavin Stevens tells him Mink is out of prison (379 ff.); killed by Mink Snopes (416).

_____: deputy to whom Mink Snopes is handcuffed (3).

Eula (86) Varner Snopes (4): marries Flem Snopes (4); a year older than Gavin Stevens (114); tale of her affair with Hoake McCarron repeated by Ratliff (116 ff.); takes annual vacation with daughter at same time De Spain leaves town (135); according to Ratliff, wants Gavin Stevens to marry Linda (139); dies (141); commits suicide by pistol (146).

Linda (86) Snopes (4) Kohl (102): daughter of Eula Varner Snopes (4); lives with Flem Snopes; married; in Spanish Civil War; husband killed; she deafened; fought on communist side (93); gets petition to have Mink Snopes released (102); spends afternoons in drugstore with Gavin Stevens (134); after time in Seminary, enters University of Mississippi at Oxford; with husband, fights in Spanish Civil War (141); leaves her estate in will to Flem Snopes (143); goes to Greenwich Village (151); does not want to marry Barton Kohl, but lives with him (161); according to Gavin Stevens, knows she is not Flem Snopes's daughter (162); before going to Spain with Barton Kohl to fight with Loyalists, marries him (164); gives Gavin gold lighter with initials G. L. S. (175); tells Gavin that Hoake McCarron is her father (175); blown up while driving ambulance in Spain; deafened (192); communicates by written notes (199); has dinner with Mallisons (216-217); drives Flem Snopes around country after bank closes (219); after Gavin takes her to bootlegger, drives there with Flem every Wednesday (221-222); meets with two Finnish communists; begins to visit black schools (222); then tries to improve black education by putting white teachers in classrooms (225); called "nigger lover" (226); anti-semitic and anti-communist sidewalk slogans appear (228); gives up campaign and teaches children in black churches on Sunday mornings (229); investigated by F. B. I. (233 ff.); has not learned lip reading (236); offers sex to Gavin (238); says she lost her communist party card (240); asks Gavin if he ever had sex with her mother (241); says she loves him (241); goes to Pascagoola to work in shipyard (246); when Gavin visits her, takes him to hotel (249); asks him to marry someone other than her (252); sends him back to Jefferson (253); returns to Jefferson in fall 1945

(350); walks a great deal (353 ff.); asks Gavin to get Mink Snopes out of jail; apparently knows Flem's role in the extra sentence (368); will pay $250 every quarter to Mink provided he stays out of Mississippi (370); finds Mink after he kills Flem (416); buys new car (419); attends Flem's funeral (420); intends to drive alone to New York; deeds house and land to De Spains (421); orders her new Jaguar as soon as she knew Gavin could get Mink the pardon (425); gives Gavin an envelope full of money for Mink; leaves him (426).

Hoake (135) McCarron (4): suitor of Eula Varner (4); tale of his affair with Eula Varner told by Ratliff; father of Linda Snopes (116 ff.); only child of widow in Tennessee; attends fancy gentleman's school (125); has arm set by Will Varner and leaves town next day; returns a month later and sends note to Eula (126); appears at Linda's wedding (169); takes her to dinner at Club 21; brings her back and leaves (174-175).

Will (4) Uncle Billy (16) Varner (4): owner of village store; justice of the peace (16); orders Mink to pay $18.75 for cow and, since he does not have that amount, to work it out (17); offers to lend Mink the money to redeem cow from Houston so that he can begin plowing his own land (19); pays Houston the money and returns cow to Mink; threatens to jail Mink if he sets foot on Houston's land (20); 40 at time Eula becomes pregnant (124); sets McCarron's broken arm after his affair with Eula (126); a founder of Sartoris bank (135); uses stock in bank to get presidency for Manfred de Spain and vice presidency for Flem Snopes (137-138); backs Clarence Snopes for election to Congress (296-297); announces Clarence Snopes's withdrawal from Congressional race (315).

Jody Varner (4): son of Will Varner (4); tells Linda the history of Mink Snopes (367).

_____ Houston (7): Jack Houston's young wife; killed by stallion (7) four years earlier (10).

_____ : black owner of scrub bull; paid fifty cents fee by Mink Snopes (8).

Henry (14) _____ : black man who feeds Houston's beef herd (9).

Yettie (50) Snopes (10): Mink's wife (10); writes to husband in Parchman (50); while Mink is in prison, returns to her folks and dies (93).

_____ Snopes (10): daughter of Mink Snopes (10); moves away while father is in prison (93).

_____ Snopes (10): daughter of Mink Snopes (10); moves away while father is in prison (93; eventually madam of whorehouse to which Mink first goes (290).

_____ : Mink's grandfather; owned 10-gauge shotgun (38).

_____: unidentified man who gives Mink Houston's message to get his cow (10).

Nub (14) Gowrie (10): Mink said he sold his cow to him (10); sells whisky; lives in Beat Nine (61).

_____: wife of black man who feeds Houston's cattle; cooks for Houston (10).

Lon (20) Quick (17): constable in Frenchman's Bend (16).

_____: two professional cattle buyers brought in to judge value of Mink's cow (16-17); set value of cow at $37.50 fifty cents (17).

_____ Varner (17): Will Varner's father; one of Forrest's cavalrymen (17).

Lump Snopes (27): replaces Flem as clerk in Varner's store (27).

_____: mail carrier who gives Mink Snopes ride to Jefferson; knocks him down after being accused of stealing his $5 (31); takes Mink back to Frenchman's Bend (38); takes note from McCarron to Eula Varner (126).

Solon Quick (31).

Vernon Tull (31).

Ike McCaslin (31): junior partner in hardware store in Jefferson (31); refuses to lend two buckshot shells to Mink (32); owner of hardware store (323).

Walter Ewell (31).

V. K. (52) Vladimir Kyrilytch (157) Ratliff (32): sewing-machine agent; owns restaurant (32); with partner Grover Winbush, beaten out of it by Flem Snopes (57); narrates section three (52 ff.); signs petition to release Mink (103); narrates part six (109 ff.); repeats history of Eula's affair with McCarron (116 ff.); buys Old Frenchman place from Flem Snopes with others (137-138); drives Flem Snopes to Varner's store (142); to his home (144); wears tie for first time when he goes with Gavin Stevens to New York for Linda's wedding (165); buys tie in New York (167-168); now 40 (169); goes with Gavin Stevens to Saratoga to see where his ancestor decided to stay in the New World (177); good cook; keeps house by himself (206); makes plan to defeat Clarence Snopes in Congressional race (315), by getting dogs to wet legs of his trousers (317); now sells radios (321); signs petition to release Mink (376); telephones Gavin from Parchman that Mink is out without money (376); says Linda has finished killing her mother's husband (377); accompanies Gavin Stevens to find Mink (427 ff.); suggests to Gavin that Linda knew all the time what would happen when Mink was released and that Flem knew it too (430-431); and that her motive was to avenge Eula (431); drives Gavin back to town after he gives money to Mink (434).

_____: ticket seller at movies in Jefferson (33).

Manfred (56) de Spain (34): mayor of Jefferson; owns automobile (34); lover of Eula Varner Snopes (86); first sees Eula Snopes in Jefferson; graduate of West Point; son of Confederate Cavalry officer; fought in Cuba (127); president of Sartoris bank (128); leaves Jefferson for good after Eula's death (141, 146).

_____: president of Bank of Jefferson; owns White Steamer (34).

Colonel (34) _____ Sartoris (34): rich bank president; had law passed banning automobiles from Jefferson (34); dies after grandson drives car into ditch (135, 189).

_____ Buffaloe (34): made homemade automobile, first in Jefferson (34).

Lucius Hogganbeck (35): owns automobile jitney (34).

_____: night telegraph operator in Jefferson (36).

Hub (52) Hubert (103) Hampton (53): sheriff (40); "a meat-eating Hard-Shell-Baptist deacon" (53); takes Montgomery Ward Snopes to jail (59); dead before Mink is released (102).

Euphus Tubbs (60): jailor handcuffed to Mink Snopes (41); tells Montgomery Ward Snopes that Hampton found liquor in his shop (60).

_____: Mink Snopes's lawyer appointed by court (42); tells Mink what he must do to be paroled (43-44); goes to judge to have Mink sent to Jackson instead of Parchman (45-46).

_____: turnkey who rescues lawyer from Mink (45).

_____: District Attorney who prosecutes Mink (46).

_____: deputy sheriff handcuffed to Mink; takes him to Parchman (47).

_____: warden of Parchman when Mink arrives (49).

Mrs. _____ Tull (50).

Montgomery Ward (52) Snopes (58): runs a pornographic picture peep show in Jefferson (52); expects Flem to usurp his business; surprised when Lawyer Stevens and Hampton break in (58); knows Flem planted whisky in his shop (60); out of jail on bond posted by Flem (61); after trip to Memphis with Clarence Snopes, returns to jail (63); sentenced to two

368

years in Parchman (63); narrates part four (65 ff.); sets internal date 1923 when he is sentenced to Parchman (66); bargains with Flem about task he is to perform at Parchman (67 ff.); threatens to resume pornography after Parchman (68); submits when Flem threatens him with evidence of sending pornography through mail (69); his assignment: to enter Parchman and prevent Mink's pardon in five years; realizes that Flem is a virgin; half-brother of Clarence Snopes (71); visits Reba Rivers's whorehouse (75); was in Y. M. C. A. during WW I (76); gives Reba $10 for herself and Minnie; gives her $40 to send to his great-uncle Mink Snopes in Parchman (82); meets Mink in Parchman and tells him that Flem wants him out (83); begins to persuade Mink to escape dressed as a woman (85 ff.); in 1948, in Los Angeles engaged in motion picture industry (367-368).

Judge (52)   Long (52): sentences Montgomery Ward Snopes to two years in Parchman (63).

Gavin (77) Stevens (53): lawyer; county attorney (52); with Hub Hampton, first to catch Montgomery Ward Snopes in pornography business (55); talks with Chick when Linda Snopes returns to Jefferson (109 ff.); M. A. Harvard, Ph. D. Heidelberg (116); helpless rival of Manfred de Spain for Eula Varner Snopes; tries to fight him at Christmas Ball (129); brings suit against De Spain to impeach him; asks father "What must I do now, Papa?" leaves next morning for Germany (130); in early spring of 1914 (131), expresses admiration for German "Aryan" culture, especially music (131-132); joins French army; admits he was wrong about Germans (132); attracted to Linda Snopes (133); wants to get Linda out of Jefferson and Mississippi and safely married (137); orders college catalogues for Linda Snopes (138); appointed by Will Varner trustee for Linda; has Eula's monument made in Italy (147); weeps after the unveiling (150); says Linda knows she is not Flem Snopes's daughter (162); visits her in New York (163); goes with V. K. Ratliff to New York for Linda's wedding (164-165); tells V. K. that Barton Kohl is dead (178); meets Linda at airport in Memphis when she returns from Spanish Civil War (179); served in Y. M. C. A. in WW I (180); refuses to give F. B. I. message to Linda (236); advises her to give him her communist party card and to leave Jefferson (236); refuses to marry Linda (238); tells her she does not have to leave town but that she must if he tells her again (240-241); contemplates telling F. B. I. that Flem has the communist party card (242 ff.); chairman of draft board (245); visits Linda in Pascagoola (247); married to Melisandre Backus Harriss (254); tells Res Snopes to give hog away (342); returns booby trap .22 to Res Snopes; forces Snopes to deed disputed land to Essie Meadowfill so that she can marry Smith; sell land and buy farm (348 ff.); calls his wife Milly (363); flashback: knows what Mink will do as soon as he gets near Flem (268); yet agrees to help Linda get him out of jail (369); arranges for warden to give him $250 provided he get out of Mississippi; $250 each quarter to an address outside of Mississippi for the rest of his life (369-370); gets petition for release signed (370-371); does not tell Flem (370); tells sheriff that Mink is coming to Jefferson (377-378); tells Flem that Mink is out of prison (379); feels guilty (381); calls friend in Jackson about Mink (387); refuses to tell Linda about Mink's intent (390); translates "the Old Testament back into the classic

Greek of its first translating" (392); by Sunday afternoon, says Mink is dead (393); but knows he is not (394); on Wednesday, gets call from friend telling him that Mink bought a pistol Monday morning, but that it will not work; tells his friend that it already has (395); takes money from Linda for Mink (426); as he starts to search for Mink, tells Ratliff, "I've just committed murder" (427); finds Mink in cellar of old house; gives him $250 from Linda (432).

Grover (52) C. (68) Winbush (52): night marshal who wrecks Montgomery Ward Snopes's pornographic photo business (53); once owned cafe with Ratliff; beaten out of it by Flem Snopes (57); purchased pornographic photo from Montgomery Ward Snopes (68).

_____: two men who rob Uncle Willy Christian's drugstore (55).

Uncle Willy Christian (55): owner of drugstore; robbed (55); dead by 1937 (201).

_____ Rouncewell (59): boy; sees and reports two robbers (55-56).

_____: black who fires furnace in Baptist church that Flem now attends (57).

_____: preacher in Baptist church (57).

Clarence Egglestone Snopes (61): state senator; once constable of Frenchman's Bend; once pistol-whipped man (61); put in state legislature by Will Varner, Flem Snopes, and Manfred de Spain; discovers prostitutes in Gayoso Avenue, Memphis (62); takes Montgomery Ward Snopes to Memphis for two days; returns (62-63); prefers "nigger" houses to white prostitutes (70); half-brother of Montgomery Ward Snopes (71); bets on Virgil Snopes's ability to take care of two prostitutes in succession (74); beaten in race for Congress (102, 295); now a senator (296); withdraws from Congressional race and disappears from Will Varner's picnic (297); his career sketched (298 ff.); as constable, harries blacks (299-300); joins Ku Klux Klan (300); becomes Klan officer (301); denounces Klan after announcing candidacy for state legislature and wins liberal vote (301-302); joins Silver Shirts (303); refuses to run for lieutenant governor because he wants to be sent to Congress (305); uses Devries's record in leading black unit in battle against him in Congressional race (312); at Will Varner's picnic, withdraws from race and retires from politics (315).

_____: man pistol-whipped by Clarence Snopes (61).

Mrs. Euphus Tubbs (63): puts Montgomery Ward Snopes to work in kitchen (63).

Homer Bookwright (63).

Hunter Killegrew (64): deputy who takes Montgomery Ward Snopes to

Parchman (64).

_____ Snopes: father of Montgomery Ward Snopes; first cousin of Flem Snopes (68).

_____ Winbush (69): wife of Grover C. Winbush (69).

Virgil Snopes (71): son of Wesley Snopes (71); with Fonzo Winbush rents room in Reba Rivers's whorehouse when they attend barber college in Memphis (72); takes care of two prostitutes in succession (73).

Wesley Snopes (71): father of Virgil Snopes (71); found in cottonhouse with 14-year-old girl; tarred and feathered out of town (71).

Fonzo Winbush (71): nephew of Grover C. Winbush (71); with Virgil Snopes, rents room in Reba Rivers's whorehouse when they attend barber college in Memphis (72).

Reba Rivers (72): two hundred pounds; madam of whorehouse (72); offers to let Montgomery Ward Snopes be her "landlord," her pimp (78).

Lucius Binford (72): Reba Rivers's former pimp; now dead (72).

Minnie (72)_____: maid in Miss Reba's whorehouse (72); wears hat all the time (75), because Ludus, her husband, hit her with an iron and almost took her ear off (80).

Captain (75)_____ Strutterbuck (75): a client of Reba Rivers, in both wars--Spanish-American and WW I; about 50 (75).

Thelma (75)_____: one of Reba Rivers's whores (75); new at Miss Reba's (77).

Ludus (80)_____: Minnie's husband (80).

Q'Milla Strutterbuck (81): maker of money order Strutterbuck gives to Miss Reba (81).

I. O. Snopes (83): Clarence's father (83); sent back to Frenchman's Bend by Flem Snopes (152).

Wallstreet (83) Panic (153) Snopes (83): not really a Snopes; runs wholesale grocery (153); at Flem's funeral; now very successful in wholesale groceries; lives in Memphis with family (420).

Admiral Dewey Snopes (83): not really a Snopes (83, 153).

Eck Snopes (83): father of Wallstreet Panic and Admiral Dewey Snopes; not realy a Snopes (83).

_____ Snopes (87): Eck Snopes's mother; had Eck by another man (87).

_____ Snopes (87): husband of mother of Eck Snopes; titular father of Eck Snopes (87).

_____: biological father of Eck Snopes (87).

Ab Snopes (87): evicted by Will Varner (123); lives two miles out of Jefferson (152).

Vardaman Snopes (87).

Bilbo Snopes (87).

Byron Snopes (87): bank clerk who absconds with bank's money (152). flees to Texas; sends four children back to Jefferson (298).

_____ Snopes (88): Mink Snopes's mother; now dead (88).

Barton (157) Kohl (102): Linda Snopes's husband; killed in Spanish Civil War (93); Greenwich Village poet (109); sculptor, not a poet; shot down in aeroplane (110); a Jew (102); a communist (161); marries Linda Snopes before they go to fight, in 1936, in Spain for Loyalists (164).

_____: Mink Snopes's uncle (89).

_____: ten other convicts in Mink's work crew who plan escape (94).

_____: present warden of Parchman (96).

Shuford H. (101) Stillwell (96): one of ten convicts; escapes (96); sends Mink threatening notes (98); killed when an abandoned church in San Diego collapses (101).

Jake Barron (97): convict killed in the escape (97).

Captain (97)_____ Jabbo (97): guard who kills Jake Barron (97).

_____: chief of police in San Diego (101).

_____ Snopes: woman who raised Mink after his mother died; takes him to church every Sunday and Wednesday (99); second wife of Mink's father (104).

_____ Snopes (99): Mink Snopes's father (99).

_____: Governor of Mississippi (97).

_____: Clarence Snopes's grandfather; Mink's oldest brother (102).

_____: Flem Snopes's grandfather (102).

372

_____: District Attorney; signs Mink's petition (103).

Hubert Hampton Jr. (103): present sheriff; signs Mink's petition (103).

_____: truck driver who picks up Mink Snopes after his release (104).

Chick (109) Charles Mallison (179): makes anti-semitic remark about Kohl; now student at Harvard (110); jealous of Uncle Gavin as Linda returns to Jefferson (112-113); 19 years old (116); attends unveiling of Eula's monument (148); narrates part eight (179); 5 years old in 1919; accompanies Gavin to meet Linda in 1937 (179); serves in WW II 1942-1945 (186); makes long tirade on Bayard Sartoris's shame and guilt about twin's death (189 ff.); goes with Gavin to meet Linda in Memphis (192); says Linda will marry Gavin (204); narrates part nine (205 ff.); returns to Harvard; worries over Gavin marrying Linda (205); after graduation, attends Harvard Law Scool; has A. M. (207); visits Europe (208); tirade on communism (210 ff.); falls in love with Linda (218-219); recognizes that Gavin will not marry her (219); spends last year of law school at University of Mississippi (244); narrates part eleven; in Army; takes flight instruction from crop duster (254); bombardier, not a pilot (256); returns from WW II September 1945; shot down; prisoner of war in Germany (294); major when discharged (320); waits for Linda to return; spent ten months in German POW camp (352).

Bookwrights, Binfords, Quicks, and Tulls (117): suitors of Eula Varner in Frenchman's Bend, according to Ratliff, at time of McCarron affair (117).

Tulls, Bookwrights, Turpins, Binfords, and Quicks (119): another of Ratliff's catalogues of Eula Varner's suitors at time of McCarron affair (119).

Theron Quick (120): one of Eula's suitors, laid out with the buggy whip (123); leaves town after announcement of her wedding to Flem (126).

_____ McCarron (125): Hoake McCarron's mother (125); widow (127).

Herman Bookwright (126): one of Eula's suitors; leaves town after announcement of her wedding to Flem (126).

Odum Bookwright (127): fleeced by Flem Snopes with salted ground with Ratliff and Armstid (127); buys Old Frenchman place (138).

_____ Rouncewell (128): owner of Commercial Hotel; ousted by Flem Snopes (128).

_____ Rouncewell (128): his wife.

Maggie (206) Mallison (187): Gavin Stevens's sister (129); Chick's mother (187).

_____ Mallison (187): husband of Gavin's sister; takes Gavin home after fight with Manfred de Spain (129); goes to Miami after Christmas for horse racing (207)

_____ Snopes (128): from Frenchman's Bend takes over tent and restaurant from Flem as he becomes superintendent of power plant (128).

_____: city auditor who, two years in a row, collects from Flem for missing brass (129).

Judge (130) _____ Dukinfield (130): excuses himself from De Spain trial; appoints Judge Stevens (130).

Judge (130) _____ Stevens (130): settles De Spain case (130).

_____ De Spain (135): Manfred de Spain's father (127); a founder of Sartoris bank (135); lawyer (153).

Bayard Sartoris (183): grandson of banker; grandfather dies in his car (135); in training in RFC in 1917 (183); returns to Jefferson in 1919; buys fast car (188); twin of John (190).

_____: black boy who buys Flem Snopes's cap (135).

Henry Armstid (138):with V. K. Ratliff and Odum Bookwright purchases Old Frenchman place from Flem Snopes for $200 mortgage on farm (138).

_____ Armstid (138): wife of Henry Armstid (138).

Mrs. _____ Ledbetter (142): purchases sewing maching from Ratliff (142).

_____: lawyer in Oxford who writes Linda's will (144).

Mrs. Will Varner (144).

_____: Methodist preacher; baptised Eula; presides at Eula's funeral (146).

_____: black driver of Flem's car; takes Linda to Memphis for train to New York (148).

_____ Snopes (152): four half-Indian children of Byron Snopes (152).

Wat, Watkins Products Snopes (154): carpenter; rebuilds Flem Snopes's mansion (154); rebuilds old Compson carriage house for Flem

Snopes (328); builds veterans' housing for Flem Snopes on old Compson place; thought to be Flem Snopes's partner; calls it "Eula Acres" (333).

Doc   Meeks (154): owns patent medicine truck (154).

_____: Flem Snopes's black cook (154).

_____: Flem Snopes's black yardman and chauffeur (154).

_____: black coachman for Colonel Sartoris (156).

_____: black chauffeur for Manfred de Spain (156).

Nelly Ratliff (162) Ratcliffe (165): married first V. K. Ratcliffe (165).

Vladimir Kyrilytch Ratcliffe (162): V. K. Ratliff's ancestor (162).

Myra Allanovna (167): sells tie to Ratliff (167-168).

Calvin Bookwright (173): Jefferson bootlegger (170).

_____: young couple that take Linda's New York apartment when she and husband go to Spain; newspaperman (171).

_____: Army nurse, lieutenant; visits Jefferson in 1919 (179).

Tug Nightingale (181): son of cobbler in Jefferson; got almost to fourth grade (181); good with horses and mules; housepainter; about 30 in 1916; enlists in Army; father throws him out (184); made cook; last to return to Jefferson in 1919 (186).

_____Nightingale (181): cobbler in Jefferson; Hard-Shell Baptist; widower (181); opposes son enlisting in WW I (184); dies in 1917 (187).

_____: principal who tells Mr. Nightingale that Tug should quit school (181).

_____Dilazuck (181): owner of livery stable (181).

Lonzo Hait (181): horse and mule trader (181).

Pat Stamper (181): famous horse and mule trader (181).

Captain (183)   McLendon (183): organized Sartoris Rifles in 1917 (183); later relieved of command (185).

John Sartoris (183): in training in RFC in 1917 (183); shot down and killed in July 1918 (189); twin of Bayard (190).

Crack (184)_____: elected First Sergeant in Sartoris Rifles (183).

_____ McLendon (184): mother of Captain McLendon; close to two hundred pounds (184).

Joanna Burden (185).

Skeets McGowan (187): soda jerk in Uncle Willy Christian's drugstore beaten by Tug Nightingale after teasing him (188).

_____ Du Pre (189): Bayard Sartoris's aunt (189).

Narcissa Benbow Sartoris (189): wife of Bayard Sartoris (189).

Melisandre (194) Milly (362) Backus (194) Harriss (195) Stevens (254): given books of poetry by Gavin Stevens (194); married to New Orleans underworld character (195); after death of husband, takes children to Europe (196); marries Gavin Stevens (254); called Aunt Em by Chick (357) and Milly by Gavin (362).

_____ Harriss (195): marries Melisandre Backus; New Orleans underworld character (195); converts Backus farm to horse farm (196); killed in New Orleans barber chair; .38 caliber pistol (196).

_____ Backus (195): father of Melisandre; drinks and reads Latin poetry (Horace); dies (195).

_____: black who drives Melisandre Backus to town (195).

_____: nurse in Backus-Harriss home (195).

_____ Harriss (196): son of Melisandre Harriss (196); tries to kill Argentine steeplechaser who wants to marry his sister; enters Army after his murder attempt (255).

_____ Harriss (196) _____: daughter of Melisandre Harriss (196); marries Argentine (255).

_____: caretaker of Harriss place (196).

Benbow Sartoris (206): good bird-shot (206).

Luther Biglin (206): best bird-shot in county (206); self-appointed bodyguard for Flem Snopes; jailor under Sheriff Ephriam Bishop (408); in WW II, joins Marine Corps; almost no vision in right eye; shoots left handedly (408-409); thinks that Snopes will make him rich if he saves him (409).

_____ Spoade (206): had been at Harvard with Gavin in 1909 (206).

_____ Spoade (206): his son; friend of Chick Mallison (206).

_____: Finn; escaped from Russia; settles in Jefferson; takes over Nightingale's cobbler shop (213).

_____: another Finn; escaped from Russia; settles in Jefferson; becomes tinsmith (213).

_____ De Spain (215): Major [Cassius] de Spain's mother (215).

Jakeleg Wattman (220): bootlegger (220).

_____: black man who works for Wattman (221).

_____: black principal of school Linda visits (223); asks Gavin to dissuade Linda; gives speech on white-black relations (224).

_____: black senior woman teacher (223).

_____: woman who sweeps away words "nigger lover" from Linda's sidewalk (226-227).

_____: president of the board of supervisors (227).

_____ Gihon (233): Federal officer (233) investigating Linda as a communist; visits Gavin Stevens (234); wants her to name fellow communists (235).

_____: Gavin's friend in Pascagoola; lawyer; gets Linda an apartment (246).

_____: crop duster who teaches Chick to fly (254).

_____: Argentine cavalry officer; wants to marry Harriss girl; almost killed by her brother; marries her (255).

Rafe McCallum (255): horse trader (255).

_____: pickup truck driver; gives Mink Snopes lift after release from jail (259).

_____: black man in store at which Mink stops (259); drives Mink to nearby crossroads (262).

_____: proprietor in store at which Mink buys food and drink after release (259).

Beth Holcomb (265): woman who hires Mink to rake her yard for a meal he does not want (265).

J. C. (265) Joe (279) Goodyhay (265): lay preacher; former Marine sergeant (267); religious fanatic (271); promises to restore Mink's stolen $10 (274); tells congregation about battlefield visit from Jesus (280 ff.); three times denies Christ (280-281); asks congregation to give Mink $10 (282).

377

_____: other worker for Goodyhay; called "Dad" (266); robs Mink of $10 (273).

_____ Goodyhay (267): Goodyhay's wife; ran away with potato chip salesman while he was in Pacific (267).

_____: potato chip salesman (267).

Albert (274)_____: man who helps Goodyhay load truck (274).

_____: man and wife who take Goodyhay and Mink Snopes to church on Sunday (276).

_____: black woman at Goodyhay's church (277).

_____: ex-whore at Goodyhay's church (277).

_____: her husband; commanded an infantry platoon (277); committed suicide (279).

_____: black man in Marines with Goodyhay (277); beheaded by Japanese in WW II (278).

_____: soldier carried by Goodyhay (281).

_____: man in Goodyhay's congregation; gives Mink $10 (282).

_____: man in Goodyhay's congregation; drives Mink to Memphis (282).

_____: policeman; wakes Mink in Memphis (287).

_____: second policeman; wakes Mink in train station (288).

_____: black store owner; sells Mink animal crackers (290).

_____: two men in pawnshop where Mink buys pistol (291).

Plexiglass, Plex, Harold Baddrington (294): pilot of Chick's plane (294).

Orestes (Res) (322) Snopes (294): installed by Flem Snopes in rebuilt old Compson carriage house; turns Compson place into hog lot (328); goes to Gavin for advice about hog; gives him $5 (342); rigs .22 rifle to shoot Meadowfill so that it would look as though Smith shot him (346 ff.).

Doris Snopes (298): youngest brother of Clarence Snopes; almost burned at stake by Byron's children (298).

_____: Clarence Snopes's lieutenant in rough gang; savaged by Clarence when he becomes constable in Frenchman's Bend (300).

Colonel _____ Devries (308): Clarence Snopes's opponent in Congressional race (307); much decorated in WW II; commands black infantry outfit; loses leg; awarded Congressional Medal of Honor (308); elected to Congress (315).

_____: black sergeant who serves with Devries (308).

_____: black soldier from Arkansas; saves Devries and black sergeant (309).

_____: nurse in hospital where Devries is patient (309).

_____: twin boys of Colonel Devries's sister (315); help V. K. Ratliff defeat Clarence Snopes in dog-wetting scheme (316-317).

_____: Colonel Devries's sister (315).

Res Grier (316): swapped dog from Solon Quick (316).

_____ Littlejohn (316).

Quentin Compson (322): oldest son; suicide at Harvard by drowning (322).

Benjy Compson (322): set himself and house on fire; died; placed in asylum, but brought home by Jason when mother complained (322).

Candace Compson (322): marriage broke up; disappeared (322).

Quentin Compson (322): Candace's daughter; father unknown; ran off with carnival (322).

Jason Compson (322): places Benjy in asylum; brings him home because mother whines; with insurance, builds house for mother and self; keeps original lot; buys golf course; works in Ike McCaslin's hardware store now run by Earl Triplett whom Jason eliminates; purchases golf course (pasture) originally sold to send Quentin to Harvard; launches rumor that it will become air-training field (323); tricks Flem Snopes into buying golf course and paying off mortgage on remains of old Compson place by suggesting it be called Snopes Field; Air Force locates field elsewhere (324-325); tries to have Gavin find a flaw to get property back when he realizes that Flem will profit by converting golf course to housing project (327).

_____ Compson (322): Jason's mother (322).

Earl Triplett (323): runs McCaslin's hardware store; eliminated by Jason Compson (323).

_____ Compson (323): Jason's father (323).

379

_____ Compson (325): Jason's ancestor; governor (325).

_____ Compson (325): Jason's ancestor; brigadier general (325).

_____ Meadowfill (327): owns small portion of land next to old Compson place (327); retired saw-mill operator (328); buys wheelchair and retires to it (329-330); deeds land to daughter; hopes to sell land to oil company but refuses to in order to thwart Flem Snopes (335); refuses Flem's offer of free land to thwart sale (336)1 fires .22 at hog (337).

_____ Meadowfill (328): his wife.

Essie (329) Meadowfill (328) Smith (348): his daughter; high-school valedictorian; earns highest grades ever; offered $500 scholarship from president of Bank of Jefferson (328-329); refuses scholarship; wants to borrow $500 to install bathroom (329); 9 years old in 1934 (334); engaged to McKinley Smith (339); marries him (348); is pregnant (361).

_____ Holland (329): president of Bank of Jefferson; offers $500 scholarship in memory of son (328-329); installs bathroom in Meadowfill house; gives Essie job in bank for life (329).

_____ Holland (329): son of bank president; Navy pilot; killed in WW II (329).

_____: paralytic woman whose wheelchair Meadowfill buys after her death (329).

_____: black man who helps Res Snopes install fence (330).

Mohataha (334): Chickasaw matriarch; deeded land to Quentin Compson in 1821 (334).

Quentin Compson (334): original Compson in Jefferson; deeded land by Mohataha (334).

_____: man from oil company approached by Flem Snopes about Meadowfill's land (335).

_____: boy hired by Meadowfill to bait yard with garbage (337).

McKinley Smith (339): Marine corporal (338); engaged to Essie Meadowfill; son of east Texas tenant farmer (339); builds house in Eula Acres; does work himself (340); marries Essie Meadowfill (348).

_____ Smith (339): his father.

_____: professional carpenter who helps Smith (340).

_____: manager of Rose Hill where Gavin and Melisandre live (358).

380

_____: vice president in Snopes's bank (364).

Ephriam Bishop (370): alternates terms as sheriff with Little Hub Hampton (370).

_____: foreman of grand jury that indicts Mink (370).

_____: Harvard classmate of Gavin; signs petition to release Mink (371).

_____: warden of Parchman at time of Mink's release (374).

_____: two sisters; run Holston House; one married young; descendants of Alexander Holston (383).

Alexander Holston (383): one of the founders of Jefferson (383).

_____: trusty at Parchman (384); killed wife with ball-peen hammer; lay preacher (385).

_____: turnkey at Parchman (384).

_____: Gavin's friend from Harvard; plantation near Jackson (387).

Quick, Tull, Turpin (388): family names in Frenchman's Bend (388).

_____: black family near Jefferson with whom Mink picks cotton (399); man confirms that Linda is deaf (401).

Colonel [John] Sartoris (406): Confederate officer; built railroad (406).

_____: black boy on bicycle; gives Mink directions (408).

Mrs. Luther Biglin (408): wife of Luther Biglin; neice of husband of Sheriff Ephriam Bishop's wife's sister; knows that husband is Flem's bodyguard (408).

Mrs. Ephriam Bishop (408): wife of sheriff (408).

_____: her sister (408).

_____: husband of sister of Mrs. Bishop (408).

Mrs. _____ Biglin (408): mother of Luther Biglin; sister of rural political boss (408).

_____: rural political boss; uncle to Luther Biglin (408).

_____: doctor in Parchman whom Mink questions about

deafness (413).

Mrs. Will Varner (417): second wife; about 25 (417).

_____: Will Varner's grandson; courts grandfather's second wife before their marriage (417).

_____ Turpin (418): draft evader in Frenchman's Bend (418).

_____: Baptist minister; conducts Flem Snopes's funeral (420).

_____: sister of old Major [Cassius] de Spain; lives in Los Angeles with daughter; deeded De Spain house by Linda (422).

Allison (429) _____: her daughter; 60; retired principal of grammar school (422).

_____: young man; delivers Linda's new British Jaguar (423).

A 29 *The Reivers*

The idea for this novel was conceived as early as May 3, 1940; first four chapters typed by July, 1961, then called *The Horse Stealers: A Reminiscence*; completed August 21, 1961; published June 4, 1962. Portions of Chapters 5, 6 and 7, "The Education of Lucius Priest," published in *Esquire*, 57 (May, 1962), 109-116; a portion of Chapter 4, "Hell Creek Crossing," received by Harold Ober on December 6, 1961, was published in *The Saturday Evening Post*, 235 (March 31, 1962), 22-25, with short introduction by Faulkner; revised excerpts from pp. 236-303 entitled "William Faulkner Reading from *The Reivers*. . . April 19, 1962," published in *Faulkner at West Point*, eds., Joseph L. Fant and Robert Ashley (New York: Random House, 1964), pp. 8-46.

Pagination, in parentheses, to the following edition (New York: Random House, 1962), 305 pp., and to the following reissue (New York: Vintage Books, 1966), paperback.

Lucius Priest [III] (12): narrator (3); his family "cadet branch" of the McCaslin-Edmonds family (18).

Lucius (34) Priest [II] (12): narrator's grandfather (3); as he makes up his mind to go on trip with Boon, realizes he is leader, boss, master (53); tries to establish alibi with Ned (54-55); tells cousin Zack Edmonds that he intends to stay with cousin Ike McCaslin before he leaves on trip (63); with Boon, leaves for Memphis in May 1905 (71 ff.); after they cross Hell Creek Bottom, relieves Boon as driver (94); experiences "smell" as he enters Miss Reba's whorehouse (99); very impressed with Minnie's gold tooth (100); learns that Mr. Binford is Miss Reba's pimp (113), and lover for five years, whose only vice is horse racing (114); gives treatise on mules, rats, cats, dogs, and horses (121-123); homesick (154); upset by learning too rapidly about life and sex (155); hits Otis when he tells him of Corrie's beginnings as a whore (157); hand cut on Otis's knife (158); afraid when sheriff Butch begins to bully Corrie (174); feels that innocence and childhood are gone forever (175); lets name *Everbe* slip to Boon (212); loses first heat in race because Ned is disqualified (236-237); during second heat, seems to lose as crowd breaks into fight (238-239); heat cancelled (241); goes to stay with Uncle Parsham on Ned's instructions (244); tells Uncle Parsham of desire to own pack of beagles; suddenly cries and is comforted by Uncle Parsham (246-247); sleeps with him (251); homesick again (252); after he hears about Boon hitting Corrie, goes to town and hits him (259-260); wins final heat (273); refuses share in Miss Reba's winnings on race; takes it finally for Ned or Uncle Parsham (279); tells Corrie that her last sex with Butch was all right (280); races Coppermine; wins (273); races Coppermine for fourth time (295); loses (297) because Ned threw race by not letting horse smell sardines (296); after escapade, instead of whipping by father, gets lecture by grandfather (302 ff.).

Boon Hogganbeck (3): six feet four inches (4); wants to shoot Ludus (5); assistant to Mr. Ballott; on night duty (7); very poor shot (10); sets internal date, 1905 (13); fires five shots at Ludus; misses (14-15); says

Ludus insulted him (15); sometimes boasts of Indian blood; sometimes denies it; two hundred and forty pounds (19); adopted by Edmonds and De Spain at 12 years of age; takes care of General Compson when he becomes senile (22); has room in Commercial Hotel (24); becomes fascinated with automobile (27); becomes dean of Jefferson motor-car drivers (29); drives to Memphis to get grandfather's [Lucius Priest I] car (31); gets keys to car and takes Lucius Priest [II] with him (33); becomes Priest's driver (36); transferred to night shift (37-38); as family prepares to go to Grandfather's funeral, anticipates week's free use of automobile (45); teaches Lucius Priest [II] to drive (50-52); decides to take him on trip (50 ff.); shaves and dresses for trip (57); pays $6 for help crossing Hell Creek Bottom (91); announces that they will stay in a "kind of boarding house" in Memphis (95); before they enter Miss Reba's whorehouse, gives Lucius Priest [II] keys to car and his wallet less $6 (98); tries to prepare Lucius not to tell his folks what he is about to learn (104-105); jealous when Corrie wants to telephone Sam for help to get horse to Parsham (132); with Sam and Corrie, walks horse to railroad boxcar (139); with Ned and Lucius, boards train to Parsham (165); restrains himself while sheriff Butch badgers Corrie (172 ff.); furious at notion of Corrie quitting being a whore (197); said by Ned to have hit Corrie and whipped Butch; now arrested in Hardwicke (255); in jail for third time (275) for fighting with Butch (277); released; makes excuse for Corrie's last sex with Butch (298); calls her his wife; fought Butch for calling her a whore; they return to Jefferson (299); marries Corrie and has child (304-305).

Maury (5) Priest (12): narrator's great-grandfather (3); Ned's betting agent in mule racing (123).

Lessep (53) Priest (12): younger brother of Lucius Priest [II] (4).

Maury (53) Priest [II] (12): younger brother of Lucius Priest [II] (4).

Alexander (30) Priest (12): younger brother of Lucius Priest [II] (4).

John Powell (4): head hostler (4); owns .41 calibre revolver, which he bought from his father on twenty-first birthday (6); black (10).

Son Thomas (4): youngest driver in livery stable (4).

Ludus (5)   : one of Boss Priest's drivers (10).

Luster (6)   : works in Boss Priest's livery stable (6).

Gabe (6)   : blacksmith.

          Powell (6): John Powell's father; sells son revolver (6).

Mrs. (7)   Powell (7): wife of John Powell (7).

          Ballott (7): white stable foreman (7).

Dan Grinnup Grenier (8): hanger on at livery stable; descendant of Louis Grenier (8).

Louis Grenier (8): came to Mississippi in 1790's; founded Jefferson (8).

_____ Grinnup (8): idiot nephew or cousin of Dan Grinnup (8).

Mrs. _____ Ballott (8): first wife of Mr. Ballott; daughter of Dan Grinnup (8).

_____ Grinnup (8): father of Dan Grinnup (8).

_____ Hampton (10): sheriff; grandfather of present sheriff (10).

_____: daughter or wife of tenant farmer; Ludus's new girlfriend (10).

Mack Winbush (13): lives near Jefferson (13).

Uncle Cal Calvin Bookwright (13): whisky maker (13).

Isaac McCaslin (14): owner of hardware store (14); grandson of Lucius Quintus Carothers [McCaslin] (31); lives alone in room over hardware store (54).

Hub Hampton (14): "Little" Hub Hampton; present sheriff (14).

_____: black woman whose buttock Boon's bullet creased (14).

Doc (15) _____ Peabody (15).

_____ Christian (15): owner of drugstore (15).

Judge (15) _____ Stevens (15).

_____ Lessep (43): grandfather of Lucius Priest [II]; father of his mother; great-great-grandfather of Lucius Priest [III]; dies in Bay St. Louis (18).

Zachary Edmonds (18): son of McCaslin Edmonds (18); called Cousin Zachary by Lucius [II] (59).

McCaslin Edmonds (18): Isaac McCaslin gives plantation to him on twenty-first birthday (18).

Major _____ de Spain (18): owner of hunting camp (19).

General (18) _____ Compson (18).

_____: Boon Hogganbeck's grandmother; daughter of Chickasaw; married white whisky trader (19).

Issetebbeha (19): Chickasaw chief (19).

Thomas Sutpen (20).

Manfred de Spain (21): banker; "sold lease, land and timber" (21); owns E. M. F. racer; mayor of Jefferson (25).

Walter Ewell (21): hunter (21).

Bob Legate (21): hunter (21).

Sam Fathers (21): half black, half Chickasaw Indian [sic] (21).

Lucius Quintus (31) Carothers McCaslin (22): grandfather of Ned McCaslin (31); arrived in Mississippi in 1813 from Carolina (61).

Tennie's Jim (22)_____: grandfather of Bobo Beauchamp (22).

Boss (34) Lucius (39) Quintus Carothers (285) Priest [I] (34): grandfather of Lucius Priest [II]; buys auto (23); banker; president of Bank of Jefferson (25); buys Winton Flyer; then White Steamer (28); spits tobacco juice from moving car; hits his wife (39-40); arrives at track as Lucius wins last heat (274); has recovered automobile (275); marries Sarah Edmonds in 1869 (285); agrees to final race to determine who buys or owns Coppermine (295); takes toddy before getting dressed each morning (302).

Flem Snopes (24): banker; murdered ten to twelve years ago by kinsman (24).

_____: mad kinsman who kills Flem Snopes (24).

Little Chicago (24): brassy haired woman who leases Commercial Hotel (24).

Mrs. _____ Rouncewell (24): owner of hotel once called Commercial Hotel (24).

Colonel (25) _____ Sartoris (25): president of Merchants and Farmers Bank (25); horses bolt at automobile; has ordinance passed prohibiting cars in Jefferson (27-28).

_____ Buffaloe (25): mechanic (25); takes Memphis car apart and reassembles it; then builds his own automobile (27).

_____: owner of car from Memphis (26).

Sarah (32) Edmonds (285) Priest (12): grandmother of Lucius Priest

[II]; can not stand smell of gasoline (28); married in 1869 (285).

_____ Wordwin (29): cashier in grandfather's [Lucius Priest I] bank; goes to Memphis to return automobile [Winton Flyer] to town (29).

Ned (30) William (129) McCaslin (30): coachman for Lucius Priest [I]; dies at 74; born in McCaslin back yard in 1860 (30); mother was natural daughter of Lucius Quintus Carothers [McCaslin] and slave woman (31); rides in car only once (36); hides in car under tarpaulin as Boon and Lucius [II] leave for Memphis (69-70); leaves Boon and Lucius at Miss Reba's (98); turns up that night with horse (115); has swapped car for horse; is captivated by Minnie's gold tooth (116-117); plans to race horse at Parsham; intends to win back automobile (120); once had racing mule (120 ff.); admits horse is stolen (125); gets horse into boxcar with help of others (150); Mason (167); trains horse (168 ff.); influences horse by something he puts on its muzzle (182); plans to lose first heat and win next two (221); disqualified in first heat because he released horse too soon (236-237); arrested after second heat; after giving Lucius small packet, tells him to stay with Uncle Parsham (239); appears with horse next morning (252); tells Boss Priest and Lucius [II] that he used sardine to win race (286); tells story of swap of horse for automobile (287 ff.); throws last race by not letting Coppermine smell sardines (296).

Delphine (30) McCaslin (30): Ned's present wife; one of four; cook for Sarah Edmonds Priest (30).

_____: natural daughter of Lucius Quintus Carothers McCaslin and slave woman; mother of Ned McCaslin (31).

_____: female slave and concubine of Lucius Quintus Carothers McCaslin; grandmother of Ned McCaslin (31).

Aunt Callie (34) _____: black servant of Priests (34).

Allison (34) Lessep (43) Priest (12): mother of Lucius Priest [II]; wife of Maury Priest (34).

_____ Lessep (44): maternal grandmother of Lucius [II] (44).

Louisa (47) Edmonds (59): called Cousin Louisa by Allison Priest (47).

_____ Rouncewell (47): oil company agent in Jefferson (47).

_____: Rouncewell's black employee; pumps gasoline (48).

Carothers Edmonds (61).

_____ Ballenbaugh (69): giant; displaces Wyott from his ferry and store (73).

_____ Wyott (69): family friend of Priests (69).

387

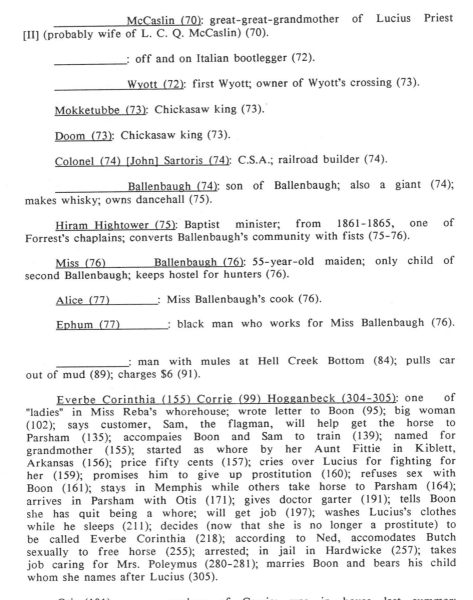

_____ McCaslin (70): great-great-grandmother of Lucius Priest [II] (probably wife of L. C. Q. McCaslin) (70).

_____: off and on Italian bootlegger (72).

_____ Wyott (72): first Wyott; owner of Wyott's crossing (73).

Mokketubbe (73): Chickasaw king (73).

Doom (73): Chickasaw king (73).

Colonel (74) [John] Sartoris (74): C.S.A.; railroad builder (74).

_____ Ballenbaugh (74): son of Ballenbaugh; also a giant (74); makes whisky; owns dancehall (75).

Hiram Hightower (75): Baptist minister; from 1861–1865, one of Forrest's chaplains; converts Ballenbaugh's community with fists (75–76).

Miss (76) _____ Ballenbaugh (76): 55-year-old maiden; only child of second Ballenbaugh; keeps hostel for hunters (76).

Alice (77) _____: Miss Ballenbaugh's cook (76).

Ephum (77) _____: black man who works for Miss Ballenbaugh (76).

_____: man with mules at Hell Creek Bottom (84); pulls car out of mud (89); charges $6 (91).

Everbe Corinthia (155) Corrie (99) Hogganbeck (304–305): one of "ladies" in Miss Reba's whorehouse; wrote letter to Boon (95); big woman (102); says customer, Sam, the flagman, will help get the horse to Parsham (135); accompaies Boon and Sam to train (139); named for grandmother (155); started as whore by her Aunt Fittie in Kiblett, Arkansas (156); price fifty cents (157); cries over Lucius for fighting for her (159); promises him to give up prostitution (160); refuses sex with Boon (161); stays in Memphis while others take horse to Parsham (164); arrives in Parsham with Otis (171); gives doctor garter (191); tells Boon she has quit being a whore; will get job (197); washes Lucius's clothes while he sleeps (211); decides (now that she is no longer a prostitute) to be called Everbe Corinthia (218); according to Ned, accomodates Butch sexually to free horse (255); arrested; in jail in Hardwicke (257); takes job caring for Mrs. Poleymus (280–281); marries Boon and bears his child whom she names after Lucius (305).

Otis (101) _____: nephew of Corrie; was in house last summer; lives on Arkansas tenant farm (95, 99); tells Miss Reba that Mr. Binford took him to race track instead of zoo (111); used to watch Aunt Corrie as prostitute through peephole (143); charges boys five cents and men ten cents to watch Corrie as prostitute (156–157); hit by Lucius [II] when he tells of Corrie's beginnings as whore (157); not 10 but 15 years old (158);

disappears from Parsham (198); had stolen Minnie's gold tooth while she was asleep (200); found at Parsham (203).

Theophilus McCaslin (96): with General Forrest's brother, almost captured Yankee general in Gayoso Hotel in Civil War (96).

Miss Reba (98)   : madam of Memphis whorehouse (98); threatens to throw Mr. Binford out for using word *whore-hopping* to Lucius (108); after he leaves, says she can not do without him (113); for third time tells Boon to marry Corrie (135); her house is on Catalpa Street (139); arrives in Parsham with Minnie; registers as Mrs. Binford (199); sends Butch packing (210-211).

Minnie (100)   : black maid at Miss Reba's (99); has gold tooth (100); married twice (135); arrives in Parsham with Miss Reba (199); Otis stole her gold tooth (200); tooth restored (278).

              Binford (99): Miss Reba's "landlord" (99); tells Lucius that Boon is whore-hopping (108); fights with Reba at dinner; leaves (111-113); Miss Reba's pimp and lover; only vice is horse racing (113-114).

Vera (101)   : one of Miss Reba's whores; visiting her folks in Paducah; Boon and Lucius use her room to change (101).

              : another prostitute at dinner in Miss Reba's; wears red dress (109).

              : another prostitute at dinner; wears pink dress (109).

Birdie Watts (110): madam of whorehouse across street from Miss Reba's (110).

              : man who jumps switch and removes car (117); white man with whom Bobo gets mixed up (287 ff.).

              McCaslin (120): Cousin Zack Edmonds's uncle (120) [Zack Edmonds's literal uncle was either Uncle Buck or Uncle Buddy, who are great-uncles; perhaps F. means L.Q.C. McCaslin.]

Colonel (181)   Linscomb (181): rich white man in Parsham; owns blood horse that twice has defeated Ned's horse (119, 128); arrives at racetrack (268); a lawyer (284).

              Van Tosch (269): owner of horse that Ned acquires (128); from Memphis (269).

Sam (131) Caldwell (152): flagman on train to New York; customer of Corrie (130); agrees to put horse in boxcar to Parsham (135); walks with Boon and Corrie to railroad (139); attends race (235).

              : railroad division superintendent; uncle of Sam (130).

_____: Minnie's two husbands (135).

_____: policeman they meet on way to railroad (140).

Aunt Fittie (143)_____: woman Otis lives with in Arkansas (143); makes Corrie a whore after her mother dies (156).

Charley (148)_____: switchman in railroad yard; helps load horse (143).

_____: grandmother of Corrie (155).

_____: mother of Corrie (156).

_____: conductor on train to Parsham (164).

_____: engineer on train to Parsham (164).

_____: other railroad man on train to Parsham (164).

Lycurgus (168) Briggins (247): 19-year-old black youth; meets horse in Parsham (165); grandfather Parsham Hood is Mason (167); recovers Minnie's gold tooth (282).

Uncle Parsham Hood (168): old black man; meets Ned, Lucius, and horse in Parsham; Mason (167); picks teeth with gold toothpick like grandfather (247).

Mary (248) Briggins (247): Uncle Parsham's daughter; mother of Lycurgus (171).

Butch (172) Lovemaiden (192): man with loud voice; almost as big and as ugly as Boon; sheriff; calls Boon Sugar Boy; holds Corrie by wrist (172); racist bully (173); returns in evening (206); tries to make Corrie leave with him (208-209); sent packing by Miss Reba (210-211); after Ned's arrest, says race will continue at second heat tomorrow (241); forces sex with Corrie; beaten by Boon (255).

_____: doctor who treats Lucius's hand (188).

_____: iron-gray woman at doctor's (189).

George Peyton (194): bird-dog fancier (194).

Virgil (208)_____: clerk in hotel in Parsham (195).

_____: black waiter in hotel in Parsham (195, 197).

Jackie (201)_____: whore in Miss Reba's (201).

_____: black cook in hotel in Parsham (203).

_____: two strangers who talk to Boon morning of race (215).

McWillie _____ (225): black youth who rides other horse (223).

_____: black stableman at Colonel Linscomb's (226).

Walter (226) Clapp (241): trainer of other horse (226); Akron (227); Acheron (236).

Bobo Beauchamp (229): cousin of Lucas Quintus Carothers McCaslin Beauchamp; motherless; raised by Aunt Tennie; came to Memphis three years earlier; used to work for man that owned Coppermine knows where auto is (229); gets mixed up with white man to whom he owes money (287); steals Van Tosh's horse (288).

Lucius (Lucas) Quintus Carothers McCaslin Beauchamp (229).

_____ Edmonds (229): mother of Sarah Edmonds Priest (229).

Aunt Tennie (229).

_____: spinster aunts of Lucius Priest [II] (234).

Ed (266) _____: judge of race; night telegraph operator at depot (235).

_____ McDiarmid (235): judge of race; runs depot eating room (235).

_____: steward and marshal of race; shoots quail for market; now out on bail in homicide (235).

_____: volunteer who replaces Ned as starter (237).

_____ Poleymus (254): man with Butch; arrests Ned (239); constable of the Beat (242).

_____ Poleymus (257): wife of constable (257).

_____: deputy to Poleymus; drives car (259).

_____: second man with Colonel Linscomb; declares second heat suspended; third heat will win all (269).

_____: Colonel Linscomb's chauffeur; McWillie's father (275);

_____ Linscomb (277): wife of Colonel Linscomb (277).

_____ Parsham (281): original family after which town was named (281).

_____: Colonel Linscomb's maid (284).

391

_____ Priest (285): father of Boss Priest; color sergeant; shot in Civil War (285).

_____: white man to whom Bobo Beauchamp owes money (287).

_____ Priest (285): mother of Boss Priest; died 1864 (285).

Miss (303) _____ Rhodes (303): teacher of Lucius Priest [II] (303).

_____: nurse to Boon's baby (304).

Lucius Priest Hogganbeck (305): child of Boon and Everbe (305).

Writing and publishing history appears before each story.

Pagination, in parentheses, to the following edition (New York: Vintage Books, 1981), 716 pp., ed. Joseph Blotner, paperback edition; (New York: Random House, 1979), 716 pp., ed. Joseph Blotner, and to the following reissues (London: Chatto and Windus, 1980), 716 pp. For Miss Zilphia Gant, see A 10 above; for Idyll in the Desert, see A 9 above.

"Ambuscade"

Written in the spring of 1934; first published in *The Saturday Evening Post*, **207 (September 29, 1934), 12-13, 80, 81; revised for** *The Unvanquished*, **1938.**

Bayard (4) Sartoris (9): narrator; 12 years old (3); son of John Sartoris (4); with Ringo, sits and observes as father, Joby, and Louvinia prepare to bury silver (6); feels he must watch Loosh (7); after hearing Loosh tell of approach of Yankees, tells Miss Rosa (8-9); with Ringo, watches road for Yankees; falls asleep and dreams of destruction of house; sees Yankee in road (9); with Ringo, runs to house; takes musket; shoots at Yankee (10); tells Granny, "We shot the bastud;" hidden by Granny under her skirts (11); mouth washed with soap by Granny for saying "bastud" (16).

Loosh (3): slave; announces that Vicksburg has fallen and Yankees are at Corinth (3); son of Louvinia (7); husband of Philadelphy; at night, rides mule toward Corinth; returns after dark next day; announces that they will be free (8).

Philadelphy (3): slave of John Sartoris (3).

John (4) Sartoris (9): father of Bayard; away at war in Tennessee (4); returns riding Jupiter; with son and slaves, builds pen in creek bottom for livestock (5); announces that Vicksburg has fallen; after burying silver, leaves (6).

Ringo (4) Marengo (6): slave companion to Bayard (4); agrees that they must watch Loosh (7); with Bayard, watches road for Yankees (9); with Bayard, shoots at Yankee (10); hidden by Granny under her skirts (11); mouth washed with soap by Granny for saying "bastud" (16).

Louvinia (4): slave (4); wife of Joby; mother of Loosh (7).

Rosa (5) [Millard]: narrator's grandmother (4); after Ringo and Bayard fire at Yankee officer, hides them beneath her skirts (11); lies to protect the boys (12); offers Yankee colonel drink of milk (14-15); after he leaves, accuses Ringo and Bayard of cursing; admits lying; kneels and prays with them; washes their mouths with soap (16).

Joby (5): slave (5); with Loosh, loads wagon with wood (7).

Sergeant (12)   Harrison (13): Yankee sergeant; announces that boys shot a horse, not a man (12).

_____: Yankee colonel (13); knows that Granny is hiding boys under skirts; takes her word that they are not there (13).

_____: Yankee general referred to by Sgt. Harrison (13).

"Retreat"

Written in spring, 1934; first published in _The Saturday Evening Post_, **207 (October 13, 1934), 16-17, 82, 84, 85, 87,89; revised for** _The Unvanquished_, **1938.**

Bayard (28) Sartoris (20): narrator (17); accompanies Granny to Memphis in wagon (20); now 14 (22); takes Sartoris dirt with him (23); after Yankees steal their mules, with Ringo, steals old white horse and tracks them (26); father finds him (27); returns home with father (32); Yankees set house on fire (34-35); calls Yankees "bastuds" (36).

Rosa (19) [Millard]: Granny (grandmother of narrator); plans to take trunk of silver to Memphis; plans digging up trunk (17); says she dreamed that a black man, whom she knows, goes to where silver is buried and points at it; will not reveal name (18); orders Joby and Loosh to carry trunk upstairs to her room (19); insists on taking musket with them; leaves with Joby, Bayard, and Ringo (20); on journey, refuses to sleep in houses; sleeps rather in bed of wagon by trunk (23); John Sartoris's mother-in-law; ignores warning not to go to Memphis (24); tries to beat off Yankees who steal her mules (25); returns with strange horses in wagon; buries trunk again (32); says she "borrowed" the horses (33); says Loosh showed Yankees where silver is buried (34); calls Yankees who burned Sartoris, "bastuds" (36).

Ringo (17): slave (17); son of Joby; brother of Loosh (18); accompanies others in wagon to Memphis (20); shares Bayard's Sartoris dirt (23); tracks mules with Bayard (26); found by John Sartoris (27); returns home (32); calls Yankees who burned house, "bastuds" (36).

Louvinia (17): slave (17).

Joby (17): slave (17); with Loosh, digs up trunk of silver; carries it to Granny's room (18-19); drives wagon (20); sleeps under wagon with musket (23).

Loosh (17): slave (17); with Joby, digs up trunk of silver (18); after Yankees burn house, says he has been freed; leaves with Philadelphy (35).

Colonel (22) John (17) Sartoris (20): voted down to major by his own men (21); returns and raises a cavalry unit; receives title of colonel (22); finds son and Ringo (27); takes Ringo and Bayard back home (28 ff.); as they ride, comes upon Yankee troop; bluffs them; takes their pants and boots (30); returns home with boys (32); sitting on porch when Yankees ride up (33); escapes riding Jupiter bareback (34).

Mrs. (20)   Compson (20): gives basket of food and bottle of wine to Granny (23).

Uncle Buck [Theophilus] McCaslin (20): makes   speech   about   John Sartoris (21).

_____: Captain of CSA company in Jefferson (21).

_____: man who succeeds John Sartoris as colonel (21).

_____: Confederate officer; warns them not to try to reach Memphis (24).

_____: Rosa's sister in Memphis (24).

_____: five Yankee soldiers who steal Rosa's mules (25).

_____: Yankee captain of troop John Sartoris captures (31).

Uncle Few Mitchell (34): a loony (34).

Philadelphy (35): slave; wife of Loosh; leaves with him (35).

"Raid"

Written in late spring of 1934; first published in *The Saturday Evening Post*, **207 (November 3, 1934), 18-19, 72, 73, 75, 77, 78; revised for** *The Unvanquished*, **1938.**

Bayard Sartoris (44): narrator;   walks   to   Jefferson   (four   miles); returns with hat, parasol, and hand mirror; after house is burned, lives in Joby's cabin (37); leaves with Granny (38-39); for several nights, they hear ex-slaves passing in road (40-41); reaches bridge as it is about to be blown up by Yankees (48-49); wagon and horses washed into river (50-51); rescued by Yankees (51).

Rosa (46) [Millard]: narrator's   grandmother;   writes   note   to   Mrs. Compson; borrows hat, parasol, and hand mirror from Mrs. Compson (37); leaves with Ringo and Bayard to find silver and stolen mules (38-39); insists on driving "borrowed" horses (39); stops at Hawkhurst (42); after they are rescued from river, asks to see Colonel Dick; taken to his tent (51); asks him for return of silver and mules, "Old Hundred" and "Tinney" (52); sends half the blacks home (55); arrives home with mules and horses; kneels in road and prays because she lied (57).

Mrs (37)   Compson (37): lends Granny hat, parasol, and hand mirror (37).

Ringo (37): slave (37); walks to Jefferson with narrator (37); takes over in requisitioning mules and food (54).

Louvinia (37): slave (37); wife of Joby (38).

Colonel Nathaniel G. Dick (37): Ohio cavalry; in "Ambuscade" knew Ringo and Bayard were hiding under Rosa's skirts (37); promises to restore silver and mules (52).

Joby (38): slave (38).

Uncle Buck [Theophilus McCaslin (38).

Loosh (38): slave; son of Joby and Louvinia; has run off (38).

_____: white woman and child; watch Granny and boys pass her burned-out house (40).

_____: slave woman with baby who falls behind others; rides in wagon until she reaches creek bottom; leaves them there (41).

Denny (42) [Hawk]: uncle to narrator; now dead (42).

Jingus (42): slave of Hawks (42).

Denny (42) [Hawk]: cousin of narrator; 10 years old (42); tells them about Drusilla's rescue of horse Bobolink (44).

Drusilla (Dru) (43) [Hawk]: cousin of narrator; best woman rider in country (44); wears pants; calls Bayard, John Sartoris; threatens to kill horse rather than let Yankees take it (44); describes slaves walking along road "Going to Jordan" (44-45); wakes boys at night to hear slaves moving along road; long speech about passing of old order; tells Bayard to tell his father that she wants to ride with his troop (47).

[Colonel] John Sartoris (44).

Gavin Breckbridge (44): engaged to Drusilla; killed at Shiloh (44).

_____: Yankee major; tries to have Drusilla turn ex-slaves back (45).

Louise (46) [Hawk]: called Aunt Louise by narrator; mother of Drusilla (46).

_____: orderly in Colonel Dick's tent (52).

Philadelphy (52): slave; wife of Loosh (52).

_____: sergeant who, on Colonel Dick's order, gives Granny ten trunks of silver and one hundred and ten ("Old Hundred" and "Tinney") mules (52-53).

_____: Lieutenant who participates (53).

_____: officer; gives them forty-seven more mules (54).

_____: final Yankee officer that Ringo talks out of horses (56).

_____: sergeant (56).

Captain (56)   Bowen (56): Union army officer (56).

"Skirmish at Sartoris"

Written late in 1934, and originally entitled "Drusilla;" first published in *Scribner's Magazine*, **97 (April, 1935), 193-200; revised for** *The Unvanquished*, **1938.**

Bayard (63) Sartoris (67): narrator (58); 15 at time (59); does not tell father that Drusilla wants to ride in his troop (60).

Colonel (67) John (Johnny) (59) Sartoris (67): father of narrator; leader of cavalry troop; has carpet bagger voting box (58); after war, returns with Drusilla (61); lives in cabin with Bayard and Drusilla (62); busy protecting Jefferson from carpetbaggers (66); tells two Burdens that there never will be an election with blacks voting (68); kills Burdens (70); with derringer, after letting them shoot first (71); not married to Drusilla (72).

Drusilla (58) Hawk (67): before Christmas, 1864 (58); cuts hair short; wears shirt and jeans pants the day she learned of Gavin Breckbridge's death; does not cry; wants to ride in John Sartoris's troop (59); disappears from house (60); lives openly in John Sartoris's troop; visits her mother; not ashamed (61); after war, returns with John Sartoris; sleeps behind quilt in same cabin (62); after Mrs. Habersham extends sympathy, runs to Louvinia's cabin; shocked that people will think that she and John Sartoris were cohabiting; cries in Louvinia's arms (65); beaten by ladies and her mother; made to wear a dress (67); not much older than Bayard [II] (68); says that she never lived with John Sartoris (68); wedding set for day of election (70); appointed voting commissioner by John Sartoris (71); not married to John Sartoris (73).

Louisa (58) Hawk (61): called "Aunt Louisa" by narrator (58); lives at Hawkhurst, Gihon County, Alabama; sends letter to Granny (59); earlier letter announces that Drusilla left home; wife of Dennison; mother of Drusilla and Denny; in letter, says that Drusilla and John Sartoris are living in "a word" that she would not repeat; that John Sartoris and Drusilla are not blood kin; writes third letter to Mrs. Compson after Drusilla and John Sartoris return home (61); letter calls on Mrs. Compson to do something about John and Drusilla living together (62-63); arrives from Alabama (65); with trunk full of Drusilla's dresses; in mourning (67); refuses to speak to anyone but Denny (68); asks John Sartoris if he will marry Drusilla (69).

Mrs. (58) Martha (64) Habersham (58): leads female delegation that comes out to Sartoris to save Drusilla's honor (63); approaches Drusilla to rescue her (64).

Ringo (59): slave companion to Bayard Sartoris; 15 years old (59).

[Rosa Millard]: grandmother of narrator; now dead (59).

Dennison (59) Hawk (67): uncle of narrator; husband of Louisa; father of Drusilla and Denny; killed at Shiloh (59).

Gavin Breckbridge (59): killed at Shiloh (59); fiance of Drusilla (60).

_____ Sartoris: dead wife of John Sartoris; cousin of Drusilla; mother of Bayard Sartoris (61).

Mrs. (61) _____ Compson (61): receives letter from Aunt Louisa; brings it to Sartoris; refuses to get out of surrey (62).

Louvinia (62): slave; wife of Joby (62).

Joby (62): slave; husband of Louvinia; father of Ringo (62).

_____ Compson (62): husband of Mrs. Compson; locked up as crazy long ago for shooting sweet potatoes off heads of black children with rifle (62).

_____: Mrs. Compson's black driver (63).

Cassius Q. Benbow (66): Uncle Cash; Acting Marshal of Jefferson; planning to be elected Marshal of Jefferson; formerly slave driver of Benbow's carriage (66).

_____ Benbow (66): white family name in Jefferson (66).

_____ Burden (66): carpetbagger from Missouri; to organize blacks to vote (66); dares John Sartoris to stop election (68); killed by John Sartoris (70).

_____ Burden (66): other carpetbagger from Missouri (66); killed by John Sartoris (70).

Dennison (69) (Denny 66) Hawk (67).

George Wyatt (71): tries to hold Druisilla; holds Bayard from entering hotel where John Sartoris kills Burdens (71).

_____: black porter in Holston House (71).

Mrs. (71) _____ Holston (71): owner of Holston House (71).

398

_____: northern white man with blacks after killing (71).

_____: the sheriff (72).

"The Unvanquished"

Written in September, 1934; first published in *The Saturday Evening Post,* **209 (November 14, 1936), 12-13, 121, 122, 124, 126, 128, 130; retitled** *"Riposte in Tertio,"* **and revised for** *The Unvanquished,* **1938.**

Ab Snopes (74): leaves for Memphis with mules; returns, having sold them for $450, $50 a mule; constantly chews; claims to have served in John Sartoris's troop (74, 76); tells Rosa Millard (Granny) about Grumby's Independants (93); persuades her to "requisition" Grumby's thoroughbred stallion and three mares; promises her $1500 for them (94).

Ringo (74): slave companion to Bayard Sartoris (74); helps Granny burn out U. S. brand on stolen mules (75); reconoiters for Granny to U. S. Army troops to find mules (77); procured Army letterheads that Granny uses to requisition mules; writes orders for mules (79); signs order to give mules to "Miz Plurella Harris" (80); usually goes with Ab Snopes to sell mules (81); decoys Yankees (82-83); appears with "borrowed" buggy and drives Granny and narrator home (83); past 15 years old (85); draws picture of Sartoris house before it was burned (87); says Ab Snopes told Yankee officer where the mule pen was (92).

Joby (74): slave; father of Ringo (74).

[Bayard] Sartoris (76): narrator (74); past 15 years old (85); tries to disuade Granny from trying to get Grumby's horses (94-95); finds Granny murdered (96).

Rosa Millard (77): grandmother of narrator (74); requisitions Yankee mules by forging papers; burns out U. S. brands (75); has sold one hundred and five mules back to Yankees (76); for $6720.65 dollars (76); keeps record of mule raids on U. S. Army on window shade (78); with narrator, abandons wagon and hides in woods (82); returns home; on Sunday, goes to church (83); confesses to congregation that she has sinned (85); then distributes mules and money to members of congregation (86); after Yankee officer takes remaining mules, takes Ringo and narrator to church; confesses to sinning not for gain but for justice and to feed God's creatures (92, 93); agrees to Ab Snopes's plan to requisition Grumby's horses, so that she can give John Sartoris $1500 when he returns to rebuild plantation (94); thinks they will not hurt a woman (95); killed by Grumby (96).

Colonel (77) John Sartoris (76): narrator's father; tells Ab Snopes to look out for Granny when he is away (74).

Colonel G. W. Newberry (77): Yankee commander of Illinois infantry (77).

399

Colonel (79)_____ Dick (79): Yankee colonel; gives Granny first order to requisition mules and silver (79).

_____: two men who help Ab Snopes requisition mules (80).

Mrs. (80)_____ Compson (80): Jefferson lady; lends hat and parasol to Rosa Millard (80).

Denny (81) [Hawk]: narrator's cousin (81).

_____: Yankee officer who comes after Granny (83).

_____ Fortinbride (83): Methodist, private in Sartoris's regiment; wounded; lay minister (84).

Dr. (84)_____ Worsham (84): former Episcopal minister in Miss Rosa's church (84).

Loosh (85): slave; feeds John Sartoris's dogs (85).

Louvinia (85): slave.

_____: Yankee lieutenant; about 40 (87); orders men to search Sartoris for mule pen; someone (Ab Snopes?) told him where it is (88-89); takes remaining mules from lot (90); gives Granny voucher for $10 for fence he threw down (91).

_____: Confederate captain with Uncle Buck McCaslin (87).

Uncle Buck [Theophilus] McCaslin (87).

Louisa (93) [Hawk]: narrator's aunt (93).

Drusilla (93) [Hawk]: disappears from home; rides with John Sartoris's troop (93).

_____: black man burned to death by Grumby's men (93).

_____ Grumby (93): leader of Grumby's Independents, fifty or sixty men; pillagers (93); kills Rosa Millard (96).

"Vendee"

Written in September, 1934; completed October 18, 1934; first published in The Saturday Evening Post, **209 (December 5, 1936), 16-17, 86, 87, 90, 92, 93, 94; revised for** The Unvanquished, **1938.**

Bayard (109) Sartoris (117): narrator (97); wants to borrow pistol from Uncle Buck McCaslin; starts in search of Grumby (99); finds Grumby's horses in Ab Snopes's lot (100); tracks Grumby for about two months (102); cleanses Uncle Buck's wound (106); they find Ab Snopes lying on ground tied to a sapling (107); beats up Ab Snopes for sending

Granny to Grumby (109); with Ringo, continues to track Grumby (110); finds black man hanged by Grumby with warning note; and another warning by stranger (111); Grumby turned over to them by stranger (111-112); with Ringo, kills Grumby; nails his hide to cotton compress where he killed Rosa Millard; cuts off right hand and nails it to a board on Rosa Millard's grave (115-117).

Rosa Millard (98): narrator's grandmther; now dead (97); killed by Grumby (100).

_____ Fortinbride (97): stops other preacher from giving graveside sermon; gives sermon, a tribute to Granny, after burial (98).

Ab Snopes (97): found tied hand and foot by narrator and Ringo (107); beaten by Bayard; whipped by Ringo (109); leaves Ringo and Bayard to take Uncle Buck home (110).

Ringo (97): slave companion to Bayard Sartoris; as they search for Grumby, finds several men in a house (103); whips Ab Snopes for his part in Rosa Millard's death (108); with Bayard, continues to track Grumby after Uncle Buck and Ab Snopes return home (110); with Bayard, kills Grumby; nails hide to cotton compress where he killed Rosa Millard; cuts off right hand and nails it to board on Rosa Millard's grave (115-117).

_____: preacher from Memphis or somewhere; selected by Mrs. Compson to preach at funeral (97).

Mrs. (97) _____ Compson (97): arranges for strange preacher to preach at Rosa Millard's funeral (97).

Uncle Buck (98) [Theophilus] McCaslin (98): has rheumatism; will not let others spell him from shovelling earth into Rosa Millard's grave (98); when narrator tries to borrow pistol, says he is going with them (99); says that Ab Snopes will lead them to Grumby (101); shot by stranger (106); wounded arm makes him sick (107); says Ab Snopes made two mistakes: "being born too soon and dying too late" (108); arm gets worse; goes home with Ab Snopes (110).

John (116) Sartoris (117): Bayard's father (98); looking for Ringo and Bayard (116).

Yance (100): slave; helped Ringo and narrator build pen (100).

_____ Grumby (100): kills Rosa Millard (100); leaves note on hanged black man warning Ringo and Bayard (111); killed by Bayard and Ringo (115-117).

_____: woman at Ab Snopes's cabin; says he has gone to Alabama (101).

_____: young boy abused by Grumby (102).

401

_____: woman abused by Grumby (102).

Matt Bowden (114): stranger who appears in camp as they search for Grumby (103); says Grumby killed one of his blacks; is headed for Alabama; is going to recover stolen horses (104-105); warns them to take their revenge on Ab Snopes and to ignore Grumby (105); shoots Uncle Buck in arm (106); adds another warning note to Grumby's (111); finally turns Grumby over to Ringo and Bayard (111-112); throws gun to Grumby; leaves with Bridger (113).

_____: one of Grumby's men captured by stranger (104).

_____: black man killed by Grumby (105).

_____: black man hanged by Grumby (111).

_____ Bridger (112): one of Grumby's men with stranger when Grumby is turned over to Ringo and Bayard (111-112).

Drusilla (116) [Hawk]: with John Sartoris, looks for Bayard and Ringo (116).

Louvinia (116): slave.

Joby (116): slave.

"Fool about a Horse"

Written probably about March, 1935; first published in *Scribner's Magazine*, **100 (August, 1936), 180-186; revised for** *The Hamlet*, **1940.**

_____: narrator (118); with father, sets out from town with mother's separator money (119-120); $27.65 (121); 12 years old (126); watches "new" horse lose its color in rain; wakes father to see horse (132).

_____: narrator's father (Pap) (118); prides himself on his "eye for horse flesh" (118-119); swaps several items to Beasley Kemp for a horse that he got from Pat Stamper; lives in Frenchman's Bend (119); stung to horse trading by Jody Varner's history of the horse (122); decides to trade horse back to Pat Stamper (123); halts outside town; sends son in to buy saltpeter, tar, and a fish hook; goes to Pat Stamper (124); says he must trade such a spirited horse (125); trades horse and mule for a team of mules (126); when mules collapse, sends son for whisky returns to Pat Stamper to trade for original team; offers four dollars and mules (129); thrown twice by horse; after drinking, takes separator out of wagon and returns to town; returns without separator; gets bottle of whisky from Stamper; drives off with new horse and mule (130-131); drunk, sleeps in wagon bed in rain; awakened by son; discovers that Stamper traded his original horse back to him (132).

Vynie (118) _____: narrator's mother (Mammy) (118); took four years to save separator money from egg and quilt money (121); cries when Pap returns without separator (133); leaves on mule leading horse; returns with separator but no team (133).

Pat Stamper (118): horse trader (118); never bought horse or mule outright; swaps for them (123); insists on trading Pap team for team (125); trades team of mules for Pap's horse and mule (126); when Pap returns, says he traded original horse; offers another horse with original mule; offers very fat horse (130); it is the original horse, dyed black and inflated by means of a hand pump valve behind leg (132-133).

Beasley Kemp (118): trades horse to Pap (118); paid Herman Short $8 for horse last summer (122).

Anse Holland (118): "Old Man Anse Holland" (118).

_____: neighbors who look at horse (119).

Uncle Ike McCaslin (121): owns hardware store (121).

_____ Varner (120): owns store in Frenchman's Bend (120).

Jody Varner (122): says Herman Short swapped Pat Stamper buckboard and set of harness for horse five years ago (122).

Herman Short (122): swapped Pat Stamper buckboard and harness for horse (122).

Jim (130)_____: black assistant to Pat Stamper (123); has given mules just enough stimulant to reach town (129).

_____ Hoke (123): owns pasture (123).

Doc (129)_____ Peabody (129): owns store; sells whisky (129).

Odum Tull (133): brings Vynie and separator home in wagon (133).

"Lizards in Jamshyd's Courtyard"

Begun as early as late 1920's as "Omar's Eighteenth Quatrain;" on sending schedule May 16 or 27, 1930; first published in *The Saturday Evening Post*, **204 (February 27, 1932), 12-13, 52, 57; revised for** *The Hamlet*, **1940.**

_____: narrator (135).

_____: builder of Old Frenchman Place (136).

_____: English architect; laid out grounds of Old Frenchman Place (136).

_____ Varner (136): present owner of Old Frenchman Place

(136); owner of store in Frenchman's Bend (138); politician; veterinary; Methodist lay preacher (139).

Henry Armstid (136): has been digging on Old Frenchman Place for a week; people come to watch him (136); at first attacks viewers; then ignores them (137); flashback: poor farmer; with Suratt and Tull, watches Flem Snopes dig at night (142); begins digging before Uncle Dick starts to dowse (144); threatens others (145); will not tell others how many coins his sack holds (146); gives Flem Snopes $1000 note secured by a second mortgage on farm (149-150); never admits to being fleeced; keeps digging (151).

_____ Armstid (137): wife of Henry Armstid; brings food to him in field in which he digs (137).

_____ Armstid (138): their children; four of them under 6 years old (138).

_____: northerner who wants to buy goats (most likely fictional) in Suratt's plan to fleece Flem Snopes (138).

Flem Snopes (138): runs Varner's store; buys goats from at least two goat breeders (139); gives Suratt $21 for contract he paid $20 for (140); buys Old Frenchman Place from Varner [sic] (140); begins digging at night (142); says he wants to sell Old Frenchman Place; wants $3000 for it (149).

_____ Suratt (138): fooled by Flem Snopes; sewing machine agent; drives buckboard; trades in land, livestock and farm tools; reaches Varner's store every six weeks (138); says he plans to sell one hundred goats to northerner in order to sucker Flem Snopes into buying them (139); after selling $20 contract to Flem Snopes for $21, gives extra dollar to children; believes legend that Old Frenchman Place has hidden treasure (140); part owner of restaurant in Jefferson; when he learns that Flem Snopes bought Old Frenchman Place from Varner, visits him at Varner's (141); with Armstid and Tull, watches Snopes digging at night (142); says they must get Uncle Dick to find buried treasure (143); as they dig, Uncle Dick senses someone watching them; hears horse galloping away (146); sack he finds contains $25; they feel that they must buy Old Frenchman Place (146-147); next day, visits Flem (147); teases Flem about goats (148); offers to buy house and gardens of Old Frenchman Place (149); gives Flem Snopes note for $1000, secured by lien on his half of restaurant (149-150); realizes he has been fleeced by old salted-ground trick when he discovers that the oldest coin in his sack was minted in 1896 (151).

_____: small boy questioned by Suratt (140).

_____: boy and girl to whom Suratt gives dollar (140).

_____: Suratt's brother-in-law; part owner of restaurant (141).

Vernon Tull (142): well-to-do bachelor; with Suratt and Armstid, watches Flem dig at night (142); his sack contains $25 (147); gives Snopes note for $1000 (149); realizes he has been fleeced when he discovers that the oldest coin was minted in 1901 (151).

Uncle Dick (143)_____: uses divining rod; hired by Suratt and others (143); aged; lives alone in swamp; sells charms; eats frogs and snakes; says that Henry must stop digging so that he can work (144); with forked peach branch, finds coins with which Flem has salted the earth (145); as they dig, senses another watching them; finds two more sacks of coins (146).

Eustace Grimm (147): watches Suratt and others as they dig; some kind of kin to Snopes (150).

Lon Quick (147): lives in Frenchman's Bend (147).

_____Quick (147): son of Lon Quick (147).

Mrs. (147)_____Littlejohn (147): owns boarding house in Frenchman's Bend (147).

"The Hound"

On sending schedule November 17, 1930 entitled "Hound;" first published in *Harper's Magazine*, 163, (August, 1931), 266-274; reprinted in *Doctor Martino and Other Stories*, 1934; revised for *The Hamlet*, 1940.

Ernest (157) Cotton (152): fires gun; kills man (152-153); bachelor; hears man's dog baying at night (153); has "never known a negro himself;" goes after dog to silence it; finds body of man he shot (154); puts body in hollow tree; stands on it to press it down; almost trapped in tree with body; finally climbs out (155); as he tries to sleep, hound begins to howl again (156); when men discuss Houston's disappearance, says they are better off without him (157); had won suit against Houston for wintering his hog; awarded a dollar (158); finds dog at night; shoots it, but can not find body; throws shotgun into slough; goes home to bed; returns to Varner's store; denies ownership of shotgun which was found by a black (159); watches buzzards circle over body; that night, hears hound howling again; takes axe; as he starts to chop down hollow tree, dog attacks him; wounds dog with axe; removes body from tree trunk (160-161); drags body to stream; as he hurls it in with one limb missing, dog again attacks; returns to tree to get other limb; attacked again by dog; arrested by sheriff at tree (162); tries to commit suicide by wedging neck and throwing body out of car (163); in jail, says it would have been all right if body had not come apart (164).

_____Houston (156): man killed by Cotton (153); bachelor (156).

_____Varner (152): owns store (152).

405

_____: sheriff; fat; says that Houston did not run away (156); arrests Cotton (162).

_____: first man at Varner's store (156).

_____: second man at Varner's store (156); raises questions about Houston's disappearance, his horse, his dog (158).

_____: third man at Varner's store (156).

_____: fourth man at Varner's store (157).

Joe (163) _____: deputy sheriff; drives sheriff (158).

_____ Snopes (159): clerk in Varner's store; gives shotgun back to Cotton; it was returned by black who found it in slough (159).

Vernon Tull (159): identifies shotgun as Cotton's (159).

_____: black squirrel hunter; finds Cotton's shotgun (159).

_____: second deputy (162).

_____: doctor; treats Cotton after suicide attempt (163).

"Spotted Horses"

This story was conceived as early as late 1926 in a work then called *Father Abraham* (eventually published in 1983); recast under the title "As I Lay Dying," some years later, and still later as "Abraham's Children;" probably by November 23, 1928, it was submitted to *Scribner's* under the earlier title, "As I Lay Dying;" rewritten under title "The Peasants," it was again submitted to *Scribner's*; it was revised and renamed "*Aria Con Amore*," and sent to *The Saturday Evening Post* on February 3, 1931; a final revision under title "Horses," was finished by February 20, 1931; first published in *Scribner's*, 89 (June 1931), 585-597; revised for *The Hamlet*, 1940.

[V. K. Suratt]: first-person narrator (165); sells sewing machines (174); jumps out window of room when horse enters (175); helps carry Henry Armstid into Mrs. Littlejohn's (176); admires Flem's ability to beat neighbors in trades and schemes (183).

Flem Snopes (165): (twins mentioned [165]); marries Eula Varner; goes to Texas (166-167); returns with stranger and about twenty-four Texas ponies (167); no one knows if he owns these horses (168); after all, denies he owned any of them (181); when Mrs. Armstid asks for her money, says the man from Texas took it with him; gives Mrs. Armstid sack of candy for "the chaps" (182).

Jody Varner (165).

Uncle Billy (166) Will (177) Varner (166): owns store in Frenchman's Bend; father of Jody (166); veterinarian; called to tend Armstid (177).

Eula Varner Snopes (166): "that gal of Uncle Billy Varner's;" sister of Jody; youngest one; suitors are many; outwait each other; fight; as suitors flee to Texas, marries Flem Snopes (166); goes to Texas with him; returns with baby (167).

_____ Snopes (167): Eula's baby (167).

_____: stranger; Texan; accompanies Flem and spotted horses (167); starts auction of spotted horses (168); catches one and displays it (168-169); eats gingersnaps (168); gives Eck Snopes horse to start bidding (170); sells all horses for $3 or $4 each (171); after Henry hits his wife with rope, leads him out of lot; gives $5 to Mrs. Armstid; after Henry gives $5 to Flem, says Flem will give money back tomorrow (173).

Mrs. (167) _____ Littlejohn (167): owns boarding house in Frenchman's Bend (167).

Eck Snopes (168): cousin of Flem Snopes (168); given horse to start auction (170); buys another; recovers one that broke its neck (180).

Henry Armstid (168): starts to bid on spotted horses (170); bids their last $5 for horse; threatens others if they outbid him (171); tries to get his horse out of lot with wife to help; hits wife because she can not hold horse in corner (172); takes $5 bill from wife; gives it to Flem Snopes (173); while others go to buy ropes, enters lot alone; leaves gate open; spotted horses escape (174); overrun by horses; injured; carried to bed in Mrs. Littlejohn's (176-177); screams as Will Varner begins to tend him; leg broken (178).

Mrs. Henry Armstid (169): earns money by weaving at night (170); convinced that Snopes will not return her money (179); asks Flem for the money (182).

_____ Armstid (170): children of Henry Armstid (170); oldest a girl about 12 (178).

Ina May Armstid (179): oldest of Armstid children; takes care of younger children (179).

Ad (175) Snopes (173): son of Eck Snopes; buys more gingersnaps for man from Texas (173); horse jumps over him twice (174-175).

I. O. Snopes (174): clerk in Varner's store (174).

Mrs. (174) _____ Bundren (174): customer of the narrator (174).

Vernon Tull (175): overrun by Eck Snopes's spotted horse (176).

407

Mrs. Vernon Tull (175): his wife (175).

                    Tull (176): three daughters of Vernon Tull (176).

                    : Mrs. Vernon Tull's aunt (176).

Lon (180) Quick (177): helps carry Henry Armstid to Mrs. Littlejohn's (177).

                    Winterbottom (177): at Mrs. Littlejohn's when Henry Armstid is carried in (177).

Ernest (177)   : at Mrs. Littlejohn's (177).

                    Durley (177): at Mrs. Littlejohn's (177).

                    Samson (180): lives near Frenchman's Bend (180).

                    Freeman (180): lives near Frenchman's Bend (180).

"Lion"

Written about March, 1935; first published in *Harper's Magazine*, **172 (December, 1935), 67-77; revised for "The Bear" in** *Go Down, Moses*, **1942**

Quentin (186)   : first-person narrator; just 16; goes to Memphis with Boon to buy more whisky (184); placed on stand in hunting Old Ben by Ike McCaslin (191); returns to woods with Boon to hunt squirrels (198); realizes that the woods will never be the same (199); finds Boon under gum tree (200).

Boon Hogganbeck (184): with narrator, sent to Memphis for more whisky; part Indian (184); about 40 years old; works for Major de Spain; later marshal at Hoke's (185); vies with Ad to get Lion to sleep with him (186); after purchasing the suitcase full of whisky, buys bottle for himself; drinks it all before they return to Hoke's (188); can not shoot; once shot a black man and wounded a black woman (189); returns to camp from hunting Old Ben, badly wounded and carrying Lion; goes on mule for doctor (194-195); kills Old Ben with knife; returns with doctor (196); after Lion's death, gets quite drunk (197); now marshal at Hoke's (198); sits under gum tree full of squirrels, hammering at "his broken gun" (200).

Major [Cassius] de Spain (184): sends Boon to Memphis for more whisky (184); after Lion's death, never returns to hunt (197).

                : Boon Hogganbeck's grandmother; a Chickasaw woman, niece of the chief (184).

                : Chickasaw chief (184).

Ad (185)_____: black camp cook (185); vies with Boon to get Lion to sleep with him (186).

Uncle Ike McCaslin (186): good hunter (186); instructs narrator as he puts him on stand (191).

_____: conductor on log train (187).

_____: brakeman on log train (187).

_____: news butch (188).

_____: man in uniform in washroom (188).

_____: waitress in restaurant; tells Boon he can not drink there (188).

_____: black man shot in face by Boon (189).

_____: black woman accidentally shot by Boon (189).

_____: narrator's father (193).

Theophilus McCaslin (194): uncle Ike's grandson [Note!] (194).

_____: doctor who tends Lion (196).

_____: Major de Spain's secretary (198).

"The Old People"

Written about May-June, 1939; it was first published in *Harper's Magazine*, 171 (September, 1940), 418-425; reprinted in *O. Henry Memorial Award Prize Stories of 1941*, selected and edited by Herschel Brickell (Garden City, New York: Doubleday, Doran and Company, Inc., 1941), pp. 155-169; revised for *Go Down, Moses*, 1942.

Sam Fathers (201): teaches narrator to hunt; marks his face with blood when he kills first deer (201); part black, part Chickasaw; past 70; has no children (202); teaches narrator the woods to hunt (203-204); tells narrator stories about The People (204); flashback: after Jobaker's death, asks to live in the big bottom (205); stays in hunting camp all year (206); initiation to manhood ritual by killing first buck (207); at sight of great buck, salutes him, "Oleh, Chief, grandfather" (214).

_____: first-person narrator (201); 12 years old; shoots first deer (201-202); taught the woods and to hunt by Sam Fathers (202-203); 9 at time Sam Fathers goes to live at the hunting camp (205); now 12 (209); with Sam Fathers, sees the great buck (210); tells his father (212).

Jimbo (202)_____: beats hounds back (202).

Boon Hogganbeck (202): beats hounds back (202); faithful to narrator's father and Major de Spain; absolutely dependent on them for his very bread (203).

_____: narrator's father (202); tells son that he experienced the same sight of the big buck with Sam Fathers after he killed his first deer (212).

Major [Cassius] de Spain (202): owns hunting camp (202).

Walter Ewell (202): rifle never misses (202); shoots small buck (211).

_____: narrator's grandfather (202).

Ikkemotubbe (Doom) (202): grandfather of Sam Fathers; son of sister of Issetibbeha; ran away to New Orleans as a youth; returned seven years later; poisons puppies; after Moketubbe's abdication, becomes The Man; also said to be Sam Fathers' father (203).

Issetibbeha (202): Chickasaw chief; uncle of Ikkemotubbe (202).

_____: sister of Issetibbeha; mother of Ikkemotubbe (202).

Chevalier Soeur-Blonde de Vitry (202).

_____: slave woman; Sam Father's grandmother [?] (202); pregnant with Doom's child; married to slave and sold with him and son to narrator's great-grandfather (203).

Moketubbe (202): head of Chickasaw clan (202); abdicates after Doom kills another puppy (203).

_____: 8-year-old son of Moketubbe; dies suddenly (202).

_____: male slave married to Sam Fathers's mother; sold with wife and Sam to great-grandfather of narrator (203).

_____: narrator's great-grandfather (203).

_____: Boon Hogganbeck's Chickasaw grandmother (203).

Jobaker (204) Joe Baker (210): full Chickasaw friend of Sam Fathers (204); disappears; presumed dead; grave not found (204-205).

Uncle Ike McCaslin (205): hunter (205).

Uncle Ash (205)_____: cook in Major de Spain's camp (205).

"A Point of Law"

Written probably by mid-August, 1939; sent to agent January 4, 1940; first published in *Collier's*, **105 (June 22, 1940), 20-21, 30, 31; revised for**

Go Down, Moses, **1942.**

Lucas (213) Luke (214) Beauchamp (221): black   farmer;   sharecropper
on Roth Edmonds's land; moonshiner (213); does not want daughter to
marry George Wilkins; wants to drive George Wilkins off Edmonds place;
at least 60; becomes a "nigger" when he tells Roth Edmonds of George
Wilkins's still; says he never had anything to do with whisky (214);
follows Nat at night; dismantles still and hides it (215); wakes to find
George Wilkins's still on back porch; arrested and brought before federal
commissioner (216); learns that "a man's kinfolk can't tell on him in
court" (218); says he is going to let Nat and George Wilkins get married
(219); three weeks later, they come to trial (220); produces marriage
certificate for George and Nat dated October of the previous year (221);
watches George Wilkins take his mare and put her in a spring wagon
(223); when he learns that George Wilkins has spent the money on a still,
tells him where to hide it (224).

Nat (213) Nathalie Beauchamp Wilkins (221): Lucas's   daughter,   black
(213); follows father; learns where he hides his still; arrested by sheriff
(216); negotiates for well, stove, and repair of back porch before agreeing
to marry George Wilkins (220); marries George Wilkins (221); youngest and
last child of Lucas Beauchamp (222).

[Mollie] Beauchamp 221): wife of Lucas (213).

Roth (213) Carothers (214) Edmonds (213): Lucas's   landlord;
quick-tempered; calls sheriff about George Wilkins's still (215).

George Wilkins (213): sharecropper   on   Roth   Edmonds's   land;
moonshiner; rival to Lucas (213); arrested by sheriff (216); says it was
Nat's idea to put still and whisky on Lucas's back porch; hoped to
convince him to lend them money and let them get married (219); marries
Nathalie Beauchamp; borrows Lucas's mare (221); spends money Lucas gave
him to fix porch (223) to buy another still (224).

_____Beauchamp (221): daughter of Lucas who has a child
(214).

_____: Lucas's grandchild (214).

Zack (222) Edmonds (214): father of Roth Edmonds (214).

_____: sheriff (215).

_____: deputy sheriff (216); plump voluble man; describes the
finding of the two stills (217).

Tom (218)_____: federal commissioner (216); says Nat can testify
against George and George against Lucas (218).

Judge (218)_____Gowan (218): federal judge (218); dismisses case
against Lucas and George (222-223).

Henry (221)_____: deputy marshal at court (221).

_____: clerk who signed wedding certificate (222).

_____: U. S. Attorney (222).

_____: man who sells George second still (224).

"Gold is Not Always"

Written before mid-February, 1940; first published in *The Atlantic Monthly,* **166 (November, 1940), 563-570; revised for** *Go Down, Moses,* **1942.**

Lucas (226) [Beauchamp]: black; at least 60; asks Edmonds to lend him $300 to buy divining machine (226-227); after failing to persuade salesman to use machine on an equal share basis, offers to swap mule for it; swaps Edmonds's mule for machine (229); signs bill of sale for mule (231); sends George to town for fifty silver dollars to salt the earth and trick salesman (233); finds first batch of salted coins; as salesman gets excited, bargains for half of what they find, the bill of sale for mule, and bill of sale for divining machine (235-236); gets what he wants; tells George Wilkins to take mule back to Roth Edmonds (236); now rents divining machine to salesman for $25 a night; wears heavy gold watch chain and expensive beaver hat (237).

_____: salesman; not yet 30 (226); sells divining machines (227); from St. Louis (228); tells Edmonds he bought mule from Lucas (231); rents machine to Lucas for $25 a night (233); tricked by Lucas with salted earth; agrees to give bill of sale for the divining machine next morning (236); tricked by Lucas (237).

Roth (236) Edmonds (226): Lucas's landlord; refuses to lend Lucas money (226) discovers mule missing; tracks mule (229); finds Lucas and George Wilkins with divining machine; tells Lucas to return mule to stall by sunup (231); when Lucas finally tells him of salesman renting machine, orders him out of commissary; never to return (237).

_____: two white strangers reputed to have dug up $22,000 in buried treasure (227).

_____ Edmonds (227): Roth Edmonds's father (227).

George Wilkins (228): Lucas's son-in-law (227).

Dan (230)_____: black stableman for Edmonds (229).

Oscar (230)_____: black stableman for Edmonds (229).

_____: sheriff in Jefferson (230).

412

"Pantaloon in Black"

Written before March 18, 1940; first published in *Harper's Magazine*, **181 (October, 1940), 503-513; revised for** *Go Down, Moses*, **1942.**

Spoot (249) Rider (238): black man at wife's grave; grieving; shovels dirt into grave; over six feet; more than two hundred pounds (238); head of mill gang; returns home after funeral (239); rents house from white landlord; now 24; very strong; marries Mannie; reforms life; repairs house; on wedding night builds fire on hearth in imitation of Lucas Beauchamp (240); has vision of dead wife; she fades (242); tries to eat, but can not; walks; sleeps on ground; arrives at mill (243); eats from fireman's bucket; goes to work (244); angry with God (245); picks up huge log with bare hands and heaves it from truck (245-246); goes to bootlegger for jug of whisky (246); after he drinks, says, "Try me, big boy" (247); continues to drink; vomits three times (248); goes to his aunt's house; defies God; returns to sawmill after midnight; continues to drink; joins dice game (250); catches white night watchman cheating at dice; kills him by cutting throat with razor (251); lynched by hanging with bell rope in black schoolhouse (252); tears jail cell door off its hinges; says he is not trying to escape; subdued by fellow black prisoners (255).

Mannie Rider (238): dead wife of Spoot Rider (238); appears to Rider after burial; then fades (242).

_____: member of Rider's sawmill gang; offers to take shovel from him (238).

_____: Rider's aunt; raised him (238); exhorts him to seek God's help (249); locked up with him in jail (254).

_____ Rider: Rider's parents (238).

Acey (239) _____: one of Rider's mill gang; tries to persuade him not to go home: "She be wawkin yit" (239).

Carothers Edmonds (240): landlord from whom Rider rents house (240).

Lucas Beauchamp (240): Edmonds's oldest tenant; built fire on his hearth forty-five years ago (240).

_____: black fireman at sawmill (243); gives lunch bucket to Rider (244).

_____: white foreman at mill (244).

_____: men in Rider's gang (244).

Uncle Alec (249) _____: husband of Rider's aunt; brings lunch to him day after funeral (245); tries to get him to return and not drink (248).

_____: white bootlegger or moonshiner from whom Rider buys whisky (246).

_____ Birdsong (252): white night watchman; carries pistol (250); says Rider is drunk; orders him away; cheats at dice; killed by Rider; throat cut with razor (251).

_____: sheriff's deputy who tells wife of lynching of Spoot Rider; says blacks are not human (252).

_____: wife of sheriff's deputy (252).

_____: forty-two Birdsongs; some of whom lynch Rider (252).

_____ Mayfield (252): sheriff (253); with deputy, arrests Rider (254).

_____ McAndrews (253): owner or manager of mill (253).

_____ Ketcham (254): jailor or turnkey (254).

"Go Down, Moses"

Written before July 19, 1940; first published in *Collier's*, **107 (January 25, 1941), 19-20, 45, 46; revised for** *Go Down, Moses*, **1942.**

Samuel Worsham (256) (Butch 258) Beauchamp (256): black prisoner; 26 years old; raised by grandmother; sentenced to death under another name; dies in electric chair for killing policeman (256); flashback: mother dies in childbirth; caught breaking into store; hits policeman; knocked out by policeman; escapes from jail; disappears (258); only child (261).

_____: armed guard outside cell (256).

_____: census taker (256).

_____: policeman killed by Samuel Worsham Beauchamp (256).

Mollie (257) Molly (264) Worsham Beauchamp (257): grandmother of Samuel Worsham Beauchamp; visits Gavin Stevens; intuitively knows her grandson is in trouble; asks Gavin Stevens to find him; sister of Hamp Worsham (258); over and over throughout, says Roth Edmonds sold her grandson into Egypt (264); before grandson's funeral, asks Wilmoth if he is going to give an account of funeral in paper (266).

Carothers (Roth) Edmonds (257): landlord of Mollie Beauchamp (257); had earlier ordered Samuel Worsham Beauchamp off his place (259).

Gavin Stevens (257): county attorney; prematurely gray; Phi Beta Kappa, Harvard; Ph. D. Heidelberg; translates Old Testament back into classic Greek (257); agrees to try to find Samuel Worsham Beauchamp

414

(258); visits editor of county weekly; lives in boarding house (259); takes up collection around square to bring Beauchamp's body home for burial to please Mollie Beauchamp (262-263); visits Miss Worsham's house that evening (263).

Hamp Worsham (258): Mollie Beauchamp's brother (258).

_____: District Attorney (258).

_____ Beauchamp: Mollie Beauchamp's daughter; mother of Samuel Worsham Beauchamp: dies in childbirth (258); oldest daughter (261).

_____: Samuel Worsham Beauchamp's father; now in jail for manslaughter (258).

_____: sheriff (259).

_____: grandfather of Miss Worsham (260).

_____ Wilmoth (260): editor of county weekly; very fat; gives Stevens press release about Samual Worsham Beauchamp (259).

[Lucas] Beauchamp (259): Mollie's husband (259); has money in bank (261).

_____ Rouncewell (259): owner of store broken into by Beauchamp (259).

Miss (260) Belle (266) Worsham (260): quite old; thin; erect; visits Gavin Stevens about Mollie Beauchamp; lives alone in house her father left her; she and Mollie grew up together; born in same month (260); says Mollie wants to bring body home (261).

_____ Worsham (260): father of Miss Worsham (260).

_____ Worsham (260): wife of Hamp (260); tremendous; in bright turban (263).

_____: parents of Mollie Beauchamp and Hamp Worsham; slaves; belonged to Miss Worsham's grandfather (260).

_____: warden at Joliet (260).

_____: District Attorney in Chicago (260).

_____: lawyer in Chicago who defends Samuel Worsham Beauchamp (260).

_____: black undertaker in Joliet (262).

_____: undertaker's men who lift casket out of train (265).

415

"Delta Autumn"

Written perhaps before May, 1940; received by Harold Ober December 16, 1940 first published in *Story*, **20 (May-June, 1942), 46-55; revised for** *Go Down, Moses*, **1942, and part of it was revised for** *Big Woods*, **1955.**

Uncle Ike (267) McCaslin (268): hunter for fifty years (267); while others set up tent in camp, swims horses across river (272); flashback: at 12, shoots first buck; face marked with blood by Sam Fathers in initiation to manhood ritual (273); owns house in Jefferson; had wife and children once [Note!] (274); stays in bed when others leave on first day in camp; is given envelope by Boyd to give to woman (276); gives envelope to her (277); discovers she is black; tells her to go away (278); tells her to go up North and marry a man of her own race; insists that she take Boyd's money (279); says Boyd shot a doe (280).

Don Boyd (268): son of Ike's old companion; driver of car; brakes suddenly; just past 40 (268); war hero in WW I (269); gives Ike an envelope of money to give to woman (270); father of her child (277); had seen her by side of road when he braked suddenly (278).

Will (269) Legate (268): son of Ike's old companion (268); teases Don Boyd about his affair with black woman (268-269).

_____: light colored black woman that Don Boyd met year before (268); comes to camp; carries baby; Boyd's child; Boyd's mistress; spent week with Boyd last November and lived with him six weeks in New Mexico (277); agreed that affair was over; was by side of road when Boyd saw her and braked; wrote to him; letter returned unopened; teaches school (278); takes money when Ike insists; leaves (279).

[Theophilus] McCaslin (269): Ike's father (269).

Isham (273) _____: oldest black servant in camp (273).

_____: youngest black servant in camp; stokes stove during night (273).

Major _____ de Spain (273): owner of hunting camp (273).

Sam Fathers (273): half Chickasaw Indian, half black; grandson of a chief; taught Ike McCaslin to shoot; marks his face with blood of first buck killed (273).

_____: grandfather of Sam Fathers; Chickasaw chief (273).

_____ McCaslin (274): Ike's wife (274).

_____ McCaslin (274): Ike McCaslin's children [Note!] (274).

_____: niece of Ike McCaslin's dead wife; keeps house for him (274).

_____: niece's family (274).

_____: black man who brings Boyd's mistress to camp in boat; her cousin (277).

_____: child of Boyd and black woman (277).

_____: black woman's aunt in Vicksburg; takes in washing (278).

_____: black woman's father; now dead (278).

"The Bear"

The first version of this story, "Lion," appears to have been written about March, 1935; first published as "Lion" in *Harper's Magazine*, 172 (December, 1935), 67-77. "The Bear" appears to have been started in the summer of 1941, as Faulkner revised material from "Lion" to become "The Bear" in *Go Down, Moses*, 1942. It was first published as "The Bear" in *The Saturday Evening Post*, 214 (May 9, 1942), 30-31, 74, 76, 77, two days before *Go Down, Moses and Other Stories* was published on May 11, 1942. Parts of "The Bear" were used in *Big Woods*, 1955.

_____: 10-year-old boy (281); on stand with Sam Fathers; senses presence of bear, Old Ben (282-283); with Sam, hunts bear on mule; finds tracks (284); next day, senses that bear is looking at him (285); tells Sam about bear; recognizes fear; next year in June, 11 years old (286); leaves camp each morning to search for Old Ben (287); leaves camp with no gun but only a compass (288); leaves watch, compass, and stick; relinquishes completely to wilderness; finds Old Ben's print (289); sees bear (290); two or more years pass; 14 now; has killed first buck; has had face marked with blood by Sam; now an excellent woodsman (290); sees Old Ben again (291); returns alone in April with fyce to hunt Old Ben (291-292); brings bear to bay with fyce; drops gun and rescues fyce as bear disappears; tells Sam that he did not shoot the bear either (292); thinks of Old Ben, Sam Fathers, and a mongrel dog who have taught him "humility through suffering and pride through the endurance" (294).

_____: father of boy (281); after boy brings Old Ben to bay but fails to shoot him, reads him Keats's "Ode on a Grecian Urn;" says Keats was talking about Truth (293-294); tells his son, "Courage, and honor, and pride and pity, and love of justice and of liberty. They all touch the heart and what the heart holds to becomes truth as far as we know truth" (295) [John Keats to Benjamin Bailey, 22 November 1817: "I am certain of nothing but of the holiness of the Heart's affections and the truth of Imagination-- what the imagination seizes as Beauty must be truth--whether it existed before or not--for I have the same Idea of all our Passions as of Love they are all in their sublime, creative of

417

essential Beauty."]

    Major (281) [Cassius] de Spain (281).

    General [Jason Lycurgus] Compson (281): brigade commander in 1865 (286).

    Tennie's Jim (282).

    Sam Fathers (282): son of slave woman and Chickasaw chief (282); says they do not have the dog yet (284); tells boy that bear will run over him because he knows he is the weakest (285); tells boy that gun keeps him from seeing bear (288); tells boy to be scared but not afraid (288); marks boy's face with blood after he kills first buck (290).

    _____: slave; mother of Sam Fathers (282).

    _____: Chickasaw chief; father of Sam Fathers (282).

    Uncle Ash (282): black cook in hunting camp (283).

    Walter (284) Ewell (287): hunter (287).

    Boon Hogganbeck (287).

    _____: boy's grandfather (289).

"Race at Morning"

Probably written in September, 1954; first published in *The Saturday Evening Post*, **227 (March 5, 1955), 26-27, 103, 104, 106; revised for** *Big Woods*, **1955.**

    _____: first-person narrator (296); can not write; 12 years old (296); does not go to school (297); hunts deer with Ernest (298); as he and Ernest try to jump bayou, they hit a vine and are flung backward (302); sights deer (305); says Ernest forgot to load his gun (306); returns to camp (307); after others leave camp, stays on with Ernest; adopted (informally) by Ernest (309); says Ernest removed shells from gun before shooting at deer (310).

    Ernest (296)_____: deaf; wears hearing aid without batteries (297); removes shells from gun (305); fires another three shots at deer (306); widower (308); says boy narrator is going to school next year (309).

    Roth Edmonds (296): hunter (296).

    Willy Legate (296): hunter (296).

    Walter Ewell (296): hunter (296).

    Simon (297)_____: black cook in hunting camp (297).

Uncle Ike McCaslin (297): hunter (297).

_____: narrator's mother went off with "Vicksburg roadhouse feller" (307).

_____: Vicksburg roadhouse feller (307).

_____: father of narrator (307).

_____: Ernest's wife now dead (308).

"Hog Pawn"

Written perhaps in October, 1954; it was sent to Harold Ober in January, 1955, who sent it out to magazines, but it was rejected; revised for *The Mansion*, **1959.**

Chick (327)_____: narrator, mostly third person, but speaks of "we" (311); nephew of Gavin (313); converts to first-person narrator (321); ex-soldier; major (326).

Otis Meadowfill (311): very unpleasant (311); retires to wheel chair (312); has flurry of taking two baths a day after bathroom is installed; reverts to one a week (313); can not sell property to oil company because he is on relief; tries to deed property to Essie; cannot because of legal technicality (314); finds Snopes's hog on property (316); takes .22 caliber rifle to hog; shoots hog with tiny shot (317); shot as he raises screen to shoot hog (324); blames McKinley Smith; not hurt by tiny shot (325).

_____ Meadowfill (311): wife of Otis Meadowfill; a "gray drudge" (311); refuses to leave house (313).

Essie Meadowfill (311) Smith (327): Otis Meadowfill's daughter; plain and mousey; valedictorian of high school class; highest grades; $500 scholarship; has job with telephone company; asks banker who gave $500 scholorship to lend her the money to put in a bathroom in house because all three (father, daughter, mother in that order) bathe in same water each Saturday night (311-312); meets Marine sergeant at bus stop (318); introduces him to father as her fiancee (319); marries him (327).

_____: banker; gives annual scholarship in memory of only son, Army pilot, killed in Pacific in WW II (311); lends money to Essie (312).

_____: son of banker; Army pilot; killed in Pacific in WW II (311).

McKinley Smith (319): demobilized Marine sergeant from Korean War (312); son of Arkansas tenant farmer; starts to build house (319); rents land to raise cotton (320); marries Essie Meadowfill (327).

419

_____: paralytic woman, now dead, from whose family Otis Meadowfill buys wheelchair (312).

Gavin (313)_____: uncle of narrator; advocates that wife and child kill Otis Meadowfill (313); advises Snopes to give hog away; wonders how, by giving hog away, Snopes can convince Meadowfill to sell land (322); waits in car outside Meadowfill's house (323); enters house and sees Meadowfill shot with tiny pellets as he raises screen to shoot at hog (324); takes booby trap to Snopes and forces him to deed his strip of land to Essie Meadowfill and release Meadowfill's land for sale (326); gives deed to Smith; tells him to marry Essie (327).

_____Snopes (314): owner of land adjacent to Meadowfill's; bachelor; oil company wants to buy his land, but can not without Meadowfill's permission (315); offers to release property with no charge to Meadowfill; frustrated in trying to get Meadowfill to sell land for gas station; lets hog wander to Meadowfill's orchard (316); hopes that Meadowfill will kill hog and so enable him to force Meadowfill to sell land to oil company and let Snopes sell his (318); stops letting hog into Meadowfill's orchard (320); goes to Gavin for legal advice about hog for $5 (321); gives hog to McKinley Smith; sets booby trap rifle to hit Meadowfill; intends McKinley Smith to be blamed (325).

_____: oil company's purchasing agent (315).

_____: small boy; owner of .22 caliber rifle; browbeaten out of it by Meadowfill (317).

_____: newsboy hired by Meadowfill to lace orchard with garbage to lure hog (318).

_____: carpenter who helps McKinley Smith build home (320).

_____: Baptist minister who marries Essie Meadowfill and McKinley Smith (327).

"Nympholepsy"

An expansion of "The Hill," written early in 1925; first published by James B. Meriwether in *Mississippi Quarterly*, 26 (summer, 1973), 403-409, and then in *A Faulkner Miscellany*, ed., James B. Meriwether (Jackson: University Press of Mississippi, 1974), pp. 149-155.

_____: wheat farmer (331); sees woman in distance; lust overtakes him (332); feels an "imminent Presence" about him; falls from log into river (334); in water, feels a female body; sees her climb opposite bank; removes shoes; pursues her across wheat field (335); loses her; grieves; Presence leaves him; walks to town (336).

_____: woman seen in distance by wheat farmer (332).

"Frankie and Johnny"

Written about 1925; first published by James B. Meriwether in *Mississippi Quarterly*, **31 (summer, 1978), 454-464.**

Frankie (339) Frances (343)_____: infant girl; daughter of prize fighter (338); as Johnny tries to pick her up, fights with him (339); kisses him; agrees to be Johnny's girl (340); pregnant; morning sickness (345); tells mother that she does not need Johnny or her (347).

_____: Frankie's father; prize fighter; drowned trying to save fat woman (338).

Frances (344)_____: Frankie's mother (338); seems to be a prostitute (342); leaves with boy friend for weekend (344).

_____: fat woman saved from drowning (338).

Johnny (339)_____: fellow of Frankie; tries to pick her up; fights with drunk (339); asks Frankie to be his girl (340); has job in garage (342).

_____: drunk who tries to interfere between Frankie and Johnny (339).

_____Ryan (340): policeman who knew Johnny's father (340).

_____: Johnny's father (340).

"The Priest"

Written about 1925; first published by James B. Meriwether with introduction and editorial corrections in *Mississippi Quarterly*, **29 (summer, 1976), 445-450.**

_____: completes novitiate; to be confirmed [?] tomorrow; hopes that his sexual desires will be chastened (348); aware that his fellow seminarians talk about women (349-350); walks streets wondering how many girls he sees have lovers (350); hopes to find relief from bodily desires in ordination; prays in garbled Latin (351).

Father (349)_____Gianotti (349).

"Once Aboard the Lugger" (I)

Written perhaps as early as 1926 or 1927, but certainly by November 23, 1928; first published in *Contempo:A Review of Books and Personalities*, **1 (February 1, 1932), [1]-4.**

_____: first-person narrator (352); goes ashore with captain and black cook (354); digs in sand dune (356); finds sacks and carries them to ship (357).

421

Joe (352)_____: older brother of Pete; about 35; owns boat (352).

Pete (352)_____: Joe's younger brother; about 19 (352); seasick (353); refuses to go ashore (354); finally comes ashore with black cook (357).

_____: captain; teetotaler (352).

_____: black cook; hides whisky (352); says nothing on land can bother him because he has medicine; has charm (356).

"Once Aboard the Lugger" (II)

Written about 1928; first published in *Uncollected Stories of William Faulkner.*

_____: first-person narrator; crew of lugger (359); after cargo is unloaded and captain revives, ordered to carry cook and Pete to galley; engineer (366); after hauling dead bodies, drinks and gets sick (366-367).

_____: black cook on lugger (359); shot by man with Alabama accent (362).

Pete (359)_____: Joe's brother (359); knocked out by man with Alabama accent (363).

Joe (359)_____: Pete's brother; owner of boat (359).

_____: captain of lugger; works on pump with narrator (359); knocked out by man with Alabama accent (361); recovers (365).

_____: one of two men in strange boat that approaches (359); has Alabama accent; shoots black cook (360); red haired (362); tries to blame killing of cook on Italian (363); slaps Italian after he kills Pete (364).

_____: one of two men; high voice (360); Italian (363); when Alabaman says he killed cook, cries; shoots Pete in head (364).

_____: priest (363).

"Thrift"

On sending schedule February 14, 1930; first published in *The Saturday Evening Post,* **203 (September 6, 1930), 16-17, 76, 82 and included in** *O. Henry Memorial Award Prize Stories of 1931,* **ed., Blanche Cotton Williams (Garden City: Doubleday, Doran and Co., 1931), pp. 153-169.**

Willie (397) MacWyrglinchbeath (382): first-class air mechanic; AWOL for three weeks; instead of going on leave to England for week (382); name not on pay list; tries to collect pay; arrested; hoped to get flying pay by joining bomber squadron (383); originally enlisted in infantry; limps; applies for transfer to Flying Corps for money; to disqualify himself for infantry service, burns foot; is transferred to Flying Corps as third-class air mechanic (384); insists on proper spelling of name (385); sends pay home to neighbor; promoted to second-class mechanic; then to first-class mechanic (386); then promoted to corporal; takes airplane up without lessons (387); crashes plane; arrested; sent back to England to school of aeronautics; becomes sergeant pilot (388); agrees to insurance scheme with officer pilot (390); promoted to sub-altern; DSO & MC twice over (393); refuses commission (395), because he would lose money in accepting (396); armistice; returns home (396-397).

_____: squadron commander's orderly (396).

_____: lawyer consulted by Mac (398).

"Two Dollar Wife"

Originally entitled "The Devil Beats His Wife," and then "Christmas Tree," and once "Whoopee," begun shortly before December 25, 1927; revised late in 1933 or early in 1934, and rewritten probably in the spring-summer, 1935; it was first published in *College Life*, 18 (January, 1936), 8-10, 85, 86, 88, 90.

Maxwell Johns (412): after sewing Doris's dress, leaves needle in chair (413); suspended from Sewanee; has license to marry Doris (414); plays craps; wins $140; refuses to sell license to Hap White; offers to shoot dice with Journstadt: the license against his full flask of whisky (417); loses (418); bullies Peter into getting him a jar of moonshine (419); bribes Justice of the Peace; marries Doris (421).

Doris Houston (412) Johns (421): starts to marry Maxwell Johns; changes mind (414); leaves car; walks toward club; picked up by another car (415); marries Maxwell Johns (421).

_____ Houston (412): mother of Doris (412).

_____: black maid in Houston house (412).

Walter Mitchell (413): races other car (413); stops car; offers others a drink (414).

Lucile (413)_____.

_____ Johns (414): father of Maxwell Johns; office in Cotton Exchange (414).

_____: black janitor in Cotton Exchange; lends Max two dollars to buy wedding license (414).

_____ Houston (415): father of Doris.

Hap White (415): fat youth (416).

_____ Journstadt (415): Princeton man (415); wins license in crap game (418); drinks heavily of moonshine (420).

_____: Journstadt's aunt (415).

Peter (418)_____: black cloakroom attendant at Club; pours corn whisky (416); lends his dice (418); gets whisky for Max (419).

_____: Justice of the Peace; marries Maxwell Johns and Doris

Houston (421).

Dr. (422)   Carberry (422): removes needle from baby's throat (422).

_____ Houston (422): infant child of Mrs. Houston; swallows needle left in chair by Max (422).

"Afternoon of a Cow"

Written before June 25, 1937; it was translated into French by Maurice Coindreau; first published as *"L'Apres-midi d'une Vache,"* **in** *Fontaine,* **27-28 (June-July, 1943), 66-81; first published in English, under pseudonymn Ernest V Trueblood, in** *Furioso,* **2 (summer, 1947), 5, 8, 9, 10, 13, 16, 17; material used in** *The Hamlet,* **1940, Chapter Three, part two.**

Bill Faulkner (424): tries to get cow out of gully (429-430); she falls on him; covered with cow dung (430); strips naked by watering trough and washes himself as Oliver rinses him (433).

Ernest [V. Trueblood] (424): first-person narrator; has been writing Faulkner's novels and short stories for years (424).

Oliver (424)   : black servant of Bill Faulkner; reports boys have set pasture on fire (424).

Malcolm   (424): Bill Faulkner's son (424).

James Faulkner (424): Bill Faulkner's nephew (424).

_____ Faulkner (424): Bill's brother; father of James (424).

_____: Bill Faulkner's cook; mother of Grover (424).

Grover (Rover) (424): son of Bill Faulkner's cook (424).

Mrs. Bill Faulkner (426): keeps flower beds and rose garden (426).

"Mr. Acarius"

Written shortly before February, 19, 1953 under the title "Weekend Revisited;" posthumously published in *The Saturday Evening Post,* **237 (October 9, 1965), 26-27, 29, 30, 31.**

Mr.   Acarius (435): visits doctor (435); abases himself (436); asks to be sent to sanatorium (438); sent there; saturates himself in alcohol for four days (439); returns to sanatorium (440); goes to Miller's room; leaves by window; climbs down fire escape (447-448); stopped by police; taken home by his doctor; throws liquor away (448).

Ab (435) Cochrane (442): Mr Acarius's doctor; former classmate and fraternity brother (435); tells Acarius to take mistress; get married; get drunk (436); accompanies Acarius to sanatorium (439).

Dr. (439)   Hill (439): superintendent of sanatorium (439).

_____: houseman (440).

_____: elevator man (440).

Goldie (441)   : nurse in sanatorium (440); from Alabama (441); brings Acarius small whisky to induce him to eat (444).

_____ Miller (442): male patient; undresses Acarius and puts him to bed (440); calls lobby and has Judy Lester sent to Acarius's room (442).

Judy Lester (442): girl friend of Watkins; smuggles two pints of whisky into sanatorium in brassiere (442); another bottle taped to thigh (443).

_____ Watkins (442): patient in sanatorium; at least 60 (442); falls down flight of stairs (447).

_____: orderly who brings Acarius's supper (444).

_____: nurse who relieves Goldie (444).

_____: another nurse; wears pince-nez (446).

"Sepulture South: Gaslight"

Written shortly after September, 1954, and titled once "Sepulchure South: In Gaslight," and "Sepulchure South: Gaslight," it was first published in _Harper's Bazaar_, 88 (December 1954), 84-85, 140-141.

_____: narrator (449); oldest child (451); as a child, terrified at thought of death; 14 at time of grandfather's death (452); proud of his grandfather (453).

_____: narrator's grandfather; dies (449); laid out in CSA uniform with three stars (450).

_____: narrator's father (449).

Liddy (449)   : black cook for narrator's family (449).

_____: narrator's grandmother; died seven years ago (449).

_____: black cook before Liddy (449).

Arthur (449)   : Liddy's husband (449); carries notice of grandfather's death from door to door (450).

426

_____Wedlow (450): jeweler; inscribes notice for grandfather's funeral (450).

_____: husband of Liddy's predecessor (450).

_____: narrator's mother (450).

_____: sister of narrator's mother (450).

_____: husband of sister of narrator's mother; from Memphis (450).

Charles (450)_____: brother of narrator's father (450).

Alice (450)_____: wife of brother of narrator's father (450).

Maggie (451)_____: sister of narrator (451).

_____: other children in narrator's family (451).

_____: father of grandfather; great-grandfather of narrator (451).

Rodney (451)_____: uncle of narrator; youngest brother of narrator's father; bachelor; traveling salesman from St. Louis (451).

Simon (452)_____: servant of narrator's family; drowns puppies (452).

Sarah (452)_____: wife of Simon (452).

_____: eight pallbearers; friend's of narrator's father (452).

_____: three CSA veterans, honorary pallbearers (452).

_____: preacher at funeral (454).

_____: undertaker at narrator's grandfather's funeral (454).

"Adolescence"

Written in early 1920's, and dated June 20 to November 23, 1923; first published in *Uncollected Stories of William Faulkner.*

Mrs. Joe Bunden [I] (459): small woman with enormous dark eyes; wife of Joe Bunden [I]; during pregnancy, wants twins; bears Juliet; Cyril; Jeff Davis; Bud (459); and Joe; dies in childbirth of Joe (460).

Joe Bunden [I] (459): after first wife dies, remarries; sends daughter, Jule, to his mother (460); with Lafe Hollowell, killed at his still by revenuers (470).

Juliet (459) Jule (460) Bunden (459): daughter of Joe Bunden [I] (459); hates step-mother; sent by father to grandmother (460); at 12, climbs faster than a boy; swims naked in pool; flat body; sees boy watching her swim; he joins her (461); sleeps naked by him (462); during winter, hunts with Lee; in spring they swim naked together (463); lies naked with him under horseblanket (464); discovered and beaten by grandmother (465-466); says she will kill father rather than return home with him (467); says hates grandmother (468); after grandmother hits her with stick, takes stick; breaks it; throws it in fire; rides horse to town (469); gives brother Bud food and money; watches him leave (472); despairs (473).

Cyril Bunden (459): son of Joe Bunden [I]; elected to state legislature (459).

Jeff Davis Bunden (459): son of Joe Bunden [I]; hanged in Texas for stealing a horse (459).

Bud Bunden (459): later professor of Latin (459) in small mid-western university (460); after father's death, goes to Jule (471); takes food and money from her and goes away (472).

Joe Bunden [II] (460): son of Joe Bunden [I] (460).

Mrs. Joe Bunden [II] (460): second wife; "tall angular shrew;" beats husband with stove wood; hates Jule (460).

Mrs. Alex (467) Bunden (463): mother of Joe Bunden [I]; brings up Juliet (460); discovers Juliet and Lee naked under horseblanket (465); hits Jule with stick (466); grows old (467); says that Joe has found husband for Jule (468); few days later, tells Juliet that father is dead (470).

Lee (462) Hollowell (465): boy who watches Juliet as she swims naked; joins her (461); sleeps naked by her (462); caught so by her grandmother (465); son of Lafe Hollowell (466); disappears after his father's murder (470).

Lafe Hollowell (466): father of Lee (466); killed by revenuers (470).

_____: nine children of Juliet's grandmother (467).

Alex Bunden (467): Juliet's grandfather (467).

Deacon Harvey (470): sends revenuers to Lafe's still (470).

"Al Jackson"

Written late winter, 1925; first published in *Uncollected Stories of William Faulkner.*

William Faulkner (476): first-person narrator (474); denies that

Spearhead Jackson shot blacks; says it was Jack Spearman shooting Swedes in Minnesota for a dollar a head (478).

_____: pilot of boat (474).

Al Jackson (474): descendent of "Old Hickory" (474); shy; takes courses during war to cure shyness (477).

_____ Jackson (474): Al Jackson's mother; increased church attendance three hundred percent with secret recipe for communion wine (474).

_____: Al Jackson's mother's father (474).

_____: father of pilot (474).

_____ Jackson (474): "Old Man Jackson" (474); eats library paste; wears raincoat when he takes a bath; raises sheep in swamp; alligators eat them; equips them with false horns; sheep lose legs; grow scales; tails broaden like beavers' tails; lose wool (475).

_____: twelve sons of "Old Man" Jackson (475).

Claude Jackson (476): always after women; catches sheep-alligators by swimming; turns into shark; goes for fat blond ladies (476).

Elenor (476) Perchie Jackson (477): elopes with tin pedler [sic] (477).

_____: tin pedler with whom Elenor Jackson elopes; afraid of water (477).

Spearhead Jackson (477): hanged on British frigate in 1799; slaver; throws slaves overboard (477).

Jack Spearman (478): according to Faulkner, shot Swedes in Minnesota for one dollar a head (478).

Sam Jackson (478): mysterious Jackson (478).

_____: old moonshiner; will not discuss Sam Jackson (478).

Herman Jackson (478): has passion for education; admitted to university; makes pearl buttons from fish scales; dies after convulsion (478).

"Don Giovanni"

Probably written in winter and early spring, 1925; first published in *Mississippi Quarterly,* **32 (summer, 1979), 485-495 with introductory note by James B. Meriwether. Faulkner used parts of it and transformed characters from it in several of his novels, including** *Mosquitoes, Pylon,* **and** *The Hamlet.*

Herbie 486) _____: married young to plain-faced girl; now 32; widower; wholesale buyer of women's clothing; thinning hair (480); fantasizes about conquest of a woman (481); goes to Morrison for advice (482); goes on date; returns three hours later (484); tells man at typewriter about failure on date (485); loses girl he planned to seduce (486); loses $10 that he gave to taxi driver; thrown out by man at typewriter (487); phones Morrison to explain what he learned about women; woman answers phone and says, "You tell 'em, big boy; treat 'em rough." (488).

_____: wife of Herbie; now dead (480).

_____ Morrison (481): friend of Herbie (481).

_____ Steinbauer (486): girl Herbie hopes to seduce (483); dumps him at dance hall for another man (486).

_____: man; types; collarless (481); tells Herbie to leave (487).

_____: taxi driver (485).

_____: large man with whom Miss Steinbauer dances (486).

_____: waiter at dance hall (486).

_____: woman with Morrison when Herbie phones (488).

"Peter"

Written about 1925; first published in *Uncollected Stories of William Faulkner.*

_____: first-person narrator (489).

Peter (489) _____: child; says his brother is white; has no "paw;" face "like cup of milk with dash of coffee in it" (489).

_____: Peter's younger brother; white (489).

_____ Spratling (489): artist friend of narrator (489).

_____: friend of Peter; Chinese (489); sexually eager for Peter's mother (490).

Mabel (493) _____: Peter's mother; prostitute (489); light-colored black woman (493).

_____: man with Peter's mother (489).

_____: man Peter calls Eagle Beak; sleeps with Peter's mother; brings Peter candy (490).

_____: "the other one;" used to sleep with Peter's mother; brought him nothing (490).

_____: large black man whom Peter calls "Baptis';" gave Peter a top (490).

_____: neighbor boy who can spin top (490).

Euphrosy (491)_____: prostitute (491).

Joe Lee (493): beats prostitute Imogene; according to Peter, has killed three [prostitutes?] (493).

Imogene (493)_____: prostitute beaten by Joe Lee (493).

_____: another prostitute; says Mabel ought to beat Peter (493).

"Moonlight"

Written perhaps as early as 1919, or 1920-1921, and at latest June 20 to November 23, 1923; reworked in 1935; it anticipates some scenes in _Soldiers' Pay_ and some characters in "Hair;" it was first published in _Uncollected Stories of William Faulkner._

_____: youth; with corn whisky in shirt; approaches his uncle's empty house in dark (495); whisky taken from father's cask (496); has received note from Susan; flashback: earlier while petting Susan in hammock, discovered by Mr. Burdett; kicked out of hammock and kicked again (497); 16; broods on being kicked; virgin; refuses to accompany Skeet to black prostitute; breaks into empty house (498); sends Skeet to fetch Susan after he drinks (499); first-class scout (500); just wants to seduce Susan; is willing to marry her afterward; tries to get her to drink; kisses her (501); tries to take her into his uncle's house for sex (502); after she refuses, thinks "all I wanted was just to seduce somebody" (503).

_____: youth's uncle; away on summer vacation (495); still young (499).

_____: youth's aunt (495); still young (499).

_____: youth's father; thinks cask of corn whisky is hidden in attic (496).

_____: youth's mother (496).

Susan (497)_____: sends note to youth (467); reed thin; refuses to drink; kissed by youth; wants to go to movies (501); refuses to enter his uncle's house for sex (502); says she might tomorrow night (503).

431

Mr. (497)   Burchett (497): Susan's guardian (497); finds Susan and youth necking in hammock; kicks him (497-498); at least 40 (498).

Skeet (497)   : friend of youth; 16 (498); frequents black prostitutes (498); drinks youth's whisky and goes to fetch Susan (499); brings Susan to youth; gets another drink (500).

Mrs. (497) Etta (501) Burchett (497): guardian of Susan (497).

Dr. (498)   West (498).

Mr.   Hovis (498).

"The Big Shot"

Written before January 23, 1930; first published in *Mississippi Quarterly,* **26 (summer, 1973), 312-324. It anticipates parts of** *Sanctuary* **and** *Absalom, Absalom!*

Don Reeves (504): newspaperman; tells narrator story (504).

          : first-person narrator (504); tells Martin of Dr. Blount's suicide (521).

Dal (516) Martin (504): has built town; now runs it; calls someone to have Popeye released (507); born and raised on Mississippi farm; tenant farmer; sent by father to house of owner; repulsed; hides in woods (507-508); never approaches the boss again [See below]; imitates his speech and gestures; marries; has child; proprietor of cross-roads store (509); merchant; can not read or write; plays poker with boss (510); beats him; pours his drinks; sells store and moves to town at 48 (511); a millionaire; driven to office by daughter; reads of debutantes; staffs house with black servants (513); places daughter in Catholic convent (514); dreams of having daughter attend annual Chickasaw Guards ball (515); visits Dr. Blount (516); to have him invite daughter to ball (516-517); offers him check; Blount refuses him (517); does not want daughter to date bums (518); offers to build art gallery named for Blount's grandfather if daughter is invited to ball; Blount agrees (519); when Blount tells him he wants to call off agreement, refuses; after refusing $50,000 in bonds, from Blount threatens to tell newspapers (520); after Blount's suicide, daughter is invited to ball; finishes the gallery (521); after Govelli tells of Popeye's running a woman down, arranges to get him out of town (524); learns that the woman that Popeye ran over is his daughter (525).

          Govelli (504): bootlegger (504); tells Martin Popeye killed woman in automobile accident (524).

Popeye (504)   : dead face; falsetto voice; car full of liquor; runs red light; almost hits policeman; draws pistol on crowd (504); has killed one man; arrested; had previously been in jail for killing a man; hophead; would not or could not drink (505); not convicted because of Martin's influence (506); source of cocaine (snow); Italian (507); kills

432

Martin's daughter in automobile accident (515).

_____: pedestrian whom Popeye almost hits (504).

_____: Popeye's aged mother; lives in Pensacola (505).

_____: policeman who arrests Popeye (505).

_____: two reporters (505).

_____: man killed by Popeye (505).

_____: turnkey whom Popeye threatens to kill (506).

_____: Popeye's lawyer (506).

_____: person whom Martin calls to have Popeye released (507).

_____ Martin (508): Dal Martin's father (508).

_____: owner of plantation on which Martin was raised; tells Martin never to come to front door again (508).

_____: black servant at plantation house (508).

_____ Martin (508): sister of Dal Martin (508).

_____ Martin (508): sister of Dal Martin (508).

_____ Martin (508): brother of Dal Martin (508).

Mrs. Dal (516) Martin (509): Dal Martin's wife (509); keeps books for store (510); dies (512).

Wrennie (523) Martin (509): Martin's child (509); daughter (511); at 18, drives father to office (512); at 17, tells father she dates boys from best familes (513); attends (for two months) convent in Washington (514); returns home after illness; resumes social life; tells father that she dates best families (518); arrested after refusing to accept ticket after traffic violation (522); says she was with Jerry Sandeman; says she does not want to go to ball (523); killed by Popeye in street accident (525).

Sandeman, Blount, Heustace (512): important family names (512).

Tony (513)_____: Italian who keeps house for Martin after his wife dies (512-513).

_____: Tony's wife (512).

433

Dr. Harrison Blount (516): Flag-corporal of Chickasaw Guards; bachelor, 40; in charge of annual ball (516); refuses to invite Martin's daughter (517); agrees to invite Martin's daughter to ball in return for Martin's building art gallery and naming it for Blount's grandfather; consults woman (519); asks Martin to let him out of agreement; offers Martin $50,000 in bonds (520); when Martin refuses, commits suicide (521).

Mrs. (516) _____ Blount (516): Harrison Blount's mother (516).

_____: Blount's secretary (517).

Red (518) _____: Martin does not want daughter to date men like him (518).

_____ Monk (518): Martin does not want daughter to date men like him (518).

_____: Blount's grandfather (519).

_____ Windham (519): one of the architects who design Blount Memorial Gallery (519).

_____ Healy (519): one of the architects who design Blount Memorial Gallery (519).

_____: woman Blount consults about gallery (519).

_____: black butler in Martin's house (520).

_____: lawyer; manages Blount's estate (521).

_____: detective who returns summons to Martin (522).

_____: rookie policeman; gives Martin's daughter summons and arrests her (522).

_____ Hickey (522): police supervisor (522).

Jerry Sandeman (523): according to Wrennie Martin, man who was with her when traffic violation occurred (523).

_____: policeman; helps Wrennie Martin change tire when she is killed by Popeye (524).

"Dull Tale"

Written before November 14, 1930, a revision of "The Big Shot," which was first published in *Mississippi Quarterly*, 26 (summer, 1973), 312-324.

Dr. (526) Gavin (545) Blount (526): president of the Nonconnah Guards; refuses to accept money from Dal Martin to have his daughter invited to the Nonconnah Guards Ball (528); slight, smallish man, dapper dresser; 40; bachelor; lives with grandmother; an only child; mother dies in childbirth (530); crouches in closet after his father humiliates him; has crying fits; dreams; becomes ill (531); inherits father's practice; in WW I; picks fight with larger man; is beaten (532); asked to be and is transferred to another hospital; likes the smell of old female flesh; holds chairmanship of Nonconnah Guards for twelve years; this position is "another linen closet;" Flag-Corporal of the Guards (533); fears leaving his office to drive home (534); calls Dal Martin back (535); after next interview, agrees to invite Martin's daughter (542); considers reneging on agreement, paying off the contractors; removing name from list (542); visits Martin (543); tries to back out of ageement; offers $50,000 in bonds and motgage on house to get out of ageement (544); takes back bonds; commits suicide (545).

Dal Martin (526): visits Dr. Blount; a politician (526); talks to Dr. Blount about his daughter attending the Nonconnah Guards annual ball (527); says he can do anything in that town (Memphis); offers Dr. Blount cash; is refused (528); comes from southern Mississippi; had once owned grocery store; when called back by Dr. Blount, offers to build a new armory for Guards (535); flashback: born to Mississippi tenant farmer; youngest of six children; sent to house of owner of plantation; repulsed; hides in bushes; never speaks to the boss again [See below.] (536); watches and imitates him; swears he too will be rich; can not read; memorizes accounts; dictates them to wife; plays poker with boss at night; does not drink; beats boss at poker; moves to Memphis; owns store (537); becomes contractor with political influence (538); offers another bribe to Dr. Blount: to build an art gallery and name it after his grandfather (540-541); tells Blount to take daughter's name off list (544-545); refuses bonds; (internal date December 2, 1930) invitation finally arrives after Blount's suicide (545).

Laverne (545) Martin (527): Dal Martin's daughter; goes to nightclubs every night (527); dates sons of best families; owns own car (538); picks up young man; taken to Washington, D. C.; put in school (539); stays three weeks; loses fifteen pounds; returns home (540); leaves house at night (544); returns from ball disappointed (546).

_____ Martin (527): dead wife of Dal Martin (527); flashback: can read and write; keeps books for store (537).

_____: Dr. Blount's grandfather (530); first major of Guards (533); killed in Forrest's command in Civil War (534).

_____: Dr. Blount's grandmother; an invalid of 90 (530).

_____: maiden sister of Dr. Blount's father (530); (532).

Dr. _____ Blount (530): Dr. Blount's father; bluff; loud; an inferior successful doctor (530).

_____ Blount (530): Blount's mother; dies in childbirth (530).

_____: man Dr. Blount fights (532).

_____: woman Dr. Blount consults about Martin's offer of money to have daughter invited to ball (534); sick; advises him to remove Martin's daughter's name from list, and let Martin build the gallery (542).

_____ Martin (536): five brothers and sisters of Dal Martin (536); two older bothers; two older sisters;

_____: owner of land Martins live on (536); tells Dal Martin never to come to front door again (536); plays poker with Martin (537).

_____ Martin (526): father of Dal Martin (536).

_____ Martin (526): mother of Dal Martin (536).

_____: black servant of owner of land Martins live on (536).

_____: black servant in Martin's home (538).

Harrison Coates Jr. (538): dates Martin girl; dismissed from Sewanee (538).

Hack (539) Sandeman (538): dates Martin girl (538).

_____ Sandeman (538): dates Martin girl (538).

_____ Heustace (538): dates Martin girl (538).

Harrison Coates, Sr. (538).

_____: mother superior in school Martin girl attends (540).

_____: Dal Martin's grandfather; killed in Civil War (540).

_____ Windham (541): architect for Blount Memorial Art Gallery (541).

_____ Healy (541): architect for Blount Memorial Art Gallery (541).

_____: Dr. Blount's great-grandfather (542).

"A Return"

Another story of about nine pages, "Rose of Lebanon," with characters named Gavin Blount, Randolph Gordon, and Lewis Randolph was submitted to a magazine on November 7, 1930. A story entitled, "A Return," and containing similar material was sent to Faulkner's agent on October 13, 1938. First published in *Uncollected Stories of William Faulkner*.

_____: black boy; gives Charles Gordon's bouquet to Lewis Randolph (547).

Charles Gordon (547): December, 1861; meets Lewis Randolph's carriage with bouquet; escorts her to ball at Nonconnah Guards Armory in Memphis (547); marries her as he leaves for Civil War (550); wounded; recovers; killed: shot breaking into chicken-roost (555).

Lewis Randolph (547) Gordon (550): female; comes from Mississippi to attend ball at Nonconnah Guards Armory in Memphis (547); smuggled on to troop train; rides to Nashville with soldiers; marries Charles Gordon (550); tells mother she is pregnant (551); after mother's death, ekes out living on land; carries derringer (556) fires derringer at Yankee soldier; kills him; buries body (557); teaches son to read and write (559); refuses to go to Memphis with him (562); 19 years older than son; refuses son's offers of help; becomes ill; agrees to go to Memphis with son; has saved every cent he gave her in shoebox (564); stops car at bungalow; insists son buy it for her (565); lives there; proposed to by both Gavin Blount I and Charles Gordon (566); at dinner, prompted by Gavin Blount's speech about Yankees, throws soup at him; points knife and utters the same obscenity she used on Yankees (572); afterwards insists on going home (573).

_____ Randolph (547): mother of Lewis Randolph; accompanies daughter to Memphis (547); falls in hole she dug to bury trunk of silver; breaks hip (553-554); dies three nights later of pneumonia (554).

_____ Randolph (547): father of Lewis Randolph; organizes a company of infantry in December 1861 (547); supposedly killed in Civil War; body never found (553); in Rock Island prison (POW) (554); returns without teeth or hair (557); lives like an animal; disappears (558).

_____ Randolph (553) Gordon (552): listener to whom Lewis Randolph tells of the ball; 6 years old when she begins to tell of ball (548); son of Lewis Randolph (549); at 45, on business trip to New York, recalls rebel yell (549); at 69, banker (555); receives letter from paternal grandparents (559); goes to live with them (560); but decides not to; starts out on his own in Memphis (561); starts work in cotton compress; discovered by grandparents; taken to their home; refuses their offer of schooling; says he aims to get rich by his own work (562); after a year, returns to bring his mother to Memphis; gives her $200 when she refuses to go to Memphis (562-563); sends money home regularly; goes home; gives mother $1200; prospers; marries; has children (561); a millionaire; refuses inheritance from grandfather; endows refuge for childless women with it (564); persuades 90-year-old mother to come to town for dinner by telling her there is an eligible bachelor who wants to marry her (569).

Gavin Blount [I] (548): Chairman of committee and Major of battalion of Nonconnah Guards (548); dead seven months after start of Civil War (549); body found (553); had proposed to Lewis Randolph (566).

_____: father of man Randolph Gordon meets in New York (550).

_____: man Randolph Gordon meets in New York (550).

_____ Mullen (550): had been in Forrest's command (550).

_____: southern youth killed by sheriff in '78 in Kansas for shouting rebel yell (550).

_____: sheriff who kills southern youth (550).

_____: private (a minister) who marries Charles Gordon and Lewis Randolph (550).

_____: black midwife who delivers Randolph Gordon (553).

_____: neighbor who invites Lewis Gordon and her mother to live with them (553).

Joanna (554): slave; black nurse to Randolph Gordon (553).

Will (554): slave of Randolphs (554).

Awce (554): slave (554); dies (564).

_____ Gordon (555): Charles Gordon's father (555); lives in Memphis (558).

_____ Gordon (555): Charles Gordon's mother (555); invites Lewis Gordon and son to live with them; invites Randolph Gordon to live with them; rich (559-560.

_____: man; kills Charles Gordon as he breaks into chicken-roost (555).

_____: three ex-slaves who remain with Lewis Gordon (555),

Gavin Blount [II] (566): bursts into Randolph Gordon's office and demands to be told about Lewis Randolph (556); great nephew of Gavin Blount [I]; doctor; sick; lives with two maiden aunts (566); visits Nonconnah Guards club every day; 41; Chairman of Guards for seventeen years; lives in past; infatuated with story of Lewis Randolph (567); wants Randolph Gordon to bring his 90-year-old mother to Guards Ball (568); says he can not marry because Lewis Ranndolph would not have him (569); at dinner, makes speech about Yankees in Civil War (571); has soup thrown at him by Lewis Gordon (572); gets pistol from Randolph Gordon; leaves (573-574); does not use pistol; returns it; sends note that Gavin Blount has bested Charles Gordon because Lewis Gordon threw soup at him (574).

_____: Yankee soldier at whom Lewis Gordon fires gun (557).

Mrs. Randolph Gordon (563): wife of Randolph Gordon (563).

_____ Gordon (570): son of Randolph Gordon (563, 570).

_____ Gordon (570): daughter of Randolph Gordon (563, 570).

_____: 14-year-old black youth who takes Awce's place (564).

Melissandre (Lissy) (564): daughter of Joanna and Awce; servant of Lewis Gordon (564).

_____: proprietor of store; sends Randolph Gordon news of his mother (564).

Lucius (565)_____: Randolph Gordon's black chauffeur (565).

Mrs._____ Gillman (565): friend of Lewis Gordon; lives in Holly Springs (565).

_____ Blount (566): father of Gavin Blount [II]; physician (566).

_____: two maiden aunts with whom Gavin Blount lives (566).

_____ Sandeman (567): chairman of Guards before Blount (567).

_____ Heustace (567): chairman of Guards before Sandeman who followed Gavin Blount [I] (567).

_____: secretary to Randolph Gordon (569).

Henry Heustace (569): friend of Randolph Gordon (569).

Mrs. Henry Heustace (569).

_____: couple; guests at Gordon's dinner (570).

_____: female guest of Randolph Gordon's son at dinner (570).

_____: male guest of Randolph Gordon's daughter at dinner (570).

"A Dangerous Man"

On sending schedule February 6, 1930; also titled "Dangerous Man;" first published in *Uncollected Stories of William Faulkner.*

_____: narrator (575).

_____ Bowman (575): takes pistol to help Stowers (575); wants to shoot drummer on sight; wants to fight him (576); express agent; thick build; shows no age; might be 38 (577); owns two dogs (578); drinks white whisky with wife (579); fights with wife over dogs and Joe's bedroom; kills robber; gets $5000 reward (579); once owned restaurant at station; desires children (580); washes dogs despite his wife; reads *The Ladies Home Journal* (582).

Zack Stowers (575): has pistol; asks for Bowman's help when man insults wife (575); fights with drummer who insults wife (577).

_____: drummer; insults Mrs. Stowers; tall (575).

Mrs. Zack Stowers (575): insulted by drummer (575).

_____: drummer's friend; short (575).

Mrs. _____ Bowman (575): Bowman's wife (575); runs office; looks like a handsome and prosperous washerwoman (578); fights with husband over dogs in Joe's bedroom (579).

_____: two bystanders who hold Stowers (577).

Joe (579) _____: grown nephew of Bowman; father (577); adopted (578).

_____: Joe's child (577).

_____: Joe's wife (578).

_____: narrator's aunt (578).

Minnie Maude (578) _____: lives at Mrs. Wiggins's boarding house; 22 years old; ticket seller in Rex theatre (580).

Mrs. _____ Wiggins (578): runs boarding house (578).

_____: Bowman's cook (578); black (582).

_____: Mrs. Wiggins's cook (578).

_____: robber; killed by Bowman (579).

_____: locomotive engineer (580).

Wall (580) _____: enters express office while Bowman is delivering express (580); ladies' man having affair with Mrs. Bowman (581).

"Evangeline"

On sending schedule July 17, 1931; once titled "A Dark House;" first published in the *Atlantic Monthly*, 244 (November, 1979), 68-80.

440

_____: first-person narrator (583); enters Sutpen's house despite dog and finds occupant for last forty years kept alive by aged black Sutpen (594); newspaperman (595); gets past dog and enters Sutpen's house (596); follows aged black woman upstairs (597); finds Henry Sutpen (598); returns to house; dreams that Henry confessed killing Bon and said he was his brother; watches house burn (606); opens locket found in ruins; finds picture of Bon's first wife in it (608); sees that Bon's marriage to a black has compounded the bigamy and was cause for Henry to kill Bon (609).

Don (583)_____: an architect and amateur painter (583).

Colonel (587)_____ Sutpen (583): bought land and brought foreign architect to build house (583-584); dies in 1870; coffin thrown in ditch when mules bolt; buried in family plot (584); stops duel between Henry and Bon (589); after war breaks out, raises regiment; appoints himself colonel; marches to war (590).

_____: foreign architect brought to Mississippi by Sutpen (583-584).

Judith Sutpen (584) Bon (585): daughter of Colonel Sutpen; a widow without having been a wife; buries father in family plot; after his death, waits for husband to return from Civil War (584); blonde; during war stays with mother (587); engaged to Charles Bon; refuses to send back ring (588); marries Bon (590); after war is declared, her nature begins to change; after mother dies, stays in house alone with slave; finds picture of first wife on Bon's body; hammers locket shut; sends letter, then money, to first wife (601); then brings her to live in Sutpen's house (602); after she leaves, sends letter to Henry (603); he returns and she dies (604).

Henry (585) Sutpen (584): son of Colonel Sutpen (584); same age as Charles Bon; school mates at University of Mississippi; brings Bon home on weekends (586); goes with Bon to New Orleans; returns in three weeks; tries to make Judith send back ring; refuses to say why he opposes wedding; refuses to speak with Bon; has row with father about Bon coming for Christmas (588); after aborted duel, leaves for three years; returns in uniform (598); returns after war, with Charles Bon's body (591); once horsewhipped a newspaper man (595); found by Don in bed in Sutpen's house; had collapsed in garden (598); flashback: goes to New Orleans with Bon; discovers that he already has a wife; gave Charles Bon his chance (never explained) (600); goes to war (599-600); it is implied that Henry killed Bon (601); has lived in house for forty years (604); in narrator's dream, confesses that he killed Bon; says Bon was his brother (606); kills Bon after he discovers that his first wife is black (608).

_____ Sutpen (584): wife of Colonel Sutpen; dies in 1863 (584).

Charles Bon (585): husband of Judith Sutpen (584); from New Orleans

(585); same age as Henry; at University of Mississippi; visits with Henry (586); an orphan (587); visits guardian; takes picture of Judith; leaves her a ring; estranged from Henry; does not speak (588); after aborted duel with Henry, leaves; graduates; wedding set for one year; returns to hotel in town for wedding (589); married to Judith after a meeting with Henry; after marriage, rides off with Henry to Civil War (590); body returned by Henry; killed by last shot in war (591); given chance by Henry; lies to him; goes to war (600).

Raby (603) Sutpen (585): black; great-grandmother; light colored; sits in chair by cabin; supervises others who work (586); when Judith dies, lays her out in coffin (592); part Indian; part Sutpen (595); tells narrator to go away (596); shows Don the dying Henry Sutpen; says she carried him from garden to bed (598); tended him for forty years; says he is her brother (604); sets fire to house (606).

Sibey (586)   .

Abum (586)   .

Rose (586)   .

_____: Bon's slave; brings Judith flowers and a letter from Bon once a week (587).

_____: Charles Bon's guardian in New Orleans (587).

_____: slave woman; daughter of Raby Sutpen (591); goes to Sutpen's house; observes blacks burying Judith; sees another face in house after burial (592); is grandmother; finds locket among ruins of house (608);

_____: black woman and two black men from family three miles away (592).

_____: man who finds German shepherd dead in ditch; treed by another dog as he tries to investigate Sutpen house (593).

Mrs. Charles Bon (599): Charles Bon's first wife in New Orleans (599); visits Sutpen's house; visits Charles Bon's grave (602-603); stays a short time; leaves (602-603); black (608).

_____: black woman servant of Bon's first wife (602).

_____ Bon (602): Charles Bon's son; about 9 years old (602); born after Charles and Judith were married (606).

"A Portrait of Elmer"

Written in middle 1930's with various titles: "Elmer," "Portrait of Elmer Hodge," and "Growing Pains;" first published in the *Georgia Review*, 33 (fall, 1979), 534-564, with an introduction by Joseph Blotner. (See

442

Elmer **above.)**

Elmer (610) Elly (621) Hodge (611): young artist in Paris; from Texas; last of children (610); understands no Italian; has been in jail with Angelo in Venice (611); flashback: met Myrtle in Houston, Texas; has bastard son (612); has come back; a veteran of WW I; penniless; asks Myrtle to marry him (613); flashback: at 5, home in Johnson City, Tennessee burned (614); sleeps naked with sister Jo (615); gets water color set in mail from sister Jo (616); 14 in fourth grade; develops "fine sexless passion for the teacher;" infatuated with schoolboy (616); returns to teacher; walks her home (616-617); invited to her house; flees as she makes sexual overtures to him (618); at 15, borrows cup of sugar from Velma; first stirrings of sex; chases her to barn (619-620); leaves parents in Houston to go to war; returns; finds real estate agent there (620); visits parents who constantly move; learns that mother is dead (621); does not tell father about Myrtle; leaves father; visits mother's grave (622); back to present: at 18, in Houston, meets Ethel; has sex; when she becomes pregnant, offers to marry her; she refuses; travels north (624); drifts for several years; in Michigan lumber camp, begins drawing portraits; at 19, tells men about Ethel (625-626); enlists in Canadian Expeditionary Force with cook (626); fears hand grenades (627); wounded in back when one explodes; spends months recovering; returned from England (628); sees sister Jo in New Orleans (629); prevented by crowd from reaching her (630-631); sent by doctor to New York to have spine fixed (634); now has money; buys new set of paints in New York before going to Paris (635); takes cab to Hotel Leutitia (636); moves to rooms (637); does not use oils; buys water colors; goes to Meudon and paints landscapes (638); rises from table with Angelo; rushes back to hotel to use toilet; learns that Myrtle and her mother are in his room; reaches toilet; can not find paper after he relieves himself; uses his landscape painting to clean himself (638-640).

Angelo (610)   : Italian; speaks Italian to Elmer (610); has been with Elmer for two months (623).

          Hodge (611): Elmer's mother (610); dies (621); seems to be still living while Elmer is at war (632-633).

          Hodge (611): Elmer's father (610); inherits $2000; buys house (632); good cook (633).

          Hodge (611): brother of Elmer (610, 614); oldest son; leaves family for Saint Louis (615).

          Hodge (611): brother of Elmer; second son; disappears in Paris, Tennessee (615).

Jo (614) Hodge (611): Elmer's sister; sleeps with him (614); disappears when family moves to Jonesboro, Arkansas (615).

Myrtle Monson (611): Elmer's girl friend; rich (612-613); taken by mother to Europe to school (613).

Mrs. _____ Monson (611): Myrtle's mother; rich (613).

_____ Hodge [?] _____: Elmer's bastard son (612).

Ethel (623) _____: mother of Elmer's son (612); two years older than Elmer (623); when parents leave, talks to Elmer of sex and marriage; becomes pregnant; refuses to marry Elmer; is going to marry Grover (624).

_____ Monson (612): Myrtle's father; owns oil wells (613).

Gloria (614) _____: entertainer in New Orleans nightclub; having an affair with Mr. Monson (614).

_____: man with cruel heavy face; owns livery stable; gives Hodge boy job (615).

_____: Elmer's teacher; middle-aged virgin (616); saves wrapping paper for Elmer to paint on; stops Elmer from walking her home; asks him to come to house at night (617); makes sexual overtures; he flees (618).

_____: boy with whom Elmer becomes infatuated at 14; trips Elmer up (616).

Velma Merridew (619): 16-year-old girl from whom Elmer borrows cup of sugar (619); runs to barn; found by Elmer (619-620).

Mrs. _____ Merridew (619): Velma's mother (619).

_____: real estate agent in Houston (620).

_____: "Jewess;" gives Elmer letter from parents (620).

_____: Ethel's family (624).

Grover (624) _____: man Ethel is going to marry (624).

_____: cook in lumber camp; enlists in Canadian Expeditionary Force in WW I; made a corporal and cook (626).

_____: Canadian sergeant-major; teaches Elmer about hand grenades (627).

_____: Canadian soldier killed when Elmer fails to throw grenade (627).

_____: aviator in hospital with Elmer; broke back; both feet burned off (628).

_____: fat woman in canteen; Elmer's patron (628).

444

_____: her husband; dollar-a-year man (628).

_____: fat man in New Orleans selling Liberty Loan Bonds (629).

_____: young soldier at Liberty Bond speech (629).

_____: Jewish man at Liberty Bond speech (629).

_____: two prostitutes in Paris (631).

_____: American consul in Venice; gets Elmer out of jail (632).

_____: three men; dig oil well in Hodge's chicken yard (634).

_____: doctor in New Orleans; sends Elmer to New York (634).

_____: cook whom Hodge senior hires; "a lean yellow woman no longer young;" sleeps with Hodge senior (635).

_____: young woman in New York; sells Elmer set of paints (635).

_____: proprietor of artist supply store (635).

_____: cab driver in Paris (636).

_____: woman in Paris; rents rooms to Elmer (637).

_____: obese man with mop in Paris (637).

_____: waiter (638).

"With Caution and Dispatch"

Written perhaps as early as 1932; revised in 1939; first published in *Esquire*, **92 (September, 1979), 51-58, with an introductory note by Rust Hills.**

_____: general (642).

_____: A.D.C. to general (642).

_____: aerdrome colonel (642).

_____: adjutant (642).

_____ Britt (643): flight commander; MC, Mons Star, DFC; Gallipoli ribbon; commander of B flight (643); thinks that Sartoris was afraid to go to France (660); explains everything that happened (660-661).

[John] Sartoris (642): Mississippian in British service in WW I (642); in Britt's flight; on air mission (643); almost collides with Camel (644); makes emergency landing in field (645-646); instead of going back to aerodrome as ordered, decides to go to London (647); arrives at Broadlands for new Camel (648); takes plane to fly back to squadron in France; refuses command to land; heads for France (649); hits heavy rain; flies across channel (649-650); almost hits Brazilian ship; crashes on ship (651); locked in cabin (652); goes to sleep; awakened; put off ship into longboat (654); transferred to destroyer (655); foreshadowing of his death on July 5 (657); sleeps again; wakened by PM first lieutenant; taken ashore; thinks he is in Scotland (657-658); landed in France; almost 21 (659); broods over fact that they thought he was afraid; sent to airfield; gets new Camel; flies back to squadron with Atkinson in another Camel (661); dogfights Atkinson; flies ahead of Atkinson toward aerodrome (662); crashes plane (663).

_____ Atkinson (644): in B flight with Sartoris (644).

_____ Sibleigh (645): British flight commander (645).

_____ Tate (645): British flight commander (645).

_____: private who comes to crash scene (646).

_____: corporal who comes to crash scene (646).

Harry (646) _____: captain with black eye patch (646).

_____: major; observer (646).

_____: colonel who orders Sartoris to report to his aerodrome after landing (647).

_____: Liverpool boatswain (652).

_____: officer on deck of Brazilian ship; orders plane pushed overboard (652).

_____: two marines who wake Sartoris; one chief warrant officer (654).

_____: officer on destroyer who takes Sartoris to captain (655); wears Victoria Cross (656).

_____: captain of destroyer (655).

_____: boatswain on destroyer (655).

_____: steward on destroyer (656).

446

"Snow"

Written before February 17, 1942; revised by July 22, 1942; once included in the short story, "Beyond;" first published in *Uncollected Stories of William Faulkner*.

_____: child who questions father about Germans (665).

_____: father (665); architect on Pearl Harbor Sunday; late 30's; in WW I; subaltern of engineers; had seen woman who slew German fifteen years ago; flashback: becomes first-person narrator (666).

_____: wife of architect (665).

General (665)   von Ploeckner (665): Nazi   governor;   slain   by mistress; Prussian; stabbed to death (665); fourth man on mountain (670); client of Brix; sends Brix telegram; "The Big Shot;" arranges Brix's wedding (672); from Milan; with Brix and Hiller and Mrs. Brix climbs Bernardines (673); pulled from ledge when Mrs. Brix falls; after Brix's death, leaves on train with Mrs. Brix (674).

Mrs.   Brix (672): mistress of Nazi (665); stabbed him to death (666); Swiss; in funeral procession (667); wife of dead man (670); climbs Bernardines with Brix, Hiller, and Big Shot (673); falls over edge, pulling Big Shot and Brix with her; after Brix's death, leaves on train with Big Shot (674); in spring, when snow melts, returns to find Brix's body with Hiller (674-675); after funeral, leaves on train (676).

Don (666)   : companion of narrator; from California; big (666); sees funeral with field glasses (667); questions man about death (669-670).

_____ Brix (672): man to be buried (667); fell from mountain; guide (670); flashback: receives telegram night before wedding day; from The Big Shot; climbs Bernardines with him, Mrs. Brix, and Hiller (673); pulled from ledge when Mrs. Blrix falls; cuts rope; falls to death (674).

_____: priest in funeral procession (667).

Papa (672)   Grignon (672): man at funeral (669); mayor (672).

Emil Hiller (672): peasant at funeral (669); guide (670);

_____: woman who knits in bar (671).

_____: waiter with rotten teeth (671); tells Don and narrator of the accident (672 ff.); lived in Chicago sixteen years (675).

_____: daughter of Mrs. Brix's mother's half-sister (673).

Index of Titles

"A Bear Hunt," in *Big Woods*, 337

"The Bear," in *Go Down, Moses*, 241

"The Bear," in *Uncollected Stories*, 417

"The Beggar," (See "New Orleans," in *New Orleans Sketches.*)

"The Beggar," (See "New Orleans," in "Royal Street.)

"Bench for Two," (See Pennsylvania Station.")

"Beyond," in *Doctor Martino and other Stories*, 157

"Beyond the Gate," (See "Beyond.")

"The Big Shot," in *Uncollected Stories*, 432

Big Woods, 337

"Black Music," in *Doctor Martino and Other Stories*, 160

"Bourbon Street," (See Jealousy.)

"Brooch," (See "The Brooch.")

"The Brooch," in *Collected Stories*, 295

"Built Fence," (See "A Justice.")

"Built a Fence," (See "A Justice.")

"By the People," in *Mademoiselle*, 341

"Carcassonne," in *These 13*, 132

"Centaur," (See "Centaur in Brass.")

"Centaur in Brass," in *Collected Stories*, 282

"Chance," in *New Orlean Sketches*, 8

"Chartres Street," (See "Mirrors of Chartres Street.")

"Cheest," in *New Orleaqns Sketches*, 6

"Christmas Tree," (See "Two Dollar Wife.")

"The Cobbler," in *New Orleans Sketches*, 8

"The Cobbler," (See "New Orleans," in *New Orleans Sketches.*)

"The Cobbler," (See "New Orleans," in "Royal Street.")

Collected Stories of William Faulkner, 275

"The Cop," (See "New Orleans," in *New Orleans Sketches.*)

"The Cop," (See "New Orleans," in "Royal Street.")

"Country Mice," in *New Orleans Sketches*, 11

"A Courtship," in *Collected Stories*, 289

"Crevasse," in *These 13*, 119

"Damon and Pythias Unlimited," in *New Orleans Sketches*, 4

"Dangerous Man," (See "A Dangerous Man.")

"A Dangerus Man," in *Uncollected Stories*, 439

"A Dangling Participle from Work in Progress," (See *Notes on a Horsethief.*)

"Dark House," (See "A Dark House.")

"A Dark House," (See *Light in August,* "Evangeline," and *Absalom, Absalom!.*)

"Death Drag," in *Doctor Martino and Other Stories*, 152

"A Death Drag," (See "Death Drag,")

"Death-Drag," (See "Death Drag.)

"Delta Autumn," in *Go Down, Moses*, 247

"Delta Autumn," in *Uncollected Stories*, 416

"The Devil Beats His Wife," (See "Two Dollar Wife.")

"Divorce in Naples," in *These 13*, 131

"Doctor Martino," in *Doctor Martino and Other Stories,* 149

Doctor Martino and Other Stories, 149

"Don Giovanni," in *Uncollected Stories*, 429

"Dr. Martino," (See "Doctor Martino.")

"Drouth," (See "Dry September.")

456

Index of Characters

Eight of Faulkner's short stories appear in the published work as short stories in at least two different places. (Many other short stories were revised and used as parts of novels as they were published.) Most of these short stories appeared for the second time in *Uncollected Stories of William Faulkner*, edited by Joseph Blotner. In this index, I have used the following abbreviations to indicate these double appearances: *Big Woods* = BW; *Collected Stories* = CS; *Go Down, Moses* = GDM; *New Orleans Sketches* = NOS; and *Uncollected Stories* = US. The rest of the index should be self-explanatory. Page reference is to the first page in this volume on which the story or novel appears.

Abe

>Flags, 49

Abum

>"Evangeline," 440

Acarius

>"Mr. Acarius," 425

Acey

>Go Down, Moses, 217
>"Pantaloon in Black," GDM 238
>"Pantaloon in Black," US 413

Ad

>"Lion," 408

Adams

>Town, 343

Adams Mrs. Eve

>Town, 343

Adams Theron

>Town, 343

Aelia, Princess

>Mayday, 33

Andrew

Elmer, 48

Andrews

"Fox Hunt," 150

Angelique

Fable, 315

Angelo

"Portrait of Elmer," 442

Anse

Sound and Fury, 65

Antonio ('Tono)

"Jealousy," 5

Armstead

Intruder, 253

Armstid

As I Lay, 95
Father Abraham, 41
Hamlet, 201
Light in August, 133
"Lizards," 403
"Shingles," 277
"Spotted Horses," 406

Armstid (five children of Henry)

"As I Lay," 45

Armstid, Mrs.

"Shingles," 277

Armstid (female)

Hamlet, 201

Armstid, Henry

> "As I Lay," 45
> Father Abraham, 41
> Hamlet, 201
> "Lizards," 403
> Mansion, 363
> "Spotted Horses," 406
> Town, 343

Armstid, Mrs. Henry

> "As I Lay," 45
> Father Abraham, 41
> Hamlet, 201
> "Lizards," 403
> Mansion, 363
> "Spotted Horses," 406
> Town, 343

Armstid, Ina May

> "Spotted Horses," 406

Armstid, Mrs. Lula

> As I Lay, 95

Armstid, Mrs. Martha

> Light in August, 133

Arthur

> "Mississippi," 333

Arthur

> "Sepulture," 426

Ash, Uncle (Old Man Ash)

> "A Bear Hunt," CS, 279
> "The Bear," GDM, 241
> "The Bear, US, 417
> Go Down, Moses, 217
> "The Old People," GDM, 239
> "The Old People," US, 409

Atkins, Miss

> Light in August, 133

Atkinson

>Pylon, 167

Atkinson

>"With Caution," 445

Awce

>"A Return," 436

Ayers, Freddie

>"Yo Ho," 12

Ayers, Major.

>Mosquitoes, 35

Backhouse (See Backus)

Backus (father of Melisandre)

>Mansion, 363
>Town, 343

Backus, Melisandre (See also Harriss, Stevens)

>Mansion, 363
>"My Grandmother Millard," 296
>Town, 343

Backus, Philip St-Just (Backhouse)

>"My Grandmother Millard," 296

Baddrington, Harold (Plexiglas, Plex)

>Mansion, 363

Baird, Dr.

>Soldiers' Pay, 17

Ballenbaugh

>Reivers, 383

Ballenbaugh

>Reivers, 383

Ballenbaugh, Boyd

    "Hand upon Waters," 265

Ballenbaugh, Miss

    Reivers, 383

Ballenbaugh, Tyler

    "Hand upon Waters," 265

Ballott

    Reivers, 383

Ballot, Mrs. Grinnup

    Reivers, 383

Baptis'

    "Peter," 430

Barbour

    "Uncle Willy," 284

Barger, Sonny

    "Uncle Willy," 284

Barr, Captain

    Music," 63

Barron, Homer

    "Rose for Emily," 121

Barron, Jake

    Mansion, 363

Bascomb (Damuddy)

    Sound and Fury, 65

Bascomb, Maury L.

    "Appendix: Compson," 79

Sound and Fury, 65

Basket, Herman

    "A Courtship," 289
    "A Justice," 123

Basket, John

    "A Bear Hunt," BW, 337
    "A Bear Hunt," CS, 279

Beal, Colonel

    Fable, 315

Bean, Captain

    "Uncle Willy," 284

Beard

    Sound and Fury, 65

Beard, Virgil

    Flags, 49

Beard, W. C.

    Flags, 49

Beard, Mrs. W. C.

    Flags, 49
    Light in August, 133

Beatty

    "Turnabout," 155

Beauchamp (family name)

    Town, 343

Beauchamp

    "Go Down, Moses", US, 414
    "A Point of Law," 410

Beauchamp, Amodeus McCaslin

> "The Bear," GDM, 241
> Go Down, Moses, 217

Beauchamp, Bobo

> Reivers, 383

Beauchamp, Callina

> "The Bear," GDM, 241
> Go Down, Moses, 217

Beauchamp, Henry

> "Fire and Hearth," 234
> Go Down, Moses, 217

Beauchamp, Hubert Fitz-Hubert

> "The Bear," GDM, 241
> "Delta Autumn," GDM, 247
> Go Down, Moses, 217
> "Was," 233

Beauchamp, James Thucydus (See also Jim, Tennie's Jim)

> "The Bear," GDM, 241
> "The Bear, US, 417
> "Delta Autumn," GDM, 247
> "Fire and Hearth," 234
> Go Down, Moses, 217
> "The Old People," GDM, 239
> Reivers, 383

Beauchamp, Lucas Quintus Carothers McCaslin

> "The Bear," GDM, 241
> "Delta Autumn," GDM, 247
> "Fire and Hearth," 234
> Go Down, Moses, 217
> "Go Down, Moses," GDM, 119
> "Go Down, Moses," US, 414
> "Gold Is Not Always," 193
> Intruder, 253
> "Pantaloon in Black," GDM, 238
> "Pantaloon in Black," US, 413
> "A Point of Law," 410
> Reivers, 383

469

Beauchamp, Molly (Mollie) Worsham

"Delta Autumn," GDM, 247
"Fire and Hearth," 234
Go Down, Moses, 217
"Go Down, Moses," GDM, 119
"Go Down, Moses," US, 414
Intruder, 253
"A Point of Law," 410

Beauchamp, Nathalie (Nat) (See also Wilkins)

"Fire and Hearth," 234
Go Down, Moses, 217
"A Point of Law," 410

Beauchamp, Philip Manigault

Fable, 315

Beauchamp, Samuel Worsham

Go Down, Moses, 217
"Go Down, Moses," GDM, 119
"Go Down, Moses," US, 414

Beauchamp, Sophonsiba (Fonsiba)

"The Bear," GDM, 241
"Fire and Hearth," 234
Go Down, Moses, 217

Beauchamp, Tennie

"The Bear," GDM, 241
"Delta Autumn," GDM, 247
"Fire and Hearth," 234
Go Down, Moses, 217
Reivers, 383
"Was," 233

Beauchamp, Terrel (See also Terrel and Turl)

"The Bear," GDM, 241
"Delta Autumn," GDM, 247
"Fire and Hearth," 234
Go Down, Moses, 217
Intruder, 253
Town, 343
"Was," 233

Beauchamp, Tomasina (Aunt Tomy and Tomy)

"The Bear," GDM, 241
"Fire and Hearth," 234
Go Down, Moses, 217

Bedenberry, Brother

Light in August, 133

Benbow (family name)

"Skirmish," 397
Town, 343
Unvanquished, 185

Benbow, Judge

Absalom, 175
Hamlet, 201
Unvanquished, 185

Benbow, Belle Mitchel (see also Mitchell)

Flags, 49
Sanctuary, 103
Sanctuary: Original, 85

Benbow, Cassius Q.

"Skirmish," 397
Unvanquished, 185

Benbow, Francis

Flags, 49

Benbow, Horace

Flags, 49
Sanctuary, 103
Sanctuary: Original, 85
"There Was a Queen," 153

Benbow, Julia

Flags, 49
Sanctuary: Original, 85

Benbow, Narcissa (see also Sartoris, Narcissa)

Flags, 49

"Pantaloon in Black," US, 413

Birdsong, (Preacher)

Town, 343

Bishop

Town, 343

Bishop, Ephriam

Mansion, 363

Bishop, Mrs. Ephriam

Mansion, 363

Black

"Death Drag," 152

Blair

"Fox Hunt," 150

Blair, Harrison

"Fox Hunt," 150

Blair, Mrs. Harrison

"Fox Hunt," 150

Blair, John

"Artist at Home," 294

Blair, Mrs. (John's mother)

"Artist at Home," 294

Blake, Jim

"Hand upon Waters," 265

Bland

"Ad Astra," 115

Bland, Gerald

    Sound and Fury, 65

Bland, Mrs. (called Semiramis)

    Sound and Fury, 65

Bledsoe

    Wild Palms, 193

Bledsoe, Sergeant

    Fable, 315

Bleyth, Captain

    Soldiers' Pay, 17

Bleyth, George

    Elmer, 25

Blount (family name)

    "Big Shot," 432

Blount, Gavin (I)

    "A Return," 436

Blount, Dr. (father of Dr. Gavin Blount)

    "Dull Tale," 434
    "A Return," 436

Blount, Mrs. (mother of Dr. Gavin Blount)

    "Dull Tale," 434

Blount, Dr. Gavin

    "Dull Tale," 434
    "A Return," 436

Blount, Dr. Harrison

    "Big Shot," 432

Blount, Mrs. (mother of Dr. Harrison Blount)

"Big Shot," 432

Blum, Major

Fable, 315

Bob

"Sunset," 9

Bogard, H. S.

"Turnabout," 155

Bolivar, Dick

Hamlet, 201
"Lizards," 403

Bon, Charles

Absalom, 175
"Evangeline," 440
Unvanquished, 185

Bon, Mrs. Charles

Absalom, 175
"Evangeline," 440

Bon, Charles Etienne Saint-Valery

Absalom, 175
"Evangeline," 440

Bon, Judith Sutpen (Mrs. Charles) (See also Sutpen, Judith)

"Evangeline," 440

Bond, Jim

Absalom, 175

Bonds, Jack

"A Bear Hunt," CS, 279

Bookwright

"By the People," 341
"Tomorrow," 266

Bookwright

Intruder, 253

Bookwright (female)

"Tomorrow," 266

Bookwright

Town, 343

Bookwright, Calvin (Cal)

Mansion, 363
Reivers, 383
Town, 343

Bookwright, Herman

Mansion, 363

Bookwright, Homer

Mansion, 363
"Shall Not Perish," 281
"Shingles," 277

Bookwright, Odum

Hamlet, 201
Mansion, 363

Bookwright, Mrs. Odum

Hamlet, 201

Bookwrights (suitors of Eula Varner)

Mansion, 363

Bouc, Pierre (Piotr) (See also Piotr)

Fable, 315

Bowden, Matt

>Unvanquished, 185
>"Vendee," 400

Bowen, Captain

>"Raid," 395
>Unvanquished, 185

Bowman

>"Dangerous Man," 439

Bowman, Mrs.

>"Dangerous Man," 439

Boyd

>"Brooch," 295

Boyd, Mrs. (mother of Howard)

>"Brooch," 295

Boyd, Amy (Mrs. Howard)

>"Brooch," 295

Boyd, Don

>"Delta Autumn," US, 416

Boyd, Howard

>"Brooch," 295

Bradley

>Wild Palms, 193

Bradley, Mrs.

>Wild Palms, 193

Brandt, Dr.

>Flags, 49

Breckbridge, Gavin

"Raid," 395
"Skirmish," 397
Unvanquished, 185

Bridesman

Fable, 315

Bridger

Unvanquished, 185
"Vendee," 400

Briggins, Lycurgus

Reivers, 383

Briggins, Mary

Reivers, 383

Britt

"With Caution," 445

Brix

"Snow," 447

Brix, Mrs.

"Snow," 447

Broussard

Mosquitoes, 35

Brown, Joe (See also Burch, Lucas)

Light in August, 133

Brownlee, Percival

"The Bear," GDM, 241
Go Down, Moses, 217

Brummage, Judge

Mansion, 363

Bryan (last name)

    Elmer, 25

Buchwald

    Fable, 315

Buck

    Flags, 49

Buckner, Billie (Bill)

    Wild Palms, 193

Buckner, Buck

    Wild Palms, 193

Buckworth

    Wild Palms, 193

Bucky

    "Yo Ho," 12

Bud, Uncle

    Sanctuary, 103
    Sanctuary: Original, 85

Buffaloe, Joe

    Mansion, 363
    Reivers, 383
    Town, 343

Buford

    Light in August, 133

Bullitt, R. Q. (Bob)

    Pylon, 356

Bullitt, R. Q. (Bob)

    Pylon, 356

Bullitt, Mrs. R. Q.

    Pylon, 356

Bunch, Byron

    Light in August, 281

Bunden, Alex

    "Adolescence," 923

Bunden, Mrs. Alex

    "Adolescence," 923

Bunden, Bud

    "Adolescence," 923

  Bunden, Cyril

    "Adolescence," 923

Bunden, Jeff Davis

    "Adolescence," 923

Bunden, Joe [I]

    "Adolescence," 923

Bunden, Mrs. Joe [I]

    "Adolescence," 923

Bunden, Joe [II]

    "Adolescence," 923

Bunden, Mrs. Joe [II]

    "Adolescence," 923

Bunden, Juliet (Jule)

    "Adolescence," 427

Bunden, Mrs.

    "Spotted Horses," 406

Bundren, Addie (Mrs. Anse I)

As I Lay, 193

Bundren, Anse

As I Lay, 193

Bundren (Mrs. Anse II)

As I Lay, 193

Bundren, Cash

As I Lay, 193

Bundren, Darl

As I Lay, 193
"Uncle Willy," 613

Bundren, Dewey Dell

As I Lay, 193

Bundren, Jewel

As I Lay, 193

Bundren, Vardaman

As I Lay, 193

Burch, Lucas (See also Brown, Joe)

Light in August, 281

Burchett

"Hair," 262

Burchett, Mrs.

"Hair," 262

Burchett

"Moonlight," 931

Burchett, Mrs. Etta

"Moonlight," 931

Burden, Beck

    Light in August, 281

Burden, Calvin [I]

    Light in August, 281
    "Skirmish," 854
    Unvanquished, 395

Burden, Calvin [II]

    Light in August, 281
    "Skirmish," 854
    Unvanquished, 395

Burden, Evangeline

    Light in August, 281

Burden, Joanna

    Light in August, 281
    Mansion, 778

Burden, Juana (Mrs. Nathaniel I)

    Light in August, 281

Burden, Nathaniel

    Light in August, 281

Burden, Mrs. Nathaniel [II]

    Light in August, 281

Burden, Sarah

    Light in August, 281

Burden, Vangie (Evangeline)

    Light in August, 281

Burgess

    Sound and Fury, 126

Burgess

    Sound and Fury, 126

Caldwell, Sam

   Reivers, 823

Callaghan

   "Fox Hunt," 319

Callaghan

   Wild Palms, 412

Callaghan, Miss

   "Uncle Willy," 613

Callicoat, David (See also Ikkemotubbe)

   "A Justice," 257

Callie, Aunt

   Reivers, 823

Cap'm

   "Once aboard Lugger (II)," 911

Carberry, Dr.

   "Two Dollar Wife," 915

Carl

   "Divorce," 276

Caroline

   "Mississippi," 716

Carruthers, Miss

   Light in August, 281

Carter

   "Black Music," 341

Caspey (See also Strother)

   Flags, 95
   "There Was a Queen," 325

Chlory

    "Beyond," 332

Christian, Hoke

    "Uncle Willy," 613

Christian, Walter

    Town, 733

Christian, Willy (Bubber, Uncle Willy)

    Mansion, 778
    Reivers, 823
    Town, 733
    "Uncle Willy," 613

Christian, Mrs. Willy

    "Uncle Willy," 613

Christmas, Joe (See also McEachern)

    Light in August, 281

Church, Mrs.

    "That Will Be Fine," 620

Cinthy

    Light in August, 281

Clapp, Walter

    Reivers, 823

Clarissa

    "Knight's Gambit," 582

Clay, Beulah

    Sound and Fury, 126

Clefus

    Town, 733

Clytemnestra (Clytie) (See also Sutpen)

    Absalom, 372

Coates, Harrison Jr.

    "Dull Tale," 939

Coates, Harrison Sr.

    "Dull Tale," 939

Cochrane, Dr. Ab

    "Mr. Acarius," 919

Cofer

    Wild Palms, 412

Colbert

    "A Courtship," 624

Colbert, David

    "A Courtship," 624

Coldfield (family name)

    Absalom, 372
    Requiem, 659

Coldfield, Ellen (See also Sutpen)

    Absalom, 372

Coldfield, Goodhue

    Absalom, 372

Coldfield, Mrs. Goodhue

    Absalom, 372

Coldfield, Miss

    Absalom, 372

Coldfield, Mrs.

    Absalom, 372

Coldfield, Rosa

Absalom, 372

Coleman, Mrs.

Soldiers' Pay, 30

Collier

"Turnabout," 329

Collyer

Fable, 676

Compson (family name)

"Mississippi," 716
Requiem, 659
"Skirmish," 854
Town, 733
Unvanquished, 395

Compson, Benjamin (Benjy) (See Compson, Maury)

Compson, Candace (Caddy)

"Appendix: Compson," 161
"A Justice," 257
Mansion, 778
Sound and Fury, 126
"That Evening Sun," 265

Compson, Caroline Bascomb

"Appendix: Compson," 161
Mansion, 778
Sound and Fury, 126
"That Evening Sun," 265
Town, 733

Compson, Charles Stuart

"Appendix: Compson," 161

Compson, Jason Lycurgus [I]

"Appendix: Compson," 161
Mansion, 778
"A Name for the City," 655
Requiem, 659

Compson, General Jason Lycurgus (II)

Compson, Mrs. Jason Lycurgus (II) (wife of General)

Compson, Jason Richmond

Compson, Jason Lycurgus (sometimes called Jason IV)

Compson, Maury (Benjamin) (Benjy)

Compson, Mrs. (not wife of General)

Connors, Buck (II)

Town, 733

Conventicle

Fable, 676

Cook, Celia

Unvanquished, 395

Cooper

Pylon, 356

Cooper, Minnie

"Dry September," 269

Cooper, Mrs.

"Dry September," 269

Cotton, Ernest

"Hound," 873

Cowan, Mrs.

"Hair," 262

Cowrie, Captain

Fable, 676

Crack

Mansion, 778

Crain, Amos

"Artist at Home," 634

Crain, Mrs. Amos

"Artist at Home," 634

Crain children

"Artist at Home," 634

Cranston, Lily

 "Doctor Martino," 315

Crawfish-ford (Crawford)

 "A Justice," 257

Crawford, Dr.

 "The Bear," GDM, 521
 Go Down, Moses, 468

Crenshaw, Jack

 Town, 733

Crowe

 Wild Palms, 412

Crump, Lucas

 Idyll, 207

Cunningham, Sergeant

 "Victory," 234

Daingerfield, Miss

 Sound and Fury, 126

Daisy

 "The Bear," GDM, 521
 Go Down, Moses, 468

Damuddy (See Bascom, Damuddy)

 Sound and Fury, 126

Dan

 "Fire and Hearth," 506
 Go Down, Moses, 468
 "Gold Is Not Always," 888

Dandridge, Maggie (See also Stevens)

 Intruder, 545

Davy

    "Leg," 344

Deacon

    Sound and Fury, 126

Demarchi (See also De Marchi)

    Fable, 676

De Marchi

    Fable, 676

De Mont (male) (See also Dumont)

    Fable, 676

De Mont, Marthe, Magda (See also Dumont)

    Fable, 676

De Montigny, Captain

    Fable, 676

De Montigny

    Wild Palms, 412

de Montigny, Paul

    "Elly," 338

Depre, Mrs. Virginia Sartoris (See also DuPre, Sartoris)

    Requiem, 659

DeSpain (family name)

    "Mississippi," 716
    Town, 733

de Spain, Major Cassius

    Absalom, 372
    "Barn Burning," 592
    "A Bear Hunt," BW, 723
    "A Bear Hunt," CS, 600

"The Bear," GDM, 521
"The Bear, US, 900
"Delta Autumn," GDM, 537
Go Down, Moses, 468
Hamlet, 430
Intruder, 545
"Lion," 880
"The Old People," GDM, 517
"The Old People," US, 882
Mansion, 778
Reivers, 823
"Shall Not Perish," 605
Town, 733
"Wash," 335

de Spain, Lula, (Mrs. Cassius)

"Barn Burning," 592
"A Bear Hunt," CS, 600
Hamlet, 430

De Spain (mother of Cassius)

Mansion, 778

De Spain (daughter of Cassius) (married name unknown)

"A Bear Hunt," CS, 600
Mansion, 778

de Spain, Major Manfred

"A Bear Hunt," BW, 723
"Delta Autumn," US, 897
Mansion, 778
Reivers, 823
"Shall Not Perish," 605
Town, 733

de Spain, Mrs. [Manfred?]

"A Bear Hunt," BW, 723

De Spain, (son of Manfred)

"Shall Not Perish," 605

Despleins, Jules

Pylon, 356

"Snow," 967

Doshey (family name)

    Hamlet, 430

Dough, James

    Soldiers' Pay, 30

Downs, Mrs.

    Intruder, 545

Drake

    Requiem, 659
    Sanctuary: Original, 174

Drake

    Requiem, 659
    Sanctuary: Original, 174

Drake

    Requiem, 659
    Sanctuary: Original, 174

Drake, Hubert (Judge)

    Requiem, 659
    Sanctuary, 211
    Sanctuary: Original, 174

Drake, Hubert, Jr. (Buddy)

    Requiem, 659
    Sanctuary, 211
    Sanctuary: Original, 174

Drake, Temple (See also Stevens)

    Requiem, 659
    Sanctuary, 211
    Sanctuary: Original, 174

Dukinfield, Judge

    Mansion, 778
    "Smoke," 562

Town, 733

Dukinfield, Emma

"Smoke," 562

Dulcie

Wishing Tree, 91

Dumont (male, See also Demont)

Fable, 676

Duncan, Demon (see also Ginsfarb)

"Death Drag," 322

DuPre (husband of Jenny)

Flags, 95
"There Was a Queen," 325
Unvanquished, 395

DuPre, Virginia Sartoris (Jenny) (See also Depre,
Sartoris)

"All Dead Pilots," 243 (as Mrs. Virginia
Sartoris)
Flags, 95
Mansion, 778
Requiem, 659 (as Depre)
Sanctuary, 211
Sanctuary: Original, 174
"There Was a Queen," 325
Town, 733 (as sister of Bayard),
Unvanquished, 395

Durley

"Spotted Horses," 875
Ed

"Mirrors," 4
Ed

Mosquitoes, 35

Ed

Reivers, 383

Ed

    Soldiers' Pay, 17

Edmonds (family name)

    Town, 343

Edmonds, Alice

    "The Bear," GDM, 241
    Go Down, Moses, 217

Edmonds, Carothers (Roth)

    "Delta Autumn," GDM, 247
    "Fire and Hearth," 234
    Go Down, Moses, 217
    "Go Down, Moses," GDM, 249
    "Go Down, Moses," US, 414
    "Gold Is Not Always," 412
    Intruder, 253
    "Pantaloon in Black," GDM, 238
    "Pantaloon in Black," US, 413
    "A Point of Law," 410
    "Race at Morning," BW, 338
    "Race at Morning," US, 418
    Reivers, 383
    Town, 343

Edmonds, Carothers McCaslin (Cass)

    "A Bear Hunt," BW, 337
    "The Bear," GDM, 241
    "Delta Autumn," GDM, 247
    "Fire and Hearth," 234
    Go Down, Moses, 217
    "The Old People," GDM, 239
    Reivers, 383
    Town, 343

Edmonds, Mrs. McCaslin

    Go Down, Moses, 217
    "Was," 233

Edmonds, Louisa

    Reivers, 383

499

Edmonds, Mrs.

   Reivers, 383

Edmonds, Zachary (Zack)

      "Fire and Hearth," 234
      Go Down, Moses, 217
      "Gold Is Not Always," 412
      Intruder, 253
      "A Point of Law," 410
      Reivers, 383

Edmonds, Mrs. Zack

      "Fire and Hearth," 234
      Go Down, Moses, 217

Egbert

   Wishing Tree, 47

Ek

   "Liar," 10

Elma, Miss

   Town, 343

Elnora (See also Strother)

      "All Dead Pilots," 243
      Flags, 95
      Sanctuary: Original, 85
      "There Was a Queen," 153

Elys, Princess

   Mayday, 33

Emmeline

   "That Will Be Fine," 287

Emmy

   Soldiers' Pay, 17

Ephraim

    Intruder, 253

Ephum

    Reivers, 383

Ernest

    "Race at Morning," BW, 338
    "Race at Morning, US," 418

Ernest

    Father Abraham, 41
    "Spotted Horses," 406

Ernie

    "Fox Hunt," 150

Ethel

    Elmer, 25
    "Portrait of Elmer," 442

Eunice (See also McCaslin)

    "The Bear," GDM, 241
    Go Down, Moses, 217

Eunice

    Flags, 49

Euphrosy

    "Peter," 430

Eustace

    Flags, 49

Ewell (family name)

    "Mississippi," 333

Ewell, Bryan

    "Error," 269

Ewell, Walter

  "A Bear Hunt," BW, 337
  "The Bear," GDM, 241
  "The Bear, US, 417
  "Delta Autumn," GDM, 247
  Go Down, Moses, 217
  Mansion, 363
  "The Old People," GDM, 239
  "The Old People," US, 409
  "Race at Morning," BW, 338
  "Race at Morning," US, 418
  Reivers, 383

Ewing, Ira (I)

  "Golden Land," 298

Ewing, Ira (II)

  "Golden Land," 298

Ewing, Mrs Ira (II)

  "Golden Land," 298

Ewing, Mitch

  "Hair," 262

Ewing, Samantha (I), [Mrs. Ira (I)]

  "Golden Land," 298

Ewing, Samantha (II) (See also April Lalear)

  "Golden Land," 298

Ewing, Voyd,

  "Golden Land," 298

Exodus

  Wishing Tree, 47

Experience

  Mayday, 33

Frances (mother of Frances-Frankie)

"Frankie and Johnny," 421

Frank

Sanctuary, 103
Sanctuary: Original, 85

Frankie

Flags, 49

Frankie (See also Frances)

"Frankie and Johnny," 421
"New Orleans," NOS, 3
"Royal Street," 13

Franz

"Ad Astra," 115

Fraser

"A Bear Hunt," BW, 337
"A Bear Hunt," CS, 279
"Monk," 263

Fraser, Adam

Intruder, 253

Fraser, Doyle

Intruder, 253

Frazier (family name)

Town, 343

Frazier, Judge

"Tomorrow," 266

Fred (I)

"That Will Be Fine," 287

Fred (II)

"That Will Be Fine," 287

Freeman

    Hamlet, 430
    "Spotted Horses," 406

Freeman, Mrs.

    Hamlet, 201

Frony (See also Gibson)

    "Appendix: Compson," 79
    Sound and Fury, 65
    "That Evening Sun," 126

Frost, Mark

    Mosquitoes, 35

Gabe

    Reivers, 383

Galwyn of Arthgyl

    Mayday, 33

Gambrell, C. L.

    "Monk," 263

Gambrel, Mrs. C. L.

    "Monk," 263

Gant, Eunice

    Town, 343

Gant, Jim

    Miss Zilphia Gant, 83

Gant, Mrs. Jim

    Miss Zilphia Gant, 83

Gant, Zilphia

    Miss Zilphia Gant, 83

507

Gargne

Fable, 315

Gargne, Mrs.

Fable, 315

Garraway

Town, 343

Garraway

Town, 343

Gary, Dr.

Soldiers' Pay, 17

Gatewood, Jabbo

Town, 343

Gatewood, Uncle Noon

Town, 343

Gavin (See also Stevens, Gavin)

"By the People," 341
"Hog Pawn," 419
"A Name for the City," 305

Gawtry, Steve

"Fox Hunt," 150

Gene

Sanctuary, 103
Sanctuary: Original, 85

Genesis

Wishing Tree, 47

George

"Divorce," 131

508

George

    Hamlet, 201

George

    "Leg," 162

George

    "That Will Be Fine," 287

George

    Wishing Tree, 47

Georgie

    "That Will Be Fine," 287

Gianotti, Father

    "The Priest," 421

Gibson, Dilsey

    "Appendix: Compson," 79
    Sound and Fury, 65
    "That Evening Sun," 126

Gibson, Frony (See also Frony; married name unknown)

    "Appendix: Compson," 79
    Sound and Fury, 65
    "That Evening Sun," 126

Gibson, Roskus

    "A Justice," 123
    Sound and Fury, 65

Gibson, T. P.

    "Appendix: Compson," 79
    Sound and Fury, 65
    "That Evening Sun," 126

Gibson, Versh

    Sound and Fury, 65
    "That Evening Sun," 126

Gibson, Will

"Liar," 10

Gihon,

Mansion, 363

Gihon, Danny

"Pennsylvania Station," 293

Gihon, Mrs. Margaret Noonan

"Pennsylvania Station," 293

Gillespie

As I Lay, 95

Gillespie

Wild Palms, 193

Gillespie, Mack

As I Lay, 95

Gilligan, Joe (Yaphank)

Soldiers' Pay, 17

Gillman

"Country Mice," 11

Gillman

"Country Mice," 11

Gillman

"Country Mice," 11

Gillman

Light in August, 133

Gillman, Mrs.

"A Return," 436

Ginotta

Mosquitoes, 35

Ginotta

Mosquitoes, 35

Ginotta, Joe

Mosquitoes, 35

Ginotta, Pete

Mosquitoes, 35

Ginsfarb (See also Demon Duncan)

"Death Drag," 152

Gloria

Elmer, 25
"Portrait of Elmer," 442

Goldie

"Mr. Acarius," 425

Gombault, Pete (Uncle Pete)

Requiem, 307
"Tall Men," 278
Town, 343

Goodwin, Lee

Requiem, 307
Sanctuary, 103
Sanctuary: Original, 85

Goodwin (?) Ruby Lamar (see also Lamar and Ruby)

Sanctuary, 103
Sanctuary: Original, 85

Goodyhay, Brother Joe (J. C.)

Mansion, 363

Goodyhay, Mrs. Joe

    Mansion, 363

Gordon

    Mosquitoes, 35

Gordon, Charles

    "A Return," 436

Gordon (father of Charles)

    "A Return," 436

Gordon, Mrs. (mother of Charles)

    "A Return," 436

Gordon, Lewis Randolph

    "A Return," 436

Gordon, Randolph

    "A Return," 436

Gordon, Mrs. Randolph

    "A Return," 436

Gordon (son of Randolph)

    "A Return," 436

Gordon (daughter of Randolph)

    "A Return," 436

Govelli

    "Big Shot," 432

Gowan, Judge

    "Fire and Hearth," 234
    Go Down, Moses, 217
    "A Point of Law," 410

Gower

Wild Palms, 193

Gowrie (family name)

Intruder, 253
Town, 343

Gowrie (bootlegger)

Town, 343

Gowrie, Amanda Workitt

Intruder, 253

Gowrie, Bilbo

Intruder, 253

Gowrie, Bryan

Intruder, 253

Gowrie, Crawford

Intruder, 253

Gowrie, Forrest

Intruder, 253

Gowrie, N. B. Forrest (Nub)

Intruder, 253
Mansion, 363

Gowrie, Vardaman

Intruder, 253

Gowrie, Vinson

Intruder, 253

Grady

Pylon, 167

Gray, Simon

    "Victory," 113

Green, Captain

    Soldiers' Pay, 17

Greenleaf

    Intruder, 253

Grenier (family name)

    Town, 343

Grenier, Dan (See also Dan Grinnup)

    Reivers, 383

Grenier, Louis

    "Hand upon Waters," 265
    Intruder, 253
    "A Name for the City," 305
    Reivers, 383
    Requiem, 307

Grier (narrator)

    "Shall Not Perish," 281
    "Shingles," 277
    "Two Soldiers," 280

Grier, Ek

    "By the People," 341

Grier (Maw)

    "Shall Not Perish," 281
    "Two Soldiers," 280

Grier (Pap)

    "Shall Not Perish," 281
    "Shingles," 277

Grier, Pete

    "Shall Not Perish," 281
    "Two Soldiers," 280

Grier, Res

Mansion, 363

Grierson (father of Emily)

"Rose for Emily," 121

Grierson, Emily

"Rose for Emily," 121

Grignon, Papa

"Snow," 447

Grimm

Hamlet, 201

Grimm

Light in August, 133

Grimm, Eustace

As I Lay, 95
Hamlet, 201
"Lizards," 403

Grimm, Mrs. Eustace

Hamlet, 201

Grimm, Mrs. Fite

Hamlet, 201

Grimm, Percy

Light in August, 133

Grinnup

Reivers, 383

Grinnup

Reivers, 383

Grinnup, Dan (See also Dan Grenier)

Reivers, 383

Grinnup, Lonnie

"Hand upon Waters," 265
Intruder, 253

Grove

Light in August, 133

Grove, Lena

Light in August, 133

Grove, McKinley

Light in August, 133

Grove, Mrs.

Light in August, 133

Grove, Mrs. McKinley

Light in August, 133

Grover (Rover)

"Afternoon of a Cow," 425

Grover

Elmer, 25
"Portrait of Elmer," 442

Grumby, Major

Hamlet, 201
Unvanquished, 185
"Unvanquished," 399
"Vendee," 400

Grummet

As I Lay, 95

Gualdres, Captain Sebastian

"Knight's Gambit," 270

Gus

    "Country Mice," 11

Habersham (family name)

    Town, 343

Habersham

    Unvanquished, 185

Habersham, Miss Emily

    Town, 343

Habersham, Miss Eunice

    Intruder, 253
    Town, 343

Habersham (father of Eunice)

    Intruder, 253

Habersham, Mrs.

    "Two Soldiers," 280

Habersham, Mrs. Martha

    "Skirmish," 397
    Unvanquished, 185

Habersham, Dr. Samuel

    Intruder, 253
    "Mississippi," 333
    "A Name for the City," 305
    Requiem, 307
    Town, 343

Habersham (son of Dr. Samuel)

    "A Name for the City," 305
    Requiem, 307

Habersham, Mrs. (Chickasaw woman)

    "A Name for the City," 305
    Requiem, 307

Had-Two-Fathers (See also John Had-Two-Fathers and
Fathers, Sam)

"Red Leaves," 119

Hagood

Pylon, 167

Hait, Lonzo

Mansion, 363
"Mule in Yard," 287
Town, 343

Hait, Mrs. Manny

"Mule in Yard," 287
Town, 343

Haley

Hamlet, 201

Haley, Lem

"Liar," 10

Halladay, Jim

Intruder, 253

Halliday

Light in August, 133

Hamblet, Jim

Absalom, 175

Hamp

Wild Palms, 193

Hampton

Reivers, 383

Hampton, Hope

Hamlet, 201
Intruder, 253

Hampton, Mrs. Hope

    Intruder, 253

Hampton, Hubert Jr. (Hub)

    Mansion, 363
    Reivers, 383

Hampton, Hubert Sr. (Hub)

    Mansion, 363
    Town, 343

Hank

    Pylon, 167

Hanley

    Fable, 315

Harker

    "Centaur," 282
    Town, 343

Harker, Otis

    Town, 343

Harmon, Mrs.

    "Liar," 10

Harper

    "Turnabout," 329

Harris

    "Barn Burning," 275

Harris

    "Death Drag," 152

Harris

    Elmer, 25

Harris

    Hamlet, 201

Harris

    "Honor," 165

Harris

    "Rosary," 7

Harris, Mrs.

    "Rosary," 7

Harris

    Sanctuary, 103
    Sanctuary: Original, 85

Harris, Elmer

    "Black Music," 160

Harris, Meloney

    Flags, 49

Harrison, Sergeant

    "Ambuscade," 393
    Unvanquished, 185

Harriss

    "Knight's Gambit," 270
    Mansion, 363

Harriss, Miss

    "Knight's Gambit," 270
    Mansion, 363

Harriss, Max

    "Knight's Gambit," 270
    Mansion, 363

Harriss, Mrs. Melisandre Backus (See also Backus, Stevens)

> "Knight's Gambit," 270
> Mansion, 363

Harry (Mistairy)

> Fable, 315

Harry (See also Dr. Henry Wilbourne)

> Wild Palms, 193

Harry

> "With Caution," 445

Harvey, Deacon

> "Adolescence," 427

Hatcher, Louis

> Sound and Fury, 65

Hatcher, Martha

> Sound and Fury, 65

Hawk, Dennison (I) (Uncle Denny)

> "Raid," 395
> "Skirmish," 397
> Unvanquished, 185

Hawk, Dennison (II) (Denny)

> "Raid," 395
> "Skirmish," 397
> Unvanquished, 185
> "Unvanquished," 399

Hawk, Drusilla (See also Sartoris, Hawk, Drusilla)

> "Raid," 395
> "Skirmish," 397
> Unvanquished, 185
> "Unvanquished," 399
> "Vendee," 400

Hawk, Louise (or Louisa)

>"Raid," 395
>"Skirmish," 397
>Unvanquished, 185
>"Unvanquished," 399

Hawkshaw, Henry (See also Stribling)

>"Hair," 125
>"Dry September," 128

Head, Sydney Herbert

>Sound and Fury, 65

Healy

>"Big Shot," 432
>"Dull Tale," 434

Henderson, Mrs.

>Soldiers' Pay, 17

Henri

>Fable, 315

Henry

>Elmer, 25

Henry

>"Fire and Hearth," 234
>Go Down, Moses, 217

Henry

>Mansion, 363

Henry

>"A Point of Law," 410

Henry

>Requiem, 307

Henry

    Soldiers' Pay, 17

Henry

    Sound and Fury, 65

Henry, Unc

    Flags, 49

Heppleton (male)

    Flags, 49

Heppleton, Joan

    Flags, 49

Herbie

    "Don Giovanni," 429

Hestelle

    "Mississippi," 333

Het (Old Het)

    "Mule in Yard," 287
    Town, 343

Heustace (family name)

    "Big Shot," 432

Heustace

    "Dull Tale," 434

Heustace

    "A Return," 436

Heustace, Henry

    "A Return," 436

Heustace, Mrs. Henry

    "A Return," 436

Hickey

"Big Shot," 432

Hightower

Light in August, 133

Hightower, Mrs.

Light in August, 133

Hightower, Gail (I)

Light in August, 133

Hightower, Rev. Gail (II)

Light in August, 133

Hightower, Mrs. Gail (II)

Light in August, 133

Hightower, Hiram

Reivers, 383

Hill, Dr.

"Mr. Acarius," 425

Hiller, Emil

"Snow," 447

Hilliard

Unvanquished, 185

Hines, Eupheus (Uncle Doc)

Light in August, 133

Hines, Mrs. Eupheus

Light in August, 133

Hines, Milly

Light in August, 133

Hipps, Buck

>Father Abraham, 41
>Hamlet, 201

Hoake

>Hamlet, 201

Hodge (brother of Elmer)

>Elmer, 25
>"Portrait of Elmer," 442

Hodge (brother of Elmer)

>Elmer, 25
>"Portrait of Elmer," 442

Hodge (father of Elmer)

>Elmer, 25
>"Portrait of Elmer," 442

Hodge (mother of Elmer)

>Elmer, 25
>"Portrait of Elmer," 442

Hodge, Elmer (Ellie)

>Elmer, 25
>"Portrait of Elmer," 442

Hodge, Jo (Jo-Addie)

>Elmer, 25
>"Portrait of Elmer," 442

Hogben

>Wild Palms, 193

Hogganbeck (family name)

>"Mississippi," 333

Hogganbeck, Boon

>"A Bear Hunt," BW, 337
>"The Bear," GDM, 241
>"The Bear," US, 417
>"Delta Autumn," GDM, 247

Go Down, Moses, 217
Intruder, 253
"Lion," 408
"Mississippi," 333
"The Old People," GDM, 239
"The Old People," US, 409
Reivers, 383
Town, 343

Hogganbeck (father of Boon)

"The Bear," GDM, 241
Go Down, Moses, 217

Hogganbeck (mother of Boon)

"The Bear," GDM, 241
Go Down, Moses, 217

Hogganbeck, David

"A Courtship," 289

Hogganbeck, Everbe Corinthia (Corrie)

Reivers, 383

Hogganbeck, Lucius (Butch, Luke)

"A Bear Hunt," BW, 337
Mansion, 363
Reivers, 383
Town, 343

Hogganbeck, Lucius Priest

Reivers, 383

Hogganbeck, Mrs. Lucius

"A Bear Hunt," BW, 337

Hogganbeck (3 children of Lucius Hogganbeck)

"A Bear Hunt," BW, 337

Hogganbeck, Melissa

"Knight's Gambit," 270
Town, 343

Hoke

    "Fool about a Horse," 402

Holcomb, Ashley

    Town, 343

Hollcomb, Beth

    Mansion, 363

Holland

    Mansion, 363

Holland

    Mansion, 363

Holland

    "Tomorrow," 266

Holland, Anselm (I) (Anse)

    "Fool about a Horse," 402
    Hamlet, 201
    "Smoke," 261

Holland, Anselm (II) (Young Anse)

    "Smoke," 261

Holland, Cornelia Mardis

    "Smoke," 261

Holland, Virginius (Virge)

    "Smoke," 261

Hollowell, Lafe

    "Adolescence," 427
Hollowell, Lee

    "Adolescence," 427

Holmes, Jack

    Pylon, 167

Holmes, Miss

    Sound and Fury, 65

Holston (family name)

    "Mississippi," 333
    Town, 343

Holston, Alexander

    Absalom, 175
    "Hand upon Waters," 265
    Intruder, 253
    Mansion, 363
    "A Name for the City," 305
    Requiem, 307
    Town, 343

Holston, Dr.

    "My Grandmother Millard," 296

Holston, Mrs.

    "Skirmish," 397
    Unvanquished, 185

Hong Li

    "Royal Street," 13

Hood, Parsham Uncle

    Reivers, 383

Hooper

    Mosquitoes, 35

Hope

    "Turnabout," 155

Hope, L. C. W. (Claude)

    "Turnabout," 155

Hopkins

    Sound and Fury, 65

Horn

    Fable, 315

Horse (See also Casse-tete)

    Fable, 315

Houston

        As I Lay, 95
        Flags, 49

Houston

    "Two Dollar Wife," 424

Houston, Mrs.

    "Two Dollar Wife," 424

Houston, Jack

        Hamlet, 201
        "Hound," 405
        Mansion, 363
        Town, 343

Houston, Lucy Pate (Mrs. Jack)

        Hamlet, 201
        Mansion, 363

Houston (father of Jack)

    Hamlet, 201

Houston, Mrs. (mother of Jack)

    Hamlet, 201

Houston, Zack

        Town, 343
Houston, Letty Bookwright (Mrs. Zack)

        Town, 343
Hovis

    "Moonlight," 431

Hunger

    Mayday, 33

Hurtz

    Pylon, 167

Hurtz, Mrs.

    Pylon, 167

Ike

    "Hand upon Waters," 265

Ikkemotubbe (See also David Callicoat)

    Absalom, 175
    "Appendix: Compson," 79
    "The Bear," GDM, 241
    "A Courtship," 289
    Go Down, Moses, 217
    Intruder, 253
    "A Justice," 123
    "A Name for the City," 305
    "The Old People," GDM, 239
    "The Old People," US. 409
    Reivers, 383
    Requiem, 307
    Town, 343

Imogene

    "Peter," 430

Ingersoll, Robert

    "Beyond," 157

Ingrum

    Intruder, 253

Ingrum, Willy

    Intruder, 253

Irey

    Fable, 315
    Notes on a Horsethief, 301

Isham

"Delta Autumn," GDM, 247
"Delta Autumn," US, 416
Go Down, Moses, 217

Isom

"All Dead Pilots," 117
Flags, 49
Sanctuary, 103
Sanctuary: Original, 85
"There Was a Queen," 153

Issetibbeha

"The Bear," GDM, 241
"A Courtship," 289
Go Down, Moses, 217
"A Name for the City," 305
"The Old People," GDM, 239
"The Old People," US, 409
"Red Leaves," 119
Reivers, 383
Requiem, 307
Town, 343

Ivor

Elmer, 25

Jabbo, Captain

Mansion, 363

Jack

"Honor," 165

Jack

"Uncle Willy," 284

Jackie

Reivers, 383

Jackson (Old Man Jackson)

"Al Jackson," 428

Jackson, Al

> "Al Jackson," 428

Jackson, Art

> Pylon, 167

Jackson, Claude

> "Al Jackson," 428

Jackson, Elenor (Perchie)

> "Al Jackson," 428

Jackson, Herman

> "Al Jackson," 428

Jackson, Mrs.

> "Al Jackson," 428

Jackson, Sam

> "Al Jackson," 428

Jackson, Spearhead

> "Al Jackson," 428

Jake

> "Beyond," 157

Jake

> "Death Drag," 152

Jake

> "Kingdom of God," 7

James, Colonel

> Fable, 315

Jameson, Dorothy

> Mosquitoes, 35

Johnny

>"Frankie and Johnny," 421
>"New Orleans," NOS, 3
>"Royal Street," 13

Johns

>"Two Dollar Wife," 424

Johns, Doris Houston (Mrs. Maxwell Johns)

>"Two Dollar Wife," 424

Johns, Maxwell

>"Two Dollar Wife," 424

Jonas

>Go Down, Moses, 217
>"Was," 233

Jones

>"Death Drag," 152

Jones

>Sanctuary: Original, 85

Jones, Dr.

>Flags, 49

Jones, Herschell

>Sanctuary, 103
>Sanctuary: Original, 85

Jones, Januarius

>Soldiers' Pay, 17

Jones, Melicent

>Absalom, 175
>"Wash," 335

Jones, Milly

>Absalom, 175

"Wash," 335

Jones-Sutpen

    Absalom, 175
    "Wash," 335

Jones, Wash

    Absalom, 175
    "Wash," 335

Jordan, Mrs.

    "That Will Be Fine," 287

Journstadt

    "Two Dollar Wife," 424

Jubal

    "Mountain Victory," 163

Judith

    "Knight's Gambit," 270

Jug

    Pylon, 167

Julio

    Sound and Fury, 65

Junkin, Professor

    Sound and Fury, 65

Jupe

    Light in August, 133

Kauffman, Julius (I)

    Mosquitoes, 35

Kauffman, Julius (II)

    Mosquitoes, 35

Kaye, C. Major

    "All Dead Pilots," 117

Kazimura

    "Golden Land," 298

Kemp, Beasley

    "Fool about a Horse," 402
    Hamlet, 201

Kennedy, Watt

    Light in August, 133

Kenny

    Sound and Fury, 65

Ketcham

    Go Down, Moses, 217
    "Pantaloon in Black," GDM, 238
    "Pantaloon in Black," US, 413

Killebrew, Miss

    Town, 343

Killegrew

    "Shall Not Perish," 281
    "Shingles," 277
    "Two Soldiers," 280

Killegrew, Mrs.

    "Shingles," 277
    "Two Soldiers," 280

Killegrew, Hampton

    "Knight's Gambit," 270

Killegrew, Hunter

    Mansion, 363

King, Alvina

>"Doctor Martino," 149

King, Louise

>"Doctor Martino," 149

"Kitchener," (Kit)

>"All Dead Pilots," 117

Kneeland

>Town, 343

Kohl, Barton

>Mansion, 363

Kohl, Linda Snopes (Mrs. Barton Kohl) (See also Snopes, Linda)

>Father Abraham, 41
>Mansion, 363

Kyerling, R

>"All Dead Pilots," 117

Labove

>Hamlet, 201

Labove (female)

>Hamlet, 201

Labove

>Hamlet, 201

Lafe

>As I Lay, 95

Lafe

>Elmer, 25

Lafe

    "Liar," 10

Lalear, April (See also Ewing, Samantha)

    "Golden Land," 298

Lallemont, General

    Fable, 315

Lamar, Ruby (See also Ruby)

    Sanctuary, 103
    Sanctuary: Original, 85

Landry, Sergeant

    Fable, 315

Lapin

    Fable, 315

Laura, Miss

    Sound and Fury, 65

Lawington, Miss

    As I Lay, 95

Leblanc

    Pylon, 167

Ledbetter, Mrs.

    Mansion, 363
    Town, 343

Lee, Joe

    "Peter," 430

Legate, Bob

    Reivers, 383

Legate, Will (Willy)

>"Delta Autumn," GDM, 247
>"Delta Autumn," US, 416
>Go Down, Moses, 217
>Intruder, 253
>"Race at Morning," BW, 338
>"Race at Morning," US, 418

Legendre, Dr.

>Pylon, 167

Lena, Missy

>Unvanquished, 185

Leonard

>Hamlet, 201

Leonora

>Pylon, 167

Lessep

>Reivers, 383

Lessep

>Reivers, 383

Lester, Judy

>"Mr. Acarius," 425

Levine, Gerald David

>Fable, 315

Levine (father of Gerald)

>Fable, 315

Levine, Mrs. (mother of Gerald)

>Fable, 315

Levitt, Matt

>Town, 343

Loosh

"Ambuscade," 393
"Raid," 395
"Retreat," 394
Unvanquished, 185
"Unvanquished," 399

Lord of Sleep

Mayday, 33

Lorine

"Uncle Willy," 284

Lorraine

"Appendix: Compson," 79
Sound and Fury, 65

Lorraine

Sanctuary, 103
Sanctuary: Original, 85

Lothair

"Knight's Gambit," 270

Louis

Sound and Fury, 65

Louisa

"That Will Be Fine," 287

Louisa

Wild Palms, 193

Louisa (II)

"That Will Be Fine," 287

Louvinia

"Ambuscade," 393
Flags, 49
"My Grandmother Millard," 296
"Raid," 395

Luke

    Sanctuary, 103
    Sanctuary: Original, 85

Luluque

    Fable, 315

Luster

    Absalom, 175
    "Appendix: Compson," 79
    Sound and Fury, 65

Luster

    Reivers, 383

Mabel

    "Peter," 430

Mac

    Pylon, 167

Mac
    Sound and Fury, 65

McAndrews

    Go Down, Moses, 217
    "Pantaloon in Black," GDM, 238
    "Pantaloon in Black," US, 413

McCallum (family name)

    Town, 343

McCallum

    Hamlet, 201
    Intruder, 253

McCallum

    "Knight's Gambit," 270

McCallum

    "Knight's Gambit," 270

547

McCallum, Anse

  Hamlet, 201

McCallum, Anse (I) (Old Anse)

  "Tall Men," 278

McCallum, Mrs. Anse (I)

  "Tall Men," 278

McCallum, Anse (II) (Buddy)

  "Tall Men," 278
  Town, 343

McCallum, Mrs. Anse (II) (mother of twins)

  "Tall Men," 278

McCallum, Anse (III) (twin of Lucius)

  "Tall Men," 278
  Town, 343

McCallum, Lucius (twin of Anse)

  "Tall Men," 278

McCallum (Old Man Hundred and One)

  Hamlet, 201

MacCallum (father of Virginius I)

  Flags, 49

MacCallum, Henry

  Flags, 49

MacCallum, Jackson

  Flags, 49
  "Tall Men," 278 (as McCallum)

MacCallum, Lee

  Flags, 49
  "Tall Men," 278 (as McCallum)

548

MacCallum, Raphael Semmes (Rafe)

> As I Lay, 95
> Flags, 49
> "Knight's Gambit," 270
> Mansion, 363" (as McCallum)
> "Tall Men," 278 (as McCallum)

MacCallum, Stuart

> As I Lay, 95
> Flags, 49
> "Tall Men," 278 (as McCallum)

MacCallum, Virginius (I)

> Flags, 49

MacCallum, Virginius (II) (Buddy)

> Flags, 49
> Intruder, 253

MacCallum, Mrs. Virginius (I)

> Flags, 49

MacCallum, Mrs. Virginius (II)

> Flags, 49

McCannon, Shrevlin (Shreve) (See also MacKenzie, Shreve)

> Absalom, 175

McCarron (father of Hoake)

> Hamlet, 201

McCarron, Mrs. Allison Hoake

> Hamlet, 201
> Mansion, 363

McCarron, Hoake

> Hamlet, 201
> Mansion, 363
> Town, 343

McCaslin (family name)
    "Mississippi," 333
    Requiem, 307
    Town, 343

McCaslin

    Reivers, 383

McCaslin, Amodeus (Uncle Buddy)

    "The Bear," GDM, 241
    "Delta Autumn," GDM, 247
    "Fire and Hearth," 234
    Go Down, Moses, 217
    "The Old People," GDM, 239
    Unvanquished, 185
    "Was," 233

McCaslin, Carolina (Callina)

    "The Bear," GDM, 241
    Go Down, Moses, 217

McCaslin, Delphine (Mrs. Ned)

    Reivers, 383

McCaslin, Eunice (See also Eunice)

    "The Bear," GDM, 241
    Go Down, Moses, 217

McCaslin, Isaac Beauchamp (Ike, Uncle Ike)

    "A Bear Hunt," BW, 337
    "A Bear Hunt," CS, 279
    "The Bear," GDM, 241
    "Delta Autumn," GDM, 247
    "Delta Autumn," US, 416
    "Fire and Hearth," 234
    "Fool about a Horse," 402
    Go Down, Moses, 217
    Hamlet, 201
    Intruder, 253
    "Lion," 408
    Mansion, 363
    "The Old People," GDM, 239
    "The Old People," US, 409
    "Race at Morning," BW, 338
    "Race at Morning," US, 418
    Reivers, 383

551

Reivers, 383
"Retreat," 394
Unvanquished, 185
"Unvanquished," 399
"Vendee," 400
"Was," 233

McCaslin, Theophilus

"Lion," 408

McCaslin, Thucydides (Thucydus) (See also
Thucydides)

"The Bear," GDM, 241
Go Down, Moses, 217

McCord

Wild Palms, 193

McDiarmid

Reivers, 383

McEachern, Joe (See also Joe Christmas)

Light in August, 133

McEachern, Simon

Light in August, 133

McEachern, Mrs. Simon

Light in August, 133

McGinnis, Darrel

"Turnabout," 155

Macgowan, Skeet

As I Lay, 95

McGowan, Skeets

Intruder, 253
Mansion, 363
Town, 343

McKellogg

"Two Soldiers," 280

McKellogg, Colonel

"Two Soldiers," 280

McKellogg, Mrs.

"Two Soldiers," 280

MacKenzie, Shreve (See also McCannon, Shreve)

Sound and Fury, 65

McKie

"Crevasse," 119

McLan

"Victory," 113

McLendon, Jackson

Town, 343

McLendon, Captain John

"Dry September," 128
Light in August, 133
Mansion, 363

McLendon, Mrs. John

"Dry September," 128

McLendon, Mrs. (mother of Captain John)

Mansion, 363

McNamara

"Damon and Pythias," 4

McWilliams

"Knight's Gambit," 270

McWillie

    Reivers, 383

MacWyrglinchbeath, Willie

    "Thrift," 422

Madden, Rufus

    Soldiers' Pay, 17

Magda (See also Marthe, Demont, Dumont)

    Fable, 315

Magdalen

    "New Orleans," NOS 3
    "Royal Street," 13

Maggie

    "Sepulture," 426

Maggie

    Wishing Tree, 47

Mahon, Donald

    Soldiers' Pay, 17

Mahon, Rev. Joe

    Soldiers' Pay, 17

Mahon, Margaret Powers (Mrs. Donald) (See also Powers)

    Soldiers' Pay, 17

Malcolm

    "Afternoon of a Cow," 425

Mallison, Charles Jr. (Chick)

    "By the People," 341 (as Charles)
    "Hog Pawn," 419
    Intruder, 253
    "Knight's Gambit," 270

Marge

> Sanctuary, 103
> Sanctuary: Original, 85

Marguerite

> "Knight's Gambit," 270

Marina, Angelo

> Elmer, 25

Mark

> Mayday, 33

Markey, Robert

> "Knight's Gambit," 270

Marsh

> "Two Soldiers," 280

Martel, General

> Fable, 315

Martha

> Elmer, 25

Martha

> Wild Palms, 193

Marthe (See also Magda, Demont, Dumont)

> Fable, 315

Martin (brothers and sisters of Dal Martin)

> "Big Shot," 432
> "Dull Tale," 434

Martin (father of Dal Martin)

> "Big Shot," 432
> "Dull Tale," 434

Memmy (See also Bill and William)

>"Mississippi," 333

Merridew

>"Uncle Willy," 284

Merridew, Mrs.

>"Uncle Willy," 284

Merridew, Mrs.

>"Portrait of Elmer," 442

Merridew, Velma

>"Portrait of Elmer," 442

Metcalf

>Light in August, 133

Middleton, Captain

>Fable, 315

Midgleston, Mrs. Martha

>"Black Music," 160

Midgleston, Wilfred

>"Black Music," 160

Mike

>Sound and Fury, 65

Milhaud, Madame

>Fable, 315

Millard

>"My Grandmother Millard," 296

Millard, Rosa

>"Ambuscade," 393
>Hamlet, 201

Mitchell

> "Liar," 10

Mitchell, Mrs.

> Soldiers' Pay, 17

Mitchell, Belle (I) (See also Benbow)

> Flags, 49
> Sanctuary, 103
> Sanctuary: Original, 85

Mitchell, Belle (Little Belle)

> Flags, 49
> Sanctuary, 103
> Sanctuary: Original, 85

Mitchell, Uncle Few

> "Retreat," 394
> Unvanquished, 185

Mitchell, Harry

> Flags, 49
> Sanctuary, 103
> Sanctuary: Original, 85

Mitchell, Hugh

> Hamlet, 201

Mitchell, Walter

> "Two Dollar Wife," 424

Mohataha

> Mansion, 363
> "A Name for the City," 305
> Requiem, 307

Moketubbe

> "A Courtship," 289
> Go Down, Moses, 217
> "The Old People," GDM, 239
> "The Old People," US, 409
> "Red Leaves," 119

Reivers, 383

Monoghan, Buck

"Ad Astra," 115
Fable, 315
Flags, 49
"Honor," 165

Monckton

"Divorce," 131

Monk

Pylon, 167

Monk

"Big Shot," 432

Monson (father of Myrtle)

Elmer, 25
"Portrait of Elmer," 442

Monson, Mrs. (mother of Myrtle)

Elmer, 25
"Portrait of Elmer," 442

Monson, Myrtle

Elmer, 25
"Portrait of Elmer," 442

Montgomery, Jake

Intruder, 253

Mooney

Light in August, 133

Moore,

Flags, 49

Morache

Fable, 315

562

Murry

"Mississippi," 333

Myers, Al

Pylon, 167

Myrtle

Flags, 49

Myrtle

Sanctuary, 103
Sanctuary: Original, 85

Myrtle

Sound and Fury, 65

Nancy (See also Mannigoe)

Requiem, 307
"That Evening Sun," 126

Natalie

Sound and Fury, 65

Nate

"Hand upon Waters," 265

Ned

"Mississippi," 333

Nelson, Callie, (Cal'line)

Soldiers' Pay, 17

Nelson, Corporal Loosh

Soldiers' Pay, 17

Newberry, Colonel G. W.

Unvanquished, 185
"Unvanquished," 399

Nightingale

>Mansion, 363

Nightingale, Tug

>Mansion, 363

Nunnery, Cedric

>Town, 343

Nunnery, Mrs.

>Town, 343

Odlethrop, Mrs.

>"Monk," 263

Odlethrop, Stonewall Jackson (Monk)

>"Monk," 263

Odum, Cliff

>Hamlet, 201

Oliver

>"Afternoon of a Cow," 425

Ord,Matt

>Pylon, 167

Ord, Mrs.

>Pylon, 167

Oscar

>"Fire and Hearth," 234
>Go Down, Moses, 217
>"Gold Is Not Always," 412

Osgood

>Fable, 315

Otis

>Reivers, 383

Ott, Jimmy

    Pylon, 167

Otto

    "Kid Learns," 9

Owl-by-Night

    "A Courtship," 289

Pain

    Mayday, 33

Painter

    Idyll, 101

Paoli

    "Knight's Gambit," 270

Pap

    Sanctuary, 103
    Sanctuary: Original, 85

Parker

    Sound and Fury, 65

Parsham (family name)

    Reivers, 383

Parsons, Maurice (See also Priest, Maurice)

    Town, 343

Parsons, Sally Hampton (Mrs. Maurice) (See also Priest, Sally Hampton)

    Town, 343
Patterson (boy)

    Sound and Fury, 65
Patterson, Mr.

    Sound and Fury, 65

Patterson, Mrs.

Sound and Fury, 65

Paul

Fable, 315

Peabody (family name)

Town, 343

Peabody, Dr.

"A Name for the City," 305
Requiem, 307

Peabody, Doc (sells whisky)

"Fool about a Horse," 402

Peabody, Dr. Lucius Quintus (I) (Loosh)

As I Lay, 95
"Beyond," 157
Flags, 49
Hamlet, 201
Mansion, 363
Reivers, 383
Sound and Fury, 65
Town, 343

Peabody, Mrs. Lucius (I)

Flags, 49
Peabody, Dr. Loosh (II)

Flags, 49

Pearson

"Tall Men," 278

Peebles, E. E.

Light in August, 133

Pete

"Home," 8

Pete (bootlegger's younger brother)

>"Mississippi," 333
>"Once aboard Lugger (I)," 421
>"Once aboard Lugger (II)," 422

Pete

>Pylon, 167

Pete

>Requiem, 307

Pete

>Wild Palms, 193

Peter

>"Peter," 430

Peter

>"Two Dollar Wife," 424

Pettibone

>Absalom, 175

Pettigrew

>"Beyond," 157

Pettigrew, Thomas Jefferson

>"A Name for the City," 305
>Requiem, 307

Pettigrew, Mrs (mother of T. J.)

>"A Name for the City," 305
>Requiem, 307

Peyton, George

>Reivers, 383

Philadelphia

>"My Grandmother Millard," 296

Philadelphy

>"Ambuscade," 393
>"Raid," 395
>"Retreat," 394
>Unvanquished, 185

Philip

>"Elly," 159

Philip

>"Golden Land," 298

Phoebe

>"The Bear," GDM, 241
>Go Down, Moses, 217

Picklock

>Fable, 315

Pinckski

>"Pennsylvania Station," 293

Pinkie

>"Artist at Home," 294

Piotr (See also Bouc, Pierre)

>Fable, 315

Plexiglas (Plex) (See Baddrington, Harold)

Ploeckner

>Flags, 49

Polchek

>Fable, 315

Poleymus

>Reivers, 383

Poleymus, Mrs.

    Reivers, 383

Pomp

    Light in August, 133

Popeye (See also Vitelli)

    "Big Shot," 432
    Requiem, 307
    Sanctuary, 103
    Sanctuary: Original, 85

Pose

    "Hand upon Waters," 265

Potter, Jack

    "Cheest," 6

Powell (father of John Powell)

    Reivers, 383

Powell, John

    Reivers, 383

Powell, Mrs. John

    Reivers, 383

Powers, Margaret (Mrs. Richard) (See also Mahon)

    Soldiers' Pay, 17

Powers, Richard

    Soldiers' Pay, 17

Priest (father of Boss Priest)

    Reivers, 383

Priest (mother of Boss Priest)

    Reivers, 383

Priest, Alexander

    Reivers, 383

Priest, Allison Lessep

    Reivers, 383

Priest, Lessep

    Reivers, 383

Priest, Lucius Quintus Carothers (I) (Boss)

    Reivers, 383

Priest, Lucius (II)

    Reivers, 383

Priest, Lucius (III)

    Reivers, 383

Priest, Maurice (See also Parsons, Maurice)

    Town, 343

Priest, Maury (I)

    Reivers, 383

Priest, Maury (II)

    Reivers, 383

Priest, Sally Hampton (Mrs. Maurice) (See also Parsons, Sally Hampton.)

    Town, 343

Priest, Sarah Edmonds

    Reivers, 383

Pritchel, Wesley

    "Error," 269

Provine

    "A Bear Hunt," BW, 337

571

Provine

    "A Bear Hunt," BW, 337

Provine

    "A Bear Hunt," CS, 279

Provine, Lucius (Luke, Butch)

    "A Bear Hunt," CS, 279

Provine, Mrs. Lucius

    "A Bear Hunt," CS, 279

Provine (children of Lucius Provine)

    "A Bear Hunt," CS, 279

Provine, Wilbur

    Town, 343

Provine, Mrs. Willbur

    Town, 343

Pruitt

    "That Will Be Fine," 287
    "Tomorrow," 266

Pruitt, Mrs.

    "That Will Be Fine," 287
    "Tomorrow," 266

Pruitt, Rufus

    "Tomorrow," 266

Quentin

    "Lion," 408

Quick (family name)

    Hamlet, 201
    Mansion, 363

Quick, Ben

> Hamlet, 201
> "Tomorrow," 266

Quick, Isham

> "Tomorrow," 266

Quick, Lon (I) (Big Lon)

> As I Lay, 95
> Hamlet, 201
> "Lizards," 403
> "Spotted Horses," 406

Quick, Lon (II) (Little Lon)

> As I Lay, 95
> "Lizards," 403
> Mansion, 363

Quick, Solon

> Mansion, 363
> "Shall Not Perish," 281
> "Shingles," 277

Quick, Mrs. Solon

> "Shall Not Perish," 281

Quick, Theron

> Mansion, 363

Quicks (suitors of Eula Varner)

> Mansion, 363

Quinn, Dr.

> Sanctuary, 103
> Sanctuary: Original, 85

Quistenberry, Dink

> Town, 343

Quistenberry, Mrs. Dink

> Town, 343

Rachel

Flags, 49

Rachel, Aunt

"That Evening Sun," 126

Ralph

Wild Palms, 193

Randolph (father of Lewis Randolph Gordon)

"A Return," 436

Randolph (mother of Lewis Randolph Gordon)

" A Return," 436

Rastus

"Music," 63

Ratcliffe

Town, 343

Ratcliffe

"A Name for the City," 305
Requiem, 307
Town, 343

Ratcliffe, Mrs. Nelly Ratliff

Mansion, 363
Town, 343

Ratliff, Vladimir Kyrilytch (V. K.)

"A Bear Hunt," BW, 337
"A Bear Hunt," CS, 279
"By the People," 341
Flags, 49
Hamlet, 201
"Lizards," 403
Mansion, 363
"Spotted Horses," 406
Town, 343

Ratliff (V. K.'s father)

Hamlet, 201

Ratliff, Vladimir Kyrilytch (ancestor)

Mansion, 363
Town, 343

Ray

Elmer, 25

Red

"Big Shot," 432

Red

Requiem, 307 (as Alabama Red)
Sanctuary, 103
Sanctuary: Original, 85

Redlaw

Flags, 49

Redmond, Ben

"Mississippi," 333
Requiem, 307
Unvanquished, 185

Reed, Susan

"Hair," 125

Reeves

"Turnabout," 155

Reeves, Don

"Big Shot," 432

Reichman

Mosquitoes, 35

Reinhardt,

"Honor," 165

Rideout, Dr.

>"Fire and Hearth," 234
>Go Down, Moses, 217

Rider, Mannie

>Go Down, Moses, 217
>"Pantaloon in Black," GDM, 238
>"Pantaloon in Black," US, 413

Rider, Spoot

>Go Down, Moses, 217
>"Pantaloon in Black," GDM, 238
>"Pantaloon in Black," US, 413

Rider (Spoot's parents)

>"Pantaloon in Black," US, 413

Ringo (See also Marengo)

>"Ambuscade," 393
>"My Grandmother Millard," 296
>"Raid," 395
>"Retreat," 394
>"Skirmish," 397
>Unvanquished, 185
>"Unvanquished," 399
>"Vendee," 400

Rittenmeyer, Ann

>Wild Palms, 193

Rittenmeyer, Charlote (I)

>Wild Palms, 193

Rittenmeyer, Charlotte (II)

>Wild Palms, 193

Rittenmeyer, Francis (Rat)

>Wild Palms, 193

Rivers, Lee

>Soldiers' Pay, 17

Rogers, Ken

>"Liar," 10

Rogers, Mildred

>"Honor," 165

Roland

>"Knight's Gambit," 270

Roscius (Roskus)

>"The Bear," GDM, 241
>Go Down, Moses, 217

Rose

>"Evangeline," 440

Rosie

>"That Will Be Fine," 287

Ross, Frank

>"Brooch," 295

Ross, Martha (Mrs. Frank)

>"Brooch," 295

Rouncewell

>Go Down, Moses, 217
>"Go Down, Moses," GDM, 249
>"Go Down, Moses," US, 414

Rouncewell

>Mansion, 363

Rouncewell
>Mansion, 363
>Reivers, 383

Rouncewell, Mrs.

>Mansion, 363
>Reivers, 383

Town, 343

Sartoris [father of John (I)]

"There Was a Queen," 153

Sartoris [mother of John (I), Bayard (I), Virginia]

Flags, 49
"My Grandmother Millard," 296
"There Was a Queen," 153

Sartoris (mother of narrator of "My Grandmother Millard")

"My Grandmother Millard," 296

Sartoris [wife of Bayard (II)]

Flags, 49

Sartoris [wife of John (I); mother of Bayard (II)]

"Skirmish," 397
Unvanquished, 185

Sartoris [daughter of John (I)]

Flags, 49
"Mississippi," 333

Sartoris [daughter of John (I)]

Flags, 49
"Mississippi," 333

Sartoris [daughter of John (I)]

"Mississippi," 333

Sartoris, Bayard (I)

Flags, 49
Unvanquished, 185

Sartoris, Bayard (II)

"All Dead Pilots," 117
"Ambuscade," 393
"The Bear," GDM, 241
Flags, 49
Go Down, Moses, 217

583

Sartoris, John (I)

> Absalom, 175
> "Ambuscade," 393
> "Barn Burning," 275
> "The Bear," GDM, 241
> Flags, 49
> Go Down, Moses, 217
> Hamlet, 201
> Light in August, 133
> Mansion, 363
> "Mississippi," 333
> "My Grandmother Millard," 296
> "Raid," 395
> Reivers, 383
> Requiem, 307
> "Retreat," 394
> "Shall Not Perish," 281
> "Skirmish," 397
> Sound and Fury, 65
> "There Was a Queen," 153
> Town, 343
> Unvanquished, 185
> "Unvanquished," 399
> "Vendee," 400

Sartoris, John (II)

> "The Bear," GDM, 241
> Flags, 49
> Go Down, Moses, 217
> "There Was a Queen," 153

Sartoris, John (III) (Johnny)

> "Ad Astra," 115
> "All Dead Pilots," 117
> Flags, 49
> Mansion, 363
> Sanctuary: Original, 85
> "There Was a Queen," 153
> Town, 343
> "With Caution," 445

Sartoris, Lucy Cranston

> Flags, 49

Sartoris, Narcissa Benbow (See also Benbow, Narcissa)

> Flags, 49
> Mansion, 363

585

Semmes

>   "The Bear," GDM, 241
>   Go Down, Moses, 217

Sethynnen ap Seydun Seidl

>   Mayday, 33

Shack

>   Sanctuary, 103
>   Sanctuary: Original, 85

Shegog, Rev.

>   Sound and Fury, 65

Short, Herman

>   "Fool about a Horse," 402
>   Hamlet, 201

Shumann, Dr. Carl

>   Pylon, 167

Shumann, Mrs. Carl

>   Pylon, 167

Shumann, Jack

>   Pylon, 167

Shumann, Lavern

>   Pylon, 167

Shuman, Roger

>   Pylon, 167

Sibey

>   "Evangeline," 440

Sibleigh

>   Fable, 315
>   Flags, 49

"With Caution," 445

Sickymo

"The Bear," GDM, 241
Go Down, Moses, 217

Simmons

Sound and Fury, 65

Simms

Light in August, 133

Simon (See also Strother)

Flags, 49
"There Was a Queen," 153

Simon

"Race at Morning," BW, 338
"Race at Morning," US, 418

Simon

"Sepulture," 426

Simon (father of Ringo)

Unvanquished, 185

Simpson

"Liar," 10

Skeet

"Moonlight," 431

Skipworth

Intruder, 253

Skipworth, Mrs.

Intruder, 253

Smith, Lieutenant

Fable, 315

Smith (father of McKinley)

Smith, Mrs.

Smith, Essie Meadowfill (Mrs. McKinley Smith)

Smith, McKinley

Smith, Ronnie Boyce

Smitty

Snopes

Snopes

Snopes (second Snopes in Frenchman's Bend)

Snopes (wife of second Snopes in Frenchman's Bend)

Snopes (third Snopes in Frenchman's Bend)

Snopes (fourth Snopes in Frenchman's Bend)

Snopes (The actual schoolmaster)

Snopes (daughter of Ab)

Snopes (daughter of Ab; old maid)

Snopes (four children of Byron)

Snopes (older brother of Colonel Sartoris Snopes)
(probably Flem Snopes)

Snopes (sister of Colonel Sartoris Snopes)

Snopes

Snopes (titular but not biologic father of Eck)

Snopes (son of Eck)

Snopes (Flem's grandfather)

Snopes (brother of Flem)

Snopes (child of I. O.)

Snopes (infant child of I. O.)

Snopes, Eckrum (Eck) (father of Wallstreet Panic and
Admiral Dewey)

    Father Abraham, 41
    Hamlet, 201
    Mansion, 363
    "Spotted Horses," 406
    Town, 343

Snopes, Mrs. (mother of Eck)

    Mansion, 363
    Town, 343

Snopes, Mrs. Eck (I)

    Father Abraham, 41
    Hamlet, 201
    Town, 343

Snopes, Mrs. Eck (II)

    Hamlet, 201

Snopes, Eula Varner (Mrs. Flem Snopes)

    "Centaur," 282
    Father Abraham, 41
    Flags, 49
    Hamlet, 201
    Mansion, 363
    "Spotted Horses," 406
    Town, 343

Snopes, Flem

    As I Lay, 95
    "By the People," 341
    "Centaur," 282
    Father Abraham, 41
    Flags, 49
    Hamlet, 201
    "Lizards," 403
    Mansion, 363
    Reivers, 383
    "Spotted Horses," 406
    Town, 343

Snopes, I. O.

    Father Abraham, 41
    Flags, 49

Hamlet, 201
Mansion, 363
"Mule in Yard," 287
Sound and Fury, 65
"Spotted Horses," 406
Town, 343

Snopes, Mrs. I. O. (I)

Flags, 49
Hamlet, 201
Town, 343

Snopes, Mrs. I. O. (II)

Hamlet, 201
Town, 343

Snopes, Isaac (Ike)

Hamlet, 201

Snopes, Launcelot (Lump)

Hamlet, 201
"Hound," 405
Mansion, 363

Snopes, Lennie

"Barn Burning," 275

Snopes, Linda (See also Kohl) (child of Eula Varner
Snopes)

"Centaur," 282
Father Abraham, 41
Flags, 49
Mansion, 363
"Spotted Horses," 406
Town, 343

Snopes, Mink

Hamlet, 201
Mansion, 363
Town, 343

Snopes, Montgomery Ward (son of I. O.)

Flags, 49
Mansion, 363

Town, 343

Snopes, Net

"Barn Burning," 275

Snopes, Orestes (Res)

"Hog Pawn," 419
Mansion, 363

Snopes, St. Elmo

Hamlet, 201

Snopes, Vardaman (son of I. O. and second wife)

Mansion, 363
Town, 343

Snopes, Virgil

Mansion, 363
Sanctuary, 103
Sanctuary: Original, 85
Town, 343

Snopes, Vynie

Hamlet, 201

Snopes, Wallstreet Panic (Wall)

Hamlet, 201
Mansion, 363
Town, 343

Snopes, Mrs. Wallstreet Panic

Town, 343

Snopes, Watkins Products (Wat)

Mansion, 363

Snopes, Wesley

Mansion, 363

Snopes, Yettie (Mrs. Mink)

Hamlet, 201

Starnes, Joe

 "Liar," 10

Starnes, Mrs. Joe

 "Liar," 10

Starnes, Sophie (Sophy)

 "Hair," 125

Starnes, Will

 "Hair," 125

Starnes, Mrs. Will

 "Hair," 125

Stefan

 Fable, 315

Steinbauer

 Mosquitoes, 35

Steinbauer, Genevieve (Jenny)

 "Don Giovanni," 429
 Mosquitoes, 35

Stevens (family name)

 Requiem, 307
 Town, 343

Stevens

 "Hand upon Waters," 571

Stevens (murdered infant)

 Requiem, 307

Stevens (parents of Gowan Stevens)

 Requiem, 307
 Town, 343

Stevens (mother of Maggie and Gavin)

Town, 343

Stevens, Bucky

Requiem, 307

Stevens, Captain

"Error," 269
"Tomorrow," 266

Stevens, Gavin (See aso Gavin)

"By the People," 341
"Error," 269
Go Down, Moses, 217
"Go Down, Moses," GDM, 249
"Go Down, Moses," US, 414
"Hair," 125
"Hand upon Waters," 265
"Hog Pawn," 419
Intruder, 253
"Knight's Gambit," 270
Light in August, 133
Mansion, 363
"Monk," 263
"A Name for the City," 305
Requiem, 307
"Smoke," 261
"Tall Men," 278
"Tomorrow," 266
Town, 343

Stevens, Gowan

Requiem, 307
Sanctuary, 103
Sanctuary: Original, 85
Town, 343

Stevens, Judge Lemuel

Mansion, 363
Reivers, 383
"Rose for Emily," 121
Town, 343

Stevens, Melisandre Backus Harris (Mrs. Gavin,
Milly) (See also Backus, Harris)

"By the People," 341

Mansion, 363

Stevens, Temple Drake (Mrs. Gowan) (See also Drake, Temple)

Requiem, 307

Stillwell, Shuford

Mansion, 363

Stokes

"A Justice," 123

Stone

Town, 343

Stone

Town, 343

Stovall

"That Evening Sun," 265

Stowers, Zack

"Dangerous Man," 439

Stowers, Mrs. Zack

"Dangerous Man," 439
Straud, Dr.

Flags, 49

Stribling, Henry (Hawkshaw) (See also Hawkshaw)

"Dry September," 128
"Hair," 125

Strother, Caspey (See also Caspey)

Flags, 49
"There Was a Queen," 153

Strother, Elnora (married name unknown) (See also Elnora)

"All Dead Pilots," 117

Sutpen (family name)

Sutpen (father of Thomas Sutpen)

Sutpen (mother of Thomas Sutpen)

Sutpen, Clytemnestra (Clytie) (See also Sutpen, Raby)

Sutpen, Ellen Coldfield (Mrs. Thomas Sutpen) (See also Coldfield, Ellen)

Sutpen, Eulalia

Sutpen, Henry

Sutpen, Judith (See also Bon, Judith Sutpen)

Sutpen, Raby

Sutpen, Colonel Thomas

Terrel (Tomys Turl) (See also Beauchamp, Terrel, and Turl)

"The Bear," GDM, 241
"Delta Autumn," GDM, 247
"Fire and Hearth," 234
Go Down, Moses, 217
Intruder, 253
Town, 343
"Was," 233

Thelma

Mansion, 363

Thelma Frances

Mosquitoes, 35

Theodule

Fable, 315

Thisbe, Aunt

"Fire and Hearth," 234
Go Down, Moses, 217

Thompson

"Landing in Luck," 1

Thompson

Light in August, 133

Thompson, Roz

Light in August, 133

Thoms, Captain Joe

"Mississippi," 333

Thorndyke

Town, 343

Thorpe

Fable, 315

Thorpe

"Tomorrow," 266

Thorpe

"Tomorrow," 266

Thorpe

"Tomorrow," 266

Thorpe

"Tomorrow," 266

Thorpe, Buck (Bucksnort)

"Tomorrow," 266

Three Basket

"Red Leaves," 119

Thucydides (Thucydus) (See also McCaslin)

"The Bear," GDM, 241
Go Down, Moses, 217

Tim

"Liar," 8

Tim

Mayday, 33

Tobe

Flags, 49

Tobe

"Rose for Emily," 121

Tobe

Soldiers' Pay, 17

'Toinette

"All Dead Pilots," 117

605

Tull, Eula

    As I Lay, 95
    Hamlet, 201
    "Spotted Horses," 406
    "Two Soldiers," 280

Tull, Kate

    As I Lay, 95
    Hamlet, 201
    "Spotted Horses," 406
    "Two Soldiers," 280

Tull, Odum

    "Fool about a Horse," 402

Tull, Vernon

    As I Lay, 95
    Hamlet, 201
    "Hound," 405
    "Lizards," 403
    Mansion, 363
    "Shingles," 277
    "Spotted Horses," 406
    Town, 343
    "Two Soldiers," 280

Tulls (suitors of Eula Varner)

    Mansion, 363

Turl (See also Terrel and Beauchamp, Terrel)

    "The Bear," GDM, 241
    "Centaur," 282
    "Delta Autumn," GDM, 247
    "Fire and Hearth," 234
    Go Down, Moses, 217
    Intruder, 253
    Town, 343
    "Was," 233

Turpin (draft evader)

    Mansion, 363

Turpin (family name)

    Flags, 49
    Hamlet, 201

Varner, Jody

    As I Lay, 95
    Father Abraham, 41
    "Fool about a Horse," 402
    Hamlet, 201
    Light in August, 133
    Mansion, 363
    "Spotted Horses," 406
    Town, 343

Varner, Maggie, (Mrs. Will; first wife)

    As I Lay, 95
    Father Abraham, 41
    Hamlet, 201
    Mansion, 363
    Town, 343

Varner, Will (Uncle Billy)

    As I Lay, 95
    "By the People," 341
    Father Abraham, 41
    Flags, 49
    "Fool about a Horse," 402
    Hamlet, 201
    "Hound," 405
    Intruder, 253
    Light in August, 133
    "Lizards," 403
    Mansion, 363
    "Shingles," 277
    "Spotted Horses," 406
    "Tomorrow," 266
    Town, 343

Varner, Mrs. Will (second wife)

    Mansion, 363

Vatch

    "Mountain Victory," 163

Velma

    Elmer, 25

Venturia, Juan

    "Rosary," 7

Vera

    Reivers, 383

Vernon

    "Death Drag," 322

Vernon

    Sound and Fury, 65

Vidal, Francois

    "Mountain Victory," 163

Vidal, Mrs. Francois

    "Mountain Victory," 163

Vines, Deacon

    Light in August, 133

Vinson

    Miss Zilphia Gant, 83

Vinson, Mrs.

    Miss Zilphia Gant, 83

Virgil

    Reivers, 383

Vitelli, Popeye (See also Popeye)

    "Big Shot," 432
    Requiem, 307

Von Ploeckner, General

    "Snow," 447

Vynie

    "Fool about a Horse," 402

Waldrip

    "Honor," 165

Waldrip, Mrs. Vernon

Wild Palms, 193

Wales, Sells

"Mississippi," 333

Walker, Ed

Sanctuary, 103
Sanctuary: Original, 85

Walker, Mrs. Ed

Sanctuary, 103

Walkley

"Victory," 113

Wall

"Dangerous Man," 439

Wall, General (Confederate)

Town, 343

Wallace, Captain

"Sunset," 9

Waller, Hamp

Light in August, 133

Waller, Mrs. Hamp

Light in August, 133

Walter

Mosquitoes, 35

Walter

Mosquitoes, 35

Walthall, Parson

Sound and Fury, 65

Whitfield, Rev.

    As I Lay, 95
    Hamlet, 201
    Requiem, 307
    "Shingles," 277
    "Tomorrow," 266

Whittington

    Hamlet, 201

Widrington

    "Black Music," 160
    Town, 343

Widrington, Mrs.

    "Black Music," 160
    "Carcassone," 132
    Town, 343

Wiggins, Mrs.

    "Dangerous Man," 439

Wilbourne

    Wild Palms, 193

Wilbourne, Dr.

    Wild Palms, 193

Wilbourne, Dr. Henry (Harry)

    Wild Palms, 193

Wilbourne, Mrs.

    Wild Palms, 193

Wildermark

    Town, 343

Wilkie

    Sound and Fury, 65

Wilkins, George

    "Fire and Hearth," 234
    Go Down, Moses, 217
    "Gold Is Not Always," 412
    "A Point of Law," 410
Wilkins, Nathalie Beauchamp (Nat) (See also
Beauchamp, Nathalie)

    "Fire and Heath," 234
    Go Down, Moses, 217
    "A Point of Law," 410

Wilkins, Mrs.

    Unvanquished, 185

Wilkins, Profesor, Judge

    Unvanquished, 185

Wilkinson

    "Appendix: Compson," 79

Will

    "A Return," 436

Willard

    Soldiers' Pay, 17

William (See also Bill, "Memmy")

    "Mississippi," 333

Willow, Colonel

    Absalom, 175

Willmoth

    Go Down, Moses, 217
    "Go Down, Moses," GDM, 249

Wilson, Sergeant

    Fable, 315

Winbush

    Hamlet, 201

Winbush, Mrs. (mother of Grover Cleveland)

    Town, 343

Winbush, Fonzo

    Mansion, 363
    Sanctuary, 103
    Sanctuary: Original, 85

Winbush, Grover Cleveland

    Hamlet, 201
    Mansion, 363
    Town, 343

Winbush, Mrs. Grover Cleveland

    Mansion, 363

Winbush, Mack

    Reivers, 383

Windham

    "Big Shot," 432
    "Dull Tale," 434

Winterbottom

    Hamlet, 201
    Light in August, 133
    "Spotted Horses," 406

Winterbottom, Mrs.

    Flags, 49

Winword, Colonel

    Father Abraham, 41

Wiseman, Mrs. Eva

    Mosquitoes, 35

617

Worsham, Samuel

> Go Down, Moses, 217
> "Go Down, Moses, GDM, 249
> "Go Down, Moses," US, 414

Worthington, Mrs.

> Soldiers' Pay, 17

Wright, Doc

> Sound and Fury, 65

Wyatt

> "Rose for Emily," 121

Wyatt, Captain (named Wylie in Sartoris)

> Flags, 49

Wyatt, George

> "Skirmish," 397
> Unvanquished, 185

Wyatt, Henry

> "Delta Autumn," GDM, 247
> Go Down, Moses, 217

Wyatt, Sally

> Flags, 49

Wyatt, Sophia

> Flags, 49

Wylie, Captain (See Wyatt, Captain Flags, 95.)

Wylie

> "Mississippi," 333

Wylie, Ash (I)

> "A Bear Hunt," BW, 337